Ballet under Napoleon

ALSO BY IVOR GUEST

Napoleon III in England
The Ballet of the Second Empire
The Romantic Ballet in England
Fanny Cerrito
Victorian Ballet Girl
Adeline Genée
The Alhambra Ballet
La Fille mal gardée (editor)
The Dancer's Heritage
The Empire Ballet
A Gallery of Romantic Ballet
The Romantic Ballet in Paris
Dandies and Dancers
Carlotta Zambelli
Two *Coppélias*
Fanny Elssler
The *Pas de Quatre*
Le Ballet de l'Opéra de Paris
The Divine Virginia
Letters from a Ballet-master
Adeline Genée: a pictorial record
Adventures of a Ballet Historian
Designing for the Dancer (contributor)
Jules Perrot
Gautier on Dance (ed. and trans.)
Gautier on Spanish Dance (ed. and trans.)
Dr John Radcliffe and his Trust
Ballet in Leicester Square
The Ballet of the Enlightenment

1. Zephyr in Gardel's *Le Retour de Zéphire*. Water colour by an unidentified artist, probably depicting André Deshayes as Zephyr and, upper left, Jean Aumer as Apollo. (© Harvard Theatre Collection)

Ballet under Napoleon

Ivor Guest

For Ann

First published in 2002 by Dance Books Ltd
The Old Bakery
4 Lenten Street
Alton
Hampshire GU34 1HG

ISBN:1 85273 082 X

A CIP catalogue record for this book is available from the British Library

Printed and bound in Great Britain by the Charlesworth Group

Contents

Illustrations

Frontispiece

Between pages 112/113

a chariot drawn by horses), by Pierre-Luc-Charles Ciceri. (Bibliothèque-Musée de l'Opéra: © Cliché BNF Paris)

58. Playbill for the last performance at the Salle Montansier, 13 February 1820, the night of the assassination of the Duc de Berry. (Bibliothèque-Musée de l'Opéra: © Cliché BNF Paris)
59. The carriage of the Duc de Berry turning from the Rue de Richelieu into the Rue de Rameau. The side door, outside which he was assassinated, is just beyond the sentry box. (Simond, *Paris de 1800 à 1900*)
60. The assassination of the Duc de Berry. (Musée Carnavalet: © MVP/ negative Desgraces) Louvel is seen being apprehended as if he had been running towards the Rue Lully. In fact, he tried to escape in the other direction.
61. The death of the Duc de Berry. Oil painting by François-Barthélémy Michel. (Musée Carnavalet: © MVP/negative Joffre) Since the ballet is shown still in progress, this must be seen as the Duke being attended to shortly after he was brought into the little salon.

Illustrations in the text

1. A typical example of Gardel's painstaking revision of the text of a scenario, in this case the opening of his unperformed *Guillaume Tell*. (Archives Nationales, AJ[13] 1023)
2. A petition by the senior dancers in support of Joly, with whom they took class. Note the embracing signatures of Auguste Vestris and Mlle Chameroy. (Archives Nationales, AJ[13] 83)
3. Playbill for the first performance of *Achille à Scyros*. (Bibliothèque-Musée de l'Opéra)
4. The Comte de Luçay's report to Napoleon, seeking approval of the estimate for Henry's ballet, *L'Amour à Cythère*, with the endorsement of the Emperor's approval, granted at Munich on 27 October 1805, just five weeks before the Battle of Austerlitz. (Archives Nationales, AJ[13] 91)
5. Playbill for the second performance of *Le Retour d'Ulysse*. (Bibliothèque-Musée de l'Opéra: © Cliché BNF Paris)
6. A letter from Noverre to Louis Duport's brother, written after Louis Duport had secretly left Paris for Vienna in 1807. 'Please let me know in secret of his arrival so that I can write to him and, reminding him of my friendship, open my heart to him by telling him of the dangers that might result from a liaison [i.e. that with Mlle George] that is destroying his health and his talent.' (Archives Nationales, AJ[13] 84)
7. Playbill for the first performance of Nina. (Bibliothèque-Musée de l'Opéra: © Cliché BNF Paris)
8. Playbill for the first performance of *Flore et Zéphire*. (Bibliothèque-Musée de l'Opéra: © Cliché BNF Paris)

Acknowledgements

Over the four years or thereabouts that this book has been in the making, and indeed for many years earlier as I began to gather the material on which it is based, I have incurred countless debts of gratitude. Since my narrative is set in Paris, and more particularly in its opera house, it is only right that I should begin by expressing my gratitude to the librarians and staff of the Bibliothèque de l'Opéra, and in particular to the three successive Librarians who have been at its helm since I first entered through its doors in 1946: the late André Ménetrat, Martine Kahane and Pierre Vidal. My thanks are due, too, to the staff of the Archives Nationales, which contain a veritable treasure-house of documents relating to the Opéra during the period covered in this book.

Among those in other libraries and museums in which I have delved for material, I must record my thanks to Jean-Marie Bruson of the Musée Carnavalet, who helped me locate several prints that have added a vivid touch of actuality; Madeleine Nichols, Curator of the Dance Collection of the New York Public Library for the Performing Arts, which holds a number of important documents relating to the period; and Annette Fern, Research and Reference Librarian of the Harvard Theatre Collection.

I must also thank, most warmly, David Garforth, who gave willingly of his time to play through for me the manuscript full-scores of some of Gardel's ballets to give me a flavour of the musical accompaniment; Hugh Cobbe of the British Library, who identified a surprising number of Haydn borrowings (listed here in an appendix); my French colleague, Marie-Françoise Christout, who answered a great variety of questions that came up in the course of my research and was not stumped once; and fellow historians and enthusiasts, Knud Årne Jurgensen, Gunhild Oberzaucher-Schüller, Maria Ratanova, Marian Smith and Jean-Louis Tamvaco.

A special mark of appreciation is due to Séverine Darroussat who, in the course of her research into the work of the sculptor François-Nicolas Delaistre, rediscovered his bust of Pierre Gardel, which had lain forgotten and gathering dust beneath the eaves of the Opéra. Illustrated in these pages, this portrait in stone brings its subject most vividly to life, and surely deserves to be rescued from its dark and lonely corner and given a public place of honour at the Opéra alongside other great figures of its history.

I have also to thank Richard Ralph, who has most painstakingly read the final draft and made numerous suggestions that have smoothed a few rough edges in the text; my publisher, David Leonard of Dance Books, for his friendship and support; and Rodney Cuff, whose editorial skill has added a touch of polish to these pages. For any infelicities that may remain, the responsibility is mine.

And finally I have to acknowledge the encouragement of the person who has shared with me the whole process of this book's creation – my wife Ann, to whom the text was read aloud chapter by chapter as it emerged from my word-processor, in an attempt to achieve that easy readability which must be an objective of any self-respecting historian. It has been my incredible good fortune to share my life with one who understands the commitment that a work of this scale demands, and it is to her that these pages are lovingly dedicated.

Ivor Guest
Holland Park, February 2001

Introduction

Between the Ages of the Enlightenment and Romanticism lies a span of some three decades, during which the ballet, that most ephemeral of theatrical arts, flourished almost miraculously in a Europe riven and scarred by revolution and war. Against such a turbulent background, when the fabric of the Old Régime disintegrated and the Napoleonic adventure ran its destructive course, ballet in Paris grew to maturity. In 1789, although its independence from the opera had been attained, it was still a comparatively minor form of entertainment, akin to a silent form of *opéra-comique.* But by 1815 it had shown itself capable of handling serious, even grand, subjects, and had established its claim to be ranked alongside opera on terms of near equality.

Notwithstanding the excesses of the Revolution and the ravages of war, Paris was still revered as a focus of European culture, and in no other art was its superiority so unchallenged as in ballet. The Opéra was still accepted without question as the fountain-head from which the Western world sought guidance in matters of technique and taste concerning the ballet; and the credit for this was due in very large part to the guidance of one man, Pierre Gardel. Gardel directed the ballet there from his appointment in 1787 until his retirement forty years later in 1827, laying much of the foundation that was to underpin the great development of ballet in the glow of Romanticism.

Strangely, considering the attention that has been given in recent times to the development of ballet, this period has so far escaped detailed examination by historians. For the Romantic ballet that followed had such a dazzling effect on the audiences of its time, and on the imagination of later historians, that it might have appeared to a casual outsider to have emerged as a sudden emanation. But of course this was not so. Romanticism was only the shining façade of a structure whose foundations had been laid long before, and that had appeared to an earlier generation hardly less gloriously in Neo-Classical guise.

The young Romantics sneered at the Neo-Classical style of their forbears, but during the Revolution and the Empire that style had a ringing relevance. With Napoleon's fall this relevance disappeared, and the younger school of writers and artists, calling themselves Romantics, embarked on a frenzied search for novel sources of inspiration that were to give the world a dazzling new crop of masterpieces in every field of art. However, in the cold light of history, the achievements of the Neo-Classical phase of ballet are not to be ignored; and it is a purpose of this book to bridge the gap in our knowledge and understanding of the antecedents that led up to, and significantly contributed to, the extraordinary flowering of ballet in the glow of Romanticism.

The ballet in its Neo-Classical guise, over which Pierre Gardel presided, was itself rooted in a long and intricate tradition. It traced its origins back to the courtly diversions during the Italian Renaissance and the more complex spectacles that developed in the courts of the Valois and Bourbon kings of France. Its acceptance as a theatrical art based specifically on dance and pantomime, however, was much more recent. The court ballet, as it had developed by the reign of Louis XIV in the seventeenth century, had been a composite form, in which dance was combined with singing and declamation. But when the wars that beset France towards the end of that King's reign imposed a régime of austerity, dance as a spectacle shifted from the court to the theatre with the creation of the 'Académie Royale de Musique' (more familiarly known as the Paris Opéra). There it developed as a distinctive component of French opera; and before long no important opera would be considered complete without its ballet. Subsequently, in the second half of the eighteenth century, ballet underwent a momentous change. It established itself as an independent form by allying dance with pantomime, rather than being merely a decorative feature within an opera. There thus emerged a virtually new theatrical form: the ballet-pantomime, or the *ballet d'action*, in which the dancers themselves assumed the task of conveying the narrative.

By welcoming this form as a permanent feature of the repertory offered at the Opéra, Paris was only giving its seal of approval to a development that had been intermittently tested elsewhere since the early years of the century. Inspired by accounts of the pantomimes of ancient Rome, a number of far-seeing ballet-masters had been experimenting independently with the use of pantomime to convey narrative; and in 1760 Noverre had cogently set forth the principles of this new form in a work that was immediately granted the status of a classic, his *Lettres sur la danse et les ballets*. Shortly after its publication, Noverre became ballet-master at the court of Württemberg, where, in the course of several seasons, he put his ideas into practice by producing a number of ballet-pantomimes for the reigning Duke. His company there was headed by the most celebrated dancer of his time, Gaétan Vestris, on leave from the Opéra, who was so overwhelmed by the impression he made in the rôle of Jason in *Médée et Jason* that on his return to France he produced his own version of that ballet before Louis XV.

Some years later, in 1776, at the behest of Queen Marie-Antoinette, Noverre was appointed ballet-master at the Opéra, where he produced a series of *ballets d'action*. Unfortunately, he was regarded as an interloper by the resident assistant ballet-masters, Dauberval and Maximilien Gardel, who considered the post to have been rightfully theirs. In time they succeeded in easing out Noverre; shortly afterwards Dauberval resigned, which left Maximilien Gardel in sole charge. In his brief career Maximilien Gardel produced a number of lighter *ballets d'action*, mostly versions of popular *opéras-comiques*. These too proved highly popular, and formed the mainstay of the ballet repertory when the Revolution broke. By then, however, Maximilien Gardel was dead and had been succeeded by his younger brother, Pierre.

When the story of the ballet at the Paris Opéra is taken up in this book, Pierre Gardel, now thirty-five, is at the peak of his creative power, with three major ballets already to his credit, all based on themes taken from classical antiquity: *Télémaque*, the story of Telemachus, son of Ulysses, and his love for the nymph Eucharis on the island of Calypso; *Psyché*, which told of Cupid's wooing of the beautiful Psyche and the latter's torments at the hand of a jealous Venus; and *Le Jugement de Pâris*, the legend of the golden apple awarded to Venus by the shepherd Paris.

It was a very promising beginning, but the Revolution had reached its most menacing phase. The Reign of Terror had begun, and so uncertain was the political climate that no institution could be regarded as secure, let alone one that owed its foundation to a royal patent. By Gardel and his dancers – as indeed by everyone else in the strife-torn city – the future could only be contemplated with foreboding.

1

Surviving the Terror

By the autumn of 1793, when the principals of the Paris Opéra could at least congratulate themselves on achieving their long-held ambition to control the artistic policy of their theatre, France had struggled through four increasingly turbulent years of Revolution. Since the fall of the Bastille on 14 July 1789, the changes had been so drastic and far-reaching that the days when they had been proud to call themselves pensioners of the King had become but a distant memory, not untinged perhaps with regret. For there must have been some who, in secret thoughts too dangerous to admit openly, hankered after what seemed a happier, calmer, more stable time, when a comfortable retirement on a pension was the anticipated reward for years of loyal service.

All that had now been swept away. Though it had been welcomed in a wave of popular euphoria, the Revolution had not produced the promised golden age of liberty and fraternity. At first, few tears had been shed at the dismantling of an ineffective regime that was already faltering under the dead-weight of privilege and social abuse. But since that heady summer of 1789 the Revolution had lurched from one crisis to another, at the mercy of events and of a growing urge to abolish anything associated with the past. It was still too soon to judge whether it was succeeding in its historic task, not just of reform in the sense of replacing what was rotten, but of virtually building anew the very structure of society. However, for ordinary citizens concerned with their own livelihoods, life was hard, often desperately hard.

The 350 souls (or thereabouts) employed by the Opéra – singers, dancers, musicians, machinists, tailors, costumiers, administrators, clerks, concierges, down to the humblest of all, the nocturnal character known as Maroudin the German whose function was to destroy the rats – could, on the whole, count themselves fortunate. At least they enjoyed regular employment, although their salaries had not kept abreast of inflation and on one occasion, in 1791–2, had even been abated. The daily routine of the dancers, like that of the musicians and singers, had not been affected; the round of classes, rehearsals and performances had continued, the only concession to outside events being the dilution of the regular repertory with hastily got-up productions of a propagandist nature.

The danger that the Opéra might have been swept away as a trapping of the monarchy had been averted when the Assembly had recognised its importance in propagating the national culture. When Louis XVI found he could no longer cover the Opéra's chronic deficit, the Commune of Paris had assumed responsibility. For many years the leading artistes had been eager to administer the Opéra themselves, but the grant of a franchise to Francoeur and Cellerier in 1792 had dashed their hopes. However, the growing difficulties that overwhelmed those two *entrepreneurs* emboldened the artistes to renew their efforts. By the summer of 1793 the Opéra was in such a plight that they had little difficulty in convincing the Commune that the Directors were in breach of the terms of their franchise. Salaries and suppliers' bills were unpaid, the stock of scenery, costumes and props had been woefully depleted, and – most serious charge of all – the Directors had been culpably dilatory in purging the repertory of works that offended republican principles.

To their surprise perhaps, the artistes found an unexpected, if somewhat dubious, ally. Several members of the Commune were inclined to press for the abolition of the Opéra, but the influential figure of René Hébert, publisher of the scurrilously outspoken news-sheet, *Le Père Duchêne*, surprisingly spoke out in its defence. 'The Opéra,' he declared, 'has been the hotbed of the counter-revolution, but it ought to be encouraged all the same because it supports a large number of families and nourishes arts of entertainment.' The General Council of the Commune responded by dispossessing the Directors, invoking the recently enacted Law of Suspects. Accordingly Francoeur was arrested and imprisoned, Cellerier being fortunate to evade the net. As a provisional measure, the Commune appointed a committee of six artistes to administer the Opéra under its supervision. Chosen presumably for their republican leanings, they included only one dancer, Nivelon; the others were Rey and Rochefort, representing the orchestra, Lasuze, the chorus master, the singers Laïs and Rousseau, and Cavailhès, formerly a member of the chorus and now on the administrative staff. Castil-Blaze was probably not far from the truth in describing them as 'true *sansculottes*',[1] Laïs being the most rabid of them all. These artistes hurried to the Hôtel de Ville to assure the Commune of their revolutionary zeal, and enthusiastically complied when called upon to sing the *Marseillaise*.

One who was rightly put out by being excluded from the list – not

[1] Castil-Blaze, *Académie*, II, 21.

because he identified himself with the *sansculottes*, but by right of seniority – was Pierre Gardel, the *maître des ballets*. Gardel had spent his entire career in the service of the Opéra. He had been trained from childhood in the noble genre by his brother Maximilien, who was then understudying Gaétan Vestris and expecting to succeed him. On being appointed *maître des ballets*, Maximilien began to make use of his younger brother as his assistant, and when he died unexpectedly from the effects of a minor accident – he had trodden on a chicken bone and his leg turned gangrenous – his sibling stepped into his shoes without much opposition. By 1793 Pierre Gardel had been ballet-master for six years, having established an unassailable reputation with three major ballets produced in quick succession: *Télémaque* and *Psyché* (1790) and *Le Jugement de Pâris* (1793), which were to form the bedrock of the ballet repertory of the Opéra over the next quarter-century.

For him now to be passed over in the appointment of the Artistes' Committee was deeply galling to his professional pride; for in his eyes no dancer, and certainly not Nivelon, had served the Opéra more loyally and more effectively than he. Often without adequate help and at the risk of endangering his health by overwork, he had not only replenished the repertory, but had raised the standards and discipline of the ballet through a most difficult period, and had given it a prestige that he could justly claim it had never enjoyed before.

Not only was there justice in his claim to a seat on the Artistes' Committee, but he may have been in a position to press his claim through the powerful Committee of Public Safety, which was then governing the nation in the name of the Convention. However Gardel engineered his appeal, it was successful, for within a few weeks, on 8 October, an order was issued reconstituting the Artistes' Committee. Now his name was included at the head of the new list in place of Nivelon's. Surprisingly, Laïs was also dropped, Guichard, the *chef de chant*, being appointed in his place. Rey, Rochefort and Lasuze remained; and Berthélémy, the costume designer, was brought in. To these were added two administrators: Bralle, the Inspector-General, and Watteville, the new Secretary-General.

To give the dispossessed Directors their due, they had maintained the numerical strength of the opera and ballet companies and the orchestra, and when the leading artistes took control, Gardel still found himself at the head of a fine body of dancers. By long tradition, the upper ranks, or the *sujets* as they were collectively called, were graded into three genres: the *noble* or serious, the *demi-caractère*, and the *comique*. The company as a whole was organised in a hierarchy that extended from the *premiers sujets*, through two grades of soloists, known as *remplacements* and *doubles*, to the *choeur de la danse* as the *corps de ballet* was then still called.

Traditionally the number of *premiers sujets* was restricted to one of each sex in each of the three genres, although there had been recent precedents for exceeding this establishment when in danger of losing an exceptionally promising young dancer. In 1793 there were in fact just three male *premiers sujets*, but no less than five on the female side. The three men at the top of the tree were Pierre Gardel himself, Auguste Vestris and Louis Nivelon, all dancers of very considerable experience.

At thirty-five, Gardel was two years older than his two colleagues. His tall, elegant figure and noble allure had singled him out for the *noble* genre from the very beginning of his training. Historically this genre held pride of place among the three, claiming descent from the style that had been honed at the courts of Louis XIV and his predecessors, and thereafter nourished at the Opéra by a succession of eminent professionals, most notably Louis Dupré, Gaétan Vestris, and Maximilien Gardel. In 1793 Pierre Gardel himself represented this genre, with no contender or successor in sight, but in recent years it had been noticed that he had been making what seemed to some a misguided attempt to extend its boundaries. With the change in composition of the opera-going public resulting from emigration and the growing influx of *nouveaux riches*, public taste had been weaned away from the *noble* genre by the extraordinary virtuosity of Auguste Vestris, who had revolutionised and given a new dimension to the *demi-caractère*. In the words of an observer writing some fifty years later:

> Gardel, who for years had been admired in the *noble* genre, which he danced with great purity, took it into his head to turn his hand to the *danse élevée*. Vestris's daring leaps and dazzling pirouettes had been giving him sleepless nights, his dreams being cruelly disturbed by the echo of applause given to his fortunate comrade. He tried to compete, and had the mortification of being vanquished. And to add to his anguish, he sprained his back so badly that he lost both the heart and the capability to start afresh.[2]

Never before in the history of ballet had there been such a virtuoso as Auguste Vestris. Before his extraordinary physical prowess, even the glory of his father, once acclaimed as '*le dieu de la danse*', had paled. By

[2] Touchard-Lafosse, IV, 19-20. According to a request for a benefit that Gardel made in 1806, the accident had occurred during the thirtieth performance of the opera *Panurge*, which took place on 26 March 1786. (Arch. Nat., AJ^{13} 82)

1793 Auguste, now thirty-three, was no longer the youth who had conquered Paris with an unbelievable range and command of technique, but he had developed astonishingly as an artist. His physical powers, perhaps somewhat tamed but hardly noticeably diminished, were now complemented by a dramatic talent that seemed to grow with every new rôle he undertook in the ballet-pantomimes that were becoming so popular.

The third male *premier sujet* was Louis Nivelon, a finely proportioned man but smaller in build than his two companions. It had been his misfortune to be an exact contemporary of Auguste Vestris, for, although by nature and physique a *demi-caractère* dancer, he had been constrained to represent the *comique* genre so as to qualify for the top rank. Without such impossible competition he might have fulfilled the promise of his youth, when he had been Guimard's favourite partner, and taken his place at the top of his profession. Nevertheless, he had not become bitter, but had come to terms with his lot, remaining steadfastly loyal to the Opéra and, such was his good nature, being constantly imposed upon.

The shift in popularity from the *noble* to the *demi-caractère* was also perceptible among the *danseuses*. Of the five *premiers sujets*, it was the *demi-caractère* Marie Miller who held the senior position. She had been the most outstanding of an exceptionally gifted clutch of young dancers who had emerged in the last years of the Old Régime. 'A nymph barely nubile, a quasi-vaporous sylphide' was how one man remembered her from the days of his youth. Many years later, this memory was to be 'rekindled in more ways than one by the celebrated Taglioni,' for she was not naturally endowed with that 'feminine charm or exquisite figure which adds such a seductive allure to a ballerina's talent, and indeed which is frequently a substitute for non-existent talent.' In short, Marie Miller was not a dancer who aroused carnal desire; her supremacy was founded securely on her artistry. She had a profound musicality, which gave her style a fluency and a poetic quality that inspired one admirer to imagine 'wings on her shoulders, and a soul in her feet'.[3] No less impressive was her interpretative gift; she could convey with equal effect an astonishingly wide range of emotions – innocence, dream-like spirituality, coquetry, abandon, sensuality, pleasure and joy. And no dancer could have a stronger commitment to her art; she was quite exceptionally reliable, and, unlike some of her colleagues, was never suspected of feigning an indisposition.

She had entered Gardel's life after being spotted dancing at Nicolet's theatre as a child. Recognising her promise, he had taken her under his

[3] Touchard-Lafosse, IV, 13-15.

wing, training her with such care and devotion that in 1789, three years after her début, she succeeded to the coveted position of *premier sujet* in the *demi-caractère* genre that had become vacant on Guimard's retirement.

At that time Gardel himself was at the threshold of his career as ballet-master, and it was for her that he went on to create the principal rôles in his first three ballets. As Eucharis in *Télémaque*, as the eponymous heroine of *Psyché* and as the shepherdess Oenone in *Le Jugement de Pâris*, she established an uncontested supremacy. Still only twenty-three in 1793, a long and distinguished career lay ahead of her. Her relationship with Gardel was already very close; the pupil had become the muse, and now a more intimate relationship was developing.

Among the women, as with the men, the *noble* genre had declined somewhat in status. Its last great exponent had been the majestic Anne Heinel. She had been difficult to replace, but after a few years a successor had been found in Victoire Saulnier, a pupil of Maximilien Gardel. The former Director of the Opéra, Antoine Dauvergne, dismissed her as 'a beautiful woman but a mediocre dancer',[4] but there was no doubt of her commanding presence. While she had revealed her talent as a mime in three important rôles which Gardel created for her – Calypso in *Télémaque* and Venus in both *Psyché* and *Le Jugement de Pâris* – it was most particularly the sight of her tall and shapely figure, displayed to full advantage in the flimsy attire then coming into fashion, that drew gasps of admiration whenever she entered the stage.

Her colleague in the *comique* genre was Marie-Eve Pérignon, still attractive at the age of thirty and a firm favourite with the public. In terms of service, she was the senior female *premier sujet*, a hard-working, highly dependable dancer whose talent drew a warm testimonial from Noverre.[5]

In the lower ranks were to be found a number of names that were of interest for past achievements or future promise. Among the senior soloists, or *doubles*, was Alexis Huard, who had had a narrow escape when the opera house in the Palais-Royal had been burnt to the ground in 1781. Also at that rank were Anne-Jacqueline Coulon, who had had a long and seemingly stable relationship with Pierre Gardel and borne him two children before they separated, and two recently promoted dancers who were shortly to fulfil their promise, Emilie Collomb and Clotilde Malfleuret. Further down the hierarchy, at the level of junior soloist or *remplacement*, were to be found the senior comic dancer, Charles Beaupré, the future

[4] Arch. Nat., O[1] 619 (42). List of Committee Members [August 1788].

[5] Noverre (1804), IV, 99.

choreographer Louis Milon, and an exceptionally talented youth, André Deshayes, whose father and teacher directed the Opéra's School of Dance.

The School of Dance had long been an integral part of the Opéra. For many years under the old regime it had occupied rooms in the building known as the Magasin in the Rue Saint-Nicaise, but the Republican government had expropriated this as former royal property. It was, in any case, convenient to find premises closer to the Opéra itself, by the Porte Saint-Martin, and the School had moved to rented property available nearby. It still remained modestly staffed, Jacques-François Deshayes being supported merely by two assistant teachers, Béguin and Jacques-Charles Joly, both active members of the *corps de ballet*.

Under the newly introduced Revolutionary calendar, the seven-day week had been replaced by the ten-day *décadi*, and classes were now held on four days in each *décadi*. Standards had noticeably risen since Deshayes had taken over, and the short period when the School was situated at No. 16 Carré Martin was marked by the arrival of several promising pupils, including among the boys Louis Duport, Louis Henry, Arnaud Léon and the future teacher, Georges Maze. More than ever before, the School of Dance was becoming a nursery of professional talent in which young dancers were being trained in the more arduous technical skill that the developing art of ballet was now demanding, but even so there was no perfection class yet.

Neither was pantomime yet included in the curriculum, even though it was now a major feature of ballet. Evidence is scanty as to how those dancers who were assigned rôles in narrative ballets were coached, but the most credible inference is that the pantomime sections were carefully taught and rehearsed by the choreographer before the dances were set. It must be remembered that on the Parisian stage of that time pantomime was an accepted form of expression, appreciated not only by the select public of the Opéra but also by less sophisticated audiences through the influence of the *Commedia dell'Arte* at the Comédie-Italienne and pantomimes given at the minor theatres. This popular connection suggests that pantomimic acting was essentially realistic, employing gestures that were easily understood by the uninitiated spectator, but there was also another influence. At the Comédie-Française at that time, a more natural style was developing under the influence of the tragedian Talma and, in the lighter works of the repertory, was beginning to supplant the formalised delivery and gestures of the older school. It was significant that one of Talma's teachers, Dugazon, had laid particular stress on the impor-

[6] Higgins, 29.

tance of pantomime – the relevance of gesture, the art of reacting to others and of listening, which was 'the acme of silent playing, the triumph of intelligence and the most abundant source of sensitivity'[6]. Such essential precepts were surely absorbed by Gardel, Milon and other French choreographers of the period, who created their works in the warm glow that Talma's genius was shedding upon the dramatic stage.

* * *

In that summer of 1793 the political scene could hardly have been more unsettled. Indeed, it had become difficult to discover in whose hands lay the real source of power. In theory at least, the National Convention, whose elected representatives held their sessions in the Tuileries, was the rightful embodiment of the nation, and had recently completed its task of drawing up a Constitution. But in the Hôtel de Ville sat a grimmer, more dangerous gathering – the members of the Commune of Paris who, backed by the National Guard and the amorphous mob of *sansculottes* from the working-class districts, had more than once launched insurrections that had driven the Revolution into another, more extreme phase. Another potent source of influence was the political club, notably those of the Jacobins (used by Robespierre and others as a testing ground for sessions in the Convention) and the Cordeliers. Thus the power that a government needs to govern was at the mercy of outside influences, as the events of that summer all too clearly revealed.

So much had happened since the year had dawned. The King had been guillotined in January. Shortly afterwards war had been declared on the European powers that were openly hostile to the Revolution; Belgium was annexed in the first onslaught, but the early gains of the French armies were to be as quickly lost. Within its borders, France had been riven by revolt, most dangerously by the insurrection in the Vendée, which would take years before being finally extinguished. Meanwhile in Paris the Revolution was moving inexorably towards its terrible climax. Power was shifting away from Danton, the powerful demagogue who led the comparatively moderate Girondist element in the Convention, towards the inscrutable figure of Robespierre and the Jacobins. As the year drew to its close, the nation was becoming cowed by fear – fear for the future, fear also of the ultimate, and often capricious, sentence of the guillotine that was casting its malign shadow over the city as the number of its victims mounted.

[7] Prudhomme, V, 154.

The Reign of Terror had begun. Even his fellow deputies in the Convention seemed mesmerised by fear of the man who held the reins of power. From time to time Robespierre attended the Opéra, arriving without formality and being ushered into a narrow box, protected from scrutiny by a grill. Whenever his presence became known, a chill spread over the audience, and even the *filles d'Opéra*, who were usually so vivacious and merry, became staid and serious. For it was a brave soul who dared to laugh in Robespierre's hearing.[7]

Yet life went on, with ordinary folk going about their daily business as best they could and taking care not to be suspected of the new social crime of incivism. Happily, the dancers of the Opéra were to survive the difficult months that lay ahead, although many must have lost friends to execution, often on the flimsiest of evidence.

In this they could have counted themselves lucky, for the Opéra had been a royal institution, as its former name of 'Académie Royale de Musique' had clearly proclaimed, and its public had been overwhelmingly aristocratic. Now the royal stigma had been removed and it had become simply the 'Opéra National', administered under the supervision of the Commune of Paris. This new connection had produced one beneficial effect. Gone were the days when, under the benevolent rule of the King through his Intendant of the Menus-Plaisirs, the leading artistes could intrigue and impose their will on the Director. Now, in the words of Castil-Blaze, who had access to many older contemporaries with first-hand experience of those times, the situation was very different:

> The members of the Commune exercised an absolute and arbitrary power over the performers and staff, ruling them through a regime of fear. The Opéra ran admirably. No one was paid, but everyone was at his post on time. Singers launched into their parts with full voice, and dancers leapt with agility notwithstanding colds and sprains. Prosecutor Chaumette, J.J. Le Roux, Henriot and Hébert, the members of the Commune specially charged with the over-all supervision of the theatre, allowed no excuse, and a performer who was indisposed, even with a doctor's certificate, might be placed on the list of suspected persons as a trouble-making conspirator who was depriving the chiefs of the Republic of their accustomed pleasures and the *sansculottes* of the free performances that were often on offer.[8]

Among that quartet of municipal heavyweights, the most to be feared

[8] Castil-Blaze, *Académie*, II, 11.

was Hébert, a rabble-rouser who took a pernicious delight in frightening the personnel of the Opéra by taking out of his pocket a list of twenty-two names, accompanied by the threat: 'One of these days I'll send you to the guillotine to teach you a lesson in civism. Only two reasons are holding me back: first, that you are not worth the trouble, and secondly, that I need you to entertain me.'

Charles Beaupré, who was as irrepressible off stage as on, managed to get hold of this dreadful document by some absurdly specious argument while Hébert was drunk, and lost no time in destroying it. Hébert's only reaction was to prepare another list, which Beaupré was again able to steal, and then a third, which was happily to remain a dead letter until the time came for Hébert himself to be removed.

It was not unknown for the Opéra's new masters to wander backstage and invite themselves into the dressing-room of some dancer or singer, expecting to be received with the hospitality they considered to be their due. It was understood that a meal would be offered them, and after thus rubbing shoulders with their theatrical friends, the councillors would depart without a thought for who would pay for the food and wine. These repasts were provided by Mangin, the *limonadier* of the Opéra, who ran the Café de l'Opéra next door to the theatre – a kind-hearted man who understood the plight of the needy artistes and had 'the good taste not to ask [them] for payment which he would never have dared demand from the *sansculottes* for fear of the scaffold.'[9]

The artistes, now that they were responsible for running the Opéra, knew full well that the price of safety was to be wholeheartedly supportive of the Revolution, in appearance at least. The Opéra was then situated in the staunchly republican section of Paris known as Bondy, stretching northward from the Boulevard Saint-Martin to the city's northern boundary, and on 30 September it was felt appropriate to make a formal show of civism by ceremonially burning, in the presence of the local worthies, all the papers that could be found bearing the insignia of royalty. A formal minute of the occasion was even prepared and lodged with the Commune as a pledge of loyalty; among those present at this *auto-da-fe* were Gardel, Vestris, Huard and Goyon.[10]

Another forced opportunity to display their civism followed a few weeks later when the busts of two recent martyrs of the Revolution were installed in a pompous ceremony on the boulevard before the Opéra. To music by Gluck, Gossec and Grétry, these busts were publicly unveiled and

[9] Castil-Blaze, *Académie*, II, 16-7.

[10] Arch. Nat., AJ[13] 60. There is no evidence to show what was destroyed, but it is possible that the records of the Académie Royale de Danse were thrown into the flames then.

borne into the theatre, to be installed on the stage, one on either side of the proscenium. One of these martyrs was Marat, the most violent of the *enragés*, who had been assassinated in his bath by Charlotte Corday; the other, Le Peletier, was also a victim of an assassin's dagger, but had been dispatched in the more elegant surroundings of a restaurant. Neither had any connection with the arts to which the Opéra was dedicated,[11] but political considerations demanded that the busts should remain, casting their stony glances on the animated scenes being conjured up between them.

Compared with other theatres, the Opéra managed to remain surprisingly aloof from the political turmoil of 1793. From time to time, its directors were obliged to stage ephemeral revolutionary pieces, but apart from a few operas that were proscribed as glorifying monarchs, enough of the old repertory remained to give a modicum of continuity and artistic quality to the programmes. On the other hand, the ballet repertory remained virtually intact, one of Gardel's three great ballets – *Télémaque*, *Psyché* and *Le Jugement de Pâris* – invariably sharing the bill with the stirring stage representation of the *Marseillaise*, *L'Offrande à la Liberté*.

The fact that Gardel created nothing new in the autumn and winter of 1793 was no indication that he was in disfavour. Money was short, and expensive productions could not be afforded. Also, he had been virtually without an assistant since Sébastien Gallet had departed early in 1792; for Jacques-François Deshayes, who had been prevailed upon to help out, apparently without remuneration, also had his duties at the School of Dance to attend to and could not have been very effective. It was only in September 1793 that an assistant ballet-master was engaged, a much older man than Deshayes.

Jean-Baptiste Hus, known in the profession as 'Hus *père*' to distinguish him from his adopted son Eugène, was an experienced ballet-master of a generation earlier than that of the man he was to serve. Among his teachers he could claim the great Louis Dupré, and as a composer of ballets he had a wealth of experience, notably in Lyons, where he had succeeded Noverre after the latter's move to Stuttgart, and more recently in Bordeaux. He had also worked for the Comédie-Française.

With Gardel presumably occupied with other duties, Hus was given the task of showing his mettle with a short and inexpensive creation. Entitled *Les Muses, ou le Triomphe d'Apollon*, this one-act anacreontic ballet was presumably an entirely new work, for it was dutifully dedicated to 'my

[11] Le Peletier's name, however, was to be more permanently associated with the Opéra's history in the next century. When a new opera house was required after the assassination of the Duc de Berry in 1820, the site chosen fronted on the Rue Le Peletier.

brave brothers-in-arms, the *sansculottes'*. It is not clear whether this was intended to imply that old Hus had been present at the Fall of the Bastille or some other great exploit in the streets of Paris, or was merely paying lip service to the Commune, for the published programme lacked a preface which might have thrown further light on his revolutionary background.

The music for this ballet, which does not appear to have survived, was attributed to Charles Ragué, an amateur composer whose modest reputation otherwise rests mainly on a few charming but unremarkable pieces for the harp. Dramatically, the action was minimal. It opens with a scene showing shepherds and shepherdesses preparing to offer sacrifices to Apollo. A band of rustic shepherds arrives, led by Pan (Goyon), whose pipes are snatched away by the mischievous shepherdess Silvie (Collomb), who refuses to give them back unless he agrees to take her and her companions to the Festival of Apollo. So off they all go to Parnassus, where Apollo (Aug.Vestris) descends in a *gloire*[12] and the Muses are summoned to dance before him. The climax is reached when Melpomene, the muse of tragedy (V. Saulnier I), enters brandishing a crown and a dagger. Apollo commands her to trample the crown underfoot, and in a tableau alluding to the abolition of the monarchy, places a wreath of oak leaves upon her brow. With happiness and concord thus restored (a result that had hardly been achieved outside the Opéra's walls), Apollo is hoisted skyward in his *gloire* as the Muses and the mortals bow in homage.

In those disturbed times the press gave very little space to the affairs of the Opéra, but a brief account of this ballet found its way into the *Journal de Paris* a few days after its first performance on 12 December 1793.[13] The writer found several of the scenes 'very pleasing', although the action seemed 'a little dull' and not always easy to follow. The dancers, however, acquitted themselves well, and Vestris surpassed himself. That comment apart, no description of the dances appears to have survived. Presumably the two couples who featured among the shepherd folk in the opening scene – Louis Nivelon and Elisabeth Duchemin, and young André Deshayes and Alexandrine Hutin – were briefly prominent in the opening dances; but Hus's main effort was concentrated on the dances for the Muses, which formed the ballet's concluding *divertissement*. It was at this point that the leading dancers made their appearance: Saulnier as Melpomene, Miller as Terpsichore, Clotilde as Clio, Pérignon as Thalia and Coulon as Calliope. Among the others there were two interesting new-

[12] A *gloire* was a piece of theatrical machinery that could be lowered from the flies to the stage, or raised *vice versa*, for the entrance or exit of an artiste representing a celestial character such as Jupiter, Minerva or Venus. It was usually decorated to represent a cloud.
[13] *Journal de Paris*, 14 December 1793.

comers: Saint-Romain[14] as Erato and Aimée (who was to marry Auguste Vestris)[15] as Euterpe.

Despite this display of talent, the ballet was dropped after its third performance four days later, disappearing, along with its choreographer, of whom no further mention is to be found in the records of the Opéra. Perhaps only the composer, Ragué, emerged with any feeling of achievement, small though it was. His only other works for the theatre were two *opéras-comiques* for the Comédie-Italienne, one of which had been dropped after its first performance, and the other given only twice. So he alone could consider *Les Muses*, with its three performances, as a relative success. It was at least a personal record!

* * *

During the last three months of 1793, Gardel's three major ballets had, along with Hus's small contribution, shared the honours with the stirring representation of the *Marseillaise*, *L'Offrande à la Liberté*. The increasing toll of the guillotine did not interrupt performances at the Opéra; by a fortunate chance the executions of Marie-Antoinette and the former Duc d'Orléans, or Citizen Philippe Egalité as he had chosen to be known, took place on days when the Opéra did not give a performance.

However, on 10 November the Opéra was closed 'on account of the Festival of Liberty and Reason taking place at the former Metropolitan Church', as the Cathedral of Notre Dame had been renamed. Planned as a demonstration of the de-Christianising policy of the revolutionary government, the ceremony required the involvement not only of the orchestra of the Opéra, but also of its singers and dancers. These included Auguste Vestris and Sophie Chevigny, who were 'forced to dance in

[14] She may have been a daughter of the Mme Saint-Romain who ran one of the most popular gambling saloons in the Palais-Royal. A product of the School of Dance, she was engaged at the Opéra as a *double* in 1792, but remained for only a year. She married a musician named Mées, and continued her career in the provinces and abroad. Their daughter Angélique had a more distinguished career as a ballerina in Romantic times.

[15] Mlle Aimée's full name was Anne-Catherine-Frédérique Augier. Born in about 1774, she entered the Opéra in 1793. She married Auguste Vestris in about 1795, but the marriage came to grief when Vestris became enamoured of Louise Chameroy. Mlle Aimée attempted suicide, but was soon dancing again. She remained a member of the Opéra ballet until 1809, the year of her death. Capon's statement in his book on the Vestris family that she was the mother of Armand Vestris is incorrect, for the latter was born in 1787, when Aimée was only thirteen. She could, however, have been the mother of another of Vestris's sons, Bernard-Marie-Firmin Vestris, who was born on 13 January 1796; but even he may have been the product of an extra-marital liaison. Bernard (or Bernardo as he later called himself) was a minor choreographer who worked mainly in Italy. He married a Garcia, and died in Milan on 11 May 1845.

the Choir of the High Altar',[16] and the soprano Marie-Thérèse Maillard, who had been persuaded to represent the Goddess of Reason.

For Mlle Maillard the experience was an unpleasant ordeal. A confirmed royalist at heart, she had to keep her disgust to herself. When Laïs first recommended her, she had begged to be excused, but Chaumette had intervened to exert more powerful persuasion, resorting to a barely veiled threat.

'Very well, citizeness,' he told her, 'but if you refuse, you can't complain if we treat you as an *ordinary mortal*'.[17]

In the event it proved to be 'a chaste ceremony – sad, dry and boring'.[18] The weather did not help. There was a biting chill in the morning air when a convoy of open carts arrived to take the participants to the *ci-devant* Cathedral, the women shivering in their thin dresses and everyone required to wear a red woollen Phrygian-style bonnet, which at least kept the head warm. The focus of the secular oratorio was a Temple of Reason, hurriedly constructed of wood, set up in the Chancel. From this Mlle Maillard made her entrance, clad in a sky-blue cloak over a plain white dress, to listen to a Hymn to Reason (written specially for the occasion by Marie-Joseph Chénier to music by Méhul) as a troupe of young girls walked in procession before her.

Since pressure of business had prevented the members of the Convention from attending the ceremony, Mlle Maillard – a striking figure with her hair loose about her shoulders – was noisily conveyed through the streets to the Tuileries, to be borne aloft into the Convention chamber in the middle of a debate. There Chaumette welcomed her with such a flowery oration that the Convention acclaimed on the spot his proposal to dedicate Notre Dame to the Cult of Reason.

It was a festive occasion, but not an unruly one. Much less orderly was the scene enacted at the Convention the following day, when a mob of *sansculottes* turned up, many of them wearing pillaged church robes in which they proceeded to dance the *Carmagnole*.

Mlle Maillard was by no means the only Goddess of Reason. Another was the delectable young dancer, Angélique Aubry, whom a connoisseur was later to recall having seen 'seated on the High Altar in the guise of Liberty – a liberty taken to such a length that you could see through her costume as clearly as I can see the sculpted figure of St Peter on the chan-

[16] Bournonville, 650, apparently recording the reminiscences of Pierre Laurent.

[17] Castil-Blaze, *Académie*, II, 23.

[18] Michelet, book XIV, chapter III.

cel wall.'[19] It is possible that Mlle Aubry portrayed Reason when, on 30 November 1793, the personnel of the Opéra celebrated a Festival of Reason under the direction of Gardel at the Church of St. Roch, which had been transformed into a Temple of Philosophy.

Meanwhile the war was going badly. Military reverses and the defection of General Dumouriez to the Austrians were heavy blows, but even more wounding to French pride was the occupation of Toulon by the English. Honour was only saved when, some months later, the enemy forces were ejected by the brilliant efforts of a young Corsican artillery major named Buonaparte. At last Paris had cause for rejoicing, and in March 1794 this victory was commemorated at the Opéra by a one-act historical cantata with music by Rochefort.

* * *

As the Reign of Terror mounted in ferocity, those with political connections had good reason to be anxious for their safety. Gardel was no longer just a dancer and composer of ballets, but a prominent member of the Opéra's governing Committee, and with others jointly responsible for its policy. So when an official messenger called on 11 March 1794 to serve a summons to attend the Committee of Public Safety 'without delay ... to give such information as is required in the interests of the State',[20] he might have been understandably nervous as he hurried to the Tuileries, where that feared and all-powerful body settled the nation's destiny and the fate of so many of its citizens. The possibility of his being accused of some offence against the Revolution may well have crossed his mind. There is no record of what transpired at his interview, but the date of the summons suggests it was connected with reports, received that same day, of an insurrection being planned by the Cordeliers.

The Cordeliers represented the far left of the political spectrum. In contrast to the other revolutionary clubs such as the Jacobins, they provided the voice and the driving force of the embittered working class, the *sansculottes*. They controlled the sections into which Paris was divided, and exercised a dominant influence on the Commune. Their ability to call out a mob had been demonstrated all too often by disturbances that shattered the fragile calm of the city. Marat had been a dominant member until his assassination in the summer of 1793, and the leading figures were now the two politicians most closely involved with the Opéra, Chaumette and Hébert. But on this occasion the discovery of the planned

[19] Touchard-Lafosse, *Pudeur*, IV, 174.

[20] Arch. Nat., F^7 4715. Summons dated 21 Ventôse, Year II (19 March 1794).

insurrections was to seal their fate: less than two weeks later they and many of their followers were taken to the guillotine.

Gardel may have been given a fright, but the summons was more likely connected with a new production to be presented at the Opéra. This materialised three and a half weeks later, on 5 April 1794, under the title *La Réunion du 10 août*. Described as a '*sansculottide*' and dedicated to 'the people', it reproduced one by one the various stages of the ambulatory Festival of Republican Reunion which, eight months previously, had wound its way through the streets from one historical revolutionary site to another: the Place de la Bastille, the Boulevard des Italiens, the Place de la République, the Place des Invalides and finally the Champ de Mars, where a large crowd had foregathered to swear an oath to defend the Constitution.

The stage version at the Opéra could only be a pale reflection of the original, but it was remarkable for Gardel's dance scenes. There was nothing conventionally balletic about his dances, which portrayed army gunners, market porters and their women, and ordinary villagers, but the entrance of the porters had caused a storm of delight, for never before had working men been depicted so sympathetically on the stage:

> May we be forgiven [wrote the critic of the *Journal de Paris*] for recalling that in former times – that is, four or five years ago – it was not possible to present such persons on the stage unless to demean them. In this piece, on the other hand, their everyday clothes and movements are faithfully reproduced, with no attempt at caricature, and such a realistic rendering only adds to the interest. Seeing a man whose life is wholly dedicated to useful work taking part in a recreation that does not come to him naturally, we may smile at his gaffes, but after a moment's reflection his impetuosity and lack of concern for the conventions command our respect and add to the general rejoicing in which he is taking part.[21]

* * *

There was no more celebrated theatre architect living than Victor Louis. The Grand Théâtre he had designed for Bordeaux was, as it still is, one of the greatest monuments of that beautiful city, but the theatre he built in Paris shortly before the Revolution for Marguerite de Montansier, director

[21] *Journal de Paris*, 21 Germinal, Year II (10 April 1794).

of a nation-wide theatrical empire, was architecturally of lesser merit. This was due to circumstances beyond his control: not only was he given a more restricted budget, but the works had to be completed in a matter of months. Furthermore, the site on the Rue de la Loi (as the Rue de Richelieu had been renamed) facing the Bibliothèque Nationale, while being ideally central, was restricted. Nevertheless, although its exterior was plain and severe, the auditorium was beautiful, and the stage spacious and equipped with the latest machinery, including novel facilities for raising and lowering cloths without winding them on rollers. The dimensions of the theatre indicated the purpose for which Mlle Montansier intended to use it, as did the statues of comedy, tragedy, music and dance that were placed in niches cut in the proscenium arch on each side of the stage.

The theatre had been opened in August 1793, and Sébastien Gallet had staged a suitably revolutionary ballet, *La Fête civique*, for the occasion. But for all her protestations of loyalty to the Republic, Mlle Montansier suffered from the irredeemable handicap of having enjoyed the favour of Marie-Antoinette. Covetous eyes were soon directed towards her new theatre, and the infamous Hébert launched a venomous attack on her in *Le Père Duchesne*. Ranting that every stone of the building was 'cemented with the blood of the people', he called for her arrest as a suspected person. This tirade was soon echoed by his colleague, Chaumette, who denounced her for building the theatre not only with funds deriving from the former Queen, but worse still, with British gold, and with the ulterior motive of setting fire to the Bibliothèque Nationale across the street!

In the highly charged political atmosphere of the time, these attacks led to Mlle Montansier's arrest and the closure of her theatre. The authorities seemed in no hurry to bring her to trial, which may have saved her life, but not her theatre. For before she was freed in August 1794, it had been compulsorily acquired by order of the Committee of Public Safety for the use of the Opéra.

For the Opéra, this move solved a long-standing problem. For the past thirteen years, it had been situated – very inconveniently, as all were agreed – some distance to the north of the centre of Paris, alongside the Porte Saint-Martin. This had come about through an unfortunate accident of timing. When the previous theatre in the Palais-Royal had burned down in 1781, the Treasury was in a parlous state, and the erection of a suitable permanent theatre to take its place could not be contemplated. Consequently it had been found expedient to take advantage of an offer from a speculator-architect to construct a provisional theatre by the Porte Saint-Martin at only a fraction of the cost of rebuilding it in the Palais-Royal. The inconvenience of the new site very quickly became apparent, and over the years a number of proposals for a move had been made but not followed through. More recently, Francoeur and Cellerier had hopes that the former royal stables and riding school might be assigned to them, only to see them commandeered instead for the National Assembly.

All through the winter and into the spring and summer of 1794 the political scene was in a perpetual state of flux. In the Convention the two opposing factions, the extremist group known as the Montagnards and the more moderate Girondins, faced one another in bitter and unresolvable enmity. Increasingly the nation became ruled by a policy of fear, with the guillotine claiming more and more victims, often several tumbril-loads in a day. Not even members of the Convention were exempt; in October, twenty-one leaders of the Girondins were taken to the scaffold, and in the following April the charismatic Danton was executed. The toll rose alarmingly in the summer of 1794 until the tide suddenly turned against the Terror's evil genius. During a single extraordinary day, all the pent-up resentment against Robespierre surfaced, courage returned to the Convention, and the fear he had sown in its members' hearts vanished. He was guillotined the next day, and after a few more executions, the frightful blood-letting ceased.

It had taken several months, from the day when Montansier's company vacated their theatre to its reopening as the Opéra's eighth home, for the necessary repair and conversion works to be carried out. When the Opéra gave its first performance there on 7 August 1794, the façade bore prominently its new official name, 'Théâtre des Arts', and to everyone's delight, the public discovered that the pit had been raked and provided with benches for the first time. This was a long-overdue innovation, for not only had the jostling and discomfort of the standing spectators provoked fights and other disturbances, but even in the quieter moments an unceasing rumble had risen from the pit as its occupants shuffled to and fro in their efforts to gain a better view. Certainly, there still remained an undercurrent of chatter from the boxes and elsewhere, for absolute silence had not yet become a rule of correct behaviour; but the spectator intent on enjoying the opera or the ballet to the full was certainly much better off.

In the aftermath of Thermidor – the month of Robespierre's fall – the flame of the Revolution continued to burn, but with a less lurid hue. As a sop to the *sansculotte* element, production of patriotic pieces continued, and two works of this kind followed in quick succession. The first, a one-act opera by Grétry called *Denys le tyrant*, was about a king who became a pedagogue, and introduced dancers portraying pupils disrespectfully leaping on to his shoulders and trying to bring him down. This bit of horseplay was about the only point of interest in an otherwise dull and soon forgotten little work.

La Rosière republicain, also by Grétry, was hardly more remarkable. The explosion of a powder magazine at Grenelle caused its first performance to be cancelled, and alterations had to be made at the behest of the Committee of Public Safety. Its plot reflects the process of de-Christianisation that still remained official policy. The setting is a closed church, before which a group of women, gathering in the hope of hearing mass, fall to their knees and begin to pray. The church door then opens to reveal the statue of Reason, in whose honour a hymn is sung to the accompaniment of the Opéra's new organ, which was being played for the first time. Finally a priest joins in the popular celebrations, throwing off his soutane to reveal the costume of a *sansculotte*. And who better to represent this character than that confirmed republican, Laïs, holding aloft the red bonnet of Liberty as he makes a dashing exit to present it to the Pope! The final ballet was as long as the rest of the piece, but it was

> pleasing and full of very ingenious ideas .... One very merry scene was that of two nuns who are making their way to the church to hear Mass, and a citizen who tries to bar their way, in which, not without some difficulty, he is successful. Little by little [the nuns] become infected by the rejoicing around them ... and finally they join in the *Carmagnole*.[22]

The two nuns were enchantingly played by Pérignon and Duchemin; they came on, very solemn and demure, but were soon carried away when Auguste Vestris came bounding out of the wings at his most ebullient to tempt them into sharing the happiness of the people. It was an innocent scene, which caused little offence and for some at least banished for a few minutes thoughts of the harsh conditions of the world outside.

[22] *Journal de Paris*, 4 September 1794.

2

A Still-born Revolutionary Ballet

'Authors of operas worked hard for the *sansculottes*,' remarked Castil-Blaze in his history of the Opéra. 'But why did choreographers do nothing but compose *divertissements* for those operas and paraphrase patriotic songs in *entrechats*? Why was there not at least one great Republican ballet?' He then proceeded to offer an explanation, which he may have had from Pierre Gardel himself, whom he acknowledged among those who had provided him with information:

> At the unanimous request of men of power and champions of Liberty, Citizen Gardel had composed *Guillaume Tell*, a ballet-pantomime in three acts which had great merit from the points of view of drama, the variety of its episodes, its dances, costumes and scenery, and was more highly regarded by its creator than his other works. The scenario was submitted to the Committee of Public Safety, who accepted it with unanimous enthusiasm. Its production called for an expenditure of 50,000 francs, and this sum was promptly placed at the disposal of the directing municipality. It would have been impossible to act more swiftly or generously. But alas, when the time came to construct Gessler's palace and William's cottage, the 50,000 francs had vanished. Two weeks later the money was replaced, only to be purloined by the same hands, and no one was curious or indiscreet enough to try and trace it to the new shelter where it had been placed. So with the money gone, there could be no Swiss hero and no ballet, and *Guillaume Tell* returned to its author's portfolio.[1]

There can be little doubt that the money that was paid twice over to the Commune from government funds was misapplied, probably as handouts for stirring up insurrections in the streets.

Since the power of the Commune disappeared with the fall of Robespierre, *Guillaume Tell* was probably conceived by Gardel in 1793. At

[1] Castil-Blaze, *Académie*, II, 42.

that moment the figure of William Tell, the inspirational hero of Swiss legend who led the revolt against the Habsburg oppressors in the fourteenth century, offered a striking parallel with the situation in which France now found herself, facing an Austrian army encamped on the frontier with the declared aim of restoring the Old Régime.

French theatre-goers were already familiar with the legend. Some thirty years before, Lemierre had written a tragedy which the Comédie-Française had been forced by public demand to revive in 1790, and the following year Sedaine provided Grétry with a libretto for an *opéra-comique* that enjoyed similar success at the Comédie-Italienne.

Fired with revolutionary idealism and with the expectation of powerful support from the Committee of Public Safety, Gardel had set to work with a will on his own adaptation. Three versions of his scenario that survive in the papers of the Opéra[2] attest to his painstaking method of working out in advance the fine detail of the pantomime.

With its fast-moving action, a suspense maintained until the very last scene and the touching depiction of the love that bound Tell and his family, it might have enjoyed even greater success than either the tragedy or the *opéra-comique* and become a mainstay of the Opéra's ballet repertory. Certainly it would have lasted longer than the hastily got-up revolutionary spectacles on which Gardel was to waste so much of his energy at this stage of his career. If he could have successfully interwoven passages of dance into the complex pantomime, it might even have surpassed his three neo-classical masterpieces in popularity and longevity, not only because it brought on to the stage characters with whom all levels of the public could identify, but because it would not have suffered when Neo-Classicism went out of fashion.

Being a highly proficient musician, Gardel must have given careful thought to the music that would accompany the action. Had he followed the same procedure as in his earlier ballets, he would have required a score made up largely of various numbers selected by himself, particularly for the dramatic high-points. One can only conjecture whom he might have chosen as his collaborator: Méhul, perhaps, with whom he had already worked closely, or Grétry, who was also well-known to him, and from whose *opéra-comique* he could have borrowed some melodies to help the audience follow the pantomime.

Gardel's professional concern for the musical side of his work is apparent in the opening paragraph of his scenario, where he gives specific directions for the overture:

[2] Arch. Nat., AJ^{13} 1023.

> The overture must express, first, the peace that reigned in the three cantons of Uri, Schwyz and Underwalden before Gessler's arrival; secondly, the Governor's tyranny; thirdly, the storm; fourthly, the complaints of the oppressed population; and fifthly, the joys of tranquillity.

The curtain then rises on the first act to reveal a Swiss valley, with a castle on the mountainside in the middle distance. This is the seat of the hated Gessler, the tyrannical Governor who rules the land on behalf of the Habsburg Emperor. In the foreground is a fine mansion belonging to the Swiss patriot Stouffacher,[3] and to the left, on a small eminence, is a farmhouse. Gessler finds the sight of the prosperous mansion offensive. True to his vicious character, he turns out the owner and his wife and expropriates it. Leaving his soldiers to pillage it, he returns to his castle. William Tell is then seen approaching from the mountains, accompanied by his wife and son. There follows a sentimental scene in which Tell and his wife seek likenesses of each other in the little boy's features; they kiss him tenderly, believing him to be asleep, and are embarrassed when they realise he has been awake all the time. Tell, an expert archer, gives the boy a lesson in the use of the bow.

A happy band of harvesters then arrives. Their working day is over, and the farmer, Henry de Melchtal, provides a meal to reward them for their labours. Young William makes off with the reed pipe belonging to one of the harvesters, and, from a spot where he believes himself to be unobserved, tries to play it. The villagers are mystified as to the source of the sound, but Tell, who has espied the little rascal, pulls him from his hiding place and delivers him up to the judgement of the elders. The boy is ordered to stand on the table and play the *chant des vaches*.[4] Several of the cowherds get up and dance to this ancient folk tune, after which the boy joins his parents in a 'picturesque' *pas de trois*, 'entirely in the Swiss character', as Gardel specifies. Another popular dance follows – a type of *Bödele* – to be performed in clogs and with poles that are struck against one another in time to the music.

These festivities are broken up by Gessler. Tell manages to conceal his

[3] Werner Stauffacher and Arnold of Melchthal (Stouffacher and Arnoul de Melchtal in the scenario) are historical characters who distinguished themselves in the revolt leading to the liberation of the three cantons in 1307. The names of Tell and Gessler appear in no records and are probably legendary. The story of William Tell can be dated back to the fifteenth century, and was given its present form by the historian Tschudi, a century later.

[4] This echoed a scene at the beginning of Grétry's *opéra-comique* in which Tell's son is seen sitting on the mountainside playing on his pipes the *Ranz aux vaches* which Swiss cowherds play when tending their cattle. Grétry based this number on the version given in Rousseau's *Dictionnaire de musique*.

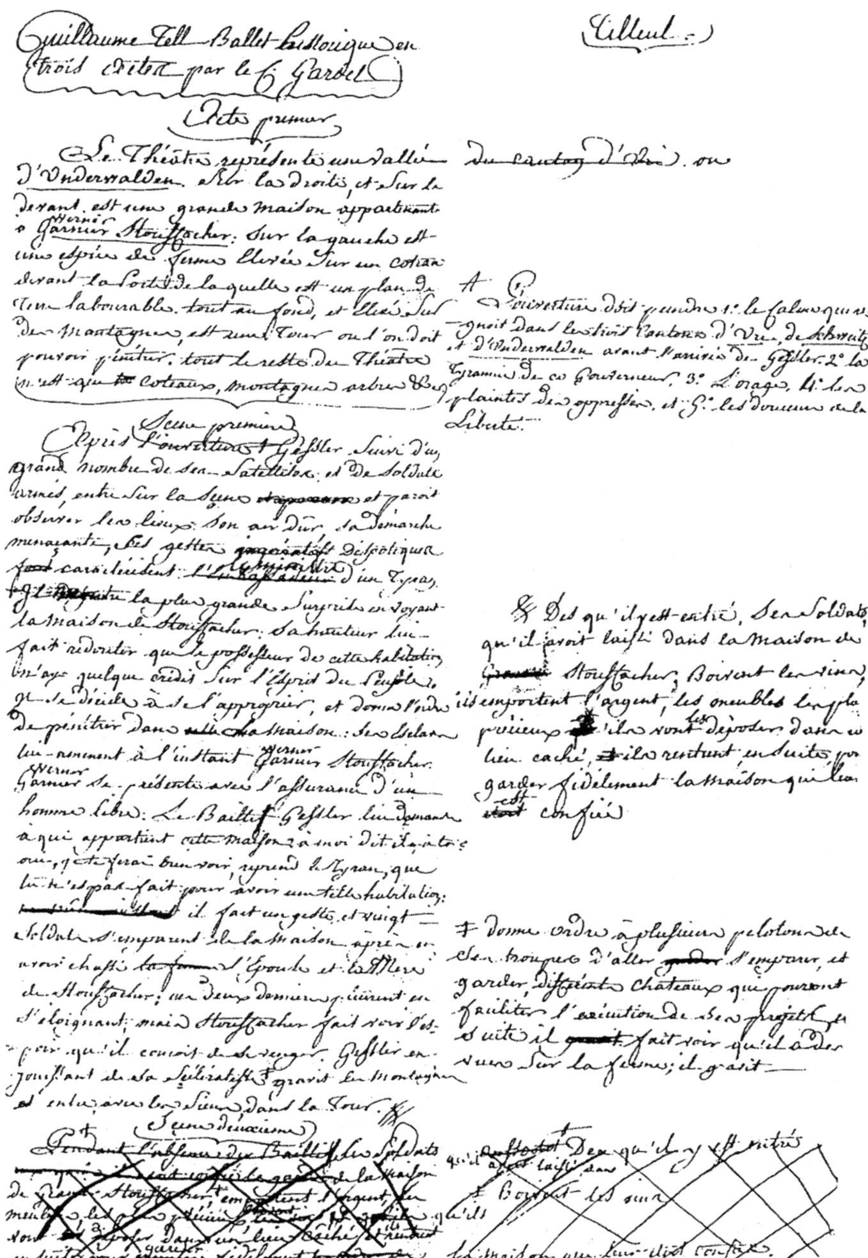

Guillaume Tell Ballet historique en trois actes par le C. Gardel

Tilleul

Acte premier

Le Théâtre représente une vallée du canton d'Uri ou d'Underwalden. Sur la droite, et sur le devant, est une grande maison appartenant à Werner Stouffacher: sur la gauche est une espèce de ferme élevée sur un coteau devant la porte de laquelle est un plan de terre labourable. tout au fond, et élevé sur des montagnes, est une tour où l'on doit pouvoir pénétrer. tout le reste du Théâtre n'est que coteaux, montagnes arbres &c.

A. L'ouverture doit peindre 1° le calme qui régnoit dans les trois cantons d'Uri, de Schwitz et d'Underwalden avant l'arrivée de Gessler. 2° la tyrannie de ce Gouverneur, 3° l'orage, 4° les plaintes des opprimés, et 5° les douceurs de la Liberté.

Scène première

Après l'ouverture Gessler suivi d'un grand nombre de ses satellites et de soldats armés, entre sur la scène et paroit observer les lieux. Son air dur, sa démarche menaçante, ses gestes despotiques caractérisent [illegible] d'un Tyran. Il [illegible] la plus grande surprise en voyant la maison de Stouffacher. Sa hauteur lui fait redouter que le possesseur de cette habitation n'ait quelque crédit sur l'esprit du peuple. Il se décide à se l'approprier, et donne l'ordre de pénétrer dans la maison: ses soldats lui amènent à l'instant Werner Stouffacher. Werner se présente avec l'assurance d'un homme libre. Le Bailli Gessler lui demande à qui appartient cette maison? à moi dit-il [illegible] oui, je te ferai bien voir, reprend le Tyran, que tu n'es pas fait pour avoir une telle habitation: il fait un geste, et vingt soldats s'emparent de la maison après en avoir chassé la femme, l'épouse et la mère de Stouffacher; ces deux dernières pleurent en s'éloignant; mais Stouffacher fait voir l'espoir qu'il conçoit de se venger. Gessler jouissant de sa scélératesse gravit la montagne et entre avec les siens dans la tour.

& Dès qu'il y est entré, ses soldats qu'il avoit laissé dans la maison de Stouffacher, boivent le vin, ils emportent l'argent, les meubles les plus précieux ils vont les déposer dans un lieu caché, ils rentrent ensuite pour garder fidèlement la maison qui leur est confiée.

‡ donne ordre à plusieurs pelotons de ses troupes d'aller s'emparer, et garder, différents chateaux qui pourront faciliter l'exécution de ses projets; ensuite il fait voir qu'il a des vues sur la femme; il gravit —

Scène deuxième

A typical example of Gardel's painstaking revision of the text of a scenario, in this case the opening of his unperformed Guillaume Tell. *(Archives Nationales, AJ[13] 1023)*

anger, but as he leaves he fixes Gessler with a scornful glare. Melchtal tells his son Arnoul to plough the field in front of the farmhouse. Coveting the powerful team of oxen, Gessler orders his men to seize them. As an officer proceeds to cut the traces, Arnoul, in desperation at the threat to his livelihood, strikes him with his staff. Fearful of the consequences, Melchtal advises his son to make himself scarce. Gessler, having learnt of the assault, returns with a band of soldiers. Melchtal refuses to disclose his son's whereabouts, and is thereupon blinded. On this horrific climax the act closes, with the old man being half-carried back to his farmhouse by his daughters.

Act II is set in the town square of Altdorf, with Lake Lucerne seen in the background. Tell and Stouffacher meet, and are sharing their outrage at the Governor's brutality when Arnoul enters with the news of his father's blinding. The old man himself then enters with his daughters, and on being informed of the identity of the two men with his son, leads all three to the front of the stage and, taking three swords from beneath his doublet, makes them swear to deliver their cantons from the monstrous oppressor. This tableau, which Gardel specifically directed was to reproduce faithfully the attitudes of the characters in David's celebrated painting of the Horatius brothers, was a moment that was no doubt to be frozen in a tableau long enough to make the reference clear.

The scene has been observed by a squad of Gessler's soldiers, too few to risk trying to make an arrest, for the square is now beginning to fill with townsfolk. Arnoul harangues the people, who respond by swearing to overturn the Governor. Gessler himself arrives with a strong troop of soldiers, but has no cause to arrest any of the three men, as they are not bearing arms. For a moment he seems thwarted, but his anger returns; to show who is the master, he has his cap placed on a pole in the middle of the square. He then issues an order that every passer-by must pay the same respect to the cap as is due to his own person, and sentries are posted to see that this order is carried out. Tell finds it hard to credit such an act of folly, and when Gessler orders him to comply, he responds by shooting the cap off the pole with an arrow. Gessler orders Tell to be arrested and taken to the scaffold. The people are dumbfounded. Tell's wife tries to snatch her husband from his guards. Young William clasps his father's knees, sobbing. Tell lifts him into the air, 'darting a terrible look at the tyrant. Tell's wife trembles, the Governor pales, and the populace ... freezes in a state of terror at this tableau.'

Gessler judges it prudent to pardon Tell, but demands proof of his skill with the bow. Tell must shoot an arrow into an apple placed on his son's head. Tell would rather die than take such a risk of injuring his son, but can only comply when Gessler's men seize the boy and threaten to do him harm. There are tearful moments as Tell's wife hands over the boy, and Tell leads him to a tree, where he blindfolds him and cautions him to remain perfectly still. Gessler hands Tell his bow and arrows. As he places the apple on the boy's head, and noticing that Gessler's attention has been momentarily diverted, Tell conceals a second arrow in his clothing, with a clear indication of its purpose, should he injure his son. After a short prayer, Tell looses an arrow, which finds its mark with unerring accuracy.

There is a moment of joyful relief, but it is short-lived, for Gessler has perceived the concealed arrow. Too proud to deny its purpose, Tell is seized and taken to a boat, where he is lashed to the mast. He is to be incarcerated in the Tower of Küsnacht at the far end of the lake. As the boat departs, his wife is restrained from throwing herself into the water only by the tearful protestations of her son.

For Act III the action has moved to the area around Tell's house, which stands to the left of the stage and is to be so constructed, according to Gardel's direction, as to allow the audience to observe what is happening inside. The lake is seen in the background, and jutting into its waters is an enormous rock at the foot of a massive cliff. In another note for the composer, Gardel specifies that the orchestra must convey 'the uttermost depths of grief with affecting tones,' as Tell's wife, her hair loose, and weeping copiously, is accompanied to her home by her friends. Once inside, she cradles her little boy to sleep, and watches over him while a terrible storm breaks outside. The boat in which Tell is being taken to the fortress comes into view, tossing on the troubled surface of the lake. Tell is the only experienced sailor among the occupants; to save all aboard from certain disaster, Gessler has Tell's bonds removed so that he can take the helm. Skilfully Tell steers the boat towards the shore. Taking advantage of a moment when Gessler and the guards lose their balance at a great clap of thunder, he leaps on to the rock, at the same time pushing the boat away with his foot. It seems inevitable that the frail craft must be smashed to pieces with the loss of all aboard. Tell's wife, who has witnessed this scene, is overcome with joy. She runs out with her son, but the cliff separates her from her husband. Standing on the rock, Tell takes out his horn and sounds the signal for the cantons to rise in revolt. Answering calls inform him that his summons has been heard, and that the fight for liberation is about to begin.

But Gessler and his men have survived, and Tell's wife and son return to be faced by the tyrant. They seek shelter in their house, but Gessler locks the door against them and orders his men to set it on fire. Tell's wife retreats before the advancing flames. Her first thought is for her boy; she protects him from the flames as best she can, and in desperation places him in a bucket, which she lowers into the indoor well, tying the rope around her waist. Outside, Gessler, while giving orders to his men as they engage in battle with the Swiss, contemplates the pleasurable prospect of his enemy returning to find his home and his family destroyed.

The great battle swings this way and that until finally one of Tell's arrows finds its mark in the tyrant's breast. Tell returns to the remains of his home to find his wife safe, but no sign of his beloved boy. His wife then shows him the rope around her waist, and with it he pulls up the bucket, with his son inside unharmed. A desperate remnant of Gessler's forces makes a last effort to kill Tell, but with redoubled strength he floors them all. The battle now reaches its final phase. Gessler's soldiers are routed, and the infamous Tower of Küsnacht bursts into flames. Amid general rejoicing, 'Tell, in the centre of the stage, with his arm linked with his wife's and his son on his shoulder, places his foot on Gessler's corpse. All the inhabitants of the reunited cantons form a tableau in the presence of their prisoners, uttering a warning to make all tyrants tremble: "Victory is ours!"'

The scenario is all that has survived of Gardel's conception. The only indication of the dance passages is the description of the dances in the first act. It is known, however, that Gardel was contemplating two ballet insertions, but the scenario is silent about the other one, which was undoubtedly to take the form of a celebratory *divertissement* at the end.

Nor is it known how he proposed to cast the characters. No doubt he would have reserved the part of Tell for himself had the ballet been produced promptly, but by 1801 he may have had Auguste Vestris in mind. Marie Gardel would have been the certain choice for the part of Tell's wife; their son would presumably have been played by a talented child. An experienced mime, such as Milon or Goyon, would have been needed for the major rôle of Gessler, and Beaupré might have been cast as Henry de Melchtal, with Nivelon or André Deshayes as Arnoul.

But all this is conjecture. There is more evidence of how the ballet might have looked, for Gardel's descriptions of the scenery are specific enough to stir one's imagination. The last act, with the burning of Tell's house, must have posed a daunting challenge for Degotti (who had succeeded Pâris as chief scene designer) and his colleague, the machinist Boullet, and one can only regret that they were never allowed to put their combined ingenuity to the test.

*   *   *

Production of the ballet had first been aborted by the chicanery of the Commune. It then languished during the Reign of Terror. It was clearly not abandoned, but shortage of funds and the general uncertainty resulted in one delay after another. The earliest mention of *Guillaume Tell* in the surviving records of the Opéra appears in a minute of its Committee dated 28 November 1795. Referring to an earlier decision, it directed that *Guillaume Tell* and the opera, *Hécube*, were to be the first new works to be staged, the latter to be given priority because the recent revival of *Psyché* was drawing good houses.[5] These plans failed to materialise, and the summer of 1797 found Gardel pressing the Artistes' Committee to make decisions with a view to 'purifying the Opéra'. In particular he advised that a revival of *Le Jugement de Pâris*, with some additions, could be ready in two months' time, and *Guillaume Tell* a month after that.[6]

By April 1798, nearly a year later, *Tell* was still not ready, no doubt for the usual reason: lack of funds. A new administration had by then been installed, and it was noted that the designs for the scenery of *Tell* had all been outlined on cloths, and two-thirds of the sets were finished. When the Government Commissioner overseeing the Opéra requested a plan of action to place before his Minister, Gardel's hopes rose, and the list of productions that was consequently drawn up included the ballet of *Guillaume Tell*.[7]

However, economies were needed to bring order to the affairs of the Opéra; the scenery budget for *Tell* was reduced by 15 per cent, and not until November 1799 was Gardel authorised to begin work, with a view to the ballet being given at the end of the year.[8] But by that time Gardel had become preoccupied with another new ballet, *La Dansomanie*, and nearly two more years were to elapse before the question of *Tell* came up again.

In the summer of 1801 the plans for the coming winter included two new ballets by Gardel, *Daphnis et Pandrose* and *Achille à Scyros*.[9] However, neither of them could be ready in time, so *Tell* resurfaced to fill the gap. That August, Gardel's scenario was considered by the Opéra's new Selection Jury, which made no decision, taking the view that ballet-panto-

[5] Arch. Nat., AJ[13] 48 (I). Extract from Committee minutes, 7 Frimaire, Year IV (28 November 1795). The minute was signed by, among others, Gardel, Vestris and Nivelon. Milcent's *Hécube* was to be more fortunate than *Guillaume Tell*, being eventually produced in 1800.

[6] Arch. Nat., AJ[13] 48 (II). Note for the Committee, 23 Prairial, Year V (11 June 1797).

[7] Arch. Nat., AJ[13] 44. Report to Minister of the Interior, and Committee Minutes dated 27 Germinal, Year VI (16 April 1798).

[8] Arch. Nat., AJ[13] 51. Minutes of Meeting of the Administrators, 1 Frimaire, Year VII (22 November 1799).

[9] Arch. Nat., AJ[13] 51. Bonet to Minister of the Interior, 29 Prairial, Year IX (18 June 1801).

mimes did not fall within their remit.[10] This seems to have cleared the way for *Tell*, the production of which was re-costed to include nearly 130 costumes, with a maximum limit of 32,000 francs. It was reported that the scenery would take about two months to complete, and then the ballet could be presented very quickly.[11]

But once again *Tell* was to be shelved. Gardel was now working on other, newer projects, and was perhaps losing interest. Also, times had changed. The coming to power of Napoleon Bonaparte signalled not only a change of régime, but the introduction of a new political philosophy. Republican France had now become an autocracy, and the image of a people struggling to free itself from foreign domination no longer accorded with the official line.

Many years later, in 1812, Gardel would present his scenario to Napoleon, who was mildly attracted by the subject but preferred an alternative proposal: for a ballet based on the biblical story of the Prodigal Son. By then nearly twenty years had passed since Gardel had begun work on the story of the Swiss liberator, and with a disappointed sigh of resignation he finally brought himself to accept that this long-cherished project would remain unrealised.

[10] Arch. Nat., AJ^{13} 44 (IV).

[11] Arch. Nat., AJ^{13} 51. Note by Cellerier, written in Fructidor, Year IX (August/September 1801).

3

Rays of Hope in Difficult Times

In 1800, thinking back over the previous seven years, Gardel was to feel the need to explain his lack of productivity after the extraordinary explosion of creative energy that had produced three great ballets in rapid succession in the early years of the Revolution.

> Since 3 March 1793 (old style), when I presented my last work, the ballet *Pâris*, [he confessed] I have remained in a state of apparent idleness. Often have I lost hope; my friends complained, and others accused me of sterility. I faced my despair by making excuses, which were quite lame, and responded to my friends' complaints by giving reasons, good ones, for such idleness, leaving everyone else free to speak and write as they wished (which they did).[1]

This was a *cri de coeur* from a man who was first and foremost a creative artist. Certainly there lay behind him seven frustrating years of apparent sterility; but if we take a broader and kinder view, idleness was the last failing he could be accused of. For in those seven years of unprecedented political and social instability he had made a vital, even indispensable, contribution to his art. Not only had he preserved the ballet of the Opéra intact, but he had raised its quality and prestige to such a peak that the public's appreciation of the ballet disturbed the delicate balance that bound singers and dancers at the Opéra in a common endeavour.

Vested with an executive authority that went far beyond the duties he had taken on when originally appointed ballet-master, he must have found himself at times quite overwhelmed by administrative and financial worries. But being in the forefront of those principal artistes who had long pressed for the responsibility of administering their own theatre, there was little else he could honourably do but follow where his ambition and his destiny led him.

What neither he nor anyone else could have foreseen at the outset were

[1] Preface to the programme of *La Dansomanie* (Paris, 1800).

the financial consequences that followed in the wake of the Revolution. The Artistes' Committee had first been entrusted with running the Opéra in 1793. Their first year, which coincided with the Terror, had closed with a large deficit, mainly because of unforeseen increases in costs, although salaries had not kept up with inflation. When the régime of the Artistes' Committee was renewed in 1794 with a monthly subsidy of 30,000 *livres*, the Government authorised the raising of a loan of 500,000 *livres* to clear outstanding debts, increase salaries, and pay for new productions. Gardel then nobly placed his purse where his heart lay, contributing 10,000 *livres*, as did Marie Miller; while his colleague, Nivelon, who was apparently more flush, pitched in with double that sum.

The régime of the Artistes' Committee was interrupted in the summer of 1796 when the Government appointed four independent directors, headed by one La Chabeaussière, to take over. A year later that team was dismissed and the Artistes' Committee reinstated, only to be again deprived of its functions when it became hopelessly insolvent in the spring of 1798.

Those were times of incessant political turmoil and uncertainty, with the nation still at war with at least one of the great European powers. Although the Reign of Terror had ended with the fall of Robespierre in July 1794, there was no immediate return to stability. Shorn of many of its members, who either had been guillotined or were languishing in prison, the Convention was still committed to the Revolution.

That winter, however, the extremism that had so frequently turned political debates into a life-and-death struggle began to abate – not that calm returned to the long-suffering city. The power of the Commune may have been destroyed, but misery and famine continued to haunt the more densely populated districts, and the spectre of mob violence could still be aroused. In April 1795 the Convention was again invaded by a mob, which was ejected, happily without bloodshed, by the National Guard; and a few weeks later the dreaded tolling of the tocsin announced a more dangerous uprising, which was only quelled with the help of the Army. The intervention of professional troops introduced a new force on the political scene, as was unmistakably demonstrated a few months later when the new Constitution was being introduced. In a day of bitter street fighting, the scales were turned in the Convention's favour by a volley of grapeshot, fired on the order of General Bonaparte at an armed band standing defiant on the steps of the Church of Saint-Roch. Thus, in blood, was the new régime of the Directoire inaugurated; it would last four years, its end being eventually brought about by the very soldier who had assisted so dramatically at its birth.

* * *

In the summer of 1794, when the Opéra moved to its new quarters in the Rue de la Loi, it found itself much closer to the epicentre of political turmoil; but its doors were never broken by disturbances, and its regular round of performances continued virtually undisturbed. The cooler political temperature following the fall of Robespierre was welcomed by the growing majority who preferred their arts to be unalloyed by partisan propaganda; while for the artistes themselves, particularly the principals, political feelings were subsumed to their professional calling.

The Artistes' Committee was not slow to recognise this change, and in the spring of 1795 it was complimented for having 'cast off the yoke of vandalism' and 'brought back several masterpieces such as *Castor et Pollux, Iphigénie en Aulide, Oedipe à Colonne*'.[2] The ballet was not overlooked either, and in that same year four old favourites were revived: *Le Déserteur* (last given in 1791), *La Chercheuse d'esprit* and *Mirza* (last given in 1792) and *Psyché* (last given in 1793).

Performances did not always pass without incident. Although the installation of benches in the pit had gone some way to restore calm in that part of the house, politically inspired interruptions had not altogether ceased. The famous revolutionary piece, *L'Offrande à la Liberté*, was still a regular item in the programmes, but the *Marseillaise* no longer aroused unanimous enthusiasm. The Jacobin Club had been closed towards the end of 1794, and early in 1795 there began to be heard another song, *Le Reveil du Peuple*. This had been adopted by the counter-revolutionary faction that was now coming into the open and flexing its muscles through street gangs of young toughs from the *jeunesse dorée*, known in the argot of the time as *muscadins*.

The strength of this reaction was demonstrated at the free performance on 14 July 1795. *L'Offrande à la Liberté* was included in the programme as a matter of course, and during the first verse of the *Marseillaise* a woman's voice was heard, shouting 'Bread!' in the shrieking tones of those *sansculotte* furies who not long before had made their influence felt in the galleries of the Convention and the Jacobin Club. This immediately sparked vociferous calls for *Le Reveil du Peuple*, which so startled the unfortunate singer that he dried up completely. That song was

[2] *Journal des théâtres et des fêtes nationales*, 9 Ventôse, Year III (10 March 1795).

then duly given to appease the audience, but when the first singer reappeared to sing the *Marseillaise*, he was so nervous that he sang off-key, drawing such a storm of protest that the curtain had to be lowered. Feelings were still high after the interval, and when the orchestra struck up the overture to *Télémaque*, such a clamour arose from the upper tiers that some of the ladies in the boxes took fright and began to leave. However, calm was eventually restored after *Le Reveil du Peuple* was sung once more, amid angry protests from above at the presence of *aristos*.[3]

Audience participation of this sort, which was a feature of theatregoing during the Revolution, had been almost unknown, at least at the Opéra, under the Old Régime. Since then the social structure had been virtually overturned. The Opéra had been seriously affected by the disappearance of the aristocracy, which in earlier times had formed the backbone of its audience and been a main source of its income. In those more carefree times, its affairs and productions had aroused an interest within society that was fed not only by serious and often lengthy analyses of new operas and ballets, but also by tittle-tattle about the singers and dancers. That society had now vanished. Of course there was still food enough for gossip, for others had risen to take the place of the aristocratic protectors of old; but frivolity had disappeared in the sterner morality of the Revolution. Also, public attention focused on weightier matters, and the newspapers and journals had little space for anything other than political and military news.

Thus, apart from attracting accounts of its propagandist offerings, the Opéra found itself no longer newsworthy at a time when it had been reduced to a state of near stagnation. The lack of firm direction and above all a chronic shortage of funds meant that new productions figured low in the list of priorities. The Opéra was thus forced to live on its fat – on favourite operas that could be revived without offending republican sentiment, and on the fortuitously strong repertory of ballet-pantomimes. *Télémaque*, *Psyché* and *Le Jugement de Pâris* consequently accumulated an extraordinary tally of performances in these few years.[4] But not a single opera or ballet[5] was created in 1795 or 1796; not until 1797 would a new opera – Grétry's *Anacréon* – be presented, and Paris was to wait two years longer before seeing a new ballet.

[3] Anon, *Paris pendant...1795*, III, 152-9.

[4] In the 10 years 1789–98, a total of 886 ballet performances were given, of which three works by Pierre Gardel accounted for 486 and seven by Maximilien Gardel for 364. The ballets most frequently performed were *Psyché* (224), *Télémaque* (187), *Mirza* (79) and *Le Jugement de Pâris* (75).

[5] A 'new *divertissement*' was given four times in 1794, but it had no title, and apparently never received a notice in the press.

It would hardly be fair to suggest that Gardel was suffering from 'choreographer's block'. The efforts to stage *Guillaume Tell* – a major project by any standard – consumed much of his energy throughout these years of apparent creative inactivity. Further, by his own admission this was not the only ballet scenario he had sketched out, for in the preface to *La Dansomanie* he admitted to having conceived several other projects for new ballets which 'lie in my portfolio groaning at being wasted'. But between the solitary task of composing a scenario and the practicalities of setting the action and devising the dances lay a barrier which, it seemed, he was unable to cross.

Whether this was because of external circumstances or caused by some psychological impediment, he did not divulge. But certainly he had his worries, in common with his fellow dancers. Under the Old Régime, not only was there no shortage of funds for new productions, but successful dancers such as himself were financially secure, their lives uncomplicated by politics. Now much of that stability had been pulled from under their feet. That the Opéra itself had survived was something to be thankful for, but Gardel had suffered heavily from the Revolution, losing 6,000 francs a year when pensions paid from the royal treasury were abolished.[6] Outwardly he accepted this with little complaint, but it nevertheless rankled. He had further suffered from the privations and effects of inflation that were the common lot of those who lived through the Revolution.

Gardel also had domestic concerns. His affair with Anne-Jacqueline Coulon[7] had cooled long before, and they had separated in 1789. Their two children, then aged five and two, had no doubt remained in their mother's care, but Gardel continued to fulfil his paternal responsibility towards them. By the end of 1793 Mlle Coulon was nearing the end of her career and finding it difficult to make ends meet, but her desperate plea to the Artistes' Committee to be promoted to *premier sujet* fell on stony ground.[8] Gardel had meanwhile turned for companionship to his former pupil, Marie Miller. Their relationship blossomed into love, and on

[6] This sum was made up of three pensions: 1200 francs as *danseur des ballets du Roi*, 500 francs as an academician, and 4300 francs granted to him by order of the King in 1785. The second pension was paid to him as a member of the Académie Royale de Danse. Although that Academy had ceased to be active some years before the Revolution, pensions continued to be paid to surviving Academicians until 1789.

[7] Guest, *Enlightenment*, 306–7. The note given there on Gardel's first family requires correction in that he and Mlle Coulon apparently never married, although the latter is described in the baptism certificates of the two children as Gardel's 'spouse'.

[8] Arch. Nat., AJ^{13} 54. Mlle Coulon to Committee, *'primedi nivôse, an II'*. She held the rank of *remplacement* in the *noble* genre until 1799, when she was demoted to *double*; she retired in 1801.

25 November 1794 she presented him with a daughter, Rose. They were married a year later on 24 December 1795, and another child, Achille, was to be born to them on 6 February 1800. It was to be an ideally happy marriage, a partnership in the truest sense.

* * *

Although the ballet repertory had been stagnating for want of funds, the strength of the ballet personnel was fully maintained throughout the 1790s, partly because of the lack of alternative opportunities at a time of war, when it was well nigh impossible to leave the country.

The male establishment of *premiers sujets*[9] remained unchanged, with Gardel representing the *noble* genre, Vestris the *demi-caractère*, and Nivelon the *comique*. The lion's share of the burden was shouldered without complaint by Vestris, now in his thirties and still brimful of vigour. Nivelon had passed his prime and would retire in 1799, while Gardel himself was increasingly troubled by injury and retired as a dancer at his own request in July 1796, voluntarily renouncing part of his salary, although continuing to appear in mime rôles.

Among the ladies of the ballet, Marie Gardel, *née* Miller, was the only one to have been appointed *premier sujet* before the Revolution. Her supremacy was not in jeopardy: not only was she the muse and companion of Pierre Gardel, but her artistry was beyond compare. However, coming rapidly into prominence behind her was a clutch of exceptionally talented young dancers, each determined to reach the uppermost rung of the ladder. By a curious coincidence, as if setting them apart as a group, their names all began with the same letter – Collomb, Chevigny, Clotilde, Chameroy – but each was a distinctive artiste in her own right.

The oldest was the diminutive Emilie Collomb. Born in 1768, she was already twenty-one at the outbreak of the Revolution. She was almost certainly trained from childhood by Jacques-François Deshayes, for she had begun her dancing career at the age of thirteen at the Comédie-Française, where he was ballet-master. It was he who signed her engagement there as a solo dancer in 1786; two years later she succeeded Mlle Mozon as *première danseuse*. For a dancer, the Comédie-Française was a modest arena by comparison with the Opéra; but at least she was not lost among a crowd, and she managed to catch the eye of Noverre when he

[9] The term *premier sujet* to denote a principal dancer was beginning to fall into disuse, giving way to *premier danseur* (in Years V, VI, VII and XI) or *danseur seul* (Year VIII) before the adoption of *premier artiste* first in Year IX, and then regularly from Year XII.

was in Paris in 1788, seeking dancers for the forthcoming London opera season. That trip to England was a turning point for her. For the first part of the season, before the arrival of Saulnier and Guimard, she was featured as principal ballerina, appearing in ballets by Noverre himself (*La Fête provençale*) and Didelot, and even being given a benefit – hopefully, early enough in the season for her to be paid before the theatre burnt down and the management went bankrupt.

It was undoubtedly this London success that led to her début at the Opéra as a *double* in January 1791. Three years later she was promoted to *remplacement* in the *comique* genre, her ambitions already fixed on succeeding Mme Pérignon, the *premier sujet* in possession. Her physique was ideal for her genre: Noverre described her as 'small of build', with stocky little legs that moved 'with infinite brilliance and facility', and as having a manner of dancing infused with an infectious sense of fun that was seductively appealing.[10]

Sophie Chevigny, whose forte was the *demi-caractère* and whom some saw as the most promising talent among this little band, was four years younger. Her principal teacher had been Favre-Guiardele, and she had acquired her early stage experience as a solo dancer at the Ambigu-Comique before entering the Opéra as a *double* in 1790 at the age of eighteen. She made a favourable impression on Gardel when she created the rôle of Flora in *Le Jugement de Pâris* in 1793, and the following year was raised to the intermediate rank of *premier sujet remplaçant*, understudying Marie Miller. Noverre was to describe her as 'attractive and engaging ... from every point of view':

> Her dancing is perfect, her execution lively and brilliant. The formation and linking of her steps are correct and well defined; she has strength and grace, and, as a dancer, combines all the qualities and charms that her art demands. But Nature has not been content with endowing her with grace, vigour and agility; it has been lavish with other gifts: a noble countenance framing two lovely eyes that can express anything at will; mobile features ideal for conveying any passion; gestures which are eloquent because they come from the soul and are perfectly performed whatever the meaning or emotion to be depicted. As an outstanding mime she is not to be overlooked. Her speech has no need of a tongue, for she can declaim without recourse to her voice.[11]

[10] Noverre (1807), II, 161.
[11] Noverre (1807), II, 160–1.

Early in September 1791 she made her début as a mime in Guimard's old rôle of Mélide in *Le Premier Navigateur*, astonishing the audience by her power of expression. Nearly a year later, as Psyché, the most testing of rôles, she revealed the full extent of her promise. No other dancer, wrote one critic, combined

> such nobility of bearing, such charm in her dancing, and such expression in her gestures and, most particularly, in the play of her features, which at all times reveal whatever she has to convey. We had foretold that she would develop into one of the most distinguished talents in this genre, and already, with her career hardly begun, she is justifying this prediction.[12]

Among those who were smitten with her attractions was Jacques Cellerier, a previous director of the Opéra. His liaison with Chevigny was to be productive in more ways than one: as an architect specialising in theatres, he was no doubt a wise and valuable adviser, and he also fathered her child.

Younger still, and by common consent the most beautiful of the four, was the tall and elegant Clotilde, who chose to be known professionally by her first name alone.[13] As a child she had been a pupil of Pierre Gardel, but her parents, under the belief that he was neglecting her, removed her from his class and placed her under the elder Vestris to be trained specifically in the *noble* genre. Under his auspices she made her début in a *pas* inserted in Gluck's opera, *Iphigénie en Aulide*,[14] on 11 March 1793, and a few days later appeared in *Le Jugement de Pâris*. Accounts of her golden-haired and 'well-busted'[15] beauty had preceded her appearance, but the precocious polish of her technique made no less an impression. The Opéra at once engaged her as a *remplacement*, and a year later raised her to *premier sujet* in the *noble* genre on the retirement of Victoire Saulnier.

The rôles of Calypso in *Télémaque* and Venus in *Psyché* and *Le Jugement de Pâris* thus fell into her lap. Of these three classic parts, the Venus of *Psyché* was by any yardstick the greatest challenge, and that which

[12] *Chronique de Paris*, 21 July 1792.

[13] A number of variants in the spelling of Clotilde's family name (Mafleur-ai, -oy, -et) are to be found in both archival and printed material. I have chosen to follow the spelling she adopted when signing her contract in Year VIII: Mafleuret.

[14] This was no doubt the *pas* that became celebrated in the *noble* genre as *Le Prix de la danse*. Composed for the 1793 revival of *Iphigénie*, it was most probably danced to the *passepied* at the end of Act II. It is not to be confused with the *pas* of the same name that Gardel created in Spontini's *La Vestale* in 1807.

[15] *Affiches*, 11 March 1793.

earned her the greatest triumph. One admirer, seeing her in her youthful prime, declared that she was the only dancer who played it with true understanding:

> She expresses all its passions, whether gentle, stormy or violent, to perfection. She has grace, softness, vigour and energy, making full use of her eyes and displaying her beautiful figure in a myriad of ingeniously varied attitudes. And how well she handles the progression from stillness, becoming more and more animated, as she works herself up into the most violent rage against the audacious mortal who has dared to compete with her beauty! She is a goddess indeed; it can be sensed in the pleasure she feels at her revenge. She is drawn to gloat at the terrible sight of the torments being endured by her victim. Her anguish is calculated, as if she wishes to savour the very sensation of death. She is Venus personified, utterly engrossed with her captive prey.[16]

Again it was Noverre, writing a decade later, who summed up the essence of her style. To him she was

> the very image of the lovely Diana of antiquity. Her execution is perfect, and her vigour uncommon for a woman of her height. She covers the stage with ease; there is grace in her arms, and her extensions are appropriate to one of her majestic build. Her dancing has nobility and assurance; and although she has no need to work further to perfect her technique, one could wish she might acquire the expressiveness that is so necessary for the great rôles offered by history, mythology and the poets. With such a beautiful appearance, who could represent them better and more energetically than the Dlle Clotilde. But she still has to work at conveying feelings and passions which, personally, she is so capable of inspiring.[17]

For more than quarter of a century her supremacy in the *noble* genre was never challenged. She was to become one of the glories of the Napoleonic ballet, her statuesque beauty reflecting perfectly the Neo-Classical style that was so much in fashion in all forms of art. Not since the days of Anne Heinel had a serious dancer possessed such a majestic allure.

[16] *Courrier républicain*, 4 Nivôse, Year V (12 December 1796).
[17] Noverre (1807), II, 158.

Finally, there was the baby of this little band, as yet only briefly glimpsed. Adrienne Chameroy, a pupil of Pierre Gardel, had entered the School of Dance in 1785 at the age of six, and made her first stage appearance the following year in the opera *Roland*. Six years later in 1790, Gardel created especially for her the rôle of Cupid in *Télémaque*, which she played with 'great finesse'.[18] She was the most promising young pupil in the School of Dance, and was engaged in the *corps de ballet* as a figurante the following year. Wisely, whoever was responsible for her training, probably Gardel himself, withdrew her from public gaze in 1792, and four more years were to pass before, at the age of 16, she was formally engaged as a *double*.

Any ballet-master at any time would have been proud to offer such an array of talent as was then assembled under Gardel's banner, and to have nurtured it through a period of such stringency and hardship. The scale of his achievement was now becoming apparent as this remarkable new generation of dancers emerged to share the stage with the amazing Vestris and that epitome of technical purity, Marie Gardel. In a few years there would even be talented young men striving to emulate Vestris, but for the moment that old master remained without a potential rival, and it was on the little band of nascent ballerinas that attention was focussed. They were thoroughbreds all, each a distinct individual to be recognised instantly from the crowd: the tiny, agile Collomb with 'her laughing features and mischievous eyes', the expressive Chevigny, ablaze with 'all the fire of a consummate actress', the imperious Clotilde commanding the stage like a goddess of old, and 'that good-hearted, pretty Chameroy'.[19] It was on them that the future of the ballet would largely depend, if only stability would return.

[18] *Journal de Paris*, 26 February 1790; *Mercure de France*, 20 March 1790.
[19] Baron, 253, 275, 277.

4

The Shifting Balance of Power

The new regime of the Directoire soon turned their attention to the ailing Opéra, replacing the Artistes' Committee by an administrative committee under the chairmanship of a minor playwright, La Chabeaussière. This new management lasted less than a year, but left one achievement to be remembered by: the first significant operatic creation for many a year, Grétry's *Anacréon*. It proved an unqualified success, in which Gardel's ballet revealed the captivating talent of the youngest of the little band of ballerinas, Louise Chameroy. For her he had created a sensational solo to unaccompanied clarinet, in which her delicate footwork echoed the virtuosic trills of the musician. Recalling it many years later, Castil-Blaze wondered why no one else had made use of the same formula: 'that dialogue, at once melodious and mute, that *ad libitum, a piacere*, in which musician and dancer teased one another with their respective difficulties in a duet remarkable for the rapport, relish and elegance displayed in their repartee, was worth a fortune.'[1]

The impact of Gardel's inserted ballet led the *Journal de Paris* to make an impassioned appeal to dance lovers who had gone into hiding during the Terror and were now nervously beginning to emerge. 'They will be amazed,' the writer told them, 'by the number of excellent principals who have been formed and who are unknown to them. The zeal of the director of this department [Gardel] has not slackened; he has succeeded in saving it from disruption, and with the result that each of the newly promoted principals ... is given encouragement as well as being trained in the correct principles of the art.'[2]

As Director of the Opéra, Gardel had been exercising an authority that no ballet-master before him had enjoyed, and from this his dancers reaped a significant benefit. Among the four emerging young ballerinas there was great rivalry; they seemed to lose no opportunity to give proof of zeal.

[1] Castil-Blaze, *Académie*, II, 61.

[2] *Journal de Paris*, 19 January 1797.

A prime example of this was Sophie Chevigny's achievement when, on a summer evening in 1797, she twice stepped into the breach. First, she triumphantly danced Clotilde's *Prix de la danse* solo in *Iphigénie en Aulide*, that most noble of *pas* that strictly lay outside the scope of a *demi-caractère* dancer such as herself. In the same performance she took over the rôle of Psyche at very short notice. Gardel was quick to express his gratitude. Her performance of a *pas* conceived in the *noble* style was proof, he wrote to her, that 'nothing is impossible for true talent,' but it was her interpretation of Psyche that had impressed him most. 'Bless you,' he added. 'It is by such examples as this that the arts will be preserved and prosperity restored to us as artistes, and to you will belong the glory of having played your part.'[3]

When control of the Opéra was returned to the Artistes' Committee in the summer of 1797, Gardel set to work with a will on a revival of *Le Jugement de Pâris*, which had been out of the repertory since 1794. Because the scenery stock had been so much depleted in the previous few years, more than 50,000 francs had to be spent on restoring the sets and costumes. One scene – the palace that Juno conjures up before Paris's eyes – had been completely renewed by the architect Alexandre Brogniart, who had redesigned the interior of the Théâtre des Arts before the Opéra moved in. Gardel also took the opportunity to tighten the action through a few cuts.

The public was enraptured at the return of this old favourite, and the theatre was almost uncomfortably full for the first performance on 16 March 1798. Vestris and Marie Gardel appeared in their original rôles of Paris and Oenone, but in the other parts there were many new faces, including the statuesque Clotilde in Saulnier's former rôle of Venus; Alexandrine Hutin, who was shortly to leave to accept an engagement in Spain; and Emilie Collomb as the lively shepherdess in the first act.

* * *

The School of Dance, which had been moved to premises in the Rue des Filles-Thomas near the new opera house, had meanwhile declined into a state of near inactivity. It was disastrously understaffed, and its director, Jacques-François Deshayes, was not only underpaid, but could not give it his undivided attention now that he was also serving as assistant ballet-master. By the end of 1796 its ineffectiveness was causing such concern that the Minister of the Interior, Pierre Bénézech, proposed the establish-

[3] Arch. Nat., AJ[13] 48 (II). Gardel to Chevigny, 12 Thermidor, Year V (30 July 1797).

ment of a new School of Dance, staffed by no fewer than three teachers of sufficient standing to warrant salaries at *premier sujet* level.[4] It was certainly a most commendable proposal, envisaging an extension of the School's existing purpose from merely producing figurants for the *corps de ballet* to training soloists as well. There were, however, two obstacles: firstly, the Opéra lacked the funds to launch such an expensive project, and secondly, the new School would be in direct competition with teachers who prepared dancers privately for their débuts.

It transpired that the Minister had someone in mind to take charge of the revitalised School, and it probably needed no great insight to conclude who this person might be. Now approaching seventy, and with his creative career behind him, Jean-Georges Noverre had returned to France in need of employment to augment his diminished resources. As well as making a claim against the Opéra for money due to him from the past, he had expressed a desire to direct the School. That claim may have given him some bargaining power, for in the spring of 1797 the Minister authorised a monthly payment to him of 200 francs 'pending the reactivation of the School of Dance'.[5]

Unfortunately the plans for the School had not progressed when La Chabeaussière's direction failed. Financial control of the Opéra was then passed to a Temporary Liquidator, who demanded to be satisfied as to Noverre's qualifications for the post, and in June there was a further setback when Bénézech was dismissed. Then another complication arose: the Opéra's records were in such disorder that the papers whereby Noverre's claim could be verified could not be found. Only with difficulty was he able to settle for a sum of 3000 francs, payable by instalments over four years. Even then he would have to wait until 1800 before receiving the first payment – a miserly 600 francs, which he grumbled was wholly inadequate to get him out of his difficulties.[6]

Jacques-François Deshayes died at the age of fifty-eight, after an illness of several months, on 8 April 1798. Noverre was then firmly under the belief that a commitment existed to his succeeding to the post of Director of the School, subject only to the formality of his being considered suitable – surely, he must have thought, a foregone conclusion. But in the meantime the new Minister had asked Gardel to submit a report on the School, suggesting that he should do this in concert with Noverre.

[4] Arch. Nat., AJ[13] 48 (II, Brumaire, Year V).

[5] Arch. Nat., AJ[13] 48 (II, Germinal). Bénézech to Administrators of the Opéra, 27 Germinal, Year V (16 April 1797).

[6] Arch. Nat., AJ[13] 46 (II). Noverre to Minister of the Interior (Lucien Bonaparte), 17 Frimaire, Year IX (8 December 1800).

When this report reached the Minister's desk at the end of April, it was signed by Gardel alone. It turned out to be little more than a factual report on the existing state of the School, and contained no reference to the proposals discussed with Noverre eighteen months before. Gardel reported that the School catered for up to sixty pupils of both sexes and was staffed by one teacher and an assistant or *prévôt*, who received annual salaries of 1200 and 600 francs respectively. He went on to say:

> Its regulations are concerned primarily with the maintenance of order, decency and good manners. It is very useful, not for perfecting a *premier artiste* – there are too many pupils for this to be possible – but for forming excellent figurants, providing them with the knowledge and understanding of their craft that distinguish the personnel of the Opéra, and also for training the youngsters up to a certain standard. It is from this School that the Opéra draws numerous dancers for its ballet. It is there that leading teachers seek out young persons with a natural potential for this difficult art. It was from there that Vestris the father took Mlle Rose, a perfect dancer now in London, and it was there that I noticed the potential talent of my wife and Citizenesses Collomb, Chameroy, Hutin, Saulnier, Millière and Delisle and Citizens Laborie, Deshayes *fils*, etc., etc., etc. This, Citizen Minister, is why the School is useful. I might add that the principal towns in the Departments, and even abroad, have dancers who came from the School.

Gardel realised that he had to explain why Noverre had not been consulted. 'First of all,' he wrote, 'he is always far away in the country, and then, since he has never visited the School, he certainly could not have been of any use to me.'[7] It seems that Gardel made no effort to contact Noverre, who may even have been lodging within walking distance of the Opéra, in the Rue de Maïl, from which address he wrote less than three weeks later to ask the new Directors to recommend him for the post of Director of the School.[8]

The chips were down, with Gardel seeing Noverre as a threat to part of his empire, and the latter openly staking his claim after preparing his ground by inspiring a laudatory account of his reforms of ballet that had appeared in the *Courrier des spectacles* little more than a week before his application.[9]

[7] Arch. Nat., AJ^{13} 49 (II). Report dated 11 Floréal, Year VI (30 April 1798).
[8] Arch. Nat., AJ^{13} 49 (II). Noverre to Directors, 29 Floréal, Year VI (18 May 1798).
[9] *Courrier des spectacles*, 20 Floréal, Year VI (9 May 1798).

For the moment, however, the School continued as before under the supervision of Gardel, who now busied himself with a search for a teacher of some standing whose appointment might lessen the need for an expensive new Director. And before the summer was out, a suitable candidate had appeared in the person of François Malter, a member of a family long renowned in the annals of the Opéra. Three of his uncles, each known by a descriptive epithet, had adorned the ballet in the first half of the previous century, the oldest having entered on his career a year before the death of Louis XIV and the youngest being the last Doyen and President of the Académie Royale de Danse before it had faded out of existence around 1778.[10] François Malter was a Malter on his mother's side; his father's name was Duval, but he had called himself Malter since entering the Opéra in 1766. He never reached the top rank as a dancer, but became a teacher just in time to be elected to the moribund Académie.

When it came to making the appointment, Gardel apparently had no difficulty in swaying the choice in favour of Malter, who was engaged as a teacher on 1 December 1798. However, the proposal to upgrade the School had not been entirely abandoned, and a year later Noverre was given the title 'Head of the School of Dance'.

The revised regulations for the School were approved on 23 October 1799. Noverre was to be provided with a staff of two teachers to conduct the classes, a *prévôt répétiteur* to assist them and provide violin accompaniment, and an *avertisseur* or beadle. The number of pupils was reduced to 48, divided equally between the sexes, the boys attending class in the morning and the girls in the afternoon. Pupils were obliged to attend classes until the age of sixteen, and were forbidden to take classes elsewhere. They were also forbidden to appear on any stage other than the Opéra without authorisation, and were required to appear at the Opéra whenever needed at a fee of two francs per performance. Individual progress was to be monitored every quarter, and at the end of the year the pupils were to be taken to the Opéra to display their talents before a panel consisting of the Directors, the ballet-master and the *premiers artistes*, with four prizes being awarded to the most gifted.[11]

Noverre's duties were largely supervisory, although he was required to compose and rehearse '*pas d'ensemble*, solo *entrées* and *corps de ballet* work' for the teachers, and to attend auditions and the annual display at the Opéra. How seriously he devoted himself to this task the records do not

[10] Malter I (*le Diable*) entered the Opéra in 1714; Malter II (*l'Oiseau*) made his début in 1722 and died in 1775; and Malter III (*l'Anglais* or *la petite Culotte*) made his début in 1734 and died in 1788 or 1789.

[11] Arch. Nat., AJ[13] 44.

reveal; but, whatever the reason, his appointment was not renewed at the end of Year VIII in September 1800. From then on Gardel resumed responsibility for the School, at first with the title of Inspector, and later as Director.

The principal teachers in Year VIII were Malter and Jacques Lebel, a cousin of Dauberval. A third teacher, François-Louis Berton, was given charge of the children's class. The only other member of the staff was Béguin, the beadle.

Malter remained attached to the School for seven years before his eyesight began to fail. He continued to receive his salary for two years more, at the end of which he broke his leg and had to be retired with a lump-sum gratuity. He had little means, his annual income of 610 francs being the sole means of support for himself, his ailing wife and two sisters. Gardel made a compassionate plea on his behalf. Recalling how the famous Malter brothers of old had been distinguished by their nicknames, he suggested that their nephew might claim to be known as Malter the Unfortunate. The Opéra responded favourably; for each of the few years that remained to him, the last of the Malters received a bounty of 390 francs.

* * *

In common with many of his colleagues, Gaétan Vestris had lost his pensions and most of his savings in the Revolution, but he had at least preserved his honour by refusing offers to dance in enemy territory,[12] preferring to remain in Paris and share the privations of his family and friends.

At the age of nearly seventy, the old man was still in remarkably good shape, and on 17 January 1799 he was honoured with a special performance for his benefit. To mark the occasion, his son Auguste revived Noverre's *Annette et Lubin* with himself and Sophie Chevigny in the title rôles and with his father playing the Lord of the Manor. The action was adapted to include the stately *Menuet de la cour* from *Ninette*, in which old Vestris was partnered by his daughter-in-law, Aimée. His entrance in formal court dress was a moment to be cherished, stirring many a nostalgic memory. As he began to move, the years seemed to slip from his shoulders. 'A man in the springtime of life,' wrote an eyewitness, 'could not have presented a more supple or more graceful bearing.'[13] His mas-

[12] Pougin, 100, quoting a petition, dated 1 Nivôse, Year IV (21 December 1796), by the artistes of the Opéra to the Director-General of Public Instruction requesting compensation.
[13] *Courrier des spectacles*, 10 Pluviôse, Year VII (30 January 1799).

tery of the measured *noble* style of his youth seemed undimmed; it was a lesson in perfection, in which 'mediocrity has no place because even the slightest fault and the tiniest neglect becomes all-apparent, which no doubt explains why [that style] has been abandoned and why this celebrated dancer has no successor.'[14]

When the minuet drew to a close, a storm of applause broke out from all parts of the house. But there was more to come, for the dancers had planned their own tribute. As Vestris stood alone in the centre of the stage, the principals entered one by one, wearing costumes of characters with which they were associated, to bow before him in homage: first the ladies, Marie Gardel, Emilie Collomb, Marie-Eve Pérignon; then Milon as the Grand Cousin in *Le Déserteur*; and finally Gardel himself, attired as the Deserter. With each entrance, the applause seemed to redouble. Vestris was unprepared for such a thunderous display of affection, and tears were coursing down his cheeks as Gardel placed a wreath on his brow.

Gaétan's son Auguste was by nature inconsiderate and headstrong, and in his desire to play Lubin opposite his beloved Louise Chameroy he had thoughtlessly forgotten that the part was one of those that had devolved upon Marie Gardel on the retirement of Mlle Guimard. Mme Gardel only learnt of his intention indirectly, but charitably chose not to make an issue of it, although she could not forbear chiding young Vestris in private for his discourtesy in not approaching her beforehand.[15]

In the event *Annette et Lubin* caused little stir and disappeared after a few performances, and the incident was soon forgotten. Of course, Mme Gardel knew all about Auguste Vestris's roving eye, and that he was besotted with Chameroy. His promiscuity was notorious, but this new liaison was more serious than most of his passing fancies, for in addition to the physical attraction there was an artistic bond between them, which Noverre was perceptive enough to note when analysing her merits as a dancer:

> She competed, to advantage, with Vestris, who was her favourite partner; she had the same strength, the same skill, the same vigour, the same brilliance. And she had the advantage of her sex, namely an indefinable quality that places a priceless value on all that pretty women do and say, for they alone have the art of embellishing imperfections and giving beauty a new brilliance.[16]

[14] *Journal de Paris*, 20 Nivôse, Year VII (20 January 1799).
[15] Bibl.-Mus. de l'Opéra. *Dossier d'artiste*, Pierre Gardel, 283. Letter dated 17 Floréal, Year VI (9 September 1798).
[16] Noverre (1807), II, 155.

Their affair had a strong element of professional partnership, and early in 1798 it came to the notice of the police that the couple, tempted by the lure of English gold, were planning to slip out of the country to dance at the Opera in London. An agent was instructed to investigate, and after a visit to Vestris filed his first report:

> On the orders of the Minister ... I called at Vestris's residence ... From my conversation with him, and the openness with which he responded, I need more time to satisfy the Minister ... With regard to Citizeness Chameroy, I shall take the necessary steps ... I am aware of the intimate relationship between these two artistes, and there is reason to believe that they might escape together.

Warned of the consequences, the couple then wisely disengaged themselves, although the agent was not convinced that they had been permanently frightened off, as his second report warned a week later:

> After further enquiries, there is reason to believe that Vestris and Chameroy, artistes of the Opéra, will not be escaping together to go abroad. It would appear that there are strong reasons of interest that bind Vestris to his father. However, I am not going by appearances, *and since Vestris's conduct towards his wife is not that of an honest husband*, his infatuation with Chameroy and the debts for which he is continually being hounded, may possibly lead him to do something rash.[17]

Vestris, who spent his money as it came and was chronically in debt, was particularly susceptible to temptation. The state of war between France and England did not prevent agents of the London Opera from coming to Paris to offer the most tempting terms, and towards the end of 1799 a police informer reported that:

> a certain Frederici [*sic*] had arrived in Paris to engage Vestris and Chameroy for London, but the engagement did not materialise. The contract was held by Perrégaux. The matter was brought to the attention of the Minister of the Interior and the First Consul. Gallini was also in Paris, and has not been out of the Opéra since his arrival and is also trying to entice away several artistes.[18]

[17] Fribourg, citing Arch. Nat., Archives de la Police Générale, 453 (Vestris-Chameroy). Reports of Agent No. 6, 6 and 14 Pluviôse, Year VI (25 January and 20 February 1798).

[18] Fribourg, citing Arch. Nat., Archives de la Police Générale. Report on '*les Embaucheurs*'. Vicenzo Federici was the conductor of the orchestra of the King's Theatre for the seasons of 1798/99 and

* * *

Another ballerina renowned for her beauty was Mlle Clotilde, whose appeal was unfortunately marred at close quarters by a skin complaint that troubled her for a number of years. The powerful body odour she exuded may have been a symptom; all efforts to conceal it with a generous application of musk were apparently of little avail. In the summer of 1799 her doctors prescribed a cure at Bagnères-de-Luchon, a small spa near the Pyrenees, and the Opéra gave her four months' leave to take the waters before making a few guest appearances in Bordeaux.

At Bagnères, whether through misfortune or in a foolish moment, she became embroiled in an adventure that could have had the direst consequences. On the day she took the waters, the little town was invaded by royalist insurgents. An armed band broke into her bedroom, ordering her at pistol-point to give them one of her dresses to be made into a flag. Terrified out of her wits, she handed over a white dress she had worn for a ball the previous evening.[19]

The use to which this dress was put became widely known at Bagnères, and when the uprising was quelled, she was accused of having welcomed and collaborated with the invaders. She was taken in charge and interrogated on suspicion of being implicated in the plot, but her explanations were accepted and she was allowed to proceed to Bordeaux. Her problems were not yet over, for she there found herself once again under arrest. This time her investigators were not fully satisfied, and she was provisionally released on condition that she reported to the police every three days. This respite gave her time to alert the Opéra of her plight, and the Director sought the aid of the powerful Minister of Police, Fouché. As a result she was speedily released, but doubts about her loyalty lingered, and on her return to Paris she was for a time kept under observation.

She could certainly count herself lucky, for the royalist uprising had been far from a minor incident, and General Bernadotte, the Minister for War, was in no mood to be lenient. He had even specifically mentioned her in his report:

1799/1800. Giovanni or John Gallini (1728–1805), a Florentine dancer who settled in London, became involved with the King's Theatre in a number of capacities – dancer, ballet-master, stage-manager and manager. His connection with the theatre ended when it burnt down in 1789, but this report makes it clear that he was still being useful ten years later. Jean-Frédéric Perrégaux was a leading banker who was to be one of the founders of the Bank of France and to be ennobled by Napoleon.

[19] These facts are based on a letter she wrote to the administration of the Opéra on 22 Fructidor, Year VII (9 September 1799). It was published in *Le Moniteur* on the 1st supplementary day, Year VII (18 September 1799).

> Calm has been re-established in the departments of the Midi ... A large number of noblemen and priests were found among the rebels, disguised as peasants. The leaders and the principal hangers-on of the royalist rebellion we have just crushed included men who had been condemned to death or to the irons for the basest and most infamous crimes, and the most shamefully notorious prostitutes. In the commune of Bagnères-de-Luchon ... a few women, headed by one Clotilde, a dancer of the Paris Opéra, were prominent among the creatures of the monarchy, offering them white plumes and a white flag, for which this girl had provided the material as well as cutting it out and embroidering *fleurs de lys* on it, an act which she is now saying was forced upon her. She has been brought before the Military Commission. And to think that for the past five years people like this have been considered honest folk *par excellence*![20]

In all probability she was not the innocent victim caught up in events that she had made herself out to be to the authorities, for once back in Paris she apparently maintained her connections with elements hostile to the Republican government. In the last months of the Directoire there was a stir of undercover activity by various elements hostile to the régime, and towards the end of 1799 it came to the notice of the police that:

> the Dlle Clotilde of the Opéra has been reported as receiving visits from a large number of Chouans. A man who has alternately taken the names of Legris, Lenoir and Leblanc has been observed; he has just left for Dreux and is to return in four or five days. He will be kept under close observation and run to earth.[21]

It must have been the final crushing of the Chouan revolt in the first year of Napoleon's Consulate that put an end to her meddling in politics. The incident at Bagnères had in no way affected her stage career, but she was now to exchange one form of notoriety for another. The royalist suspect faded into the past as she acquired a reputation as one of the most lavishly protected women in Paris.

[20] Report dated 15 Fructidor, Year VII (2 September 1799), published in *Coureur des spectacles*, 5 September 1844.

[21] Aulard, *Consulat*, I, 264, citing Arch. Nat., F7 3844. The Chouans were royalist rebels who fought a long campaign in north-west France, particularly in the Vendée, and were only finally defeated in 1800.

Her earliest protector had been a merchant named Gelot, whose mistress she became soon after her début at the Opéra, and who was probably the father of her elder daughter, born in the summer of 1795. Some years later she was to charm a more sensitive soul, the composer Boïeldieu, who in 1802 went so far as to marry her, although the union lasted only a few months. Her unfortunate ailment did not seem to deter men from finding her irresistible, for her conquests became legendary. The incredibly wealthy Prince Casimir Pignatelli, Marquis de Morel, Comte de Flandre et d'Egmont, provided her, if reports are to be believed, with an annual income in excess of a million francs as well as a fabulously furnished mansion in the Rue de Menars and the most splendid carriages to be seen at Longchamps. The Spanish admiral, José de Mazarredo, was said to have added another half million to her income, and yet another admirer was reputed to be paying 100,000 francs just for the privilege of sitting at her side when she dined.

These golden years came to an end long before she retired in 1818, and she would be remembered for her unique contribution to the *noble* genre, of which she was the last great exponent, and not for the notoriety of her private life.

* * *

The collapse of the Artistes' Committee in March 1796 had been largely brought about by the financial stringency that had dogged the Opéra throughout the Revolutionary years. When their régime was restored in the summer of 1797 after the dismissal of La Chabeaussière, they were authorised to raise a loan of 240,000 francs in shares of 5000 francs each, bearing interest at 6 per cent. Several of the senior artistes took them up in lieu of arrears of salary due to them, Gardel and his wife again giving proof of their commitment to the theatre they served. It was to be an unfortunate investment. Less than half of the loan had been taken up when their administration collapsed; no repayments had been made out of the receipts, and their investment was worth no more than 40 per cent of its face value.

With needs that were more than could be met out of diminishing resources, the situation had gone from bad to worse. It had been impossible to afford money to renew the stage (an urgent enough need, for already several dancers had fallen and injured themselves), and a shortage of rope to maintain the stage equipment presented an even greater danger. Salary increases were no longer possible. Some artistes and employees had taken a second occupation to make ends meet, but others, less fortunate, were driven to sell possessions to maintain an acceptable standard of living. The administration then began to delay payment of bills, with the consequence that the Opéra's suppliers became increasingly restive. The Opéra finally closed when the stock of candles became exhausted and the supplier refused to make further deliveries until his account was settled.

The Artistes' Committee had lost its credibility. Matters came quite suddenly to a head. One evening in March 1798 only a third of the chorus reported for duty; many of the musicians were absent earning ready money by playing in a concert, and the firemen, stage hands and military guard were all withholding their services. All these misfortunes came to haunt the individual members of the Artistes' Committee, who found themselves the butt of insults and even physical assault, from which not even the Government Commissioner was spared.

One of the last straws had been a demand from Auguste Vestris that the first performance of the revival of *Le Jugement de Pâris* should be given for his benefit. The Committee had little choice but to agree, requiring only that payment of the net receipts should be spread by instalments over the first five performances of the revival.

No doubt Gardel and the others who had subscribed to the loan to keep things going saw Vestris's demand as a shameful act of disloyalty, not to say blackmail, but they were in no position to risk the public odium that would fall on them if the Opéra were to lose its greatest dancer. That Vestris was very unsettled they were well aware, and the action he might take were he thwarted could not be contemplated.

In the death-throes of the Artistes' Committee there had been another disruptive factor. A conflict had arisen between the opera and the ballet that seemed to threaten the fundamental structure of the Opéra. Ironically, the problem lay in the fast-growing popularity of the ballet. Perhaps because so much of the operatic repertory had had to be abandoned as offending Revolutionary principles, while Gardel's mythological ballets aroused no such objections, the balance between the two departments had swung preponderantly in ballet's favour. Gardel and his followers pressed their advantage, no doubt with insufficient regard for the singers' feelings, and certainly to the disquiet of many of the older members of the public.

The singers' point of view was forcefully put in the *Censeur dramatique*:

> Partisanship and personal interest are not open to reason, and once passions are unleashed, rival elements, instead of striking a balance

where each acts as a counterweight to the other, become intent only on destroying one another, and in the end both are destroyed.

All the crises and incidents that usually precede a total collapse have followed one another at this theatre. Observers who like to compare a small institution with the world at large might have seen what has been taking place at the Opéra as a microcosm, and an exact one at that, of the consequences of our great Revolution.

Two rival factions have arisen, motivated, as I can well believe, by the sole desire of pleasing the public and gaining its favour. But in the manner of achieving that end, they lost their way, and the laudable spirit of emulation that should have guided them turned into a dangerous rivalry. And to such hapless machinations was added blind greed, a shameful and muddled love of gain. From that moment, self-interest, resentment, persecution, plots, intrigues, vengeance, and finally hatred and all that follows in its dreadful wake took hold of the Théâtre des Arts. Its activities ground to a halt, and despair set in. That fine establishment was destroyed, and the taste of the public led astray and even corrupted. Expenditure increased to a frightening extent; at the same time the public began to stay away, receipts became insufficient, and the Government was unable to clear an exorbitant deficit. The end was virtual bankruptcy, and today every artiste can see for himself that, by setting his sights too high or making excessive pecuniary demands, he has only added to the general collapse.[22]

The writer of these lines attributed the collapse to the introduction of *ballets d'action*. Such productions incurred enormous expenditure, and he cited as an example the ruin of Noverre's great patron, the Duke of Württemberg. But he had to admit that the opera company had sunk to a level of abject mediocrity. In the recent revival of *Alceste*, Gluck's music had been overpowered by the lavish staging, and everyone had noticed that the loudest applause had been for the dancers.

The extent to which the opera company had become demoralised by the preponderance of the ballet was revealed in an article in the *Courrier des spectacles*, which explained that the ballet's extraordinary rise was due to the leadership of its ballet-master, Gardel:

a master of untiring zeal with a passion for his art and an inspired gift for scholarly and bold creations, [who] for several years has presented a

[22] *Censeur dramatique*, 7 Germinal, Year VI (27 March 1798).

talented team of such perfection at the Opéra that any further improvement seems impossible ...

The opera company, on the other hand, hidebound by routine, has looked on passively at the achievements of the ballet and produced only a very small number of remarkable artistes, who possess natural talent but, with a few exceptions, are inferior to the leading singers in Europe ...

The ballet attracts talent from every quarter, ... encourages its own talent and increasingly offers opportunities to artistes who are willing to work.

The ballet-master runs a school from his residence that is always open to the dancers of the Opéra, both male and female. Several other artistes do likewise, and there is one school in particular that caters for child beginners.

The opera company, far from gathering talent that might be useful and necessary, discourages its own singers and turns away applicants. Offering no basic training, practice or coaching, it is declining day by day...

The ballet, which is constantly kept in training, is growing richer in talent at every level, even at Vestris's; it produces *remplacements* and *doubles* who are always on hand to please the public, which rewards their zeal with ovations that urge them to make further efforts and even on occasion to surpass themselves.

The opera company, although reduced in number, allows several of its principals to languish in inactivity ... who, through coming seldom before the public gaze, are coolly received, which is adversely reflected in their performance ... Such are the grievous consequences that result from the apathy and inactivity of the opera company. By taking the opposite course to that of the ballet, it has arrived at the opposite destination. This explains why the one has attained a degree of perfection which merits its current flattering preponderance, while the other has sunk into a wretched decline. This is the cause of all the clamour and prejudice against the ballet which is blindly shared by so many. Such people claim that the public favours the ballet too much, and that this misplaced favour must inevitably bring about the Opéra's ruin; and that it is bad policy to allow what ought to be an accessory feature to destroy its primary purpose. It follows, in their eyes, that if the Opéra is to be restored to its former splendour, the ballet must be downgraded ... It is only just and reasonable that the Opéra should regain its former brilliance ... But it would be against all reason and good sense to contend that the Opéra can only be resurrected on the ruins of the ballet,

> when it ought to be adding to [the ballet's] glory and making it an integral part of the whole, like the orchestra and the stage machinery. For what the Opéra needs is a nicely adjusted combination of competition and fusion between its various elements.[23]

The truth of the matter was that ballet had come of age, and would no longer accept a status inferior to that of the opera. This was both the legacy of the régime of the Artistes' Committee and the personal achievement of Pierre Gardel. In 1799 it was to be officially enunciated in the preamble to the new Regulations for the School of Dance that 'the dance is no longer regarded as an accessory, and that it contributes, as a separate entity, to the delights of the stage, to the success of the Opéra, and to the variety that determines the taste of the public.'[24]

* * *

The collapse of the Artistes' Committee was a scandal of such major proportions that an enquiry into its causes was unavoidable. Louis Francoeur, who had served Dauvergne as his deputy for five years and had himself directed the Opéra at a very difficult time, was selected to conduct an investigation and, in the interim, to keep the Opéra running on a provisional basis. He was appalled at what he discovered. The Opéra had been bled, as he put it, by 'shameful trafficking'; the costumes were in tatters, the scenery store had been pillaged and the stock had diminished to only a fraction of its worth a few years previously. The debt stood at nearly 700,000 francs, and even the Government subsidy was in arrears.

He lost no time in making economies where he could, taking steps to reassure the worried personnel and to keep them gainfully and happily employed. Some of the savings were achieved by reducing the chorus and the *corps de ballet*, but at the same time he introduced salary increases that were long overdue. The three disaffected singers Chéron, Rousseau and Laïs were placated and returned to the fold. While it was not possible to enrich the much depleted opera repertory overnight, a revival of Gluck's *Alceste* was presented in December 1798 with impressive new ballet scenes, arranged for the most part by Gardel with his accustomed flair. A *pas de deux* to a musical insertion from Haydn inspired an analysis rare for that time in the pages of the *Courrier des spectacles*:

[23] *Courrier des spectacles*, 3 Germinal, Year VI (23 March 1798).
[24] Arch. Nat., AJ[13] 44.

> How unfortunate it is that the description of choreographic works can never be made perfectly intelligible, despite efforts to explain them in detail. Generally speaking, music owes its character to the way in which the harmonious parts of a composition are assembled, linked, selected and contrasted. The art of the dance only truly reaches a degree of perfection when the choreographer adapts every nuance of the music to the steps, attitudes and groups he creates. Thus one dancer will express one part of a song or simple melody with light steps; at the same time another will interpret another part of the same song by different steps, while yet another will follow every measure, every modulation of the accompaniment. All the ballets of Citizen Gardel possess this essential merit; they all offer a perfect harmony; they have the priceless advantage of making palpable, as one might say, the beauties of the music, transforming them into well-thought-out tableaux; in short, this choreographer adds body, colour and action to the ideas of the musician. He has just given further proof of this by making use of one of Haydn's most pleasing and cleverest andantes. The alternating *piano* and *forte* passages which give this piece its charm are respectively rendered by the Citizenesses Gardel and Collomb, each in her own manner, while the variations and even the repeats are in turn represented by Citizenesses Millière and Louise.
>
> This entire dance scene compels admiration, particularly for the precision and the individual nuances of style with which each dancer colours her performance – the lightness, rapidity and delicacy of Citizeness Gardel, the force, aplomb and accuracy of Citizeness Collomb, and the volubility, symmetry and precision of Citizenesses Louise and Millière. Such are the distinctive characteristics of the parts that make up the whole of this charming ballet.[25]

Elsewhere in this opera the strength of the ballet company was impressively displayed by Louise Chameroy, who was featured in two *pas de deux*: one arranged by Auguste Vestris, in which she danced with Emilie Collomb, and the other, a virtuosic display devised by Gardel, which she performed to the first movement of Viotti's Third Violin Concerto, partnered by a young man of whom much more would be heard – Jean Aumer.

In the months that followed, *Télémaque* and *Psyché* continued to draw good houses, with Vestris featured in both. The latter ballet had an excep-

[25] *Courrier des spectacles*, 14 and 15 Frimaire, Year VII (4 and 5 December 1798).

tionally strong cast, with the incomparable Marie Gardel as Psyche, Chevigny as Terpsichore, Clotilde as Venus, and, as Zephyr, a promising young dancer coming into notice, Charles Saint-Amant. In another popular ballet, *Le Déserteur*, a newcomer of a different genre was making his mark as a comic mime in the rôle of Montauciel – the Swiss-born Isaac Branchu, a pupil of Milon.

* * *

During the period of retrenchment in the summer of 1798, there could be no prospect of augmenting the company, and débuts were out of the question; but in the case of one brother and sister an exception was made, perhaps at the pressing request of their teacher. Their names would have meant nothing to the public. They were the children of a little-known Italian ballet-master by the name of Carlo Taglioni, who at no small sacrifice had brought them to Paris to perfect their dance studies under Jean-François Coulon. Filippo was not yet twenty; his sister Luigia only thirteen. Coulon was an inspired choice, made perhaps on the recommendation of Gardel, by whom he had been employed in his early days to help with private coaching. Although not yet officially on the Opéra's books, Coulon was now fast becoming celebrated on his own account. He was a hard taskmaster; when the two young people were presented to him, he warned Filippo that he would need 'eyes, ears and great perseverance' to succeed. A word with Gardel must have made the début possible, although in the circumstances no promises could be given that an engagement might follow.

Nevertheless, Coulon's influence may have enabled Filippo to dance with the *corps de ballet* before his formal début took place. In later years Filippo would often describe how he got his first chance. One of the male dancers was taken ill seconds before he was to make his entrance. The orchestra had already begun the introduction. Drastic action was called for, and Marie Gardel, who happened to be in the wings, thrust Filippo on to the stage, hissing in his ear: 'Now take your chance!' He could only do his best, but fortunately he had memorised the *pas* well enough to perform it in a more than acceptable fashion. Mme Gardel no doubt brought the lad's achievement to her husband's notice, and this fortunate incident could well have smoothed the way for the début of the two young Taglionis on 18 September 1798.

A début was a rarity at the Opéra that summer, a circumstance from which the young couple benefited by receiving an unusually long notice in the *Courrier des spectacles*:

> Citizen Taglioni already displays a sound training; he even performs a few difficulties with considerable ease. His figure is supple and well formed; perhaps a few complicated steps need to be more cleanly performed, but that will be remedied by further training of this interesting pupil, who appears to be devoting himself to the *demi-caractère*, his style being very similar to Saint-Amant's. What is particularly remarkable is an excellent aplomb not usually found in a débutant.
>
> That the Citizeness Taglioni did not display similar aplomb was perhaps due to her great nervousness. This pupil is very young, yet her talent is already much advanced: her extensions are bold, smooth and delicate, her steps positive yet not stiff; she is already performing several difficult steps without faltering. Her arms are graceful, and betray nothing of the effort in her dancing. She is small of stature, but supple and light; and she holds her balance with ease, which already denotes a certain degree of skill. This young person made her début in a *pas* which comes very close to being in the grand serious genre, but we have doubts whether that genre is really suitable for one of her stature.[26]

For both brother and sister the début was a success, but it took place at a time when Francoeur was struggling to put the Opéra back on the rails. New engagements were out of the question, and the Taglionis were faced with the choice of remaining in Paris in the hope that something might turn up, or going back to Italy and abandoning all hope of a career at the Opéra. The decision was to wait, and wait they did for a full year, for it was not until September 1799 that the two youngsters were offered engagements as *doubles*, each with an annual salary of 2000 francs.

Remaining in Paris for a year with no money coming in must have been a considerable strain on the family's resources. In addition to their living expenses, there had been Coulon's fees to pay, and what could be afforded presumably had to be sent to Italy to support Carlo's wife and younger children. When at last the salaries of Filippo and Luigia began to be paid, the family was considerably in debt, and in the summer of 1800 Filippo had to assign a year's salary to clear a debt of 1775 francs owed to their landlord for 'the lodging of Charles my father, myself Philippe and Louise my sister, and for the food of Louise Taglioni.'[27]

In the long run, neither of the Taglionis would settle at the Opéra.

[26] *Courrier des spectacles*, third supplemental day, Year VII (20 September 1798).

[27] Arch. Nat., AJ[13] 51 (Thermidor, Year VIII). Agreement dated 10 Thermidor, Year VIII (7 August 1800).

Filippo left in 1802 with a contract as leading dancer in Stockholm, while Luigia, or Louise as she was known in Paris, remained until 1806. Neither would rise above the rank of *double*, but a higher destiny awaited Filippo: he was to return in 1831 in the post of ballet-master, serving his miraculous daughter, 'Marie *pleine de grâces*', who would cast such a potent spell over the audiences of the Romantic generation.

But that day lay far in the future. For the present, the Taglionis were small fry.

5

Milon Passes His Test

Did Gardel look back with regret to the more carefree days of his youth when assisting his brother in his ballet-master's duties? No doubt he had served him with a devotion that transcended what a master would normally require of his apprentice; and when, after his brother's death, he had taken his place, he must have felt the loneliness of his situation and yearned for someone to assist him as he had served his brother.

During his first eleven years as ballet-master, he had been unlucky in the assistants who had been brought in to help him. None had stayed long. Pierre Laurent, who succeeded the ineffectual Favre, came closest to fulfilling his requirements, but he returned to his native Copenhagen before the Terror. Sébastien Gallet, who followed him, was too established a choreographer to accept subservience, while the equally experienced Jean-Baptiste Hus was old and at the end of his career. Jacques-François Deshayes, who gallantly agreed to assist when times were hard, was probably of little help, being occupied at the same time with his duties at the School of Dance.

If anything was to be learnt from experience, it was that an outsider was unlikely to provide the sort of help that Gardel needed. Of the five assistants who had come and gone, only Laurent had had experience of the Opéra and its ways. And when the solution to the problem was eventually found, the choice fell, most happily as it turned out, on a dancer approaching retirement who had spent almost his entire working life at the Opéra and, as well as being a well-trained dancer, had revealed a remarkable talent as a mime.

Louis-Jacques Milon was born in 1766, and as a child of twelve had been brought to Paris by his widowed mother. They had settled in the Boulevard du Temple, not far from the Théâtre des Elèves de l'Opéra, which opened shortly after their arrival. Fascinated by its colonnaded front, young Milon had somehow managed to wheedle himself inside, spending more and more of his time hanging around, awestruck, at the rehearsals for the opening. The piece being prepared was a five-act pantomime, *La Jérusalem délivrée*, based on Tasso's epic, and when children were sought to play Saracens on the city walls, the boy was conveniently at hand to be enlisted. For him it was a game, and every night he gave his all to the great battle. One evening, however, when Jerusalem was being attacked, he was stunned by a misdirected sword. When he regained consciousness, he was consumed with rage and threw himself at the enemy with such fury that he knocked down the three flats that constituted the city walls. He had to be dragged out from under the wreckage, and after being given first aid, taken home, where he lay in bed for two months before he was fit again.

This unlucky adventure left him as stage-struck as ever, and by the age of fourteen he was playing pantomime and comedy, dancing and generally making himself useful at the Variétés Amusantes. His vocation was now turning towards the dance, and he entered the ballet company of the Opéra. His was no meteoric rise: after being trained he passed many years in the ranks before rising to the junior soloist level of *double* in 1791; and not until 1799 was he promoted again, to become a *remplacement* in the *noble* genre, at which level he would remain until his retirement as a dancer in 1800.[1]

Many years later, an obituarist would describe him as 'a pupil of the old school' in whom his teachers had instilled 'correctness, precision and grace'. These were the qualities most particularly associated with the *noble* genre, and if the term 'celebrated' used to describe those teachers is to be taken at its face value, it may be assumed that he had studied under the elder Vestris or Maximilien Gardel. But it was apparently not so much technical deficiency that hindered his advancement as his height and lack of good looks. As a result he was forced to spread his gifts beyond the genre for which he had been trained, becoming in the process equally useful in the virtuosic and expressive *comique* genre. In one sense this versatility may have been a disadvantage, but it did draw him down a different path, enabling him to specialise in dances that relied on characterisation, and above all to build up a reputation as a mime who could play serious and character parts with equal effect. Three rôles in particular were to be long remembered after he retired: two of them comic – Bertrand in *Le Déserteur* and Don Quixote in his *Noces de Gamache* – and the other in the *noble* genre, Mentor in *Télémaque*. The remarkable understanding of character that he displayed as a mime would be further revealed when he embarked on a new career as a choreographer.

The seeds of Milon's ambitions in this direction must have been germinating for some time. During his years as a dancer he had had ample

[1] *Corsaire*, 17 November 1824.

opportunity to observe Gardel at work, certainly a most valuable experience; but at that time there was no precedent for a novice choreographer to try his hand on the stage of the Opéra, and his contract would have prevented him from exercising his talents elsewhere without consent. With his dancing career nearly over, the need to supplement the small pension he could expect on his retirement was becoming pressing. Although his wife, who had danced at the Opéra from 1777 to 1794, was in receipt of a pension, it brought in only 500 francs a year because she had never risen above the *corps de ballet*.

The confusion that followed the collapse of the Artistes' Committee in the summer of 1798 now worked to Milon's advantage, for it enabled him to negotiate an arrangement whereby he could accept an offer from the Ambigu-Comique, Audinot's old theatre on the Boulevard du Temple. Although Audinot himself, who had been Maximilien Gardel's father-in-law, had retired, the policy of presenting pantomimes with a dance content had continued, and the post of ballet-master had become vacant. That the Opéra raised no objection to Milon's trying out his choreographic skill on another stage suggests that Gardel sanctioned it as a means of giving him a trial without commitment. He was not taken off the Opéra's strength, and was apparently only seconded to the Ambigu-Comique.

His first task there was to arrange the dances in Pixerécourt's five-act pantomime, *Le Château des Appenins*, for which he was rewarded with an ovation no less warm than that given to the work's author when it was presented in December 1798. His dances had been placed in a fête at the end of the first act, opening with a stately minuet performed by his wife and Antoine Corniol. This austere opening was the prelude to a rare treat for the audience, the first appearance on the stage of two extraordinary children, plucked out of the School of Dance no doubt with the blessing of Gardel: Louis Duport and his sister Minette, aged fifteen and fourteen respectively.

Milon's reward for this initial success was to follow it with a ballet of his own: *Pygmalion*, presented at the Ambigu-Comique some six months later on 8 May 1799. Working within a modest budget, he had to eschew spectacle and startling stage effects. All, therefore, would depend on the choreography, the alternation of his mime scenes and dances, and of course the performance of his dancers. His choice of a well-known theme was perhaps to be expected, but he had the happy inspiration of layering it with the charming conceit that Cupid's realm was divided between the spirits of constant and inconstant love, the two rival bands being presented forging their arrows in the opening scene.

After this introduction, Delphide, a young shepherdess, enters with her companions to gather flowers. She is followed by the lovesick Pygmalion, who teasingly snatches away her bouquet, which he refuses to return unless she agrees to place it before Cupid's statue as an offering. When she refuses, Cupid lets loose one of his darts. Believing a thorn has pricked her, Delphide is overcome by languor and allows Pygmalion to lead her to the statue. There her companions discover Cupid himself, apparently asleep; they are tempted to clip his wings, but he slips from their grasp. A rival swain, Palemon, then appears to pay court to Delphide. Supported by the inconstant spirits, his courtship prospers, and he and Delphide carve their names on a tree. Pygmalion is plunged into despair. After Delphide is borne away by the inconstant spirits, the constant spirits console Pygmalion by offering him the prospect of the arts to compensate him for his disappointment; placing a chisel and mallet in his hands, they conjure up a vision of the delights of sculpture.

The second scene finds Pygmalion in his studio. Among his works is a statue of a young woman of surpassing beauty, Galatea. To the familiar strains of the air *Que de grâces, que de majesté* from Gluck's *Iphigénie en Aulide* (which Gardel had so effectively used in *Le Jugement de Pâris*), he clearly establishes that he is infatuated with his creation. Despairingly, he invokes the aid of Venus, beseeching her to bring it to life. The goddess hears his plea, and descends to touch the cold marble and warm it into living flesh. Cupid appears to bless the union of Pygmalion and Galatea, and the ballet closes with celebratory dances.

The reception must have surprised even Milon himself. The *Courrier des spectacles* gave it exceptional coverage, devoting no less than four articles to it before the end of the month. Its critic was unsparing in his praise. *Pygmalion*, he wrote, had proved that good taste had at last prevailed at the Ambigu. It 'was not one of those bizarre creations of the imagination monstrously concocted out of the marvellous and the Romanesque, but a subject founded on fable that sweeps along with an action both ingenious and wholly anacreontic. It gives rise to allegories that are easy to follow and very delicate, and to tableaux of unmatched freshness and finesse.'[2] Milon's groups were a feast for the eyes, and it was hard to imagine that the addition of dialogue could have made the various scenes and situations any more expressive.

In retrospect, the casting of the characters might have seemed like the raising of a curtain on the future. In the rôle of Pygmalion Milon had

[2] *Courrier des spectacles*, 20 Floréal, An VII (10 May 1799).

cast Isidor,[3] a young dancer with the physique of a Greek god, whose fine technique was matched by his sensitivity as a mime. As if to emphasise Pygmalion's fidelity to his ideal, the two female rôles of Delphide and Galatea were played by the same dancer, a young girl announced simply as Citizeness Emilie, who 'left nothing to be desired in expression, suppleness and lightness'. Emilie, a dark-haired beauty with large expressive eyes who had just turned fourteen, was the much younger half-sister of Mme Milon. This was to be Paris's first sight of her; a few years hence, admitted to the Opéra under her family name of Bigottini, she would begin her rise to fame as the greatest dancer-actress of her generation. Representing the two aspects of love were the wonder-children, Louis and Minette Duport, their promise excitingly evident in their 'unusual finesse and lightness', their aplomb and their musicality.[4]

Milon was also fortunate in his collaborators. His composer, François-Charlemagne Lefebvre, who would work with him on other ballets, produced a score that opened with an evocative passage descriptive of a sunrise. No less impressive were Simon-Frédéric Moench's sets, 'perfectly lit' by the standards of the time, which inspired an unusually informative description in the *Courrier des spectacles*:

> The first [scene] represents the gardens of Amathus, where two forges are manned by the little amorets. The second is very original: a studio of considerable size, stretching straight back from the spectator's viewpoint. This is an unusual conception, for most recent perspectives have been designed to be viewed diagonally. The architectural style is simple and sober, as one would imagine the interior of a studio to be. In the third scene the conch-shell on which Venus makes her descent is supported but not surmounted by clouds; on each side are amorets holding streamers, and the space between is a sky whose misty hue blends all the better with the sky of the backcloth and is pleasingly reflected.[5]

A spectator who cared little for melodramatic pantomimes but who had been reluctantly persuaded to go to the Ambigu was overwhelmed by the warmth of feeling shown in Milon's choreography. 'What he has given us,' he wrote, 'is not just a simple ballet, but a rare confection of grace, freshness, delicacy and sentiment on a subject that, taken on its own, is dry and unrewarding.' Paris quickly became aware of this minor

[3] André Isidor Carey, to give his full name, was the father of Gustave and Edouard Carey, who were to distinguish themselves as dancers in Romantic times.

[4] *Courrier des spectacles*, 22 Floréal, Year VII (12 May 1799).

[5] *Courrier des spectacles*, 22 Floréal, Year VII (12 May 1799).

masterpiece, and such was the demand for admission that it was necessary to arrive very early in the day to be sure of securing a place; for 'our fashionable ladies', it was explained, 'are discarding old habits to go there and honour Milon's triumph with their presence.'[6]

In July Milon was rewarded with a benefit performance for which several of his senior colleagues at the Opéra gave their services. Consequently some of the promising young dancers of the original cast had to be given the evening off. Auguste Vestris, no less, condescended to play Pygmalion, while Marie Gardel assumed the part of Galatea in a costume over-decorated with gilt and spangles. Beaulieu took the part of Palemon, and Adrienne Chameroy lent her dazzling beauty to the rôle of Venus. However, the public was not deprived of seeing the promising children: deservedly, little Emilie Bigottini was left with the rôle of Delphide, while the Duport children delighted the audience once again as the two aspects of love.

The proceeds of this evening must have been a welcome addition to Milon's finances, but his real reward, upon which he had set his heart, followed on 23 September 1799, when he was formally engaged as second *maître de ballet* at the Opéra with a salary of 5000 francs.

* * *

While Milon was enjoying the fruits of his new-found vocation at the Ambigu, Francoeur was energetically tackling the problem of bringing order to the Opéra. He pruned the chorus and the *corps de ballet*, and made a start on renovating the repertoire, even if new works came rather slowly. By the end of 1798 two new operas by Kalkbrenner had been produced. Both were quickly forgotten, but more successful was Méhul's opera *Adrien*, which was produced in June 1799 – too late, alas, to save Francoeur, who was summarily dismissed a few months later. The Opéra then closed, and was dark for more than two months.

Francoeur's successors were named as 'the Citizens Devismes and Bonet, one-time members of the Convention'. In fact only one of them, Joseph Bonet, had been a *Conventionnel*, in which capacity he had voted for the death of Louis XVI. His partner, Devismes, had never been active in politics, but to many of the older habitués his name was familiar, for he was none other than the former De Vismes du Valgay who had briefly directed the theatre with such headstrong energy in the late 1770s. Now, older and maybe a little wiser, he was returning to the scene of his

[6] *Courrier des spectacles*, 10 Prairial, Year VII (30 May 1799).

younger days determined, on being given a second chance, to make his mark. His mind was as brimful of ideas as ever, but he needed a steadying hand, which was perhaps why he had been given an associate. Bonet had no experience in administering a theatre, but as a member of the upper house of the legislature, the Council of Five Hundred, and a friend and cousin of the influential politician Cambacérès, he was presumably given a watching brief to ensure a measure of financial control. If this was Bonet's function, he certainly fulfilled it, for he would remain at the Opéra's helm for more than seven years, bringing to it at last a much-needed measure of stability.

With the new administration in the saddle, and encouraged by a stream of announcements that Devismes issued through the press, hopes were raised that the Opéra's fortunes were on the rise. In the programming, Gardel's *Guillaume Tell* was high on the list of priorities, and a revival of Maximilien Gardel's *Mirza* was also in contemplation. The recollection that the latter ballet had contained a concert scene in which the heroine, with the unseen assistance of a soloist in the orchestra pit, had to enchant the guests by her skill on the harp, had given Devismes a brain-wave. This scene could be adapted as a framework for presenting unknown singers and instrumentalists who, as he put it, would compete for public acclaim in a kind of theatrical Olympic games. It was a wild idea; mercifully – no doubt as a result of a strong objection by Pierre Gardel to his brother's ballet being thus mutilated – wiser counsels prevailed, and no more was heard of it.

The way was thus open for Milon to begin work on *Héro et Léandre*, his first ballet specially composed for the Opéra, which was first shown to the public on 4 December 1799. Once again his inspiration had alighted on a tale from classical antiquity. As told by Ovid, Leander was a young man from Abydos who nightly swam the Hellespont to Sestos to keep a tryst with Hero, a priestess in the Temple of Venus, who, from the top of a tower, guided him with a flaming torch. But there came the day when Leander was drowned in a sudden storm. At the sight of his lifeless body, Hero threw herself from the tower to perish, with him, beneath the waves. For the plot of his ballet Milon elaborated this theme to add dramatic effect, but enough of its essentials remained for the audience to follow the action.

The title rôles were confided to the two dancers who reigned supreme at the Opéra, Auguste Vestris and Marie Gardel. The first meeting of the doomed lovers is shown as taking place during a festival in honour of Venus. Leander falls hopelessly in love, and taking advantage of a moment when they are alone, declares his passion. Hero, loath to incur her goddess's wrath, rejects him. Cupid (M. Duport) then agrees to assist Leander in his suit; disguised as a young boy, he presents Hero with a bouquet, requesting her to offer it to Venus on his behalf. Charmed by the boy's good looks and modest demeanour, Hero embraces him and is rewarded with a kiss, which kindles a disturbing emotion.

The festival is later interrupted by Cupid, now no longer disguised, who complains that the proceedings are unworthy of his mother, Venus. By a stroke of magic he transforms two Phrygian girls into the goddesses Juno (Mimi Saulnier) and Minerva (Clotilde), while Hero herself becomes Venus, and Leander assumes the guise of Paris. The apple that is to be the prize for the famous contest of beauty is no sooner placed on Venus's altar than a dove flies down and bears it away – a clear sign of the goddess's displeasure. As night falls, the lovers swear fidelity.

Oblivious to the passing of time, they realise that the boat that is to carry Leander back to Abydos has already set sail. Leander realises what fate would be in store for Hero should they be discovered together. To save her from disgrace, he dives into the water, oblivious to the violent storm that is brewing. Amid flashes of lightning he disappears beneath an enormous wave. Hero swoons, believing him drowned, but all ends happily. The sea-goddess Amphitrite brings Leander back to life, Neptune (Goyon) emerges from the sea bearing him in his arms, and the ballet closes with an apotheosis in which the gods descend to earth to give the lovers their blessing.

The ballet's success was not for a moment in doubt. It was to survive until 1802 – not a long life by comparison with the ballets of Gardel, but an honourable one. Although staged at very little cost, it made use of almost the entire company: apart from the eleven rôles, the programme listed sixty-five dancers, including *sujets* such as Beaupré who appeared as Pan, Branchu and Beaulieu leading the fauns, and Mlles Pérignon and Collomb playing nymphs. Allowed to present the company at full strength, Milon could have no cause to complain of being short-changed, and he must have been gratified to read the long and careful review that appeared just two days later in the *Courrier des spectacles*:

> This ballet, which is arranged with the greatest good taste, is full of charming details ... One can hardly think of a more ingenious idea than to have Cupid arrange a festival in honour of Venus by evoking that time when Paris awarded her the apple, and particularly to ensure Leander's triumph by casting him, at Hero's side, as the shepherd of Mount Ida. It is also a very nice tribute to the choreographer of *Pâris*, and more particularly, in view of the basic plot, a real stroke of genius,

> as is also the martial dance for Minerva. This *pas* is superbly crafted, and its performance by Clotilde is beyond description. For the vigour and precision of her virile, bold, even majestic interpretation and the beauty of her presence, this rôle ... is one of the finest of all she has so far taken on ...
>
> The two principal rôles are played by Vestris and Mme Gardel. It is impossible to describe how natural is their acting in even the slightest situations ... Even when performing steps that require exceptional strength in the scene when Cupid introduces the Phrygian girl into the games, Vestris does not lose sight of the character of his rôle: at this point Leander, although bewitched by the charms of the new beauty, keeps his gaze fixed on Hero – the meaning could not be more clearly conveyed. As for Mme Gardel, her sadness and despair is conveyed just as skilfully as her astonishment and joy when the gods bring Leander back from the dead. Here the very slightest nuances are depicted with admirable precision.
>
> Minette Duport was quite astonishing. In this story Cupid, now no longer a child, is played as a serious character; as the years have gone by he has become more skilled and more cunning, and Minette has caught the character to perfection. Furthermore, this is a major part, for it is he who holds the thread of the action; and it demands all the intelligence that Minette has put into it.[7]

Milon had been wisely economical in constructing his plot, keeping his characters to a minimum and the action simple. Indeed, it came across so clearly that one critic went so far as to suggest that the practice of distributing a printed programme might be abandoned as being an insult both to the expressive skill of the actors and to the intelligence of the spectators.[8]

Seldom had a new ballet cost so little. Only 3353 francs had been spent on the scenery, most of which was assembled from what was available in the store. The first set consisted of bits and pieces from *Le Jugement de Pâris*, *Le Premier Navigateur* and *La Caravane du Caïre*, and a few seacloths painted for the doomed *Guillaume Tell*. Only the statue of Venus and Hero's tower were new. For the scene when the lovers are overtaken by the approach of night, a blue gauze was prepared to produce the effect of dusk, and several existing cloths had to be repainted for the storm.

It was for this last scene that Milon had been most explicit in his scenic requirements:

[7] *Courrier des spectacles*, 15 Frimaire, Year VIII (6 December 1799).

[8] *Gazette national*, 8 December 1799.

> Night falls gradually – very noticeably, but very gently. The moonlight pierces the clouds, which gradually disperse to reveal [the moon] in all its brilliance. As the scene proceeds, the moon completes its circuit. A few clouds appear on the horizon. The sea begins to turn rough. Leander climbs a rock and dives into the water. The waves rise, and Leander is seen, appearing and disappearing. The darkness is total. Nothing is to be seen except during the flashes of lightning. A terrible wave throws Leander up as high as possible and casts him down again into the depths. A very loud thunderclap is preceded by a brilliant flash, which must clearly reveal Leander at the moment he is on the crest of the wave. Another thunderclap breaks near Hero. She falls senseless on a rock, as though struck.[9]

For his musical collaborator, Milon had remained loyal to Lefebvre, with whom he had worked on *Pygmalion*. The score was very largely a *pot-pourri* of extracts from the works of other composers, but several of Lefebvre's original passages were praised, notably the effective overture, an expressive adagio and a march (although this may have been taken from Mozart's *Die Zauberflöte*). In his score Lefebvre hinted at the identity of the composers, whose pieces he had indicated by their initials: L, Hd, M^{ini}, M, P, G. Some of these borrowings are recognisable. L was no doubt Lefebvre himself. Hd, of course, was Haydn, a favourite source with ballet-masters, and whose symphonies provided material for three passages in Act I.[10] M^{ini} was for Martini and M for Mozart. Martini's delightful song *Guarda mi un poco* accompanied the tender moment in the night scene when Leander removes Hero's veil, the melody being played on the horn with much feeling by Frédéric Duvernoy. Two borrowings from Mozart were detected, a march and the 'Letter' duet from *Le nozze di Figaro*. P and G may have respectively included Pleyel or Piccinni, Grétry or Gossec. There was one other borrowing, which was not accorded an identifying initial: the strikingly effective music for the storm, which made the greatest impression of all, had been taken from Vogel's opera, *Le Toison d'or*.[11]

[9] Arch. Nat., AJ^{13} 55.

[10] Symphony No. 85 (*La Reine*), fourth movement, *presto*; Symphony No. 97 (*Miracle*), second movement, romance, *allegretto*; Symphony No. 90, second movement, *andante*.

[11] *Gazette nationale*, 16 Frimaire, Year VIII (7 December 1799), and *Courrier des spectacles*, 15 Frimaire, Year VIII (6 December 1799).

* * *

When the curtain had first risen for *Héro et Léandre*, Paris was in the grip of a new mood of excitement. Less than a month before, a momentous event had taken place that for many seemed to presage at last a return to order and stability. Few tears had been shed when the régime of the Directoire had been swept away in a *coup d'état* by the military hero of the hour, Napoleon Bonaparte, who had made himself virtual dictator of France with the title of First Consul.

Already it was becoming clear that the Revolution was over. On the occasion of the revival of Gluck's *Armide* a few days before the première of Milon's ballet, the added confidence aroused by the recent events was reflected in a display of finery among the audience such as had not been seen for many a year. To one sanguine observer, the jewels that sparkled that evening in the candlelight of the boxes seemed to reveal an art-loving race that had rediscovered its former glory, and to hint at prosperity to come from expansion of trade in the growing expectation of an early end to the war.[12]

[12] *Courrier des spectacles*, 3 January 1800.

6

La Dansomanie

At last the Opéra seemed to be settling down and even beginning to prosper. Thanks to the conciliatory efforts of Francoeur, the clash between the opera and the ballet, which had brought down the Artistes' Committee, had lost its edge. Even the singers were beginning to accept that the dance had 'attained such a degree of excellence as to entitle it to be classed among the fine arts and ... share in the nation's glory'.[1]

That winter, lovers of the dance were well catered for. A month after *Héro et Léandre* came a revival of Gluck's *Armide* with new *divertissements* by Gardel. The most successful of these was danced to Haydn's 'beautiful romance' (probably the second movement of Symphony No. 85), which had inspired the choreographer to new heights. A critic wrote:

> The way in which the groups were arranged and linked together, and their variety, were enchanting. Everything in it is simple, offering tableaux that surprise and captivate the senses. There is no confusion, no trace of effort; the thing pleases, you are unaware of all the effort that must have gone into it, and the standard of the performance was fully worthy of the composition.[2]

* * *

For more than half a century the ballet of the Opéra had passed through a golden age dominated by the extraordinary dynasty of Vestris, and there was still no sign of a challenge to the family's pre-eminence. The career of the elder Vestris was already enshrined in legend, but his sceptre had passed to his son, Auguste, who in his fortieth year was giving little sign that his powers were on the wane. Such was the influence of his technical achievement on public taste and on the younger generation of male dancers that the once-dominant *noble* style had paled before the

[1] *Année théâtrale*, Year IX, 61.

[2] *Courrier des spectacles*, 13 Nivôse, Year VIII (3 January 1800).

virtuosity of *demi-caractère*. Many saw that as an exciting advance in technical accomplishment, but others were not to be dazzled and tried to see his contribution in a more sober perspective. As one such objective commentator recorded:

> The old habitués reproach [Auguste Vestris] for having distorted the *noble* genre. But those who are more modern in their tastes are charmed by the mixture of nobility and grace, line and lightness, which he has artistically introduced into his steps and attitudes. For our part, however, we fear he might be debasing his great gifts when we see him being so prodigal with *tours de force*, and jumping and pirouetting more often than dancing.[3]

Now word was going round that there was another generation in the offing. A son of Auguste was being carefully schooled behind closed doors by both his grandfather and his father, and showing such precocious promise that the family had decided he was ready to be presented to the public. But they were only to be given a foretaste, following the precedent set when Auguste himself had first appeared at the age of twelve and had then been withdrawn for his skill to be perfected before being formally launched on his career three years later.

The origins of young Armand were shrouded in mystery. That he was the son of Auguste was not in question, but the identity of his mother remained a tightly kept secret. So far as was known, Auguste had been married once only, in 1795 or thereabouts to the dancer Mlle Aimée. But she was only nine years old when Armand was born, and could not have been his mother. All that could be said was that the boy had come into the world in 1787, when Auguste was a randy young virtuoso taking his pleasure when and where he willed within the ballet company and no doubt without.

The Vestris blood flowed no less thickly in Armand's veins, and illegitimacy was no barrier to his assuming the cloak of the great dynasty of the dance. By the spring of 1800 he had grown into a tall, handsome lad of thirteen, whose progress had satisfied the stringent demand of his grandfather that a public viewing of his extraordinary skill would not shame the family honour. The moment was right for the Opéra too, whose new Directors were more than usually receptive to new ideas. Excited by the unprecedented prospect of three generations of Vestrises appearing in the same performance, they enthusiastically agreed to the boy's début. Of

[3] *Année théâtrale*, Year IX, 60.

course, a price had to be paid, for old Gaétan was fully aware of the commercial value of the family name, and he was in need of money. And no doubt it was arranged in advance that the Minister of the Interior would give his approval to one-third of the receipts of the three début performances being paid to the head of the family as an honorarium.

As was to be expected, the house was packed on the first performance of the series on 6 March 1800. The moment for which everyone was waiting arrived in the bazaar scene of Grétry's *La Caravane du Caïre*, a scene frequently used for a début that required the insertion of another composer's music to suit the needs of the débutant. And what an experience it was for those present that evening when the elder Vestris,

> the patriarch of the dance, wearing a white-plumed hat in the style of Henri IV, appeared on the scene of his former glory to guide his grandson's first steps and, so to speak, install him on the field of honour. Age has not dimmed the nobility, majesty and grace that characterised his talent, but on this occasion, contenting himself by displaying to the public once more the beautiful vestiges that remain, he basked in his descendant's glory. Dancing talent is the family prerogative, a title of nobility which he was the first to bring to his house.[4]

For a boy of thirteen, Armand's performance was a revelation. Devoting more than half a column to his début, the critic of the *Journal de Paris* gave an impressive account of his technique:

> This young man combines the styles of his two able teachers. A precise technique, strength and boldness of his extensions, the rapidity of his movements, accurate timing, and above all an aplomb that is unbelievable in one so young – these are the advantages with which he presents himself on the stage. But in addition to these he has grace, a very fine set of the head, charming arms, and generally a stance that allows his body to betray no trace of the effort that has gone into the steps.
>
> The audience voiced its admiration with a long and resounding ovation. The pupil has chosen the most difficult style of all if it is to be practised in its fullest purity and carried to perfection – the genre known as the *grand sérieux*. His features appear to suit him to it, and furthermore, this young man has a manner of walking that is noble without affectation and controlled without being stiff. He has already

[4] *Journal des débats*, 5 March 1800.

> conquered great difficulties, among others that of being able to recover his balance without effort.[5]

It would have been churlish to hold his precocious virtuosity against him, but the eminent critic Geoffroy felt constrained to add a word of warning about the direction that theatrical dancing was then taking:

> French dancers enjoy a supremacy in the theatres of Europe similar to that of Italian singers, but their art, which over a long period of time has been brought to a pitch of perfection, is now on the point of being distorted and debased by a mania to astonish rather than to please, and to make difficulty an end in itself. The dance is the most mechanical of all the fine arts, appealing least of all to the intelligence. One might even say that it only becomes an art when it speaks, that is to say when it depicts the emotions through the movements of the body. The dancer is descending to the level of a fairground performer if his steps express nothing at all, and if his skill is limited to jumping a little higher or turning longer on one foot than anyone else.[6]

In his début performances young Armand showed beyond all doubt that he was a prodigy in the true family tradition; and the authority for the honorarium that his grandfather had demanded was promptly signed by the Minister of the Interior, Lucien Bonaparte, and delivered to the Directors.[7]

Armand did not have to wait as long as his father to be taken into the company. The fact that the Vestris family needed money like everyone else was no doubt the reason for this dispensation. Armand's service at the Opéra commenced some six months later, at the beginning of Year IX, but for the first two years it was only on a temporary basis; not until September 1802 did he become fully-fledged with the rank of *double*.

The young man and his family seem to have expected a rapid rise to *premier sujet*, and by the autumn of 1803 both he and his father were thoroughly disgruntled. Feelers had already been sent out to other opera houses, and when there seemed to be a real chance of securing an engagement, Armand himself wrote to Bonet, complaining of broken promises and asking to be released.[8]

Bonet replied the next day accepting his resignation, without compen-

[5] *Courrier des spectacles*, 17 Ventôse, Year VII (8 March 1800).

[6] *Journal des débats*, 17 Ventôse, Year VIII (8 March 1800).

[7] Arch. Nat., AJ^{13} 51. Minister to Administrators, 15 Germinal, Year VIII (5 April 1800).

[8] Arch. Nat., AJ^{13} 86. Armand Vestris to Bonet, 10 Vendémiaire, [Year XII] (3 October 1803).

sation, but that did not end the matter. What Armand and his father wanted was promotion, as became clear some weeks later when Auguste disclosed to Bonet that La Scala, Milan, had made Armand an offer to replace Deshayes:

> I would have felt entirely free to advise him to accept were I only to consider the administration's attitude towards him, but the interest which Mme Bonaparte has apparently deigned to show in him makes it particularly incumbent on me to do nothing without her consent, or her permission. Therefore I beg you, Monsieur, to kindly explain my feelings to the Prefect so that he can make a decision, either to grant my son the position he is seeking, and to which I believe his talents entitle him, or to give him formal notice and so leave him free to enter into the engagement he has been offered, particularly since he is required to be in Milan on 1 December.[9]

The Prefect presumably spoke to Josephine Bonaparte, for it was decided that the Opéra should not give in to pressure, and Auguste was curtly informed that he was entirely free to sign a contract with La Scala.

With that, the habitués of the Opéra were to be deprived of a third generation of the family of Vestris, as Armand Vestris left Paris to embark on a distinguished career as dancer and choreographer in the opera houses of Milan, Lisbon, London and finally Vienna, where he died in 1825 at the age of thirty-nine. In Lisbon he was to fall in love with a fellow dancer, Julie Petit, whom he courted and won against the formidable competition of the French military governor, General Andoche Junot, but the marriage failed to produce a fourth-generation prodigy.

* * *

Now that the horrors of the Terror were receding, the social life of Paris was beginning to revive. Many who had gone into hiding emerged, and some who had emigrated even ventured to return. In this climate of relaxation, dancing became a safety valve, and balls proliferated all over the capital, catering for every class of society, high, middle and low. The most exclusive were those known as *bals à la victime*. That ubiquitous social observer, Sébastien Mercier, asked:

[9] Arch Nat., AJ[13] 86. Auguste Vestris to Bonet, 20 November 1803. The Prefect of the Palace had become the official responsible for supervising the Opéra in January 1803 when it became an appanage of the First Consul's household.

Will anyone in future years believe it, that persons whose parents perished on the scaffold have been arranging, not solemn days of mourning on which to indulge their grief over recent cruel bereavements, but days set aside for dancing when all present waltzed, ate and drank to their hearts' content? To be admitted to this feasting and dancing, it was obligatory to produce a certificate that one had lost a father, mother, husband, wife, brother or sister under the knife of the Guillotine. The death of a collateral was not an entitlement to attend such a revel.'[10]

The shock of the Revolution, and the social re-orientation resulting from the emigration and rise of new wealth, had brought about a noticeable shift, an *embourgeoisement* in fact, in the forms of social dancing. While the minuet was tainted as being redolent of the Old Régime and scorned as hopelessly outdated, the gavotte had managed to preserve a certain vogue. But it was another dance, the waltz, more popular in origin and spurned by some as indelicate because the man held his partner close by the waist, that was fast becoming the rage in the public balls.

Among the hundreds of dance halls, the music from which hovered in the street air until the early hours, was the richly appointed Wauxhall in the Rue de Bondy, whose proprietor was a former dancer of the Opéra, Jacques-Charles Joly. Joly had joined the Opéra ballet in 1787, at the age of about sixteen, and had quickly made himself useful, despite his humble standing in the company. Until September 1793 he had performed the duties of *répétiteur* to the *premiers sujets*. Then, through some mischance, his career was abruptly interrupted when he was denounced and arrested under the infamous Law of Suspects. Four years later, when his replacement at the Opéra departed, he asked for his job back; but for some reason his application was ignored, although at the pressing request of the *premiers sujets* he began working with them again without reward, in daily expectation of being re-instated.

Presumably they saw that he was remunerated; they certainly valued his services, for in May 1798, after the Artistes' Committee had collapsed, they presented a petition recording his selfless efforts and his lack of means. This petition has a poignant interest that has no bearing on poor Joly's problem: prominent among the signatures were those of Auguste Vestris and his beloved Louise Chameroy, the latter's scratchy signature comfortably resting, as if in an embrace, within her lover's proprietary flourish.

[10] Mercier, 339.

Certificats des 1ers Sujets de la danse du Théâtre des Arts.

Nous soussignés certifions et reconnoissons la juste et équitable demande du Cen. Joly pour sa place de Répétiteur, dont nous ne pouvions nous passer vû les différents changements de pas à prendre suivant les circonstances. en foy de quoy nous lui avons délivré le présent certifficat pour lui servir et valoir ce que de raison. Donné en notre Théâtre le vingt floréal an sixième de la République française une et indivisible.

A petition by the senior dancers in support of Joly, with whom they took class. Note the embracing signatures of Auguste Vestris and Mlle Chameroy. (Archives Nationales, AJ[13] 83)

Vestris, in the full pride of mature manhood, was now basking in his glory, both upon the stage and in society, and his arrogant figure was caught by two celebrated artists of the time. In an aquatint by Debucourt, he appears not in a balletic pose, nor even in theatrical costume, but standing aloof from the main figures, superbly dressed in the latest fashion and preening himself in a mirror. The print is enigmatically entitled *The Orange, or the modern Judgement of Paris* – not apparently alluding to Gardel's ballet, for the man holding the orange is the artist's son and the others, one imagines, friends of the family. The identification of the figure by the mirror as Vestris is endorsed on a copy in the Bibliothèque Nationale, and there is no reason to doubt it.

Vestris also featured in a caricature by Isabey, entitled *Le Petit Coblentz* and drawn about the time of Bonaparte's *coup d'état*, when royalists were still hopeful that the General might play a similar rôle to that of General

Monk, who had restored Charles II of England. The scene is the Boulevard des Italiens, which was then the haunt of royalist sympathisers: the political reference is emphasised by the title, Koblenz being the border town where, in the early years of the Revolution, an army of emigrés had assembled in the vain hope of marching back to Paris in the wake of the Austrian and Prussian forces. In Isabey's drawing, Vestris, recognisable by his much caricatured simian features, is seen quizzing an approaching couple – the singer Garat and Julie Récamier, one of the leading hostesses of the Directoire – while in the background are three men upon whom the royalists innocently believed they could rely: General Joachim Murat, and that wily diplomat and former bishop, Talleyrand, behind whom can be recognised the lean and inscrutable features of the man of destiny, Bonaparte.

* * *

In contrast to the ebullience and flamboyance of Vestris, Gardel was a man of sober and industrious disposition. Utterly dedicated to his art, he was almost totally absorbed by his duties at the Opéra, and most of all by his creative urge as a maker of ballets. Belonging to a generation that had grown up in a more regulated society, he was a firm believer in tradition, which at times led him to ignore the changing attitudes that had been seeping into the public consciousness. An example of this was his insistence that only the accredited ballet-masters had the right to present ballets at the Opéra, a stance that in time would alienate certain younger dancers with choreographic ambitions and their supporters. It was in the nature of a person in his position of authority to hold himself aloof, but nevertheless he was a man of feeling with a genuine concern for his dancers. In all his forty years at the helm, he never lost their respect. A man of serious interests, he was seldom seen in the fashionable salons of society, although he had friends and acquaintances in literary and musical circles.

He was a private man, of whom little was known concerning any interests outside the theatre and the studio at his home where he gave private coaching. He was, however, very proud to have been elected to a learned society, the Société Philotechnique,[11] and announced his membership on the title page of several of his ballet programmes. This might have puzzled those who knew him only as a man with an obsessive commitment to

[11] The Dance Collection of the New York Public Library possesses, among its Gardel material, Admiral Guillaud's recommendation for Gardel's election, dated 12 Germinal, Year VI (1 April 1798).

the dance. But perhaps to his friends there was no mystery; he was fascinated by the mechanics of the human frame, and particularly by the ability to spin. The skill of pirouetting, which had been so much developed in his own lifetime, may have led him to imagine a ballet performed by mechanical puppets. His pupil Emile Collomb wrote in her diary:

> Rumour has it that M. Gardel is working on a new ballet which will have the title, *Les Toutous (sic) et les girouettes*. The costumes and shoes have already been prepared. A very skilful mechanic has very skilfully adapted little steel points, very light and very solid, by which 37½ turns can be made in 15 seconds.[12]

He was happiest, it seems, in the company of his family and his friends, many of whom were, of course, dancers. No trace of scandal ever sullied his name. Widely respected for his integrity, he could also inspire affection, as was touchingly expressed in a simple verse found among the papers of Emilie Collomb:

> *Excellent ami, bon époux,*
> *Dans sa maison la gaîté brille.*
> *Quand il est au milieu de nous,*
> *Nous nous croyons de la famille.*[13]

He had now come to realise that *Guillaume Tell*, which he had struggled for so long to bring to fruition, had lost its political relevance. In the early months of 1800 Bonaparte had come to grips with the nation's problems with an energy that astonished even his admirers. As the foundations of the new régime of the Consulate were laid, it soon became clear that there would be no resurgence of Jacobinism, nor was the monarchy to be restored. France's new master was to be his own man; the Revolution was over.

Guillaume Tell was not formally withdrawn from the Opéra's list of future plans, but Gardel had already moved on to a new subject. The Parisians' mania for dancing in the last years of the Directoire had sown a fertile seed, and in his painstaking way he had constructed a tongue-in-cheek scenario with a contemporary setting. Two of his drafts survive: the first peppered with revisions and lengthy interpolations that reveal

[12] Bibl.-Mus. de l'Opéra, Fonds Collomb, 23. Forget to Collomb, 27 August 1804.
[13] Musée-Bibl. de l'Opéra, Fonds Collomb, 5. 'Excellent friend and good husband,/ His house shines with gaiety./ When he is in our midst/ We feel we are members of the family.'

the meticulous way in which he built up the detail of the action, and the second, with further last-minute revisions, endorsed with the certificate of acceptance, signed by Devismes and dated 4 Nivôse of Year VIII – Christmas Day 1799.[14]

It was entitled, from the outset, *La Dansomanie*, and modestly described as 'a *folie-pantomime* in two acts'. Since it was so different from his earlier ballets, Gardel felt that a note of justification was called for. To those who had wondered why he had not presented a new ballet for more than six years, he explained that he had not lost his ability to create and that during that time four of his ballets had been accepted by different administrations.[15] He touched briefly on the reasons for his apparent lack of creativity during the Revolutionary years: the demand for revolutionary spectacles, the lack of funds, and the administrative burden that he had to bear. Only now, with Devismes and Bonet firmly installed, could he feel free to concentrate his mind and effort on creative work, and this farcical comedy, which the Directors may have read with some surprise – 'a bit of fun, a mere trifle', as he called it, thought up merely to display the talents of his dancers – no doubt reflected an exhilarating sense of relief.

La Dansomanie was first performed on 14 June 1800. The First Consul was unable to attend, being engaged elsewhere on the nation's business: a month previously, he had left Paris to lead an army across the Alps to force peace on France's most powerful continental enemy, Austria. By coincidence, on the very evening when a full house was enjoying the first performance of this new ballet, the Austrian army conceded defeat after the battle of Marengo. News of the French victory would not reach Paris until several days later, but no sign of anxiety tempered the enthusiasm of the audience. They were transported by the ballet's light-hearted magic right from the opening strains of Méhul's overture and kept laughing until the curtain finally fell to a storm of applause.

The *dansomane* of the title is M. Duléger (Goyon) a rich landowner with an obsession for dancing. He is first seen tripping down a hillside, returning from a morning walk with his young son (Simon). Once inside his house, he decides to give the boy a dancing lesson. His dim-witted servant Pasmoucheté (Branchu) imitates him behind his back until Mme Duléger (Clotilde) arrives and puts a stop to his clowning. It is now time for the Dulégers' morning cup of chocolate, and while they are partaking of refreshment their neighbour Colonel Demarsept (Auguste Vestris) ap-

[14] Arch. Nat., AJ[13] 1024.

[15] *Guillaume Tell* was, of course, one; the others no doubt included *Daphnis et Pandrose* and *Achille à Scyros*, which were among the works accepted for production in the summer of 1801.

[16] The specification for the scenery required a built *pavillon* which could be opened to the audi-

pears in the garden outside.[16] He has fallen in love with their daughter Phrosine (Mme Gardel), who is in her room upstairs; and, unobserved by her parents, he attracts her attention. She is not insensitive to his declaration, and tells him she will give him her reply in writing. Meanwhile the Dulégers have finished their chocolate, and Pasmoucheté comes to remove the crockery. He too has become touched by his master's folly, and in an attempt to perform a couple of *jetés battus* and an *entrechat* he knocks over the table with the crockery. He falls to his knees to apologise, coming down heavily on his master's toes. Duléger is on the point of dismissing him for his clumsiness, but his anger vanishes when he learns how the accident occurred.

At this juncture Mme Duléger returns to speak to her husband about their daughter's future, but his attention is entirely taken up with trying to learn the steps that Pasmoucheté is demonstrating. Meanwhile Phrosine has written the promised reply and placed it under the wing of her pet dove, which flies across the stage to her lover's house. Delighted at reading that his proposal has been accepted, Demarsept prepares to ask for her hand. But just as he is about to set out, accompanied by his English servant (F. Taglioni), Flicflac (Milon), a dancing master, arrives with his assistant Brisotin (Beaupré) to give Duléger his dancing lesson. Noticing Demarsept hovering in the garden outside and Phrosine anxiously watching him, Mme Duléger realises that her daughter is in love.[17] Meanwhile, Duléger is asking Flicflac whether he has anything new to show him. Flicflac then demonstrates (to quote Gardel's own words) 'the new double, triple and quadruple *temps de cuisse*, steps in which the legs are thrown forward one after the other, pirouettes on the *cou de pied*, waltzes, arabesques, and finally all those steps that make our social dances look ridiculous and all too often disfigure the dancing in our theatres.'

Duléger then asks Flicflac to give Phrosine her dancing lesson, and master and pupil dance the latest ballroom rage, the Vestris Gavotte. Duléger is transported, and the Colonel deems the moment propitious to ask for her hand. Phrosine is all a-twitter. But Duléger is annoyed at the

ence's view by being raised several feet above stage-level and provided with 'doors sufficiently wide so as to enable the audience to see what is going on inside'. (Arch. Nat., AJ[13] 55. Scenery estimate.)

[17] The conductor's score at this point (No.11, bars 7 to 30) describes the mime of Phrosine and her mother, which was set strictly to the music: DEMARSEPT: *A mon bonheur ne soyez point contraire* (bars 7–10). Mme DULEGER: *Oui, c'est lui que j'entends pour gendre* (bars 12–14). *C'est lui que ma fille a choisi* (bars 15–17). *Confirmez les voeux les plus doux* (bars 24–26). ALL: *Confirmez les voeux les plus doux* (bars 28–30).

interruption of his dancing lesson, and impatiently demands to know whether Demarsept can dance the Vestris Gavotte. Thinking the question of no importance, Demarsept admits that he cannot do so, only to be told that there can be no question of Phrosine marrying a man who does not dance better than she. The lovers and Mme Duléger are aghast. They try to make the *dansomane* see sense, but to no avail. Demarsept cannot understand such a ridiculous turn of events, but while Duléger is practising his steps before a mirror, Mme Duléger tells the young couple not to despair, for she has a plan.

After Mme Duléger has taken Flicflac aside to make arrangements for a fête, Duléger welcomes a group of peasants who have come to dance for him. A young couple (Chameroy, Beaulieu) come forward to ask him to sign their marriage contract. The *dansomane* evinces no interest until his servant gives them a sign that they should dance. At this he is so excited that he showers them with banknotes. The act ends with the arrival of a shoe-seller. Among his wares is a pair of shoes marked with the name of Vestris. He tells the *dansomane* they are not for sale, but is persuaded to part with them at a price he cannot refuse. The shoes turn out to be too small for the *dansomane*, but with great difficulty he manages to squeeze his feet into them, convinced that something of the great dancer's magic will rub off on them. Finally he limps back towards his house, as the peasants trickle away homeward.

The second act opens with preparations for the fête. After making sure that everyone knows their part, Mme Duléger carefully adjusts Phrosine's dress so as to conceal another costume which she is wearing underneath it. Duléger, who is not in the secret, then comes into the garden walking painfully in Vestris's shoes. He is astounded by all that is going on around him, until his wife reminds him that it is his birthday. The festivities then begin with the bringing on of a large chest, from which springs a Jack-in-the-box who turns out to be his son. The child performs a Savoyard dance to his father's delight, and is then joined by two of his young cousins in a *pas de trois*.

There follows the main *divertissement* that has been planned by Mme Duléger and Flicflac. Three groups of dancers enter in turn to demonstrate their national dances before the Duléger family: one in Chinese costume, the next dressed as Turks and the last appearing as Basques. The leader of the Turks (Flicflac in disguise) announces that they have come to compete for the hand of his daughter. The *dansomane* delightedly acquiesces. The Chinese open the contest; their leader (Pasmoucheté) makes a great impression on Duléger, and Phrosine becomes noticeably nervous. Then comes the turn of the Turks, but their contribution is not to the *dansomane*'s liking. Finally it is the turn of the Basques, who carry the day. Unnoticed, Phrosine has discarded her outer dress and slipped away to join Demarsept, who has been cast as the leading Basque. Carried away, Duléger grabs his wife's hand, thinking it is his daughter's, and offers it to the Basque. Mme Duléger laughingly confesses to her ruse, which has turned out so successfully. Duléger is in no way put out, and gives the young couple his blessing – on condition that they will dance for him again.

It was a ballet to place in the annals beside that other comic masterpiece, Dauberval's *La Fille mal gardée*. By comparison the story of *La Dansomanie* might appear more contrived and certainly a little far-fetched, but the characters were, as in the earlier ballet, ordinary everyday people living in a recognisable countryside setting. It was also very much a ballet for its time. Although its setting was contemporary, it had no political message apart from reflecting France's growing stability in the first year of Bonaparte's Consulate.

The Duléger family were not aristocratic but gentry, living in comfortable style and surrounded by a docile and contented peasantry. It might have been imagined that the *dansomane* was one of those *nouveaux riches* who had acquired his property from some dispossessed emigré – in fact, a man very much of his time, *un bourgeois vivant noblement*. As for the hero, Demarsept, he had been promoted in the course of the ballet's gestation from being a 'young officer', as described in the first draft, to an 'Infantry Colonel'. Maybe Gardel thought this a more appropriate description, considering that the rôle was entrusted to the forty-year-old Vestris. It must also be remembered that colonels were younger in those days of war, and Demarsept could well have been a young hero who had served in Bonaparte's Army of Italy; rapid promotion was not unusual at that time, when the officer class, formerly reserved to the nobility, was opened to all.

Demarsept's English postillion, or 'jockey', was originally planned as a more important rôle, for in Gardel's first draft he was to lead an English contingent to open Mme Duléger's fête. France having been at war with the English for some years, a touch of caricature would not have come amiss; and Gardel had planned to make the most of this comic potential by showing the *dansomane* disgusted by their galumphing dances and raucous music. But on second thoughts he decided to cut this section, and poor Filippo Taglioni saw his rôle as John shrink into insignificance.

The only critic to have any reservations about the ballet was Geoffroy of the *Journal des débats*, who found it overlong but short on action, although he admitted it made full use of the dancers. It was indeed a feast of dancing. The Savoyard *divertissement* of the first act opened with a brilliantly witty character dance for three gossiping women, played by Chevigny, Pérignon and Collomb. It was a perfect little cameo, a lively bacchanalian frolic – 'the very intoxication of popular joy', as Geoffroy was to write on seeing it again five years later.[18] The other highlight of the first act was a *pas de deux* for a betrothed couple, charmingly portrayed by Adrienne Chameroy and a rising young dancer, Jean-Baptiste Beaulieu.

The contemporary setting and the *dansomane*'s obsession led Gardel to feed his imagination on the social dances of the time. Boasting more than a century of tradition, the gavotte had assumed a classical status in the ballroom, and Gardel had seized on this to make the Vestris Gavotte a main feature of his plot; but much more daring was a moment when the dancers circled the stage in couples to the infectious rhythm of the more intimate dance that was beginning to infiltrate society: the waltz. Mme Duléger's fête, however, had to be opened in a more formal manner. Since the entertainment had been planned as a surprise for her husband, he could not be her partner, and Gardel resolved this problem by adding a rôle for himself, that of the hostess's brother. It would be quite in character to show them as familiar with the manners of the Old Régime, and he therefore inserted at this point a formal minuet. Many of those present at the first performance would have realised what was in store on hearing the opening bars of the celebrated *Menuet de la cour*,[19] which the elder Vestris had danced at his benefit only a few months before. Dancing a minuet was second nature to Gardel, and there is no doubt that what he and Clotilde danced at this juncture was stylistically authentic and in no way a caricature. Even to younger eyes there was something indescribably impressive in this re-creation of 'the graces of the former Court – the unfurling of the figures, the dignity of the carriage, and the modesty of the attitudes that characterise this noble dance, now a somewhat outmoded monument to our former gallantry.'[20]

Gardel was to continue to perform the minuet in *La Dansomanie* for a number of years, partnered first by Clotilde and later by Victoire Saulnier the younger, whose costume was shortened to display her elegant footwork. But eventually, in 1809, it was dropped, conceivably because he considered that none of the younger dancers could do justice to the male

[18] *Journal des Débats*, 23 August 1805, commenting on a later performance by Chevigny, Aimée Vestris and Mlle Favre-Guiardele.

[19] Dr Tilden D. Russell has identified the music as being by Grétry, composed originally for the ballet of the nymphs of Diana in Act I of the opera, *Céphale et Procris* (1775).

[20] *Gazette nationale*, 27 Prairial, An VIII (16 June 1800).

part. As Geoffroy explained in 1805, the new generation was being trained with qualities different from those that had distinguished their predecessors:

> Today's dancers are more skilled in jumping, they rise much higher, and they perform steps requiring greater skill, ability and strength, but I feel that the stately minuet was more suitable for the entertainment of a high society who were not brought up to jump, and for whom the sole purpose of dancing was to present oneself well and display one's grace.'[21]

After the minuet Gardel had remained discreetly on stage as an onlooker until the Jack-in-the-box scene. The moment when the *dansomane*'s son sprang out was the cue for Gardel to bring out his violin, on which he proceeded to play a solo while the boy and two girls danced a noble and elegant *pas de trois*.[22] For many years this remained a major feature of the ballet, but when Gardel discontinued his appearances, there was no other dancer with the musical talent required. The violin solo[23] was thereafter played by a distinguished instrumentalist from the orchestra pit – first Rodolphe Kreutzer (to whom Beethoven was to dedicate one of his violin sonatas) and then François Habeneck.

The dances of the three national contingents presented a challenge to Gardel's ingenuity, which he met with great skill. Not once did the audience's attention wander, for the theme of rivalry for Phrosine's hand was being constantly alluded to in the pantomime between the *dansomane* and his daughter until the moment when the brilliant Basque dancer was revealed to be Demarsept himself. It was now that the Vestris Gavotte was performed by the gallant Colonel and Phrosine, the latter still unrecognised by her father, who is filled with delight at such a perfect display.

When Gardel, who had remained on stage until the end of the ballet, came forward to acknowledge the ovation given him as the ballet's author, it was impossible to decide who were applauding him more, the public or his comrades. His musical collaborator, Etienne Méhul, was also given a call; his score was almost entirely original, the only insertion, apart from the minuet, being the rondo for the Basque dance, which had been composed by Pierre Gavaux.

[21] *Journal des débats*, 24 May 1805.

[22] Later reviews, referring to the dancers in this *pas de trois* being goddesses and nymphs, suggest that it was adapted for three girls. In 1824 it was referred to as the *pas des trois cousines*.

[23] According to a note in Berchoux (156), the piece that Gardel played at this point came from Langlé's *opéra-comique*, *Corisande*, premiered at the Opéra in 1791.

The ballet was unequivocally a most brilliant success, but those of a more conservative frame of mind were a little disconcerted that such a rollicking comedy should be presented on the august boards of the Opéra. Was it prudent, wondered Geoffroy, for a dancer in the employ of the Opéra to ridicule the craze for dancing and stress the frivolous side of an art on which that theatre depended so heavily for its prestige?[24]

Others, however, were not bothered. The *Courrier des spectacles* considered it 'as perfect of its kind as *Télémaque*, *Psyché* and *Pâris* were in theirs'.[25] Another writer in the same journal commented that 'the serious nature ... of Citizen Gardel's other creations led us to feel he might find it difficult to come down from Olympus and mingle with mere mortals, but he has proved that if Terpsichore has found her Quinault in him, she can now equally well hail him as her Molière'.[26] Praise could hardly go further, but the applause and laughter that had punctuated the performance from beginning to end provided its own justification.

The ballet was performed with two superb sets, the scene-change between the acts being executed with commendable speed. In charge of this aspect of the production was Degotti, working closely with the machinist, Boullet. Where possible it was accepted practice to use material made for works no longer in the repertory, care of course being taken as far as possible to avoid recognition. In preparing his estimate, Degotti had proposed using part of a stock set known as 'the pleasant countryside scene', which reduced the cost for the first act to below 2200 francs. For the second act he offered an option: either having a completely new set, which would cost about 7500 francs, or using the garden set from Méhul's *Adrien*, which would effect a saving of about 2500 francs. One way or other, it was not an expensive production, although nobody complained of penny-pinching.

An amusing feature of the first act was the flight of the dove from Phrosine's first-floor room, bearing a letter to her lover's house on the other side of the stage. No suitably trained bird was available, and so, relying on his ingenuity to meet Gardel's requirements, Degotti rigged up a wire on which a painted wooden bird could be propelled from one side of the stage to the other. This worked smoothly enough until one evening in November 1801 when it stuck in mid-flight and remained embarrassingly suspended. Vestris, from his end, then tugged at the wire so hard that it snapped and the bird fell like a stone on the stage. It was finally the

[24] Geoffroy, V, 261-2.

[25] *Courrier des spectacles*, 15 June 1800.

[26] *Courrier des spectacles*, 19 June 1800. Quinault wrote libretti for many of Lully's operas.

dansomane himself who, disregarding the plot, took the initiative to deliver the note!

A mere nothing (to quote its author) though it might be, *La Dansomanie* was to have a special significance in the history of French ballet. As the first truly comic ballet to be presented on the Opéra stage, it expanded the horizons of the art not only by adding variety to the repertory but also in giving greater scope to the dancer-mime. Significantly, it was the comic rôles that made the most impression – the *dansomane*, his imbecile of a servant and the dancing-master's assistant. Jean Goyon as the *dansomane* was on stage virtually throughout the ballet, not for a moment departing from the spirit of his part and seizing every opportunity of raising a laugh. In the words of Geoffroy, he acted with 'a comic verve that not every speaking actor possesses'.[27]

The ballet maintained its popularity for more than quarter of a century. It passed its hundredth performance in January 1807, and its two-hundredth in May 1819; when it was last performed in 1826, it had been given 245 times. During those years only *Psyché* was more frequently performed, and even as late as 1824 *La Dansomanie* was being praised as 'the most original and witty *ballet de genre* in the entire repertory'.[28]

As time passed, those who had created the leading rôles inevitably handed on their mantles to others. Jean Goyon remained the archetypal *dansomane*. His fitness was somewhat precarious, and in February 1801 Gardel was thinking of asking Milon to take over the part. However, at that time Milon was heavily occupied with the early performances of his *Noces de Gamache*, and the singer Garat had come to his rescue, successfully pleading with Bonet not to overburden him. Milon did, however, play the part a few times in 1802 when Goyon was laid low by a painful bout of sciatica, but the latter soon returned to continue performing it until shortly before his death in 1815. The rôle was then taken over by Simon Mérante.

Advancing years eventually took their toll of Vestris too. Shortly before Vestris finally relinquished the rôle of Demarsept, Beaulieu, who was making a strong claim to succeed him, was struck by an illness to which he succumbed in 1811. Later, the rôle suited the young *danseur noble*, Albert, to perfection.

In time the seemingly ever-youthful Marie Gardel also retired, although Paris was to be treated to a last glimpse of her 'fascinating light-

[27] *Journal des débats*, 23 August 1805.
[28] *Journal de Paris*, 24 June 1824.

ness' and her distinctive *pas glissés* when she came out of retirement in 1819 to play Phrosine at her husband's benefit performance. After her, the part was danced by Fanny Bias and Amélie Legallois.

Clotilde abandoned the rôle of Mme Duléger in 1804, high-handedly informing Bonet that she would no longer appear in *La Dansomanie*. Bonet threatened her with a fine, and she called on him in high dudgeon. Bonet's request to put her refusal in writing did not improve the atmosphere, and she haughtily retorted that she never replied to administrators except by word of mouth. She was engaged to dance, she told him, not to play mother parts, which she had only done in the past out of the kindness of her heart.[29] The part of Mme Duléger was then taken over by Mimi Saulnier.

One of the final performances of this popular ballet was remarkable for the appearance of several dancers in rôles they had created twenty-four years before. It was given on 27 February 1826 for the benefit of the singer Mme Branchu, whose late husband had been the first Pasmoucheté. Sophie Chevigny was among those taking part, and Charles Beaupré returned to reveal vestiges of his former ebullience in his old rôle of the dancing-master's assistant; but the main attraction of this performance was the appearance, as Demarsept, of Auguste Vestris, who at sixty-seven was reported to have 'acted adequately for his age'.

* * *

'*Dansomanie*' was also an appropriate term to embrace the great swell of popularity that supported the claim of the ballet to be accepted as an equal partner with the opera, and in the summer of 1800 its enhanced standing was acknowledged by the provision of a separate retiring room for the dancers. Known as the Foyer da la Danse, it was situated on the first floor, facing north on to the Rue de Louvois. No pictorial record of this room survives, and memories of it gradually faded after the theatre was demolished in the 1820s. But it has a claim to be remembered as the forerunner of the cosy Foyer de la Danse of the Opéra Le Peletier, immortalised in paint by Eugène Lamy, and the august chamber that is today's Foyer, situated like a holy-of-holies behind the stage of the Palais Garnier.

[29] Arch. Nat., AJ^{13} 86. Bonet to Prefect of the Palace, 25 Ventôse, Year XII (15 March 1804).

7

Milon in the Ascendant

That summer a glow of optimism and hope seemed to hang in the air above Paris. Stirring reports from the battlefront were fostering new hopes of peace, and Paris seemed to be recovering its former gaiety. Carnival, which had been banished during the Revolution, was celebrated once again by the grace of the First Consul; and the Mardi Gras procession and the masked balls at the Opéra were revived to universal delight. There was racing again at Longchamp, and the theatres were full. At the Opéra, audiences were revelling in *La Dansomanie*; the Opéra-Comique was echoing to the refrains of Boïeldieu and Cherubini, and at the Ambigu-Comique the comedian Corsse was sending audiences into gales of laughter with his comic creation of Madame Angot, the very personification of the *nouveau-riche*. For the first time for many years there was much fun to be had in Paris.

Under its new Directors, the Opéra seemed to have overcome the doldrums of the 'nineties, and the popularity of ballet remained as high as ever. Having successfully launched *La Dansomanie*, Gardel found himself free to indulge his inspiration with new ideas. While he had not given up hope for his *Gauillaume Tell*, he was now turning his attention to planning another major work, based on the classical story of Achilles at Scyros. This, however, was still very much in its early stages, and it was convenient to allow his assistant, Milon, to have the next turn.

Milon was happy to revive his *Pygmalion*, which had had such a striking success at the Ambigu-Comique the year before, earning him the coveted post of second ballet-master at the Opéra. At the Ambigu it had been something of a family affair, with his wife dancing a minuet and her half-sister Emilie taking on the dual rôle of Delphide/Galatea. Now turned sixteen, Emilie was considered too young and inexperienced to be similarly featured at the Opéra, where the public expected to see at a première, not fledgling children, but dancers of tried skill and renown in which that theatre was so rich. So, when *Pygmalion* was offered in the grander surroundings of the Théâtre des Arts on 20 August 1800, during a sweltering heatwave, the cast of characters was headed by Vestris and Marie Gardel.

Vestris had already been seen as Pygmalion in a single appearance for Milon's benefit. Having discovered a penchant for acting, he relished parts with a dramatic content, and Pygmalion, who is driven out of his mind when Inconstant Love leads his beloved to prefer his rival, was just that – 'one of those crazy characters that [he] seems to play better than anyone else.' His rendering of even the most delicate feelings astonished this critic for its 'energy, pathos and truth'[1], but another found his grimacing a little too much to take.[2]

Marie Gardel, although she had appeared as Galatea at Milon's benefit, was now given the rôle of Delphide as one more suitable to the *demi-caractère* style. The part of Galatea was allocated to a younger beauty, Louise Chameroy, now accepted as Vestris's preferred partner, and Venus was portrayed by Mimi Saulnier. Beaulieu retained the minor rôle of Palemon, while also in their original parts were the two children who represented the contrasting aspects of love, Louis and Minette Duport – the former, now seventeen, already recognised as 'a really precious acquisition, both in the dance and in pantomime'.[3]

Although this was not his first production for the Opéra, Milon was nonetheless apprehensive, feeling that he still had to justify his appointment as second ballet-master. For him much would depend, not only on the impression the ballet would make on the public, but also, as he must have been acutely aware, on the relationship he had to establish with Gardel. His decision to dedicate the ballet to his superior was not so much a fawning tribute as a politic statement conveying a message of intended loyalty. He frankly admitted that, being at the threshold of what was virtually a new career, he was still unsure of himself, and that he had taken Gardel as his sole model. This first effort was offered, therefore, as 'a tribute of friendship and gratitude owed by a disciple to his master'. This was nicely put, and entirely sincere, for Milon did not, nor ever would, have any ambition to replace Gardel, with whom he was to maintain a smooth and happy relationship for the next twenty-six years.

The action of the ballet remained unchanged from the original production at the Ambigu. Milon, it was believed, had recognised that the opening scene, which introduced the two aspects of love, might appear weak. He had accepted this as a challenge and left it as it was, allowing it to be judged on two counts: first, as a flight of his imagination, and then, on his

[1] *Courrier des spectacles*, 3 Fructidor, Year VIII (21 August 1800).

[2] *Année théâtrale*, Year IX, 215.

[3] *Courrier des spectacles*, 9 Fructidor, Year VIII (27 August 1800).

skill and taste in attaching it to the ancient fable as told by Ovid in his *Metamorphoses*. In the result, the manner in which the two parts were interwoven revealed 'the touch of a master', every scene seeming 'incomparably fresh'. All through the 'allegory of two Cupids of opposing natures', the audience was held spell-bound and in a state of delighted amusement and anticipation of the familiar myth that was to be retold in the second act.'[4] In both scenes there were moments when the memory of some great painter was awakened: of Leonardo, at the moment when Delphide and the nymphs chase the inconstant Cupid in an attempt to clip his wings, and of Fragonard when Pygmalion pays homage to the statue of Cupid.

Another critic presented a different view, judging the ballet more severely by the higher standards expected at the Opéra:

> The absence of action, the complete lack of connection between the two acts, the longueur of some of the scenes and the monotony of certain situations were recognised as perceptible faults. But everything that related to the art of composing dances was deservedly applauded. Indeed, it was that part which offered the most successful tableaux, and the most ingeniously arranged scenes.'[5]

The second act, set in Pygmalion's workshop and played before a set originally painted for an unproduced opera, attracted less comment. Had it not been for the introductory scene, wrote a more supportive critic, *Pygmalion* 'would have been nothing but a pantomime – in a word, it would not have been a ballet any longer',[6] and this no doubt was a good reason for Marie Gardel choosing to play the part of Delphide.

The music which Lefebvre had written and arranged for this ballet was a considerable factor in its success. At the time it was considered outstanding, both in the passages accompanying the pantomime scenes – the 'declamatory' part, as one writer put it, for which the *airs parlants* had been judiciously selected – and, in a more general sense, considered as a whole. It was full of interesting contrasts of melody and harmony, and inspired one critic who used his ears as well as his eyes to write a rare assessment of the qualities needed in a conductor for the ballet:

> The heavy burden borne by the conductor at a ballet performance may not be sufficiently appreciated. It is here that he has to display excep-

[4] *Courrier des spectacles*, 9 Fructidor, Year VIII (27 August 1800).
[5] *Année théâtrale*, Year IX, 215.
[6] *Courrier des spectacles*, 9 Fructidor, Year IX (27 August 1800).

> tional understanding. Long experience is not an insignificant factor in bringing the dancing as a whole to perfection. He alone must know a principal dancer's strengths and weaknesses, and how to carry the work along in such a way as to support the steps and meaning of the dancing. Without for a moment losing his place in the score, he must keep his eye on those on stage, judge the tempi necessary to accompany their steps, shorten or lengthen pauses as required, mark the entrances, indicate to the musicians so rapidly as to be imperceptible to the audience, passages to be passed over or repeated, and have a feeling for the groups and in general the overall design and details of a ballet with as much precision and perception as that of the choreographer himself. The performance of an opera enables a conductor to be judged as a musician, but the performance of a ballet demands many other qualities that will be admired by those who enjoy observing the difficulties of an art and award praise to those who overcome them.[7]

Although by all accounts a worthy addition to the repertory, *Pygmalion* seems to have lacked the substance or the appeal to survive long in the repertory. Not only did it have to compete with more substantial ballets – Gardel's great triptych of *Télémaque*, *Psyché* and *Pâris*, not to mention *La Dansomanie* – but it was more vulnerable to the need to make room in the repertory for new works. Thus *Pygmalion* was eventually sacrificed, disappearing after its sixteenth performance in May 1802, neither unmourned nor, one hopes, forgotten by those who had enjoyed its delicacy of composition, which had first announced the arrival of a major choreographer.

* * *

That summer a prodigal son, André Deshayes, returned to the Opéra, richer by many guineas after a successful season at the King's Theatre in London. He may not have been welcomed with the enthusiasm that his talents alone might have entitled him; with the state of war existing between England and France, an escapade of that nature was unlikely to endear him either to the authorities or to his fellow dancers.

He would also have had before him the example of Alexis Huard, a dancer of no mean technique, possessing 'surprising agility, aplomb and strength',[8] who a year before had decamped to Madrid to take up an

[7] *Courrier des spectacles*, 13 Fructidor, Year VIII (31 August 1800).

[8] *Courrier républicain*, 4 Nivôse, Year V (24 December 1796).

engagement as ballet-master and principal dancer. Huard had been driven to this extremity by finding himself unable to pay his debts. The cause of his ruin had been the fall in value of assignats, and the advance he received from Spain enabled him to pay off his creditors. But even though he had not gone to an enemy country, he lost his pension rights by resigning.[9]

However, while Huard had been nearing the end of his career, young Deshayes could confidently look ahead to a glowing future, and was well aware that lusher fields awaited him if Paris were to prove difficult.

The Opéra had been his nursery. His father, Jacques-François Deshayes, a nephew of the celebrated actor, Préville, had at one time concurrently held the posts of Director of the School of Dance and ballet-master of the Comédie-Française, and there was never any question but that young André and his elder brother would follow in the family profession. André was admitted as a pupil at the School of Dance in March 1785, at the age of nine. He could have had no better teacher than his father, who had seen to it that he was introduced to the stage at the age of six or seven, dancing on the boards of the little Théâtre de Beaujolais in the gallery of the Palais-Royal and what in later years he used to call the Panthéon, by which was presumably meant the Petit Panthéon, a public ball that was converted early in the Revolution to become the Théâtre du Vaudeville.

In 1787 André and his brother were inscribed among the dancer-figurants of the Comédie-Française, and in his childhood days he also occasionally took part in performances at the Opéra. By 1789 he was a growing lad of twelve and already showing remarkable promise. It became a great source of pride that he had been among the last group of dancers to be invited to perform before the King and Queen at Versailles before the Old Régime was shattered by the Revolution.

He was taken on to the payroll of the Opéra as a figurant in 1792. While his elder brother joined the army and was lost to the dance, he himself went on from strength to strength. He rose rapidly through the hierarchy, being promoted to *double* in 1794 and to *remplacement* two years later. His exceptional gifts soon began to be recognised, and in the autumn of 1796, when Vestris was away dancing for Dauberval in Bordeaux, he was given opportunities he could hardly have expected so soon and found himself flattered as a potential rival of the great man. Of course, when Vestris returned, such opportunities dried up, but Deshayes' ambition had been whetted.

Indeed, such was its extent that he had even been tempted into signing

[9] Arch. Nat., AJ^{13} 68 (V).

a contract with Sébastien Gallet, who was gathering a company for the London opera season due to open in the winter of 1797. Wisely he had decided at the last minute against taking such a risk, being joined in this decision by Sophie Chevigny, who had also signed a contract. Having demonstrated his loyalty, he seemed destined for promotion in due course to *premier artiste*; but, to everyone's surprise, in March 1798 he suddenly left the Opéra, seeing it perhaps as 'a sinking ship' under the disintegrating control of the Artistes' Committee. Meanwhile he had formed a romantic attachment for another dancer of the Opéra, Elisabeth Duchemin, who resigned several months later and was to become his wife.

Emboldened by the relaxation of the political situation, Deshayes accepted an engagement at the Teatro de los Caños del Peral, Madrid's opera house, for the season of 1799. From there, after short engagements in Marseilles and Montpellier, he made his way to London, where he made his English début in the congenial company of other expatriate dancers: Charles Didelot and Mlle Rose (now his wife), the Labories and Marie-Louise Hiligsberg.

But he soon began to have doubts about the wisdom of leaving the Opéra; he turned down lucrative proposals for the following season, and in August made his way back to Paris with the expectation of being readmitted to the Opéra. However, he had not counted on the resentment still felt among the dancers at Didelot's and Laborie's defections from the Opéra 'at a time when their emigration could have ruined that fine institution.'[10] On his return to France he was shocked to find himself arrested and thrown into gaol – according to his account, in the very tower of the Temple where Marie-Antoinette had been incarcerated. His crime – that of having gone to Madrid and London, the latter then an enemy capital, without a passport – was not all that grave. The financial director, Cellerier, was able to obtain the approval of Lucien Bonaparte, the Minister of the Interior, for him to be readmitted to the fold, and furthermore to be promoted to *premier artiste* in the *noble* genre, sharing that rank as a male dancer only with Auguste Vestris.

His escapade did, however, give rise to some lurid rumours that were still circulating a couple of years later, and certainly caused no harm to his growing reputation. It was then being whispered that he had been 'convicted during the time of Robespierre of an attempt to emigrate to

[10] Such feeling was still strong at the end of 1802 when, during the brief period of the Peace of Amiens, Didelot and Laborie were reported to be making overtures to return to the Opéra. 'Foreign states have been savouring their talent,' commented one paper, 'and it would only be just that they should enjoy the fruits of their old age there. Deserters, take note!' (*Journal de Paris*, 16 November 1802.)

England. He was condemned to the guillotine; but afterwards pardoned, on condition of dancing, during the whole of one season, without fee or reward, before *le peuple souverain*.[11]

Such rumours were no doubt unfounded, but Deshayes may have fallen foul of the authorities through his friendship with Louis Boisgirard, who as a royalist agent had abetted the dramatic escape of Captain Sidney Smith. Smith was regarded as an important prisoner, having been instrumental in blowing up half the French fleet during the Siege of Toulon in 1793. He had later been captured off the coast of France, and had languished in prison for two years before making his escape. Boisgirard, who was picked up by the police soon afterwards, had been using the Opéra as his cover, although it does not appear that he was actually employed there. Deshayes met him when he was briefly imprisoned in the Temple, and was able to arrange for him to be released and engaged at the Opéra as a figurant.[12]

It must have seemed that Deshayes had reached the pinnacle of his ambition, but ill luck and his difficult character were to make his stay at the Opéra short-lived. When he returned in the title rôle in *Télémaque* on 17 October 1800, he was visibly 'nervous, as if realising he was being reproached for having been absent so long'. At the next performance three days later, 'Vestris's rival', as he was already being called in some quarters, seemed more confident, although he was criticised for trying a little too hard to emulate 'the tedious difficulties that are too much in fashion', rather than relying on the more refined qualities of the *noble* style for which he was naturally suited.[13]

His next rôle was Zephyr in *Psyché*, a part he had previously played with success. The ballet had been given an impressive new set for Venus's bath scene, painted in a single month by an artist named Robert. For Deshayes this was a very special occasion, for the two male *premiers sujets*, Vestris and himself, would be appearing together. Vestris, playing his original part of Cupid, was in top form that evening, clearly unafraid of competition. In a great display of speed and daring he gave his all, but when the two danced together they seemed so perfectly matched that it was hard to decide to whom to award the palm: to the senior for his vigour or to the junior for his gentler style.

[11] Lemaistre, 190–1.

[12] Deshayes himself is the authority for his relationship with Boisgirard (Bibl.-Musée de l'Opéra, Dossier d'artiste, Deshayes). The name Boisgirard appears among the figurants in the company lists of the Opéra for the years XI to XIII (1802–5). For his career in London, see Guest, *Romantic Ballet in England*, 28, 85.)

[13] *Courrier des spectacles*, 30 Vendémiaire, Year IX (22 October 1800).

Some weeks later, dancing in the same ballet, Deshayes slipped and fell. According to him,[14] a charlatan from the pit then jumped on to the stage and calmed the audience, which included Mme Bonaparte, by announcing that he would cure the dancer. He proceeded to remove Deshayes' shoe, and rubbed the injured foot with his own, muttering some apparently mystical words. This may not have done much harm, but Deshayes, who had no more dancing to do, unwisely continued his rôle until the end of the ballet. In fact his injury proved much more serious than he had realised. It was thought he had skidded on a slippery patch, left by a member of the public who had been allowed on to the stage before the ballet. The next day, the First Consul, having heard of the accident from his wife, sent his personal surgeon, Dr Yvan, to see what he could do, but without much avail. The unfortunate Deshayes was unable to walk for five months, and after that only with the aid of crutches. It was fourteen months before he was fit enough to dance again, a period of inactivity bitterly hard to endure for a young man to whom the pinnacle of his profession seemed within his grasp. The experience would leave him scarred by a deep-seated resentment, as the powers at the Opéra were to discover.[15]

* * *

With the repertory enriched by two new ballets, the activity of the Opéra turned to the production of a major opera, *Les Horaces*. Based on Corneille's tragedy, the libretto had previously served an opera by Salieri, which had been a failure, and was now resurrected with a new score by Bernardo Porta. The librettist, Nicholas Guillard, who had a number of operas already to his credit, including Gluck's *Iphigénie en Tauride*, was an experienced figure whose suggestions bore some weight at the Opéra. He was also a great admirer of Gardel, whose martial dance for the Scythians in *Iphigénie en Tauride* had given him the idea of staging the celebrated combat scene between the two sets of brothers, the Horatii representing Rome and the Curiaces representing Alba, for six dancers without orchestral accompaniment. The combat was of course to be set by Gardel, who probably also arranged the tableau of the Horatius brothers, swearing their oath, faithfully reproducing the celebrated painting by David.

14 The story of the charlatan was recounted by Deshayes in some biographical notes of his career (Bibl.-Musée de l'Opéra, Dossier d'artiste, Deshayes).

15 The presumed cause of the accident had been suggested in the *Courrier des spectacles* (13 December 1800), which had probably been read by Deshayes, sowing the suspicion in his mind that the Opéra had been at fault.

First given on 20 October 1800, Porta's *Les Horaces* made only a marginally better impression than Salieri's. The mimed combat scene unfortunately fell rather flat; the sudden silence from the orchestra pit disconcerted the audience.

Porta's *Les Horaces* did not vanish from history quite without trace, for the evening of the first performance had been selected by a band of Jacobin conspirators for an attempt on the First Consul's life. His decision to attend the performance had been known for some time; on being told of the plot, he had decided not to alter his plans but to entrust his safety to the efficiency of the police. The chorus of the oath was to be the signal; some of the conspirators would then extinguish the lanterns in the corridors, others would cause a diversion by throwing fire-crackers from the upper tiers, shouting 'Fire!' while an armed band, taking advantage of the panic, would burst into Bonaparte's box and kill him. However, the plot was betrayed, and the police moved in to arrest the conspirators with such quiet efficiency that not only were they taken completely by surprise and offered no resistance, but the audience was unaware that anything untoward had occurred.

Much more serious in its consequences was another attempt on Bonaparte's life two months later. Police spies had overheard whispers that a plot was being hatched for the evening of 24 December, when Bonaparte would again be attending the Opéra, to hear Haydn's oratorio, *The Creation*. The theatre was inspected from attics to basement and found secure, and once again the First Consul decided against changing his plans.

His route to the Opéra was short and direct: the consular carriage would leave the stables in the inner courtyard of the Tuileries (the Caroussel), turn into the Rue Saint-Nicaise and continue north on the Rue de la Loi. No details of the plot had come to the ears of the police, and no one had noticed a strange contraption on a small cart in the Rue Saint-Nicaise as Bonaparte's carriage drove swiftly past followed by a mounted escort. Seconds later an enormous explosion left a toll of dead and wounded lying in the street. The little cart had carried an 'infernal machine' consisting of an iron-hooped barrel filled with nails and gunpowder, and its intended victim had escaped destruction through the luckiest of chances. Josephine had decided to change her shawl at the last minute; briefly delayed, Bonaparte had set off alone, leaving the womenfolk to follow in another carriage. His own carriage had emerged from the Tuileries at a greater speed than usual, catching the bomber unawares. It was shaken by the explosion, and some of the mounted escort had been caught in the blast, but the coachman was ordered to drive on.

Meanwhile, in the Opéra, the performance had already begun when the explosion was clearly heard above the music. A shock of apprehension and fear spread through the audience. Ten minutes or so passed before the suspense was broken. Then the door of the empty box was seen to open and Bonaparte came forward, calm and smiling as if nothing had happened, accompanied by four of his generals. The house at once broke into an emotional burst of cheering. Many women were weeping tears of relief, and their menfolk were still visibly shocked. In face of such a demonstration, even Bonaparte's composure for a moment gave way.

* * *

Meanwhile, Gardel's *Dansomanie* had paved the way for an even more rollicking comic ballet on which Milon was now at work, *Les Noces de Gamache*. Its derivation from two chapters in Cervantes's great novel, *Don Quixote*, gave it a veneer of respectability and no doubt helped it on the way to acceptance. From the long sequence of adventures featuring the maniacal Knight of the Doleful Countenance and his comic squire, Sancho Panza, Milon had selected the predicament of Quiteria, whose father, the landlord of an inn, plans to marry her to the rich Camacho, and the successful ruse of her poor sweetheart Basilius, who by feigning death wins her for himself. Milon described his ballet as a *'ballet-pantomime-féerie'*, but it was really more of a *'folie'* and therein lay the secret of its long popularity. His scenario was packed with incident and detail, but no one complained that it was hard to follow or confusing. Wisely, Milon had followed Cervantes's story, adding little in the transcription that was not to be found elsewhere in the novel.

The curtain rose to reveal the Spanish village where Laurenzo (Goyon) keeps his inn. His daughter Quitterie[16] (Chevigny) is in love with Basile (Aug.Vestris), but he is poor and her father has plans to marry her to the wealthy Gamache. After sending Basile packing, Laurenzo and Gamache (Lebel) discuss the terms of the marriage contract over generous draughts of wine. When Laurenzo becomes drowsy, Gamache turns his attention to Quitterie, but she scorns him and slips away to keep a tryst with Basile. As daylight fades, Don Quixote (Aumer) and his squire, Sancho Panza (Beaupré), make their appearance, the Don being under the delusion that he has arrived at a castle. Taking Laurenzo to be its noble owner, he falls to his knees before him. In his drunken stupor, Laurenzo bids them enter. Sancho follows his master, imitating his char-

[16] In describing this ballet, I have adopted the spelling of the names of the characters as they appear in the scenario, with the exception of that of Don Quixote.

acteristic walk, but, before he can reach the door, is set upon by a band of youths who draw him into a game of blind man's buff and abandon him clutching the stump of a tree. Famished, Sancho makes his way into the inn, only to find that dinner is over!

During the night Don Quixote is unable to sleep for thoughts of Dulcinea, the ideal lady of his confused imagination to whom his exploits of knight-errantry are dedicated. He takes a walk outside, gazing at her medallion. Sancho then appears, complaining that he has gone without his supper. His master believes he wants to admire his lady's portrait, and when Sancho becomes angry at being misunderstood, orders him to kneel down and beg the lady's pardon. They retire for the night, but Sancho cannot sleep for hunger pains. He slips out and finds the larder. Meanwhile, Quitterie has crept out too, to keep an assignation with Basile, who acquaints her with the ruse he has devised to thwart the plan to marry her to Gamache. They are interrupted by a noise, which also wakes Don Quixote, who takes it as a sign that a new adventure is about to begin. Quitterie has to pass the Don's bed on her way back to her own; under the delusion that she is Dulcinea, he clasps her in his arms and expresses his passion. Meanwhile, Sancho, who has assuaged his hunger and is trying to wash his hands, has got one of them stuck in a pitcher. Unable to break it without waking everybody up, he remembers the tree-stump. At that moment Don Quixote emerges from the inn in pursuit of Quitterie, and Sancho, mistaking him for the tree-stump in the dark, breaks the pitcher over his head. Horrified when he realises what he has done, he takes to his heels, leaving his master in the belief that evil spirits and giants are attacking him. Slashing right and left with his sword, he eventually realises he is alone, and concludes that his enemies have fled and that he has won a great victory. By now everyone has been woken up by the clatter. Laurenzo is convinced that Don Quixote is mad, and the latter is only calmed down when the villagers invite him to attend the wedding party of Gamache and Quitterie. They all disperse. As Basile then enters, looking very conspiratorial and carrying a black mourning robe and a sheaf of cypress leaves, the act closes.

For the second act the scene has moved to the countryside, where the wedding party is in progress. Don Quixote and Sancho arrive, the one enjoying the festive atmosphere, but the other only interested in what there will be to eat. As part of the festivities, a character dressed as an armed knight challenges any comer to single combat. The Don accepts, and Sancho finds himself also challenged by the knight's equerry. In a desperate attempt to avoid such an encounter, he bumps into his master and falls flat on his face. This makes him so angry that he attacks the equerry, and in the course of the rumpus knocks down both his master and the knight with whom he is duelling. Sancho is now angrier than ever, and the villagers can only appease him by awarding him the prize. But now it is Don Quixote's turn to be angry; he draws his sword and cravenly Sancho begs forgiveness and hands over the prize to his master.

Quitterie and Gamache then arrive, accompanied by the Mayor, but before they can proceed to their wedding, Basile appears swathed in the black cloak. He makes a great fuss, berating Quitterie for being unfaithful, and with a dramatic gesture, appears to thrust his sword into his chest. Everyone is aghast as he falls to the ground. Quitterie is in tears, and even her father is affected, but Gamache is unmoved. As for Don Quixote, he is quite carried away at having witnessed such a heroic act. He feels Basile's pulse, dolefully announces that there can be no hope for the poor lad, and proposes that he should marry Quitterie *in extremis*. Gamache very reluctantly gives his consent after it has been explained to him that when Basile breathes his last, Quitterie will be free to marry him. But as soon as the couple are pronounced man and wife, Basile springs to his feet and announces that it has all been a trick. Gamache turns on Don Quixote, who draws his sword and chases him into the wings. Meanwhile Sancho has run off to gorge himself on cakes and wine. The Don returns, still in pursuit of Gamache, and is only with difficulty persuaded out of his murderous intent. Sancho then comes waddling back, his stomach swollen with all the food he has stuffed into it, with the remains of a half-eaten cake sticking out of his mouth. In this state the girls force him to dance, and the revelry is still continuing when the curtain finally falls.

Certainly the comedy was very much broader than that of *La Dansomanie*, and not surprisingly a few eyebrows were raised. Geoffroy of the *Journal des débats* looked back to the days when the Opéra left 'farces and other nonsensical pieces' to the minor theatres, preferring to preserve its dignity intact. 'But now it is not so proud and is even becoming human, and perhaps a little too human. With so many ways of appealing to the public, it should leave it to others to make people laugh.'[17] Geoffroy would in time recover from his shock; twelve years later he was recognising *Les Noces de Gamache* as a minor classic, 'a ballet-pantomime that might be compared to a painting by Teniers in which burlesque farce alternates with the most graceful of scenes'.[18]

Other critics, however, took this novel introduction of knockabout comedy more in their stride. The *Mercure* had noted that certain 'delicate

[17] *Journal des débats*, 30 Nivôse, Year IX (20 January 1801).
[18] *Journal de l'Empire*, 21 December 1812.

connoisseurs' had criticised the rôle of Sancho Panza for containing too much clowning, but was sure that 'even the most woeful [would] perhaps admit to having laughed and been disarmed.'[19] The *Journal de Paris* was not at all shocked by this 'burlesque ballet'; nothing could be crazier or merrier, even though it was 'a curious sort of spectacle, put on with intent to attract all who love art and gaiety.'[20] Most enthusiastic of all was the *Courrier des spectacles*, for whom no subject could have been better chosen. 'One cannot help wondering,' wrote its critic, 'what happy circumstance has led us to discover in a ballet what we have been looking for in vain in modern comedies, namely a well-ordered plot, a logical action, and characters that are sustained throughout'.[21]

Milon had drawn his characters superbly well, making the most of the foibles of Don Quixote and Sancho Panza. Jean Aumer proved himself a memorable Don Quixote. 'His lean body, his pallid, elongated visage, his grave and melancholy air all made it possible to recognise the Knight of the Doleful Countenance as seen in engravings and as described by the immortal Cervantes,' wrote Geoffroy.[22] The *Courrier des spectacles* thought him 'extremely funny', while Beaupré was 'Sancho Panza in the flesh, making you laugh out loud at his grotesque appearance, his gluttony and his clowning',[23] even if his final appearance with half a cake sticking out of his mouth seemed to overstep the bounds of good taste. How unrestrained was the 'knockabout' by-play between Aumer and Beaupré was to be demonstrated a few months later when the former accidentally wounded his colleague with his lance and drew blood. The only disappointment was that their two steeds, Rosinante and Dainty, appeared only momentarily at the back of the stage.

As Quitterie, Sophie Chevigny presented a character that was endearingly naïve, while Vestris, playing Basile, was as ebullient as ever. Goyon's rôle as Laurenzo was less prominent, although he had his moment in the first act when getting progressively intoxicated as his discussion with Gamache proceeded. Gamache was little more than a foil for the other characters, and not even Dauberval's cousin, Lebel, could make much out of the part. The scenario did not list the names of all who participated in the first performance, but among the anonymous children was a twelve-year-old girl known only as Emilie, who in later years, as Emilie

[19] *Mercure de France*, Pluviôse, Year IX (January/February 1801).
[20] *Journal de Paris*, 30 Nivôse, Year IX (20 January 1801).
[21] *Courrier des spectacles*, 30 Nivôse, Year IX (20 January 1801).
[22] *Journal des débats*, 30 Nivôse, Year IX (20 January 1801).
[23] *Courrier des spectacles*, 3 Floréal, Year IX (23 April 1801).

Leverd, was to become celebrated as an actress of the Comédie-Française.[24]

The first dance in the ballet came, as a natural insertion, early in the first act, during the tryst of the two lovers. Quitterie is playing with a ribbon when Basile steals up to her unawares and tries to snatch it away. Sensing her displeasure, he takes up his guitar and soon has her dancing to her favourite melody. This *pas de deux* had germinated in Milon's mind some time before when he, Gardel and Chevigny had been dining with the Spanish ambassador, and a young relative of the host had enchanted them in a Spanish dance with castanets. Both Gardel and Milon vowed to stage it at the Opéra, and it was Milon who had that privilege in *Les Noces de Gamache*. Someone, who may have heard the story from him, thought it too good to be forgotten, and many years later wrote it up for a theatrical journal:

> Vestris and Mlle Chevigny made it all the rage. The modest grace of the poses was found especially enchanting by the public, which was under the illusion that still prevails today, that such dances must necessarily be *décolletées*. This *pas* contributed to the ballet's success. It is a shame that it has not been preserved, for today [that is, 1841] it would provide a contrast that would be instructive for some and charming for others. Perhaps M. Milon still has the music in his rich portfolio.[25]

Another choreographic highlight was a *pas de trois* in the wedding scene; much praised for its design, it was danced by young André Deshayes, as a troubadour, with Marie Gardel and Adrienne Chameroy. This preceded the last dance of all, reserved for the two principals, Vestris and Chevigny, who brought the festivities to their climax with a brilliant *fandango*, 'a sort of Spanish minuet, much livelier and gayer than the ordinary minuet', as Geoffroy rather quaintly observed. Here Vestris was very well served by Milon, being given several 'amazing entrances'. He was also very conspicuous in the general dancing at the end; 'in order to leave the audience with a wonderful image in their mind's eye of his talent and his great superiority, [he] performed perilous jumps and bounded with such vigour that his head was forever rising above the other dancers like that of Diana surveying the nymphs of her suite'.[26]

General comments on the production were on the whole very favourable. B***, writing in the *Courrier des spectacles*, thought it 'praiseworthy

[24] Castil-Blaze, *Académie*, II, 79-80.
[25] *Courrier des théâtres*, 22 January 1841.
[26] *Journal des débats*, 30 Nivôse, Year IX (20 January 1801).

both as a whole and in every detail'. The *Journal de Paris* agreed, commenting that the composition of the dances had added greatly to Milon's reputation. Only Geoffroy remained difficult to please; the dances, he thought, were attractive enough, but they had nothing to distinguish them from any other ballet at the Opéra; indeed they seemed even 'more ordinary and less meaningful', and too prodigal for a village wedding.[27]

Lefebvre's score, much of it a patchwork, attracted little attention, and was considered hardly more than adequate, the judgements ranging from 'mediocre' to 'suitable and well adapted to the action'.

However, none of these reservations detracted from the ballet's success with the public, and at the end, when he was announced as the author and brought on to take his call, Milon was given a rousing ovation that visibly overwhelmed him. There could be no doubt that the ballet would become a sure favourite, as indeed it did. In its first two years it was performed more frequently than any other ballet, even *Psyché*; it reached its hundredth performance in December 1806, and retained its place in the repertory until 1820. In 1841, twenty-one years later, it was to be thought worthy of revival, with Georges Elie and Jean-Baptiste Barrez as Don Quixote and Sancho Panza, and Maria [Jacob] as Quitterie, but the world had moved on and it had lost its bite. Although Théophile Gautier gave it a kindly notice, it had little appeal for a public so besotted with the marvels of the new school of Romanticism.[28]

[27] *Courrier des spectacles, Journal de Paris, Journal des débats*, 30 Nivôse, Year IX (20 January 1801).
[28] *Presse*, 23 January 1841.

8

Three Young Dancers: Two Losses and a Gain

Mozart had now been dead ten years. There must have still been a few older habitués of the Opéra who remembered him from that unhappy summer in Paris in 1778 when he lost his mother and supplied Noverre with music for *Les Petits Riens*. Although none of his operas had been staged in Paris, awareness of his genius had been growing in musical circles, and from time to time notices of ballets had drawn attention to passages borrowed from his works. Considering the dearth of novelties during the Revolution and the Directoire, it was not all that surprising that his operas remained unperformed, and allowing for that, the decision in 1801 to stage a version of *Die Zauberflöte* at the Opéra was not too belated.

However, doubts had been expressed as to whether a faithful staging with a French text would appeal to the Paris public, and of course an adjustment would have to be made to accommodate a ballet. This was the background against which emerged, under the title *Les Mystères d'Isis*, a virtual parody of the original *singspiel*, written with the best of intentions of making it palatable to Paris, and with its music chopped about to include extracts from *Don Giovanni*, *Le nozzi de Figaro* and *La clemenza di Tito*, not to mention a couple of insertions from symphonies by Haydn. The change of title was not only fair to the memory of Mozart, but also indicated a significant change of focus from Masonic rites to pharaonic Egyptian mysteries.

Up to a point those responsible for the adaptation achieved their purpose, for the work, first presented on 20 August 1801, would hold its place in the repertory until 1827. The inserted ballet was a significant factor in its success, Gardel's evocation of a great ceremony in worship of the goddess Isis being so impressive that the Director, Bonet, paid an unprecedented tribute to him in an open letter to the press:

> I owe you a *formal* acknowledgement of *my* particular satisfaction with the way in which you have handled the production of *Les Mystères d'Isis*, and I hasten to *express it publicly*.

> Art cannot go further than your skilful depiction of the brilliant splendour of the cult of Isis, showing us the *august* mysteries once celebrated at Memphis, crowned with such innocent grace and such impressive majesty.
>
> Should the production of this opera add to the glory of this establishment, the principal credit will be yours for the taste you have displayed in assuring its success.
>
> Please inform the dancers on my behalf how pleased I was by their brilliant showing in the performance of *Les Mystères d'Isis*.[1]

This great ballet scene formed the climax of the opera. All Gardel's unerring taste and choreographic skill had been brought to bear to present a display of feminine grace and dexterity and male vigour and lightness such as could be seen only at the Opéra. It reached its climax with Vestris delivering himself of a salvo of amazingly steady pirouettes, but younger dancers, notably Saint-Amant and Beaulieu, were also given prominence to display their virtuosity. And for the audience's delight, Gardel had a special surprise up his sleeve.

With tongue in cheek he had devised a *pas d'égyptiens* in which his most promising pupil, Louis Duport, gave a brilliant impression of the grotesque style of the Italians. This was no doubt a parody of a small troupe of Italian dancers that had been billed at the Théâtre de la Société Olympique a month before. Their entire performance seemed to consist of repeated *écarts*, jumps, and even *doubles tours en l'air* (which had not at that time been seen at the Opéra), but performed with all-too-visible preparations and heavy landings and presented with a complete lack of artistry. They had no success, and after a few performances returned to Italy; but they did at least inspire Gardel to show how a young dancer with impeccable technique and striking allure could adopt the grotesque style in a way that was in good taste without in any way diminishing its content of virtuosity.[2] Although there was apparently a touch of parody in the general dance into which Duport's solo was inserted, Gardel had made a conscious effort to add historical verisimilitude by studying the ancient Egyptian collection in the Louvre. Not everyone appreciated his erudition, but an English visitor, writing to a friend *à propos* recent archaeological discoveries, added as an afterthought: 'I suppose you know

[1] Letter dated 4 Fructidor, Year IX (22 August 1801), published in the *Journal de Paris* of 9 Fructidor, Year IX.

[2] The ballet-master of the Ambigu-Comique, Richard, presented a parody of Gardel's ballet in the melodrama *Le Jugement de Salomon* in January 1802.

that in the *Mystères d'Isis* at Paris, there is an entire ballet copied from the 'Obelisks' – all the dancers [form hieroglyphic poses]'[3]

It was in *Les Mystères d'Isis* a year later that Jean Coralli made his début in a *pas de deux* with his wife Teresa. As his name implied, Coralli was of Italian extraction, although born in Paris. He claimed to have been trained at the Opéra, but he was more likely a private pupil of Gardel or Coulon. At the time of his début he was already twenty-three, and was clearly being introduced to the public not as a prospective addition to the company, but as a special favour from Gardel that would give him that cachet of approval so valuable to a dancer at the outset of his career. The couple acquitted themselves well enough; Coralli's physical strength was impressive, but his aplomb in *tours de force* was found a little lacking.[4] After this single appearance, he departed to continue his career abroad. It would be more than twenty years before he returned to Paris. By then his dancing career would be over, but he was to repay his small debt to the Opéra many times over when he became its principal ballet-master in the palmy years of the Romantic ballet.

* * *

During the summer of 1801, hopes began to rise of an end to the hostilities with England, and on 1 October, to widespread relief, the preliminaries of peace were signed. Although details of the peace treaty still remained to be settled, there was cause for celebration, and little more than a month after Mozart, so to speak, had entered the portals of the Opéra, a one-act pastiche of an eighteenth-century opera-ballet, *Le Casque et les Colombes*, was presented with music by Grétry and dances by Gardel. No more than an anacreontic conceit about Venus's efforts to persuade Mars to abandon his warlike ways and bring peace to the world, it was never intended to be anything but a *pièce de circonstance*, and it disappeared after a few performances, leaving barely a memory in the minds of those who had sat through it.

This was among the pieces on offer to a veritable invasion of English visitors who were now pouring into Paris, which had been out of bounds to them for so long. Generally the ballet appealed to them more than the opera, and a knowledgeable and exceptionally observant English lady, Mary Berry, recorded in her diary some revealing impressions of two vis-

[3] Berry, II, 237. Sir Harry Englefield to Mary Berry, 18 February 1803. As originally written, the passage ended: "all the dancers were" followed by four pictograms in the hieroglyphic style.
[4] *Courrier des spectacles*, 7 Fructidor, Year X (25 August 1802).

its to the Opéra that she made during this brief interlude of peace. She dismissed the opera as 'always a dull thing', but had to admit that 'the dancing is certainly more *marvellous* than ever,' although with the qualification: 'I do not think it more pleasing.' She continued:

> In the first ballet [in the opera *Anacréon*] there was only one *entrée* of men, three together, all the rest were women, of whom six were capital dancers; but the women now dance in the style of men, that is to say, with all the difficult steps and *tours de force* possible. A long *pas de deux* was performed with such a perfect *ensemble* and precision, that one was obliged to rub one's eyes to feel sure it was not two machines moved by the same strings.

The ballet that followed was *Télémaque*, which she considered to be 'not half so well given as by D'Egville in London.'[5] She was experienced enough to perceive that Vestris was not ideally suited to the rôle of Telemachus.

> He is still marvellous and has movements that nobody else ever had, but he is grown so much thicker that his figure looks *écrasé* and his head too large; his wig was bushy light hair, curled all over. Mdlle Clotilde was Calypso, and at first I did not much admire her figure, which is remarkably tall, but when she came in dressed for hunting, she was the exact copy of the statue called the *Diana Caciatrice*, the drapery of which is open just above the knee, and in my life I never saw such perfect legs, nor legs so perfectly resembling those of the Apollo, into the attitudes of which they fell a thousand times. All the other women dancers were dressed in one petticoat of white muslin, or something as thin, with another drapery of the same stuff arranged in various ways about half as long as the first, but both allowing the whole form to be fully perceived up to the waist, covered with flesh-coloured *tricot*. Some of them had no covering above the waist but flesh-coloured *tricot*, with some little scrap on one shoulder.[6]

On her next visit, Miss Berry saw *Psyché* with Marie Gardel and Saint-Amant as Psyche and Cupid. Her description of it as 'a long pantomime, little dancing, but admirable in its way', suggests she found it overlong.

[5] This was a production by J.H.d'Egville of his teacher Dauberval's version of *Télémaque* during the London season of 1799, and revived in 1800 and 1801.
[6] Berry, II 137–8 (entry of 16 March 1802).

Nevertheless, there was plenty in it to admire: 'the scene of Psyche ascending the rock, of her being carried off in the clouds by Cupid [it was, in fact, Zephyr], and of her torments in Tartarus; of her toilet and her lesson of dancing given by Terpsichore.' She then went on to make an interesting general comment on the superiority of the Paris ballet. 'In all the ballets here,' she wrote, 'even when there are not many *entrées* of the principal dancers, the *remplissage* of figurants, &c. is never tiresome, because it is done with a grace and a perfection of execution which exists here, and here only.'[7]

A few days later her path again crossed that of Vestris, not this time in his stage persona but as a social celebrity. The occasion was a grand ball given by the fabulously wealthy Prince Demidoff, and she was somewhat taken aback by the sight of Vestris taking part in a quadrille. 'Vestris's figure was curious,' she recorded; 'his coiffure was one of those bustling, frizzed and powdered heads which were worn about twenty years ago, and in dancing, showers of powder came out of it, and it flapped up and down in the most ridiculous manner.'[8]

* * *

The continuing absence of Deshayes, who was still recovering from his fall of the year before, was to be another dancer's opportunity. Charles Saint-Amant was altogether an easier character than the discontented invalid: open, without a trace of jealousy in his nature, and popular with his comrades. In November 1801 he appeared in the title rôle of *Télémaque*, making an excellent impression by his thoughtful interpretation. His was not the only cast-change that evening, for there was also a new Eucharis – Marie Millière, who caught the eye of one critic in a *pas* performed to what he called 'Garat's romance'.[9]

That autumn, when the weather turned cold, the Opéra was smitten by one blow after another. Bonet was almost at his wit's end. Among his singers, Laïs had a nervous breakdown, Mme Branchu lost a child, Mlle Armand was down with a heavy cold, Mlle Maillard had a sore throat, Chéron had dysentery, and Adrien a fever. Nor were the dancers in any better state. Mme Gardel had a miscarriage, Chevigny was suffering from gout in her knee and was about to undergo a dental operation, Beaulieu

[7] Berry, II 161–2 (entry of 29 March 1802).
[8] Berry, II 174 (entry of 2 April 1802).
[9] Pierre Garat was the greatest concert singer of his day. He had made his reputation at the court of Louis XVI, and this romance may have been one of those that had so delighted Marie-Antoinette.

had a sore throat, and Saint-Amant, who was never robust, was also on the sick list. Deshayes had not yet recovered, and to cap it all, Vestris and Chameroy were away dancing in Bordeaux and Montpellier.[10] Both *Les Mystères d'Isis* and *La Dansomanie* had to be taken off. 'As you will see, I am having great difficulty in keeping things going,' Bonet told the Minister. 'To attract the public I have had no alternative but to have Mlle Bigottini make her début in the ballet.'[11]

But how fortunate he was to have young Bigottini up his sleeve! The hastening of her début was of course an unexpected boon to her, but for the public it was to reveal a talent that would be considered extraordinary in an experienced artiste. Of the two pantomime rôles in which she was to be tested, that of Psyche was the most daunting in the entire repertory, requiring its interpreter to express an astonishing range of feelings and emotions, and pitting her against the ballerina for whom it had been created, Marie Gardel.

Although announced as only fifteen, Emilia Bigottini was in fact two years older – perhaps a deliberate falsehood by the administration to stimulate the indulgence of the public. She was the child of the celebrated Harlequin of the Comédie-Italienne, Francesco Bigottini, by his second marriage, and had a half-sister, Louise, twenty years her senior. Louise had been a useful member of the Opéra ballet from 1777 until her retirement in 1794. She never rose out of the *corps de ballet*, remaining a figurante until the end, but the lack of advancement had not diminished her commitment to her profession, for she assiduously took classes from the Hennequin brothers to whom dancers went in pre-Revolutionary times to improve their suppleness and strengthen their backs and legs.[12] Now long retired, she was happily married to Louis Milon, who had been responsible for Emilie's training.

Emilie had thus grown up in a theatrical environment, among family traditions rooted in both the Commedia dell'Arte and the Opéra, where her brother-in-law Milon had the reputation of being one of the most versatile mime artistes. He was a man of imagination and, as his adaptation from *Don Quixote* bore witness, well-read – as were most choreographers at a time when it was incumbent on them to prepare their own scenarios. Under his auspices Emilie had first faced an audience across

[10] In his letter to the Minister, Bonet wrote that they were in London, but in fact they were enjoying a triumph in Bordeaux in *La Fille mal gardée*.

[11] Archives de l'Opéra, quoted in *L'Intermédiaire*, 568 (12 December 1891), 1043–4. Bonet to Minister of the Interior, 9 Brumaire, Year X (30 October 1801).

[12] Anon., *Vol plus haut*, 128.

the footlights at the Ambigu-Comique in 1799, in the double rôle of Delphide and Galatea in his *Pygmalion*.

The decision to launch her in the part of Delphide on her début on 27 October 1801 gave her the advantage of a trial in a familiar rôle before she faced the more daunting challenge three weeks later on 19 November, when she appeared as Psyche, supported by Saint-Amant as Cupid and Beaulieu as Zephyr.

As her performance as Psyche unfolded, it became increasingly evident that a star of dazzling brilliance had risen in the firmament of ballet. What was so extraordinary was the completeness of her talent. As the *Courrier des spectacles* pointed out, it was rare to find talents for dance and pantomime so happily combined as they were in 'this new *actress*' – a term for which the writer made no apology, seeing her as 'an actress in the true sense, even in the least significant situations'. Indeed, she seemed blessed with every attribute that could be desired: 'noble features, the most expressive eyes, a beautifully placed head, a tall and slender figure, an easy gait, and arms that are amazingly graceful'.

The scene in the second act when Psyche wakes to find herself in an enchanted palace, whither she has been spirited at Cupid's bidding, was regarded as one of the most difficult exercises in the art of pantomime, so varied are the emotions that have to be conveyed. Her fears, her wooing by the invisible Cupid, and the dramatic scene with Venus who appears disguised as her mother – all presented a formidable challenge, but the young dancer concealed any difficulties 'with an extremely delicate touch'. Her gestures were astonishingly precise, her whole bearing revealing a sensitivity that was all the more effective for being so natural. 'It is qualities such as these,' commented the critic of the *Courrier des spectacles*, 'that make one fully realise the value of good training,' a nice tribute to her teacher, Milon.

Also in this act was the celebrated scene in which Psyche is instructed in the various characters of the dance by the muse Terpsichore, 'perhaps the greatest masterpiece in the entire field of dance':

> Here the very art of the dance has to be displayed; proficiency must be proved in every genre. But mere proficiency is not enough, for this passage permits no mediocrity in its performance.[13]

[13] This, and the quotations in the two preceding paragraphs, are from the article by B*** in *Courrier des Spectacles*, 30 Brumaire, Year IX (21 November 1801). (*Psyché* is described in detail in Guest, *Enlightenment*, Chapter 17.)

In this scene, Bigottini was joined by Clotilde as Terpsichore. To see them together was a moment to remember:

> On one side we have Mlle Clotilde, a beauty renowned both for the regularity of her features and for the nobility of her bearing, demonstrating to her young pupil all the secrets of her art, and on the other, Mlle Bigottini, attentive and docile, repeating every step and every movement of her model with fluency and precision. The illusion is complete: we see the Muse of the Dance instructing the youngest of the Graces.[14]

By nature and build Bigottini was a *demi-caractère* dancer, but here she seized the opportunity of showing that the division into genres need not be exclusive, and that it was possible for a dancer to excel in both the *noble* and the *demi-caractère*, and even in the *comique* genre too. That she had made her point was proved by the applause that echoed the flattering compliment paid by Terpsichore to Psyche in the choreography.

The third act brought further ovations. In the apotheosis, when Psyche casts herself at Jupiter's feet in gratitude for her deliverance, she once again displayed that sure theatrical sense that had made the evening so memorable. 'Here,' wrote her admirer in the *Courrier des spectacles*, 'Mlle Bigottini invested her walk, the placement of her head and arms, and her features with such a glow of natural happiness as to throw into the shade the glory of divine majesty. And such perfection distinguishes the début performances of a girl who is not yet sixteen!'[15]

In the festive scene that brought *Psyché* to its close, her dancing again revealed the finish and accuracy of her technique, and the consistency of her interpretation:

> While her feet are performing the most brilliant difficulties, the rest of her body, and her arms in particular, retain their fluency and grace. She holds that charming *équilibre* that follows a pirouette with equal aplomb and lightness. But to the more graceful [i.e. *noble*] genre she adds energy, investing her steps with bold extensions that mark the style of Mlles Clotilde and Saulnier, and it is that quality above all that makes one feel that Mlle Bigottini will one day be one of the greatest pillars of the dance.[16]

[14] *Mercure de France*, Nivôse, Year X (December 1801/January 1802).

[15] *Courrier des spectacles*, 20 Frimaire, Year X (11 December 1801). Bigottini was in fact seventeen.

[16] *Courrier des spectacles*, 30 Brumaire, Year X (21 November 1801). Notice signed B***.

All in all, it was an extraordinary achievement. She had exceeded every expectation: 'grace, suppleness, strength, and profound insight, whether depicting astonishment, fear, joy or sadness – she [had] it all.'[17]

Had she appeared ten years earlier, she might have expected a rapid ascent to the uppermost rank, but by 1801 the company was exceptionally rich in talent, and she had to wait longer for promotion. She was admitted into the company as a *double*, and only two years later would be promoted to *remplacement* in the *demi-caractère* genre. But long before she eventually attained the rank of *premier sujet* in 1812, she had earned the affection of the public as a principal in her own right.

* * *

The doctors had now pronounced André Deshayes fit enough to resume his career. As a *premier sujet*, he had a presumptive right to a creation, and the Opéra may have felt a degree of responsibility for his accident. To mark his return, therefore, Gardel devised a one-act *divertissement*, *La Vallée de Tempé*, which he subtitled, in a graceful allusion to the dancer, *Le Retour de Zéphire*. Its plot quite openly alluded to Deshayes himself, whose performance as the god of the winds in *Psyché* had become a golden memory during his enforced absence. The ballet is set in the valley of the river Tempe, with the mountains of Pelion and Ossa rising up on either side in the distance, and a Temple of Apollo prominent in the foreground. A happy band of shepherds and shepherdesses are dancing without a care in the world. But the sky darkens, and they are scattered by a violent storm. Zephyr (Deshayes) is injured, and the rural divinities, Flora (Chevigny), Pomona (Collomb) and Ceres (M. Saulnier), bedraggled and bemoaning the disaster to their crops and flowers, come to implore the assistance of Apollo. That god (Aumer) answers the summons and agrees to send his son Aesculapius (Victor), the great healer, to tend to Zephyr's wounds. Completely restored, Zephyr is welcomed to health, and the ballet concludes with a brilliant *divertissement*.

It was not a ballet to be taken very seriously, although it was to be remarkably long-lived. One of its claims to be remembered lay in the score by Daniel Steibelt, who had forborne to interpolate any borrowed melodies.[18]

Reporting on the first performance on 3 March 1802, the *Mercure de*

[17] *Courrier des Spectacles*, 20 Frimaire, Year X (11 December 1801).

[18] The claim that it was the first wholly original ballet score to have been heard at the Opéra seems to ignore Rochefort's music for *Bacchus et Ariane*, which had attracted attention for that very reason ten years before.

France merely remarked that 'it managed to interest the public without anyone bothering to write about it.'[19] That was not quite accurate, for Geoffroy gave it a fair hearing in the *Journal des débats*. He considered the idea of solemnising the return of a dancer excessive and even unseemly; it was in any case an 'insipid adulation, harmful even to [Deshayes], for artistes are too much inclined to puff themselves up with empty pride that can only stifle their talent.' But the dancing, he conceded, was quite another matter:

> What is totally delightful is the performance, the design of the dances, the aspect of the various groups, and the combination of talents that Citizen Gardel has succeeded in bringing into play with such artistry and taste. If *Le Retour de Zéphire* has nothing to say to the intellect, one's eyes are enchanted by the sight of proud Diana, played by Clotilde, giving an archery lesson to two nymphs, of Terpsichore whom one could not fail to recognise in the form of Mme Gardel, of laughing Flora whose light and lively graces are brought to life by the dancing of Chevigny, of benevolent Ceres whose gentle majesty is drawn to perfection by Saulnier, etc. And among those goddesses of the first order can be espied a host of lesser divinities of the countryside who, while they do not raise their legs quite so high, are no less supple, charming and sensual. And let us not forget Zephyr himself, the god of the festivity, whose slender figure, interesting features and graceful movements delight the audience, and who, through the elegance of his attitudes and the delicacy and smoothness of his dancing, seems to make up for what he lacks perhaps in strength.[20]

Relations between Gardel and Deshayes were already strained. Towards the end of March, Cellerier, who had taken over responsibility for running the Opéra following Bonet's resignation in December, was surprised to receive a letter from the young dancer, tendering his resignation. Soundings that Cellerier then made led him to suspect that Deshayes had accepted an engagement in London and had no intention of working out his period of notice.

This was extremely inconvenient in view of Deshayes' position in the company, but it also highlighted a problem that had become increasingly acute: the activity of foreign agents who hovered like wasps around the Opéra, trying to entice dancers with offers far more lucrative than any-

[19] *Mercure de France*, Germinal, Year X (March/April 1802).
[20] *Journal des débats*, 24 Ventôse, Year X (15 March 1802).

thing the Opéra could match. The Ministry of the Interior had specifically prohibited provincial theatres from making offers to dancers on the Opéra payroll, but little could be done to curb the activities of agents from London or Berlin, for example. Cellerier's first thought was to beseech Comte Roederer, the Councillor of State, to take some sort of action to prevent Deshayes from leaving, perhaps by seeking the intervention of the ambassadors. But there was a problem as far as England was concerned, for although the peace treaty had been signed at Amiens at the end of March, no ambassador had yet arrived in Paris.

Deshayes, by now thoroughly disaffected, tried to justify his action to Cellerier. His medical expenses during his long recuperation had been very heavy, and he had convinced himself that he was entitled to the performance bonuses, or *feux*, which he would have received if the accident had not occurred, arguing that his injury had been caused by 'excessive zeal' in the line of duty. He alleged that he had refused offers at a much higher salary from various European countries. He was also upset at not being cast in any of the leading rôles in the *noble* genre, and at having to take on rôles belonging to other genres. And then, he added, there was the matter of the indifference with which he had been received at the time of his return.

A few weeks then passed without any further development. Cellerier may have hoped that the storm had blown over, but it had not. In May, Deshayes' anger and frustration exploded in an unpleasant incident, which Cellerier described in vivid detail to Roederer, the Counsellor of State:

> The most indecent scene took place this evening at the theatre. Citizen Deshayes buttonholed me to tell me he would be playing the part of the Deserter on Sunday. I replied that Citizen Gardel was to play it at the request of his comrades. Citizen Deshayes then claimed that, as a *premier danseur*, he would not allow anyone else to play it. I pointed out that Citizen Gardel had obtained from the Minister the right to keep the pantomime rôles that suited him, of which there were at most only two, the Deserter and the Concerto in *La Dansomanie*.
>
> I will not expound on the lengths to which Citizen Deshayes went in his insolence. He abused me so coarsely that I was obliged to have him removed from the theatre by a guard and taken to the Police Station. There, in the presence of Citizen Gardel and two officers, and after a lively exchange of words in which Citizen Gardel was as cool as ever, we managed to make Citizen Deshayes see reason, and Citizen Gardel agreed to give up the part for the sake of peace.

> Citizen Deshayes' conduct has revolted all his comrades; his insolence and his threats are a scandal that calls for him to be punished as an example to others. No one sets more store by Citizen Deshayes' talent than I, and it is with regret that I am reporting the offence he has committed, but, Citizen Counsellor of State, I should forfeit the respect and the authority which are so necessary to maintain discipline in an establishment placed under my direction were I not to request the greatest severity to be applied towards an artiste who has dared to conduct himself so outrageously towards his administrator...
>
> Citizen Deshayes' conduct pains me all the more in that it is to me that he owes his return to France, his release from imprisonment, and his place at the theatre, and that I have always held him in great affection. But his lack of gratitude is notorious, and does not extend to me alone; the Citizens Vestris and, in particular, Gardel, to whom he owes his talent, have even greater cause for complaint.[21]

Deshayes' letter of explanation had been written about two weeks before this incident, and had been forwarded to Roederer. There could be no question of paying *feux* for performances in which he had not taken part, but in a final effort to secure Deshayes' services, Roederer offered to increase his salary to the figure that Vestris was receiving – a rise of 3000 francs to 15,000 francs. This was coupled with a warning that, if he persisted in his intention to go abroad, he would not only lose his ranking and the rewards that went with it, but would be treated as having left the Republic as a 'fugitive'. He was also informed that he would not be granted a passport.

Deshayes was not to be so easily deflected from his purpose, for his services were indeed in great demand. He made it clear that his resignation stood, and by September, when six months had passed since his notice of resignation had been served, there was little the Opéra could do. His departure, wrote Cellerier, was 'very annoying. He is the only *premier danseur sérieux* we have. His talents have endeared him to the public, and his place will be difficult to fill. I have written to the Minister of the Interior, who, now that he is charged with the interior police, will, I believe, have the means to prevent Citizen Deshayes from obtaining a passport.'[22]

It was now inevitable that the Opéra would lose him. Bent on exploiting his talent to best advantage, Deshayes had no difficulty in negotiating

[21] Arch. Nat., AJ[13] 45. Cellerier to Roederer, 1 Prairial, Year X (21 May 1802).

[22] Arch. Nat., AJ[13] 45. Cellerier to Fourcroy, who had just succeeded Roederer, 30 Fructidor, Year X (17 September 1802).

an engagement to head the ballet at La Scala, Milan, for the approaching Carnival season, being joined there a few months later by his wife. And from Milan he would go to London, where he was to pass the greater part of a long and distinguished career as dancer and ballet-master.[23]

* * *

On 15 July 1802, Pierre Gardel was given a well-deserved and somewhat belated benefit. Dance was of course the main focus of the programme, and two ballets were given, separated by an *opéra-comique* 'to give the eyes a rest, and the dancers time to recover their breath'. The first of these was *Le Jugement de Pâris* with Deshayes, and the evening concluded with a revival of Gardel's brother's ballet, *Ninette à la cour*, which was to be memorable for the participation in the opening scene of Antonio Franconi's trained circus horses. It went without saying that the public found them a great improvement on the wickerwork animals that had been used in the original production. The scene itself had also been completely rearranged to Méhul's *La Chasse du jeune Henri*, and as one critic wrote:

> no illusion could be more ravishing than the introduction of these horses in the various incidents of a stag hunt that form the greater part of the first act. Imagine Méhul's superb hunt music ... set in action and, as one might say, transcribed into a poem, and you will have an idea of a scene which is so true to life that it surpasses anything that has been seen before at the Opéra. The passage of these horses through the forest, the action of the huntsmen in pursuit of the stag, their coming to rest to give signals, and the fanfares of the hunting horns produced an effect which aroused the greatest enthusiasm.[24]

It was a nice tribute to his deceased brother, but it did not earn the ballet a place in the repertory, for Franconi's horses could not be engaged for regular performances. Without that novelty, the action of the ballet lacked substance and its music sounded thin and old-fashioned to the ears of a later generation.

[23] His links with Paris were by no means cut completely. In 1816 he was appointed dancing-master to the King's pages and teacher of theatrical deportment at the Royal School of Music, a post he held until his death. In 1824 Charles X appointed him dancing master to the royal princes.

[24] *Courrier des spectacles*, 28 Messidor, Year X (17 July 1802). Gardel was to produce *La Chasse du jeune Henri* again in May 1826, but on a more modest scale, using eight dancers and a stag trained by Franconi.

* * *

A strange, disturbing rumour was floating around the Opéra as the spring of 1802 approached. Auguste Vestris and Louise Chameroy had been absent for some weeks, dancing in Bordeaux, and it was whispered that both had met with a sudden end. How this story originated, let alone the details of the supposed tragedy that had taken place on 'the banks of the Garonne',[25] was a mystery. It was soon shown to be without foundation.

But more serious was the discovery of a plot to organise a hostile reception when the couple were to reappear at the Opéra. The police discovered that a large quantity of tickets had been bought up on behalf of supporters and opponents of the couple for this performance, and the Minister was assured that those responsible would be kept under strict observation.[26] The vigilance of the police was enough to prove effective, for no untoward scenes disturbed the welcome the two dancers received when they returned in *Le Jugement de Pâris* on 6 March. Nevertheless, an unmistakable antagonism had been spreading within the company, of which a visiting Russian dancer, Ivan Valberkh, became aware when he overheard one dancer commenting to another that Vestris was '*décousu*' – going to pieces.[27]

The idyll of Vestris and Chameroy was now approaching its mournful end. Not many weeks after they came back from Bordeaux, she returned to her apartment, feeling chilled and out of sorts. Her dry cough left her doctor in no doubt that she was suffering from an advanced stage of consumption. This diagnosis came as no surprise, for she had seen her father die of the same complaint when she was a child, and had long had a premonition that she would be similarly stricken. One who had followed her short career thought she had been overtaxing her strength. Her dancing, he explained, was 'more vigorous than graceful; although very delicate, she had followed her natural inclination instead of conserving her strength, and this error was partly responsible for cutting short a career which she herself said she had no hope of continuing beyond the age of twenty-four'.[28] Other friends, learning she was ill, were convinced she was a victim to fashion, remembering how, after a performance during which she had been profusely perspiring, she would put on a light muslin dress that left her neck and shoulders bare, and go out into the

[25] *Courrier des spectacles*, 17 Ventôse, Year X (7 March 1802).
[26] Arch. Nat., F^7 3830. Report of the Prefecture of Police, 14 Ventôse, Year X (4 March 1802).
[27] Valberkh, 59 (entry of 14 March 1802, old style).
[28] *Observateur des spectacles*, 28 Vendémiaire, Year XI (20 October 1802).

chilly evening air without a shawl. She was also pregnant, and gave birth to a child not long before she died.

Her death was registered by Jean Aumer and another witness on 15 October, her age being given as 24 years and 5 months. A gentle, friendly soul, she was much mourned by her fellow dancers, who made a collection to pay for her funeral. The day after her death, in the late afternoon, a sizeable gathering of mourners, many from the Opéra but not a few from other theatres, collected outside the house in which she had died, No. 8 Rue de Louvois. After the coffin, draped in white as was customary for an unmarried woman, had been placed on the hearse, the procession moved slowly off towards the church of Saint-Roch, where it was expected the coffin would be admitted. On the way the band of mourners was swollen by a number of curious passers-by. But on reaching the church they found the doors closed. Dazincourt, a distinguished actor of the Comédie-Française, called loudly for admittance. Eventually his call was heard, and the curé, the Abbé Marduel, made an appearance. Hearing the deceased's identity, he peremptorily refused permission for the coffin to be brought into his church on the ground that, being a dancer, the deceased was an excommunicant in the eyes of the Church. A reference to the recent Concordat was airily brushed aside. Another obstacle in the eyes of this unenlightened priest was that the deceased was an unmarried mother.

The situation now turned threatening, for the mourners had been joined by a large crowd only too willing to take up cudgels on behalf of the deceased. Someone called for the doors of the church to be forced and the vicarage assaulted, and a few stones were thrown. Aghast at the turn that events were taking, Dazincourt raised his powerful voice and called the crowd to order. There was an alternative plan, he told them, and the procession moved away to the Church of the Filles-Saint-Thomas, whose more liberally minded curé was standing at the door of his church when they arrived. By the time mass had been said for Chameroy's soul, night had almost fallen. The procession then reformed to accompany the coffin to the cemetery in Montmartre, passing on the way the Café Frascati, a fashionable haunt of theatre folk, where Chameroy had often supped and danced in her all-too-short heyday.

Meanwhile, the Abbé Marduel of Saint-Roch was in no mood to be charitable, and when it came to his notice that one of his choirboys had sung at the service at the Filles-Saint-Thomas, the poor lad was summarily dismissed. The incident did not rest there, for there were political repercussions. Only a few months earlier, the First Consul had succeeded in agreeing a Concordat with the Vatican. Anticlericalism was still deep-seated in a sizeable proportion of the population, and incidents such as this could only damage the spirit of co-operation with the Church that Bonaparte was anxious to foster. When news of the incident reached him, he was so incensed that he dictated an article for *Le Moniteur* condemning prejudices that could only bring the Church into disrepute and ridicule. And it was no doubt under pressure from the Tuileries that the newly appointed Archbishop of Paris, a 93-year-old cleric chosen no doubt for being pliable, ordered Marduel to go into retreat for three months and ponder Christ's message that one should love one's enemies.

Where, on this sad day, was Vestris? His name is strangely absent from accounts of the funeral and its consequences. And what became of the baby that Chameroy left behind: the fruit, presumably, of her escapade with that wayward dancer on the banks of the Garonne, and if so, not the only bastard he had fathered? One can only hope that he shed a few tears for his mistress before seeking consolation elsewhere. All too soon his roving eye was caught by the sparkling little Dutch dancer, Mlle Polly, who probably turned him down, and then it shifted, rather more seriously, to Louise Courtois, for whom he even contemplated divorcing poor Mlle Aimée.[29] But Mlle Courtois, 'the all too charming Louise', was to die in the summer of 1806; Vestris was then forty-six, and the salacious stories of his amours were dying down. Mlle Aimée died of tuberculosis in 1818, but not until 1823 was he to marry for the second time. He then chose not a seductive young dancer, but the daughter of a kindly neighbour who befriended him when his fortunes were at their lowest ebb – one Jeanne-Marie Thuiller, who to her eternal credit cared for him until he died in 1842, and who now lies by his side in the cemetery of Montmartre.

[29] Bibl.-Mus. de l'Opéra, Fonds Collomb, 22. Bonamy-Berville to Collomb, 20 August 1803.

9

Dauberval and Noverre Revived

In the progressively monarchical structure of Bonaparte's Consular regime, the Opéra was to play a significant rôle. This became apparent when, on 11 January 1803, the First Consul signed an Order placing the Opéra under the supervision of the Prefect of his Palace. Bonet was confirmed in his functions as Director, and the State was to provide a subsidy of 50,000 francs a month. For the time being Morel was left in his post as Deputy Director, concerned mainly, it seems, with artistic policy.

The First Consul and Mme Bonaparte were planning to attend the first performance following this restructuring on 12 January, and the programme had been notified to the Tuileries. It was to conclude with a new two-act ballet on which Gardel had been working for some months, *Daphnis et Pandrose*. Great was the consternation, therefore, when Gardel announced that it could not be ready in time. When notified of this hitch, Luçay, the Prefect of the Palace, peremptorily replied that the ballet must be given on the date arranged. 'This performance,' he tersely informed Morel, 'has been notified to the First Consul and Mme Bonaparte, and you must cast your thoughts back to the times of a wise and well-ordered administration, when all obstacles were swept aside and there was a will to overcome them.'[1]

But Gardel, the last man to shirk his duty, was in a real quandary and lost no time in setting the facts before Morel:

> I have just received the letter you have had the honour to send me, enclosing a copy of one you have received from the Prefect of the Palace concerning my ballet, *Daphnis*.
>
> That letter greatly distressed me because it is absolutely impossible to give the first performance of this ballet on Tuesday the 21st [Nivôse], as I had hoped, for the following reasons.
>
> 1. Mme Victoire Saulnier, one of my pupils whom I was planning to present for her début in one of the principal rôles, and who already

[1] Arch. Nat., AJ[13] 89. Luçay to Morel, 15 Nivôse, Year XI (6 January 1803).

knows it, is at this moment so ill that I no longer have any hope of seeing my work adorned by her superb physique. I, therefore, need time to teach the rôle of Dryas to Mme [Aimée] Vestris, who is very willing to take it over.

2. The ball that you are giving is depriving me of two rehearsals, those of Saturday evening and Sunday morning.

3. The terrible pressure on the stage staff (I say terrible because the staff worked sixteen hours without a break for yesterday's performance of *Oedipe* and *Pâris*) does not give our able machinist and myself all the time I need. For he only received the scenery yesterday. Finally, dear Sir, if the problem were merely whether I should sacrifice my spare time to satisfy the wishes of the Prefect and yourself, I can assure you I would gladly work into the night, but as you know that is impossible, for at the present moment my work depends more on others than on myself.

Tomorrow I shall call a meeting of the heads of the departments, and will have the honour of notifying you of the day when all my worries will be at an end.[2]

Even Bonaparte had to bow to the inevitable, and it was to Gardel's credit that his ballet was delayed by no more than forty-eight hours. Being unable to present his young pupil in this ballet was a personal disappointment, for he was on close terms with the Saulnier family, and Victoire, the youngest, was his favourite pupil. He had been living in the hope that she might have sufficiently recovered to appear in his new ballet, while at the same time worrying lest she should suffer a relapse if she returned to work too soon.[3] The rôle was in fact of secondary importance, for the action of the ballet was to fall mainly on the shoulders of Mme Gardel and Clotilde. The two notices of the ballet that appeared in the press both made a passing reference to Mlle Saulnier as one of the cast, misled by the fact that the cast list in the programme had not been corrected, and overlooking Gardel's announcement in the press that Mme Vestris would be replacing her.

Although the plot of *Daphnis et Pandrose* might appear, at first glance, to be based on Greek mythology, it had in fact been taken from a short novel by Mme de Genlis which Gardel had probably been permitted to

[2] Arch. Nat., AJ^{13} 89. Gardel to Morel, 15 Nivôse, Year XI (6 January 1803). The Victoire Saulnier mentioned is not to be confused with the dancer of the same name who retired in 1794 and may have been her aunt.

[3] *Journal de Paris*, 18 Nivôse, Year XI (9 January 1803).

read in manuscript.[4] Félicité de Genlis had been governess to the children of the former Duc d'Orléans, who had espoused the Revolution under the name of Philippe Egalité and was eventually guillotined; she had also been his mistress, bearing him at least one child. She had made her reputation as a prolific writer of novels and works on education and various other topical subjects; on her return to Paris after several years of emigration, she had been welcomed as a celebrity. She was particularly admired by the First Consul, who placed at her disposal an apartment at the Arsenal, where Gardel may have made her acquaintance at one of her celebrated 'Saturdays'. The hero of the novel, Daphnis, was clearly suggested by the legendary Sicilian shepherd – the son of Mercury by a nymph – whom Pan taught to play the flute, and who was regarded as the inventor of bucolic poetry. However, both the nymph Pandrose and Dryas, the goddess of modesty and chastity, were inventions of Mme de Genlis as, of course, was the plot itself. Nevertheless, the Oreads, who featured in it, do figure in mythology as nymphs of mountains and caves.

Gardel's ballet was based only on the first half of Mme de Genlis's mythological pastiche. Daphnis (Aug. Vestris) has fallen in love with Pandrose (Clotilde), a nymph in the service of Dryas (Aim. Vestris). Cupid (Mme Gardel), who by his very nature is the natural enemy of that goddess, takes the young man's part and assumes the form of Pandrose's friend Coronis (Millière). In that disguise he makes his way into Dryas's Temple, which men are prohibited from entering on pain of death. Within are a number of statues, one being covered by a veil. To this statue Dryas now conducts Pandrose. Removing its veil, she reveals the figure of Cupid, warning Pandrose to guard against the tricks of that wily little god, and handing her the veil that will offer protection should Cupid appear to her in one of his disguises. But Pandora fails to notice the substitution when Cupid assumes the form of her friend, and allows herself to follow the disguised god out of the temple.

The second act takes place on Mount Etna, where the Cyclops are discovered at work in the depths below, forging a thunderbolt for Jupiter. When their task is done, they disport themselves in a frighteningly grotesque dance before disappearing. Cupid then appears, still disguised, describing the delights of love to the mystified Pandrose. Strains of Daphnis's lyre are then heard; before she can escape, Pandrose finds Daphnis kneeling at her feet, declaring his love. Her first thought is to cover her head with the veil, but Cupid snatches it away, and the couple

[4] Her *Daphnis et Pandrose* was published in the *Nouvelle Bibliothèque des romans* (5th year, vol. 7: Year XI - 1803).

melt into each other's arms. Cupid consigns Dryas and the Oreads to the bowels of the earth, and the ballet ends with an apotheosis.

For the music to accompany this somewhat contrived theme, Gardel had turned to his friend Méhul, who had served him so well in *La Dansomanie*. On this occasion, however, the composer preferred to remain anonymous, forgoing the ovation that would have been his due in the customary announcement of the authors. The reason for such reticence was perhaps the extent of the musical borrowings on which Gardel had presumably insisted. The overture was ascribed in the score to 'Himmer' (Hummel perhaps?). In the first act there were borrowings from Haydn – the first movement, *presto*, from Symphony No. 67 – and horn solos and harp music respectively by Frédéric Duvernoy and Dalvimaire. Act II contained an overture by Winter, a piece by Kreutzer, a long passage from ballet music that Ernest Miller had written for Grétry's *Aspasie* (1789), and a *bourrée* from Gluck's *Echo et Narcisse*.[5]

Such success as the ballet achieved was almost entirely due to the dances, for its action was dismissed as too 'slender'[6] and too 'cold and obscure'[7] to engage the interest of a spectator on a second hearing. The only rôle of any consequence was that of Cupid, which Marie Gardel 'could not have played more intelligently, with a greater sense of mischief, or more expressively'.[8]

However, Geoffroy of the *Journal des débats* made it plain that he had not enjoyed it, and this was also the reaction of a Prussian visitor who managed to get a seat for the first night only by what he mysteriously called an 'old theatrical tactic'. This was Johann Friedrich Reichardt, who had nearly had an opera produced in Paris before the Revolution and whose opinion deserved respect. He recorded his impressions in a letter to a friend:

> *Daphnis et Pandrose*, which had been announced and postponed for months, has at last been performed ... The public and I were equally disenchanted with Gardel's choreography ... The scenario, based on an insignificant short story by Mme de Genlis, was incomprehensible; the dances were fussy and lacking in form and artistic arrangement; and Chastity was presented in long white draperies, ridiculously thrashing about among nymphs who were perhaps even less dressed than usual

[5] Bibl.-Mus. de l'Opéra, A 384.

[6] *Courrier des spectacles*, 25 Nivôse, Year XI (16 January 1803). Review by F.J.B.P.G***.

[7] *Journal des débats*, 3 Pluviôse, Year XI (24 January 1803).

[8] *Courrier des spectacles*, 25 Nivôse, Year XI (16 January 1803).

> and seemed to have no more to do than stretch their legs. The music was a sad pot-pourri in which not even the harp and horn concertos which are showered upon us nowadays had any success.[9]

At its first performance, *Daphnis et Pandrose* was well received, no doubt largely out of respect for the presence of Bonaparte, but Gardel was not blind to its faults and made a few adjustments for the second showing four days later. One of these was to replace the headwear of a group of peasant children that, on account of their resemblance to the Phrygian woollen bonnets associated with the Revolution, had 'revived memories which it is as well to try and forget'.[10] Gardel also introduced another character, Mercury, but where that god fitted into the plot was not explained. In the mythological fable Mercury was Daphnis's father, and it may be that his appearance was to add relevance to the apotheosis. But these revisions were not enough to save the ballet, and after six performances and a stage-life of less than a month it was dropped and quickly forgotten.

* * *

In January 1803 Europe was still at peace, but the euphoria that had greeted the cessation of hostilities with England had evaporated when the negotiations for a permanent treaty stalled without hope of resolution. In the spring they were finally broken off, and before May was out France was once again at war with her old enemy. Bonaparte at once responded by occupying Hanover and assembling a great army on the Channel coast, making periodic visits to inspect the preparations for an invasion. Although there was a general sense that great events were impending, the other European powers seemed for the moment undisturbed, and life in Paris continued much as before, save only for the absence of English visitors.

At the Opéra that summer there was little activity of note. Gardel's disastrous *Daphnis et Pandrose* was no more than a memory, but now it was Milon's turn to be unlucky. He had been asked to produce a new *divertissement* for a benefit performance honouring Mme Rose Vestris, sister-in-law of Gaétan and a distinguished actress of the Comédie-Française. This was to take place at the Opéra, and no doubt it was felt desirable to end the evening on a cheerful note, for such occasions could turn out to be a great trial for the audience if, as frequently happened,

[9] Reichardt, 279–80.
[10] *Courrier des spectacles*, 25 Nivôse, Year XI (16 January 1803).

more admissions were sold than there were places to fill. Where Milon got hold of the plot for his contribution was not disclosed; it was credited to him alone on the title page of the scenario, and its attribution to Dauberval by the *Journal de Paris* was almost certainly unfounded.

Lucas et Laurette, as the wretched piece was called, should have been nipped in the bud before an audience had the opportunity of seeing it. How it ever survived the rehearsal period is a mystery. One can only assume that it was not seen in advance by Bonet or Gardel, being destined for a benefit performance that was primarily a Comédie-Française affair, although taking place at the Opéra. And perhaps none of the dancers who appeared in it gave much thought to how it might appear to the audience, looking on it merely as a bit of a romp.

All the dances being placed at the end, the audience had had to sit through a complicated narrative wholly devoid of interest. Since the parts of Lucas and Laurette were played by Vestris and Marie Gardel, it was no doubt clear enough that they were a couple in love, but as the ballet proceeded it became difficult to follow the thread of the plot.

Lucas's aunt Nicole (Chevigny) favours the match, but Laurette's father Eloi (Goyon), who plans to marry her to the simpleton Nicaise (Branchu), refuses his consent. Eloi introduces Nicaise to his daughter as her future husband. She makes it clear she will have nothing to do with him, but Eloi leaves the couple alone with one another, suggesting to Nicaise that he make himself agreeable to her while he is away on a visit. Nicaise's gauche attempt to court her meets with no success, and he finally drops off to sleep. Laurette then summons Lucas, who enters under the pretence that he is selling two barrels of wine that he has found outside Eloi's house. The lovers make Nicaise remove the plug from one of the barrels and insert his finger as a tap, and there they leave him while they discuss what to do next. Of course the fool withdraws his finger, and begins to imbibe the wine. Eloi returns to find his son the worse for wear, and angrily sends him packing.

At this stage Nicole intervenes, hoping to arouse Eloi's jealousy by flirting with Nicaise, and when to her surprise that awkward youth asks her to marry him, she pretends to accept. This little subterfuge has the desired effect on Eloi, who confesses that he has long loved Nicole, to whom he proposes. But she will only accept him if he agrees to the marriage of Lucas and Laurette. At that point Nicaise arrives dressed up for his wedding, only to be disillusioned. He is then introduced to an old crone (A.J. Coulon) whom he angrily pushes away, thinking she is offering herself to be his bride – but it turns out that she is seeking a husband for her simple-minded daughter (Aim. Vestris). Since the girl is pretty, Nicaise is appeased; the three happy couples sit down to a banquet, and at long last the dances begin.

In the absurd plot of *Lucas et Laurette* there can be detected distant echoes of Maximilien Gardel's *La Chercheuse d'esprit* and Dauberval's *La Fille mal gardée*, but the success of those two works was due, in the one, to the action being taken from a well-known *opéra-comique* and, in the other, to the plot being a model of clarity, freshness and charm.

No doubt all those who took part did their best, but that was not enough. 'The ballet,' reported the *Journal de Paris* in apparently the only account of it to exist, 'had the honour, very rare at the Opéra, of receiving several salvos of whistling.' Truly there was nothing in the ballet to praise. Its scenery was 'gloomy and ill-lit', and the dances did not even deserve the epithet of 'grotesque'. The main cause of discontent was the absurd overacting of Branchu as Nicaise, 'the most revolting simpleton ever to have appeared on any stage – a crippled, twisted-limbed, skinny and pasty-faced idiot, quite unworthy of the boards.'[11]

It was given a second viewing in an ordinary performance at the Opéra the following evening, meeting with a similar reception. Now that the Opéra had been brought under Bonaparte's jurisdiction, such scandalous scenes were not to be tolerated, and the Prefect of the Palace promptly intervened. 'The ballet *Lucas et Laurette*, Citizen Director, appeared ridiculous,' he wrote. 'This work met with disfavour, its details descending to the level of the basest simplicity, I would even say triviality, when contrasted with the magnificence of the capital's leading theatre. These considerations lead me to forbid any future performances of the ballet.'[12] Perhaps Milon was lucky to survive this consular reproof.

* * *

That *Lucas et Laurette* fell by the wayside was in no way to exclude comedy from the Opéra's balletic repertory, but that type of ballet fitted more comfortably into the programmes of the more popular, commercial theatres such as the Porte-Saint-Martin.

This was the theatre that the Opéra had vacated nine years before, although until the Government sold it in 1799 it had served as a scenery store and workshop. Now, three years later, it had reopened as a theatre under private management, with melodrama as its staple fare. To stage the ballets in such productions the management had engaged Jean

[11] *Journal de Paris*, 14 Prairial, Year 11 (4 June 1803).

[12] Arch. Nat., AJ[13] 53 (IV). Luçay to Bonet, 23 Prairial, Year XI (14 June 1803).

Aumer, although he was still in the Opéra's employ. No objection had apparently been made to his working elsewhere, presumably because it did not interfere with his duties at the Opéra, where he held the modest rank of *double*. In 1802 he was already twenty-eight, and, being uncommonly tall, had no real prospect of promotion as a dancer. He had, however, seen an alternative route to success, and had undertaken a rigorous study of music and design, coupled with a wide range of reading, to equip himself as a ballet-master. His mentor was Dauberval, under whom he had danced in London in 1791; among the ballets he had seen staged by its creator there, and probably danced in, was *La Fille mal gardée*.

Not only did the Opéra raise no objection to Aumer working elsewhere on the side, but in September 1803 an impressive contingent of his fellow dancers donated their services when he was given a benefit. He had presented a revival of Dauberval's *Les Jeux d'Eglé* at the Porte-Saint-Martin the previous November, and this was given again on his benefit night with Marie Gardel and Beaulieu in the leading rôles, and Vestris, Bigottini and Saint-Amant featured in the final *divertissement*.

A month later, on 13 October 1803, the Porte-Saint-Martin presented another Dauberval ballet, none other than *La Fille mal gardée*, produced, however, not by Aumer but by Eugène Hus. That this minor masterpiece had not found its way to Paris before was not altogether surprising. It was not, of course, unknown to the powers of the Opéra, for it had provided several of the principal dancers with triumphs in the provinces, notably Vestris and Chameroy, and more recently Louis Duport and Emilie Collomb in Lyon. But the traditional monopoly of the official ballet-masters was rigid and absolute, as had been shown the year before when Roederer, the Councillor of State responsible for the Opéra, had requested that *La Fille mal gardée* should be produced there. Although it was made clear that this was the wish of Mme Bonaparte, the proposal fell on deaf ears.[13]

Thus the introduction of *La Fille mal gardée* to Paris was a very modest affair, most of the rôles being played by actors, as indeed they had been on its first production in Bordeaux. In fact, only the part of Colas was taken by a dancer, Spitalier, who alternated with another dancer, Antoine Corniol. The only other rôle requiring dancing ability was Lise, which was given to a versatile and intelligent young actress who appeared under the name of Mlle Laure.[14] For the other main part, Mother Simone as she

[13] Arch. Nat., AJ[13] 52. Roederer to Cellerier, 20 Floréal, Year X (10 May 1802).

[14] It is very unlikely, since no connection appears to have been made at the time, that she was the promising young dancer of that name, a pupil of the elder Vestris, who had disappeared from public view eight years or so before and was believed to have died.

was now called, Hus had selected an actor by the name of Hossart, explaining in a programme note that the rôle was 'a kind of caricature which, since it had been created by a man, I thought it best to leave that way.'

Nevertheless the ballet succeeded on its inherent merits, notwithstanding a ridiculous publicity stunt. Hus himself had interrupted one of the performances of Dauberval's original production in Bordeaux in 1789 to propose a toast to the Third Estate, and now another distraction, this time of a culinary nature, was offered in the harvest scene. A steaming bowl of cabbage soup was brought in, and its savoury aroma wafted across the footlights. In an all-too-obviously inspired letter published in the *Courrier des spectacles* it was reported that several expectant mothers in the audience made such a clamour to be served some of the soup that the management bowed to their demands. Two days later the same journal published a letter purporting to be from a prospective father, claiming that his wife was refusing not only her cook's soup, but also soup delivered by some of the best restaurants in town. Her state was 'truly alarming'. 'For Heaven's sake,' he pleaded, 'help us by asking ... the theatre to satisfy my wife at the first serving, and to do this as quickly as possible, for a pregnant woman's craving brooks no delay.'[15]

Neither this production of *La Fille mal gardée* nor the revival of Dauberval's *Le Déserteur* that followed was felt worthy of the theatre, and Aumer was installed officially as ballet-master while Hus moved to the Gaîté. At the same time the dance company was strengthened by two capable male dancers, Morand and Rhenon, and Marie Quériau,[16] a ballerina who had made a name for herself in the provinces as an unusually gifted dancer-actress. For her Paris début Aumer had the happy inspiration of producing *La Fille mal gardée*, and, conscious of the shortcomings of Hus's earlier production, devoted special care to producing a version more worthy of its creator. And this time there was to be no cabbage soup!

For his production, first presented on 13 May 1804, Aumer marshalled a strong cast: Mme Quériau and Morand as Lise and Colas, Rhenon as Alain, and as Mme Simone the comic dancer Fusil, who would still be remembered twenty-four years later as the best male interpreter of the rôle.[17] Mme Quériau's reputation had preceded her, and her appearance was awaited with eager interest, many of the Opéra's dancers being rec-

[15] *Courrier des spectacles*, 29 Vendémiaire and 1 Brumaire, Year XI (22 and 24 October 1803).

[16] Mme Quériau's name is sometimes spelt 'Quériaux', but I have followed the form given in pleadings in a lawsuit in which her children were involved (Arch. Nat., AJ^{13} 1039).

[17] *Courrier des théâtres*, 29 November 1828.

ognised among the audience. By this flattering court of peers she was granted a resounding triumph, setting a standard for the rôle of Lise that would not be surpassed in Paris as long as the original production continued to be given.[18]

It was largely Marie Quériau's evening, and Geoffroy wrote a vivid account of her performances:

> Mme Quériau's special talent lies in the true form of dance, the pantomimic dance. Her figure is elegant and slender without appearing skinny; she has eyes that speak to us, and features that are animated, expressive and dramatic. There is much grace in her movements and attitudes, and great mobility in her features, on which all the passions are rapidly depicted.
>
> The ballet of *La Fille mal gardée* is an old one, but none the less pleasing for that. In it are to be found all the ruses that a village swain can summon up to evade the vigilance of a stern mother. In particular there is a scene of great energy that shows how effective pantomime can be. The young girl is alone in her cottage, believing she is out of danger. Suddenly her lover bursts into view, coming out from a bundle of hay under which he has been hiding. At the sight of him the poor girl is struck speechless with astonishment and fright. The lover, whom she was formerly so happy to see, now appears to her as a serpent ready to pounce. Her efforts to get rid of him, and her struggle between modesty and love, form an original scene. On no stage could such a situation be risked by dialogue. The looks and gestures have a mute eloquence that transcends the power of words.[19]

Later Marie Quériau was seen in three other ballets by Dauberval: *Annette et Lubin*, in which she aroused general sympathy by bravely continuing after a bad fall which interrupted the performance for an anxious quarter of an hour; *Le Déserteur*, in which she gave a highly dramatic rendering as Louise, although one critic thought it somewhat excessive when she flung herself down on the stage to express despair at her lover's imminent execution; and *Les Jeux d'Eglé*.

Aumer's achievement in these few months was to reveal Dauberval's genius to Paris where, apart from Hus's less than satisfactory revival of *La Fille mal gardée*, none of his ballets had been seen before. The talent of

[18] Aumer revised the ballet to a heavily rearranged score in 1828. Paris had never seen Mme Théodore, the first Lise, in the rôle.

[19] *Journal des débats*, 15 May 1804.

Marie Quériau had been another revelation. Furthermore, the management of the Porte-Saint-Martin was deeply in Aumer's debt for the added prestige that these ballets had brought. For overnight that theatre seemed to have become almost fashionable, even respectable. Also it was laying the foundations of a reputation as a centre of the dance second only to the Opéra, whose former monopoly, abolished during the Revolution, seemed, for the time being at least, to have been abandoned.

* * *

Certainly no dancer could have been more entitled to a benefit than Auguste Vestris, and towards the end of 1803 plans were well advanced for a very special performance to be offered to his admirers in the spring. The proposal to stage a revival of Noverre's *Médée et Jason* had presumably originated from the Vestris family. Auguste's eminent father Gaétan had not only created the part of Jason in Stuttgart forty years before but, having also produced two versions of the ballet at the Opéra in the 1770s, no doubt considered he had some sort of proprietary interest in it. Now, at his son's request, he had agreed to teach the mime sections. Noverre himself, then living in retirement at Saint-Germain-en-Laye, had also given his consent. Had he been ten years younger, he would probably have insisted on being in charge; but old age had come upon him, and at the age of seventy-six he was, in his own words, 'an infirm old man'. Knowing from personal experience that outsiders, however eminent, were not welcome at the Opéra, and grateful for the opportunity of seeing his ballet given a new lease of life, he had virtually delivered the production of his ballet into the hands of Gardel and father and son Vestris.

In November the public was notified of the treat in store. Auguste Vestris was to play his father's old part of Jason, and Clotilde was to be his Medea. The puff in the press promised 'much dancing, spectacle, charming scenes, and, what will particularly please the pit, a general conflagration' at the end, that splendid finale being entrusted to the veteran chief machinist, Pierre Boullet.[20]

As far as the outside world was concerned, the preparations went ahead smoothly. The date was announced – 12 April 1804 – and tickets went on sale well in advance. As happened on such occasions, it was up to the beneficiary and his friends to fill the house for as much as could be

[20] *Journal de Paris*, 19 November 1803. Shortly after Vestris's benefit, Boullet was to be killed when he fell on to the stage while supervising the final details of Le Sueur's opera, *Ossian*. He had worked at the Opéra for 43 years, 30 of them as chief machinist.

obtained. As a result, no account was taken of the number of places available, and so wide was the network built up by the Vestris family that an enormous number of tickets was sold for admission to the pit, far more than could be accommodated. Many who had paid their 9 francs and found they could not get into the auditorium either resigned themselves to standing in one of the corridors or went out and sold their tickets to unsuspecting purchasers. The family and their friends were no doubt properly looked after, and such was the aura surrounding the Vestris name that the evening was graced by the First Consul himself.

Typically, the programme was a mixed one, with contributions from other theatres as well as from the singers and dancers of the Opéra. It opened, not very propitiously, with an insipid little opera which was loudly hissed, and concluded, after a light comedy which was listened to more politely, with the high spot of the evening, *Médée*, as it had been retitled. For this an exceptionally large cast had been assembled, Vestris and Clotilde being supported by Marie Gardel as Creusa, Milon as Creon, and almost the entire ballet company playing minor rôles or forming groups of courtiers, soldiers, priests of Hymen, common people and demons: the printed scenario listed eighty names. It seems no one was left out in this tribute to France's greatest dancer.

Putting aside the applause that was Vestris's due, *Médée* was not a success. 'No one can say it was not perfectly well composed by the celebrated Noverre,' explained Geoffroy in his review, 'but Gardel and Vestris have not improved it in their revival, and one could have wished that the author's original plan had been more closely followed.' The few survivors of those who had seen the elder Vestris's production in 1776, and the revision that Noverre had staged a few years later, would have remembered that the latter had been pruned of a lot of dances that had been added. Presumably these had now been put back, and others may have been tacked on to enable as many dancers as possible to have their turn. As it was, all the dances in the second act inordinately held up the action and weakened the dramatic effect. Also, the harrowing scene of Medea killing her sons was found too lurid for the sensitivities of the audience, coming, as it did, towards the end of a very long and exhausting evening. As Geoffroy reported, it was an hour past midnight when he staggered into the cool night air, 'suffocated, exhausted, weary, fatigued, his head in a whirl, and his mind drained.'[21]

Noverre himself, it seems, had stayed away, having abandoned Paris after three rehearsals, complaining he had been shabbily treated. *Médée*

[21] *Journal des débats*, 15 April 1804.

was after all his own ballet, and although he had been approached for his consent and invited to rehearsals, he had felt unwelcome. Perhaps he expected to be more closely involved; perhaps little effort was made to present him to the company as the eminent figure he was. No doubt most of the younger dancers had only a vague idea of who he was; in their eyes Gardel and the Vestris family were in charge, and the old gentleman no more than an invited onlooker. On the other hand, he may have interfered more than those taking the rehearsals liked. He had always been excessively touchy, with a large chip on his shoulder, and perhaps few were surprised when he walked out in a huff and was seen at the Opéra no more. A few days later, in fact on the very day of the benefit, he wrote a pained letter to Bonet:

> The ballet of *Médée* being my own property, I gave in to M. Vestris's request and consented to his reviving it for his benefit. He had promised that nothing would be neglected in reviving this work, which in times long past won brilliant successes in Paris and all the courts of Europe, and recently in St. Petersburg, staged with all the pomp that this work demands. He had even pressed me to attend the last rehearsals. I did not feel I could refuse to give such assistance as might be useful to contribute to the success of this ancient production. But boredom, disgust, the lack of respect and attention due to a man of my age and my accommodating attitude, resulted in my escaping from Paris on Wednesday morning, and the three journeys I had made proving quite pointless. I have returned to my fireside only with a bout of the shivers which I caught from the fatiguing breeze of pirouettes and the icy expressions of men and women who have no ears to hear, no eyes to see, and no souls to be moved. I make an exception of Mme Gardel, who must have been convinced by the sincerity of everything I have written to her husband about her rare gifts and her absolute honesty.
>
> I have just learned that my work did not have all the success that should have been expected. I am not surprised. What must have spoilt it were the longueurs of the fête which Gardel himself accepted, although it was not always in his power to shorten it. The action of the second act was said to drag and to lack warmth, vitality, expression – and, it has even been added, meaning.
>
> Much work, effort and trouble could have been avoided if my scenario had been followed, along with the very detailed observations I sent to M. Vestris at his request three months ago.
>
> I beg you, Sir, if you decide to continue presenting this work, which

> in the past has brought in good receipts and could still do so today if staged properly, to suspend performances for a few days and make it known that changes are being made, which are absolutely indispensable and will incur very little expense since all that needs to be done is to remove the longueurs, give the ceremonial more pomp and grandeur, attend to some minor touching-up, and in particular add more warmth to the action. I have the right to require that this work of my youth should not dishonour my old age. If you think my presence is necessary, let me know; I shall not mind dragging myself into Paris for the fourth time. I only ask that instructions be given that I am not to be kept waiting for three hours after the time announced for the rehearsals.[22]

Meanwhile, Bonet had other problems. His life was being made a misery by what he saw as a malaise of indiscipline among the artistes, many of whom considered themselves the sole dispensers of their talents, and at liberty to rearrange their activity according to their whim. Some of the dancers, he complained, were reluctant to come on early in a ballet because spectators were still taking their seats in the boxes. Others did not want to appear at the end when the public were beginning to leave and giving the impression, by the noise they made, that they were not interested in seeing them dance.

Vestris was a particular thorn in his side. On several occasions he had sent a last-minute refusal to appear, pleading pain in one of his knees. Then, just two weeks before his benefit, he had announced his intention to leave Paris once his benefit was over. Since Clotilde was at the same time threatening to go to St. Petersburg, this was the last straw for poor Bonet, who saw himself in danger of losing both his Jason and his Medea. And what made the situation especially serious was that there was no one available to teach those rôles to others: old Gaétan Vestris had only agreed to teach the mime to oblige his son, and neither Gardel nor Milon was familiar with the choreography.

Two weeks before the benefit was to take place, there seemed no chance of giving the ballet again, in which event the Opéra would be unable to recover any of the very considerable outlay on the production, for the entire net proceeds of the benefit (estimated at 32,500 francs) would find its way into Vestris's pocket. The situation was serious enough for Bonet to advise the Prefect to issue an order making the benefit conditional on

[22] *Journal de Paris*, 17 April 1804. Noverre to Bonet, 23 Germinal, Year XII (12 April 1804).

Vestris agreeing to play Jason as often as the Opéra required, and that Clotilde should be placed under a similar obligation.[23]

In the last resort Vestris was not going to endanger his benefit, but when it took place Bonet still faced the danger of losing both principals and having a wasted production on his hands. For several weeks Vestris continued to maintain his intention to retire, but finally, realising that Luçay was prepared to take a tough line, he came to heel, coming out of his sulks to play *Médée* four times more in May, and for a sixth and last time in June.

Médée was also nearly scuppered by Clotilde. She, too, had seen an opportunity of holding Bonet to ransom, demanding the right to include, in whatever work she might choose, a particularly effective *pas* created for her in Sacchini's *Oedipe à Colonne*, and threatening to withhold her services until her demand was granted. This was quite out of the question, and when Bonet could not get her to see reason, he passed the problem to the Prefect. Luçay summoned her to his office, and on her refusing to attend, ordered her arrest. This had the desired effect, and she was released the day before Vestris's benefit with a warning that she would be imprisoned for six months if she did not appear in *Médée* the next day.

Several weeks later she approached Luçay with a request to be given six months' leave of absence to accept an engagement in Italy at 30,000 francs. She told him:

> I have been to see Mme Bonaparte. She has kindly interested herself in my case, and promised to obtain six months' leave for me; she mentioned it to the First Consul, who has given his agreement, but she told me you are against it. May I suggest, Citizen Prefect, that you have not given my request proper consideration, seeing that it is for the summer when no one goes to the theatre ... Nor do I understand why you are being hard on me alone ... It is unnatural to prevent an artiste from earning money; I have worked at the Opéra for ten years, and must think of myself; I have two daughters to care for and I cannot provide them with dowries out of my paltry salary.[24]

Luçay must have made it clear that the Palace would not be interfering in the matter, for three days later Bonet notified the recalcitrant dancer that the sprain of which she had been complaining had kept her away long enough to justify her suspension. 'A leave of absence,' he reminded

[23] Arch. Nat., AJ[13] 72 (IV). Bonet to Luçay, 11 Germinal, Year XII (31 March 1803).
[24] Arch. Nat., AJ[13] 63 (xv). Clotilde to Luçay, 24 Floréal, Year XII (13 May 1804).

her, 'is at all times a favour that the management grants as a reward for long and uninterrupted service.'[25]

* * *

For the true connoisseur, a début was a special occasion, calling for both critical faculties and a prescient imagination to perceive whether, beneath nervousness and technical shortcomings that might be remedied by further training and experience, there lay an exceptional talent in the making. Fine details were discussed afterwards in the corridors; if the new dancer was lucky, a report of the event might appear in the *Journal de Paris*, whose critic was a respected expert and unfailingly just and understanding in his judgement. 1803 and 1804 saw the appearance of several young hopefuls, some just emerging from their training and presented by a distinguished teacher, and others who had already embarked on careers elsewhere and had come to Paris to obtain a final seal of approval. Among them were three young men, all destined for successful careers, and a number of interesting young women.

The most remarkable of the men was Louis Henry, who in the course of time was to achieve international renown as a choreographer, in which capacity Paris would have several opportunities to appreciate his skill. His father had been a glorified head waiter, *un officier de bouche*, in the household of the Comte d'Artois, and clearly very conscious of his dignity as a royal servant, as the regally-sounding names of Louis-Xavier-Stanislas he had bestowed on his son bore witness. Young Louis had taken up dancing by pure chance after being sent by his father on an errand to his friend Boullet, the chief machinist of the Opéra, asking the favour of a free entry. While waiting for the reply the lad had wandered off and found himself in the wings while Gardel was rehearsing a group of rather nervous children who were to be demons in his new ballet, *Psyché*, and who had to throw themselves from a rock on to a mattress. All this was too tempting for the young daredevil, who begged to join in. Amused by his fearless spirit, and noticing how trimly he was built, Gardel let him have his turn and afterwards sent him home with the offer of a place in the School of Dance. The invitation was gratefully taken up, and there, as he grew up, Louis Henry received his initial training from old Deshayes, and in due course passed into the sure hands of Coulon, who prepared him for his début in March 1803.

[25] Arch. Nat., AJ^{13} 63 (xv). Bonet to Clotilde (draft), 27 Floréal, Year XII (16 May 1804).

He was at that time nineteen, a little on the tall side,[26] good-looking and with legs so finely shaped that the painter Horace Vernet declared they were more like those of the Apollo Belvedere than any he had seen. His height and his looks made him ideal for the *noble* style; he accordingly made his début in the pantomime rôle of Telemachus, and two months later was given the honour of partnering Clotilde, who was nearly as tall as he, in that celebrated *pas* from *Iphigénie en Aulide*, *Le Prix de la Danse*.

A year later, in April 1804, Coulon presented another young pupil, Baptiste Petit. He too had remarkable qualities, particularly an unusual aplomb that was the secret of his remarkable facility for pirouettes. On this account his début created a great sensation, it being recorded that he performed 'one more pirouette than Duport, who every now and then does one more than Vestris'.[27]

He was followed, in June 1804, by Antoine Titus, another future ballet-master, who many years later would stage the first production of *Giselle* in Russia. Titus had been prepared for his début by Milon, but he was not a product of the School of Dance, having arrived in Paris with experience of dancing elsewhere. As with Henry, his natural leaning was towards the *noble* genre. His *batterie* was judged to be excellent, but the sharp eye of the *Journal de Paris* critic noticed that he was expending too much effort to excel and that his turning was a little untidy.

Henry and Baptiste Petit were rewarded according to their merits. Henry had the most rapid promotion, being engaged as *double* in 1804 and *premier sujet* in 1806. Baptiste, who became Duport's brother-in-law in 1808 by marrying his sister Minette, was also engaged as a *double* in 1804, but had to wait until 1809 before moving up the ladder to *remplacement*. He never achieved his ambition to become *premier sujet*, and, disappointed, left the Opéra in 1809 to spend most of the rest of his career in Russia and London.

On the whole, the girls were less interesting. Among the four débutantes presented in 1803, two had come up through the School of Dance. Mlle Claire (her family name was Maillard) and Sophie Delisle, whose elder sister Marie-Madeleine was already in the company, were both pupils of Coulon and made their débuts on different nights as Flore in *Le Retour de Zéphire*. They were both to be rewarded with contracts, but Sophie Delisle did not remain long at the Opéra.

The other two débutantes attracted more interest, although neither, as it turned out, had the ambition to remain in Paris. The first to appear was

26 According to Saint-Léon, his height was 5 feet 5 inches. Assuming this was expressed in French measurement, the English equivalent would be 5 feet 9 inches.
27 *Journal de Paris*, 7 April 1804.

Rose Coustou, a mature ballerina from Bordeaux, who had played Eucharis in Dauberval's *Télémaque* there in 1797 under the eye, no doubt, of Mme Théodore. For her Paris début in April 1803, she was presented in the title rôle of *Psyché*. She could hardly have chosen a more challenging part in which to face the exacting Paris public; it was a most daunting ordeal, as can be appreciated from the critical analysis of her performance that appeared in the *Journal de Paris*:

> Her pantomime seemed animated, intelligent and even moving, but the steps in Psyche's dancing lesson from Terpsichore now and then lacked the grace that comes from facility and natural agility; she seemed to prepare her *battements* and her poses with exaggerated *pliés* that savoured of the classroom and detracted from the brilliance of her performance. But it is only fair to add that, while her preparations were poorly concealed, she possesses great precision. Perhaps, and I would like to think this was so, she was forcing herself to be over-careful not to falter in a single step that is performed so perfectly by Mme Gardel.[28]

Mlle Polly, whose test followed in August 1804, also came from Bordeaux, where she had been born in the very year, 1785, in which Dauberval became ballet-master there. Her full name, Marie Polly Cuninghame [sic], suggests an English father. As a child she was taught by Jean-Baptiste Hus; and in 1798, at the age of thirteen, she had taken her first steps on the stage in two of the minor theatres of Paris, the Salle Louvois and the Théâtre des Jeunes Artistes. Two years later she went to Brussels with a small company headed by Antoine Corniol, and in 1801 became *première danseuse* in Amsterdam and at the Théâtre de la Monnaie in Brussels. In the summer of 1803 she had returned to Paris to study for two months under Gardel, making a very successful début in Paisiello's opera, *Proserpine*. Of all that year's débutantes, she was the most interesting, appearing as

> a pretty little person, who cannot be much more than four feet tall. She is not exactly a classical beauty, but her expression is bright and striking ... She excels in multiple *entrechats* and what are commonly called *tricotets*; she jumps with astonishing lightness, vivacity and daring, and we can add to her glory that she performs *jetés battus en avant* as easily as anyone else would do a simple *pas de basque*. However, she is not yet as perfect as her model [Mlle Collomb]; she gives the impression

[28] *Journal de Paris*, 24 April 1803.

> of gathering her strength in bursts, and she is sometimes lacking in grace in her arm movements and in the way she flings out her legs, but more time spent in the Temple of Terpsichore [i.e. the Opéra] would no doubt correct these minor faults.[29]

Her stay in Paris was all too short. Her tiny figure had in no way been lost on the vast stage of the Opéra, and she would undoubtedly have been a welcome addition to the company. But if a suggestion had been made for her to stay, she must have declined out of loyalty to Amsterdam, for she preferred to shine in the more modest surroundings of the Dutch city than to aspire to greater glory in Paris.

[29] *Journal de Paris*, 7 August 1803. Four old French feet was equivalent to 4 feet 3 inches. *Tricotet*, a term borrowed from the art of dressage, is a prancing step staying in place. Among the papers of Emilie Collomb is an interesting comment on Polly in a letter from a friend of Mlle Collomb: 'She has a good leg, as an administrator would say; in fact, she has quite brilliant legs, and strength in them, but that is all. You have everything she has, but she is very far from having everything you have; you are more than a match for her, for she will never have such a well-placed stance (*haut du corps*) as you have, nor does she carry her head so well, or have the expression, soul and vivacity of my friend.' (Bibl-Mus. de l'Opéra, Fonds Collomb, 22. Bonamy-Berville to Collomb, 4 August 1803).

10

The Rise of Louis Duport

In the summer of 1804 two stars rose in the firmament of France. The more brilliant shed its light upon the Tuileries, where Napoleon had assumed the mantle of Emperor of the French. The other was much more modest, rising above the Opéra to mark an event that few had expected to occur so soon – the appearance of a potential successor to Auguste Vestris.

For more than twenty years that great dancer had reigned without a rival, but his powers were beginning to diminish. A decline, formerly virtually imperceptible, was now being revealed through the technical achievements of an ardent generation of young male dancers, building upon Vestris's accomplishments in a frantic quest for virtuosity. Already his supremacy had been lightly threatened by André Deshayes and his own son, Armand, but neither had stayed long enough to dent his reputation. Now, however, another claimant had appeared in the person of Louis Duport, a young prodigy whose technical prowess was showing a truly extraordinary development.

There may be some mystery about Duport's early training. An unfriendly critic, whose sympathies were clearly with Vestris, alleged that the young dancer had been a late starter, and studied dancing for two years only. This was clearly nonsense, and Duport himself dismissed it as a joke. In fact, among those pupils of the School of Dance in 1794 who were listed as taking part in performances – *élèves faisant la service de l'Opéra* – were a 'Duport (L)' among the boys and a 'Duport (C)' among the girls.[1] It has been suggested that the male Duport may have been an elder brother of Louis, but in the absence of any other reference to a brother being a dancer, this is mere conjecture.

Louis-Antoine Duport, to give his full name, was the son of a sculptor, Joseph-Pierre Duport, and was born in 1783, assuming that his age was given correctly on the registration of his death. By the time he was eleven

[1] Arch. Nat., AJ[13] 47. Duchesne, *Calendrier historique et chronologique des théâtres pour l'année 1794 (seconde de la République)*. L and C stand for *l'aîné* and *cadette*.

his promise was already being recognised. No doubt his first teacher was Jacques-François Deshayes, but later he became a *protégé* of Milon, who chose him and his sister Minette for the rôles of Constant and Inconstant Love in *Pygmalion* when it was first staged at the Ambigu-Comique in 1799. For a short time in 1800 Louis danced at the Gaîté. These early successes were to earn both of them engagements at the Opéra as *doubles*, Minette in 1799 and Louis one year later.

Young Louis soon gave proof of an extraordinary zeal. In the winter of 1800/1, when Vestris was away in the provinces, Deshayes was injured and Beaulieu and Saint-Amant were both sick, he became for a while a sort of Jack-of-all-trades, taking on any part that was asked of him. At one performance of *Les Noces de Gamache* he had so much to do that the audience could hardly restrain their laughter when, on three or four occasions, he had to dart into the wings only to reappear moments later on the opposite side of the stage as a different character.

Gardel was quick to notice his extraordinary talent, which he exploited in the stunning Egyptian dance created for him in *Les Mystères d'Isis*. In April 1802 Duport took over the title rôle in *Le Retour de Zéphire*, and three months later was tried out as Cupid in *Psyché*, playing opposite the equally promising Bigottini. His promotion to the rank of *remplacement* followed in September.

Notices of his early appearances commented on the originality of his talent. Even though a trifle short for a *demi-caractère* dancer, it was in that genre that he was formally classified; but such was his versatility and virtuosity that he seemed equally competent in all three genres. Clearly he was a dancer in the tradition set by Auguste Vestris, who had virtually created a genre all his own in which elements of all three traditional genres could be discerned. By the end of 1803 he was being hailed as 'the white hope of the Opéra ballet'.[2] Already the memory of Deshayes was being eclipsed by this wonderboy, who was seen by one critic as

> the Zephyr depicted by the poets, barely touching the ground in his rapid flight. The suppleness of his movements, his precision in the most difficult steps, the unbelievable boldness of his pirouettes, in which Duport has perhaps no equal for the perfection and finish of their execution – all these qualities deservedly earned this charming dancer the warmest applause.[3]

[2] *Courrier des spectacles*, 16 November 1803.

[3] *Courrier des spectacles*, 12 November 1803.

All too soon the general delight that had greeted the rise of this new star was dampened by the news that he had fallen ill. The cause, according to his admirer, Geoffroy, was over-exertion that had affected his lungs. Alas, this was to prove a chronic weakness. According to Noverre, he never danced as often as the public would have wished; when he did appear, he would overtax his strength by dancing for too long, and afterwards cough up blood. He would have to learn, counselled the old ballet-master, how to moderate the fire and petulance of his dancing by 'giving up steps that are too complicated and replacing them with others of a contrasting nature that would give his *enchaînements* that *chiaroscuro* which is so essential in all the imitative arts'.[4]

His enforced absence emphasised the risks of exhaustion and injury faced by dancers of the new virtuosic school. Virtuosity was indeed nothing new at the Opéra, dating back at least 30 years to the emergence of Auguste Vestris with his exhilarating and, to all appearances, dangerous jumps and pirouettes of ever-increasing complexity. Inevitably others tried to emulate Vestris's feats, but there was much shaking of heads among those who feared that the traditional classic dance of their youth was being brought down to the level of the Italian *grotteschi*. And indeed the dangers were real: in January 1804 Saint-Amant twisted his foot after a multiple pirouette (five or six turns, according to one witness's count)[5] and was incapacitated for many months, and in October Henry 'almost broke his neck beating a series of endless *entrechats*'.[6] But even as the dangers became more apparent, no amount of grumbling could turn back the clock. Vestris was one of those rare artistes who change the course of their art, and it was the thrust of his personal example, not nostalgic recollections of the historical past, that would determine the course that ballet was to take.

For it was the toughened, forward-looking generation that survived the Revolution that produced Louis Duport, a young man of overweening ambition who cared little for the legacy of the past and was already champing at the bit to fashion the future. For the moment, however, he was being forced to rest and to bear, impatiently, many weeks of inactivity. He was well aware of the sensation he had caused, and his ambition was now focussed on making a stunning impact when he would be fit enough to dance again. It was then that the idea formed in his mind that he should appear in one of the major rôles in the repertory, Paris in

4 Noverre, *Arts imitateurs*, II, 173.
5 *Journal de Paris*, 22 January 1804.
6 *Journal de Paris*, 11 October 1804.

Gardel's *Le Jugement de Pâris*. He himself of course had no right to insist on it, but under the regulations the management had power to permit him to play it three times, and if he passed the test to their satisfaction, to require the rôle to be shared. To this Gardel was agreeable, but when Vestris adamantly refused to concede the rôle, the proposal was dropped for fear of the possible consequences.[7]

In a moment of frustration Duport then served the Opéra with six months' notice to terminate his contract, and there matters stood when, in May, he was pronounced fully recovered. There could be no question of a glittering return in the rôle of Paris, but as a conciliatory gesture the Opéra allowed him to appear in a new dance arranged by himself to the well-known melody of *Les Folies d'Espagne*. In this and in the gavotte from *Panurge*, it was observed that he had gained much from his enforced absence. Not only were his vigour, grace and aplomb unimpaired, but both his technique and his presentation had acquired a new polish. He had progressed, wrote one critic, from being merely the most skilful pirouettist of all to being the 'complete dancer'.[8]

The critic Geoffroy, who deplored the current fascination with pirouettes, welcomed this new development in a dancer whom he greatly admired. He was pleased to discover that Duport had 'succeeded in adding a previously unattained grace and precision to a style that had seemed to be all spring and steel', and that he was abandoning 'bad habits ... out of a delicate appreciation of the beauties of his art'. Nor did this critic overlook the significant fact that Duport was appearing as both executant and composer, 'dancing as a violinist might play his own music'. As a choreographer, this was a modest début, but Geoffroy noted that instead of devising 'movements that were out of the ordinary and bizarre, he had been inspired solely by a taste for beauty and decorum in his art'. And underlying Duport's performance was 'a happy fluency which is the product of hard work, but in which effort is entirely concealed so as to present an image both pleasing and full of merriment'.[9]

The impact that Duport made in the weeks following his return was extraordinary, and something of the excitement he inspired can be sensed in an account that was published some weeks later when the dancer's engagement seemed in jeopardy. It was written by an elderly man who had regularly attended the Opéra in the last years of the Old Régime. During the Revolution, he had decided not to emigrate, but to go into

[7] Arch. Nat., AJ[13] 81. Bonet to Luçay, 2 February 1804.
[8] *Courrier des spectacles*, 19 May 1804. Signed F.J.B.P.G***.
[9] *Journal des débats*, 20 May 1804.

hiding until calmer times returned. And now, in the summer of 1804, after more than ten years of self-enforced seclusion, accounts of the miraculous new dancer had tempted him to venture out and pick up the threads of his former life. Filled with golden memories of Auguste Vestris in his prime, he made his way to the Opéra, convinced he would be disappointed. But no: old loyalties were swept aside in an instant, and the idol of his youth was forgotten in his mounting enthusiasm:

> Towards the middle of the second act of [the opera] ... I heard a whisper going around, 'Now is the time for Duport'. A great hush descended. He then made his entrance, and my poor ears were assailed by such a volley of applause and bravos that I was nearly deafened. I tried to tell my neighbours, 'Give the man a chance, gentlemen, let him get on with his dancing' ... but everyone looked at me as if I were a country bumpkin. I was somewhat disconcerted, and vowed to punish this display of enthusiasm by a stern disapproval, but things took a very different turn when he began to dance. The uproar doubled in intensity, and I willingly joined in, adding my voice to the general clamour. Grace, lightness, unrestrained brilliance, charm, polish, strength, aplomb – all I could wish for was there, and no words of mine can adequately describe the pleasure it gave me.
>
> The young dancer seemed even more amazing when, after appearing first as a dancer in a troubadour *pas*, he played Zephyr in the ballet, *Pâris*, and showed himself to be a real actor. A consummate artiste, he captured the nuances that distinguished the two characters as well as one could possibly desire: first, he was the charming troubadour whose gentleness was conveyed by a combination of the majestic grace of the Spanish character with all the voluptuous passion that one requires in a lover; and then the nimble Zephyr, barely touching the stage, flitting above the flowers without bending their stems, now spinning, now rapidly taking flight, always dominating the stage, and by the unprecedented vivacity of his steps seeming to be here, there and everywhere ... Truly this young man must either be very well read, or moved by some happy instinct that is almost beyond belief.
>
> But what is absolute fact is that he aroused such enthusiasm that the audience was still applauding three or four minutes after he had disappeared into the wings. And if anything could be added to the flattering expression of the public's satisfaction and enthusiasm, it was the modesty with which he acknowledged them.[10]

[10] *Courrier des spectacles*, 30 July 1804.

Three weeks later on 11 June, Duport and his sister appeared in a benefit performance at the Porte-Saint-Martin in *La Fille mal gardée*. The following day found him suffering from a painfully swollen heel. Being listed to dance at the Opéra a few days later, he notified Bonet, Gardel and Milon that he would be unable to appear. For some reason, the powers at the Opéra suspected he was malingering, and on Luçay's instructions a doctor was sent to Duport's apartment, where he found the dancer up, 'practising and still covered with sweat'. Duport explained the problem, showing his heel, which his doctor had ordered to be covered in plaster. On the strength of its emissary's report, the Opéra concluded that he was fit enough to carry out his duties, and promptly served him with an order to dance, under threat of withholding his monthly salary.

Duport was appalled, for he considered it quite impossible to obey this peremptory summons without risk of serious injury. Realising that he was liable to arrest if he did not comply, he hastily left Paris and went into hiding, but wisely not before taking the precaution of seeking an opinion from Dr Caron, the distinguished senior surgeon of the Hôpital Cochin. Dr Caron had come to examine him in his apartment, accompanied by another doctor, and diagnosed inflammation of the tissue surrounding the Achilles tendon. Duport told him that the Opéra's surgeon had not bothered to attend him personally, but had sent a minion who seemed merely concerned with seeing whether he was mobile or confined to a chair or his bed, and did not even bother to inspect his foot. It was on the strength of that report that the Opéra had come to the conclusion that Duport's injury was feigned. The certificate that Dr Caron and his colleague delivered was cavalierly ignored. Taking this as a slur on his professional integrity, Dr Caron wrote a letter to the press not only confirming his diagnosis but also recounting Duport's version of the visit by the Opéra's representative, which drew a correction from the Opéra's surgeon declaring that he had personally examined Duport and had not sent a substitute.[11]

From his refuge in the country, Duport sent a desperate appeal to the one friend at the Opéra who could help him, Emilie Collomb. In it he complained bitterly of his salary being frozen, how he had appealed to Luçay who had not had the courtesy to reply, and how the Opéra had sent a posse of police to his home to arrest him. He told her:

> Fortunately I escaped, but without any money; and if I had had no

[11] *Journal de Paris*, 6 July 1804 (Dr Caron's letter); *Journal de Paris*, 7 July 1804 (Dr Dujandon's rejoinder). A doctor had been attached to the Opéra since Year III (1794–95), as a result of a petition from the dancers.

> other resource, I would at least have had a pleasant choice – either dying of hunger or rotting in a prison cell ...
>
> Nevertheless, as I shall soon no longer belong to the Opéra, I am putting everything out of my mind to concentrate on the duties I still have to fulfil until the expiry of my six months, but knowing for certain that the Administration is intent on arresting me sooner or later and holding on to me for a long time, I am determined not to reappear until my liberty is guaranteed *in writing* and, particularly, the month's salary that has been withheld is restored.[12]

There was more to this incident than the Opéra trying to bring a difficult employee to heel. It was common knowledge that Duport had been making demands for an increase in salary that the Opéra considered exorbitant. He was then receiving 8000 francs, a low figure by comparison with Vestris's 15,000 francs, and he freely admitted that he was claiming an increase commensurate with his situation, although not of the order of 30,000 or 40,000 francs as was being rumoured. Nor, he hastened to add, was he demanding that his sister should be engaged on the same terms as Mme Gardel. To him it was abundantly clear that he had enemies who would stop at nothing to make his life difficult. No doubt the Vestris camp was marshalled against him, and Duport suspected dirty work. More than once, he complained, obstacles seemed to have been deliberately placed on the stage to trip him.[13]

Auguste Vestris himself was a seasoned enough intriguer to keep in the background, but he did not conceal his dislike for Duport. On being asked one day what he thought of him, he casually enquired, as if he did not know:

'Of whom are you speaking?'

'Duport.'

'Ah yes,' he replied, as if searching his memory to fit a face to the name, 'Duport, that little chap who spins and spins,' scornfully accompanying his words by making little *ronds en l'air* with his finger.[14]

The Opéra's firm stand in dealing with Duport on the question of discipline was supported by a letter published in the *Courrier des théâtres*, above the signature, 'A Partisan of Order and Obedience':

> I cannot open a single newspaper without finding a letter from M. Duport. This young man desperately wants ... to be pitied as a victim of

[12] Bibl.-Mus. de l'Opéra, Fonds Collomb, 23. Duport to Collomb, 4 July 1804.

[13] Berchoux, 193.

[14] Maurice, *Histoire anecdotique*, I, 124–5.

slander and persecution ... M. Duport is certainly a very interesting dancer; he has precious gifts which time and further study will improve, and for which he has a right to the public's interest. But should not duty come before rights? An actor is subject to authority, and to regulations which he must respect. The interests of art and those of the public demand that regulations are there to be obeyed. It is only through rigorous discipline that the anarchy which has seeped into our theatres can be eradicated. It is possible that M. Duport has reason to complain of certain reproaches made by his comrades, and which he himself may have provoked, but that cannot excuse his conduct. What would become of our theatres if each actor were entitled to follow his whim in defiance of authority? I can well believe that M. Duport may have been spoilt by the excessive praise he has received, that pride may have affected his thinking, and that he may well have imagined that his success as a dancer has elevated him to a status of importance. Such vanity is found all too often in theatre folk . Certainly talent must be encouraged, and rewarded appropriately, but there is a limit to all things – and what if M. Duport really is fit, and the strain of that interesting tendon is only a pretext to obtain a convenient rest?[15]

This letter touched some raw spots on the thin skin of the young dancer. His reply, which he sent to both the *Journal de Paris* and the *Courrier des théâtres*, did not advance the dispute any further. It was published in the former paper, but the editor of the latter ignored it on the ground that it was not his paper's purpose 'to record documents relating to a dispute that ought not to exist, and which M. Duport has the power to bring to an end'.[16]

Emilie Collomb had all the necessary contacts to calm the troubled waters, and with the aid of his brother extracted an assurance that Duport's liberty would be respected and that the negotiations for a new contract would be resumed. The Opéra had no wish to lose him, nor did Duport wish to depart, provided he was remunerated according to his deserts. For the moment, however, fearful of what might happen were the negotiations to collapse, he was content to leave matters in the hands of his two trusted agents, with instructions to deal not with Bonet, whom he distrusted, but with Luçay. The Prefect's refusal to consider a higher figure than the 15,000 francs that Vestris was receiving was conceded, and terms for a three-year contract were agreed in principle.

[15] *Courrier des théâtres*, 5 July 1804.
[16] *Journal de Paris* and *Courrier des théâtres*, 7 July 1804.

Having been given a sight of the new contract in draft, Duport was now bursting to make his reappearance, and, to his mind, an appropriate occasion was only a few days away. On 14 August, Vestris, who had been on leave, was billed to make his reappearance in Grétry's opera, *Anacréon*. Duport, with a presumption that must have taken Gardel's breath away, proposed not merely that he reappear on the very same evening, but that he do so in a dance of his own composition to the most stirring number in Gluck's *Iphigénie en Aulide* – the duet for Achilles and Iphigenia, *Ne doutez jamais de ma flamme*, presumably shorn of the singing. Gardel's advice was to reject the request as setting a most dangerous precedent. He feared that

> it would very quickly contribute to the decay of French opera. It would add to ... the mutual antipathy that all too unfortunately exists between the opera and the ballet. For, once this precedent has been set, no singer will possess a single pretty number, be it a solo or a duet, that some dancer will not hasten to pilfer.

Being fully aware that Duport's ultimate aim was to displace Vestris, Gardel was faced with the delicate problem of preventing a confrontation. He went on:

> If such a contest were in the interests of the management and to the benefit of the contestants, the management should allow it. But in the present circumstances what would be the result? Humiliation and revulsion for one or the other of these two great artistes.
>
> If the management is to give full scope to the extraordinary talent that is emerging, ought it to ignore the consideration it owes to the veteran artiste who for the past thirty years has contributed to the success of the establishment and who is still capable of rendering very great services? Who can foresee the consequences of such a public challenge, in which each contestant will not fail to muster all his partisans? The [Opéra] would immediately become an arena which would be wide open to a clash of personalities and perhaps to violence.

Gardel's considered advice was that the Opéra should at all costs 'avoid a contest that might lose [it] a great dancer; or, if it were felt to further the art of the dance, or be financially desirable, then a work should be chosen that could be advantageous [to both] and not likely to do more harm than good.'[17]

Duport was insistent on having his way, putting Luçay on notice that should M. Vestris succeed in preventing me from dancing next Tuesday, I shall be unable to return to the Opéra, for after such a triumph of intrigue over justice, I would have reason to see myself as a pawn at the mercy of whoever wishes me harm.

So I shall be forced out despite your wishes, and, as you have explained to me, the wishes of the Emperor, while M. Vestris will remain.

It is not for me to judge which of the two of us dances more often and offers the greater hope for the future, either for the development of the art or in the interests of the Opéra.

But what would happen if, from what you have told me about M. Vestris, it should become clear that he only wants to make a brilliant return to obtain greater advantages and privileges which he can no longer hope for at the Opéra? In that case I would have been gratuitously sacrificed for a momentary whim and for personal interest. These, Monsieur, are the steps which you are being urged to take for the benefit and prosperity of the Opéra.

If, on the other hand, we were both to dance (and this I have no wish to avoid), there could be no objection, and both the public and the box-office would gain.

You see, Monsieur, how much it is to be hoped that the middlemen who separate you from the artistes should not be partial towards one individual or another, but be concerned solely with the matter in hand.[18]

Although terms had been agreed, the matter of the contract seemed to have dragged to a halt. Towards the end of August Duport registered a formal complaint, which was served on the Opéra by a court bailiff. He was now all the more convinced that the Opéra was dragging its feet for some nefarious purpose of its own, and to Mlle Collomb he poured out his exasperation, disclosing a secret he had no doubt been keeping very much to himself – that he was in touch with an agent of the Russian Imperial Theatres:

You must see that after this it is impossible for me to enter the Opéra. I was so shattered by the conduct of all those rogues (for I believe that Bonet was in league with them to deceive M. de Luçay) that I immediately went to see the Russian that I told you about, and if the contract

[17] Arch. Nat., AJ[13] 87. Report, Bonet to Luçay, 21 Thermidor, Year XII (9 August 1804).
[18] Arch. Nat., AJ[13] 63. Duport to Luçay, 21 Thermidor, Year XII (August 8th, 1804).

> in question had been ready, I would have signed it on the spot. It seems that M. Didelot wants to have a few *danseuses*, for there are none over there, and I shall take my sister. I am making no proposals on my behalf because they will only have to find my letter to put me into an asylum, but speaking for this gentleman, who is authorised to enter into a contract, I can inform you that you could make a clear profit of 30,000 francs, with travel expenses paid, together with everything else and other special conditions. Please reply as soon as possible if this is acceptable to you. They will give you in Paris all the safeguards and advances you can possibly need. As for me, I plan to flee next week.[19]

This rejection had struck Duport to the core, but he did not desert the Opéra. Remembering that Luçay had told him that Napoleon wished him to remain, he took what must have seemed to him the final step. 'I have written a letter to the Emperor, which reached him at Mayence,' he told Mlle Collomb:

> Apparently it interested him because, when his wife asked whether he was going to do me justice, he said, 'I shall reply to him myself and get my own back on that Prefect who has no idea how to handle artistes'. Then Mme de Luçay, to whom this remark was reported, wrote at once to her husband; or so at least I presume, since as soon as I learnt of the Emperor's flattering reply, Bonet requested a discussion and pressed me to bring my matter to a conclusion, and finally, as proof of what I am telling you, I need only say that they accept as fair what they had accepted as fair two months ago, and that it was decided to give me everything; that they had even wanted to do so at once were it not for my principle of making haste slowly, although unfortunately he had told me several times to have no hope.

Mlle Collomb's friend, Forget, also heard the story of Duport's appeal to the Emperor, who was quoted as saying 'What, more of the Prefect's stupidities?' When pressed to sign the new contract, Duport gave his word of honour to do so, but cannily, 'not wishing to behave like a child', preferred to wait until hearing the Emperor's reaction.[20] In the end he honoured his promise, the Opéra allowed his sister to remain as if nothing had happened, and all was treated as forgotten, if not forgiven.

Duport's claim to challenge Vestris for supremacy had become public

[19] Bibl.-Mus. de l'Opéra, Fonds Collomb, 23. Duport to Collomb, 23 Thermidor, Year XII (13 August 1804).

knowledge, and a satirical pamphlet made fun of the situation by imagining a meeting of the General Council of the Opéra to investigate the philosophical question of what effect rapidity or slowness of movement might have on public morals. Summoned as the defendant, Duport was put through an examination:

> Q. M. Duport, why do you allow yourself to dance differently from your predecessors?
> R. I have no idea of how my predecessors danced, because I am too young to have seen them all, and there is no written record. Furthermore, it would be difficult to preserve steps performed in the air.
> Q. Are you aware, sir, that, in accordance with *tradition*, no one before you has performed two *tours en l'air* and landed in perfect balance?
> R. No, but I do know that on one occasion when, being in the air after preparing for a turn, I was unable to hold myself back and did land in perfect balance for my own safety.
> Q. Why do you perform new steps, by which I mean steps that were unknown in the great days of the Opéra?
> R. I know nothing about the great days of the Opéra or of the old steps, but I do my best to profit, as much as I can, from the examples set by Vestris and Gardel that delight the connoisseurs.

Found guilty by the Council, Duport was forbidden to perform any new steps, under pain of having to dance between two gendarmes, each holding a ribbon attached to one of his feet to restrain him from excessive activity. As this sentence was pronounced, Duport was reported to have thrown up his hands in despair, exclaiming: 'I give up!'[21]

The long absences of Vestris and Duport that summer had had a disastrous effect on receipts, and the opportunity of recouping some of the shortfall by exploiting their rivalry was too good to miss. With Gardel's warning in their ears, Luçay and Bonet worked on their difficult charges to find a *modus vivendi* that would enable them to appear on the same evening without incurring the dangers of a confrontation. Eventually an acceptable compromise was reached, the two dancers agreeing to be fea-

[20] Bibl.-Mus. de l'Opéra, Fonds Collomb, 23. Duport to Collomb, undated; Forget to Collomb, 8 October 1804.

[21] *Journal de Paris*, 17 September 1804, quoting a pamphlet entitled *Extrait du procès-verbal de la séance du conseil-général de l'administration de l'Opéra, tenue le 27 fructidor an 12* (29 August 1804). This pamphlet suggests that Duport was the first dancer to perform *doubles tours en l'air* at the Opéra. It is possible that none of his contemporaries followed his example, for when Arthur Saint-Léon was dancing at the Opéra in 1848, the *Courrier des spectacles* (22 October 1848) went out of its way to criticise him for performing this virtuosic step.

tured in separate works: Duport would dance a *pas* in *La Caravane*, and Vestris would play the title-rôle of *Télémaque*. Their respective contributions were accepted as being sufficiently different to avoid any invidious comparison, but the public, and particularly the rival cliques, saw matters differently and were determined to muster in force to cheer their respective favourites.

On the evening of 19 October the beams of the Opéra must have shaken as they had never shaken before, and heated arguments raged both during the performance and after. In the event the honours were more or less even. In his review in the *Journal des débats* a few days later, Geoffroy called for an end to this 'regrettable rivalry'; the talents of the two dancers should be enjoyed, he said, not compared.[22]

In fact, the two dancers were never to engage in the face-to-face contest that Duport so ardently desired, whatever the frontispiece to a poem written by J. Berchoux might suggest. This depicted Vestris reclining on the ground after a fall, and offering the palm to a triumphant Duport towering above him in the flow of a pirouette; and underneath this was printed a couplet from the poem that had no basis in fact:

O Chute épouvantable et digne de mémoire!
La Parterre aussitôt proclaime la victoire.[23]

* * *

The passions that lay behind the rivalry were real and strong enough. No doubt Vestris would have preferred that Duport did not appear at performances in which he was dancing, while Duport, conscious of his physical and technical superiority, may have dreamed of just such a triumph as Berchoux was to imagine. The Opéra, of course, had to tread carefully, but the management did not concede its right to present them both on the same evening if it deemed it advisable. In fact another occasion on which the public was to be so spoiled took place a few days later. The cause of what was believed to be a snap decision on the part of the Opéra was the disappointing reception of a new ballet.

Several months earlier, Gardel had put together an inconsequential piece that might have been more accurately described as a danced interlude than a ballet. It had been given at the Palace of Saint-Cloud in the presence of Napoleon on 28 April 1804, the day that he was proclaimed

[22] *Journal des débats*, 22 October 1804.
[23] 'Oh that dreadful and memorable fall!/ The pit at once proclaims the victory.'

Emperor. Now, six months later, Gardel was to revive it for the Opéra; but, being very conscious of its transitory nature, he took the precaution of warning the public in a letter to the press to expect nothing more than a little pantomime scene arranged to introduce a dance called the *pas du schall*.

This dance was then a subject of topical interest, having been featured in a new novel, *Valérie*, that was arousing curiosity in literary salons in the early months of 1804. Interest in the book was further stimulated by the mystery surrounding the identity of the author, who, it transpired, was a Russian-born lady who had forsaken a life of pleasure for an obsession for mysticism. A prominent passage in the book was a description of a shawl dance that supposedly shed an insight into the arcane amatory delights of the East; this dance was one of the heroine's accomplishments, which a distrustful lover observed when peering through the window of a Venetian villa:

> I saw her surrounded by a number of persons who were asking something of her; she seemed to be refusing, and I said to myself, 'She does not want to dance the shawl dance because there are too many people present ...' The doors were then closed so that no one could enter the room. Lord Mery took up his violin, Valérie asked for her dark blue muslin shawl, loosened her hair from above her forehead, and covered her head with the shawl ... Those varying attitudes, some expressing fear and others depicting affecting situations, form an eloquent language steeped in movements of the soul and the passions. And when presented through a body that is pure and antique in its form, and whose power is drawn out by the expression of the features, the effect is beyond description. Milady Hamilton, who possessed those precious accomplishments, was the first to give an idea of this type of truly dramatic dance, if such it can be called ... the shawl dance, which is at the same time so ancient and so appropriate to be designed in so many different ways ...[24]

The name of Lady Hamilton was surely known to Gardel, who must have heard of the statuesque 'attitudes' that she used to perform in her drawing room before friends, making frequent use of a shawl and displaying her flowing black hair. The dance had also come to the attention of Mme de Staël, who two years before, in her novel *Corinne*, had imagined her heroine performing an expressive Oriental dance 'tracing poetic ideas

[24] Krudener, I, 82.

and sensations which, under an Eastern sky, are almost beyond the power of the most beautiful verses to describe'.[25]

This strange newly-published novel gave Gardel his inspiration for *Une Demi-heure de caprice*, which was presented at the Opéra on 23 October 1804. But what could allusively be suggested in literary form could not adequately be conveyed on the stage, and the pantomime introduction that Gardel provided to give the dance a framework was quite trite by comparison. The central character, Melzi (Mme Gardel) is a spoilt young woman ruled by her whims. Her married sister Azelaïde (M.-M. Delisle), wishing to see her settled in life, favours a suitor, Zénor (Aug. Vestris). Knowing Melzi's unpredictable character, she advises against a direct approach, first suggesting that he declare his love in writing. But when Melzi finds his note, she capriciously tears it up. Zénor is in despair, but Azelaïde has another idea. Taking up her guitar, she persuades Melzi to dance to a favourite melody. Choosing a moment when Melzi is completely absorbed, she beckons to Zénor to take over the accompaniment. When the dance ends, Melzi runs to embrace her sister only to discover Zénor standing before her. In her confusion she realises she loves him, and the ballet concludes with a short *divertissement*.

Marie Gardel, of course, was enthusiastically applauded after her *pas du schall*, but its somewhat louche origins had, as Geoffroy put it, been 'dignified', smoothed over:

> The shawl dance at the Opéra is an ingenious and refined dance of coquetry, a display of preening, or rather a study of the various ways in which a beautiful woman can drape herself in a shawl, adding to her charms by varying her costume ... The Terpsichore of the Opéra seems at first to have no other purpose but to please herself. Before a mirror she practices every possibility of manoeuvring her shawl to reveal aspects of her beauty, but by degrees her coquetry gains the upper hand. Merely finding herself attractive does not suffice, and she becomes bored by the mysteries of the shawl with nobody looking on but herself.[26]

Commenting on a later performance, Geoffroy was to add that Mme Gardel was 'more than half responsible for composing the work; it is she who gives it meaning and life; the elegance, grace and voluptuousness which she puts into her performance of the *pas du schall* is the ballet's only merit and charm.'[27]

[25] Staël, *Corinne*, I, letter 27.

But not even Marie Gardel's artistry could conceal the shallowness of the piece, and the audience gave it a cool reception. 'The public,' wrote Geoffroy, 'made it clear that it required more vivacity and action in a ballet; all that gallant and coquettish simpering seemed a little feeble'.[28]

Clearly it was not worth Gardel's time to improve this little work – in any case, he had no time to do so, being heavily involved preparing a major ballet – but at the second performance the public was compensated by what Geoffroy described as 'another caprice'.

Duport's services had been sought to rescue the ballet by dancing, in the accompanying opera, a new *pas*, conceivably of his own composition, entitled *La Réunion des genres*. As its title implied, he presented a brilliant survey of the three genres, taken in turn, with a youthful quartet of four girls, including his sister Minette and Luigia Taglioni, echoing his movements. The announcement of his appearance had an immediate effect; the public flocked to the Opéra to see him, and the storm of cheering that broke out at the end of his dance completely outshone the polite applause that followed *Une Demi-heure de caprice*. Duport was left in no doubt of his triumph, for at the end of the opera the audience shouted for him to take another call, an almost unprecedented honour. Geoffroy, interpreting this as a slap in the face for Vestris, found it excessive, observing:

> However astonishing this young dancer may be, I doubt whether he ought to have been honoured by such a distinction. Admittedly [a call] is particularly flattering at this theatre, where it is so much rarer, but if the public wants to give full rein to its enthusiasm for superior merit, there are surely kinder ways of showing it that are more honourable for being less humiliating for his rivals.'[29]

Duport may not have danced Vestris into the ground as his supporters liked to believe, but in this brilliant display of mastery he had certainly proved himself second to none in technical versatility. But in those times a dancer was also judged on another level, as a dramatic artiste, and his greatest test was still to come.

26 *Journal des débats*, 28 October 1804.
27 *Journal de l'Empire*, 29 March 1806.
28 *Journal des débats*, 28 October 1804.
29 *Journal des débats*, 28 October 1804.

11

Achille à Scyros

Since the outbreak of the Revolution, those responsible for reshaping the nation had looked back for their inspiration to ancient Rome, seeing themselves as the spiritual heirs of the grave statesmen of the Roman Republic. But when Bonaparte arrived to dissipate the threat of chaos, the emphasis shifted noticeably to a later phase of Roman history. By its very name the lifetime Consulate, as it became, stressed this indebtedness, for in substance the new régime was unashamedly an autocracy, inspired by the almost godlike figure of the Emperor Augustus. Indeed, to add strength to the Roman analogy, the Consulate was soon to be transformed into a new Empire. By 1804, when Napoleon was proclaimed Emperor, French hegemony extended halfway across Europe, and only England, it seemed, stood in the way of a *Pax Gallicus*.

In Paris all attention was focussed on the coming coronation in the cathedral of Notre Dame. Responding to an invitation that brooked no refusal, the Pope arrived in Paris to officiate, not by placing a crown on the new Emperor's head, but by endowing the ceremony with an historical echo of the coronation of Charlemagne a millennium before. Pompously celebrated on 2 December, Napoleon's coronation was the culmination of a winter of festivities. Some of these were deliberately military, but others were designed to publish abroad France's claim to be the cultural centre of the civilised world. Among the latter were the first performance of Mozart's *Requiem* under Cherubini's baton, and a profusion of ballet. At the Porte-Saint-Martin in a season of Dauberval ballets, *La Fille mal gardée* was performed more than twenty times in the last quarter of the year; at the Opéra, Gardel was to usher in the Imperial regime with an important new ballet in the Neo-Classical mould, *Achille à Scyros*.

Far from being hastily got up for the occasion, *Achille à Scyros* had for many years featured among the Opéra's future projects. That it had not been produced sooner was undoubtedly partly due to its scale and cost of production. Its plot also presented an unavoidable problem in that it demanded a dancer who could give a credible interpretation of the title rôle, a part that presented a daunting challenge on which a reputation might stand or fall. For Gardel's conception was daring in the extreme: to recount in mime and dance the ancient legend of Achilles's youth in the court of King Lycomedes disguised as a girl.

The subject had been suggested to Gardel by his friend Luce de Lancival, then Professor of Literature at the Collège Louis le Grand. Luce was no dry academic; in his spare moments he wrote for the theatre. Although he never achieved much success, he mixed in theatrical circles, where he made the acquaintance of Gardel. At that time he was engaged upon a major work, an epic poem on the subject of Achilles in Scyros. This lay in his desk unpublished for many years, and in a moment of generosity – and perhaps despairing that it might never be published – he gave a copy of it to Gardel with permission to make use of it as the basis of a ballet.

This gift was made no later than 1800, for in November of that year Degotti was consulted about the cost of staging it. He estimated this at 35,000 francs and about three months' work, on the assumption that the four exterior sets would be prepared in the Opéra's workshops and the three interiors allotted to outside scene-painters such as Jacques-Charles Protain or Moench.[1]

By the following summer, the plans had made a little progress. Méhul was now envisaged as the composer, and the ballet was mentioned in a memorandum by Cellerier, the financial director, setting out plans for the coming winter. It was then hoped that work on the production might start once the opera *Les Mystères d'Isis* had been presented. Cellerier commented that:

> the ballet of *Achille à Scyros* is a very important work on account both of its subject and of the episodes contained in it. Its settings are numerous and splendid. Precise costings have not been presented because Citizen Gardel has not yet worked out his scenario, and it is not possible to make an estimate, but it will certainly be more expensive than the ballet *Pandrose* and will therefore cost more than 46,000 francs. Another problem is that it will be difficult to produce because of the need to find a male dancer who, without appearing ridiculous, can play the rôle of Achilles dressed as a woman throughout three acts.[2]

For one reason or another, hopes of an early production did not materi-

[1] Arch. Nat., AJ[13] 51 (Brumaire). Report dated 22 Brumaire, Year IX (13 November 1800).
[2] Arch. Nat., AJ[13] 51 (Fructidor IX). Memorandum written in August/September 1801.

alise. Undeterred, Gardel tightened his plot by reducing the number of scenes to five. In the summer of 1801 there was a proposal to engage a scene-designer from Milan, Giorgio Fuentes, to work alongside or, as Gardel put it, 'in competition with' Degotti. This proposal came to naught, and the project gathered dust for three more years before the approach of Napoleon's coronation finally resuscitated it.

In July 1804 Gardel at last received official sanction to begin work on it, and orders were given for the scenery and costumes to be prepared. Only two of the sets (Act II, Scene 1; and Act III) were to be entirely new, while the others would incorporate items from stock: these included the Elysian fields set from Paisiello's failed opera, *Proserpine*, in Act I, and a palace from Cherubini's *Anacréon* in Act II. These borrowings resulted in considerable savings, but even so it would be an expensive production, the total estimate working out at 54,000 francs. The final figure was certainly higher, for shortly before the first performance Gardel rejected the Elysian fields set, making a new backcloth necessary.[3]

The scenario had now reached its final form, and, as Luce had asked, it was possible to present the ballet only a few months after the publication of the poem. The common source was the *Achilleis* of Statius, a poet of the silver age of Latin literature who flourished in the first century AD. This purported to recount the youth of Achilles before the Trojan War. Achilles's mother was the nereid Thetis, who, to subvert the prophesy that he would either meet an early but glorious death or live a long and inglorious life, had endeavoured to make him immortal by plunging him as an infant into the river Styx – leaving him vulnerable only in the heel by which she held him. To prevent him from being involved in the Trojan War, she had him disguised as a girl and introduced into the court of Scyros. There he remained concealed, his true sex becoming only belatedly known to the King's daughter, Deidamia, who would bear him a son. His identity was eventually revealed when Ulysses arrived in the guise of a merchant to seek him out. Concealed among his merchandise were some arms, which Achilles, in a moment of elated inattention, eagerly seized, thereby betraying his identity. His ardour aroused, he departed with Ulysses for Troy, where he was destined to meet his death.

By now Gardel had brought his scenario to its final form, in which it would be sent to the printers with a list of the dancers who would bring it to life on the stage. The curtain first rose to the final measures of Cherubini's overture, a stirring march to which the daughters of Lycomedes, the Scythian king, are shown entering the Temple of Minerva

[3] Arch. Nat., AJ[13] 90.

to make their offerings. As the gates close behind them, the music dies away, and to a gentler melody a chariot bearing Thetis, mother of Achilles, is seen crossing the rocky isthmus to the shore. Thetis (V. Saulnier II) steps ashore and, having dismissed her attendant nymphs, gives thanks to the Gods, imploring them to watch over the island where she will be leaving her son, and to keep her secret inviolate. Her nymphs return; finding her in tears, they endeavour to console her. Awakening, Achilles (Duport) presses his mother to explain why she has brought him here, and she discloses the fate decreed for him – her mime being augmented by the descent of a cloud with the following inscription:

> You, Achilles, are free to choose between a life long in years but deprived of glory, and a life short in days but followed by everlasting fame.[4]

Achilles chooses the path of glory. Horrified, Thetis exhorts him to spare her the grief of his early death. He hesitates, but despite her pressure, remains undecided. Only when she falls to her knees to beg him to relent does he give way to her plea. On his asking what he must do to avoid his destiny, the nymphs bring out women's clothing with which he must be disguised. He is so shocked that he tries to escape, but his mother is too quick for him. Rejecting her entreaties, he tells her he would rather drown himself than comply. Thetis then makes a desperate appeal to the Gods, and just as the Temple doors open to reveal Deidamia, the Scythian king's daughter (Mme Gardel), Cupid (V. Hullin) appears, hovering above Achilles's head. Achilles is thus smitten by Deidamia's beauty. His indignation vanishes, and to his mother's suggestion that he should remain for some time in the company of the princess and her ladies, he can do no more than blush and remain silent. In this bemused state he allows himself to be dressed as a girl. He has to be restrained from running after Deidamia and her suite; and before departing in her chariot, Thetis instructs him in the feminine graces that he must adopt.

Left alone, Achilles feels awkward in his new guise. But when Deidamia and her suite of sisters and ladies-in-waiting reappear as bacchantes for the forthcoming Festival of Bacchus, his embarrassment vanishes. He entreats them to let him join them. Deidamia is enchanted by the beauty of the newcomer, who claims to be the survivor of a shipwreck. Her father, Lycomedes (Milon), agrees that Achilles can be admitted to his daughter's suite. As Deidamia takes Achilles by the hand, she

[4] A quotation, slightly amended, from Racine's *Iphigénie* (Act I Scene 2).

winces at the strength of his grasp. She and her ladies, now joined by the disguised Achilles, then cross the rocky isthmus on their way to the Festival.

The scene changes to a grove dedicated to the worship of Bacchus. The bacchantes arrive and begin to dance around the statue of the God. The women are struck by the strength that Achilles exerts in his steps; they try to emulate him, but tire long before he does and, one by one, drop to the ground in exhaustion. Achilles alone remains awake, and there follows the central scene of the ballet, which Gardel described in sharp detail:

> Young, ardent, amorous, yet virtuous, he is overcome by such feelings as are stirred by such voluptuous moments as this. Desire and shyness, honour and ardour struggle for supremacy in his mind, leaving him in a torment of uncertainty. What is he to do? Should he take advantage of the opportunity that the object of his love is offering him? No, such a dishonourable action would be unworthy of a heart such as his. Should he reveal his sex and his love? On this he seems to have decided, but then his shyness, natural in one of his age, holds him back. Nevertheless he approaches [the sleeping form of] Deidamia, his hungry eyes feasting on the charms that her happy disorder allows him to see. Her tiny foot, her charming figure, all about her enchants and transports him. His nervousness betrays the heat of his passion; many a time he stretches out his trembling hand to take that of the charming Deidamia, and as often draws back in fear of waking her, and while his love is thus preventing him from making a violent move, Deidamia wakes. Her first thought is to throw herself into her companion's arms with all the confidence of innocent friendship. Achilles, however, reacts to this with the ardour of carnal desire. His legs give way beneath him, his heart beats wildly, his eyes gleam. Deidamia cannot understand what she takes to be fear, and presses her new friend to confide in her. Achilles hesitates, but Deidamia insists. Now nothing can hold him back. He falls at her feet and confesses his ruse, his sex, his birth, his love. Confused, shocked and all a-tremble, Deidamia runs off distraught, but Achilles, youthful and light of foot, soon catches her, takes her into his arms and kisses her. Deidamia cries out in alarm to summon her companions. She runs up the mountain path, rejecting the pursuing Achilles with gestures that convey her indignation.

The second act was played against an interior set, representing the princesses' dressing room. Deidamia enters, followed by Achilles. She is tearfully upbraiding him, while he attempts to assure her of his love. They are interrupted by the arrival of Deidamia's sisters, who have come to prepare themselves for a court function. Servants bring tunics, garlands and jewellery, which the sisters fall upon with coquettish delight. Deidamia does not share in their feelings, while Achilles's gaiety is patently forced. Presented with clothing richer even than that which he is wearing, he dresses so awkwardly that Deidamia has to make some hurried adjustments to prevent his lapse being noticed. After a dance by two of the princesses, the sisters leave. Deidamia tells them she will follow shortly. Achilles wishes to remain with her, but she insists on being left alone.

She is now overcome with shame and revulsion at having yielded to Achilles's passion. She contemplates leaving her father's roof, but thrusts that thought aside; only death can put an end to her shame. At this moment her father enters. She looks at him with tears in her eyes. He takes her in his arms and asks what is troubling her. At first she cannot bring herself to look at him, but after a moment's reflection her revulsion leads her to decide to confess. But at that very moment Achilles reappears. Unseen by the king, he falls to his knees, imploring Deidamia not to reveal his secret. Lycomedes turns and sees him. He tells his daughter that she may speak freely before her companion, and when Achilles offers to retire, insists on his remaining. Deidamia thus finds herself in an awkward predicament; if she remains silent, she will offend her father; if she speaks, she risks losing the man she now realises she loves.

The tension is broken by news that a party of Greeks has arrived and is seeking an audience. Deidamia is filled with foreboding, while Achilles has a presentiment of the glory that awaits him. Momentarily distracted, Lycomedes is pondering on the motive that lies behind this visit. Achilles takes the opportunity this gives him to warn Deidamia of the consequences of indiscretion, and is delighted to find her ready to listen to him. When the king's attention turns back to her, her revulsion has given way to love.

The scene changes to the throne-room where the court has assembled. The two visitors, Ulysses (Gardel) and Diomedes (Aumer), are introduced. They explain that they have come to seek support for the campaign of the Greeks against Troy and in particular to search for Achilles. Their mission is explained to the audience by banners borne by the Greek soldiers with such bellicose inscriptions as: 'War on the Trojans', 'Victory awaits us', 'Shame on the Laggard', 'The Oracle demands the presence of Achilles'. When Lycomedes explains that he is old and has no sons, a squad of Amazons enters carrying a banner with the words, 'Courage has no sex'.

The visitors are invited to attend a festival in their honour, which is opened by the princesses, but Ulysses is quick to notice that neither Deidamia nor her mysterious companion is taking part. To deflect suspicion, Deidamia takes up her lyre and plays a voluptuous melody. She tries to calm Achilles, for his excitement has caught Ulysses' observant eye. Deidamia hands Achilles her lyre. But carried away by the talk of war, and forgetful of his disguise, he plucks a martial air. Ulysses' suspicions are thus strengthened. Deidamia tries to distract him by pressing Achilles to dance with her, but his energy gives him away. Ulysses rises from his seat, but Deidamia summons her companions, who with arms interlocked pass in a line between them, allowing her to conceal Achilles from his view and enabling her to spirit him away. When Ulysses attempts to follow, Lycomedes restrains him. Foiled, Ulysses invites the king to be his guest at a festival on board his ship.

Act III takes place on the ship, on which a splendid tent has been erected. Both Ulysses and Diomedes are convinced that they have recognised Achilles, but they do not wish to unmask him until his martial ardour has been awakened. Ulysses has devised a plan, and hands a javelin, shield, helmet and sword to one of his officers. The flaps of the tent are then drawn aside to reveal the Greek fleet at anchor. Lycomedes and his court arrive, and the festival opens with a display of martial combat. Achilles is so carried away that Deidamia has difficulty in preventing him from going to the assistance of an unlucky wrestler. Ulysses, now certain that he has seen through Achilles's disguise, gives the order for gifts to be brought in; there are bracelets and necklaces, rich materials, musical instruments, everything to appeal to feminine taste. As Deidamia is selecting her gift, Ulysses draws Achilles's attention to the offerings. While Deidamia is thus distracted, Achilles's hand strays to the arms that have been secreted among the gifts. His eyes gleam, his body stiffens; he puts on the helmet and takes up the shield and sword. Realising the deception, Lycomedes accuses Achilles of bringing dishonour to his house and challenges him to combat. Achilles casts his weapons aside, and falling to his knees, begs forgiveness, while Deidamia uncovers her breast to her father, who backs away in horror.

In an apotheosis featuring Hymen, Cupid, the Graces, Pleasures, Games and Spirits of Laughter, Thetis returns in her conch-shell to beg Lycomedes to forgive the two lovers. Achilles casts off his female attire and is armed for battle. Thetis gives him her last blessing. The Greek army has already embarked, and the moment of parting is at hand. Achilles still hesitates to leave Deidamia, but she, with tears in her eyes, takes him in her arms in a farewell embrace. Jupiter and the Gods then appear, admiring the heroism of the lovers, and as the mortals raise their arms, the curtain falls.

Gardel found himself under great pressure in the weeks leading up to the first performance. Duport was the first and obvious choice for the part of Achilles, but the ordeal of a part to be played in female costume filled him with apprehension. Torn between his desire to take on a rôle of such grandeur and the hazard of how the audience might react, he hesitated to confirm his verbal acceptance and delayed reporting to Gardel for rehearsals. Unable to pin him down after several rehearsals had been cancelled, Bonet sought instructions from Luçay.

Further delay could not be considered, and he was authorised to replace Duport. Louis Henry was next on the list for the part; but, before he could be approached, Duport made up his mind and wrote to the Director confirming his acceptance:

> My earnest wish to offer my feeble talents to embellish the festivities of the Coronation of His Majesty the Emperor and my duty to further the interests of the Académie Impériale have led me to overlook the difficulties and disadvantages which the rôle of Achilles seems to present, and I have decided to accept it. Whatever the success of the rôle, it will at least be an honour for me to have sacrificed my personal interests to satisfy the wish of the management and the ballet-master.[5]

It had all been a most trying time for Gardel who, under pressure to have the ballet ready by the middle of December, had been unable to compose the warriors' dance he had planned as the set-piece of the final act. He had consequently been forced to substitute a somewhat similar dance, that of the Samnites, which he had arranged for the opera *Sémiramis*, whose composer, Catel, gave his consent to its being used for the first few performances.[6]

Gardel had almost driven himself into a nervous breakdown to have the ballet ready for the first performance on 18 December 1804, and he managed to meet the deadline only by means of an effort that went beyond the normal bounds of duty. When little more than two weeks were left before the première, he had written to Luçay to explain the difficulties he faced and to ensure that the Prefect appreciated his zeal in overcoming them. 'I am taking the liberty of informing you as follows,' he wrote:

[5] Arch. Nat., AJ^{13} 90. Bonet to Luçay, 27 Brumaire; Luçay to Bonet, 28 Brumaire; Bonet to Luçay, 29 Brumaire; Duport to Bonet, 29 Brumaire, all Year XIII (18, 19 and 20 November 1804).

[6] *Courrier des spectacles*, 18 December 1804. Letter from Gardel to the Editor.

1. M. Duport's four days of indecision were spent first in composing on my own, then in demonstrating what I had composed, first to M. Henry, and finally to M. Duport when he had made up his mind.
2. Until now I have not seen on the stage *any of the sets* prepared for my work.
3. Since the musicians of the Opéra are involved in preparations for the festivities attendant on the Coronation, they are unable to rehearse.

And when you add to all this the Opéra's conditions of employment that prohibit artistes dancing the next day from overtiring themselves, and the balls, and the free gala performance, you will have an idea of the delays and difficulties I have had to face. However, I have not wasted a moment, and despite an accident when I cut my leg on a piece of glass and was ordered by the doctor to rest, I appeared that same evening, last Tuesday, in *La Dansomanie*, and worked the following Wednesday and Thursday from 10 in the morning until 10 at night. At last all I could possibly do without the scenery has been done. All I now ask is to have two rehearsals with [scenery] and three with the orchestra.[7]

There had been little that Bonet or even Luçay could do to resolve the problems of the music, for the demands of the Coronation inevitably took precedence. Le Sueur, the Emperor's Director of Music, had sent Bonet what amounted to a command for instruments to be lent for the Coronation. Bonet could do no more than protest that the production of *Achille à Scyros* had been commanded by the Government and the date of the première fixed, and that a concentrated series of rehearsals was about to commence. The Coronation ceremony was to include a grand mass for full orchestra and choir by Paisiello, as well as other music by Le Sueur himself, and on 26 November Bonet was ordered to deliver a large quantity of instruments, desks and stools, which would be kept for a full week, until the day after the Coronation.[8]

At the first performance of the ballet on 18 December, the house was crowded almost to suffocation. As he entered his box, the newly crowned Emperor was acclaimed by an audience so packed with invited dignitaries that many faithful supporters of the Opéra had been unable to gain admittance. The critic of the *Journal de Paris* had to view the ballet standing

[7] Arch. Nat., AJ^{13} 90. Gardel to Luçay, 12 Frimaire, Year XIII (3 December 1804).

[8] Bibl.-Mus. de l'Opéra, Fonds Teneo, 1 (7). Copies of letters, Le Sueur to Bonet, 22 November 1804, and Grégoire, Secretary to the Emperor's Household, to Bonet, 26 November 1804.

ACADÉMIE IMPÉRIALE
DE MUSIQUE.

On commencera à 7 h. précises. --- *Aujourd'hui Mardi 27 Frim*[illegible] 13,

LES PRÉTENDUS,

Comédie-lyrique en 2 actes, paroles de *Rochon de Chabannes*, musique de *Lemoine*; suivi de la première représentation

D'ACHILLE
A SCYROS,

Ballet-pantomime en trois actes.

M.lle *VICTOIRE SAULNIER* continuera ses débuts par le rôle de *Thétis*.

CHANT : MM. *Dufrêne*, *Laforêt*, *Bertin*, *Albert* ; M.mes *Branchu*, *Armand*, *Chollet*.

DANSE : MM. *Gardel*, *Milon*, *Vestris*, *Duport*, *Goyon*, *Branchu*, *Aumer*, *Titus* ; M.mes *Clotilde*, *Gardel*, *Saulnier*, *Louise*, *Bigotini*, *Delisle*, *Vestris*, *Félicité*, *Nalei-Neuville*, *Huttin*, *Coulon*.

Nota. Le Public est prévenu de ne point acheter des Billets hors des Bureaux, parce qu'on n'en rendra point la valeur.

Prix des Quatrièmes Galeries de côté, 30 francs 60 centimes.

De l'Imprimerie de Ballard, rue J.-J. Rousseau, n.° 14.

Playbill for the first performance of Achille à Scyros. *(Bibliothèque-Musée de l'Opéra)*

up in a corridor and peering through the window of a box. Nevertheless he saw enough to appreciate the magnificence of the production and the excellence of the dancing, although Duport's dancing and his pantomime seemed to him grossly exaggerated, and his *tours de force*, however technically astounding, in questionable taste – 'more like the antics of an acrobat than the noble panache of Achilles.'[9]

Geoffroy, on the other hand, who was no doubt more comfortably accommodated, commended Gardel for producing a ballet that was of equal merit to Luce's poem, and took a much more favourable view of Duport. 'The difficulty,' he explained, 'had been to find an Achilles who did not appear ridiculous or shocking in female attire. Happily Duport's youth and vigour, added to his childlike features, removed the major obstacle to this ballet's success.'

Both in Statius's epic and Luce's poem, Achilles' passion leads him to ravish Deidamia – with a child being conceived as a result. This physical element of the story could not be ignored in the ballet, but Gardel handled it with a discretion that satisfied the great majority of spectators. The

[9] *Journal de Paris*, 19 December 1804.

seduction scene, a necessary prelude to the action that followed it, was described in some detail by Geoffroy:

> When the daughters of Lycomedes become exhausted by dancing and fall asleep, Achilles, who remains wide awake, contemplates those slumbering beauties and seems overwhelmed by the violence of his desire. This singular and explicit situation at first shocked the delicate feelings of the audience, but carried away by the charm of the dancer's performance, they soon broke into unrestrained applause at such a perfectly acted struggle between modesty and love. This struggle culminated in Achilles stealing a kiss from the lips of Deidamia, a larceny that drew from her a cry of surprise or fright. It was by toning it down in this way that Gardel translated Achilles's amorous passion, which has much more serious consequences in Luce's poem.[10]

While both Geoffroy and the critic of the *Courrier des spectacles* found the plot somewhat lacking in dramatic impact, at least the ballet was brought to an end both dramatically and choreographically on a high note. At the close some isolated whistling was heard, but this was soon drowned by the applause.

* * *

The only aspect of the ballet's production about which Gardel made no complaint in the last frantic weeks of preparation was the music. Presumably this had been under his firm control, for being a skilled musician with firm ideas for the accompaniment of both dance and mime scenes, he seems always to have collaborated very closely with his composers. It was also vital, of course, that the music should be completed before he began rehearsing the dancers.

For *Achille à Scyros* he found himself working with a composer who already enjoyed a considerable reputation in the operatic field, Luigi Cherubini. That composer's first work for the Opéra, *Démophon*, produced in 1788, had been a failure, but he had followed this in the 1790s with a number of successes at the Théâtre Feydeau, the most notable of which was *Médée*. More recently his music had been heard at the Opéra: a funeral dirge for the fallen hero General Hoche in 1797, and in 1803 a short opera-ballet, *Anacréon*, which had also proved short-lived.

Gardel had produced the ballets for both *Démophon* and *Anacréon*, and had presumably been impressed with Cherubini's skill in writing for the

[10] *Journal des débats*, 19 December 1804.

dance. The score for *Achille à Scyros* contained a fair number of insertions from other sources, which may have been requested by the choreographer. In Act I there were two borrowings from Haydn: one to accompany the arrival of Thetis and Achilles (the second movement, *scherzo*, of the Quartet op. 33, no. 3), and the other for a dance at the end (the second movement, *andante*, of the Symphony No. 94). There were also additions by Viotti (Act I, No. 4), Weigl, Catel, Righini (three pieces, including the two combats, those of wrestlers and gladiators, in Act III), Méhul and Cousineau. The last-named contributed a passage for solo horn and harp and a duet for two harps that were played on the stage. The score seems to have been skilfully crafted so that the insertions were seamlessly woven into the fabric. The critic of the *Courrier des spectacles*, who for one did not recognise them all, was nevertheless pleased that this time-honoured convention had been followed:

> Apart from two or three airs which the public was glad to hear again, it is all new; but a completely new score seems to us to be unfavourable rather than helpful for pantomime, for how better can the spoken word be replaced than by being explained by well-known and even at times hackneyed tunes? Is there anything more suitable for letting the spectator into the secret of a certain sentiment or situation than a melody that is already fixed in everyone's memory through being used before to depict a similar sentiment or situation? How well this method holds the attention and assists one's understanding![11]

As a result of a change in the Opéra's Regulations relating to the royalty rights of a composer writing for ballet, an embarrassing situation arose between Gardel and Cherubini. Under the 1798 Regulations both the choreographer and the composer were entitled to royalties on the same scale; but the new Regulations, introduced in 1801, provided that royalties due to the composer were to be payable by the choreographer.[12] Gardel would have been well aware of this, but, probably as a result of pressure from Cherubini, he had broached the subject with Luçay to see whether an exception might be made.

About a month after the first performance, prompted no doubt by Cherubini, who was expecting a payment of royalties, he put the position formally to the Prefect in the expectation of a favourable response:

[11] *Courrier des spectacles*, 19 December 1804.

[12] Arch. Nat., AJ[13] 72. Regulations of the Opéra of 29 Brumaire, Year VII (19 November 1798) and 19 Ventôse, Year IX (10 March 1801).

> You will remember, I hope, that before engaging M. Cherubini to write the music for my ballet *Achille*, I had the honour of asking you to grant him royalties as an author, and you kindly assured me that there would be no difficulty in granting this favour; you felt that a man of talent would always refuse to accept a sum from the hands of a ballet-master, and that a ballet-master could not take up four months of a composer's time when he knew that his work would be completely wasted. I therefore beg you ... to issue orders for M. Cherubini to receive the royalties which other composers have always received until now. I would be grateful if you would grant me a few moments of your time so that I can put to you a few comments on the clause in the Regulations dealing with the ballet-masters.[13]

Gardel was not granted the interview he sought. Now that the matter had progressed to a formal request, Luçay must have realised that there could be no justification for authorising an exception to the Regulations that would set an unfortunate precedent. The request was therefore rejected in no uncertain terms:

> Your request is contrary to the Regulations which lay down that the composer's rights are payable by the choreographer. The examples you quote to the contrary relate to the period before my administration and only show either that those works were produced prior to the coming into force of the current Regulations, or that your arrangements in this matter were not made in accordance with the proper procedure. Neither of these hypotheses allows me to charge the establishment with an expense for which it is not liable. If you are afraid that M. Cherubini's delicate feelings might be upset by receiving a payment directly from you, there is a course open to you, which has been followed until now, whereby your concern will be removed – namely, that you make a declaration as to the proportion of the royalties that you are abandoning to M. Cherubini, whereupon he will receive from the Cashier the sums specified on the orders of the administration and will be able to ignore, so long as you wish, the basis on which he is receiving them.[14]

There the matter must have ended, for there is no record of any further correspondence. It seems that at his earlier meeting with Luçay, Gardel

[13] Arch. Nat., AJ[13] 66. Gardel to Luçay, 4 Pluviôse, Year XIII (24 January 1805).
[14] Arch. Nat., AJ[13] 66. Luçay to Gardel, 6 Pluviôse, Year XIII (26 January 1805).

had read more into the Prefect's sympathetic words than was intended. Another possibility is that Luçay had referred the matter to Napoleon, who, not being well disposed towards the composer, had insisted on a flat refusal.

* * *

Achille à Scyros was to have received its second performance three days after the first, but the programme was changed and *La Dansomanie* given instead. This was probably caused by Gardel's having to make adjustments following suggestions that the Prefect had conveyed to Bonet. Luçay had no doubt taken stock of comments made to him during the course of the performance, and may well have had to listen to the views of Napoleon himself, who was not above considering himself an authority in theatrical matters. In his letter to Bonet, the Prefect suggested that some judicious cuts should be made to the first and second acts to tighten up the action and heighten the effect of the last act. He also passed on a general criticism that Duport's dance in the second act lacked the character that was appropriate to it:

> When Achilles is disguised as a woman, one looked in vain for the nobility that should characterise a demi-god, and even more the propriety that distinguishes the female sex which he is representing. And his movements should arouse suspicions, but not give away completely the secret of his disguise.[15]

Meanwhile, Duport had been very upset by the criticism of his own performance, and had hurriedly written a letter to the press in which he hinted at an understanding he had reached with the Prefect that he would receive a *quid pro quo* for taking on the rôle of Achilles:

> It is far from my mind to complain of criticism which has so often seen fit to draw my attention to my own faults; had it affected myself alone, I would have responded by correcting myself. But being obliged to persevere, I should inform you that what seemed to you exaggerated and excessive in a woman would only be natural in a man, and furthermore, that I have throughout followed the intentions of the choreographer, who considered that show of vigour to be necessary to enable Achilles to be recognised, as he makes clear in his scenario ... Moreo-

[15] Arch. Nat., AJ[13] 68. Luçay to Bonet, 28 Frimaire, Year XIII (19 December 1804).

ver, in deciding to accept this rôle, which I refused for a long time, I did not conceal [my concern at] the risk to which I would be exposed by the cross-dressing which he insisted upon. But the management, which was anxious to give this ballet during the Coronation festivities, pressed me, and in the circumstances I was honestly delighted to sacrifice my own interests.

Allow me also to take this opportunity of informing you that the Prefect of the Palace, who is always ready to give protection and encouragement to artistes, has kindly promised that after the production of *Achille à Scyros*, I shall be able to mount my own ballet, in which I have endeavoured to create a rôle for myself that will be within my capabilities and likely to compensate me for the reproaches I have deserved in the former work.

The sincere proofs of zeal which I have promptly given to M. Gardel allow me to hope that, far from objecting to my benefiting by this favour, he will do me the kindness to help me with his advice.[16]

Unfortunately, the effect of Duport's letter was spoilt by the appearance, in the same issue, of another letter to the Editor, signed by one Duménuet, who described himself somewhat pompously as an *'artiste chorégraphique'*, a euphemism for a ballet dancer:

I have read your article on *Achille à Scyros*. Your criticism of Duport at first seems a little exaggerated, and I know it has scandalised many people. But, on the other hand, since your fellow journalists are no less exaggerated in their praise of that young artiste, I have no qualms in acting as a counterweight.

The truth is that Achilles, when dressed as a woman, must betray his disguise by gestures that are somewhat masculine, as indeed Gardel intended they should be. However, Duport should not forget that he is playing the son of a goddess, and that it is necessary to preserve his dignity, even when disguised in a skirt. In my experience of attending the Opéra, I have seen many Pallases and Bellonas who have danced with a very bellicose allure, and could have been taken for young warriors, but none of them performed *cabrioles*. Dangerous acrobatics such as those never-ending pirouettes and flying skirts, and those enormous splits are mere carnival buffoonery, and in no way indicate a hero. The laughter they provoked sufficiently proves my point.

[16] *Journal de Paris*, 28 Frimaire, Year XIII (21 December 1804). Letter to the Editor dated the day before.

> Instead of performing *jetés en avant* and *en arrière* ... and *soubresauts*, let Duport assume proud attitudes, mark the measure with masculine precision, and above all display the vigorous *aplomb* that nature has denied to women. His dancing will then make no less a contrast with his women's clothing, and he will reveal his true sex no less effectively to the eyes of Ulysses without reminding the spectator of the bacchantes of the Grand Salon.
>
> The fault lies not, as some say, in the rôle. It is entirely up to Duport to remedy it, for having enough talent to be modest, he will surely not take offence at my remarks, and will profit from them if he sees fit.[17]

The mixed reception had unsettled Duport, who seems to have considered abandoning the rôle of Achilles. But he was talked out of it, and in reporting that he would be keeping the part, the *Courrier des spectacles* explained to its readers that

> a misunderstanding, which was soon cleared up, far from discouraging him, [had] only inflamed his zeal and redoubled his efforts. A talent as flexible and brilliant as his grows and is enriched by everything, even by a mistake. Thus the contest with two of his emulators, who had hoped to succeed him in this rôle, is indefinitely postponed.[18]

From all reports, the second performance, on 28 December, was prodigiously successful. Duport excelled himself with a display that had the audience gasping with delight. But in January he sprained his foot, and notified the Opéra that he was not in a condition to play the taxing rôle of Achilles. Bonet, ever suspicious that he might be malingering, tried to make him change his mind, but Duport was not to be hassled. 'Your wishes are my commands,' the dancer replied,

> and if it were possible to satisfy them by making my return in the ballet *Achille*, I would willingly do so. But in spite of M. Gardel's cuts, this rôle is much too fatiguing for my lungs after a month of inactivity, and I have been forced to choose *pas* that I can perform without having recovered all my strength.
>
> Apart from the pleasure it would give me to comply with your wishes by playing Achilles, I still very much want you to fulfil the promise you

[17] *Journal de Paris*, 21 December 1804.
[18] *Courrier des spectacles*, 24 December 1804.

made me regarding my own ballet, on which I count as soon as I have fulfilled the conditions you have required of me.[19]

So nearly two months passed before the third performance on 22 February. Duport had made his return some three weeks before in *Le Retour de Zéphire*, and had to be cajoled into resuming the rôle of Achilles. Geoffroy, who always had his ear to the ground, explained the background to the long interruption of *Achilles à Scyros*:

> The bills spoke of an indisposition. But those with access to the inner cabinet of the Opéra said that Achilles had withdrawn from the ballet because he disliked the part. Gardel, like another Agamemnon, had dispatched several ambassadors and made great efforts to soften the hero, who had been annoyed by the mediocre success he had obtained. During his absence, no Patrocles had dared put on ... I will not say his armour, but his tunic. Finally Duport consented to sulk no more, and to become a girl again, but upon certain conditions. However, the secret clauses of the treaty have not been published.

Seeing the ballet again, Geoffroy had had time to reflect upon its unusual nature, and his second review concentrated very much more on the details than had his first. He found the ballet 'noble and impressive', with scenes that were both pleasing to the eye and moving. Duport's bewilderment with his rôle was understandable because his efforts did not evoke the cries of admiration that usually greeted his displays of virtuosity. It was the very nature of the rôle, in Geoffroy's opinion, that defeated him.

> When a dancer becomes an actor ... he astonishes the eyes much less ... The silence in which the audience watches him is not a sign of indifference, but a mark of attention ... I know that a dancer's pride is more flattered by noisy acclaim, ... but such pride is blind. There is always more merit in speaking to the mind than astonishing the senses.

Thanks to Gardel's adjustments, Duport's interpretation had certainly developed in the right direction. Geoffroy went on:

> Duport has wisely avoided those *grands écarts* and *tours de force* which might appear too masculine in a girl's dance, but without detracting from the brusque vivacity and the kind of ardour which must charac-

[19] Arch. Nat., AJ[13] 68. Duport to Bonet, 27 January 1805.

terise Achilles. What he has been obliged to discard in his *pas* and his dancing has been compensated by the intelligence, warmth and charm of his pantomime.

In analysing the part of Achilles, Geoffroy noted that there were

> two very distinct sections in the ballet: the first presents Achilles disguised as a girl at the court of Lycomedes, while the second, in which the Greeks are looking for the young hero, sheds a martial glow over this little seraglio. This latter section has more movement, action and interest, while the first is voluptuous, but a little languid, and would gain by being shortened. The situation of Achilles being shut up with Lycomedes' daughters is a little reminiscent of the scene in *La Fille mal gardée* in which Colas finds himself shut up with Lise in her cottage, but is more lively, more natural and more theatrical. Surrounded by all those sleeping girls, Achilles has too many advantages, but what prevents him from exploiting them is first his inexperience, his modesty, his good upbringing, and secondly, his feelings for Deidamia. Tormented by desire, Achilles remains respectful, because he is in love, and so as to lead himself out of temptation's way, he wakes his mistress. One might be surprised at such reserve on the part of Thetis's son, who is usually depicted as uncompromising and dominated by his impetuous nature, but it must be remembered that Achilles, who has been brought up by the centaur Chiron, had, whatever one might say, good morals and high principles ... It is, therefore, natural that a 'well bred' young man should not take advantage of his mistress while she is asleep, but it is also quite natural that daily contact with Deidamia should result in youthful ardour overriding morality. Thus all is explained.

The rôle of Achilles was so extraordinary in conception that it is perhaps hardly surprising that critics gave little space to Marie Gardel as Deidamia, whose contribution was no less significant to the success of the ballet. It seems that she was almost beyond praise, but Geoffroy gave her a brief but less glowing accolade, recording that she

> had retained her advantages as a charming dancer by adding those of an excellent actress, full of soul and expression. Her delightful *pas* and her affecting acting lay claim to the greatest part in the ballet's success.[20]

[20] *Journal des débats*, 24 February 1805.

Writing a few months later, Geoffroy expanded on this:

> One does not know which to admire more, the grace of her dancing or the perfection of her pantomime. The latter merit is particularly appreciated in the scenes when the Greek chieftains, Ulysses and Diomedes, appear to dominate the stage. By her silent acting, and the continual concern with which she watches over her lover who is on the point of revealing his identity, she draws the eyes and attention of the spectators back to herself.[21]

Duport had clearly considered the rôle unsuitable for him from the very beginning. By delaying rehearsals while he dithered over accepting it, he had left Gardel with precious little time to mould the finer points of the part. The pantomime and the assimilation of his dances with the character needed careful attention, and in the rush to get the ballet ready he was perhaps left too much to his own devices and allowed to insert those *tours de force* that were to seem extraneous to discerning eyes. His self-centred hubris seemed to have got the better of his responsibility to Gardel.

It was presumably part of the agreement that he had struck with the Prefect, Luçay, that he should perform the rôle of Achilles six times. This he did with bad grace, thereby counteracting the favourable impression he had made at the outset. As a result Geoffroy, who had gone out of his way to be fair and understanding, remembered him as an unfortunate choice for the part: he was too short, and his surly manner made an unfortunate impression. 'His dancing was considered unworthy and comic, and one was even led to suspect that Duport, who then had ambitions to become a choreographer, was not sorry to be casting ridicule on a ballet by Gardel, a very dangerous rival for him.'[22]

On 26 April, at the seventh performance, Duport was replaced by Louis Henry, on whom great hopes had been placed. He was handsome, possessing a finely proportioned and elegant figure and a graceful and supple technique. As a mime he played the part with great skill and intelligence, giving a much more satisfactory interpretation than his predecessor. But the public was disconcerted by his height, which made him much too conspicuous when surrounded by the bevy of dancers playing Lycomedes' daughters.

It was during Henry's tenure of the part of Achilles that Gardel at last found time to complete his choreography with the warriors' dance in the

[21] *Journal des débats*, 11 July 1805.
[22] *Journal de l'Empire*, 3 December 1812.

last act. Added at the tenth performance on 9 July 1805, it was appreciated as an impressive display of male dancing of the most virile kind:

> About twenty heroes, divided into four platoons, advance, divide, separate, come together again, then seem to lose themselves in a general *mêlée*, and after this disorder, resume their ranks without confusion, draw their swords and attack one another, now all together, now by squads, and then in single combat. All this noisy pretence at fighting electrifies the mind of the hero, concealed in girl's clothing, and provides a very skilful preparation for the moment when he is exposed.[23]

The problem of seeking the ideal Achilles was not resolved until nearly a year had passed from its first performance. Then, at last, a dancer combining the right stature with the sensibility, lightness and impetuosity the part demanded was found in Charles Saint-Amant. But within a year Saint-Amant tendered his resignation. Bonet then had the idea to cast a woman in the title rôle, presumably with Mlle Clotilde in mind. Such a suggestion was wholly unacceptable to Gardel, the strength of whose reaction surprised even himself when he calmed down. In spite of this reaction, Bonet's will prevailed.[24] Although realistic enough to know when to accept the inevitable, Gardel was finding it a bitter pill to swallow, when the problem seemed to be resolved by Saint-Amant withdrawing his resignation.

He reappeared as Achilles later in the year, but his lacklustre performance was a sign that he was seriously ill, and by the summer of 1807 the search for an Achilles was resumed. Loath to see the ballet dropped, Gardel finally acceded, no doubt with heavy heart, to the proposal to present it with Mlle Clotilde as Achilles. It proved to be a great mistake, and after three performances she was relieved of what, for her, had become an unpleasant embarrassment, particularly after reading Geoffroy's scathing review:

> To show Achilles on the stage as a woman was already taking a great risk, but to present a woman as Achilles is much worse.
>
> A woman discards the grace of her sex when she tries to imitate the brusque and violent movements of us men. Such efforts only result in producing an awkward and forced manner such as always happens when one is doing something against one's nature. Mlle Clotilde is a

[23] *Courrier des spectacles*, 11 July 1805.
[24] Arch. Nat., AJ[13] 87. Gardel to Bonet, 3 August 1806.

very fine dancer in the *noble* genre, and she should not deviate from that. Vivacity, petulance and ardour do not become her style of dancing. In that bacchanal in which Achilles wears out the daughters of Lycomedes, it was the female Achilles who was the first to tire. Her dancing was full of *grand pas* and pirouettes which are not proofs of strength, being for the male dancer a relaxation rather than an exercise; it is the beaten steps, the *entrechats*, that must then dominate in Achilles's dancing, but these were beyond Mlle Clotilde's capability.

Her love scenes with Deidamia appeared a little cold, and the kiss that signals the victory over that beautiful princess was almost repellent. Nothing is more insipid on the stage than passion between one woman and another. This ballet, which is so rich, pompous and magnificent, lost all its effect through this amphibian Achilles who is neither woman nor man. Mme Gardel [as Deidamia] was, as always, perfect both in her dancing and in her pantomime, but she was completely wasted with a lover whose very nature must have cast a chill on her passions.

Mlle Clotilde made a complete mess of the moment when Achilles seizes the arms that are being offered to him, a moment which Henry used to perform with extraordinary energy. She had forgotten to remove her crown of flowers, and in her hurry to remove it, her wig nearly fell off. All these little accidents cast a chill over the action. Mlle Clotilde had covered her head with a white wig whose colour does not suit her features and her complexion. A woman playing a man invariably appears younger than her years, but Mlle Clotilde as Achilles proved the exception, giving the appearance of being older. Of all the women at the Opéra, she was undoubtedly the most suitable to play a man's rôle, and she did as well as her sex permitted, but the illusion was completely destroyed, and even while applauding her, we were bored by the falsity of this sort of imitation.[25]

Saint-Amant never recovered to play the rôle again. For want of a suitable Achilles who could compare with him, the ballet was not given again for nearly five years. It was not until 1812 that, in Albert, a dancer was found with the presence and intelligence to carry off the difficult part. When Marie Gardel retired, the rôle of Deidamia passed successively to Emilie Bigottini and Fanny Bias. The ballet survived the reign of Napoleon, and was last given in 1820 with Montjoie as Achilles. That it then disappeared was due in part to the renovation of the repertory after

[25] *Journal de l'Empire*, 18 September 1807.

Gardel's partial retirement. It suffered also from being expensive to put on, costing some 5400 francs per performance, of which 900 francs was taken up by *feux* paid to the dancers. It is not surprising, therefore, that its tally of performances fell below that of several of Gardel's other ballets. Nonetheless, it was highly regarded in its time, not only for the magnificence of its staging but as one of the finest examples of its choreographer's unmatched stagecraft when working on the grand scale.

To Lady Granville, who was mightily impressed when she saw it shortly after Waterloo, is due the last word. 'I am just come from the Opéra,' she breathlessly wrote to her sister, 'and have seen a magnificent ballet, Achille in petticoats, with people in the sea, in the air, and, in short, splendid.'[26]

[26] Granville, I, 70. Letter to Lady Morpeth, 4 August 1815.

12

Duport in the Ascendant

There is no doubt that both Gardel and Bonet found Duport a very prickly thorn in their sides, while to the young dancer the two older men represented an establishment that had become hidebound by tradition. Duport had made no secret of his ambition to become a choreographer, and he was now to advance an opinion that Gardel would take as downright heresy. The young man had also acquired the habit of dealing directly with the Prefect over the heads of the Director and the ballet-master, and in October 1804 it was to that imperial functionary that he addressed a request to be allowed to produce a ballet of his own at the Opéra. The privilege he was seeking could, he suggested, be advantageous, since it was in the Opéra's interests 'that its *maître de ballet* should no longer be any more exclusive than its *maître de musique*'.[1]

When this came to Gardel's ears, he must have begun to see Duport in a new light – not as a difficult young dancer who needed taming, but as posing a potential threat to what he contended to be the accredited ballet-masters' monopoly to compose ballets at the Opéra. That Luçay seems not to have consulted either Bonet or Gardel before replying showed how firmly control had been taken into the hands of the palace. For the reply reached Duport the very next day, bringing sweet music to his ears as he read that there was no exclusivity in staging ballets at the Opéra, and that if he had a scenario to be considered, it would be placed before the reading jury.

However, Duport's troubles were not over, for both Bonet and Gardel were members of this jury, and his original conception may well have been watered down before it was finally accepted on 24 March 1805. Certainly financial limitations must have been imposed. For an untried choreographer's work, the Opéra could hardly be prepared to lay out more than what was minimally necessary, and the final cost came to no more than 4364 francs, split between the preparation of the costumes and the adaptation of a set from existing stock. More serious, however,

[1] Arch. Nat. AJ[13] 66 (I). Duport to Luçay, 28 Vendémiaire, Year XIII (20 October 1804).

was the refusal of some of the *premiers sujets* to have any part in it, a boycott to which Duport referred with considerable bitterness in the preface to the programme:

> When they see *Acis et Galathée* the public will undoubtedly be astonished, and rightly so, that such passionate opposition should have been levelled against such a slight production, and that so many obstacles have been put in my way to prevent me from continuing with it. Certainly my enemies could not have done me greater harm than to give so much importance to a *little one-act ballet*, and to prejudice the public against it by stimulating expectations of a much worthier work.

Covert intrigues are seldom recorded, but while only Duport's word exists for this persecution, there was clearly some justification for his complaint. However, Geoffroy could not take it very seriously, writing:

> Such is the lot of nearly every author. The Opéra undoubtedly wanted to maintain the exclusive privilege of its official choreographers, and is there any group of people that does not cling to their time-honoured customs? So I do not believe in Duport's persecution, but he has certainly had a few little difficulties to face, including some sort of action in the courts: the documents of this action have filled gaps in the newspapers and fed the partisan spirit which Duport has no need to call to his aid.[2]

In the event Duport had little cause to worry, for the ballet of *Acis et Galathée* was extremely well received, and without any sign of partisanship, when given its first performance on 10 May 1805. The *Journal de Paris* paid it a rather back-handed compliment in declaring it to be 'a wild, prodigious success, due more to the obstacles which the author overcame to get his work performed than to any real merit in its composition', and summed up its virtues as 'charming scenes, perfect execution'.[3] In the *Débats* Geoffroy saw its success as proof that Duport had been justified in persevering with his efforts to compose a ballet, describing it rather curtly as 'very pleasing, lively and jolly, with not much narrative but a great deal of movement and life; no situations, but picturesque dancing throughout'.[4]

2 *Journal des débats*, 12 May 1805.
3 *Journal de Paris*, 11 May 1805.
4 *Journal des débats*, 12 May 1805.

The plot was taken from Ovid's *Metamorphoses*, and did not radically depart from the classical myth except that in the ballet it was not Acis who perished, but the cyclops Polyphemus. The curtain rose on a cheerful scene of little amorets at play near a Temple of Venus. Acis (L. Duport) enters with a hunting party, expressing his grief that Galatea seems insensitive to his love. Cupid (V. Hullin) then makes a fortuitous appearance to offer his support. When Galatea (M. Duport) makes her entry on a conch-shell, Cupid conceals Acis. The little god then proceeds to arouse her pity by pretending to be sad; he steals a kiss and brings the despairing Acis out of hiding. Galatea's modesty at first holds her back, but gradually her true feelings towards Acis are awakened. Everyone is delighted at this outcome, but the rejoicing is interrupted by the appearance of a rival for her favours, the fearsome one-eyed giant, Polyphemus (Lefebvre). He and Cupid confront one another, but his rage vanishes at the sight of Galatea. Turning his attention to her, he does his utmost to make her submit, but she eludes his grasp. When the lovers find one another, Galatea warns Acis of Polyphemus's enmity and presses him to make his escape. Polyphemus reappears. Galatea manages to calm him, and she and Acis flee. In a terrible rage, Polyphemus overturns Cupid's statue. The sky darkens, and a great storm breaks out. Pursuing the lovers, Polyphemus is about to hurl a great rock at Acis, when Galatea implores the help of Jupiter. Her prayer is granted; Polyphemus is felled by a Jovian thunderbolt and Venus (Millière) emerges from her Temple to unite the lovers.

The opening scene with the children from the School of Dance was a masterstroke. '[The] legion of little amorets perform their exercises with every possible grace,' recorded Geoffroy. 'Their movements and steps, their little games and mannerisms, all so true to nature, gave the greatest pleasure.' Geoffroy was pleased that Duport had chosen such a modest framework for his choreographic début. Dances, groups and tableaux all revealed an interesting talent. Duport had been so sparing with the pantomime action that it almost seemed that the cast was dancing all the time, with the choreographer himself 'jumping, spinning, darting here, there and everywhere, unceasingly lavishing, not the most noble and charming things in his art, but those that seem most difficult and novel and please the multitude.' He was rewarded with tremendous applause, 'more than he deserved,' in Geoffroy's opinion, but that was only to be expected from a young dancer whose virtuosity was 'perfect in the eyes of those who are not connoisseurs'. Of course, Duport had designed the main part specifically for himself, for which Geoffroy willingly forgave him:

> It is not at all Duport's fault if he abandons himself to sparkling acrobatics, if he seeks to astonish with his extraordinary turns, for that is what has created his vogue, that is what feeds it. He is only giving the public what its taste craves, and doing what he knows must be applauded. His critics deserve a little criticism themselves, for they are blaming Duport for tricks and abuses which nature has not allowed them to perform. Duport's faults are only those of an extraordinary talent.[5]

But having said that, Geoffroy gave the matter further thought, and a month later, adopting a more serious tone, warned Duport against abusing his talent. He recalled such acrobatic dancers as Furioso and Placide who had done their stunts at Nicolet's theatre in the 1780s, and reminded his readers that there were still Italian *grotteschi* who could jump higher than Duport and perform even more difficult and astonishing turns; but they

> will never be anything more than grotesque dancers in the eyes of the French, and their dancing will never be regarded as anything more than a caricature. It is in grace, expression and nobility, the beauty of attitudes, the expression of various inner feelings by gestures and movements of the body that lies the true merit of dancing. That is what makes it an art. Everything that departs from that aim, everything that goes against those principles is wrong, however difficult and astonishing it may seem to the common herd. Since Duport can do what he wants, let us hope he will never do anything but what is worthy of himself and his art.[6]

Duport had given the rôle of Galatea to his sister Minette, whom the *Courrier des spectacles* found somewhat lacking in dramatic expression, although it was perhaps her misfortune to have to compete with a child – for critics and public alike were sent into raptures by the pretty six-year-old Virginie Hullin to whom Duport had given the rôle of Cupid. Nini, as the child was affectionately called, was the daughter of his friend and fellow-dancer, Jean-Baptiste Hullin, by whom she had been trained for a professional career from the tenderest age. Geoffroy was much taken by the neatness of her steps, but what really warmed his heart were the occasional awkward moments, such as when she had to make two at-

[5] *Journal des débats*, 12 May 1805.
[6] *Journal des débats*, 9 June 1805.

tempts to extend her leg before being able to hold the required pose. 'She would have been less lovable if she had succeeded first time,' he wrote.[7] One of the most effective moments in the ballet came at the end when, after striking Polyphemus in the chest, the little girl was whisked high into the air.[8] The public took her to their hearts, and every little indication of progress was treasured: a year later the achievement of a triple pirouette was deemed worthy of record.[9]

During the rehearsal period, Duport had found himself the butt of snide remarks for selecting a fifty-year-old dancer to play the important part of Polyphemus. Milon would have been the obvious choice, but there were perhaps good reasons why he could not oblige. However, Duport was to have the last laugh, for the dancer who took the rôle turned out to be superb, both for his graceful, Herculean physique and for his dramatic miming.

The scoffers had not exaggerated Dominique Lefebvre's age. A pupil of Maximilien and Pierre Gardel, he had been first engaged at the Opéra as far back as 1770, and in 1773 had been promoted to the second level of *danseur seul et en double*. A year later he had left, 'forced out', as he put it, 'by cabals and the jealousy of M. Vestris the father'. After dancing for one season in Naples under Lepicq, he had gone to St Petersburg to enter the court ballet of the Empress Catherine, coming under the influence of Gasparo Angiolini, one of the father-figures (with Noverre and Hilverding) of the *ballet d'action*. He had left Paris before that form had become established at the Opéra, and the experience of dancing in Angiolini's ballets was his first real introduction to the art of mime.[10]

This was the turning point of his life; after leaving St Petersburg, he embarked on a career as a choreographer. Following engagements in Poland and Germany, in 1796 he found himself at La Scala, Milan, at the moment when Bonaparte's victorious Army of Italy entered the city. There he received an order from the General to mount a five-act ballet, a feat he accomplished in a burst of patriotic zeal in just ten days.[11]

Lefebvre had returned to France in the hope that the Emperor would remember his efforts and reward him by readmitting him to the Opéra.

[7] *Journal des débats*, 12 May 1805.
[8] *Courrier des spectacles*, 29 May 1805.
[9] *Journal des débats*, 4 April 1806.
[10] In 1807 he scornfully wrote that the art of mime was 'unknown even in Paris'. (Arch. Nat., AJ[13] 83. Lefebvre to the direction of the Opéra, 7 September 1807).
[11] *Il Generale Colli in Roma*, with music by Pontelibero, first performed on 23 February 1797. Known as the *Ballo del Papa*, it caused great controversy by depicting recent events, namely the fall of Mantua to Napoleon, on the stage. The choreographer himself played the rôle of Pope Pius VI, who was shown at the end of the ballet casting aside the triple crown and donning the cap of liberty.

He had learned to his surprise that instead of there being three or four official choreographers at the Opéra, Gardel was now the only one. Concluding that there must be a vacancy, he applied for a post. His request was courteously received, in a manner that led him to believe that it would be granted. But weeks passed without a further word, and he began to suspect that forces within the theatre were working against him. Gardel pointedly ignored him, and had been heard to declare that so long as he was ballet-master at the Opéra, he would never make use of Lefebvre's talent.

There must have been a reason for Gardel's dislike, if such was his attitude towards Lefebvre. Of course he already had a very competent assistant in Milon, but with Duport and Henry now clamouring to try their hand at choreography, he can have been in no mood to encourage another threat to the accredited ballet-masters' monopoly to stage the ballets.

Lefebvre had turned up just as Duport was coping with the boycotting of his new ballet by some of the *premiers sujets*. When Duport asked him if he would play the rôle of Polyphemus in *Acis et Galathée*, he was not particularly interested, for he was living comfortably enough on his savings. However, perhaps seeing the young choreographer as a fellow-victim of Gardel, he agreed to take it on, even though he had no formal engagement and would be receiving no remuneration. This was the position at *Acis's* première.

But some months later his financial security disappeared as a result of a speculation that went wrong, and he was given a year's engagement as a mime at a salary of 2000 francs. At the end of the year, in 1807, his contract was not renewed and he returned to Russia, where he became ballet-master in Moscow. He had made many friends in Paris, and early in 1809 returned there for a brief visit. Emilie Collomb wrote of their last meeting, when he called to say goodbye and did not leave until two o'clock in the morning. She felt very sad and wondered whether she would ever see him again.[12] She never did. He was still in Moscow at the time of Napoleon's entry into the city. When the Grande Armée evacuated Moscow and began its retreat, he threw in his lot with his countrymen. He was never to see his native land again, perishing in the terrible crossing of the Beresina.[13]

[12] Collomb, entry of 15 January 1809.

[13] The main source for this section is a letter of complaint by Lefebvre himself to the authorities of the Opéra, dated 7 September 1807 (Arch. Nat., AJ[13] 83). He gives the date of his leaving the Opéra as 1777, but the records (AJ[13] 15) show that he left in 1774, which tallies with his engagement in Naples for the 1774/75 season. He gave his age at the time of leaving the Opéra as eighteen, and must therefore have been born in 1755 or 1756.

The reluctance of the *premiers sujets* to take part in *Acis et Galathée* turned out to be no great handicap, for it provided several dancers who were younger or further down the hierarchy with opportunities which they must have gratefully grasped. Arnaud Léon and Jean-Baptiste Hullin took the prominent parts among Acis's hunting friends, Luigia Taglioni and Mlle Favre-Guiardele headed Galatea's nymphs, and among the cyclops were Goyon, Branchu, Baptiste Petit (who was to marry Minette Duport) and Antoine Titus. The boycott was not in fact complete, for if the *premiers sujets* were on the whole reluctant to accept rôles, some were prepared to be featured in the final *divertissement*: Saint-Amant and Marie-Madeleine Delisle appeared as Zephyr and Flora, and Chevigny and Vestris danced a remarkably explicit *pas de deux* as a bacchante and a faun.

To put together the music for his ballet, Duport sought the assistance of two musicians, Henry Darondeau and Luigi Gianella. The resultant score was full of borrowed melodies, as was noticed by the critics: Geoffroy considered this a merit, since they were well chosen and gave the ballet an old-time flavour. The *Journal de Paris* was of the same opinion, noting that they were particularly well suited to the situations they accompanied. Several of these borrowings were identified on the score: a *rondeau* by Krumpholtz; a *pastorale* by Steibelt; an andante by Ehler; an air that Jacques Schneitzhoeffer (father of the future composer of *La Sylphide*) had composed to accompany a dance in Lully's *Atys*; a melody by Dreuilh; an extract from Méhul's *Jugement de Pâris*; and the *pas russe* from *La Caravane du Caïre*. And there were no doubt other borrowed snatches to accompany moments of action.[14]

To judge from the receipts, *Acis et Galathée* was a popular addition to the repertory. Before Duport left on a four-month leave to dance in the provinces, it had been given eight times in seven weeks. His satisfaction, however, was marred by the rejection of a ballet he had submitted to the reading jury entitled *Almas et Zulima*; and his resentment mounted as he basked in the adulation of the Bordeaux public. He was due to reappear at the Opéra early in November, but the authorities were soon to learn that he was back to his old tricks again. He wanted to stage a ballet he had created in Bordeaux, called *Le Volage fixé*, for which Luçay had refused consent. Not prepared to take 'no' for an answer, he delayed his reappearance in an attempt to make the Opéra give in. An express order from Bonet was ignored, and he countered with a demand to be given two or three rehearsals of *Le Volage fixé* so that he could demonstrate its mer-

[14] Bibl.-Musée de l'Opéra, A 3991-2.

its. Finally, in desperation, Luçay asked the Minister of Police to have the recalcitrant Duport arrested.[15]

The parties had reached an impasse, and Duport, whose headstrong action and obstinacy when cornered had led to this situation, was in need of a friend who could calm him down and intercede on his behalf. Fortunately, one of the *premiers sujets*, Emilie Collomb, stepped in to play the rôle of wise counsellor, recording the crisis as it developed in her diary:

> 13 December 1805
> Duport was arrested this morning, which upset me very much, and which I considered to be very wrong. [Other means] ought to have been tried before resorting to violence. I said as much to M. Lecraicq and Bonet, who both felt it had been wrong to act so quickly ... In the evening I went ... to see Duport, whom I found with his guard. He is very offended by the measures taken against him, and he is right. Yesterday evening he gave in to everything, but today he is less disposed to do so, which does not surprise me. However, I still hope that his brother will intervene in this matter to sort it all out. Tomorrow I shall go and see M. de Luçay. The difficulty in effecting a reconciliation seems to be that neither side will give way, and yet it is necessary that they should come to a mutual understanding.
>
> 14 December 1805
> I have been to see M. de Luçay. He seemed sorry that Duport was arrested, but that is his [i.e. Luçay's] own fault, for all he had to do was to delay sending the suspension order until, after mediation, Duport's final decision would have been known. At last, after a long discussion about this matter, it was agreed that since Duport can no longer deny what he had said to the Prefect of Police and M. de Luçay, and the authorities cannot give way, Duport will dance a new *pas*, either a *pas de deux* or a *pas de trois*, and later, that is in a fortnight, his *divertissement* would be staged. I think, as I have suggested to M. de Luçay, that Duport can and must give way to this agreement; indeed he must give way somewhere if he wishes to receive his salary.
>
> 15 December 1805
> I delivered a sermon to Duport, telling him he should agree to dance once or twice before giving his *divertissement*; he knows very well that

[15] Arch. Nat., AJ[13] 81. Luçay to Bonet, 28 November 1805; Bonet to Duport (draft), undated but c. 29 November 1805; Duport to Bonet, 1 December 1805; Luçay to Minister of Police, 11 December 1805.

he must, but wants to have his salary and I do not know what else before accepting that he is in the wrong; he will not be satisfied with doing something which he has, so to speak, been ordered to do, but then how is he to demand his salary! He will give the impression of having only given way out of necessity, which is not the way to ask a favour!

16 December 1805
Hullin came while I was dining to tell me Duport had gone with Esmenard to the Ministry of Police and that Duport was going to dance once and his *divertissement* would then be given.[16]

Duport did give way a little, reappearing at the Opéra at the end of December to Luçay's great relief. The Prefect, however, was not so innocent as to believe that his difficulties would be over when he allowed *Le Volage fixé* to be staged; he was thankful for a brief respite, but realised that Duport would never be completely satisfied. In January Duport appeared in *Le Retour de Zéphire*, dancing so full out that Emilie Collomb, who was on stage with him, was quite blinded by his virtuosity:

> I do not think that any dancer, past, present or future, has danced or will dance it better than Duport. Even I, who am used to seeing him and familiar with his execution, was so overwhelmed that I was unable to look at his legs ... I thought I would die with admiration. My nerves were not strong enough to withstand the violence of my emotion. However, the pleasure of seeing him was mingled with the sad thought that poor Duport could not last long if he was so prodigal of his physical and moral strength. He dances too much and too well, and exceeds the limits that Nature has prescribed for the human race.[17]

Acis et Galathée returned to the bills on 11 March 1806, after an absence of seven months. Luçay had authorised the addition of a new *pas* for Vestris, which alluded to Napoleon's return after the winter campaign that had culminated in the great victory at Austerlitz. It was preceded by a pompously flattering introduction:

[16] Collomb, entries as given. Lecraicq was Secretary-General of the Opéra. Duport had two brothers, the one referred to being probably Auguste, who became a bassoonist at the Opéra. Esmenard wrote the words for a Fête that was then being prepared at the Opéra to celebrate Napoleon's victory at Austerlitz (see Chapter XIV).
[17] Collomb, entry of 28 January 1806.

> Mars arrives in a chariot, preceded and followed by soldiers. Pleasures, amorets and fauns press around the chariot, and the soldiers depart. Venus approaches him, while the Graces are occupied with removing his armour. Mars holds Venus in his arms. All the personages on stage pay their homage by dancing, and invite Mars to dance with Venus. They perform a *pas de deux*.[18]

Also new that evening was a *pas de bacchante* to replace the *pas du faune* which Duport and Chevigny had danced at the creation. The original dance had met with criticism for being too explicit, and Duport had rearranged it in the form of a *pas de trois*, adding a part for a satyr, who competes with the faun for the possession of some panpipes while the bacchante laughs at their antics. The choreography was extensively adjusted for Emilie Collomb, Saint-Amant and Hullin. Collomb had a personal reason to be gratified at taking over from Chevigny, for there was no love lost between the two women. Bad blood had long existed between them, and Collomb now enjoyed the satisfaction of being chosen to supplant Chevigny, albeit in only a *pas*. After dancing the *pas de trois* for the first time, and being flatteringly applauded, she described in her diary how she had refashioned it:

> In the evening I danced the *pas de la bacchante* in the ballet *Acis*, which was being given for the first time since Duport's return. This *pas* was as successful as it was when Duport danced it. In the *pas* I did not follow in the footsteps of Mlle Chevigny. To my mind one should never present the public with lascivious scenes, and I am convinced that when the *pas* was first seen, if Duport had not, by his lightness, made amends for the lasciviousness that Mlle Chevigny put into it, it would have been hissed. So I tried to give it another style. I made my bacchante lively, playful, voluptuous in a crazy way but modest in her feeling. My partner could not give the *pas* Duport's technique and strength, so I was given the technical passages and placed them at moments where my predecessor had inserted what in dance terms are called *niaiseries* [stupidities]. These changes were successful, and appreciated by the public. My bacchante benefited from being light-hearted and crazy, which was what was lacking when Mlle Chevigny had the part. At the end my *pas* had a wild success. I received compliments from everyone. Duport is in seventh heaven at the way I danced his *pas*, and does not stop talking about it. Hullin supported me very well in all our passages together, I

[18] Arch. Nat., AJ^{13} 81.

was very pleased with him, we were both very well costumed. The Empress applauded me three or four times.[19]

Collomb's success was not in doubt, although Geoffroy suggested that her execution may not have been entirely faultless. 'Her lightness and vigour are astonishing,' he wrote, 'and she gives you no time to observe whether her steps are correct and in strict time – a bacchante's intoxication excuses a few lapses.'[20]

Three days later the Emperor came to see the ballet for himself. He was not in the best of moods, and Luçay was commanded to write a stern letter to Bonet:

> Praise is due to the care with which the ballet of *Acis et Galathée* has been revived, but there are some parts of this lovely work that should be modified to meet public demand. It is generally considered to be too full of dances. The *pas du faune*, which in the early performances appeared to be in bad taste, was yesterday considered indecent. I order you to suppress it. M. Duport was severely criticised for introducing movements in his own dances that are too grotesque and cannot be reconciled with the grace which is a feature of his talent, and to which the public is so accustomed that it would not want to see him stray from his usual purity. The administration is too concerned for M. Duport's success as a dancer and choreographer not to offer advice that should assure him of the good will of true connoisseurs.[21]

Duport was so upset that his first reaction was to disobey the order; he was even prepared to refuse to dance if the *pas* were cut. However, an imperial command could not be brushed aside, and he eventually complied. In her diary entry for 1 April, Emilie Collomb recorded that 'she had danced the new *pas de trois* which Duport had substituted for that of the *bacchante*. It is very pretty, made a great impression, and as I said to my husband, was very well danced. It was given three calls after we had left the stage.'

Vestris's appearance as Mars in the introduction seems to have been received by Napoleon as a piece of unwelcome flattery. 'Mars,' wrote Geoffroy of the next performance early in June, 'no longer comes to scare away the nymphs and fauns and join in the play of the shepherds; Vestris's triumphal chariot has been suppressed as a bad joke, and Vestris

[19] Collomb, entry for 11 March 1806.
[20] *Journal de l'Empire*, 14 April 1806.
[21] Arch. Nat., AJ[13] 81. Luçay to Bonet, 23 March 1806.

has sulked and withdrawn from the ballet as if he could play no other rôle in it but that of Mars.'[22]

By July the ballet had been further revised. The *pas de la bacchante* had been toned down even more, and various other adjustments had improved the piece. Little Nini Hullin was still there to enchant the public; and 'although,' as Geoffroy remarked perhaps a little sadly, 'she has become accustomed to her part since we first saw her, she is still a marvel.'[23]

When Duport left the Opéra in 1807, *Acis et Galathée* was understandably dropped, for it was not to be expected that Gardel or Milon would keep it rehearsed. Twelve years later, in 1819, a revival was attempted with Paul and Mme Courtin as the eponymous couple, Milon as Polyphemus, Bigottini as Venus and in the rôle of Cupid, Nini Hullin's youngest sister, Joséphine. But without the guiding spark of its creator it made little impression and after four performances it was withdrawn, never to be revived.

[22] *Journal de l'Empire*, 4 April 1806.
[23] *Journal de l'Empire*, 17 July 1806.

13

Louis Henry Stakes His Claim

Difficulties with Duport tended to distract attention from other happenings at the Opéra in 1805. In fact, it was far from an uneventful year, being marked by an important operatic event, the first production in French of Mozart's opera *Don Juan*. It was also to see revivals of Milon's *Pygmalion* and Gardel's *Le Jugement de Pâris*. The latter was reduced to two acts and in the process (in response, it was believed, to a shocked reaction from Napoleon) the famous scene of Venus taking her bath was cut. Later, at the year's end, there came another ballet by an untried choreographer.

For Gardel and Milon it was to be an unproductive year. Gardel's *divertissement* in *Don Juan*, during the scene in which the statue of the Commendatore dramatically interrupts Don Juan at dinner and, unable to make him repent, consigns him to damnation, was praised for its 'wit, imagination and taste';[1] but it was poor compensation for the frustration that the demands of aspiring young choreographers caused him. Milon was even less lucky. He had been given the task of arranging the *divertissement* in the oratorio *La Prise de Jéricho*, but had been forced to make changes against his better judgement and to cut it to half its original length, which meant that he could not use Duport.

Meanwhile, on the outer Boulevards, in the theatre by the Porte Saint-Martin which had once housed the Opéra, ballet still remained part of the staple fare. There, over the past eighteen months, Aumer had embarked on a series of revivals of ballets by his mentor, Dauberval. This was a much overdue tribute to a man who had been one of the principal progenitors of the *ballet d'action* in France; for only in the previous two years had his ballets begun to be seen in Paris, and then only at the Porte-Saint-Martin. They were quite a revelation, and many may have wondered how it was that not one had been staged at the Opéra. One theatrical chronicler even alleged that they had been deliberately excluded, 'rejected by the ineptitude of the Opéra administration and the pride of the dictator

[1] *Courrier des spectacles*, 21 September 1805.

Gardel, who is not willing to share his crown.'[2] In fairness to Gardel, however, it should be added that there is no evidence that any approach was made – although, if it had, it might well have been resisted, bearing in mind Gardel's stubborn adherence to the ballet-masters' traditional monopoly. Certainly, no disrespect was intended to Dauberval. And although Aumer was now permanently engaged as ballet-master at the Porte-Saint-Martin, he still remained on the Opéra's payroll as a dancer.

In July, Aumer produced his fourth Dauberval ballet at the Porte-Saint-Martin. This was a pantomime version of Beaumarchais's comedy, *Le Mariage de Figaro*, which had been the theatrical sensation of the last years of the Old Régime. When first offered to the Comédie-Française, the play had been considered seditious, and was only eventually performed in 1784, when the grip of the royal government began to weaken. For his ballet, however, Dauberval had steered clear of political controversy by omitting the dialogue and judiciously excising certain scenes. How close Aumer's revival was to Dauberval's original can only be a matter of conjecture, for he had been just thirteen when it was last performed in Bordeaux. Describing the 1805 revival, the *Courrier des spectacles* explained that 'the foundation ... is ... Dauberval's, but it is a canvas that Aumer's talent has been able to embroider with infinite taste'.[3] However, the ballet had been originally described by Dauberval as a pantomime rather than a ballet-pantomime, and Aumer did not depart from the original scenario, since it was republished word for word for the revival. In his notice, Geoffroy explicitly recorded that it closed with a *pas* by Aumer, which may suggest that this was the only innovation. There is also no record that Aumer received any help from Dauberval, who was still alive in 1805, and it is difficult to imagine that he and Aumer were not then in touch. Dauberval was to die unexpectedly the following February while returning from one of his periodical visits to Paris.

The company with which Aumer worked at the Porte-Saint-Martin was of course considerably inferior to that of the Opéra, but it contained several competent mimes. The principal dancer was Marie Quériau, whom he chose to play Suzanne. Geoffroy thought she could profitably vary her expression a little more, and was a little put off by the way she seemed to be continuously laughing at the audience, as if inviting them to share a joke. As a dancer, her technique was not impeccable, but she was experienced enough to conceal this from all but the experienced eye. Geoffroy, however, noticed that her *épaulement* was not always sufficiently

[2] *Opinion du parterre*, III, 361–2.

[3] *Courrier des spectacles*, 20 July 1805.

effacé, and that she could not always conceal her physical effort.[4] The Figaro who played opposite her was miscast, his forte being apparently imbecile parts. In the rôles of the Count and Countess were Morand, who was both an intelligent mime and the best male dancer in the company, and Mlle Aline, whose mediocre talent as a dancer mattered little in what was mainly a pantomime part. As Cherubino, the diminutive Antoinette Santiquet was a sheer delight, imprinting the part with all the 'mischief, gaiety and vivacity' it demanded.[5]

Meanwhile at the Opéra, three of its senior ballerinas reappeared that summer after lengthy absences. Mlle Clotilde, the senior of these, had been at loggerheads with the administration for some months, but her hopes of securing a lucrative Russian engagement had collapsed. In September she rejoined the fold, reappearing as Calypso in *Télémaque* and in the celebrated *pas de deux* in *Iphigénie en Aulide* known as *La Prix de la danse* with a new partner, young Louis Henry. Although somewhat disparate in age – she was eight years his senior – the two were almost ideally matched: both imposingly tall, good-looking, elegant and proudly noble in the tranquil, unhurried grace of their movements. To connoisseurs with long memories this *pas de deux* was a joy to behold, but to a growing number it conveyed the musty fragrance of a vanished era. Even Geoffroy was forced to accept that the hallowed *noble* style was losing its appeal and its relevance:

> The noble and grave dance is the most esteemed, but not the most pleasing [of genres] for the majority of spectators. Even connoisseurs find little charm in that manner of rising, turning the leg, performing slow pirouettes and describing a circle in the air with the foot. One may doubt whether such movements are really graceful, especially for women, but the appeal of attitudes in dancing in different countries is arbitrary, just as is beauty of feature.[6]

The other two returning ballerinas, Sophie Chevigny and Emilie Collomb, had been absent for much longer through illness, and now, by force of circumstances, had become bitter rivals as a consequence of being both placed in the *comique* genre. Their careers had run very much in parallel, and they had attained the highest grade of *première artiste* at the same time, in September 1798. Chevigny had then been classified as a

[4] *Journal de l'Empire*, 25 July 1805.
[5] *Opinion du parterre*, III, 367–8.
[6] *Journal de l'Empire*, 13 September 1805.

demi-caractère dancer, while the diminutive Collomb had been placed in the *comique* category.

In 1802 Chevigny had suffered a breakdown, and not long afterwards Collomb too had fallen ill. In Chevigny's case, the Opéra had been lenient in keeping her on full pay for nearly three years before she was able to resume her classes preparatory to her reappearance. More than once there had been a question of retiring her. In 1803 she had narrowly avoided dismissal by making an appeal to the First Consul. In December 1804 she was actually struck off the roll and obtained a remission only by producing a doctor's certificate that she would soon be able to resume her activity. She claimed that she could have returned long before if Gardel had found time to arrange the little *divertissement* he had been ordered to produce for her.[7] She eventually returned as Oenone in *Le Jugement de Pâris* on 16 July.

Her colleague Emilie Collomb reappeared after an absence of nearly two years on 3 September, playing Flore in *Psyché*. Both dancers were then assigned to the *comique* genre. The reasons for reclassifying Chevigny were twofold: firstly, her physique and her ability had been adversely affected by her long absence, and secondly, there was no longer a place available in the *demi-caractère* genre, since Emilie Bigottini, Marie Gardel's *remplacement*, was the obvious contender for the succession. The situation invited trouble and gave rise to much ill feeling. Collomb, the elder by nearly four years, claimed seniority on the ground that she had never been classified otherwise, and was incensed to find Chevigny using every means to dislodge her. To support her claim for precedence, Chevigny reminded Bonet that her salary was higher than Collomb's. The latter retorted that this was so only because Chevigny had been the mistress of the former Director, Cellerier, by whom she had had a child. They also engaged in an absurd quarrel over their respective ages, each accusing the other of being older than she made out.

What Gardel thought of Chevigny has not been recorded, but among Collomb's papers is a letter from the ballet-master accusing her of having 'a proud and haughty character, and seeming to expect a friend, or *maître*, to act as servant or coachman as though he were only there to be made use of, paid, and frequently insulted.'[8]

* * *

[7] *Courrier des spectacles*, 3 January 1805. Letter from Chevigny to the Editor.

[8] Bibl.-Musée de l'Opéra, Fonds Collomb, 1.

Gardel and Milon had both been disturbed at the ease with which Duport had insinuated himself into the Opéra as a choreographer, and they now learned that another young aspirant, Louis Henry, had obtained a similar privilege. Henry's method, however, was somewhat more orthodox. He had sought the protection of one of the most powerful men in France, Jean-Jacques Cambacérès, formerly Second Consul and now Arch-Chancellor of the Empire, and the affair was arranged at the highest level over the heads of both Gardel and Bonet, the Director.

Cambacérès was homosexual and shared his palatial apartment in the Palais du Luxembourg with an elderly friend of long standing whose vacuous sayings at the dinner table were a continual source of amusement among his guests. The Second Consul's support of Louis Henry, therefore, however innocent it may have been, was bound to arouse resentment in some quarters, and the suspicion of undue influence must have come easily to mind. One who may have had particularly strong feelings in the matter was Aumer, who was ten years Henry's senior and might have justifiably felt that, personal preference apart, he had a greater right to consideration.

However, the principal objections to Henry's ballet being received came from the ballet-masters themselves, and was based on their claim of an exclusive monopoly to choreograph ballets. Gardel was adamant on this, raising the spectre of anarchy that would prevail if any of the Opéra's dancers could claim the right to produce a ballet – a claim he had successfully maintained three years earlier in quashing an application by Sébastien Gallet to produce a ballet.[9] The Opéra, he pointed out, 'is not an arena open to all and sundry, good, bad or indifferent'. Mediocrity may be tolerated among the performers, but not for a ballet-master: he 'is to some extent a teacher who must have proved his superiority as a dancer and his ability as a choreographer.'[10] When he became aware that young Henry was to be allowed to stage a ballet, he consulted Milon and the two of them drew up a joint protest to the Emperor, couched in terms of servility that had become obligatory in petitions to France's absolute ruler:

To His Majesty, the Emperor and King.

Sire,

Forgive us if we venture to distract Your Majesty's attention from those

[9] New York Public Library, Dance Collection, *MGZM.Rés.Gar P. Petition by Gardel to Pierre-Louis Roederer, Councillor of State, 22 Vendémiaire, Year XI (14 October 1802).

[10] *Courrier des spectacles*, 24 May 1805.

serious matters that weigh heavily on him, but the protection with which the Académie Impérial de Musique has been honoured imposes a duty upon us to denounce an abuse which, if not stopped, will bring about the ruin of a great nation's finest, most brilliant and most eminent theatre.

The ballet-masters have always been solely authorised to compose for the Opéra. This right has been laid down in all the Regulations. Indeed it is even imposed on them as a duty, in that they are expressly forbidden to produce the fruits of their toil on any other stage.

They were themselves selected only after a long apprenticeship, a long study of the art of dance and pantomime. This is how the Empire of Euterpe and Terpsichore has attained such a glorious peak in France as to arouse the admiration and astonishment of other nations; and this is how it can be maintained.

Today every dancer wants to be a choreographer. Duport has had a ballet performed, and now Henry is on the point of presenting a ballet which has been accepted in defiance of both the Regulations and custom.

Dazzled by the applause lavished on them as dancers, they think they know everything, and they want to do and organise everything themselves.

But can a twenty-year-old dancer acquire sufficient of those qualities that Lucian (in his *Dialogue on the Dance*) requires in a ballet-master? He will hardly have had time enough to absorb the bare mechanics of his art. Sire, would it not be ridiculous and dangerous if a common soldier, who has just learnt his drill, were to wish to have his turn to command the army?

But this is not all. These demi-gods have their hangers-on and supporters. And their supporters form pressure groups to influence the administrators. They appeal to the discontented, namely those whom the ballet-masters have forced to do their duty or whose inordinate ambition they have not satisfied. To the former they offer the promise of an easier life, and to the latter good rôles and brilliant *pas*.

What is the result? The most talented, who are concerned only with their art and have no truck with cabals and partisans, are cast aside; contractual obligations are neglected, and obedience is an unknown word.

Once a dancer has become a choreographer, he will only want to dance in his own ballets; Duport, since he began playing with Acis's crook, has already thrown aside the lance and shield of Achilles.

Sire, we have no hesitation in stating that if these abuses spread, the Académie Impériale de Musique will in a few years become disrupted: bad taste, ignorance and vanity will have been its ruin.

Only when a master has proved himself in his art can he appreciate [individual] talents, direct them to advantage, develop them, even set them in rivalry against one another, thus giving an all-embracing beauty to the whole that arouses amazement, carries you away, and frequently makes you believe in magic.

But, Sire, if we speak in this way, might we not be accused of a desire to stifle talent and prevent it from blossoming? No, we are far from wishing to work and shine in exclusivity. Ours is indeed a career that should be open to all who have the call to compose, provided they have aptitude and genius.

Every opera libretto calls for a ballet or *divertissement*, and it is there that the riches of our art and all the resources of one's training must be developed, for it is necessary to respond to the librettist when he says, 'At this point there must be some dancing.' But will his idea be realised if the sources which he has used are unrecognised?

This, Sire, is where experiments will be found to tempt our youngsters. Such experiments will be difficult and unrewarding, for it is hard to become familiar with the ideas of others. But the effort must be made.

The other theatres still offer them a vast field. Let them show their productions there, and one will soon judge whether they have made a study of foreign parts and other peoples' customs, morals and manners. Only then will they be worthy of composing for your Académie Impériale de Musique. In short, let them begin by obeying if they wish one day to have the honour to command.

As for ourselves, Sire, being free of any kind of self-interest, we have proved and will continue to prove by numerous sacrifices that we are acting solely in the interests of our art, its progress and its preservation.

We therefore await the justice that always dictates Your Majesty's commands.

We are, with the most profound respect, Your Imperial and Royal Majesty's very humble and obedient subjects,

Gardel and Milon[11]

Louis Henry was a pleasanter character by far than his colleague Duport. His openness, modesty and good manners endeared him to everyone, and particularly to Cambacérès, who no doubt enabled the Regulations to be bent to allow his protégé's scenario, at that time entitled *L'Amour et Cythère*, to be read before the jury on 5 August 1805. Objec-

[11] Arch. Nat., AJ[13] 82 (Gardel).

tions were then made on the grounds of expense and the likelihood that the *premiers sujets* would not be prepared to take part in it. Cambacérès asked Henry for his comments. Henry explained that he was asking for 1500 francs at most for garlands, masks and wings, a sum that would be recouped out of the takings on the first night. As far as the *premiers sujets* were concerned, both Mme Gardel and Clotilde had agreed to play leading rôles. He went on to say that he needed only 20 days to produce the work.

On 12 September, Cambacérès summoned Luçay to Saint-Cloud, showed him Henry's letter and peremptorily reminded him that Cambacérès needed only to give the word for the production to go ahead. Then, as if in passing, he let drop that the ballet was to be dedicated to himself, and added significantly that he would be obliged if the matter could be concluded as quickly as possible.

Luçay assured Cambacérès that he was awaiting an estimate; but when this came to hand, the costing turned out to be much more than expected – more than six times higher than the Arch-Chancellor had been informed. Called to Saint-Cloud for another discussion, Henry managed to give a satisfactory explanation to his protector, at whose request he then wrote the following letter to Luçay:

> I have the honour to inform you that Monsigneur the Arch-Chancellor has just summoned me to express his surprise with regard to my ballet, having learnt from you that the expense comes to 9000 francs. He asked me why the expense had risen so high, when I had only spoken to him of 1500 to 1600 francs. I have told him I was not consulted and that my intentions had undoubtedly been misunderstood, that I was only asking for 1500 francs for a few accessories which I would do without if that was a difficulty. Consequently he told me to let you know as soon as possible in order to set the record right.
>
> I have asked for a rainbow, a fountain, a cloud and a trap. I can do without them if necessary.[12]

Consequently, the ballet had to be reduced in scale, largely by simplifying the requirements for the scenery, but even so the cost came to nearly 8000 francs. Henry's original plan had been to feature sixty-six children, but Gardel reminded him that the maximum number of children allowed to be admitted to the School of Dance was sixty.[13] In the end, if the cast list in the programme is accurate, no more than twenty-eight would be

[12] Arch. Nat., Henry to Luçay, 2 Vendémiaire, Year XIV (24 September 1805).
[13] Arch. Nat., AJ^{13} 87.

used, among them being two little sisters named Gosselin of whom more would be heard in years to come. Whatever small annoyances were put in Henry's way, the influence of Cambacérès could not be ignored, and orders went out for the ballet to go into production.

Like Duport before him, Louis Henry had constructed his scenario, now called *L'Amour à Cythère*, around the rôle he envisaged for himself: that of Zephyr, the personification of the west wind. The modest narrative was based on no particular legend, although the personages were taken either from classical mythology or from allegory. The action took place on the island of Cythera, sacred to the worship of Venus, whose Temple was a prominent feature of the set. Venus (Clotilde) appears with her son Cupid (Rosière) and the three Graces (Aim. Vestris, Félicité, Hutin). After Cupid has been bathed at the fountain, Venus decrees that whoever drinks of its waters will fall under the sway of her child. Proof of this is provided in a *pas de deux* by a young shepherd and shepherdess (Saint-Amant, Collomb), who fall in love in the course of it. Cupid, however, is a mischievous brat, and in an attempt to curb him Venus has him secured to a post. At this point Zephyr (Henry) appears and releases the child. He has come with the disturbing news that Jupiter has decided to destroy Cupid, and that the only way to avoid such a calamity is for Venus to go to Olympus and plead with the king of heaven.

While she is away, Zephyr gives life to the flowers, first the Tuberose (V. Saulnier II), then the Violet (Mme Gardel). Cupid then amuses himself by piercing Zephyr with one of his arrows at the very moment that the Rose (Millière) is unfolding. A tender scene between Zephyr and the Rose is interrupted by a roll of thunder announcing the arrival of Mercury (Saron) to order Cupid to be handed over. But the nymphs spirit Cupid into the safety of the Temple, which not even Mercury dares enter. Mercury summons the winds to his aid, and in a titanic struggle Zephyr is overwhelmed and carried off in a cloud. Venus then returns, having been unsuccessful in her plea. At first she believes Cupid to have perished, but to her relief she finds him safe in her Temple. Thunder breaks out anew, and Jupiter himself (Lebel), still angry and inflexible, appears in the heavens. Cupid now gives himself up and throws his arms around Jupiter, who, moved by Venus's entreaties, at last relents. A rainbow spreads across the sky, and Zephyr reappears to be pardoned and united to the Rose, who is declared to be the queen of flowers.

This simple tale was performed to music by Pierre Gaveaux, a singer of the Théâtre Feydeau who had already composed several *opéras-comiques*. It was a simple, unpretentious accompaniment, which did not seem out of place. Geoffroy wrote:

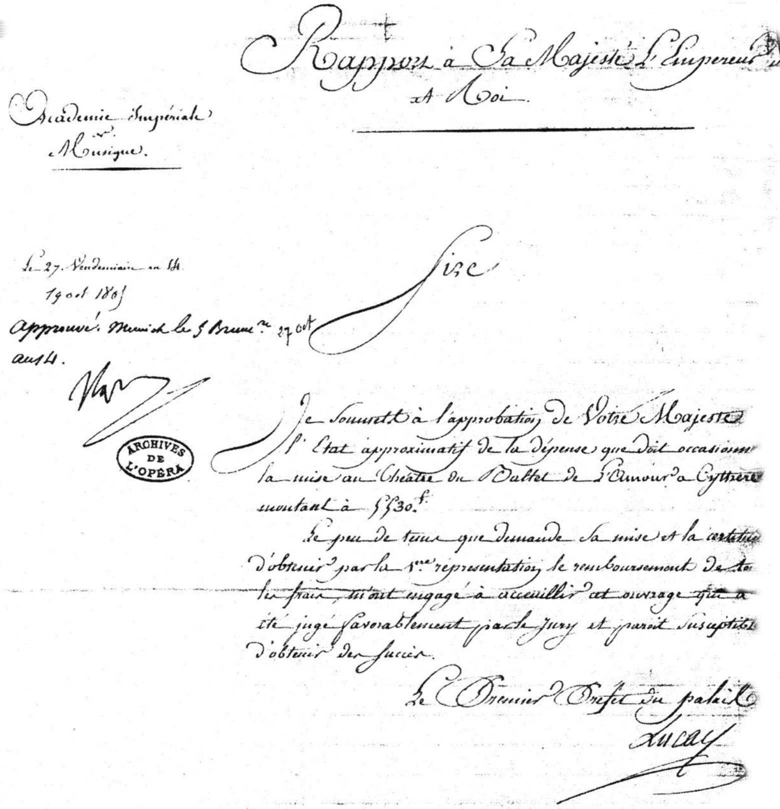

Rapport à Sa Majesté l'Empereur et Roi.

Académie Impériale de Musique.

Le 27 Vendémiaire an 14.
19 oct 1805

approuvé. Munich le 5 Brumaire 27 oct an 14.
Nap

ARCHIVES DE L'OPÉRA

Sire

Je soumets à l'approbation de Votre Majesté l'État approximatif de la dépense que doit occasionner la mise au Théâtre du Ballet de l'Amour à Cythère montant à 5530.f

Le peu de temps que demande sa mise et la certitude d'obtenir par la 1re représentation le remboursement de tous les frais, m'ont engagé à accueillir cet ouvrage qui a été jugé favorablement par le Jury et paraît susceptible d'obtenir du succès.

Le Premier Préfet du palais
Luçay

The Comte de Luçay's report to Napoleon, seeking approval of the estimate for Henry's ballet, L'Amour de Cythère, *with the endorsement of the Emperor's approval, granted at Munich on 27 October 1805, just five weeks before the Battle of Austerlitz. (Archives Nationales, AJ[13] 91)*

All through the piece his vaudevillish tunes sing to us. Their motifs are so happy and the melodies so pure that they easily linger in the memory and are always listened to with renewed pleasure. These little tunes, so well phrased, honour a musician more than grand airs in which can be found neither phrase nor lilt, and which have no other claim to respect save monotony and ennui.[14]

In estimating the time needed to stage this ballet, Henry had been true to his word: it took him just three weeks. However, the pressure had been

[14] *Journal de l'Empire*, 3 November 1805.

14

Duport's Figaro

Glory was in the air as the new year of 1806 dawned. Propitiously, the sun had shone at Austerlitz on Napoleon's greatest victory, which had humbled Austria and seemingly brought peace, for England alone now remained at war with France. After the collapse of the peace talks with the old enemy in 1803, Napoleon had begun to assemble a powerful invasion force on the Channel coast, but two years later the unsteady peace on the Continent crumbled, and it was against Austria that he had marched. When, so unbelievably soon, the news arrived of the victory at Austerlitz and the end of hostilities, Paris erupted in a paroxysm of joy.

Preparations were soon on foot to honour the Emperor's triumph. Naturally, the Opéra was to make a significant contribution to the celebrations, and Fouché, the Minister of Police, suggested that Gardel might devise a one-act scene – of an allegorical nature, he added, rather than an analogy with some great historical warrior, for any comparison could only be a feeble tribute. Dutifully, Gardel lost no time in responding to the Minister's request, and produced a script with the flattering title, *L'Homme du Destin*.

It was to open with a series of joyful dances of different nationalities, performed before the Temple of the Goddess of Peace, attended also by the Muses and by Mercury, the representative of commerce. But the sky darkens, and Discord bursts upon the scene, bringing hatred, terror, famine and pestilence in her wake. The Goddess of Peace is imprisoned in a rock surrounded by impenetrable chasms, and Demons celebrate Discord's victory with their violent dances. Jupiter, however, is offended, and summons the Gods to hear his decision 'to send to earth a man who, through his wisdom, intrepidity, justice, eloquence, magnanimity and strength, will restore peace'. Destiny is charged with forming this paragon, whom the Gods invest with the appropriate attributes. Jupiter returns to Olympus, and the hero marches forth to perform his great task. He gathers an army, but finds his way barred by Discord's threatening array. The enemy is routed, but the final battle is still to come. The hero's troops force their way into Discord's rocky realm, to which the sole access is over a rickety bridge, on which none dare venture until the hero seizes a standard and, waving it aloft, crosses to the other side. His soldiers follow, and after many dangers the Goddess of Peace is rescued. In the final apotheosis an eagle hovers above the hero's head as he is hailed by all the nations of the world.[1]

Had it been placed before the Emperor, this fawning tribute would probably have been rejected out of hand. But Fouché, who understood Napoleon better than most, had meanwhile had second thoughts. He mollified Gardel with the assurance that, had an allegory been required, his would of course have been chosen, and explained that a different kind of interlude was now being envisaged. Consequently Gardel put aside his draft, with which, truth to tell, he had not been entirely satisfied. He had certainly included all the appropriate allusions – to the Revolution and the Terror, to the emergence of Napoleon as the saviour of the nation, and, however illusory it was to prove, to the establishment of peace – but he had become conscious of its shortcomings. For one thing, his allusion to Napoleon leading his soldiers across the bridge at Lodi more than nine years before was an obvious anachronism when placed in the context of the recent campaign; and in the finale, so was the inclusion of America, which had not been discovered when the ancient gods held sway.

Napoleon returned to Paris late in the evening of 26 January 1806. The dancers of the Opéra were in high hopes that he might appear in his box two days later to see Duport in *Le Retour de Zéphire*, but they were to be disappointed – as also was Emilie Collomb, who, as she was not dancing, had reserved the box alongside the Emperor's. By then the plans for the special performance, scheduled for 4 February, were well advanced. Gardel's original project had been replaced by a laudatory spectacle with words by Esmenard and music by Steibelt. By virtue of his position, Gardel was responsible for the dances, and was also placed in general charge of the production. The piece was given no title, being announced simply as *A Fête to Celebrate the Victories*.

The auditorium that evening offered a splendid spectacle. It had been specially decorated with masses of laurel, an effect that was augmented by providing the audience with sheaves of the same plant. The house was packed, the boxes filled with 'princes, ministers, ambassadors and all the most distinguished figures in Paris whether by rank or fortune'. Outside, large crowds were gathered in the hope of catching a glimpse of Napoleon when his carriage and escort passed. He made his entrance to deafening cheers as the audience rose to their feet, dipping their sheaves in homage.

[1] Arch. Nat., AJ^{13} 1024. Draft scenario, notes and preface.

It seemed the ovation would never end, and indeed a full ten minutes passed before the audience became exhausted and settled down to watch the Fête.

When the curtain rose, a magnificent tent came into view, decorated with appropriate inscriptions, emblems and trophies. It was open at the back, revealing a panorama of the Seine from the Pont Royal to the Pont Neuf, painted with a wonderfully realistic eye for detail, down to the crowds along the river bank and in the streets, and people out on their balconies. After an opening chorus, a crowd of children carrying the inevitable laurel branches burst on to the stage from the wings, soon to be followed by troops from many different regiments, performing drill with great precision. Their display over, they were joined by their families and friends. Then, at a roll on the drums, the stage cleared, and Lainez, in General's uniform, came on to sing a stirring martial air which was taken up by the large chorus.

After this, the dancing began: a dance for two Frenchwomen, a Polish dance (Mimi and Victoire Saulnier), an exotic dance by Mamelukes (led by Beaupré and Luigia Taglioni), a dance of Turkish sultanas (featuring Mlle Clotilde), a virile dance performed solely by men dressed as Greek soldiers (commanded by Henry), and dances by Swiss peasants (headed by Vestris and Marie Gardel), Basques from Béarn (prominent among whom was Emilie Bigottini), Spaniards (led by Beaulieu) and, entering to the strains of a vielle, Savoyards (headed by Marie Millière). A special place had been reserved for the women of Strasbourg, for whom Gardel had devised a charming little scene. A group of them, finding themselves in the presence of some soldiers, are too timid to ask the officers to dance with them until one, more daring than the rest, very tentatively steps forward to make the first approach. In a twinkling of an eye, they all burst into movement, whirling round with their partners in an exhilarating waltz.

At this point Duport and his sister were to have been featured in a new *pas*, but he was not feeling well enough to appear, even for Napoleon, and so it had to be omitted. The critic of the *Courrier des spectacles* took this very much amiss, closing his review with the admonition: 'Go and hang yourself, Duport, for you were not there.'[2] In its place Mlles Chevigny, Collomb and Marie-Madeleine Delisle danced an elegant *pas de trois*. The conclusion was now at hand, and that reformed *sansculotte*, Laïs, entered to sing a hymn of thanksgiving. The stage then filled, and the curtain fell with the massed cast waving their branches of laurel to a storm of applause that must have shaken the rafters.

[2] *Courrier des spectacles*, 6 February 1806.

That evening Emilie Collomb returned home well satisfied with her performance. At the rehearsal of the *pas de trois* four days before, she had had an exchange of words with Gardel, who had reproached her for taking a class with another teacher. In reply she had chided him for having fined her, a pupil of his for fifteen years, on no less than four occasions during her recent illness. But he had now served her very well. 'The *pas* he has arranged for me is pretty,' she wrote in her diary. 'I even find it more pleasing than those of Mlles Chevigny and Delisle.'[3] From the stage she had had a good view of Napoleon, whose reaction to the tribute she described in her diary:

> The Fête is beautiful, although very inferior to what it could be, and I thought the Emperor was suffering from the praise, which, although well deserved, was certainly too direct. Heroes should be treated, like those beautiful women who attract the greatest praise, in a way that does not offend their modesty. I was enchanted that the Emperor appeared stern and even annoyed by all the adulation.[4]

* * *

Very possibly, among the pupils of the School of Dance taking part in the victory gala was a promising young pupil of Coulon who had high hopes of making his début at the Opéra. Salvatore Taglioni was a younger brother of Filippo and Luigia Taglioni, and had been in Paris for some time perfecting his technique. His début was authorised in March, but a difficulty had arisen. Everyone had assumed he would be available to accept an engagement should his début warrant it; but, only a few days before it was to take place, the Opéra learned that he had signed a contract with La Scala, Milan. Bonet saw no advantage to the Opéra in allowing the début to proceed. Not only would it be a waste of money, he told Luçay, but precious time would also be wasted in teaching him the part of Telemachus. Furthermore, it did not seem right that he should be favoured over another promising pupil, Arnaud Léon, 'a young artiste who has devoted the years of his youth to become a useful *sujet*, ... whose salary is not sufficient to pay his teacher, and who daily gives proof of indefatigable zeal'. A second grievance against young Taglioni was that he had been heard publicly running down the administration and also

[3] Collomb, entry of 1 February 1806.
[4] Collomb, entry of 4 February 1806.

Gardel, who had gone out of his way to help him. But more serious was the suspicion that he would be taking his sister with him when he left.[5]

The day before his début, Bonet extracted from him a written promise that 'when I have made my début, subject to the terms offered being acceptable to me, I will enter into an engagement with the Paris Opéra, seeing that I am not engaged for the theatre in Milan.'[6]

On the strength of this assurance, his début duly took place the next day, 29 April. As the younger brother of Filippo and Luigia, he could count on the interest of the connoisseurs. Another point in his favour was that he was a pupil of Coulon, who had been coaching him specially for the event. As was customary, he was to be given the opportunity of showing his talent as both dancer and mime: in a *pas de deux* inserted in the opera *Oedipe à Colonne*, and at the end of the evening in the rôle of Telemachus. It was an awesome undertaking for a young man of seventeen, particularly the mime rôle, in which he would inevitably be judged by the yardstick of Gardel and Vestris. Fortunately he had earlier given proof of his exceptional talent as a dancer, and the audience was in an understanding mood, making allowances for his lack of experience as an actor.

His sister Luigia, who partnered him in the *pas de deux*, had all the qualities required of a ballerina, but just lacked that touch of brilliance that arouses an audience to enthusiasm. She was, as Geoffroy remarked, the modest violet among the ballerinas. As her brother's partner, her lack of pretension served to concentrate attention on him; for his good looks, strength, aplomb, brilliant elevation and a veritable arsenal of *tours de force* made a striking impression.

Having successfully passed the test, he no doubt hoped that his troubles were over, but for some reason Luçay and Bonet placed no credence in his assurance that he was not committed to La Scala. In May he was pressing to make a second début appearance, but Bonet advised Luçay that nothing would keep him in Paris. 'He has signed a contract for Italy – I have just received certain proof of this,' he wrote. 'The reputation that M. Taglioni might gain [from the début] will be only to his advantage and will be of no benefit to the Académie.'[7] Luçay thereupon gave instructions that Taglioni was not to continue his débuts unless he signed a one-year contract at 2400 francs a year. Taglioni rejected this, and, as the Opéra had suspected, his sister gave notice within a week to terminate her own engagement.

[5] Arch. Nat., AJ[13] 86. Bonet to Luçay, draft letter, undated.

[6] Arch. Nat., AJ[13] 86 (S. Taglioni). Dated 28 April 1806.

[7] Arch. Nat., AJ[13] 86 (S.Taglioni). Bonet to Luçay, 19 May 1806.

However, Salvatore Taglioni did not appear at La Scala, and he was not seen on one of the major stages in Italy until 1808, when his long association with the royal theatres in Naples began. Meanwhile, Luigia Taglioni had left at the end of 1806, and the following year the Opéra was interested in engaging Salvatore for the post of *premier danseur noble*, which had become vacant through the resignation of Louis Henry. The salary offered was 6000 francs, which fell so far short of his expectations that the negotiations lapsed.

Meanwhile, some weeks before young Taglioni had made his single appearance at the Opéra, another interesting début had taken place at the Théâtre de la Porte-Saint-Martin. Victoria Bossi Del Caro, lately principal dancer in Vienna and one of several sisters who all became distinguished ballerinas, had come to Paris in a romantic glow of publicity. Her standing as a ballerina was beyond question, and she had studied under an impressive array of masters: Noverre, the elder Vestris, Didelot, Laborie and Gallet. Although born in Portugal, she had been brought up in England and gained her stage experience largely in London. There she had met and married Cesare Bossi, who conducted for the ballet and had composed several ballet scores. Under the harsh laws of the time, he had been imprisoned for debt in the King's Bench Prison, and she had put her wifely duties before her career in order to share his hardships. In September 1802, his spirit broken, he had died in prison. Burdened with three young children and with another on the way, she went out of her mind with grief and only recovered her reason after her child was born. Her tragedy and recovery were the stuff of romance, with such an affecting parallel with the popular *opéra-comique* by Dalayrac, *Nina, ou la Folle par amour*, that she became known in London as 'the English Nina'.[8] Happily, like Nina, she recovered, and went on to resume her career in London and Vienna.

When Paris saw her in 1806, she was probably several years past thirty. At the Porte-Saint-Martin she appeared only briefly, dancing two *pas* and playing Cherubino in Dauberval's *Le Page inconstant*. Her moving life story drew many people to see her out of curiosity, but she was not offered an engagement, even though there was a vacancy, caused just two months earlier by the untimely death of Antoinette Santiquet.

* * *

[8] *Journal de l'Empire*, 10 March 1806.

The naval disaster off Cape Trafalgar notwithstanding, the great military victories of 1805 seemed to many to offer a realistic prospect of peace, and Napoleon began to direct his mind to the affairs of the Opéra. In the early months of 1806 the Council of State ruled that the number of weekly performances should be increased from three to four, and to five in 'periods of affluence, notably during the fêtes in May',[9] and recommended that it should be the only theatre permitted to present ballets.[10]

But, as Duport was one of the first to recognise, the formal establishment of an Imperial court would provide another possible arena for his choreographic talent. Napoleon had rejected Versailles as being too extravagantly sumptuous, and was to spend the warmer months in the more intimate palace of Saint-Cloud, which was closer to Paris and had the added appeal of its association with the *coup d'état* of Brumaire. The palace had needed considerable renovation to make it habitable, and among the additions was a small theatre with two little anterooms, built behind the Orangerie.[11] The facilities of this little theatre would not allow for any spectacular scenic and mechanical effects, nor accommodate a large cast, and Duport accepted that he would have to cut his cloth to fit it. Entertainment, not spectacle, would be the order of the evening. Spurred no doubt by Aumer's recent success with *Le Page inconstant*, Duport decided to transpose Beaumarchais's comedy, *Le Barbier de Seville*, into a ballet. Gardel clearly thought it inadvisable openly to oppose a ballet in which, apparently, the court was showing an interest; when the reading jury met to listen to the scenario on 3 April, it merely made mild suggestions for improvement:

> In receiving this work, the jury wish the author to add some opportunities for dancing into the last two acts. It suggests, for example, the substitution of a dancing lesson for the music lesson. The jury also thinks that the author has relied too much on the well-known situations of the play, and that he ought to strengthen the second and third acts with a few incidents of his own invention.[12]

Presumably Duport made an effort to meet these suggestions, and on 25 April Napoleon gave it his approval.

In treating such a well-known subject, Duport was naturally hesitant

[9] Lecomte, 119. Council of State decisions, 25 February 1806.
[10] Lecomte, 106. Council of State minutes, 18 April 1806.
[11] Both the Tuileries and Saint-Cloud were renovated by the architects Charles Percier and Pierre Fontaine, who also designed scenery.
[12] Arch. Nat., AJ^{13} 66 (263). Minutes of jury, 3 April 1806.

to depart from the original plot any more than absolutely necessary. Of course, some adjustment would be necessary if the narrative was to be conveyed in pantomime. His main concern was whether Rosina's complicity in Figaro's deception of Bartholo could be mimed sufficiently delicately for her not to appear too forward or morally a trifle lax. Such misgivings were not without justification, for the comedy had been written in a cynical age, and by 1806 society had become more prim. To absolve Rosina from any deceit, Duport introduced a soubrette character, her companion Isabelle, to whom he allotted the major share of the plotting. Figaro and Isabelle thus became the principal perpetrators of the tricks that eventually lead to Rosina marrying the man she loves.

That the rôle was thus made less interesting did not appear to concern Duport. He would be giving his sister Minette the part of an unblemished but warm-blooded girl, undoubtedly more suited to her talent – for she was not a particularly strong actress and would make up for that deficiency by the 'pace and lightness' of her dancing. For the rôle of Isabelle, of equal importance in the ballet, he had a very different type of dancer in mind: his friend Emilie Collomb, a natural soubrette with an inexhaustible fund of sparkle, both in personality and as a dancer, as well as having experience and an ability to project.

Mlle Collomb, that doughty rival to Sophie Chevigny, was one of the senior members of the company, whose diary covers the period of Duport's activity as a choreographer. She was a pupil of Gardel, who found her overpowering, haughty and prone to make use of all and sundry, but nevertheless held her in great respect. Her diary entries contain a number of references to him that reveal a certain impatience with his secretiveness concerning matters which he obviously felt were not the concern of individuals in the company. Once, after a discussion with Luçay, she accused *ce coquin de Gardel* (that rascal, Gardel), not to his face, of course, but to her diary, of being devious and unhelpful. Gardel, who regarded his function as quasi-ministerial, strongly disapproved of his dancers engaging in political acts without his approval. Some six years before, shortly after Bonaparte's victory at Marengo, he had expressed his discontent when Collomb had sent some adulatory verses to the First Consul.

But the wily politician was only one aspect of Gardel's character, and when Collomb needed coaching in a *pas* she was to dance in *Achille à Scyros*, he could not have been more 'open and helpful'.[13] From her diary, Collomb comes across as an intelligent, dedicated and hard-working

[13] Collomb, diary entries of 5 and 27 November 1805, 21 December 1805 and 22 February 1806.

dancer well able to stand up for herself. To Duport she was certainly a loyal friend who uncomplainingly put up with his sulks and tantrums and, at times when he was at his most arrogant, was able to exert a much-needed steadying influence.

Apart from himself, his sister and Collomb, Duport's cast was to be enriched by three other distinguished interpreters: Jean-Baptiste Hullin, father of little Virginie, as Bartholo; Saint-Amant as Almaviva; and Baptiste Petit, who was perhaps already courting Minette,[14] as Don Basilio. In the weeks leading up to the ballet's production, Duport, Hullin and Collomb would frequently dine together, when the forthcoming ballet would be discussed at great length. In the relaxed atmosphere of a shared meal, the characters they would be playing no doubt took shape and were filled out as they imagined new details and amusing pieces of business.

To mount this ballet Duport was allotted a miserly budget of 5500 francs. There was therefore no money for new scenery, and the *divertissement* at the end had to be performed before the easily recognisable garden set from the opera *Tarare*. Also, time was very short, and a last-minute problem drove Duport into a state of panic. When it was rehearsed three days before the court performance, it was all too clear that the ballet was in no state to be presented: the last act was the source of the problem, adding nothing to the plot. The following day Duport wrote to Luçay that the ballet could not be given on the day appointed. His letter caused great consternation, for one did not cancel arrangements with the Palace at short notice, and Napoleon's ire was not to be contemplated. But somehow the difficulty was explained; the performance was postponed by two days to 22 May, and Duport was able to make his adjustments. No wonder the dancers anxiously scrutinised the Emperor's countenance to observe his reaction, as Mlle Collomb related:

> This morning we had a general rehearsal on the stage at the Opéra with the court musicians. I dined at the Opéra with Duport and his sister, and at five o'clock we left for Saint-Cloud. I acted very well and danced very well. The ballet seemed to give much pleasure. However, it was not possible to tell positively that this was so, since the Emperor did not smile for a single moment and the court observed the strictest silence. The Empress seemed to watch the ballet with interest.[15]

Whether or not Napoleon or the members of his court had been offended, the reception by the Paris public when *Figaro* was repeated at the

[14] Collomb recorded in her diary that they were married on 14 April 1808.
[15] Collomb, diary entry of 22 May 1806.

Opéra on 30 May 1806 was enthusiastic. 'A complete success,' Mlle Collomb called it:

> In spite of its rejection in the opinion of the court, it was wildly applauded, and Duport was given a call at the end of the performance. It appears that the public was generally very pleased with my dancing and my pantomime in this work.[16]

Duport was found to have taken few liberties with the general thrust of Beamarchais's plot. The first act is set in a village square on the outskirts of Seville, with Bartholo's house on the right. Count Almaviva (Saint-Amant) enters, swathed in a cloak, to express his love for Rosina, the jealously guarded ward of Dr Bartholo. Rosina (M. Duport) appears momentarily at her window before being dragged back into the house by Bartholo (J.B. Hullin). Figaro (L. Duport) then appears with some villagers, and Bartholo comes out to give orders for a fête and to instruct his ward's companion, Isabelle (Collomb), to let no one come near the house. While Figaro is overseeing the preparations, Isabelle comes out to see what is going on. Figaro flirts with her, but she pushes him away and runs back indoors. After the villagers have left, Almaviva returns. Recognising Figaro as a former servant, he is delighted to learn that he is now Bartholo's factotum. Figaro conceives a plan to assist Almaviva in his wooing of Rosina. The fête then begins, and Almaviva returns, disguised as a troubadour. While Figaro keeps Bartholo occupied, Almaviva courts Rosina. Bartholo becomes suspicious, and Figaro keeps Bartholo away from his ward by making the villagers circle around him. Before he finally breaks his way through, Almaviva has passed Rosina a note.

The scene changes to a room in the house. Figaro hides to observe how Rosina receives Almaviva's approach. Rosina enters and shows Almaviva's letter to Isabelle. Figaro then comes out of hiding, and Rosina asks him to deliver her reply. At the sound of Bartholo's footsteps, Figaro has to hide again. Bartholo enters, very much out of humour, and accompanied by his friend Don Basilio (Baptiste), who is counselling him to lose no time in marrying Rosina. Bartholo proposes to Rosina, who rejects him outright. Almaviva then makes his appearance as a drunken soldier, brandishing a billeting order. Bartholo claims he is exempt, but to no avail. Almaviva chases him with his sword, and then, sweeping into a dance, tries to pass a letter to Rosina. Bartholo attempts to snatch it away; Rosina manages to seize it but lets it drop. Pushing Bartholo aside,

[16] Collomb, diary entry of 30 May 1806.

Almaviva retrieves it and hands it to Rosina, who puts it in her pocket. After Almaviva has left, Bartholo tries to wheedle the letter out of Rosina. She tells him it is only a sheet of music, and with the help of Isabelle, Bartholo is deceived and begs forgiveness. Almaviva then enters in a new disguise, as a teacher of music and dancing sent, he says, by Don Basilio who is ill. Bartholo is taken in, believing that the young man has been sent by Don Basilio to discuss his marriage to his ward. Almaviva gives him Rosina's letter, advising him not to show it to Rosina yet. Bartholo then allows Almaviva to give Rosina a music lesson, in the course of which he explains Figaro's plan, while Isabelle distracts Bartholo's attention by dancing between them. Bartholo then asks Rosina to dance, and gradually falls asleep. When the old man wakes, some children are introduced to dance a bolero, which gives him the idea of holding a fête in his garden. Figaro is given the keys to make the arrangements.

The third act takes place in the garden. While dancing is in progress, Don Basilio makes an unexpected appearance, but is quickly got rid of by being convinced he is suffering from a contagious disease. The dancing recommences; but, seeing Rosina and Almaviva together, Bartholo realises at last that he has been tricked, and orders Almaviva to leave. Bartholo chides Rosina, who tells him she will marry whomsoever she wishes. However, when Bartholo brings out her letter, she is so upset that she gives in and agrees to marry him. Don Basilio then returns, complaining he has been tricked; but Bartholo calms him down, explaining that all is well and that he is to marry Rosina. When everyone has left, Figaro and Almaviva return, climbing over the garden wall. They come face to face with an angry Rosina, who accuses Almaviva of giving her letter to Bartholo. Contritely, Almaviva kneels at her feet, revealing his identity and assuring her of the sincerity of his love. When Don Basilio returns with a notary and a marriage contract, Almaviva, exerting his privilege as a nobleman and discreetly slipping him a bribe, orders the notary to alter the contract in his favour. So when Bartholo enters, he is presented with a *fait accompli*; he vents his fury on Don Basilio, who wryly shows him the money he has been given, but there is nothing Bartholo can do, and the ballet ends with festivities in Almaviva's gardens.

The choreography has long since been forgotten, but the programme specified a number of dances spread through the action, some arising naturally out of a situation and others actively assisting in the narrative. Act I was brought to a close by a sequence of dances including those of the villagers, a solo for Rosina in various national styles (Spanish, French, German, Italian) and a sprightly *pas de deux* for Duport and Collomb. Act II contained only two brief dance passages: a dance for Rosina during the music lesson[17] and the comical *pas de quatre* in waltz time for Almaviva, Bartholo, Rosina and Isabelle, constructed around Almaviva's efforts to pass his letter to Rosina. Most of that act was given over to pantomime, which annoyed the critic of the *Gazette de France* because it meant he had to wait until the dénouement in Act III before any real dancing took place. Then at last, at Almaviva's wedding feast, came a conventional *divertissement*, which included an amusing *bolero* for Bartholo and, of course, the inevitable display of Duport's astonishing virtuosity.

An unusual omission on the title page of the programme was the name of the composer. Duport, who would have been responsible for making arrangements for the music, may have sought the assistance of one of the composers who helped him with *Acis et Galathée* – Darondeau or Gianella. Most probably the music was the usual confection of airs from numerous sources. The reviews at the time made no mention of the score, the only clue to a borrowing appearing in the programme, where Almaviva serenades Rosina in Act I to the tune of *Daignez écouter*.[18]

In the days leading up to the first performance, Duport's detractors had been busy warning the public that it was in for a tedious evening. Such prophecies proved wide of the mark: the ballet may have had its faults, but boring it was not. The only criticism from the *Courrier des spectacles* was that it was too short, which in itself was a compliment. Its action progressed rapidly, and while no one suggested that it matched Beaumarchais's comedy for wit, a flow of amusing *lazzi* kept the audience entertained as the familiar story unfolded.

That Duport suffered from extreme exhaustion through over-exertion and generally needed at least a day to recover must have been known to the administration of the Opéra, but when this caused a last-minute change of programme on two occasions, Bonet lost patience. 'The continual postponement of your works that you cause,' he reminded Duport, 'is straining the patience of the public, whose favour you enjoy and for which you must show gratitude.'[19]

Bonet's annoyance certainly stemmed from difficulties he had had with Duport in the past, and perhaps it was at times difficult to judge

[17] Several authorities have asserted that Duport's ballet was based on J.-B. Blache's *Almaviva et Rosina* and included at this point the mirror dance that was a striking feature of the latter ballet. A study of the two scenarios shows that Duport owed nothing to Blache, and certainly no notices of Duport's ballet mention a mirror dance. For Blache's ballet, see Chapter 29.

[18] Since neither the score nor the parts are to be found at the Paris Opéra, it must be assumed that Duport took them with him when he left Paris in 1808. Scores exist both in Vienna and Stockholm, where the ballet was later revived. Ivo Cramér used the latter score for his reproduction of the ballet in the style of its period, performed at the Royal Swedish Opera, Stockholm, in 1992.

[19] Arch. Nat., AJ^{13} 73 (346-8). Bonet to Duport, 17 June 1806.

whether the dancer's excuses were genuine. Three months later the Director learned that Duport was again under the weather, when *Figaro* was already billed for the next day, 30 September. The dancer informed Gardel that he was not prepared to endanger his health, but this time he was at least willing to be helpful:

> As you are well aware, the vomiting of blood from which I suffer each time I dance makes it necessary that I should rest for at least a week. I do not know whether the management is trying to put me out of action for a long time; I do not want to believe this, but your letter which I have just received, written in spite of my communications, really leads me to this conclusion.
>
> As to *Figaro*, I have no objection to its being given, and if M. Bonet wishes to send word at once to M. Beaulieu and ask him to come to my home, Rue Montmartre, corner of Rue Feydeau, No. 161, at 11 o'clock sharp, I will arrange for Saint-Amant and Mlle Collomb to be there and we will show him the rôle of Figaro.[20]

The performance took place, apparently with Beaulieu in the title rôle. *Figaro* was given four times more before the end of 1806 and once again on 6 April 1807, which was to be its last performance at the Opéra. Although Duport served notice in September to terminate his engagement, plans for reviving *Figaro* went ahead despite his uncertain health and the absence of Hullin, who had been summarily dismissed for accepting the post of ballet-master at the Gaîté. Hullin's departure was a great blow, and December found Duport, although in considerable discomfort, working three or four hours a day with Goyon, teaching him the part of Bartholo. It was an arduous task which could not be rushed, for, as he told Picard, who by then had succeeded Bonet as Director, this was 'a much harder task in the ballet than it would have been in the comedy, since the slightest lapse of memory would destroy the entire work, which is entirely dependent on fine detail'.[21]

Disappointingly, all this effort was to be wasted; with Duport's departure only three months ahead, neither Gardel nor Milon could be expected to retain any of his ballets in the repertory. But there was another reason for its disappearance. Towards the end of September 1807, Emilie Collomb had injured her knee in practice. For many weeks she could not put any weight on her foot, and it was becoming increasingly evident that

[20] Arch. Nat., AJ[13] 69 (66). Duport to Gardel, 29 September 1806.
[21] Arch. Nat., AJ[13] 74 (387). Duport to Picard, 3 December 1806.

she might never dance again. She had been so much the life and soul of *Figaro* that perhaps it was impossible to imagine it without her.

* * *

When at long last Duport received permission to proceed with the staging of his little *divertissement* of *Le Volage fixé*, its first performance was, unusually, scheduled for a Sunday – 20 July 1806. No official explanation was forthcoming, but Geoffroy wryly suggested that since the celebrated Italian soprano Grassini would be singing on the Monday, a large house was unlikely on the previous evening, and that Duport may have himself offered to present his *divertissement* at that performance 'to uphold the honour of his countrymen'.[22]

It may have been with a view to concealing the fact that it had previously been given in the provinces that *Le Volage fixé* became the subtitle, with the piece being billed as *L'Hymen de Zéphyre*. It was a piece of very modest proportions, a 'little bit of fun' as the *Journal de Paris* called it, owing its charm to a lack of pretension and more particularly to the talented children who played Cupid and Hymen, Virginie Hullin and Mlle Rosière. The ballet indeed opened with a charming scene showing both on the stage together. Each is striving for dominion over Zephyr, and Hymen reproaches Cupid for creating mischief, counselling moderation in a slow and graceful waltz. Zephyr (L. Duport) then appears, attracted by a group of nymphs near Cupid's statue; by taking the god's place on the plinth, he kisses one of them. His presence is discovered, and he becomes enamoured with the nymph Chloris (M. Duport). But once Chloris is out of sight, he flirts outrageously with a passing group of shepherdesses. Cupid intervenes on behalf of Chloris, reproaching Zephyr for his inconstancy. Zephyr manages to slip away, but Cupid and the shepherdesses weave a net in which he is trapped. Cupid directs his arrow at Zephyr at the moment Chloris sees him. Chloris, however, is still angry with Zephyr, but he swears to mend his ways and promises to marry her. This is not to Cupid's liking, for it means that Hymen has gained the upper hand. But finally Cupid accepts the situation with good grace, and Hymen consecrates the lovers' union by placing a crown of roses on Chloris's head and proclaiming her as Flora, goddess of flowers.

All this was no more than a frame within which Duport and his sister could shine, and indeed they delighted the public as they always did when appearing together. Duport made much of Zephyr's frivolous character,

[22] *Journal de l'Empire*, 25 July 1806.

and had an effective scene at the point when Zephyr, having aroused the nymphs' resentment at his inconstancy, pirouettes his way through them in an offhand way, skilfully evading their clutches and snatching the ribbons, one by one, from their hands. Minette too was well cast as Chloris, while Emilie Collomb contributed a vivacious cameo in her portrayal of the nymph Lydie, which was to prove the last creation of her career.

Despite the individual attractions of its performers, this inconsequential ballet did little to further Duport's reputation as a choreographer. After the promise of his two earlier ballets, Geoffroy was clearly disappointed, seeing him now as no more than a lightweight. 'Duport's ballets are amusing,' he wrote. 'They lack neither movement nor variety; they are the productions of a lively and ardent young man, but one who has not yet managed to probe deeper into the science of lyric and pantomimic drama.'[23] But Geoffroy also laid a more serious charge, having recognised a number of instances of plagiarism in passages that recalled other ballets: notably, 'one of the prettiest scenes' from Milon's *Pygmalion*, 'several charming touches' from Gardel's *Jugement de Pâris*, 'a host of happy ideas' from Henry's *Amour à Cythère*. Luigia Taglioni's garland dance seemed very similar to Hebe's dance in Paisiello's opera *Proserpine*; and the incident of Zephyr and Cupid's statue inevitably awakened memories of the famous scene in Gardel's ballet when Psyché takes the place of the statue of Venus – 'except,' Geoffroy added, 'that Psyche and Venus were there better matched than Duport and his Cupid'.[24]

No composer was credited with the music, which included a rondo by Kreutzer and a borrowing from the second movement (*allegretto*) of Haydn's Symphony No. 92.

When she arrived home after the first performance, Emilie Collomb wrote an account of the ballet from a dancer's perspective:

> The ballet is only a joke, but it is pleasing and the scenes quite well arranged, though Duport was unable to take full advantage of the pretty ideas he had. He has left empty patches which cast a chill over it. His cupids, instead of having character, thrash about like mad and have no idea what they are or what they are about. The nymphs do not play a large enough part in the action at the end of the ballet when they should be busy making the net and weaving garlands; also there should be a little humorous scene when Zephyr makes up his mind about Flora; it ought to be possible and even appropriate to make a *pas*

[23] *Journal de l'Empire*, 10 July 1806.
[24] *Journal de l'Empire*, 25 July 1806.

> on the situation between Cupid and the nymphs. Duport and his sister danced well, I not too badly, and Taglioni not as well as at the rehearsal. The ballet gave pleasure; the author was called for and appeared. Duport was ready to call his sister, but that was not taken up; the public did not take the bait.[25]

There was no question but that Duport was a difficult colleague. On the last day of July, Mlle Collomb wrote: 'In the evening I was really upset. At the rehearsal Duport said some very coarse things to me which I did not deserve.' But with Duport, storms soon passed. The next day 'Duport came to have coffee in my dressing-room', and a few weeks later she had sufficiently forgiven him to lend him 500 francs.[26]

When he wanted to, Louis Duport could exert an almost overpowering charm, and indeed there was another aspect to his character that was irresistibly attractive. 'His name is associated with many acts of beneficence,' wrote a friend in a desire to put the record straight:

> Without having any children, he is a father to a numerous family. To these appealing qualities he adds very gentle manners and much natural wit that he cultivates by continuous study. That he speaks and writes well belies the malicious saying that a dancer's intelligence is to be found in his legs. To put it briefly, not content with stretching the limits of his art, composing charming ballets and performing them with a talent that leaves one at a loss for words in saying that he is the first dancer of Europe, he is still capable of being one of the best bred and most agreeable men in Paris.[27]

There were clearly two sides to this temperamental genius, and like many another, he did not fit easily within a complex organisation like the Opéra, into whose orbit he had flashed like a fiery meteor under its own propulsion. Many must have wondered how long Paris could keep him; but where else could he go?

[25] Collomb, diary entry of 20 July 1806.
[26] Collomb, diary entries of 31 July, 1 and 20 August 1806.
[27] *Opinion du parterre*, III, 271-2.

15

Two Choreographers and a Single Subject

Notwithstanding his share in the Austerlitz gala, 1806 had not opened very propitiously for Gardel. Duport and Henry were still pressing for opportunities to choreograph, and the rejection of his *Homme du destin* was an unwelcome affront to his self-esteem. Concerns such as these he would normally have taken in his stride, but he may have had other, more personal worries, to which Geoffroy alluded in his notice of a new opera, *Nephtali*, that was presented in April. This was the work of a young Italian, Felice Blangini, whose reputation hardly extended beyond those salons where the company was entertained by his graceful little ballads. However, he had had the good fortune to be in the good graces of Luçay, whose secretary had written the libretto for his opera. Gardel would have been well aware of this, and when the time came for him to arrange the dances, he had responded with a willingness that went beyond the normal call of duty, as Geoffroy thought it right to inform his readers:

> Despite having recently been dealt some bitter blows that, for a man with a long string of successes and glory behind him, must have made him exceedingly sensitive to the smallest worries, [M. Gardel] has given no further thought to personal sorrow. With the interests of the Opéra at stake, and taking no account of the extent of his responsibilities, he did not think it enough to compose the ballets, which were full of charm, but was prepared to take charge of every detail of the production and concern himself with everything else that might add interest to the action. For some little negligence had been shown in rehearsing this work of a young foreigner whose sudden favour had aroused a certain secret envy. M. Gardel, whose only thought was for the reputation of the theatre and the interests of art, devoted himself heart and soul to taking complete charge of the production, arranging the positions [of the singers], selecting the costumes and overlooking nothing that might liven up the dramatic performance. Such devotion on M.

> Gardel's part, which is typical of his character, should earn him greater respect and consideration than composing the finest ballet.[1]

It was now well over a year since Gardel had last presented a major ballet, and this may have been one of the 'sorrows' that Geoffroy had referred to. But once *Nephtali* was out of the way, Gardel was put out of his misery and at last was authorised to begin work on a new ballet. For his subject he once again turned to a work of literature. This time the narrative was not rooted in classical legend, but based on a recent work of fiction, *Paul et Virginie* by Bernardin de Saint-Pierre.

Posterity has a habit of playing tricks, and no author can ever be certain that his claim to fame will rest on the work that he himself might consider most worthy of his genius. And so, while Bernardin de Saint-Pierre considered his *magnum opus* to be his monumental *Etudes de la nature*, it was his sentimental tale of the love of Paul and Virginie, two children of nature brought up on a remote island in the Indian Ocean, that earned him his modicum of immortality. *Paul et Virginie* was appended to the third edition of the *Etudes* in 1788, and achieved an instant success that must have surprised the author himself. Published separately the following year with illustrations by Moreau *le jeune* and Joseph Vernet, it had remained a bestseller throughout the Revolution, and in 1806, carefully revised, was published in a *de luxe* edition. Long before that, in 1791, the story had inspired an *opéra-comique* by Rodolphe Kreutzer.[2] Now – inspired no doubt by the publication of the definitive edition, and possessing Edmond de Favière's libretto for the operatic version – two choreographers were about to transpose it to the ballet stage: Pierre Gardel at the Opéra and Jean Aumer at the Porte-Saint-Martin.

That *Paul et Virginie* should have inspired Gardel and Aumer independently was not entirely surprising, for the subject was then very much in the public psyche. In fact both projects were apparently already well advanced when the two men realised they would be in competition. There was also a further dimension to the situation. In April 1806 Napoleon began to turn his mind to reorganising the theatres of Paris, which he feared might become a source of political discontent. In the early years of the Revolution, the authorities had lifted all restrictions on opening new theatres and on the types of work that could be presented; but to the new Imperial régime, with its obsession for organisational tidiness in the cause of public security, such licence signalled potential danger. In the manner

[1] *Journal de l'Empire*, 18 April 1806.

[2] First performed at the Opéra-Comique on 15 January 1791.

of the time, the problem was resolved with speedy efficiency and little, if any, consultation with those who were primarily affected.

In April the Council of State agreed on two points: firstly, that having the theatres of the capital too close to one another was a potential source of unrest, and secondly, that the Opéra should be the only theatre to give ballets. The first point was based on security concerns, and the second, it seems, on the commercial need to make the Opéra more profitable or, more accurately, less of a liability on the state. Accordingly, on 8 June Napoleon signed a decree for the regulation of the city's theatres, which gave the Opéra a monopoly to present such ballets 'of a character suitable for that theatre as the Minister of the Interior should specify'. This was followed by Regulations issued by the Ministry which laid down that only the Opéra was permitted to give ballets of 'the noble and graceful kind, namely those with subjects based on mythology and history and in which the characters are gods, kings and heroes'; the only exclusion was to be ballets 'depicting country scenes or scenes of everyday life'.[3]

As this change was already in the wind, the decree would have come as no surprise to the Porte-Saint-Martin, whose Director, Dubois, had already been seeking a formula to minimise its effect on his theatre's policy regarding ballet. The lines along which his mind was working were made clear a few days before the decree in a letter to the *Courrier des spectacles* relating to Aumer's ballet, *Paul et Virginie*, which was then in rehearsal:

> *Paul et Virginie* has been billed incorrectly as a 'ballet-pantomime'. It is merely a pantomime in which dancing is only very accessory, and there is nothing about it that can justify its being called a ballet. Our intention is to revive the genre of pantomime, which is now almost forgotten, and which was very much in fashion in former times. For the past six weeks we have been busy with this work, and we hope to be able to offer it to the public shortly.[4]

This letter produced an immediate response from Gardel, who seemed particularly concerned to establish his own priority in the choice of subject:

> I would have remained silent about my ballet of *Paul et Virginie* had not M. Dubois's letter ... made me think of my enemies and the opportunity it might give them to spread a rumour that the idea of this subject (which is of course well known to everyone) only came to me after it did

[3] Minutes of a meeting of the Council of State, 18 April 1806. Decree and Regulations both dated 8 June 1806.

[4] *Courrier des spectacles*, 6 June 1806. Letter from Dubois to the Editor.

> to the authors of the work announced at the Porte-Saint-Martin. Let me just say, without casting any aspersions, that about two years ago I asked M. Kreutzer if he would object to my staging a ballet of *Paul et Virginie*. He assured me he would not, and added that if he were to be asked to write the music, the answer would be in the affirmative. I can add that the late Boullet, machinist of the Opéra, told a score of persons, who can vouch for it, that he would die content if he could stage my ballet of *Guillaume Tell* and that of *Paul et Virginie*. My work, which is a '*ballet*-pantomime', will probably be performed next Thursday at Saint-Cloud.[5]

It was a careful letter, keeping to the facts, and avoiding any reference to the reorganisation of the theatres. In his official position he was no doubt aware of what was in the wind, but he had already made known his personal view that theatres such as the Porte-Saint-Martin could be useful in providing a more appropriate testing ground for younger choreographers than did the Opéra itself.

It was now Aumer's turn to offer an explanation, for he too had his worries. Wishing to make it clear that he had in no way been underhand, he reinforced Dubois's point by very specifically referring to his new work as a pantomime:

> M. Gardel, in his reply to M. Dubois's letter, states that he has been working on *Paul et Virginie* for the past two years. From that, people might think that I am indebted either to him or to the indiscretion of his friends for the idea of my pantomime. I state *on my honour* that six weeks ago, when my work had already been read and accepted at the Théâtre de la Porte-Saint-Martin, I learned that M. Gardel was working on the same subject. I at once went to see him. I asked him to let me know whether the rumours that were circulating were true, and when he told me that he was planning to stage *Paul et Virginie*, I offered to discontinue rehearsing my own work. He was against that, telling me that the subject belonged to everyone, that he was making a one-act ballet on it which would only be performed at the Court, and that if he were to stage it in town he would put it into three acts.
>
> So I carried on, and now that all arrangements have been made for it to be presented very shortly, I am most anxious not to be accused of plagiarism. The respect and affection in which I hold, and will always

[5] *Courrier des spectacles*, 7 June 1806. Letter from Gardel to the Editor. Boullet had died in July 1804 from the effects of a fall during the staging of the opera *Les Bardes* – see Chapter 9.

hold, M. Gardel only further strengthen my desire that no such suspicion should fall on me.[6]

Gardel's *Paul et Virginie* was the first of the two versions of this tale to be seen when, on 12 June 1806, it was presented before Napoleon and the Court at Saint-Cloud. Twelve days later, on 24 June, it entered the repertory of the Opéra.

Bernardin de Saint-Pierre's story, on which both ballets were based, told of two children brought up in a state of nature by their mothers on the Ile de France, the island now known as Mauritius. Virginie is the daughter of Marguerite, whose neighbour, Mme Delatour, has a son of the same age, Paul. The two families live in idyllic harmony in the wild countryside, served by their black slaves, Domingo and Marie. The children roam free, and one day, coming across a runaway slave, they accompany him back to his cruel master and persuade him to forgive the fugitive. On their way home they lose their way. Virginie is exhausted, but they are located by their faithful dog and brought safely home by Domingo. In due course Virginie begins to enter puberty. When Mme Delatour's rich aunt requests her to return to France to share her last years, it is not she but Virginie who sails to Europe, to the great distress of those she is leaving behind, and most particularly Paul. Virginie's letters from France are not delivered, so the family does not know how badly she has been treated there, while Paul assumes she has forgotten him. They only discover that she is on her way back to the island when her ship is already standing off the coast. But before it can reach port, a violent hurricane smashes it against the rocks. Paul tries in vain to rescue her, and dies soon after of a broken heart, being survived only briefly by Marguerite and his mother.

As a contemporary observed, the scenario had cost Gardel no great effort of imagination, since it faithfully followed the libretto of Kreutzer's *opéra-comique*, even in opting for a happy ending, for it would have been unthinkable at that time to have ended a ballet with the drowning of its heroine – let alone the deaths of her lover and their grieving mothers that followed in the novel.

Gardel provided Kreutzer with a very precise specification for the overture. It was to suggest 'the dawn of a fine day, from time to time lit with flashes of summer lightning, and with distant rumbles of thunder creating a sense of foreboding that the day will not close without a storm'. At the rise of the curtain, Paul (Saint-Amant), Marguerite's son, and

[6] *Courrier des spectacles*, 8 June 1806. Letter from Aumer to the Editor.

Virginie (Mme Gardel), the daughter of Mme Delatour, are tending two large palm trees that had been planted to symbolise the love that has united them from early childhood. They engage in a playful little scene that closes with Paul climbing a tree and lowering a branch with his foot so that Virginie can pluck a juicy date. He has picked an even tastier one to offer to her, and he kisses her hand as she takes it. This scene is observed by the old slave Domingo (Aug. Vestris), who describes it to his wife Marie (Bigottini); and they in turn are observed by the children, who forgive them on condition that they teach them the *bamboula*.

This dance scene is followed by a dialogue between the two mothers (M. Saulnier as Marguerite and V. Saulnier II as Mme Delatour), who agree that the time has come for their children to marry. Lunch is then served, and the local Pastor (Lebel) arrives with a group of Creoles – another occasion for dancing. After the two mothers and the Pastor have retired to confer, Paul and Virginie are approached by an elderly black man, Zabi (Goyon), and his two children (V. Hullin, Rivière). Zabi describes the maltreatment he has received at the hands of his owner, who has sold him to another master but refuses to let him take his children with him. Paul and Virginie decide to seek out the owner and intercede with him. When the Pastor and the two ladies reappear, they are surprised not to see their children. But they are distracted by the arrival of another visitor, the island's Governor (Milon), who has brought a letter from Mme Delatour's rich aunt, inviting Virginie to France. It argues how much it is in Virginie's interest to comply, but the mothers and their slaves are heartbroken by this turn of events. At that point they realise that the children are missing. As a violent storm breaks overhead, Domingo is sent in search of them. He is undecided which way to go, but hearing the dog bark gives him the idea to fetch an article of Paul's clothing to offer to the animal as a scent.

When the second act opens, a group of slaves led by their owner, Dorval (Godefroy), are searching for Zabi. After they leave, Paul and Virginie appear, the former bearing a child balanced on each shoulder. Zabi is at the end of his strength, but they enjoy a brief rest before Dorval is heard returning. Paul boldly faces him, but it is Virginie, pleading on her knees, who persuades him not to separate the old slave from his children. At this Paul is so delighted that he kisses Virginie on the forehead. She blushes and recoils in embarrassment, strangely troubled. They now realise they are lost, but Virginie is exhausted. Paul offers to carry her on his shoulders, but she refuses out of modesty. A dog is then heard barking. Rescue is at hand, and Domingo comes into sight. From him they learn of the Governor's visit, although he conceals the plan for Virginie to go to France. The storm clouds are now gathering, and the rain has turned the river into a torrent. The problem of carrying Virginie home is solved by Zabi and his friends making a litter out of branches; accompanied by a band of rejoicing slaves, Paul and Virginie begin their journey back.

For the third act, the scene reverts to that of the first act, except that several familiar trees have been uprooted by the storm. While Marie keeps a lookout for the children, Mme Delatour weeps at the thought of losing Virginie. Soon the wanderers return, and the gifts that the Governor had brought are unpacked. A few are given away, and then Virginie picks out some tambourines, which are seized upon by the Creoles, who begin to dance. But such jollity does not dispel the sadness of the two mothers, who still have to break the news to the children. Each now leads her child into her cabin, while Domingo discovers a mirror among the gifts and can hardly contain his wonder at seeing his reflection. Paul then emerges, in a state of despair. He stands facing the two women with his arms crossed, as if frozen by shock, before bursting out in reproaches. To lose her will be the death of him, and he is determined to follow her.

At length he is calmed by the wise words of Domingo, who reminds him of his duty to stay with his mother. Drum-rolls then announce the return of the Governor to accompany Virginie to the ship. Paul's plea to accompany her is rejected, and the sound of a cannon announces that the ship is ready to sail. Paul has to be restrained as Virginie leaves, stretching out her arms towards him. His misery is compounded by the arrival of the Pastor and a band of well-wishers who have come to celebrate the marriage, for there has been no time to tell them of the change of plan. But then another, more violent storm breaks. Paul climbs a nearby rock, only to see the ship driven on to the rocks. Before the vessel goes down, Virginie is seen on the deck, with a black man at her feet begging her to let him save her. Paul dives into the water, and after a few moments of suspense, emerges bearing the unconscious Virginie in his arms. She revives, and the Governor, moved by Paul's bravery, realises that he can no longer be a party to removing Virginie from the island. He offers to endow her with a fortune so that the couple can marry.

In a note to his scenario, Gardel expressed regret at not having time to conclude the ballet with the marriage celebrations, which he had planned in the form of a magnificent fête containing dances of several different nationalities. Perhaps it was as well that time was short, for a conventional *divertissement* would have undoubtedly diminished the dramatic impact of the rescue; and Gardel may not have realised how sure was his touch in conveying the Rousseauesque sentiment and simplicity of the original tale. However, the curtailment of the fête upset the balance in that nearly all the dances were placed in the first act, which was longer than both the other two combined. The second and third acts were mainly devoted to pantomime, telling a story familiar to nearly everyone in the audience, the only danced passages being the exit of the characters at the end of Act II and the *gigue* danced by the wedding party on their arrival in Act III. Geoffroy, however, considered that the ballet was all the better for being shorn of the fête. 'M. Gardel knows his art too well to introduce his dances at the wrong moment,' he observed. 'Some might have wished the ballet to have ended with a *divertissement*, but surely the main characters were in a state of such emotion that dancing was out of the question.'[7] And after seeing the ballet a second time, the critic was even more convinced: 'It touches the heart and causes tears to flow.'[8]

Gardel need not have mourned the brilliant *divertissement*, for what he had produced was a work that respected the literary source as faithfully as could be achieved within prevailing theatrical conventions, while conveying the *couleur locale* of the tropics – not only in the scenery and costumes, but also in the action and dances. Most unusually, neither Paul nor Virginie was given a variation, the dancing being confined to character dances for the blacks, mulattos and Creoles that were inserted as occasion offered. As Geoffroy concluded:

> Never was a subject more favourable to dancing than *Paul et Virginie*. Everyone knows that blacks have a passion for dancing; it is their sole consolation, and they throw themselves into it with unbelievable ardour; the suppleness of their limbs and the vivacity of their movements have no equal ... The dances are full of taste and invention, and have a local colour that is truly novel. And strange to relate, there is not a single pirouette to be seen.[9]

All four dances that were noticed in the reviews were conceived to give an idea of the black culture of the Ile de France, even if their authenticity may have been questionable. The *pas des nègres* was probably danced by an equal number of each sex, with the men vigorously wielding batons of bamboo with great precision. The dance for Domingo and Marie was probably what the scenario referred to as the *bamboula*,[10] in which the only moment to have survived through contemporary accounts was a passage, which some found in dubious taste, when Marie scratches

[7] *Journal de l'Empire*, 26 June 1806.
[8] *Journal de l'Empire*, 29 June 1806.
[9] *Journal de l'Empire*, 26 June 1806.

Domingo's curly head. The arrival of the Pastor was followed by more dancing by the accompanying Creoles, as well as a character *pas de deux* in the *comique* style by Beaupré and Chevigny. And finally there was Domingo's dance with the mirror, full of comical *lazzi*.[11]

Since the plot would have been known to practically everyone in the audience, the casting of the title rôles was crucial to the ballet's success. There could be no question of Virginie being played by anyone other than Marie Gardel, who, at the age of thirty-six, still possessed the artistry, figure and lightness of touch to appear convincingly as a girl experiencing her first love. To Geoffroy the sensitivity, grace and delicacy of her performance was beyond compare. 'No other actress combines the modesty and chastity needed for the expression of the most tender love better than she',[12] he wrote. As Paul, Charles Saint-Amant, some nine years her junior, made a perfect companion, conveying all 'the tenderness and warmth of first love' with a moderation that was an object lesson to many of his colleagues.[13] So well did they fit their parts that no one commented on the fact that both happened to be considerably older than the Saulnier sisters who played their mothers.

The most unusual feature of the ballet lay in the sympathetic manner, albeit sentimentalised, in which the black characters were portrayed. In those days black faces were a rare sight in a European city, and the prevailing belief that the coloured races were inferior was somewhat akin to the attitude that a person's station in life was ordained by God. In colonies such as the Ile de France, the purpose of the black population was regarded as providing labour for the exploitation of the produce of the land. Bernardin de Saint-Pierre, who had spent several years there, not only had been aware of their enforced commercial contribution, but had also observed happier and more personal relationships that could be formed in a sympathetic household. Mme Delatour and Marguerite each possesses a slave who is well treated and content and has been admitted as part of the family unit; the bond between mistress and slave is shown to

[10] References to the *bamboula* can be found as far back as the early eighteenth century (Père J.-B. Labat, *Nouvelle Rélation de l'Afrique occidentale* (Paris, 1728), IV, 155)). It seems to have originated in West Africa, and apparently took its name from a type of tambourine that provided the accompaniment. It was brought by slaves to Haïti and Louisiana, and inspired one of Louis Moreau Gottschalk's most characteristic piano solos.

[11] In the mid-nineteenth century, a 'coconut dance' which purported to have been taken from a production of *Paul et Virginie* in about 1814, was taught by a dancer from the Lyons theatre named Curet and performed during the carnival festival in either Aix-en-Provence or Avignon. (François Vidal, *Lou Tambourin, musique, poésie et prose provençales* (Aix-en-Provence, 1864), brought to my attention by Professor Theresa Buckland.)

[12] *Journal de l'Empire*, 26 June 1806.

[13] *Gazette de France*, 25 June 1806.

be strong, and the slave's fidelity is a guiding theme of both the novel and the ballet.

If anything, the importance of the black characters was even more prominent in the ballet than in the novel, particularly in the case of Domingo. That rôle was given to Auguste Vestris, whose rendering became, without a doubt, the finest dramatic achievement of his career. Since the part also contained a significant amount of dancing, and dancing of a most novel character, which sought to convey the natural ebullience of the black man, he secured a double triumph, for it was observed that he never departed from the true character of his rôle. For this he was indebted to Gardel, who would have permitted no concessions in favour of classical technique.

To the Paris audience, the dances of the blacks in *Paul et Virginie* seemed 'truly local and novel', and in the course of time, as Vestris became more and more absorbed into his rôle, his performance became increasingly richer in detail and depth. Not for a moment did he seem to step out of character, not even when he had to melt into the background – as happened during a moment of repose in the *pas des nègres*, when he lay on the ground lightly tapping his tamtam. But his great moment came in the highly amusing dance with the mirror; this was full of amusing little touches 'in which Domingo contemplates himself in the mirror, hands it to his mistress, shows it off to all the blacks, and abandons himself to all the intoxication of surprise and delight.'[14] At the end, his reward was 'to be applauded as he had been in his finest days; not for a long time has a rôle brought him so much honour.'[15]

Domingo fell into the category of the devoted slave, which was an acceptable concept to the Eurocentric society of nineteenth-century Paris. The part of Zabi, on the other hand, presented the black man as a victim, which was not so palatable: it revealed the brutal side of racial relations in the colonies that those who had never come into direct contact with it preferred not to believe. Geoffroy was honest enough to call Zabi's long-drawn-out pantomime describing his sufferings at the hands of the slave-owner 'one of the most interesting scenes of the ballet ... perfectly mimed by Goyon',[16] but other observers found its realism painfully embarrassing and distasteful. Nothing, it seems, could have been more explicit than the old slave's description of his whipping almost to the point of fainting with the pain; and the sight of his lacerations, graphically painted on his body, was too much for some sensitive spectators. There can be little doubt that

[14] Courrier des spectacles, 25 June 1806.
[15] *Journal de l'Empire*, 26 June 1806.
[16] *Journal de l'Empire*, 26 June 1806.

it was this reaction that lay behind the cries of 'fairly shrill disapproval'[17] that were heard through the applause when the curtain came down at the end of the first performance at the Opéra. However, these were quickly drowned when Gardel was called to receive his ovation, not only from the public but also from several of the dancers, who rushed to embrace him.

Gardel, however, had heard the sounds of discontent, and shortened the offending scene without depriving Goyon of the effectiveness of his rôle. Indeed, the tightening made it even more impressive, for three years later Geoffroy could still speak of it as 'heart-rending'.[18] At the same time, in response to complaints that the likes of Bigottini and Chevigny had been unrecognisable, orders were given to change the make-up used by the black characters from black to a shade of brown. Thus all objections were met, and thereafter, throughout the twenty-two years that it remained in the repertory, it would never cease to appeal to the public. Until 1821, not a year went by without it being given at least one performance. When it was revived in 1826, it received 16 performances, more than in any other single year of its existence. It reached its hundredth performance on 26 April 1826, and was last given two years later.

Over the years a succession of younger dancers appeared in the principal rôles. As Paul, Saint-Amant was succeeded by Beaulieu (1808), Albert (1811), for whom a *Polacca a rondo* by Carafa was added, and Ferdinand (1813); and in the 1826 revival Lise Noblet played it in travesty. Marie Gardel's successors as Virginie were Marinette Boissière (1817) and Pauline Montessu (1826). Vestris, who had continued to play Domingo until his retirement in 1818, was succeeded by Ferdinand, but appeared in it just once more, at his benefit in 1826.[19] On that memorable evening, there were two other dancers playing the rôles they had created – Milon as the Governor and Antoine Godefroy as the slave-owner.

* * *

The Opéra had long turned a blind eye to Aumer's engagement as *maître de ballet* at the Porte-Saint-Martin. His activity there had begun modestly enough by reviving some of the lighter ballets of his teacher, Dauberval, and his first original creation, *Rosina et Lorenzo*, had caused little stir.

[17] *Journal de Paris*, 25 June 1806.

[18] *Journal de l'Empire*, 21 July 1809.

[19] August Bournonville was present on this occasion, and wrote to his father that, as Domingo, Vestris was 'still very astonishing'. (Bournonville, *Lettres*, I, 109.)

In the spring of 1806, however, he achieved his first major success with a tear-jerking melodramatic pantomime called *Jenny*, in which Marie Quériau, as the eponymous heroine, tore at the emotions of her audiences as her moods swung from the joy of motherhood to suicidal despair and back again for a happy ending. Jenny has married in secret and, unknown to her father, is the mother of a little boy. Her husband is called to the colours, and news is brought that he has been wounded in battle. Then her cottage catches fire, and although she rescues her son, the calamity reveals her secret. Her father disowns her, and she runs to her mother's grave with the intention of throwing herself off a cliff. However, in the nick of time, her husband returns.

It was heady stuff, and Mme Quériau's histrionics, enhanced by the musical accompaniment, were awe-inspiring in their emotional impact. She was by turn 'touching, terrifying, beautiful, and, to echo a tribute paid her by a dancer of the Opéra celebrated for her pantomime, sublime.'[20] News of her extraordinary performance was quickly spread by the press and by word of mouth, and within a few days queues were forming on the Boulevard several hours before the doors opened.

Two weeks later Mme Quériau was rewarded with a benefit, treating her supporters to two very contrasting interpretations: Jenny and Lise in *Le Fille mal gardée*. Recognised among the audience that evening was the doyen of ballet-masters, Noverre, now an old man of 79 but still 'full of verve, wit and taste', who was heard singing her praises.[21]

By then, Aumer's plans to stage his version of *Paul et Virginie* were well advanced. The seeds of the project could be traced back to 1795, when he was dancing at the King's Theatre, London, as a young man of twenty-one. There the ballet-master, Giacomo Onorati, had staged what was almost certainly the first balletic rendering of the novel in which Marie-Louise Hiligsberg and Victoria Del Caro were featured respectively as Paul and Virginie.[22] It may have been Del Caro's reappearance that revived his interest in the theme and spurred him to produce his own version. It was certainly a revealing coincidence that her arrival in Paris in March 1806 predated the acceptance of the scenario by only a month.

Aumer had probably marked the rôle of Paul for Marie Quériau from the beginning and, for Virginie, required a younger dancer than Del Caro, who was not after all offered a contract at the Porte-Saint-Martin. All

[20] *Courrier des spectacles*, 15 April 1806.

[21] *Courrier des spectacles*, 30 April 1806.

[22] Onorati's ballet, with music by Joseph Mazzinghi, was first performed at the King's Theatre on 26 March 1795. It was given a new lease of life after Hiligsberg revived it for her benefit performance in 1802, with Mme Laborie as Virginia.

its concern was noted when the Council of State began discussing placing restrictions on the secondary theatres. Only months before, the Porte-Saint-Martin had had complete freedom to present ballets, but now this was severely curtailed. It could justify presenting *Les Deux Creoles* only by maintaining, somewhat speciously perhaps, that it was not a ballet but a pantomime. But now the Opéra was to show its hand. In July Aumer was presented with an ultimatum: unless he resigned his post as ballet-master of the Porte-Saint-Martin and withdrew his ballets, his contract as a dancer with the Opéra would be terminated. When he sought an explanation, he was told that his choice of a subject similar to one used at the Opéra had encouraged rivalry between the two theatres and that the success of his ballets at the Porte-Saint-Martin was having an adverse effect on the Opéra's receipts. Luçay made it clear that there could be no question of rescinding the order, and with as good a grace as he could muster, Aumer bowed to the inevitable. He wrote to Luçay:

> An example had to be made, and it is I against whom the authorities strike. I do not complain, and only put it down to fate. As you have given me an order, Monsieur Prefect, I have no hesitation in obeying and giving the Opéra precedence over the Porte-Saint-Martin ... I only beg one favour – to be permitted to employ my feeble talents in the service of the Opéra as assistant to the two *maîtres des ballets*, MM. Gardel and Milon; they have more than once expressed the wish to see me reinstated. Would it not be fair to give me a little compensation for the loss I have incurred, so that I am not completely deprived of earnings? I have a ballet in three acts which I could submit within a fortnight to the jury of the Opéra.[30]

Aumer had reached his decision only after careful thought. In fact, he had delayed so long in replying that the Director began to fear that he was not prepared to give way. But in the end Aumer had realised it was in his interest to retain his position at the Opéra and the goodwill of the authorities, and the wisdom of his decision was soon to be revealed. For in 1807, in Napoleon's reorganisation of the theatres, the Porte-Saint-Martin would be closed; the ballet that Aumer had mentioned in his letter to Luçay would be accepted, and in the years ahead he was to be increasingly recognised as the main contender for the succession when the time came for Gardel and Milon to retire.

[30] Arch. Nat., AJ^{13} 79. Luçay to Bonet, 4 July 1806; Bonet to Gardel, 12 July 1806. AJ^{13} 65 (170, 171). Aumer to Luçay, n.d. and 17 August 1806.

16

Mademoiselle Aubry's Fall

Gardel could have wished for no more devoted assistant than Louis Milon. Patient and uncomplaining, this faithful servant gave his superior such constant support that one may wonder whether Gardel began to take him for granted. Milon evinced no desire to be anything but a second-in-command, and never voiced disappointment at being given so few opportunities to exercise his very considerable choreographic skill. His *Noces de Gamache* had been a popular success, but six years had now passed since it was first given, and, apart from the disastrous *Lucas et Laurette* and opportunities to arrange dances in the operas, he had remained creatively inactive. This was not, however, for want of projects, but three that he had recently proposed were modest and uninspiring: *La Naissance de Vénus*, which reached the estimate stage; *Le Pouvoir de la danse, ou la victime sauvée*, which was approved, subject to a change of title; and *Athalante*, which was returned to him with a note of certain changes required by the jury.[1]

No more would be heard of *Athalante*, because a few months later a much more promising subject fell into his hands. This was based on the story, in Homer's *Odyssey*, of Ulysses' return to Ithaca after being lost for twenty years, to discover his wife Penelope beset by an arrogant band of suitors.

The idea had originally been suggested to Gardel by Napoleon himself, but it had been passed on to Milon, presumably because Gardel was then heavily occupied with a planned revival of *Ninette à la cour* and the Emperor's suggestion could not be brushed aside. Preparations for both productions went ahead simultaneously, but the time came when a decision had to be made as to which would be given priority. Accordingly, early in October 1806 Bonet called a meeting of the Committee of Administration. When Gardel reported that he would need only a month or six weeks to have *Ninette* ready, Milon might well have feared that his ballet

[1] Arch. Nat. AJ^{13} 88: Bonet to Luçay, 27 Prairial, Year XII (15 February 1804); AJ^{13} 73 (XIV): Budget dated 12 Messidor, Year XIII (8 July 1805); AJ^{13} 66: Reading jury's report, 9 Nivôse, Year XIV (30 December 1805).

would be shelved. *Ninette*, however, required the services of from fifteen to eighteen horses, together with their riders; and Boutron, the chief machinist, drew attention to the dangerous condition of the stage, which, he pointed out, would have to be re-laid if horses were to be used. For Milon this was the saving grace; the Committee was not convinced that the expense involved for *Ninette* would be justified, and its preference for *Le Retour d'Ulysse* was intimated to the Palace with a request for instructions.

By then the resumption of hostilities made it likely that Napoleon would miss the first performance, but during the campaign he would still find time to concern himself with the affairs of his Opéra. The peace that had followed the Austerlitz campaign had not held. Shortly before the meeting at the Opéra, he had left Paris to deal with a threat posed by Prussia. Within a month he had won a decisive victory at Jena, and had proceeded in triumph to Potsdam. Among the dispatches waiting for him on his arrival was the budget for *Le Retour d'Ulysse*; and it was from Frederick the Great's Palace of Sans-Souci on 25 October that, in a letter to Fouché, the Minister of Police, he gave the order for the ballet to be produced:

> I am sending you my approval of the expenditure relating to the production of the ballet *Le Retour d'Ulysse*. Let me have a detailed account of this ballet, and attend the first performance to make sure there is nothing bad in it – you know what I mean. However, the subject seems a good one; it was I who suggested it to Gardel.[2]

In Milon's scenario, the first act opens to show Penelope (Clotilde), whose husband Ulysses, King of Ithaca, has been lost for many years, being importuned by suitors seeking her hand. She has long kept them at bay by the stratagem of telling them she must first finish her tapestry, and each night, unsuspected, unpicking the work she had done during the day. But the suitors are now becoming restive, and they coerce a soothsayer Leodes (Lebel) to announce, on oracular authority, that Ulysses is dead and that the time has come for the Queen to choose a new husband. The suitors are all buoyed up with hope, and the most ardent, Antinoüs (Aumer), boldly declares his passion. Counselled by her son, Telemachus (Saint-Amant), Penelope prevaricates and reminds them that her tapestry is still unfinished. Telemachus's tutor, Mentor (Deschamps), who is none other than the goddess Minerva in another form, now reveals to the

[2] Napoleon, *Correspondance*, XIII, 506 (Letter no. 11,079).

young prince that the oracle was false and that his father will return. Angered by Telemachus's sudden outburst of authority on receiving this heartening news, four of the suitors plot his murder.

The second act begins with Ulysses (Milon) landing at Ithaca, where his first thought is to give thanks to Minerva (Aubry), who discloses Penelope's predicament to him in a dream and warns that his son's life is in danger. Indeed, no sooner does Telemachus appear than he is set upon by four assailants. With Ulysses' aid, the attackers are driven into a grotto where, on the intervention of Minerva, they are swept to their destruction by a powerful flood that bursts from the rocks. Telemachus recognises his father, who enjoins him to strict secrecy. Minerva then transforms Ulysses into a decrepit old man, in which form he assures some passing shepherds that their king is alive. The act closes on a scene of rustic rejoicing.

In the third act Minerva surreptitiously introduces Ulysses into the palace, where he is shocked by the unseemly behaviour of the suitors towards his wife. But danger awaits, for the suitors have discovered her stratagem and force her into agreeing to choose a husband from among them that very day. In her despair Penelope is on the point of killing herself, when Ulysses, still unrecognised, comes forward to snatch the dagger from her hand, assuring her that she will see her husband again. He reminds her that in the palace is to be found the bow with which Ulysses had fought during the siege of Troy, and this he hands to Penelope with instructions to choose only a man who has the strength to string it. Meanwhile Penelope's faithful attendant Eurycleia (Chevigny) has recognised Ulysses from a scar, but he calms her trembling by swearing her to silence. Confident that they have bent Penelope to their will, the suitors now gather. They are scandalised by Telemachus's desire to invite the decrepit old man to the contest; failing to have him ejected, they shower him with insults. Penelope offers the bow to Antinoüs, the only suitor bold enough to take the test; but, unable to string it, he throws it aside. Ulysses then picks it up, and proves his superior skill. The suitors rise in fury, but Ulysses takes an arrow and kills Antinoüs. The remaining suitors rush to take up arms, but the appearance of Minerva on a fiery cloud puts them to flight and they are dispatched by a thunderbolt. All danger now over, Ulysses casts off his disguise and, reunited with his family, resumes the throne.

Great expectations were held of this stirring tale, and when the day of the première – 27 February 1807 – arrived, the Empress Josephine was in her box and the house was full to over-crowding.

As the performance drew towards its close, all involved were congratu-

30. to 32. Front and back views of the Delaistre bust, and detail showing Gardel's hair arrangement. (Bibliothèque-Musée de l'Opéra: © Séverine Darrousset)

33. Jacques-Louis David's painting *The Oath of the Horatii*, which inspired passages in Gardel's unperformed *Guillaume Tell* and his ballet for Porta's opera *Les Horaces* (1800). (Musée du Louvre: © Photo RMN Paris)
34. Jacques-Louis David's painting *The Rape of the Sabine Women*, which inspired the stirring climax of Milon's *L'Enlèvement des Sabines*. (Musée du Louvre: © Photo RMN Paris)

35. Mme Anatole in Gardel's ballet in the opera *Les Bayadères*. Painting by Sébastien Coeuré. (Collection of Jean-Louis Tamvaco)

36. Louis-Benoît Picard, Director of the Opéra, 1807–15. Drawn by Crignier, engraved by Jamont. (Bibliothèque Nationale de France: © Cliché BNF Paris)

lating themselves, with every apparent good reason, when the air was rent by a panic-stricken cry from the stage. Horrified, the audience watched as the cloud on which Minerva was making her descent tipped over in mid-air, sending the goddess tumbling on to the stage some twenty feet below. The Empress was seen to throw up her hands in distress before fainting into the arms of one of her ladies. The initial fear that Mlle Aubry, the luckless Minerva, might have been killed were removed when she picked herself up; but the effort was too much for her. Collapsing, she was carried into the wings by her comrades.

The house was in a turmoil. The orchestra had fallen silent, and angry cries of indignation could be heard above sounds of hysterical weeping. Minutes passed, the noise subsiding to an uneasy murmur, but still the audience remained as if rooted to their seats. After a seemingly interminable wait, a dancer appeared from the wings to reassure the public that Mlle Aubry's life was not in danger; she was severely injured and was receiving skilled medical attention. On that inconclusive note the première of Milon's ballet was brought to its premature close.

Had the accident occurred at the general rehearsal in the morning, it would not have had the unfortunate consequences that were to follow. But happening before a packed house, and in the presence of the Empress, it assumed the scale of a major scandal. All too unwillingly the poor victim had, so to speak, fallen to fame. When she had seen the programme she must have been flattered to find her name at the top of the cast-list, placed there not, of course, because of any prestige of her own, but because Milon had taken the view that a goddess took precedence over mere mortals. Until that evening few had heard of Angélique Aubry. Although trained in the School of Dance, she had been transferred to the opera chorus when she grew too tall for the *corps de ballet*. But recently her acting ability had been recognised and she had been given additional duties as a mime. All the same, it must have seemed unlikely that fame would ever beckon to one of such modest employ; but it had now come to her in most unwelcome circumstances, and she was even honoured with a brief but sympathetic tribute from the great Geoffroy:

> To a magnificent carriage, nobility and majesty, she added a lively gift of expression and a great talent for pantomime. The unfortunate woman so loved her art, and was so attached to her duties, that deluding herself as to the consequences of her accident, one of her greatest worries on the day after her accident was the fear of losing the rôle of Minerva.[3]

[3] *Journal de l'Empire*, 6 March 1807.

Her concern was all too understandable, for she was relying on her modest career continuing until her period of service entitled her to a pension. At the time of her accident, at the age of nearly 30, she was the sole support of her daughter Fanny, then a pupil in the School of Dance, for whose private classes she was paying out of her slender means.

Her accident and the attendant publicity made it a matter of public concern, and a medical report was circulated the very next day:

> As a result of her fall this artiste has suffered, firstly, a bruise on the forehead with slight abrasion; secondly, a fracture, with laceration and dislocation, at the lower end of the right fore-arm; thirdly, dislocation of the little toe on the same side, as well as considerable bleeding. All these injuries were accompanied by shock.
>
> In spite of all the treatment given to this artiste, it is not yet possible to give a definite prognosis on her future condition.[4]

Josephine's kind heart went out to the unfortunate victim. She at once sent a donation of 1200 francs, and at a ball at the Tuileries sought further donations from her guests. According to Geoffroy, it was on her initiative that a special performance was given at the Opéra for Mlle Aubry's benefit, for which those taking part donated their services. It was on that occasion that the second performance of *La Retour d'Ulysse* was given (this being, of course, the first performance of the complete ballet). The appearance of Minerva on her cloud must have been awaited with considerable dread, but happily good taste and prudence had prevailed, and, to everyone's relief, the new Minerva made her entrance from the wings.

The consequences of the accident were to be far-reaching. Suspicion at once fell on the newly appointed chief machinist, Gromaire – a protégé of Luçay – who virtually admitted his guilt by making himself scarce. This resulted in a hiatus in the scenic department, for his predecessor, Etienne Boutron, a man of long experience who had succeeded the almost legendary Pierre Boullet in 1804, was reluctant to return. Boutron had soon seen through the shallow, ambitious young man, who conceived not only a dislike for his superior but an ambition to displace him and assume the post of chief machinist for himself. To achieve this he had set about making life difficult for Boutron by subverting the stagehands and undermining Boutron's authority at every turn. Finally, Boutron, who was a gentle character and found it too distressing to cope with the situation,

[4] Arch. Nat., AJ^{13} 74 (X). Report by Dr Latour, 28 February 1807.

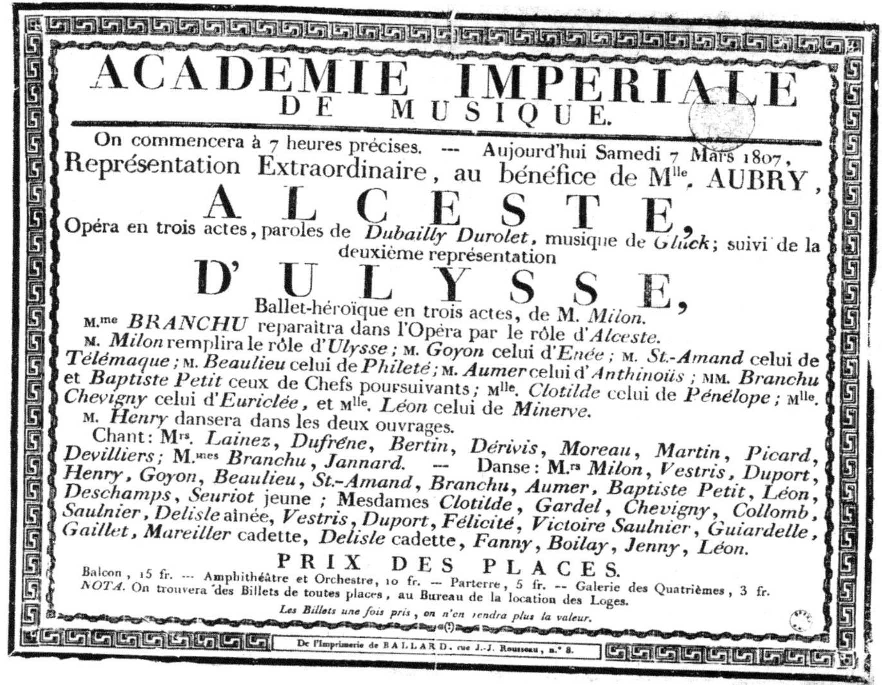

ACADEMIE IMPERIALE
DE MUSIQUE.

On commencera à 7 heures précises. --- Aujourd'hui Samedi 7 Mars 1807,
Représentation Extraordinaire, au bénéfice de Mlle. AUBRY,

ALCESTE,

Opéra en trois actes, paroles de *Dubailly Durolet*, musique de *Gluck*; suivi de la deuxième représentation

D'ULYSSE,

Ballet-héroïque en trois actes, de M. *Milon*.

Mme *BRANCHU* reparaîtra dans l'Opéra par le rôle d'*Alceste*.

M. *Milon* remplira le rôle d'*Ulysse* ; M. *Goyon* celui d'*Enée* ; M. *St.-Amand* celui de *Télémaque* ; M. *Beaulieu* celui de *Phileté* ; M. *Aumer* celui d'*Anthinoüs* ; MM. *Branchu* et *Baptiste Petit* ceux de Chefs poursuivants ; Mlle. *Clotilde* celui de *Pénélope* ; Mlle. *Chevigny* celui d'*Euriclée*, et Mlle. *Léon* celui de *Minerve*.

M. *Henry* dansera dans les deux ouvrages.

Chant : M[rs]. *Lainez*, *Dufrêne*, *Bertin*, *Dérivis*, *Moreau*, *Martin*, *Picard*, *Devilliers* ; Mmes *Branchu*, *Jannard*. --- Danse : Mrs *Milon*, *Vestris*, *Duport*, *Henry*, *Goyon*, *Beaulieu*, *St.-Amand*, *Branchu*, *Aumer*, *Baptiste Petit*, *Léon*, *Deschamps*, *Seuriot* jeune ; Mesdames *Clotilde*, *Gardel*, *Chevigny*, *Collomb*, *Saulnier*, *Delisle* aînée, *Vestris*, *Duport*, *Félicité*, *Victoire Saulnier*, *Guiardelle*, *Gaillet*, *Mareiller* cadette, *Delisle* cadette, *Fanny*, *Boilay*, *Jenny*, *Léon*.

PRIX DES PLACES.

Balcon, 15 fr. --- Amphithéâtre et Orchestre, 10 fr. --- Parterre, 5 fr. --- Galerie des Quatrièmes, 3 fr.

NOTA. On trouvera des Billets de toutes places, au Bureau de la location des Loges.

Les Billets une fois pris, on n'en rendra plus la valeur.

De l'Imprimerie de BALLARD, rue J.-J. Rousseau, n.° 8.

Playbill for the second performance of Le Retour d'Ulysse. *(Bibliothèque-Musée de l'Opéra: © Cliché BNF Paris)*

tendered his resignation. He had thus played into the hands of Gromaire, whose promotion from second to chief machinist had come as a foregone conclusion.

Boutron had retired to lick his wounds. Had it not been for Mlle Aubry's accident, he might have slipped into obscurity. But fortunately he had not lost touch with loyal friends at the Opéra, from whom he soon began to hear disturbing tales. He was at last to be drawn out of his silence by reading in a daily journal a long justification by Gromaire, blaming the accident on a couple of stagehands, whose negligence, it was asserted, was part of a plot to bring about his downfall. It was through their deliberate action that the back-cloth, which should have been drawn up as Minerva's cloud descended, had been allowed to swing forward and tip up the *gloire*, causing Mlle Aubry to fall out.[5]

At this point Boutron realised it was his duty to respond to Gromaire's allegations and to place the true facts before the public. In a letter to the

[5] *Publiciste*, 10 March 1807.

Courrier des spectacles he explained how Gromaire had consistently undermined his authority by turning the stagehands against him to achieve an ambition to be appointed in his place. Turning to what had actually happened on the evening of the accident, Boutron explained the established safety procedure, whereby the machinery to be used in the evening was tested in the morning, after which the stage would be closed until late in the afternoon. This golden rule had been broken. On the morning of the première, Milon, after finishing his rehearsal, invited Gromaire to test the machinery, and in particular the *gloire*. This Gromaire had neglected to do, but unfortunately for him several conscientious stagehands were so shocked that they told Boutron that Gromaire had said to his men: 'It is eleven o'clock. Let us go and have our dinner and say we have done the test.'

Had they done their duty, they would have discovered and rectified the fault that had caused Mlle Aubry's fall – the buckle attaching Minerva's stool to the base of the *gloire* had not been fastened. As for Gromaire's allegation of negligence against the two stagehands, Boutron pointed out that if Gromaire had noticed, as he ought to have done, that the backcloth was becoming entangled with the ropes, he could easily have stopped the *gloire*'s descent by a shouted order.[6]

Since Gromaire was very much Luçay's man, there had been little Bonet could do to prevent Boutron's earlier resignation. The accident would be Gromaire's undoing, but the Director had to tread carefully, seeing that it might be difficult to convince Luçay that his protégé was at fault. Nevertheless he did his best to protect the two stagehands whom Gromaire had implicated.

However, there were others within the Opéra whose hands were not so tied, and whose very safety depended on the expertise of the chief machinist. These were the singers and dancers, and the veteran tenor Etienne Lainez boldly took the initiative to see that something was done. Had Napoleon been in Paris, their obvious recourse would have been a direct appeal, but in his absence there was another channel to the throne. No one among the artistes was in doubt as to where the blame lay, as emerged at a private meeting which Emile Collomb recorded in her diary:

> All M. Luçay's enemies met this morning to go to the Empress to demand the reinstatement of Boutron. The meeting was held at Mlle Chevigny's. The *feuilleton* articles are, it is said, written at Lainez's.[7]

[6] *Courrier des spectacles*, 16 March 1807.
[7] Collomb, entry of 3 March 1807.

In this move to bring the scandal to the notice of the public – and to that of Luçay's master, the Emperor – the artistes had the valuable support of Geoffroy, who in his *feuilleton* hinted at the existence of a cover-up and left his informed readers in little doubt that he was pointing his finger at Luçay:

> To go by what the papers say, there is no need to worry about Mlle Aubry. She has a slight bruise on her forehead, apparently such as a child might suffer from falling down while running, a broken arm and a dislocated little toe on the left or right foot – a mere bagatelle, hardly worth thinking about. But the truth of the matter is that Mlle Aubry is in a deplorable condition. She is in great pain. New complications, such as usually follow a great shock, are reported daily, and if she survives she will lose an arm, be crippled and deprived of her livelihood, the fruits of her talent and resources of every sort. What is one to make of reports whose only purpose seems to be to distract one's attention and the pity that a misfortune such as this naturally arouses in a person of feeling? Can it be that the victim's cries are being deliberately muffled to protect the reputation of those who have sacrificed her?[8]

One result of this article was to attract public attention back to Mlle Aubry. She was indeed in a sorry state. Internal injuries and hæmorrhaging were reported on March 7; two days later the news was a little better – her arm had been reset and her temperature was falling.[9] But she was not out of danger, as the public was to read on the 21st, more than three weeks after the accident:

> Public interest in Mlle Aubry's deplorable condition is growing daily. The porter of the building where she lives is unable to cope with recording the names of all those who call to enquire after her. Sadly, we learn that her health is now giving much cause for alarm, and that to the dreaded consequences of her fall are now added a putrid fever, attacks of nerves and every sign of desperate illness. Yesterday the doctors held a conference under M. Corvisart. Apparently the treatment so far given to the unfortunate mother of a family has been approved by the leading members of the profession.[10]

[8] *Journal de l'Empire*, 6 March 1807.
[9] *Journal de Paris*, 7 March 1807; *Courrier des spectacles*, 9 March 1807.
[10] *Journal de Paris*, 21 March 1807.

Luçay was becoming increasingly annoyed by Bonet's reluctance to take action against the two stagehands whom he persisted in believing were solely responsible for the accident. Bonet, however, was anxious to avoid doing anything that might aggravate the collapsing morale of the stage staff. Another of his problems was the growing concern of the dancers for their safety. At the revival of *Psyché*, Marie Gardel had refused to set foot in a *gloire* unless the manoeuvre was personally directed by Boutron. Luçay now became alarmed, and on 22 April, fearing that things were getting out of hand, issued a formal order suspending Bonet from his functions.[11]

There was now nothing to prevent Bonet from defending himself against Luçay's accusations of covert disobedience and intrigue. In a letter to the Minister of the Interior requesting a full report, Bonet pointed out that Mlle Aubry's accident, the underlying cause of his suspension, would never have happened if the Prefect had listened to him. Also, Boutron would never have been unjustly driven to resign, and the untalented and inexperienced Gromaire would never have taken his place. Nor would Boutron have had to suffer the humiliation of returning to take charge of a disaffected staff, as he had done a week after the accident.

While all this was happening, Napoleon was many hundreds of miles away. Although he had decisively defeated the Prussian army at Jena in October, the campaign was far from over. The harsh terms imposed after Austerlitz had left Austria bitter and eager for revenge. The Russians posed another problem; it seemed that only force would make them comply with Napoleon's decrees aimed at closing all continental ports to British trade. So, with winter closing in, he had pushed eastward through the mud into Prussian Poland, bound for the Russian frontier. Early in 1807 the French clashed with a Russian army near the small town of Eylau. They suffered heavy casualties but were left in possession of the field. It was an inconclusive victory that made a spring campaign inevitable.

Napoleon had heard about 'the catastrophe to Minerva'[12] from Josephine, and no doubt received further details about the consequent scandal from the reports of his Minister of Police, Fouché. Writing to Fouché on 22 March, he expressed annoyance that 'the affair of Mlle Aubry is occupying the Parisians more than all the losses that might be suffered by the army. M. Luçay was wrong not to have shown her all the sympathy that her condition should have aroused.'[13]

[11] Arch. Nat., F[17] 1293.

[12] Napoleon, *Correspondance*, XIV, 558 (Letter no. 12,037, 1 March 1807).

[13] Napoleon, *Correspondance*, XIV, 598 (Letter no. 12,093, 20 March 1807).

Fouché continued to keep Napoleon informed, and by the middle of April, when he was indulging his new-found passion for Marie Walewska at the Schloss Finkenstein, the Emperor began to lose patience. It seems that Fouché had given him Luçay's version absolving his protégé. The Emperor wrote back:

> All these intrigues at the Opéra are ridiculous. The affair of Mlle Aubry is an accident that could have happened to the best machinist in the world, and I do not want M. Boutron to profit from it through his intrigues. Inform him from me that he must have a good relationship with his second-in-command. Would it not be said that it is not asking the impossible to move the machinery at the Opéra? I do not want M. Gromaire to be the victim of a fortuitous accident. I am in the habit of supporting the unfortunate, and certainly there is nothing but misfortune here. Three words from you will be enough to settle it all. If not, I shall sack M. Boutron and put everything into the hands of M. Gromaire.
>
> Dancers will either fly on clouds or they won't. Give support to M. de Luçay. I will see what has to be done when I am back in Paris. But bad behaviour is being pushed too far. Have a word with whoever is in charge to see that it stops.[14]

A few days later a letter from Cambacérès, the Arch-Chancellor, who had heard Bonet's side of the story, made Napoleon realise that the problem went deeper than a squabble between two machinists. With the spring campaign against the Russians looming, and 'fed up with the tiresome problems of the Opéra',[15] he decided to place the problem in Cambacérès's hands:

> I am putting you in sole charge of supervising the Opéra until my return. I do not want to hear any more about it. Impose strict discipline, see that authority is respected and that this theatre, whose purpose is to give pleasure to the capital, is maintained in its full glory.
>
> Since it is my intention that you do nothing directly, you are to use the channel of the Minister of Police, to whom I am writing, for any measures you deem necessary.[16]

Four days later, when Napoleon's letter had been delivered in Paris, Luçay issued his order suspending Bonet from his functions. Bonet at

[14] Napoleon, *Correspondance*, XV, 72 (Letter no. 12,351, 12 April 1807).
[15] Napoleon, *Correspondance*, XV, 105 (Letter no. 12, 396, 18 April 1807).
[16] Napoleon, *Correspondance*, XV, 95 (Letter no. 12,395, 18 April 1807).

once reacted by appealing both to the Arch-Chancellor and to the Minister of the Interior, requesting an investigation and that a report be sent to the Emperor. He also queried whether Luçay had power to dismiss or even suspend him without imperial sanction. Cambacérès gave Bonet his backing, and settled the matter quickly as he had been bidden. Luçay was invited to cancel the order of suspension and to specify his grievances, and on these being found insufficient to warrant dismissal, Bonet was reinstated.[17]

With matters of far greater import on Napoleon's mind, the crisis at the Opéra was a problem he could well do without. No doubt realising he had not heard the full story, and sensing that the problem was getting out of hand, he gave vent to his exasperation in a letter to Fouché, his Minister of Police:

> I am displeased with the machinations at the Opéra. Inform the Director, Bonet, that his intriguing will not succeed with me. I do not see why M. Boutron wants to prevent the others from earning their daily bread, and is being so exclusive. Pray put a stop to all that. By provoking quarrels for M. de Luçay and becoming persecutors, M. Bonet and M. Boutron will get themselves sacked. You know such methods do not succeed with me. People are not content with M. de Luçay at the Opéra; if that does not stop, I shall give them a good army man who will make them march to the beat of a drum. M. Bonet, who I suppose is at the head of all these intrigues, will have gained nothing by all this. Arrange matters so that I hear no more of it.[18]

It would take time, and radical changes, for the Opéra to settle down. Both Luçay and Bonet were to retire before the end of the year, the former being replaced in a wider reorganisation of the official theatres, and the latter resigning with the satisfaction of having gained a moral victory. In the scenic department, Gromaire formally resigned his post as chief machinist, although, somewhat surprisingly, he would later return as Boutron's second-in-command and in 1816 succeed him as chief. Boutron had, of course, been vindicated, but what secret deals and compromises secured Gromaire's eventual reinstatement the records do not reveal.

Meanwhile, poor Angélique Aubry was still receiving treatment for her injuries. The Opéra's honorary surgeon, Dujandon, attended her regu-

[17] Arch. Nat., F^{17} 1293. Luçay's order dated 22 April 1807.
[18] Napoleon, *Correspondance*, XV, 220 (Letter no. 12509, 2 May 1805).

larly at the Empress's bidding, even delaying his departure for Napoleon's headquarters to take up his duties as medical officer of the Grenadiers of the Imperial Guard. Her medical bills were paid on the Emperor's authority, and the Opéra was keeping her on full salary. It would be a year before she left her bed, and she never recovered the use of her arm. Two years after her accident, when she had completed the required length of service, she was placed on the pension list.[19]

* * *

The calamity that had interrupted the première of *Le Retour d'Ulysse* cast a cloud over the merits of the ballet. One major newspaper, the *Journal de Paris*, even failed to give it a notice apart from an account of the accident and the shock to the Empress. In *Le Moniteur*, however, Sauvo gave the ballet a balanced and not unsympathetic assessment, calling it

> a composition as sober as [Milon's] character and as modest as his talent. To arouse our interest in Ulysses' return he has not had recourse to pomp and mythological illusions, but has merely ... set the moving scenes of the Odyssey in action, following, faithfully and with good taste, in Homer's footsteps ... He has given an example of almost antique simplicity. The result is a little languid, and perhaps even a little monotonous for an audience accustomed to the ingenious magnificence of Gardel's works and the exuberant variety of the ballets of Duport. But while *Ulysse* is somewhat deficient in dancing and scenery, it surpasses nearly every other work through the interest aroused by the dramatic action and the effects of pantomime.[20]

Geoffroy for his part found the subject 'grand and magnificent', and described the ballet as 'more a silent tragedy than a pantomime. The word ballet does not suit it, there is too little dancing.' This was fair comment, for it contained only two dance passages, with Vestris and Marie Gardel being featured in the dances for the shepherds in the second act, and the Duports and Emilie Collomb appearing in a *pas de trois* in the final *divertissement*.

The most important element was the mimed action, and here Milon was in his element, for he had made a close study of pantomime and in the summer of 1804 had been placed in charge of a newly formed mime

[19] Arch. Nat., AJ[13] 75, 125; Bibl.-Mus. de l'Opéra, Fonds Teneo, 1/10.
[20] *Moniteur*, 9 March 1807.

class. His expertise and artistry in this field was attested by the fine performances of those who played the leading rôles, himself foremost among them in the central character of Ulysses. He dominated the ballet from beginning to end, his interpretation being perfectly balanced 'with just the right amount of pathos and energy, without once letting slip any of the gravity and prudence which has to remain the dominant trait of his features.'[21]

The principal female rôle, that of the long-suffering paragon of marital fidelity, Penelope, fell to the senior ballerina in the noble genre, Mlle Clotilde. She had returned after an absence of many months to be given a creation worthy of an artist of her eminence and intelligence. Her rendering presented the sad and lonely figure of the harassed queen with modesty, sensitivity and grace, and was only slightly marred by an inclination to exaggerate her gestures.

As Telemachus, Saint-Amant added to his growing list of interpretations. At this point in his career he seemed indefatigable, and his Telemachus, presented with 'extraordinary sensitivity, warmth and energy', was as ardent and vivacious as Milon could have wished.

But the passage that remained in the memory above all else was the scene in the last act between Ulysses and Penelope's confidante, Eurycleia, who, having nursed him as a child, recognises him from a scar on his leg. For this part Milon had chosen Sophie Chevigny, who was physically suited for it because she had not lost the weight she had put on during her long illness. As Noverre himself indicated, her plumper form was an asset in a rôle of a nurse:

> Great talent is not to be measured by a person's height, nor by the circumference of the waist. And furthermore, she has lost none of the dexterity and facility that come from her excellent training.[22]

Much commented upon at the time, this scene – 'a masterpiece of its kind,' according to Geoffroy[23] - was designed by Milon as a great mimic set-piece for the two of them. In his scenario, Milon was very specific about how it was to be played. The episode comes at the point after Ulysses, still unrecognised in his disguise as an old man, has prevented Penelope from killing herself and has proposed that she should invite the suitors to take part in a contest with the great bow. At this point, to quote the scenario:

[21] *Journal de l'Empire*, 6 April 1807.
[22] Noverre, *Arts imitateurs*, II, 160-1.
[23] *Journal de l'Empire*, 10 March 1807.

> [Eurycleia], who has been scrutinising this old man and comparing him with the statue [of Ulysses], is struck by the resemblance. She fetches a stool, and invites him to sit down. Hardly is he seated when she offers him a footstool. She then notices a scar that he bears; she looks at it again, becomes disturbed and begins to tremble. This sign leaves her in no doubt as to his identity, and recognising her master, she falls at his feet.
>
> Placing his hand over her mouth, Ulysses enjoins her to silence. Penelope, who has been wholly absorbed in contemplating her husband's statue ... then turns and bows to her guest before retiring to her apartment.
>
> When the Queen has left, Eurycleia gives way to her emotions. Her heart is pounding so fast she can scarcely breathe; joy, tears, love and respect for her master, all combine to hold her in a state of frenzy.
>
> Ulysses tries to calm the faithful servant's agitation. He bids her return to the Queen, swearing her to the strictest secrecy. Only with a great effort can Eurycleia bring herself to leave her master, but at last she obeys, and with her eyes fixed on him, breaks free to go to the Queen.

This scene never lost its power to move and amaze. Writing nearly fifty years later, Castil-Blaze, who had seen it in his youth, recorded the impression Chevigny had made on him:

> She attained the very sublimity of her art in playing the King of Ithaca's nurse. You have to have seen the recognition scene in *Le Retour d'Ulysse* to know what pantomime is and to have an idea of the interest that can be aroused by the *ballet d'action*. Today [he was writing in the 1850s] it is increasingly becoming a lost art, which numbers only a few rare virtuosos.[24]

In his last word on the ballet Geoffroy made an interesting comparison with Gardel's *Achille à Scyros*. Both, he observed, were

> grand ballets in the Greek style. Without claiming to make a serious comparison between these two beautiful compositions, I will merely say that in one we see a man surrounded by a company of women and in the other, a woman surrounded by a band of men. The hero of the former is a marvel of impatience and daring, while that of the latter is,

[24] Castil-Blaze, *Académie*, II, 108.

> in contrast, a model of patience and wisdom. Ulysses, after twenty years of absence, comes to deliver his wife from the violence of her suitors; Achilles, who is not yet twenty, begins by violating a young girl whom he later makes his wife. The ballet *Ulysses* is more dramatic, more varied in its incidents and its characters, and more concerned with morality and passions; the ballet *Achille à Scyros* is more descriptive, more magnificent, more brilliant, and offers a larger number of dances, games, festivities and combats. Homer, the first of the Greek poets, provided the fable of Ulysses, and if you want to appreciate this ballet, you have to read the *Odyssey* before going to the Opéra. *Achille à Scyros*, on the other hand, is taken from a French poem whose author is not a Homer, and the only homework required before seeing this ballet is to read an article in *The Dictionary of Fable*.[25]

The music for *Le Retour d'Ulysse* had been provided by Louis Persuis, who 'made a good choice of favourite and well-known melodies that fitted the situations and helped the spectator to follow them'.[26] But the most interesting borrowings, which passed almost unnoticed, were two extracts from the symphonies of Haydn: to end Act II, the fourth movement (*allegro di molto*) of No. 67, and in Act III the fourth movement (*presto*) of No. 41.

In spite of its undeniable qualities, *Le Retour d'Ulysse* was not destined for a long life in the repertory. In the year of its creation it attained a respectable total of fifteen performances, in spite of a two-month gap when Milon was incapacitated by eye trouble. Luçay was anxious to keep up the momentum of performances, and Dominique Lefebvre was called in to study the rôle of Ulysses. In fact he had only one rehearsal before Milon recovered. Lefebvre, who received no expression of regret, was offended at what he saw as a breach of courtesy.[27] But in the long run, in spite of its impressive characterisations, *Le Retour d'Ulysse* failed to appeal, and disappeared after its twentieth performance in January 1809. Perhaps the preponderance of pantomime and the paucity of its dance content told against it, and while its powerful impression was to linger in the memories of those who saw it, it was not a ballet that connoisseurs clamoured to see time and time again.

[25] *Journal de l'Empire*, 6 April 1807.

[26] *Moniteur*, 9 March 1807.

[27] Arch. Nat., AJ[13] 83. Lefebvre's letter of complaint to the Opéra, 7 September 1807. Lefebvre observed that this was the second time he had failed to play Ulysses at the Opéra, for he had previously been passed over after Gardel had relinquished that part in *Achille à Scyros* and Goyon had been given it.

17

Louis Henry Flies the Nest

Louis Henry's injury, which had interrupted his career for nine long months in 1806, marked a turning point in his career. For a dancer still in his early twenties, such a break must have seemed an eternity, but the enforced physical inactivity gave him a timely opportunity to reflect. To stave off his boredom he began to find consolation in thoughts of a creative life to come, allowing his imagination to soar as he pictured himself as a choreographer with a free hand to produce wonderful ballets. It was during these hours of reflection that his destiny was revealed, and his ambition crystallised.

In June he confided to Geoffroy that while resting his injured leg he had conceived two ballets. One was a rendering of *Paul et Virginie*, which he had wisely discarded on learning that both Gardel and Aumer were working on the same subject. The other was based on Voltaire's story *Ce qui plaît aux dames*. Knowing that Geoffroy would be sure to bring this to the notice of his readers, Henry purposely added that he would be publicly acknowledging his indebtedness to Gardel, whose favour, he was fully aware, would be indispensable if he were to stage any further ballets at the Opéra.[1]

This was easier said than done, for Gardel was not inclined to encourage another 'trial work' by an inexperienced choreographer, although he did allow Henry to arrange a *pas de trois* for his return to the stage in December. Inserted in *La Caravane*, this *pas de trois*, in which he was joined by Marie Gardel and Victoire Saulnier, representing respectively the *demi-caractère* and *noble* styles, was flatteringly received. In it the cavalier is attracted to each of his partners in turn, being first taken with the sprightlier charms of the *demi-caractère* dancer, but finally resisting her blandishments and remaining true to the *noble* dance.

The latter was the genre to which Henry was naturally suited by his physique, but his power and agility tempted him to incorporate elements that were regarded as the preserve of the *demi-caractère*. Geoffroy had

[1] *Journal de l'Empire*, 29 June 1806.

been constantly advising him to specialise exclusively in the *noble* style, but the temptation to thrill an audience by virtuosity was too much for a young man whose strength was fast returning and who was savouring the adulation of the public after a long absence. The authorities were no less aware of this dichotomy; Luçay was concerned that Henry was 'doing himself and his art a disservice by performing things that belong to the *demi-caractère* and even to the *comique*', and reminded Bonet that when Henry had been promoted to *premier sujet* at the end of 1806 it was specifically 'to preserve the beautiful character of the *noble* dance and become its model'.[2]

Henry's difficulty in identifying himself with the *noble* style in its pure form was a symptom of the times, for the boundaries between the genres were becoming blurred. But the older connoisseurs grumbled nevertheless. One wrote:

> Henry has an excellent aptitude for the serious dance, but when he strives to perform *entrechats ouverts*, pirouettes and *sautés en avant* in the manner of Vestris and little Duport, he is straying from his genre and endangering his reputation ... Those who place him in the first rank of our male dancers are either paid to flatter him at the expense of truth, or are not true connoisseurs. Henry has strength, aplomb and elevation, but his extensions do not yet have the desired grace, and his dancing as a whole lacks charm.[3]

The reference to paid flatterers was aimed at Geoffroy, whose venality was common knowledge[4] and whose articles noticeably verged on the adulatory when Henry was the subject. For Henry this favour was something of a mixed blessing, for the elderly critic's effusions annoyed a younger colleague, Jacques-Barthélemy Salgues, the owner and editor of the *Courrier des spectacles*, who, wherever Henry was concerned, was liable to strike a sour note, as if to counterbalance the gushing praise in the *Journal de l'Empire*.

Early in January 1807, without warning, Henry served notice of resignation. It soon became clear that this was a ploy to force the Opéra into giving him another opportunity to exercise his talent as a choreographer. After a few weeks' sulking, Henry withdrew his notice. A compromise

[2] Arch. Nat., AJ[13] 83. Luçay to Bonet, 10 December 1806.

[3] Rémusat, II, 120, quoting a *Revue des comédiens* of 1809.

[4] Referring to the singer François Laïs, Salgues wrote: 'He is almost the only one of the numerous singers and dancers of the Opéra who refuse to pay the tribute that his comrades pay to avoid being torn apart, ridiculed and vilified in the theatrical columns.' (*Courrier de l'Europe*, 6 July 1807).

had been arrived at whereby he would arrange a new *divertissement* in a revival of *Le Déserteur*, in which he would play the main rôle. It was no doubt cobbled together in some haste, and Salgues derived mischievous pleasure in reporting its failure, describing it as

> concocted out of ten other well-known *pas*, a sort of *pasticcio* which wore out the dancers, tired [Henry] himself and came near to fatiguing the public. How can a character who has only just escaped death and who must still be seeing those muskets levelled at his head be in a mood to dance for three-quarters of an hour? And how comes it that a soldier in gaiters dances the *Menuet de la Cour*? All this shows lack of judgement to guide the imagination, if indeed imagination is needed at all when all one is doing is to copy.[5]

Henry may well have been aggrieved that the Opéra had not given him enough time and support to prepare this *divertissement*. Certainly he now began to realise that there was no future for him there as a choreographer, at least under the existing regime. For the time being he continued as if nothing were amiss, rousing his supporters to new heights of enthusiasm, at times to the fury of the partisans of Duport. On three occasions in May he even condescended to partner a promising young pupil of Coulon who was making her début, Fanny Bias.

At the last of these performances, however, the *Courrier des spectacles* observed that he seemed 'exhausted, perhaps through overwork'.[6] This was hardly surprising, since for the past month or more he had been playing a double game. By the spring a project for a new ballet had taken sufficient shape for him to come to a secret arrangement to stage it at the Porte-Saint-Martin in the summer. There is no doubt he was fully aware that his contract at the Opéra would be at risk, just as Dubois, the Director of the Porte-Saint-Martin, must have foreseen problems ahead – remembering how, just a year before, the Opéra had forced Aumer to withdraw his ballets. Aumer, however, had seen a future for himself at the Opéra, which Henry could not. For Henry this was a desperate throw, as it would be for Dubois too, although the latter may have failed to realise the full consequences that were to follow.

Preparations for this new ballet must have begun, at the very latest, early in May. These had to be carried out without, if possible, alerting the attention of the Opéra. Nevertheless rumours soon reached Bonet's ears,

[5] *Courrier des spectacles*, 4 February 1807.
[6] *Courrier des spectacles*, 30 May 1807.

but he dismissed them, unable to believe that Henry could be so foolish as to put his engagement at risk. Before the month was out, however, these rumours were confirmed. Three days before what was to be Henry's last appearance at the Opéra, Bonet placed the matter before the Prefect, asking that appropriate measures be taken against both Henry and the Porte-Saint-Martin.[7]

By that time, rehearsals of Henry's ballet were in full swing. Geoffroy's mention of the subjects that had interested Henry during his convalescence would have prepared his readers to expect a plot based on a work of literature, as indeed was the case. Henry had been entranced by a novel called *Atala* by a rising young writer, René de Chateaubriand. Since its publication in 1801, its author had greatly enhanced his reputation with a more profound study, *Le Génie du christianisme*, which came out shortly after the Concordat with Rome and earned him Bonaparte's favour. The younger son of a noble family, Chateaubriand had emigrated during the Revolution and spent several months in North America. There he had fallen under the spell of its thick virgin forests and endless plains, and the Indian tribes that hunted and warred beyond the frontiers of the young republic of the United States. From this experience had come a vision of the ideal savage which shone through his story of Atala, a young Indian woman who befriends Chactas, an Indian from another tribe who has been condemned to be burned as an enemy. Atala contrives his escape, and together they set off through the forest. They consummate their passion; but Atala, being a Christian, has made a vow to her mother that she will never marry a heathen, and her secret sorrow drives her to take poison. She dies, and Chactas, having promised on her deathbed to seek conversion, is consoled by Father Aubry, an old priest who lives in a grotto as a hermit, ministering to the needs of a small group of Indians.

Embellished by the rich imagery of Chateaubriand's prose, this simple tale provided the basis for Henry's ballet. However, his original scenario had to undergo alterations before the production could go ahead. It was necessary to pass the censorship, then applied by the General Police, whose objections resulted in the first performance, originally announced for 28 May 1807, being postponed to 6 June. Geoffroy was sure there was an intrigue afoot to nip his protégé's ballet in the bud. 'It has been attacked – would you believe it? – on religious grounds,' he told his readers. 'Some impostors who know nothing of the ballet have called it an impious farce that casts ridicule on things sacred.' [8]

[7] Arch. Nat., AJ^{13} 74 (234). Bonet to Luçay, 26 May 1807.

[8] *Journal de l'Empire*, 8 June 1807.

The threat was serious enough for Henry to seek help from his former protector, Cambacérès, who was temporarily in charge of the Government while Napoleon was on the Russian frontier settling the fate of Europe with the Tsar. In spite of his political responsibilities, the great man found time to accommodate his young friend. A word with the Minister of the Interior to say that the inadmissible passages had been removed soon disposed of the objections, and the Porte-Saint-Martin was notified that the ballet could be performed.

How much had been excised is unknown, but in the final version of the ballet there was none of that conflict between faith and love that drives Atala to suicide in the novel. In the first reference to the ballet in the press, the *Courrier des spectacles* had jokingly imagined a white-bearded Father Aubry dancing a minuet in his cowl. That character, so central in the novel, was in the ballet reduced to a minor figure, vaguely called 'an old man', who was given no affiliation to any particular cult, Christian or otherwise.[9] With the conventional obligation to give the ballet a happy ending, Henry must have abandoned at the outset any idea of disposing of his heroine by suicide. This change brought about a fatal weakening of the plot. Indeed, in changing the title to *Les Sauvages de la Floride* and renaming the characters, Henry may have acknowledged that the ballet could hardly be called a rendering of Chateaubriand's novel.

Salgues was nonplussed by the version that finally reached the stage:

> It was hardly possible to choose a subject more resistant to the means of pantomime and dancing than *Atala*. What on earth led M. Henry to turn a sacred work into a profane *divertissement*? ... It contains grave and austere characters who cannot be made to dance. We are told that M. Henry was aware of this problem, but thought he would be able to overcome it ...
>
> To make anything out of it, he would have had to work out a new approach, invent a new plot and denouement; in other words, to write a scenario capable of arousing pleasure and interest. This M. Henry has failed to do; he has ignored poetic licence, and given thought only to the needs of the dancers. The action of his ballet is cold, methodical and lacking in interest.[10]

In the final, expurgated version of the scenario, Atala was transformed

[9] *Courrier des spectacles*, 27 May 1807.

[10] *Courrier de l'Europe*, 10 June 1807. The *Courrier des spectacles* had been forced to suspend publication at the end of May 1807, its theatrical coverage being then transferred to the newly entitled *Courrier de l'Europe et des spectacles* (referred to as the *Courrier de l'Europe* in this book).

into Omaï (Soissons) and Chactas became Atamaïde (M. Quériau), the lovers being respectively the daughter and the son of chiefs of two warring tribes. Peace is on the point of being sealed by their marriage when a disgruntled warrior, Miranda (Lefebvre), claims Omaï for himself. Hostilities break out again, and Atamaïde is seized and condemned to be burned. However, the sentence is deferred to the following day, and during the night Omaï effects Atamaïde's escape. Unnoticed, the lovers paddle down the river and take refuge from a thunderstorm in a grotto. There Omaï modestly rejects Atamaïde's ardent advances, from which she is only saved when lightning sets fire to the forest. Atamaïde believes that Omaï has been killed, but his thoughts of dying by her side are set aside by the appearance of an old man who lives in the grotto. From him Atamaïde learns that his father, whose warriors had been defeated by the old enemy, has taken refuge in the grotto. However, danger is at hand. The river fills with enemy canoes. Omaï's father and Miranda come ashore and are captured by the local Indians. In the ensuing fighting Miranda attacks Atamaïde and is killed. The two chiefs then declare peace, which is finally sealed by the union of the lovers.

Chateaubriand was probably unaware of what Henry was doing with his novel, for he had been spending the past year touring Greece and the Holy Land. He returned to Paris on the eve of the ballet's first performance, and probably made no effort to go to the Porte-Saint-Martin and see to what his work had given birth.

The easy-to-please public of the Porte-Saint-Martin was enchanted with the ballet from its very first performance. Geoffroy described its reception as 'a brilliant and complete success', adding that 'no one dared risk the slightest sign of disapproval'.[11] Even Salgues had to admit that it was 'warmly applauded',[12] which in fact was almost a foregone conclusion in view of the custom of authors filling the first-night pit with their supporters to give the public a lead. At the second performance two days later the reception was noticeably cooler, but nevertheless the ballet continued to draw good houses.

Geoffroy made little attempt to expatiate on the choreography, contenting himself with calling it 'a grand and rich composition, broad in its sweep, vigorous in its design and beautifully organised; it presents a sequence of varied scenes, warlike dances and military festivities, intermingled with joyful dances, pathos and voluptuous *pas*, all of which combined to grip and move the spectator.'[13]

[11] *Journal de l'Empire*, 8 June 1807.
[12] *Courrier de l'Europe*, 10 June 1807.
[13] *Journal de l'Empire*, 8 June 1807.

Salgues was only a shade more explicit. 'The composition of the dances,' he wrote, 'reveals more talent than does the plot. While containing nothing novel and lacking in variety, there are details that show that Henry has talent and taste.' After awarding Henry this modicum of praise, Salgues could not forbear to have a dig at Geoffroy:

> This young dancer's only fault is that he wants to fight against time, to rush things, and in particular to surround himself with imprudent and tactless flatterers who heap praise on him that is out of all proportion and not in good taste ... That a writer should pen such nonsense for a few coins is understandable, but what can an author gain from such mercenary praise? The public is not to be bought, and it is the public alone that makes reputations.[14]

An important element in the success was Henri Darondeau's score, which was described as being 'always in harmony with the situations, at times lively and animated, proud and bellicose, and sombre, touching and melancholy: it is one of Darondeau's best works'.[15]

As for his dancers, Henry can have had no complaints. Marie Quériau in the travesty rôle of Atamaïde 'might have given her features a stronger and more virile expression', but 'apart from that, the shading of her expressions and her movements convey with admirable clarity the various nuances of love, fear, surprise, terror, anger, courage and despair'.[16] She and pretty Caroline Soissons, as Omaï, made a well-assorted pair. Geoffroy paid a well-deserved compliment to the company as a whole; he was pleasantly impressed by their precision in the ensemble numbers, and singled out for special praise two of the dancers featured in the Indian dances of the first act: Simon Mérante, who showed 'great strength and aplomb in the noble dance', and Robillon, who was 'charming in the character dances'.[17]

The satisfaction of these two critics was reflected in the ballet's popularity. It was performed twenty-seven times in the space of eleven weeks, a record that would have certainly been exceeded if the Porte-Saint-Martin had not been forced to close in the middle of August.

* * *

[14] *Courrier de l'Europe*, 10 June 1807.
[15] *Courrier de l'Europe*, 10 June 1807.
[16] *Courrier de l'Europe*, 10 June 1807.
[17] *Journal de l'Empire*, 8 June 1807.

At the end of May, on Luçay's instructions, Bonet had formally required Henry to withdraw his ballet. This Henry ignored, and three months later Luçay gave orders that his salary was to be suspended until such time as he complied.[18] Henry's intransigence was to hasten his departure from the Opéra, which was no doubt what he expected; but for the Porte-Saint-Martin it was to have disastrous consequences. The growing importance of that theatre's ballets over the previous four years had strengthened the Opéra's determination to curb its activities in that direction.[19] If Dubois had assumed that the worst he could expect was some sort of fine, he was gravely mistaken. On 29 July an imperial decree limited the number of secondary theatres in Paris to four, and the Porte-Saint-Martin, not being on the approved list, was ordered to close before 15 August.

Just two days before the decree, on 27 July 1807, the first performance had been given of Henry's second ballet for the Porte-Saint-Martin, *Les Deux petits Savoyards*, a minor work based on a popular *opéra-comique* by Monsigny. To pad out a theme that had been slender even when acted and sung, Henry had introduced 'a fair and all the curiosities of the Boulevard and the Carnival – Harlequins, Pierrots, Punchinellos, conjurers, fortune-tellers, greasy poles, tilting at a ring, swings and bears'. A bear was even given quite a prominent part. One episode, in which a character turned his back to the audience and appeared to be farting at them, aroused cries of protest, and was no doubt cut at the next performance. But popular though the work was, it was lambasted by Salgues as 'the outpouring of an impoverished and sterile mind, lacking in taste, ... its situations often unintelligible by pantomime alone'.[20] The two Savoyards of the title were played by Marie Quériau and Caroline Soissons, and Mérante and Robillon were once again singled out for mention. It was certainly no failure, for between its first performance and its last, eighteen days later, it was played no fewer than fourteen times.

The actors, dancers, musicians and stage staff of the Porte-Saint-Martin all found themselves out of work. Least affected of all was Mme Quériau, who secured a lucrative engagement in Naples. For the others there was the dismal and uncertain prospect of finding employment in a market that had been arbitrarily diminished by the draconian decree. There were virtually no vacancies at the Opéra. The only Porte-Saint-Martin dancer to be admitted there was Simon Mérante, who made his

[18] Arch. Nat., AJ[13] 83. Luçay to Bonet, 20 June 1807. In 1807 Jean-Baptiste Hullin, who was ballet-master at the Théâtre du Gaîté, was also dismissed by the Opéra.
[19] See Appendix F.
[20] *Courrier de l'Europe*, 29 July 1807.

début early in 1808, becoming the first of a family that was to serve that theatre with distinction for nearly eighty years.

Henry too was out of a job, and there was no question of his seeking to be received back at the Opéra. The very idea of going cap in hand to Luçay would have been repugnant, but he was now filled with a compelling desire to seek his fortune in Italy with Marie Quériau, with whom he had fallen in love. To do this he needed a passport to leave France. Foreseeing that the Opéra, which had not formally dismissed him, would be bound to oppose any application, he decided on a clandestine flight. He managed to obtain a passport as a wine merchant's assistant, and in that guise slipped out of the country unrecognised. He and Mme Quériau probably escaped together, going first to Milan and eventually finding their way to Naples. There the management of the San Carlo welcomed him so warmly that he was emboldened to interest them in a promising young dancer he had partnered on his last appearances in Paris, Fanny Bias.

Dominique Lefebvre, who had also been appearing at the Porte-Saint-Martin, where he had played one of the Indian chiefs in *Les Sauvages de la Floride*, turned up in Naples as well. From there, some two months later, he wrote to Emilie Collomb with news of their friend Henry:

> M. Henri [*sic*] has made his début with a trifle that will not do him very much harm in the eyes of our admirers. He never wanted to be engaged without Mme Quériau as his companion. Now that the contract is signed, there is a good possibility of having Mlle Fanny as *danseuse* because, as he says, Mme Quériau is only a mime. That is true, but I do not know how this ploy by a novice will be received by the management and more particularly by Mme Quériau, who aided M. Henri's flight with all her skill at intrigue and financial means. However, I shall keep you informed how things work out, because the day after tomorrow we shall be having a little meeting with the Administrators, the Director, myself, M. Henri, Mme Quériau, in which they will be asked to develop this little argument which looks very much like a conjuror's trick.[21]

The failure of his efforts on behalf of Fanny Bias was of no great consequence to Henry, who over the next twenty-seven years was to make Italy his home and build an imperishable reputation as one of the architects of Italian ballet. His brief association with the Porte-Saint-Martin in the summer of 1807 would become especially significant in nurturing the

[21] Arch. Nat., AJ^{13} 81. Lefebvre to Collomb, 7 November 1807.

roots of his choreographic style. Trained at the Opéra in the *noble* genre that still enjoyed much of its former prestige, he would remain influenced as a choreographer by those masters from whom he had absorbed the principles of his art: Gardel, Milon, Aumer – and through the last, at one remove, Dauberval. In Italy he launched himself on his career as fundamentally a ballet-master of the French school. Among his earliest productions at the San Carlo in Naples would be two ballets, the seeds of which may have been sown in Paris: his own version of *Paul et Virginie* to the Darondeau music that Aumer had used, and a ballet about William Tell which may have reflected echoes of conversations with Gardel about his unrealised ballet on the legendary Swiss hero.

Henry would never forget his Parisian roots, and in time both the Porte-Saint-Martin and the Opéra would welcome him back as a son of France.

18

Tales of Ancient Rome

When spring came in 1807, Napoleon resumed his offensive in Poland, decisively defeating a Russian army at Friedland and advancing to the west bank of the Niemen. There, on a raft in the middle of the river, the two Emperors met to agree terms of peace. For Napoleon those days with the young Tsar Alexander seemed a crowning achievement, and on 27 July he returned to Saint-Cloud bringing, so he hoped, a final settlement of the struggle that had torn Europe apart throughout the previous fifteen years. Although many families had been bereaved by casualties of battle, Paris was in a rejoicing mood. Rumours of a chance of peace with England through Russia's mediation added to the elation. Two days of festivities were decreed, and the return of the Imperial Guard to Paris raised French pride to a new peak.

On 15 August, Napoleon's thirty-eighth birthday, the Opéra gave a free performance, for which Gardel freshened up the *pas des Sarmites* that he had originally devised for the revival of the opera *Sémiramis* five years before. Now placed as an inserted number in *La Caravane du Caïre*, it was danced by sabre-bearing Mamelukes with thrilling precision.

With final victory seemingly achieved, Napoleon turned his fertile mind to problems at home. Before leaving Poland he had dictated a warning to his Minister of the Interior: 'Peace has been made with the foreigners, and I am now going to wage war on your office.' The theatres of Paris figured high among his priorities. The secondary houses had already been reorganised; in the wake of the scandal of Mlle Aubry's fall, the Opéra too had come under Napoleon's scrutiny. It was widely felt that money was being wasted there, and that more thought should be given to appealing to the public. Another concern was whether best use was being made of existing talent, and in particular how far favour and intrigue influenced casting to the detriment of encouraging aspiring young dancers.[1]

Few were better placed than Gardel to put a finger on the causes of the Opéra's malaise. No one had longer and more wide-ranging experience

[1] *Courrier de l'Europe*, 4 August 1807.

than he of how the juggernaut of the Opéra worked. As Head of Dance he was involved in the production of both operas and ballets, but his profound musical knowledge also gave him an understanding of the problems of the orchestra. Furthermore, having been a dominant figure on the ruling Artistes' Committee during the 1790s, and for a while, during the Terror, being recognised as Director, he had first-hand experience of administering the whole enterprise. Invited to give his views on the problems affecting his own department, he responded with a memorandum that must have carried much weight:

> *Insubordination* is the root cause. The Head[2] no longer has any power or authority; the dancers know that he has power only to punish and not to reward, and so they know full well that he will not abuse the former power as long as he cannot make use of the latter.
>
> The following example is proof of what I have just stated, namely that the Head's power is non-existent.
>
> When Winter's opera *Castor* was in preparation, MM. Duport, Henry and Saint-Amant were all scheduled to dance in the last act. The day before the first performance not one of them showed up. Bonet and I made every effort to persuade M. Beaulieu to dance the *pas* of MM. Duport and Saint-Amant. M. Beaulieu was determined to do so, even though he would already be dancing himself. He learnt all the *pas*, and, thanks to his devotion to duty, the receipts were considerable. M. Bonet and I promised Beaulieu to ask for a bonus, which was a just reward rather than a favour, but we were unable to obtain anything.
>
> The permission granted to young dancers to create *ballets d'action* has been the ruin of the dance, as I had foreseen. Pray, Gentlemen, cast your eye over the attached Memorandum which Milon and I had the honour of presenting to His Majesty, and you will see there that what we predicted in Year XIII[3] has come to pass.
>
> His Majesty, who was then preoccupied with more important matters, did not concern himself with such detail. But MM. Duport and Henry have been dancing only in their own works, thus depriving my own of their talent. The combination of their appeal to the public and the perfection of their execution add greatly to the merit of their choreographic works, and mine have been severely affected by this dangerous innovation. Those gentlemen – crowing at a victory over time-honoured custom, my own rights in my works, precedent and every

[2] The terms *Chef du chant* and *Chef de la danse* appear for the first time in the Regulations of 1805.
[3] Quoted in full, supra, 311–13. Year XIII of the Revolutionary calendar commenced on 23 September 1804.

known regulation down to the present time – have used dancers without reference to me, have ordered rehearsals without my knowledge and have had artistes punished. They have even introduced [artistes] who have never been of any use to the Opéra and who drain the finances with salaries that are not earned. It goes without saying that I have not been consulted about these engagements.

Had I wanted to give full details of the abuses that exist in the organisation of the Académie Impériale de Musique, I could write a book. For example, Gentlemen, is there any need for four *maîtres de chant* when two *maîtres de ballets* suffice? Consider the difference between the tasks of these two posts. The *chefs de chant* do no more than receive from the authors [of an opera] the parts for the rôles and the chorus, distribute them to those concerned and see that they are rehearsed until committed to memory, while the *maîtres de ballets* are composers. They have to get the music done by composers who are often ignorant of this kind of work; and they have to plan their contributions so that they will bedeck the operas with pomp, grace and charm that often add to their success. Therefore, the *maître de ballets* is not only a Head [of department], but a third author. The difference would seem even greater if I were to add details, but at this point I feel I should spare you that.

I do not know whether this is the place to mention the following facts, but since this little note is written in haste, you will forgive me, Gentlemen, if I include some miscellaneous ideas of my own, which you can use as you think fit.

The programme for last Friday [included] the ballet *Le Volage fixé*, a work by M. Duport, but on the Tuesday before, HRH Prince Jérôme[4], through M. De la Flèche, requested the ballet *Psyché*, apparently so that his new wife could see it, and the very next day the First Prefect wrote that by order of the Court *Achille à Scyros* was to be given. In his annoyance at this change, M. Duport, who would have had a considerable amount of dancing to do in his own ballet, refused to dance in mine. His friend Saint-Amant did likewise, and an express order from the Minister of Police was needed to make Saint-Amant simply walk in the ballet *Psyché*. He pretended he was injured and, by defying the doctor's certificate that there was nothing wrong with him, he was responsible for His Majesty's command being jettisoned, for *Achille* was not given. Gentlemen, how can you attribute this conduct to anything but the liberty given to these young artistes to create ballets and to dance only

[4] Jérôme Bonaparte, Napoleon's youngest brother, who was then on the point of being made puppet King of Westphalia.

in their own works? By damaging my [ballets], do they not damage the receipts and consequently the establishment itself?

There are some other matters that are causing more harm to this fine establishment:

The repertoire of the Opéra, a treasure that can be regarded as a mine to be exploited, is neglected.

Performances are not well prepared.

Whether an artiste performs well or badly, or if he appears frequently or rarely, he is neither praised nor reprimanded.

If the standard of performance falls, no one complains.

We have often had occasion to point out that the programme to be given on the following day could only produce receipts of 600–700 francs, while another programme could make 4000–5000. 'What is that to you?' we have been told. 'Don't you get paid in any event?' Yes, but who is paying? The Government.

The dancers, who do not receive performance bonuses under the new system, think they are entitled not to show keenness. They dance, but choose their own *pas* and only select those that do them credit, and it is impossible to make them dance the regular *pas*, whether in an opera or in a ballet. There are a few minor drawbacks to re-establishing performance bonuses, but the accompanying advantages are so great and so real, both for the opera and the ballet, that I have no hesitation in most earnestly requesting them. It is easy to remedy small drawbacks, and it is difficult to over-estimate the advantages to this valuable establishment ...

For an establishment such as the Opéra to prosper, harmony must reign in all its parts. The opera, the ballet and the orchestra must act as one; intrigue, jealousy and egotism must cease. All acts of discipline, whether to reward or to punish, must pass through the hands of the Heads. If the Heads are not given enough power, those under them will regard them as useless and will not obey them. It is necessary to seek, discover and attract authors of great talent, men of genius; and they must be forced, by good terms, to work for the Opéra. A performance that lacks authors soon loses spectators.

Forgive me, Gentlemen, if I have stepped outside the boundaries you have set me, but you have not given me the time to be more brief.

Gardel[5]

[5] Arch. Nat., AJ^{13} 74 (XIV, 697). Dated 3 August 1807.

Presumably Gardel's memorandum was brought to the Emperor's attention, for the affairs of the Opéra were high on his agenda. By the end of August it was public knowledge that changes in the régime of the Opéra were imminent.

In what were to be the last months of Bonet's term as Director, there was little of note in the Opéra's offerings. In August Louis and Minette Duport arrived back from triumphs in Marseilles and Lyons.[6] Duport was rapturously welcomed back in Paris in his own ballet, *Le Volage fixé*, and a few days later – perhaps to Gardel's surprise – in *Psyché*, playing the part of Zephyr in each. However, before the second performance of *Psyché* he claimed to be injured, and Saint-Amant replaced him, even though he himself was suffering from a strained foot. During the first act Saint-Amant realised that he was in no condition to attempt the difficult *pas* in the act that was to follow, and in the absence of an available male substitute, Marie Delisle had to step into the breach, much to the mystification of the public. But there was compensation to come in the next act when Emilie Bigottini, who had had a child in April, returned in the rôle of Terpsichore.[7]

On 4 September the Imperial couple attended the Opéra for the first time since Napoleon's return, and the Emperor was able to see the ballet in which Mlle Aubry had been injured. Later that month came Clotilde's controversial appearance as Achilles in *Achille à Scyros*, and events that were to lead to two departures: on consecutive days Louis Duport served notice to terminate his contract, and Emilie Collomb injured her knee while exercising in the wings during a performance of *Télémaque*. Duport would move on to further triumphs elsewhere, but for Mlle Collomb this was to be a sad end to a long and distinguished career.

Napoleon's reorganisation of the four great theatres was effected by Imperial decree on 1 November 1807. Those four theatres, of which the Opéra was one, were to be placed under the supervision of an official of the Imperial household, who was to have the final word in every major decision. Napoleon had decided that changes were to be made from the top. Luçay was replaced by the Comte de Rémusat, while Bonet was succeeded by the versatile Louis Picard, whose novels and plays were to gain him election to the Académie Française with a nudge from Napoleon, and

[6] In June, at the Théâtre de la Vaudeville, Lyon, Duport had produced a successful new ballet, *La Famille des Innocents*.

[7] Bigottini had two children: a son, Charles, and a daughter, Armandine Alphonsine. The latter's father was Casimir Louis Gonzague Marie Alphonse Armand Pignatelli, Comte de Fuentes, who had formerly been Clotilde's protector.

who had additional experience as a successful theatre manager and a popular actor in light comedy.

* * *

Within a few weeks, towards the end of 1807, the repertory was enriched by two new operas, each evoking the glory that was Rome as a reflection of the French hegemony that now spread to the very borders of Russia. Judged on its music alone, the first of these, *Le Triomphe de Trajan* by Persuis and Le Sueur, produced towards the end of October, was of no outstanding merit; but the sheer magnificence of its spectacle ensured it a success that would continue for a full decade after Napoleon's fall. Nearly 100,000 francs had been spent on the production, which attained a peak of unprecedented splendour in the scene of Trajan's triumph in the second act. This was one of Gardel's most extraordinary achievements; its effect was vividly described by a visitor to Paris who sat through it, enthralled, three years later:

> So I have seen *Trajan*, so beautiful, so famous and so boring – for, to be honest, boring it is. The scene of the Triumph, though, is sheer magic, surpassing anything that can possibly be described. The depth of the beautiful set, with the more distant figures of the crowd painted on the backcloth, a daring enough process although not too shocking; the enormous number of dancers, who seem to be just rushing about the stage, although every step is pre-ordained; the nine or ten danseuses (and what danseuses! – each worth an entire ballet); the vivacity of the dances performed around the chariot and among all those horses which, under the control of Franconi himself and his riding-masters, caracole and prance as if they were in the ring; all those flowers scattered by so many pretty hands ... I assure you all this is enough to turn your head, and it defies description. You hold your breath for the twenty minutes that the scene lasts, you sit open-mouthed on the edge of your seat, and it is only when it all vanishes as in a dream and the stage empties, and the music and the applause die away – only then are you brought back, with a deep sigh, from Rome to Paris.[8]

Several weeks later, on 15 December, Gardel made another major contribution. In Spontini's long-awaited *La Vestale*, the first act ended with a

[8] Clary und Aldringen, 136–7.

long ballet, part of which survives to this day as a very rare example of his genius.

To produce ballets for two operas in the Roman style with an interval of only six weeks between them might have strained the imagination of any other choreographer, but as Salgues wrote after seeing *La Vestale*:

> M. Gardel's imagination is equal to anything. So well has he varied the processions, groups and spacing that, although we are looking at something similar, we are seeing something quite different. The arrangement of the procession is rich and full of pomp, the movements conceived with the greatest skill and the dances always relevant to the situations, for one of M. Gardel's qualities is his ability to put himself into the mind of the librettist and match his composition to the nature of each situation. His *pas* are full of expression and feeling.[9]

Geoffroy was no less complimentary. Hailing Gardel as 'the man for all operas', he appreciated the way in which he made his *divertissement* evolve naturally out of the action, and was thankful to be carried away by its exhilarating verve and gaiety after the lugubrious scenes that had preceded it.[10]

In the first act, Licinius, a young Roman general, has returned to Rome in triumph after winning a great victory in Gaul. Before leaving for that campaign five years before, he had fallen in love with Julia, whose mother had favoured the match. But being of lowly birth and fearing that her father would reject him, he had preferred to seek glory in war. In his absence, however, Julia's father has, on his deathbed, appointed Julia a Vestal Virgin. To Julia, whose vows now bind her to a life of chastity, has fallen the task of presenting the consecrated laurel wreath to Licinius. As he stands before her, he tells her he will visit her in the temple that night. Festivities then begin with marches, wrestling bouts, gladiatorial games and dances, during which the Vestals present prizes to the winners.

Gardel's *divertissement* featured two principal couples, one of the *noble* genre, Clotilde and Beaulieu, and the other of the *demi-caractère*, Chevigny and Saint-Amant. Their dances followed, in that order, an introductory dance (No. 1) by Roman warriors. The noble *pas de deux* (No. 2, noted on the rehearsal score as '*sérieux*') was to become celebrated as the finest example of that style as it had developed by Gardel's time. The *demi-caractère pas de deux* (No. 3), known as the *pas des tambours*, came

[9] *Courrier de l'Europe*, 19 December 1807.
[10] *Journal de l'Empire*, 1 January 1808.

immediately after it. Then followed two other dances, referred to respectively as the *pas des couronnes* (No. 4), which was a general dance, and the *pas de la lyre* (No. 5), arranged for two danseuses.[11] The sixth and last number of the *divertissement* brought the festivities to a close with the awarding of prizes.

Over the years ahead, the *pas de deux* in the *noble* style was performed by a succession of ballerinas, although until Clotilde's retirement in 1818 it belonged unquestionably and almost exclusively to her, and none of her successors would dim the memories she left behind. Notable among those later interpreters were Constance Gosselin, who married the dancer Anatole, Marie Taglioni, and Lise Noblet who danced it towards the end of the 1820s with August Bournonville.

Becoming known as the *pas de la Vestale*, the *pas de deux* in the *noble* style was to be noted down in a detailed verbal description, presumably at the time of the opera's creation in 1807, by Léon Michel, who in 1815 adopted the name Saint-Léon and was the father of the choreographer Arthur Saint-Léon. Léon Michel had been a figurant in the ballet company for four years before coming to Gardel's notice for his fencing skill. Some months before *La Vestale* was presented, Gardel wrote to Luçay suggesting how useful Michel could be:

> Knowing you will not mind my drawing your attention to an opportunity for improving one of the areas that contributes to the great spectacle placed under your control, I venture to place such an opportunity before you.
>
> The area of personal combat is somewhat weak for several reasons: firstly, ballet-masters are not all proficient in the handling of arms and are ignorant of all the possibilities of swordplay, and secondly, they attach too little importance to it. It is my belief, therefore, that a man who is both skilled in such exercises and a *musician*, would, if placed under the ballet-masters to compose all personal combats following their directions, be very useful in that this part would be better managed, production of works would be speeded up and the burden on the ballet-masters, who become infinitely more tired than those who are accustomed to such work, would be greatly eased.
>
> In the ballet company we have a figurant called Michel, who has all the qualities required to fill this place well. He is (1) one of the strongest in Paris, (2) an excellent musician, (3) a dancer who combines

[11] Arch. Nat., AJ[13] 91 (9). The identification of Nos. 4 and 5 follow a casting note dated 1819.

grace in his positions with good taste and a noble bearing, and (4) unassuming and honest.[12]

Luçay at once gave it his blessing, and suggested that four to six male dancers be assigned to work under Michel and be used specially in combats. For this work Michel was offered an additional 300 francs, which, after an initial hesitation, he accepted on condition he was given the title *maître d'escrime*.

To have been so strongly recommended, Michel had no doubt been advising and aiding Gardel for some time before, and his services may have been invaluable in the preparation of *La Vestale* with its wrestling bouts and feats of athletic prowess. He also had ambitions to become a teacher, and it must have been during his years under Gardel that he began to note, for use later on, dances from such works as *La Dansomanie* and *La Vestale*, to cite only those that have survived. He later became dancing master at the court of Württemberg, where he compiled a number of notebooks of exercises and dances which he used in the course of his duties of teaching the King's daughters and his own son.[13] In these notebooks he included descriptions of several dances that were current at the Opéra twenty and more years before. Among them was the *pas de la Vestale*, captured in clear technical phraseology from the first-hand experience of working with Gardel and most probably originally noted down during the period of its creation when there would have been ample opportunity to check it for accuracy.

In the later history of the *Pas de la Vestale*, two celebrated figures from the Romantic period made their appearance: Marie Taglioni and August Bournonville. Before the Revolution of 1830, the three genres were still observed at the Opéra, and in the course of her début appearances in 1827, Taglioni danced the *pas de la Vestale* with a young dancer called Pillain specifically to display her ability in the *noble* genre. At the height of her fame seven years later, on 3 May 1834, she danced it just once more at the Opéra in a benefit performance for the tenor Adolphe Nourrit.[14]

In the following day's *Courrier des théâtres* it was reported that although the ballet in Act I had been 'preserved in its original form, it was not as good as it should have been, since its movements and steps ap-

[12] Arch. Nat., AJ[13] 84. Gardel to Luçay, 1807.

[13] Bibl.-Mus. de l'Opéra, Rés. 1137 (1, 2, 3), 1140.

[14] The first three acts were given at Nourrit's benefit. *La Vestale* was billed five times more until January 1835, but on those occasions only Act II, which contained no ballet, was presented.

peared slow and cold'[15] – a revealing comment indicating the disfavour into which the *noble* genre had then fallen. Because it was a benefit performance, Taglioni had been free to choose as her partner a young dancer not on the Opéra's pay-roll, one Emile Gredelue, announced merely as 'M. Emile'. How close her version was to the one she had performed at her début, or even to that originally staged by Gardel, must be open to question, for it is quite likely that her father, Filippo Taglioni, who exclusively coached and rehearsed her, had a hand in preparing her for her performance in 1834. It has been conjectured that Gardel himself might have been lured out of retirement to revise and modernise the ballet, but bearing in mind his age and the fact that this was a one-off performance, that seems unlikely.

Bournonville's involvement in the *pas de la Vestale* began during his engagement at the Opéra in the 1820s when he danced it with Lise Noblet five times between 1826 and 1828. Gardel was active until his retirement in the summer of 1827, and there is little doubt that he himself taught and rehearsed his young Danish friend. In 1835, when Bournonville was ballet-master of the Royal Danish Ballet, he reproduced the *pas de la Vestale* for inclusion in a drama. By a stroke of fortune it has survived in the Copenhagen ballet school, where it was to be formally incorporated in the school repertory by Hans Beck. As would be expected, the two versions, Michel Saint-Léon's and Bournonville's, are remarkably similar, but comparison shows that the latter is technically somewhat less difficult. This precious survival only awaits a specialist in the dance style of the Gardel period to bring it back to life from the notes that Michel made while working under the choreographer when it was created.

* * *

Wiser perhaps and more fortunate than Henry, Aumer had judged the moment right when he gave way gracefully to the Opéra's ultimatum and broke off his connection with the Porte-Saint-Martin. He was doubly anxious not to sever relations with the Opéra: for one thing, he did not wish to lose the pension that he would receive if he were still in the Opéra's employ in 1809, and for another, a ballet of his had already been accepted by the reading jury.

The three-act scenario on the subject of Antony and Cleopatra was given a glowing report:

[15] *Courrier des théâtres*, 4 May 1834.

> The jury listened with pleasure to the reading of the scenario of *Les Amours d'Antoine et de Cléopâtre*, and unanimously approved this composition, which seemed to them full of grace and interest; the first two acts proceed very rapidly and present opportunities for very varied groups. The jury fears that the third act, being extremely tragic in character, might consequently be a little long, and want the author to shorten it. The denouement is extremely interesting and presents a magnificent spectacle.[16]

With his wide experience of the theatre, the new director, Louis Picard, not only understood Aumer's creative urge, but recognised that he was entitled to some reward for bowing to the Opéra's demand to cease working for the Porte-Saint-Martin at no little financial sacrifice. On taking over the Opéra early in November 1807, he lost no time in submitting Aumer's scenario to Luçay's successor, the Comte de Rémusat, who was delighted to receive such a promising proposal so soon after his appointment. He replied:

> It seems to me that this ballet is absolutely suitable for the Opéra. The 1st and 2nd acts in particular seem perfectly beautiful. Before he left, the Emperor ordered me to have a new ballet produced for the beginning of January. MM. Gardel and Milon have nothing ready at this moment, and since the Emperor's intentions must be carried out, I invite you to give orders at once for this ballet to be staged. I think we must be seen to be difficult concerning the acceptance of ballets by anyone other than those appointed to direct the dance department, but since M. Aumer is about to be attached to this direction, I think that the ballet-masters will look on the acceptance of his work as quite in the nature of things. Please let me have a report a week from now on what has been done to comply with the order given for staging this work.[17]

Kreutzer was chosen to write the music, and was reminded of the need to fulfil two conditions: firstly, that for the dances (as distinct from pantomime passages) the regulations prohibited the use of music that was not original; and secondly, that the orchestra could not be augmented by players from outside.[18] Kreutzer delivered his score promptly, and it was sent to be copied in the middle of December. A few days later, on the basis

[16] Arch. Nat., AJ[13] 66. Reading Jury's report, 22 April 1807.
[17] Arch. Nat., AJ[13] 92. Rémusat to Picard, 24 November 1807.
[18] Arch. Nat., AJ[13] 92. Picard to Kreutzer, 30 November and 20 December 1807.

of an estimate of 24,000 francs, Degotti was authorised to proceed with preparing the scenery.

Rémusat was still finding his feet in his new post, and doubtless saw the commission to have a new ballet ready for his master's return to Paris as a test of his competence and drive. At this time Napoleon was in Spain, where he had gone to dispose of the growing danger posed both by the Spaniards themselves and by a British expeditionary force that had established itself in the peninsula. In January the Emperor's return was almost daily awaited, and Rémusat became increasingly alarmed at the seemingly slow progress being made at the Opéra with Aumer's ballet. In December he had still expected it to be ready by mid-January, but that deadline passed and on the 23rd Napoleon returned to Paris. Six days later, Rémusat wrote nervously to Picard:

> I had asked you, Monsieur, to have the ballet *Antoine et Cléopâtre* presented during January, and I was not surprised when it became almost impossible to obey that order punctually because of the scenery and other problems; but today I am told that it will be no surprise if this work is not given until after Carnival. I confess that this would cause me great displeasure, and that I could not then avoid alleging slackness and perhaps unwillingness on the part of the Heads, who are responsible for staging this work. So please give the strictest instructions that this ballet is to be given on 16 February at the very latest.[19]

Now at last all obstacles were removed and the machine of the Opéra swung into action. The scenery was painted (bringing to notice a young artist called Isabey, who would later gain fame as a portraitist), the costumes prepared and the stage cleared for rehearsals. It probably took the methodical Aumer about three weeks to set the pantomime, arrange the dances and the groups, fit everything together and run through the entire work with the orchestra.[20] At last, to the great relief of Rémusat, it was presented to the public on 8 March 1808. It was six weeks late, but Rémusat was not chided by Napoleon, who had more pressing concerns on his mind – the Spanish war and worsening relations with Austria – and who, in fact, was never to see it.

A splendid spectacle awaited the audience as Kreutzer's overture drew to its close. The curtain rose to show the city of Tarsus, with the river

[19] Arch. Nat., AJ[13] 92. Rémusat to Picard, 29 January 1808.

[20] Bibl.-Mus. de l'Opéra, Fonds Aumer, dossier 12, in which is a timetable prepared by Aumer for the revival of the ballet at the King's Theatre, London, in 1825, with Charles Vestris as Antony, Catherine Legros as Cleopatra and Carolina Ronzi-Vestris as Octavia.

Cydnus in the background, and the stage filled with a large array of Roman soldiers. Presiding from a tribune, Antony (Aug. Vestris) receives envoys from Egypt who have come to propose a treaty of peace. The arrogant Roman refuses to heed their plea for clemency and rejects the terms. Preparations for resuming the war are well in hand when a messenger announces the approach of Cleopatra (Clotilde). The Egyptian queen glides into view, reclining, richly attired, in a splendid barge, from which she steps ashore to proceed with all regal pomp to the public square. Overwhelmed by her beauty, Antony invites her to sit by his side. Quickly forgetting his belligerent intentions, he orders the Temple of Peace to be ceremonially opened for the ratification of the treaty. During the festivities that follow, Antony's wife Octavia (Chevigny) unexpectedly appears with her two children and a contingent of troops to support him in his struggle against her brother Octavian for the domination of the Roman world. She reminds Antony of his duty as a husband and a father. He is visibly affected, but cannot resist the influence that Cleopatra already exerts on his senses. In the struggle between duty and passion, it is passion that prevails. Distraught, Octavia swoons on the temple steps.

In Act II Antony is admitted into Cleopatra's apartment, where she reproaches him for being unfaithful to his wife, and urges him to leave her, Cleopatra, to her misery. Only when he declares that it is she alone whom he loves does she confess her love for him. They celebrate with a festival of dancing, in which Antony assumes the attributes of Bacchus. The scene changes to a place consecrated to the cult of that god. Concealed among the bacchantes is Octavia, who has disguised herself in order to keep a watch over her husband. The lovers take part in the dancing, which is interrupted by the arrival of an officer bringing news that Octavian's army is approaching to avenge the insult to Octavia. Shocked and suddenly ashamed of his conduct, Antony tries to reproach Cleopatra for her charms; but her power over him is too strong. Receiving his sword and armour from her hands, he leaves to take command of his army.

When the last act opens, Cleopatra is anxiously awaiting news of the great battle between Antony and Octavian. Her confidante Charmian (Mme Elie) breaks the news that all is lost and that Antony is in flight. Soon Antony is brought in, wounded and pursued by Octavian's soldiers. Octavia, on her way to welcome her brother, pleads with his attackers to spare him. He staggers and falls; looking up, he sees her and their children, and bitterly reproaches himself for his infidelity. When Cleopatra returns, he calls down the gods' vengeance upon her. Octavia and her sons bear Antony away, and Cleopatra is left alone. Octavian (Milon) enters. Cleopatra tries to charm him, but he is not to be moved; his only interest is to take her to Rome to be ignominiously paraded in his triumph. Cleopatra then gives orders to her servants to put a prearranged plan into action, and retires. Informed that Antony is dying, Octavia leaves, soon to return with the two children. Cleopatra emerges; after listening to Antony's reproaches, she reveals the fatal asp entwined about her arm. She gazes compassionately at the children, as if foreseeing their fate, and dies. At that moment the palace bursts into flames. Seeing her brother and her sons in danger of being trapped, Octavia braves the fire to rescue them before the palace is utterly consumed.

Aumer had deliberately tampered with historical fact to give the ballet a moral message. His Antony was presented not only as a man all-consumed by a fatal passion, but also as a husband and father led astray who finally sees the error of his ways and, on the point of death, rejects Cleopatra's seductions, dying in the arms of his wife and children.

The real heroine of the ballet was Octavia, and in that rôle Sophie Chevigny gave a superlative performance that drew glowing tributes from Geoffroy. Milon had already brought out her versatility as an actress, first as the soubrette heroine of *Les Noces de Gamache* and later in the character part of Eurycleia in *Ulysse*, but the rôle of Octavia was a much more serious study, spread across all three acts of this new ballet by Aumer. Geoffroy was astonished by the way 'her face mirrors faithfully all the passions that pass across her features one after another with incredible rapidity. Tenderness, jealousy, spite, hatred, scorn could not have been more realistically or more energetically expressed. All one can say about the admirable way in which she played the rôle of Octavia is that she *created* it.'[21]

The highlight of this astonishing performance was the great mime scene in the first act, at the point where Antony has first fallen under Cleopatra's spell and is then confronted unexpectedly by Octavia and her two sons. Salgues, with Aumer's scenario to hand, described it in considerable detail:

> Octavia has effected a reconciliation between her husband and Octavian, from whom she has obtained a guard of a thousand men; she can have expected nothing but gratitude. But the services of a wife are of little account when set against the charms of a mistress. And those of Cleopatra have already triumphed. However, Antony's better nature has not been entirely subjugated. Antony cannot look on his

[21] *Journal de l'Empire*, 10 March 1808.

19

The Perfection Class

During the last years of the Bonet direction, a significant development had taken place in the training of dancers at the Opéra. In the summer of 1805, Favre-Guiardele, who had served briefly as Gardel's assistant before retiring through ill-health, had approached Luçay in the hope of being reinstated at the Opéra in a teaching post. Luçay had been receptive to his proposal for establishing an 'upper class' for the most promising pupils, and Favre, seeing a possible rôle for himself, had cunningly followed up their discussion with a letter complimenting the Prefect as though the idea had been his.[1]

It so happened that at about that time François Malter, one of the two teachers at the School, was forced by failing eyesight to retire. Gardel's first thought had been that the two classes in the School might be combined under the remaining teacher, Jacques Lebel, but at that point Favre had appeared as a possible candidate to take Malter's place. However, it then transpired that Favre had more exalted ambitions – to be given a new upper class of his own, consisting of the best pupils in the existing classes. To this Gardel was opposed, not only because he resented the interference of an outsider in matters that lay within his own domain, but also because the proposal would damage the interests of certain teachers who offered private tuition to aspiring débutants.

In his response Gardel professed to view the proposal as disgracefully unfair to his colleague Lebel, an experienced and highly regarded teacher who at that time had a number of very interesting pupils under his care. Among them were an ebullient, well-built, handsome boy called Antoine Paul, who was showing extraordinary promise, and two sisters by the name of Gosselin, for the elder of whom 'great hopes' were held. It would be a grave injustice if Favre's proposals were adopted, Gardel wrote, for Lebel would be deprived of 'the fruits of nine years of extremely hard work, which is all he has to show for his endeavours'.[2]

[1] Arch. Nat., AJ[13] 62 (289). Favre to Luçay, 3 May 1805.
[2] Arch. Nat., AJ[13] 62 (275). Gardel to Bonet, n.d. c. December 1805.

Having Luçay's ear, Favre was well able to look after himself, and left the Prefect under no misunderstanding as to the motives of those who were opposing his idea:

> M. Gardel, my friend and childhood comrade, is against the formation of this class and said to me: 'Yes, but if you are given what you are asking for, it would be the greatest injustice ever done at the Opéra.'
>
> According to what you decide, Monsieur, I shall either remain silent or will require formal proof in writing of this 'great injustice', which, considering the purity of my own intentions, can in no way affect his reputation, his authority or his interests.
>
> I also know that the *maître* [i.e. Lebel], with whom I was in full agreement, has also taken the liberty of complaining to you ... I make no comment ...
>
> Oh, Monsieur, personal interest, trivialities and false claims will dominate in this fine theatre for a long time yet! You have already had the courage to take drastic action against some of them, and it is to be hoped, for the benefit of all that is under your care, that you will have the perseverance to complete your task.[3]

In the end Gardel and Lebel had to give way, and the establishment of a *classe de perfectionnement*, as it was called, was effected by an Order dated 29 May 1806. It was to be placed under the supervision of the first *maître des ballets*, and each year the *professeur* in charge was to select the most promising pupils from the two classes of the School of Dance, and take charge of them until their débuts. He was also to coach such other pupils as the Administration might indicate. He was specifically required to so organise his classes as to form dancers of whatever genre the Opéra most needed, and to be ready to fill any vacancies in the company. Progress reports were to be submitted to the Prefect every three months. For this he was to be engaged at the handsome salary of 3000 francs a year and in addition provided with lodging.[4]

In July Favre selected nine pupils from the two classes in the School of Dance – those of Lebel and Goyon, the latter having been appointed to Malter's place a few days earlier.[5] To begin with, the perfection classes were held, not alongside the regular classes of the School in the Opéra's

[3] Arch. Nat., AJ[13] 62 (277, 278). Favre to Luçay, 31 December 1805; Lebel to Luçay, n.d.

[4] Arch. Nat., AJ[13] 62 (291).

[5] Arch. Nat., AJ[13] 87. Bonet to Luçay, 14 July 1806. The eight pupils were Auguste Toussaint, Anatole Petit, Charles Lachouque, Cézarine Launer, Louise Dupuis, Mlle Lavoncourt, Marinette Launer, Narcisse Gentil and Geneviève Gosselin.

store in the Rue des Filles St. Thomas,[6] where there was no room, but in the Salle Favart, a disused theatre which not long before had housed the Opéra-Comique.

What then transpired to complicate Favre's life can best be described in his own words:

> I was established at Favart, where for half a year I scrupulously devoted all the care and attention that lay in my power. Shortly before the lease of that theatre came to an end, and since M. de Luçay had given no thought to where I could continue with my pupils, I proposed, with the intention of saving the Administration at least 20,000 francs, that a spacious house should be rented as close to the Opéra as possible, where the singing and dance classes could be established, and which would also serve, if needed, as a general store for all the impedimenta that gets in the way of the daily activities. He instructed me to find one, went to see it and approved the lease; and for two months I supervised the works. I was bound by my engagement to live where my class was held; I engaged workmen at my own expense, and on the day before moving in, I learnt from my pupils that I had been dismissed from my post in favour of a *friend* who used to be my pupil ... so that I found myself without a job, without knowing where to live, and dismissed as if I were incompetent or even a malefactor.[7]

Bonet's reply was woundingly curt. Luçay, he informed him, had decided to replace him for three reasons: firstly, because of the bad choices he had made from among the pupils; secondly, because of the lack of results produced by his work; and thirdly, because of the impossibility of finding space to accommodate both his class and his lodging. On whose advice Luçay leaned in dismissing him the records do not reveal. But belatedly Luçay accorded Favre an interview two months after his dismissal, when he admitted that, being unable to see everything for himself, he had acted on the strength of reports. When Favre wryly commented that those who had worked against him had succeeded in their aim, the Prefect agreed that that was so. Favre appears not to have been deceived by this attempt to shift the blame, but was satisfied that Gardel 'had absolutely no knowledge of this arrangement; on the contrary, I am bound to agree that he openly declared himself in my favour for the special class;

[6] The School of Dance had been established there since 1798 or earlier.

[7] Arch. Nat., AJ^{13} 87. Favre to Bonet, 2 February 1807.

and further, I knew from persons who actually heard him that M. de Luçay had promised my place two months before my dismissal.'[8]

The 'friend who used to be my pupil', as Favre had put it, was Jean-François Coulon, who had long assisted Gardel with his teaching commitments. In February 1806, before Favre had even been appointed, Coulon had given Bonet a private demonstration by seven of his pupils, including Salvatore Taglioni and Fanny Bias. Whatever Gardel's preference may have been between the two men, it was more likely Bonet who pressed Luçay to make a change of *professeur*.

Coulon, then, took over the *classe de perfectionnement* early in 1807, and was to remain in sole charge of it for some fifteen years before sharing it with Auguste Vestris. Time was to prove the wisdom of replacing the unfortunate Favre, for Coulon quickly established his reputation as the finest and most sought-after ballet teacher of his day, forming an impressive array of dancers who would grace the stage in the decades to come. The most celebrated was a girl who would be placed in his care by her father, who had also been his pupil – Marie Taglioni.

[8] Arch. Nat., AJ^{13} 87 (737). Note by Favre.

20

Comings and Goings of Men

It was now becoming all too evident that the upper echelons of the Opéra's male dancers had been grievously depleted. Louis Henry's dismissal, the imminent departure of Duport, who was now serving out his notice with a minimum of effort, and the declining health of Charles Saint-Amant had left a void that it was imperative to fill if the balance of the company was to be preserved. Happily Auguste Vestris was still in harness, but at the age of forty-eight the years were beginning to take their toll, and he was turning more and more to mime rôles. The ferocious rivalry with Duport that had gripped the public in such a paroxysm of enthusiasm and the bitter contest that followed between Duport and Henry were now but memories. Such duels had been manna for the Opéra's treasury, but dancers with Duport's charisma were the rarest of breeds – perhaps happily for the peace and quiet of administrators. The problem facing the Opéra was very serious, and the search for young male talent became ever more urgent.

How often Picard must have wished that Duport were more amenable. He had not altogether given up hope that somehow this impetuous and unpredictable young man could be tamed, but he was probably enough of a realist not to count on it. Difficulties had come to a head in his predecessor's time. In the spring of 1807 Duport and his sister had been given three months' leave of absence. The couple failed to report back for duty at the time specified, and Duport himself did not reappear until the middle of August. Obviously disenchanted with the Opéra, he and his sister served six months' notice to terminate their engagements. On technical grounds the Opéra contended that the notice was invalid. That fundamental point remained unresolved, but for the time being neither party took further steps.

Duport's relations with Picard were not unfriendly. Picard admired him as an artiste and, being a man of the theatre, hoped he could handle him better than did his predecessor, Bonet. In their communications, by letters delivered by hand and often answered the same day, he assumed a friendly and understanding tone while being careful not to prejudice the

Opéra's contention that Duport's notice was invalid. When he had to be obdurate, he would invoke the remoter figure of his master, Rémusat.

The infrequency of Duport's appearances had long been a problem for the Opéra. In 1806 he had danced in fewer than thirty performances, and in 1807 his record was much worse: just eleven appearances. Between them, he and his sister were earning 20,500 francs a year, which over 1807 worked out at about 2000 francs for each performance. Duport was not an easy person to handle. He was known to suffer from a chronic weakness that caused him to bring up blood if he over-exerted himself, which he usually did out of his zeal to please the public; but both Bonet and Picard found it hard not to suspect that his excuses for not dancing were often invalid.

Although he made a number of appearances in the new opera *Le Triomphe de Trajan* towards the end of 1807 and was at the same time working on a revival of his ballet *Figaro*, the old pattern repeated itself in the New Year. He could hardly be blamed for *Figaro* not materialising, for this was caused mainly by Emilie Collomb's absence through injury; but once again he began to refuse to dance on the apparently specious ground that he was not well. Picard had great trouble in extracting medical evidence from him, eventually sending the Opéra's surgeon, Dujandon, to call at the dancer's apartment. It was a wasted journey: only Duport's mother was in. She told him that her son was out teaching and would not be back for several hours. Picard finally had to threaten Duport with a heavy fine if he did not promptly submit the certificate required.[1]

The information that he was well enough to go out to teach had only reinforced Picard's suspicions, as Duport realised, for he was quick to explain that his ailment was 'not of the sort that requires me to stay in bed'. To emphasise the danger of his returning too early, he added: 'Mlles Chameroy and Louise Courtois came to the Opéra a week before they died. However, I am not yet on my last legs, as those ladies were.'[2]

His appearances in *Trajan* had nonetheless taken their toll; a few days later he went down with a high temperature and took to his bed. Now that medical reports were forthcoming, Picard became concerned and even advised him against returning too soon.

But if he hoped that an understanding attitude would lead Duport to abandon his plan to leave the Opéra and improve his performance record, he was to be disillusioned. They had an inconclusive discussion, face to

[1] Arch. Nat., AJ[13] 81 (Duport folder, 98). Picard to Duport, 10 January 1808.

[2] Arch. Nat., AJ[13] 81 (Duport dossier, 111). Duport to Picard, 8 January 1808. Louise Courtois was a promising dancer who entered the Opéra in 1795 under the stage-name of Mlle Louise, rising to the rank of *double* before she died after a short illness in 1805.

face, when the Director used all his powers of persuasion to urge Duport to take a more reasonable attitude, and Duport remained as obdurate as ever. Picard was still uncertain whether Duport accepted that his notice was invalid, and towards the end of March, when the notice would have expired, he wrote asking him when and in what ballet he proposed to make his return.

From Duport's silence, Picard must have assumed that the dancer now considered his engagement terminated. A formal order was issued that his salary was to be withheld, although his name would remain on the company roll without specification of any salary.[3]

Duport's reaction was surprisingly conciliatory. He wrote a somewhat pained reply, reminding Picard that he had found his suggestions reasonable and did not think that Rémusat would make any difficulties. His letter did not specify just what these suggestions were, but no doubt Duport had proposed a new engagement. As to the contents of the order freezing his salary, he did not appear unduly concerned. He even thought it 'very fair that you should cease paying it, because I am not dancing. I refuse to take anything for March (although my resignation only expired at the end of that month), since, at your demand, I did not dance nor did I give any of my ballets during that month.'[4]

Now it was at least clear that he was not accepting the Opéra's contention that he still remained bound to that theatre after 31 March, and the very next day he put forward his requirements for a new contract. He wanted, he explained, to be able 'to retire in two years' time, since I have no hope that my declining health will allow me to complete the [length of service] necessary for my pension.' His terms were that he should be engaged at a salary of 20,000 francs, and be appointed both third *maître des ballets* at the Opéra and second *maître des ballets* of the Court. In addition, his brother was to be given a place as bassoonist in the Opéra orchestra. Finally, the Opéra was to understand that, by signing a new contract, he would be giving up between 36,000 and 40,000 francs in private tuition fees, and that he could look forward to a career as a teacher for another twenty years.[5]

Picard had to disillusion him, explaining that the Budget laid down a maximum salary of 10,000 francs for a *premier artiste*, and that a larger amount could not be given without the Emperor's express consent; that an appointment as third ballet-master was out of the question because no

[3] Arch. Nat., AJ[13] 81 (Duport dossier, 124). Director's Order, 5 April 1808.
[4] Arch. Nat., AJ[13] 81 (Duport dossier, 126). Duport to Picard, 12 April 1808.
[5] Arch. Nat., AJ[13] 81 (Duport dossier, 127). Duport to Picard, 13 April 1808.

more than two were allowed for under the Regulations; and that the position of ballet-master to the Court fell outside the Director's province.

Duport did not press the matter, and nothing further was heard of him until early in May, when a letter arrived, seemingly written to put the Opéra off the scent, from the dancer's bassoonist brother, Auguste:

> Monsieur,
>
> I have the honour to inform you that my brother, having had some reason to fear that he was about to be arrested to force him to resume his service against his will, has retired to the country, where he is now in hiding. He is busy trying to obtain his freedom, and when he has succeeded, he will let you know of his plans and renew his thanks for the interest you have always shown in him.
> I have the honour to be, with respect, your obedient
> A. Duport, the elder[6]

A few days later the news spread through Paris that Duport had disappeared, as also had Mlle George of the Comédie-Française. It was not long before it was confirmed that they had fled the country together and were on their way to St Petersburg. The flight had been instigated by the young actress and caused a great stir, since not only was she the white hope of France's leading theatre, but a few years before, still a nubile girl in her teens, she had been Napoleon's mistress. She had been coaxed into this adventure by a promise of marriage from a rich Russian nobleman, and through a friend had bought a passport for 100 francs. Duport, who had no passport, had accompanied her disguised as her maid Julie; being small and extremely handsome in a rather feminine way, he had successfully passed scrutiny.

Mlle George had signed an engagement at the Russian embassy before she set out. Whether Duport had made similar arrangements or had departed on the spur of the moment, leaving the future to chance, he found that his fame had preceded him both in Vienna and later in St Petersburg. When they broke their journey in the Austrian capital, he happily yielded to pressure to give the Viennese a taste of his talent, and in June presented a revival of his *Figaro*, having had the foresight to bring the music with him in his baggage. They then proceeded to St Petersburg, where again he found himself in demand as a celebrity of the first order, engaged at 60,000 francs for the year. As to his relationship with Mlle

[6] Arch. Nat., AJ[13] 81 (Duport dossier, 129). Letter dated 3 May [1808].

A letter from Noverre to Louis Duport's brother, written after Louis Duport had secretly left Paris for Vienna in 1807. 'Please let me know in secret of his arrival so that I can write to him and, reminding him of my friendship, open my heart to him by telling him of the dangers that might result from a liaison [i.e. that with Mlle George] that is destroying his health and his talent.' (Archives Nationales, AJ^{13} *84)*

George, the actress's memoirs and her biographers are silent, but that it went beyond mere companionship on the journey seemed to find confirmation in an unfounded report of their marriage that reached Paris in the autumn of 1809.[7]

[7] *Journal de Paris*, 9 October 1809.

In St Petersburg, in the absence of his sister Minette, he selected as his partner a delicate fifteen-year-old prodigy, Maria Danilova, whom the ballet-master, Charles Didelot, was painstakingly grooming for the fame that everyone foretold for her. With a ferocious determination that knew no rest, Duport drilled her to the point of exhaustion for the honour of appearing by his side. He seduced her too, and, fatally, she became his mistress, to be devastated when he abandoned her to return to Mlle George. When she died of consumption in January 1810, many attributed it to a broken heart.

Echoes of the furore he aroused during his three years in Russia found their way into Tolstoy's masterpiece, *War and Peace*. But unlike Mlle George, he left Russia before Napoleon's invasion and settled in Vienna, where he married an Austrian dancer, Therese Neumann. Paris never again saw him dance, for he worked out the last of his dancing years in Vienna, Naples and, briefly, London before retiring as a dancer in 1820. He then devoted his enthusiasm to theatre management with the same self-punishing zeal that he had applied to his dancing. Until 1836 he was co-director of the Vienna Opera, and after the Revolution of 1830 he was an unsuccessful contender for the post of director of the Paris Opéra. It may have been after being widowed that he returned at last to Paris to live out his retirement in the home of a nephew, a minor playwright by profession, and it was there that he died in the winter of 1853.

For the Opéra the loss of Duport, undeniably the most extraordinary dancer of his age, could hardly have been mourned by Picard or Rémusat, who had surely seen it coming. Later in 1808 Duport tried to regularise his position by applying to the French Ambassador in St Petersburg for a passport. The Opéra was consulted, and Picard, while not wishing to appear vindictive, thought it would be wrong to give him a passport that would enable him to hawk his services at great profit to himself whenever he wished. 'Since his departure,' Picard felt bound to mention in his report, 'harmony has reigned in the company, and ... the public ... no longer wants to take up cudgels, or to take sides and repeat the disgraceful scenes of former times.'[8]

His flight to Russia had also marked the end of his professional association with his sister Minette, who on 14 April 1808 married the dancer Baptiste Petit (professionally known as Baptiste). Baptiste had entered the Opéra ballet in 1804 as a *double*, and although Gardel appreciated his intelligence and his unusual ability to learn all the *pas* and rôles in the current repertory, he had not been rewarded with promotion. Shortly

[8] Arch. Nat., AJ^{13} 81 (Duport dossier, 132). Picard to Rémusat, 2 October 1808.

after his marriage, he and Minette applied for leave to dance in the provinces, and Gardel was called upon for his advice. He wrote:

> If I only had to consider Mlle Duport and the little she has contributed over a long period, I would be bound to say that several of her comrades have a better right than she to be favoured. But, turning to M. Baptiste, the very real contribution he has made, his progress and his low salary, I think it would be only just to grant him this favour as a husband and as a wedding present for them both. I would only ask that, as a mark of her gratitude, Mme Baptiste should, between now and her departure, repair some of the wrongs of Mlle Duport by enabling the administration to make more frequent use of her talent.[9]

Two months' leave was accordingly granted, being strictly limited to Montpellier and Toulouse, for Duport's flight had made the Opéra suspicious that the couple might be contemplating leaving the country. The Prefects of the two departments concerned were accordingly instructed to see that they did not stray from the route prescribed on the passports. However, they did return, and at the beginning of 1809 Baptiste was given his long overdue promotion to *remplacement* with a welcome rise in salary to 5000 francs. Unfortunately such generosity had come too late, for in June he sought permission to leave the Opéra to take up an engagement in St Petersburg, no doubt negotiated through his brother-in-law. The Opéra made no difficulties, and he arrived in Russia to dance for a salary of 7500 roubles – only a fraction of what Duport commanded for himself, but still many times more than that of the Russian dancers at his level. He and Minette probably left Russia at the same time as Duport. In 1814 Baptiste, who was seeking employment, applied to be reinstated at the Opéra, but the Opéra was not interested. He and Minette ended their dancing careers in London before retiring to Vienna, where Baptiste died in the winter of 1827, survived, it was reported, by Minette.

* * *

The ending of Saint-Amant's career was less dramatic. He too had been suffering from a recurrent illness, which had developed into tuberculosis. Gamely he had struggled on so far as his strength allowed, but as time went by his frailty became ever more apparent. Medical knowledge being what it was, the seriousness of his condition was not apparent in its early

[9] Arch. Nat., AJ[13] 85.

stages. In the summer of 1806 the doctors attributed an 'irritation of the larynx accompanied by an inflammation of the lungs'[10] to fatigue resulting from over-exertion, but no effective treatment was available to halt the onset of the disease. In time it became obvious that he was mortally ill, and in January 1809 when he called on his friend Emilie Collomb, she was appalled. 'Good God, how he is changed!' she wrote in her diary.[11] Within six months he was dead.

* * *

Duport's departure left the Opéra ballet with only two male *premiers sujets*, Vestris and Beaupré, the former still representing the *demi-caractère* genre at the spry age of forty-eight, and the latter, heading the *comique* genre, being two years older. Saint-Amant never rose above the next grade down, that of *remplacement*. His virtual withdrawal reduced the strength at that level to just one, the *demi-caractère* dancer Jean-Baptiste Beaulieu, now aged twenty-nine, who was experienced and reliable, if a trifle colourless. As a result, early advancement for a truly talented young dancer was there for the asking, and that summer of 1808 a number of contestants were shown to the public.

Among them were three young men, all born in the first year or two of the Revolution, who were to attain varying degrees of celebrity in the years to come. They were all pupils of Jean-François Coulon's perfection class, and the younger two were the first to be seen. Anatole Petit, or Anatole as he chose to be professionally known, was presented in the part of Zephyr in *Le Retour de Zéphire*, while his comrade Louis Montjoie appeared in the title rôle of *Télémaque*. Both made an excellent impression with their lightness and grace, but it was the slightly older Albert, still only eighteen, who was by all accounts the most remarkable.

Albert, whose real name was François Decombe, was the son of a retired captain of cavalry living in Bordeaux. As a boy he had wanted to follow his two elder brothers into the navy, but his father, perhaps wishing to preserve him from the dangers of the sea, had other plans – he wanted him to go into the theatre. However, although young François had a natural aptitude for the dance, he became very conscious of his height and was on the point of abandoning his classes when Vestris came to Bordeaux as a guest artist and encouraged him to continue. He then made his way to Paris, where in 1803 he managed to obtain employment

[10] Arch. Nat., AJ[13] 74 (IV). Report dated 14 July 1806.
[11] Collomb, entry of 29 January 1809.

at the Gaîté, where Eugène Hus was the ballet-master. Hus was well known in Bordeaux, where he had worked under Dauberval, and it was he who in October 1803 staged the first Paris production of *La Fille mal gardée*, in which young Albert may have taken a very modest part. Albert had not omitted to let Vestris know he was in Paris, and it was perhaps on his recommendation that he became a private pupil of Coulon. By the summer of 1808 Coulon must have realised how remarkable a pupil he was, for not only was Albert accepted for a début but he was to be presented in the very best of company, dancing in a *pas de trois* with Mme Gardel and Bigottini. That he came up to all expectations was clear from the strong mark of approval (coupled with some salutary advice not to be carried away by the vogue for virtuosity) that Salgues gave him in the *Courrier de l'Europe*:

> Apart from a few traces of provincial soil on his shoes, which will soon be washed away, M. Albert is a charming dancer whom the Opéra can be proud to have acquired. His features are pleasing, he has a slim waist and a well-turned leg; and in short, he is a dancer who will outshine the other [débutants]. He made a particular impression in one of his pirouettes. Two *entrechats droits* (I think that is the term) followed by a *rond [de jambe] en l'air* with the right leg delighted the connoisseurs. But all this was a little spoilt when, in the middle of a solo, he felt the need to imitate certain capers and *tours de bras* that are unfortunately all too common at the Opéra.[12]

Albert was clearly marked out for the *noble* genre; and when it came time to show his paces as a mime, the chosen rôle was the one Gardel had designed for himself in *Télémaque*. It was too much to expect a finished dramatic authority at a first attempt, but despite a certain exaggeration in his acting, there was no doubt that a very remarkable talent had emerged.

However pressing the need to feed this younger blood into the system, Gardel was aware of the importance of years of apprenticeship and the dangers of forcing young talent too early. It was also necessary, owing to the escalating cost of the war, to keep a close watch on expenditure. Accordingly, Albert, Anatole and Montjoie were taken into the company at the modest rank of *double*. Only time would tell whether they had the genius to restore the prestige of the male element to the level it had so recently enjoyed.

[12] *Courrier de l'Europe*, 20 July 1808. The technical terms have been left as originally printed.

* * *

While those three talented youngsters were testing their lightness and exuberance in hopeful rivalry, an old man, who was still held in awed respect as God of the Dance, lay dying in his apartment in the Rue de Hanovre. For longer than nearly anyone could remember, Gaétan Vestris had dominated his profession as had no other dancer before him or since, not even his extraordinary son Auguste. He represented the exquisite style of what older connoisseurs considered the golden age of the dance, a style that seemed a perfect blend of 'taste, grace, elegance and delicacy' and was marked by 'a purity and a finish of which no one today can have any idea'.[13] He belonged to an age when dancing was recognised not only as a sublime art of the theatre, but in a wider sense as an obligatory social accomplishment, no less essential to a gentleman's upbringing than swordsmanship. In the theatre he had not only been supreme as a performer, but had played a significant part in establishing the *ballet d'action* in France. Converted to the vision of the *ballet d'action* when dancing for Noverre at Ludwigsberg, he had returned to Paris to show off his new-found skill as an actor-dancer both to Louis XV and to the public. He had prepared the ground not only for the introduction of the *ballet d'action* at the Opéra, but also for other long overdue reforms that Noverre had called for in his famous *Lettres*. He thus became both the preserver of all that was most valuable in the venerable tradition of the noble form of dancing, and an innovator who helped pave the way for the flowering of ballet as an independent art that had taken place in the evening of his life.

He had retired as an active performer in 1780 at the age of fifty-one, but continued to teach privately until his old age. Many of the developments of technique that took place in his later years were to meet with his disapproval, for he viewed the concentration on speed and elevation and the trend towards virtuosity as decadent developments.

His domestic life had been almost ideally happy. He had sired a son who in his own way had brought added lustre to the family name, and enjoyed the satisfaction of having founded a veritable dynasty as another generation emerged to follow the family calling. He had married one of the great ballerinas of his prime, the majestic Anne Heinel, and together they had lived through good times and bad. Although some five and twenty years younger than he, it was she who died first, at the age of fifty-five in March 1808, after a long and painful illness through which he had nursed her and tended to her needs with selfless devotion, oblivious to the

[13] *Moniteur*, 30 September 1808.

strain on his own health. The effort had in fact taken a grievous toll, and shortly after losing her, he had become ill himself.

He continued to teach for as long as he was able, but as the summer wore on it was clear to his friends that he was beginning to fail. Now for the first time he began to look his age; his former sprightliness was fading by the day, although to the very end he was never anything but immaculately dressed, nor did he lose that innate nobility that had always distinguished his bearing. In his last weeks he endured much pain with extraordinary patience, remaining lucid to the last. When released from his sufferings early in the morning of 17 September 1808, a great link with the past snapped. He never wrote his memoirs; as happens with the death of an aged parent, so many precious memories that had been stored in his mind were abruptly wiped from the slate of human consciousness. But his legacy would live on in the bodies and souls of the dancers who followed him as well as in the art of dance itself, which he had done so much to perfect.

21

An Angry Mars and a Forgiving Alexander

Two years had now passed since Gardel had produced a new ballet. With Gardel's contributions to the operas *Trajan* and *La Vestale* behind him, Rémusat thought it time to remind him of his obligation to see that the repertory was regularly renewed. Two novelties, to be produced before the end of the year, were therefore required of him, and in complying with these instructions, Gardel showed that at the age of fifty he had lost none of his creative competence. He produced two new ballets, one anacreontic and the other historical, which would both survive and charm the public for several years.

It was originally planned to present *Alexandre chez Apelles* first, and Picard was instructed to proceed with its production with a view to it being given in the summer if Le Sueur's new opera, *La Mort d'Adam*, was not ready, or otherwise in the autumn. Gardel was requested not to use too many principals, in order to keep down the expenditure on *feux*, and to be sure to have understudies available so that the ballet's run would not be interrupted by 'illness, whether real or simulated'.[1]

Le Sueur's opera was not ready in time, but nor was the ballet, the estimate for which was not approved until July. Consequently it was Gardel's other project, *Vénus et Adonis*, that was given priority – a decision that may have caused Gardel to cast it in a single act rather than in two or three. Its low budget – 6000 francs compared with the 40,000 francs earmarked for *Alexandre chez Apelles* – no doubt evidenced this last-minute urgency.

Gardel's slight and inconsequential plot was familiar to an audience brought up on the classics. Venus (Clotilde) has been unfaithful to Mars by falling in love with the mortal Adonis (Montjoie). When the ballet opens, she is found pining for him. Allegorical characters representing the familiar Laughter and Games, the Graces and the Zephyrs try to distract her, but her languid mood vanishes only when Adonis returns. Their tender exchanges are interrupted by the appearance of Mars

[1] Arch. Nat., AJ^{13} 92. Rémusat to Picard, 12 April 1808. *Feux* were performance bonuses.

(Aumer) on a mountain-top. Restrained from descending to dispose of his presumptuous rival, he decides on subtler means to seek his revenge. Striking the ground with his lance, he summons up a ferocious wild boar to wreak terror and depredation in the countryside. The villagers come to beg Adonis to save them from the dreaded beast. Venus is reluctant to let him go but relents, moved by the villagers' plight. She and her retinue follow Adonis, and during her absence Mars, still in a rage, enters the goddess's deserted bower. At the sound of her approach, he hastens away. On her return, Cupid (V. Hullin) tries in vain to restore her spirits, and Morpheus descends on a cloud to drop poppies on the lids of her eyes. While she is asleep, Adonis staggers in, mortally wounded. He dies, and Venus awakes to the sobbing of her attendants. Her nymphs try to shield her from the sight of her lover's body, but she pushes them aside and gives way to her grief. Cupid flies to the mountain-top to invoke the intervention of Jupiter, who descends on a throne of clouds to bring Adonis back to life.

It was planned to present this new ballet in the presence of Napoleon, but Paris was to see little of him that summer. Early in April he had left for Bayonne to deal with the worsening situation in Spain. For months reinforcements had been pouring across the Pyrenees. In May the French Army of Spain put down an uprising in Madrid. Napoleon appointed his brother Joseph to the Spanish throne, but within ten days of entering Madrid the new monarch was forced to flee. The situation was still deteriorating in August, when more pressing concerns brought the Emperor back to Paris. After only a month's respite at Saint-Cloud, he was to set out eastwards for a conference with the Tsar at Erfurt. Paris would see him for just eleven days in November before he departed once more for Spain.

It was during those five weeks at Saint-Cloud in the summer, on 1 September, that *Vénus et Adonis* was given its first performance in the presence of Napoleon and Josephine. With not only Spain but also ominous military preparations by Austria on his mind, the Emperor was nonetheless able to concentrate his attention on the ballet. He was not impressed by Clotilde's Venus, finding her interpretation lacking in warmth; when the performance was over, he demanded to know why Victoire Saulnier, for whom he clearly had a soft spot, had not taken the part. Rémusat had to explain that Clotilde had exercised her right to it by seniority, and that there had been no way round the Regulations.

'So be it,' Napoleon replied grumpily, 'but inform Mlle Clotilde that when a character has lost her lover in such cruel circumstances, she should not appear before us with that kind of expression, hair-style and costume.'[2]

Critics did not attend court performances, at which no applause was countenanced unless initiated by the Emperor, so no serious assessment could be made until the ballet was presented in Paris. For a month that summer the Opéra was closed for the refurbishment of its auditorium. In the newly embellished surroundings – with the Imperial coat of arms surmounting the proscenium and the vaulted ceiling speckled with stars and Napoleonic bees – *Vénus et Adonis* had the privilege of being the first new ballet to be presented, on 4 October 1808. On the 31st, Napoleon came to inspect the redecoration and saw the ballet for the second time.

The enthusiasm shown when Gardel took his bow at the end of the first performance left no room for doubt that he had produced a ballet, slight though it was, of rare quality. This acclaim was echoed in the reviews. François Sauvo in *Le Moniteur* was especially enthusiastic:

> The adage, *Ut pictura poesis*, poetry is akin to painting, is frequently applied to the fine arts and literature, but there exists another art which has nothing to do with painting or poetry: namely choreography, in which the skills of designing choral works in dance, of depicting a narrative by means of pantomime, and of embellishing a drama with all the effects of theatrical magic, scenic illusion and perspective are all brought into play. This is the art that is successfully cultivated by M. Gardel, and the horizons of which he has vastly extended. The new ballet he has just composed is one of his lightest works, but not the least appealing. He seems to have composed it with an Ovid in his hand and a picture by Albano before his eyes.[3]

Interestingly, the analogy with Albano was echoed by other critics, notably that of the *Journal de Paris*, who thought the ballet 'worthy of the brushes of Albano',[4] and by Salgues, who spoke of 'a gallery of delicious freshness and striking variety, which satisfy mind, taste and eye in equal measure.'[5]

It was surely an added tribute to Gardel that, with so small an expenditure on scenery and costumes, audiences went away with such glowing impressions. In his arrangement of the dances and the pantomime, of

[2] Maurice, *Epaves*, 51.
[3] *Moniteur*, 9 October 1808. Sauvo, who was the paper's editor, wrote theatrical reviews under the signature S....
[4] *Journal de Paris*, 15 October 1808.
[5] *Courrier de l'Europe*, 5 October 1808.

The most significant divergence from Noverre's scenario lay in the relationship between Apelles and Campaspe. In Noverre's ballet the moment when Campaspe removes her veil in the studio is their first meeting, presented as a *coup de foudre* for them both. Gardel, on the other hand, made the more realistic and rational assumption that their love had had an earlier and no less intense beginning, but that some unspecified event had separated them. In both ballets Apelles was given a scene showing him pondering over the choice of an appropriate goddess in whose form to paint Campaspe's portrait: in the two versions the goddesses considered vary – Pallas, Flora, Diana, Venus in Noverre's; Diana, Terpsichore, Venus in Gardel's – the final choice in each case being, of course, Venus. Another difference was that Noverre showed Apelles working on the portrait on his own, whereas Gardel had Alexander present, admiring the artist's skill.[11]

Gardel had also discarded one member of Noverre's cast, the character of Roxane, the Persian princess whom Alexander loves and makes his queen at the end of the ballet. In Noverre's version Campaspe had been depicted as a reluctant mistress, and it was Roxane, not Hephæstion as in Gardel's scenario, who opens Alexander's eyes to the relationship between Apelles and Campaspe with the intention of disposing of a dangerous rival. Hephæstion's part had accordingly been reduced to calming Alexander's fury and inducing him to forgive the lovers. The critic of the *Journal de Paris* thought that the introduction of Roxane in Gardel's ballet might have heightened its dramatic impact, commenting that 'the jealousy of a beautiful woman is a less cold motive, and therefore a more appropriate one, than a friend's persuasion.'[12]

Nearly all the action in Noverre's ballet had been condensed into the first act, the second act being devoted to the fête and the two unions, of Apelles and Campaspe, and Alexander and Roxane. Although Noverre tried to remedy this imbalance by ending the first act with Apelles in irons, so moving the forgiveness scene to open the second act, the ballet had been generally considered to be flawed.

Gardel's treatment of Alexander's act of forgiveness, its motivation strengthened by the example depicted in the painting of Darius's family, was recognised as a point in his favour. As if remembering that Noverre had been criticised for allowing Alexander (in the person of Gardel's elder

[11] A certain E. Voïard, who had submitted an opera libretto called *Alexandre à Pella* which had been rejected by the reading jury in 1805, accused Gardel of stealing his idea. The claim was apparently ignored as being without foundation. (Archives Nationales, AJ[13] 88)

[12] *Journal de Paris*, 22 December 1808.

brother) to introduce a solo in the *noble* style into the studio scene, Gardel had presented Alexander solely as a mime character.

Gardel's *Alexandre chez Apelles* rested heavily on the shoulders of the four experienced players who took the leading parts. Auguste Vestris was Apelles, a nostalgic choice no doubt, for there must have been a few older spectators who had seen his father play the same character in Noverre's ballet. The son had now developed into a consummate actor, but was still youthful enough to be convincing as a warm and sensitive lover. As Alexander, Aumer possessed the height and personality to impose his presence with a well-judged mixture of regal nobility and energy; some thought his interpretation to be a shade too abrupt, but Geoffroy observed that Alexander had been known to be brusque and quick to fly into a rage. These two were ably supported by Milon, the most sensitive of mimes, as Hephæstion – a part with subtleties of meaning to be conveyed by looks and gestures alone that probably made it the most difficult of all. Campaspe, the sole female part, was another gift from Gardel to his wife. In Noverre's ballet, the character had been played by Guimard, and there was a certain historical justice in Marie Gardel, her direct successor as *premier sujet de demi-caractère*, being placed in her shoes. Mme Gardel was not a dancer who attracted attention by virtuosity or seductive wiles, but relied entirely on her purity of style, while in her acting she eschewed histrionics and played with a naturalness that never seemed strained or out of place. Geoffroy thought Campaspe to be one of her best interpretations. 'In no other work,' he wrote, 'has [she] had such a good opportunity for her artistry and all her grace to shine.'[13]

The commission to compose the score had been awarded to Charles Catel, a celebrated professor at the Conservatoire and the author of an authoritative treatise on harmony. He had earlier composed an opera, *Sémiramis*, which had included music for an interpolated ballet that may have impressed Gardel, its choreographer. Now he was being given his first commission for a major ballet, and he produced a score that was notable for being entirely original and containing no borrowed passages. For this reason it sounded strange to some critics. Geoffroy, for instance, dismissed it as mediocre when he first heard it, but on a second listening he was surprised to find it 'expressive, lively and faithful to the situations'.[14] Perusing the score some seventy years later, the musicologist Théodore Lajarte judged it as remarkably important considering the state of ballet music of the time, being particularly impressed by the careful

[13] *Journal de l'Empire*, 26 December 1808.

[14] *Journal de l'Empire*, 30 December 1808.

orchestration. Among its highlights he noted a solo for English horn in the first act, and a *symphonie concertante* for flute, horn, bassoon, two harps and orchestra in the second.

However, once the novelty of the work had worn off, the slenderness of its plot became more apparent. As anyone familiar with Pliny would have known, it was based on a brief anecdote that was clearly too slight to be stretched over two acts. That it survived as long as it did was itself a tribute to its choreographer, but it was also due to those who acted the principal rôles. Marie Gardel and Milon kept their parts of Campaspe and Hephæstion throughout the lifetime of the ballet; Vestris was occasionally replaced by Beaulieu; but the first Alexander, Aumer, had to relinquish the part within a few months of the ballet's creation, being succeeded first by Albert and later by Montjoie. Napoleon saw the ballet a few days after returning from Spain, and it survived in the repertory until the fateful winter of 1812.

22

Claques, Débuts and Imperial Tribute

The success of a theatrical novelty, be it opera or ballet, drama, melodrama or comedy, hung largely on the public's reception at its first performance. That was the occasion on which the critics based their reviews, and at which first impressions were made on those whose judgement was listened to in the salons. That it was possible to manipulate the reception of a theatrical work had long been understood and exploited by authors and performers alike. Before the Revolution, the Vestris family frequently mustered supporters to stimulate ovations for a member of the family or a favourite pupil. Claques of one sort of another were therefore nothing new, but the proliferation of theatres in Paris during the Revolution greatly expanded their activities, and in recent times Duport, Henry and Aumer had benefited from their services.

The ubiquitous police of the Napoleonic régime kept a close watch on the theatres for any sign of unrest, and in March 1809, following a disturbance at the Théâtre de l'Odéon, the Prefect of Police ordered an investigation into the network of claques. Remarkable for its detail, the report named the men who ran them. For most of these it was only a sideline, occupying the evening hours. The most prominent was a hairdresser named Pierre Leblond, who could call on as many as forty stalwarts to clap or whistle at a given signal from their leader. Leblond's connection with the Opéra was facilitated by the presence in his organisation of one of Milon's servants. Milon himself made use of his services, as did several of his colleagues, including Vestris, Saint-Amant, Beaupré, Milon's sister-in-law Bigottini and Mlle Rivière. Payment was made in the form of cash or of tickets, a proportion of which would be sold at a profit, or as a combination of both. According to the report, Bigottini paid 12 or 15 francs a performance, which was more than covered by her *feux*.

Another entrepreneur with connections at the Opéra was Joseph Lebrun, a journalist by day. He had only a dozen men, but with the proceeds of some of the tickets he received he was said to be able to pay his rent and his tailor. Gardel was among his clients, passing on some of his tickets – although not all, for he kept back a few to give to another provider, one Stanislas Gal, a student dentist by day. Among Gal's band was a young man employed at the Hospice Beaujon called Auguste, who can perhaps be identified with the celebrated *chef de claque* of whose services Dr Véron availed himself a quarter of a century later.[1]

The police's interest in the claques was a sign of their increased vigilance as France prepared for a resumption of hostilities. With a large French army bogged down in Spain, Austria was about to make another attempt to avenge its former humiliations. A few weeks after the report was submitted, Napoleon left Paris to take command of the Grande Armée. In May he entered Vienna as a conqueror, and at Wagram in July he won the decisive battle that led Austria to sue for peace. Throughout the spring and summer, while soldiers were dying on distant fields, there was a noticeable lull in activities at the Opéra. No new ballet would be added to the repertory until the very end of 1809; only an occasional début enlivened the evenings of the connoisseurs.

The first of these was not strictly a début, for Marie Gaillet had been in the company for six years, and had aroused the highest expectations when she had arrived in Paris from Bordeaux at the age of seventeen with the most impressive recommendations. The support of none other than Dauberval was reinforced by that of Vestris and Henry. On the strength of such credentials, Gardel sent 300 francs to bring her to Paris. Having seen her, he was moved to forecast a brilliant future for her in the *noble* genre.[2] But, for whatever reason, advancement had come to her very slowly, and by the time of her début she had been marooned at the level of *double* for four years. Dispirited, she was convinced she had been treated unfairly. In a desperate endeavour to overcome the prejudice that had been holding her back, she had been taking lessons from Vestris. This effort was to go unrewarded, for which she laid the blame squarely on the Superintendent, Rémusat, who, as she recorded,

> made it plain that she could expect no further progress unless she placed herself at his disposition, which she constantly refused to do, not wishing to owe her advancement to giving in to him. And M. de Rémusat kept his word. For so long as this man remained Intendant he took every opportunity to show his dislike by continually passing her over. He went so far in persecuting her as to withdraw the arrangement whereby she shared rôles with the elder Mlle Saulnier, by reclassifying her as a *double*.[3]

[1] *Intermédiaire* LVIII:1202 (20 November 1907), 771–6. The report is dated 20 March 1809.
[2] Arch. Nat., AJ[13] 82. Morel to Luçay, 4 Floréal, Year XI (24 April 1803).
[3] Arch. Nat., AJ[13] 82. Undated note.

Disappointed though she was, she accepted the situation and remained a loyal, hard-working member of the company, still holding the rank of *double*, until she retired with a pension at the end of 1826.

Of greater interest was the appearance of the fifteen-year-old Constance Gosselin, younger sister of an even more promising pupil who was yet to emerge. A pupil of Coulon, she made a strong impression in a solo *pas*, revealing unusual aplomb and precision for her age. Her 'graceful, elegant and smooth style'[4] offered promise of what was to come, but she was too young to be engaged, and for the time being the public would have to be satisfied with this tantalising first glimpse.

Another promising newcomer seen that summer was a pupil of Favre-Guiardele, Marinette Boissière, 'a very alert little person who appears to be happily suited to the light and jocular style of dancing'.[5]

Of the two male débutants, one was a young man who had been seen before. This was Antonin, a dancer from Bordeaux, who had made a single appearance in 1808 and, realising the moment to be premature, had returned to where he came from for further coaching. Now, a year later, he made a stronger impression, particularly by his spectacular pirouettes, for which the *Courrier de l'Europe* dubbed him 'the Duport of the provinces'. But pirouettes alone do not a dancer make, and 'no great effort was made to retain him'.[6]

The most newsworthy of all the débutants, however, was an infant prodigy, another scion of the Vestris clan. Charles Vestris, said to be only twelve, was a cousin of Auguste, the grandson of one of Gaétan's brothers – either Angiolo, who had danced in Noverre's company at Ludwigsberg in the 1760s, or Giambattista who ran the family household. Auguste Vestris had himself prepared young Charles for his début, and the family pulled out every stop to ensure a good turn-out of well-wishers and, presumably, a fair scattering of professional pairs of hands and lungs under the command of such a *chef* as Pierre Leblond. Gardel had done Charles proud by composing a *pas de trois* in which the young lad was presented in the company of his cousin Auguste and Marie Gardel; and at a later performance the boy danced a *bolero* with Chevigny.

The fruits of a most careful training were evident – precision, suppleness, lightness, aplomb, vivacity – but added to all this was a rarer quality, that of expression. The occasion inevitably recalled the early appear-

[4] *Courrier de l'Europe*, 10 August 1809.

[5] *Journal de l'Empire*, 13 July 1809.

[6] *Courrier de l'Europe*, 9 September and 17 October 1809.

thing that was not complimentary. However, reading between the lines of their reviews, the tribute did not match up to the great events it was supposed to celebrate. One critic boldly suggested that the allegory form was 'out of favour ... extremely difficult ... out-worn ... capable of presenting only an imperfect and vain image'.[10] Another found the treatment 'a little stingy ... the composition somewhat vague and obscure ... proving how difficult it is to praise a hero whose slightest actions surpass all the marvels of fable'.[11]

Kreutzer's music, particularly the dance numbers, was favourably noticed, although considered inferior to his contribution to *Paul et Virginie*.

With almost the entire ballet company involved, Gardel had been prodigal with his dances. Vestris was as active as ever, whether in pastoral or martial guise, his dancing 'always strong and measured, expressive and restrained' and marked by 'a finish and a truth of expression that are the touchstone of a great master'.[12] A highlight was a *pas de deux* by Mme Gardel and Clotilde that set the grace of Terpsichore against Bellone's forceful power. In a dance between Flora and Zephyr, performed to one of the most lyrical numbers, Chevigny was at her most coquettish, while her young partner, Albert, showed off his lightness, grace and precision. There were also martial dances, wrestling bouts in which Elie, Anatole and Michel were in evidence, and a series of military evolutions which were remembered for a stroke of Gardel's genius – the introduction of children at play, weaving in and out of the soldiers' ranks.

* * *

Gardel also had another bagatelle up his sleeve, *Vertumne et Pomone*, which was performed before the court at the Tuileries on 4 January 1810, before being shown to the public of the Opéra three weeks later on the 24th.

Based on a legend that the Latin poet Ovid included in his *Metamorphoses*, it told of the wood-nymph Pomona, whose only passion was tending her orchard, which she had fenced around to keep out prospective suitors. Not even Silenus and the satyrs could seize her. Vertumnus, a deity particularly enamoured of her, adopted another tactic, appearing before her in a variety of disguises. In the fable he finally impersonated an old woman as a means of gaining her confidence. But even in this disguise he could not persuade her to forget her pride and surrender her-

[10] *Moniteur*, 28 December 1809.

[11] *Journal de Paris*, 27 December 1809.

self to a man who truly loved her. He then resumed his original form so as to take her by force, only to discover that, confronted with his true self, she was smitten with a passion equal to his own.

For his ballet Gardel had somewhat elaborated Ovid's account. Pomona (Mme Gardel) is in her orchard, where her aged companion, Agathis (M. Launer), tells her that Vertumnus desires to see her. Frightened, Pomona runs off. Unable to understand her reluctance, Vertumnus (Aug. Vestris) decides to change his form. In turn he appears as one of a group of harvesters, a woodland creature in the suite of Pan (Albert), and as a vintager – but in each case without success. In despair, he appeals to Cupid (V. Hullin), who advises him to disguise himself as Agathis. Pomona seems to be weakening, and when Cupid conjures up a vision of Vertumnus pining on a hilltop, confesses that she loves him. Vertumnus, in his disguise as Agathis, then finds himself confronted, in Pomona's presence, by the real Agathis. So confused is Pomona that she throws herself into the arms of Vertumnus, who throws off his disguise and reveals his divine form. The ballet then closes with the customary display of dancing.

Perhaps only the appeal of Marie Gardel and Vestris in the title rôles saved the ballet from being roundly condemned. The *Journal de Paris* probably expressed the general view that the plot was both weak and obscure.[13]

François Lefebvre had put together a workmanlike score in which two borrowings were recognised by the critics: 'the fine piece from the fourth act of *Armide*'[14] and Rameau's *pas des sauvages* from *Les Indes galantes*, introduced at the end of the ballet for a brilliant *pas de trois* by Albert, Clotilde and Bigottini.

Although not savaged by any of the critics, there could be no doubt that *Vertumne et Pomone* was a failure, and it was duly consigned to oblivion after only four performances at the Opéra. Napoleon had also been unimpressed, as he made clear in a letter to Rémusat, expressing the wish for more novelties and brushing it aside as

> a cold and insipid allegory. The ballet *L'Enlèvement des Sabines* is historical, and more suitable. One should not only give mythological and historical ballets, but never allegory. I want four ballets to be staged this year. If the Sr. Gardel cannot do this, find others to present them.

12 *Courrier de l'Europe*, 1 January 1810. Signed: B.

13 *Journal de Paris*, 26 and 27 January 1810.

14 *Courrier de l'Europe*, 25 January 1810. Possibly the aria *Amour, puissant Amour, dissipe mon effroi* from Act III (not Act IV) of Gluck's *Armide*.

In addition to *La Mort d'Abel*, I want another historical ballet more analogous to present circumstances than *L'Enlèvement des Sabines*.[15]

* * *

At a first reading it might have seemed strange that Napoleon considered *Vertumne et Pomone* as allegory rather than myth, but maybe Gardel had an eye to the forthcoming event that was already being talked about in court circles – the forthcoming marriage of the Emperor to a princess of one of Europe's ruling dynasties, from which an heir to the Imperial throne was to be expected. For Napoleon the divorce from Josephine, pronounced in January 1810, had been a very painful sacrifice, not unmixed with guilt, and Gardel's attempt at a compliment, if so it was, had fallen flat. The choice of a bride was made in February when, accepting that the Tsar would never approve a marriage to his sister, the Emperor made a formal request for the hand of the young Hapsburg archduchess, Marie-Louise. Events then moved swiftly, and in the spring the marriage was celebrated and France was given a new Empress.

A somewhat uneasy peace had settled over Europe, with Austria humbled, Prussia for the time being quiescent and Russia withdrawn into isolation. Spain remained a worrying sore, but though no solution was in sight, it seemed, for the time being, to offer no threat. France's main enemy was still the intransigent English. So that summer Paris was occupied with happier prospects as Napoleon wooed his new bride and displayed her to his court and his people. It was to catch this mood of celebration that Gardel prepared his next major ballet, for which he had chosen, as its subject, the exploits of the mythological hero Perseus. Planned as a dazzling spectacle that would exploit the marvels of the machinist's art, *Persée et Andromède* was allocated in March 1810 an unprecedented budget of 80,000 francs.

Napoleon had originally instructed Rémusat to make sure it would be ready by Easter Monday, 23 April, when he planned to bring his bride to the Opéra for the first time.[16] Other more pressing matters then intervened, and the occasion was postponed *sine die*. A few weeks later, Picard enquired of Rémusat whether the date could be fixed, and was told that it could not be earlier than 15 May.[17] The ballet was eventually announced for Friday 8 June 1810.

[15] Napoleon, *Lettres inédites*, II, 11–12. To Rémusat, 13 February 1810.
[16] Napoleon, *Correspondance*, XX, 292 (Letter no. 16305, 2 March 1810.)
[17] Bibl.-Mus. de l'Opéra, Fonds Teneo, 1/13. Rémusat to Picard, 10 April 1810.

But at the last minute Napoleon's plans changed, and his visit to the Opéra was moved to the following Tuesday. Perhaps because it made little difference to him whether he would be attending the first or the second performance, the arrangements to present the ballet on the 8th were not changed, the Imperial visit being scheduled for the 12th. This came as a blow to Gardel, who had set his heart on offering his new ballet as a personal tribute to his sovereign. Napoleon's cool reaction to *Vertumne et Pomone* had shaken his self-esteem; and the fact that no objection had been made by the Palace to the new ballet being first given in the absence of the Imperial couple suggested, in the sensitive state he was in, a further lack of confidence. Picard conveyed Gardel's despair to Rémusat, who shrugged it off as presumptuous to think that the Emperor's plans could be varied to suit his ballet-master's convenience, writing:

> Do you really imagine, my dear Director, that the Emperor's wishes must give way to the ideas of authors and the speculations of theatre directors? Gardel is mad when he talks of his besmirched reputation; another fine ballet from him will only add to his reputation, and will not be prejudiced just because Their Majesties have not attended the first performance. Suppose that they do not come either to the second or the third – would you then not give it at all? Besides, why should the Opéra lose its outlay on it? Will that make any difference to the ballet? No, no, my friend, try and have more confidence in the appeal of the great enterprise you administer and put your mind at rest regarding its success. To sum up, the Emperor's order is quite clear: the ballet must be given on Friday, and all will be well.[18]

So the ballet went ahead as planned in the absence of the Imperial couple, but before the more fashionable audience that habitually attended the Friday performances. Napoleon and Marie-Louise did attend the second performance, and presumably Gardel soon regained his sense of proportion.

While his choice of theme may have been influenced by the implications for the future of Napoleon's marriage to Marie-Louise, the conception and scale of the ballet were such that it stood to be assessed on its merits. Inevitably the scenario would be compared with the libretto that Philippe Quinault had written for Lully's lyric tragedy *Persée*, created at the Opéra in 1682. Presumably Gardel had carefully studied this when

[18] Arch. Nat., AJ13 93. Rémusat to Picard, 5 June 1810.

preparing his own narrative, which in its final form bore the stamp of his personal skill in devising a narrative for pantomime.

The action begins in the square outside the palace of King Cepheus of Ethiopia. The goddess Juno (V. Saulnier II) emerges from her Temple, furious that the Queen, Cassiopeia (Chevigny), has dared to build a palace more magnificent than her own. To exact her revenge she summons up the three Gorgons. Headed by Medusa, these frightening creatures (S. Mérante, Branchu, Anatole) emerge from the earth and are commanded to lay waste the land of Ethiopia. As Juno returns to her temple, they depart to carry out their evil task.

Perseus (Aug. Vestris) then enters in a sombre mood, expressing his love for Andromeda and his jealousy of his rival Phineas. When Phineas (Albert) enters, Perseus can barely restrain himself at the sight of his arrogance. After Phineas has announced he is to marry Andromeda, the two men are on the point of coming to blows when the King (Milon) and the royal family approach. It is clear that Andromeda (Mme Gardel) does not share her parents' happiness, and her tears at the sight of Perseus betray her true affections. Cassiopeia is visibly troubled. The square then fills, and the marriage festivities begin with bouts of strength, a contest for a prize for dancing and an archery competition. Finally Perseus and Phineas dance together, each attempting to outshine the other. Perseus is adjudged the finer dancer, and Andromeda cannot conceal her pleasure when she presents him with the victor's laurel.

When the festivities are over, the royal party proceeds to the Temple to beseech the blessing of the Goddess on the couple. The king is on the point of joining their hands when Perseus gives in to his despair. Shaken out of her fatalism, Andromeda refuses to continue with the ceremony. Phineas challenges Perseus to fight. However, before they can set to, the town is struck by an earthquake. The stage fills with terrified Ethiopians fleeing from the Gorgons. One old man looks back and is turned to stone. Amid the general panic, only Perseus remains calm. He declares himself ready to deliver the kingdom from this frightful danger, and demands the hand of Andromeda as the price of his valour. Despite Phineas's objection, the promise is given.

When the second act opens, Andromeda is walking alone in the royal gardens, bowed down with worry for Perseus's safety. She throws herself at the feet of a statue of Jupiter to implore his intervention. At that moment Perseus appears. She confesses her love; filled with joy, Perseus leaves to confront the Gorgons. Andromeda returns to the palace in tears.

The scene changes to a forest overlooking the sea, the stage being filled with people fleeing from the danger that threatens. Perseus enters, his calm yet warlike demeanour contrasting with the general panic. He is seeking the monster when Mercury appears to advise him against underestimating the power he is to face. Jupiter, he tells him, has decided to supplement his strength with arms of divine power, and Perseus is equipped with a sword from Vulcan's forge, wings like Mercury's own for his heels, Pallas's buckler and a helmet from Pluto's armoury that will make him invisible at will. Left on his own, Perseus is pondering on his course of action when Juno appears behind him, calling to the Gorgons and berating them for their laxity in carrying out her commands. She indicates Perseus to them, and conceals them in the forest. While Perseus is sensing the divine power of his new arms, he catches sight of the Gorgons and rushes towards them. Juno watches the scene with growing anxiety. Perseus's slaying of Medusa takes place off-stage, and he makes a triumphant reappearance astride the winged horse Pegasus, who has burst forth from the blood of Medusa. As the horse leaps over a rock, the fountain of Hippocrene miraculously gushes from it. Her anger now aroused, Juno calls upon Neptune's aid. From the boiling waters the sea-god emerges in a chariot drawn by four sea horses, with a retinue of Tritons and Nereids and other marine divinities borne on their shells. Neptune grants Juno's request, and on the shells appears the message: 'Andromeda shall die'.

Act III opens in a courtyard of the palace grounds, where the people are rejoicing at the death of Medusa. Only Phineas appears discontented, leaving no doubt that he is contemplating some mischief at the forthcoming wedding. But while Perseus's return is awaited, a band of Tritons burst in and seize Andromeda. Cassiopeia desperately tries to defend her daughter, even offering to take her place, but to no avail. When Perseus returns, he finds Cassiopeia weeping in despair. Learning what has happened, he flies to Andromeda's rescue.

The scene changes to a seashore dominated by an enormous rock overhanging the sea. The Tritons enter, bearing Andromeda, whom they chain to the rock. As a band of Ethiopians attempt to rescue her, a fearsome sea monster rises from the water to seize his prey. Andromeda faints in horror. Perseus comes flying in on Pegasus, and, seeing the monster on the point of devouring Andromeda, descends with the speed of lightning. His spear finds its mark, and as the wounded monster charges him, he dismounts and draws his sword. In the bitter struggle that ensues the sea turns red with blood, but the monster seems impervious to the blows of Perseus's weapon. In desperation, Perseus holds up the shield bearing Medusa's severed head. Immediately the monster is turned to stone; the sea becomes calm, and Andromeda is released and restored to her parents.

For the apotheosis a brilliant palace – painted by Isabey, and the only entirely new set in the ballet – descends to hide the scene of Andromeda's torment, and the gods of Olympus come to celebrate the marriage of the hero and his beloved. At Jupiter's wish, Juno presides and a great celebration ensues, with Hebe dispensing nectar, Zephyr refreshing the air with his breezes and Flora scattering her scents. After the happy pair have danced before the gods, Hymen and Cupid offer gifts, the Graces bedeck them with garlands and Jupiter assigns to Cassiopeia and Andromeda a rank among the constellations.

Despite the aversion to allegory that Napoleon had expressed a few months earlier, Gardel was not deterred from choosing a hero whose legendary exploits suggested an obvious parallel with contemporary history. For Perseus could indeed at that time be seen as a figure of Napoleonic grandeur, triumphing over awesome perils and sealing his final victory with marriage and the blessings of the Olympian deities. Perhaps it would be pressing the analogy too far to see the sea monster as a reflection of the English maritime power that still held out in its opposition to French hegemony in Europe. What was, of course, permissible was the reference to the hero winning his bride. This had been deemed in bad taste in January when Josephine's plight was uppermost in Napoleon's mind, but was appropriate in June when a seemingly rejuvenated Emperor sat in his box with his radiant young wife.

By the Tuesday the dancers were already aware of the complimentary reviews of the première, and performed with heightened confidence. Vestris's Perseus added to his growing reputation as a dancer-actor with two particularly memorable moments. The first was in Act I, when he is unable to contain his despair during the wedding ceremony; the other was at the end of Act II when, armed for the duel with the sea monster, he learns for the first time of Andromeda's love and is filled with renewed ardour. Of Marie Gardel's rendering of the princess, little was written beyond generalised references to her energy, grace and dignity. She was no doubt as perfect as ever, but what may have been lacking in her portrayal, although no one had the courage or the heart to voice such heresy, was warmth and passion. These were the two qualities that marked the greatest actress among the dancers of that time, Sophie Chevigny, who was unforgettable in the rôle of Cassiopeia. The scene following Andromeda's abduction by the Tritons was a set-piece of immensely powerful pantomime, the action of which Gardel had prescribed in great detail in his scenario:

> Cassiopeia tries to defend [Andromeda]. Despair, tears, prayers make up for her flagging strength; she pleads to take her daughter's place, or at least to accompany her, but all to no avail. Several Tritons from across the water have already borne Andromeda away, while others hold back her unfortunate mother. At last her strength fails her, and she falls, as if lifeless, to the ground. In this cruel situation the Tritons abandon her.
>
> Cassiopeia comes to her senses and opens her eyes. It is as if she is waking from a dream, with no recollection of what has occurred. Why is she lying on the ground, alone and so weak? Thoughts such as these, as her gestures reveal, flash through her mind. At last she rises to her feet, stretching out her arms as if seeking help.
>
> At this moment sounds of rejoicing are heard, and Perseus appears, surrounded by an immense crowd bearing him in triumph. Everyone around him carries a palm or a laurel wreath, which are offered to him as they dance; they press around him admiringly, the whole scene expressing the joy and gratitude they feel for the hero. This only adds to the poor queen's delirium, and she stands as if affixed. Noticing her, Perseus quells the crowd's enthusiasm. He hastens towards her and throws himself at her feet. Utterly distraught, Cassiopeia looks about her with unseeing eyes, as if unaware of the crowd, even of Perseus. She puts a hand to her forehead, then turns her head involuntarily towards the distant shore, where ... Andromeda is seen being carried off by the Tritons. Quick as lightning, Perseus flies in pursuit, followed by the crowd. This reaction restores Cassiopeia's memory of her distress. With loosened hair, and a wild look in her eyes, she walks towards the palace, crying and calling for help, her gestures revealing the disorder of her mind.
>
> The disturbance brings on several personages of the court. The king himself arrives. The effect on him of his wife's madness is beyond description. Cassiopeia points frantically to his daughter in the distance. For a moment he is overcome by despair, but paternal love gives him added strength and he sets off after her, followed by the queen and the court.

The power of Chevigny's silent rendering of a mother shocked out of her mind by the apparent loss of her daughter was by all accounts a *tour de force*, which Geoffroy for one found infinitely more interesting than the appearance of that 'masterpiece of the machinist's art', the awesome sea monster.

Albert had a somewhat thankless part as the villain, Phineas, but did not allow that to restrain the excellence of his dancing. In the dance contest with Perseus, in which the latter – a little unconvincingly, considering Vestris's age – carried off the prize, Geoffroy wryly commented that 'to be more faithful to the scenario, [he] should not have danced so well'.[19]

Another indispensable member of the cast was the horse that portrayed Pegasus, on which Perseus rode in the last act to rescue Andromeda. The scene demanded no ordinary animal such as might be found in one of the stables of the capital, but an exceptionally splendid creature trained to an infinite degree so that, equipped with wings attached to its flanks, it would convey an illusion that it was capable of flying even if it did not actually do so. For this passage, Vestris had to allow a stand-in to take over, for the Opéra had contracted with the Franconi brothers to supply, at a fee of 100 francs a performance, their most celebrated steed, well-known to audiences of the Cirque Olympique as 'Zéphire', with a Franconi or one of their most able riding-masters in the saddle.[20]

Geoffroy was sure that both the scale and the effect of the spectacle surpassed anything that had been seen on the stage before. Gardel, Boutron, Degotti and Isabey, he averred, were much more skilful thaumaturges (Geoffroy's word) than Torelli and other Italian magicians of stagecraft who had dazzled the Paris audiences in the time of Louis XIV. Nevertheless, the spectacle of the ballet's dramatic climax was marred by an unfortunate error of the designer, for Geoffroy and many others on the audience's right were unable to see the chained Andromeda on her rock and, what was worse, Perseus's fight against the sea monster.[21]

To provide music to accompany this great work, Gardel had renewed his collaboration with the composer who had served him so well ten years before in *La Dansomanie* – Etienne Méhul. His score for *Persée* was widely praised. He had borrowed several passages from his *opéra-comique Ariodant* (1799),[22] and a rondo from a sonata by Steibelt;[23] Geoffroy also recognised some familiar melodies by Gluck.[24]

If any of the cast was irreplaceable, it would have been Chevigny. Few dancers were more conscientious than she, and when she failed to appear

[19] *Journal de l'Empire*, 11/12 June 1810.

[20] Arch. Nat., AJ[13] 93. Contract dated 1 June 1810. Franconi had also supplied horses for *Fernand Cortez*.

[21] *Journal de l'Empire*, 14 June 1810.

[22] Castil-Blaze, *Académie*, II, 130.

[23] *Le Diable boiteux*, 16 October 1823.

[24] *Journal de l'Empire*, 14 June 1810.

at the fourth performance there was much surprise and concern. Happily, she had not been taken ill, and some days later she honestly explained what had happened in a letter to the press. She had been in the country on the day in question, and thought she had left enough time to be driven back to Paris, when someone told her the performance had been cancelled. When she realised that this person was mistaken, it was too late and she had to be replaced by Mimi Saulnier. Napoleon's all-seeing police soon heard all about it, and the daily bulletin placed before the Emperor the next day recounted the incident, adding that she had been 'at her country place at Vincennes with a young man of 24, a person little-known'.[25] For her it proved an expensive oversight, costing her a fine of one month's salary.

For all its scenic splendours and illusions and the efforts of the dancers, *Persée et Andromède* had a comparatively short existence. After five performances in June, it was not given again until January 1811. In that year it had fourteen performances; then came another interval between April and October, and it was billed for the last time in January 1812. Perhaps it was never consciously dropped, but was rather pushed aside by other ballets that entered the repertory, being allowed to languish through a combination of circumstances – the effort of keeping such a complex work in production, the growing disfavour of heroic subjects, the approaching retirement of some of the principal players, and perhaps not least, the difficulty of replacing 'Zéphire'.

[25] Lecomte, 133.

23

L'Enlèvement des Sabines

In the morning of 19 October 1810, Jean-Georges Noverre died in the fullness of age at his home in Saint-Germain-en-Laye. His ballets had long since ceased to be performed, but his ideas on his art were still honoured as fundamental authority. Only three years before, he had published an expanded version of his writings under the title *Lettres sur les arts imitateurs*, and in his latter years he had been compiling a dictionary of dance, which was unfinished at his death. In his long lifetime he had seen an old world pass and a new age dawn in which he, in common with so many of his contemporaries, had lost his savings and perhaps felt a little lost himself.

Vivid among his memories was that of a bright-eyed archduchess to whom he had given dancing lessons many years before in Vienna. Later, as Queen of France, she had eased him into the post of ballet-master at the Opéra and in grimmer times been brutally sacrificed to the blade of the guillotine. And in the last year of his life there had come to Paris as consort of France's new ruler another young Austrian princess, Marie-Louise, upon whom hopes rested, as formerly they had upon her aunt, Marie-Antoinette, that she would produce an heir.

Gallantly wooed as Josephine never was, Marie-Louise was given her first taste of the Paris ballet when, at Napoleon's side, she was dazzled by the marvels of *Persée et Andromaque*. For all the difference in their ages, it was proving a happy match, and it soon became known that she was with child. During the months of her pregnancy, Napoleon went several times to the Opéra on his own; but she was not to be deprived altogether of such pleasures, for by her husband's command the first performance of Milon's *L'Enlèvement des Sabines* was to be presented for her benefit in the court theatre at Fontainebleau. Pillaged during the Revolution, this ancient palace had been restored to much of its former glory and, following a tradition of the Old Régime, was now beginning to be used again for autumn visits of the Napoleonic court. The transportation of dancers, musicians and ancillary personnel, with all their paraphernalia of costumes, props, instruments and scenery, for a single performance would be a most challenging logistical exercise, not least because the caravan was to travel through the night.

The date fixed was Sunday 4 November 1810, the performance being planned to round off a day of festivities centred on the baptism of twenty-seven boys, all sons of courtiers, to whom Napoleon and Marie-Louise would stand as god-parents. All the arrangements hung together, and as the day approached no hitch could be contemplated without the fear of incurring the Emperor's wrath. But almost at the last minute, to the horror of Rémusat, on whom responsibility rested, came news that Marie Gardel, who, as was her due, was playing a pivotal rôle, was injured. No understudy had been coached, and it seemed that the programme might have to be changed. In a state of great alarm, Rémusat wrote to Picard:

> Please, I beg of you, give orders so that, come what may, the performance will go ahead. M. Courtin[1] writes that Mme Gardel will do all she can and that I shall be advised later if it is impossible for her to take part. This is quite unacceptable. I cannot say to the Emperor on the eve of the performance: 'Mme Gardel injured herself last Tuesday, and since she is unable to dance, you will have no performance.' It would be utterly inconvenient if she cannot; the rôle must be given to someone else – nothing must prevent the programme as announced. Have you advised Milon to shorten his ballet? See that he well understands that if it is too long, it will be judged bad, and what good will that do?[2]

Whether or not Milon adjusted her part at the last minute, Marie Gardel did not let Rémusat down, although the effort was to cost her dear: it would be nearly three weeks before she could resume her activity at the Opéra.

Much more dramatic was a last-minute catastrophe, discovered only when the heavily lumbered caravan reached its destination on the morning of the performance. Because the contractor had failed to provide a wagon capacious enough to take the costumes and accessories, the head tailor had had to pack the costumes in a leather trunk strapped to the outside of one of the carriages. The night was dark and stormy, and the deluging rain never let up. Security had been lax, and at one of the stops along the way thieves had made off with the thirty-two costumes for the Roman and Sabine soldiers, leaving the trunk half-open so that some of the other costumes in it were drenched. Rémusat was hastily informed,

[1] Secretary of the Opéra, and husband of the dancer Alexandrine Rivière.
[2] Bibl.-Musée de l'Opéra, Fonds Teneo 1/13. Rémusat to Picard, 31 October 1810.

and orders were given for new costumes to be made on the spot. The storerooms of the palace were ransacked for suitable material; as many needlewomen as could be found were pressed into service under the supervision of the head tailor. In just four hours new costumes were run up; though no doubt lacking the splendour of the stolen ones, they saved the day.[3]

Cynical observers might have found an historical parallel between the incident of the rape of the Sabine women by the early Romans and Napoleon's demand for the hand of the Archduchess Marie-Louise to ensure the continuation of his dynasty, but this was certainly far from Milon's intention. Napoleon had indeed been contemplating divorce from Josephine that previous summer, but he did not reveal his intention until the end of November, by which time Milon's scenario had been completed and the costing of the scenery requirements was well under way.

It had been priced at the modest figure of 6480 francs on the basis of using existing pieces of scenery: for Act I, a backcloth from *La Prise de Jéricho* (1805) and part of a set from *Ossian* (1804); for Act II, Scene 1, the mountain backcloth from *Aspasie* (1789) and the forest cut-cloths from *Alvire et Evelina* (1788); for Act II, Scene 2, the Temple of Diana from *Alceste* (1776); and for Act III, the fortifications from *Horatius Coclès* (1794) and tree-pieces from *La Mort d'Adam* (1809). Later on, when the time came for an estimate, Degotti, officially designer-in-chief, was passed over because Napoleon had lost patience with him on account of his tardiness, and the responsibility of designing the production was delegated to the more businesslike Jean-Baptiste Isabey. Isabey's estimate, submitted in February 1810, amounted to 22,000 francs, suggesting that the Opéra had decided to be more generous in the allocation of funds.[4]

For Milon the lengthy gestation of *L'Enlèvement des Sabines* must have been a source of great frustration, for not only did he have to yield priority to Gardel, but preparations were continuously being interrupted for operas needing ballet scenes. For Catel's *Les Bayadères*, presented in August 1810, both Gardel and Milon were required to contribute ballets, Gardel's being particularly important and unusual in consisting largely of a sequence of ensembles with practically no *pas seuls*. In March 1811, to commemorate the birth of a son to Napoleon and Marie-Louise, Gardel was called upon to devise a *divertissement* on the theme of Diana and Endymion for a one-act allegorical tableau by Kreutzer, *Le Triomphe du mois de mars*. The next diversion was Fiocchi's opera *Sophocle*, produced in

[3] Arch. Nat., AJ^{13} 76. Report by the Inspector of Costumes to Picard. Castil-Blaze, *Académie*, II, 131–2.
[4] Arch. Nat., AJ^{13} 93.

April, in which the contributions of Gardel and Milon were by common consent the only parts that were at all memorable. After that Gardel was required to produce new ballets for a revival of Gluck's *Armide* in June. No wonder Milon had to wait nearly eight months before his *Enlèvement des Sabines* could be presented on the stage of the Opéra.

His scenario was based on an historical event that took place early in the history of Rome. As chronicled by the historian Livy, Rome was at that time faced with a pressing need to increase its population if it was to expand; and the reluctance of neighbouring communities such as the Sabines and the Caeninians to allow their women to choose Roman husbands was a major obstacle. Romulus, Rome's first king, therefore announced a festival to which the Sabines and other neighbouring folk came in large numbers. While the celebrations were at their height, the young Roman males burst through the crowd and carried off the young women. In time most of the women lost their resentment and settled down with their Roman husbands, but their bereft families demanded vengeance. In the tribal wars that followed, the Sabines alone remained undefeated, and their fierce struggle against the Romans was only brought to an end when the Sabine women thrust their way between the lines of the warring armies to make an appeal for peace that could not be ignored. The two tribes then joined forces, and the size of the Roman state was doubled at a stroke.

Milon's ballet opened with Romulus (Milon) presiding over a parade of his Guards, who are expressing their sorrow at being wifeless. Assuring them that he is trying to persuade the neighbouring communities to agree to intermarriage with Romans, Romulus announces that the Sabines and the Caeninians will be attending a festival to honour the gods. The stage then begins to fill with the Caeninians, the first visitors to arrive, led by their king, Acron (Godefroi), who is accompanied by Clelia (Mme Gardel), daughter of one of his courtiers. They are impressed by the grandeur of the city, but when Romulus offers an alliance to permit intermarriage, it is rejected. Romulus conceals his anger and turns to receive the Sabines and their king, Tatius (Goyon). He requests the hand of Tatius's daughter, Hersilia (Clotilde), but is met with a refusal. Still dissimulating, he enters the Temple to consult the god. When he emerges, he instructs his captains to carry out certain secret orders at a given signal. While the Sabine and Caeninian women are happily dancing in the square, this signal is given and the Roman soldiers burst among them and seize them. Romulus's friend Tribunus (Aug. Vestris) carries off Clelia, while Romulus himself seizes Hersilia despite Tatius's resistance. Acron attacks Romulus, but is disarmed. The young women are then taken to the Temple of Juno, while Romulus invites the two kings to accept the will of the gods and consent to the alliance he has proposed. They withdraw in indignation, threatening to burn Rome to the ground. The women are then placed under the care of the priests, and the Roman army marches off to give battle to the Caeninians.

In the second act the action moves to an enclosure in the Temple grounds. The captive women are led in, and the High Priest (Lhuillier) tries to calm their fears. Hersilia and Clelia are contemplating escape. There is general indignation at the sight of an inscription reading 'Romulus orders the marriage of the Sabine women to the Romans'. Hersilia persuades the women to refuse to marry without their parents' consent, and to pull down the offending inscription. At that moment, Tribunus comes to announce the Roman victory. The priests offer up thanks before leading the crestfallen women into the Temple. Clelia, however, is waylaid by Tribunus, who professes his love so passionately that she finally yields. Hersilia emerges from the Temple and reproaches Clelia. In vain Tribunus tries to appease Hersilia; Clelia, torn between two loyalties, follows Hersilia into the Temple. When Romulus returns victorious, the Caeninian women, recognising their relatives among his prisoners, plead for their freedom. Romulus agrees only in the case of those whose daughters marry Romans. Clelia is willing, and the other Caeninian women yield, to be bitterly reproached by the Sabines for betraying the common cause. The High Priest then consults the auguries, and the sight of two doves flying side by side in the sky is interpreted as a sign that the gods approve the marriages. Most of the Sabine women are persuaded; consenting to take Roman husbands, they enter the Temple for the ceremony.

The third act opens in the interior of the Temple. Hersilia and a few Sabine women who are still resisting are told to await the arrival of Romulus. He then enters, expressing a wish to speak to Hersilia alone. Declaring his love, he begs her to share his crown, but she is not to be persuaded. He then pulls aside the curtain concealing the sanctuary and reveals those Sabine women who have already married Romans. Hersilia resists his attempt to conduct her to the altar. Brandishing a dagger, she threatens to kill herself should he persist in his violence. He disarms her at the very moment when a deputation from the Sabines is announced. Romulus is not to be shaken from his decision that the Sabine women who have married Romans must remain in Rome. The women are in despair, for they realise that this means war. Hersilia alone keeps her head, summoning her companions to join her in separating the opposing armies and calling on them to lay down their arms.

The scene changes to the ramparts of Rome, with the Citadel and the Capitoline Hill to the right and the city gate to the left. Tatius, the Sabine king, is planning a counter-attack. The sentry at the gate is felled, and a party of Sabines climbs the wall to take the Citadel and open the gate. The Romans are taken by surprise, and battle is joined. Hersilia and her companions, their hair loosened, come running in to place themselves between the combatants. She stays Romulus's arm as he aims a deadly blow at Tatius, at the same time begging her father to accept the Romans not as enemies but as husbands and fathers. Her wishes are respected; Romulus and Tatius make peace, and with her father's consent Hersilia agrees to marry Romulus. In an explosion of joy, the ballet closes with a feast of dancing.

Milon's choice of theme reflected the current fascination with ancient Rome, there being obvious parallels with Napoleonic France and its expansionist foreign policy. The incident of the Sabine women, of course, predated by many centuries the age of the Caesars that was now the more obvious point of comparison, but such a minor anachronism did not detract from its relevance to French eyes, for Romulus was as good a forerunner of Napoleon as Augustus. In other circumstances it might have been presented as an act of brigandage, but to a régime that derived its inspiration from military adventure, such an interpretation was no longer permissible.

Be that as it may, the tale had been woven into the legend of Rome. On the passing of the Roman Empire many centuries later, it had been transmitted to the Western civilisation that was now, to the French way of thinking, represented by the establishment of Napoleon's new order. It was on this hypothesis that Milon's ballet was based, presenting the incident as one that was both historically justifiable and, far from being a rape in the accepted sense, was finally sealed by a consent that was willingly given.

When it was presented at the Opéra on 25 June 1811, more than seven months after it had been given before the court, Milon must have been well content. The wealth of dramatic detail in the plot required that a high proportion of the performance time had to be taken up with scenes of pantomime, which was Milon's forte; but at appropriate moments he had interwoven dances with such skill that no one complained of *longueurs*.

The dances in the first act came naturally during the festivities for the peoples of the neighbouring tribes. There was first a stirring military dance by four male soloists supported by fifteen men from the corps de ballet. Tribunus then invited the Sabines and Caeninians to join in the general rejoicing, selecting Clelia and two Sabine women to dance with him. Performed by Vestris and Mme Gardel, Emilie Bigottini and Louise Launer, this was a passage of great brilliance. Although he was now fifty-one, Vestris threw off pirouettes with the most daring panache, quite oblivious that the audience was on tenterhooks lest he should come a cropper, as seemed inevitable right up to the very last moment when, miraculously, he held his balance. This was followed by a general dance, violently interrupted when Romulus sent in his soldiers to seize the women. The act then closed with a dramatic rendering of the famous incident of the 'rape', containing references to Poussin's painting of the incident that hung in the Louvre. In it was a passage between Tribunus and Clelia, who have fallen in love at first sight, played with great sensitivity by Vestris and Marie Gardel. After that came the impressive mime scene – 'a veritable *jeu de théâtre*', Geoffroy called it[5] – with Chevigny as a Sabine woman preferring death to dishonour. Entering with eyes blazing, she is prevented only after a fierce struggle from plunging a dagger into her breast.

The second act was more intimate in scale, treating of the consequences of Romulus's defeat of the Caeninians, and the effect on the Sabine women of the augury of the doves. The scene of the mass marriage of the Sabine women was movingly impressive as, with heads and shoulders covered by red veils, they performed 'a kind of sad, slow and forced dance that well [expressed] the violent effort they had to make to marry their abductors'.[6] As Hersilia, the Sabine heroine who almost alone displays a heroic resistance to the Romans, Clotilde dominated the stage with her 'nobility and energy', particularly in a great scene with Chevigny when she vented her fury on the young Sabine, who in her eyes is guilty of a treacherous love.

A principal source of Milon's inspiration was, of course, David's great canvas *The Intervention of the Sabine Women*, painted in 1799 and already hanging on the walls of the Louvre. From it the setting of the last act can be imagined, for behind the mass of combatants crowding the forefront of the scene rises the citadel and, on the summit of the Capitoline Hill, the Temple of Juno. David showed the two kings in attitudes that Milon may well have copied for his ballet; and separating them, with arms outstretched, is the leader of the Sabine women. 'M. Milon,' recorded a critic, 'did not lose sight of his model, David's Romulus; and Goyon imitated the Tatius of the Louvre, just as Mlle Clotilde rendered the beau idéal of the

[5] *Journal de l'Empire*, 27 June 1811.
[6] *Journal de l'Empire*, 27 June 1811.

Hersilia that we admired at the Salon. But the military details of the third act seem a little niggardly for such a decisive event.' However, if the opposing ranks seemed a little sparse, the splendour of the costumes made up for it, although at the expense, as that same critic observed, of historical accuracy:

> As for the scenery, it possesses a simplicity quite in keeping with the first age of Rome, when those celebrated warriors used a sheaf of hay for their standard. But the costumes seemed to strike a discordant note, offering too great a contrast with the coarse clothing that was worn by the earliest inhabitants of the Tiber. But this observation, which echoes criticisms made of David's painting, is refuted by the need for artists to seek the beau idéal in historical paintings rather than to express actual settings and costumes as in the pictures of David Teniers. Furthermore, in Paris, where, as Voltaire has said, 'everything is depicted in terms of beauty', it would have been impossible, even ridiculous, to show early Romans clad in wretched woollen material and the Sabines no less coarsely garbed.[7]

The composer of the music, Henry-Montan Berton, was a newcomer to ballet, but already well known as a prolific composer of *opéras-comiques*. In accordance with the practice of the time, his score for *L'Enlèvement des Sabines* contained numerous borrowings from other composers. In addition to snatches from Monsigny, Sacchini and Gluck were melodies, too good not to be used again, from three of his own works: *Montano et Stéphanie, ou la Folle soirée* (1799), the finale from which accompanied the scene of the Sabines scaling the walls to surprise the Romans; *Aline, reine de Golconde* (1803); and *Françoise de Foix* (1809). These were skilfully woven into the score, but a less happy insertion was the well-known song *La Charmante Gabrielle*, which accompanied the scene of Romulus declaring his love for Hersilia in the second act. This was widely criticised as being unsuitable and in poor taste; the composer accepted the rebuke and replaced it with something more appropriate. The music for the dances, on the other hand, was wholly original, as the Regulations prescribed. It was, however, considered rather severe, which one critic justified by explaining that 'the sweet and, one might say, effeminate music of today's dances can have no relation to the earliest times of Roman civilisation'.[8]

A companion piece to *Le Retour d'Ulysse* as a serious pantomime-ballet

[7] *Courrier de l'Europe*, 22 July 1811.

[8] *Courrier de l'Europe*, 29 June, and 5 and 27 July 1811.

on a classical theme, *L'Enlèvement des Sabines* was to survive for longer than the earlier work and to accumulate a greater tally of performances. Its choreographer could well have been satisfied with its success. In his position as second *maître de ballet* he had few opportunities of staging major works, but being a modest man with no particular desire to undertake the administrative burden that Gardel bore, he was generally satisfied with his lot, although in the intimacy of his family he may at times have allowed a mild grumble to pass his lips.

In his quiet way he could stand up for himself, but his wife, who was a Bigottini with hot Italian blood coursing through her veins, was quick to support her nearest and dearest if she felt they were being unjustly treated. That summer her headstrong nature had led to an unfortunate incident arising out of a conviction that her sister, Emilie Bigottini, was being deprived of promotion to *premier sujet* because the incumbent in the *demi-caractère* genre, the forty-one-year-old Mme Gardel, showed no sign of relinquishing it. So obsessed did Mme Milon become with her sister's plight that she began to utter derogatory remarks during performances.

Her behaviour soon became more than a joke, and Marie Gardel felt obliged to put a stop to it. She therefore posted some of her friends close to Mme Milon to report what they overheard. After just three performances she had collected enough evidence on which to base a formal complaint to Picard:

> When, at the most recent performance of *Le Devin du village*, Mme Gardel made her entrance, some strangers, mistaking her for Mlle Bigottini, who had danced the *pas* the time before, said: 'What a delightful dancer Mlle Bigottini is!' At this, Mme Milon turned to them and replied: 'You must be seeing things to take that woman to be my sister. Well, I should be most annoyed if there was any resemblance. And what is more, she takes care to prevent my sister from dancing.'
>
> On Sunday, when the curtain rose on *Paul et Virginie*, Mme Milon said to a stout woman sitting next to her, in a voice loud enough to attract the audience's attention to her outburst: 'Look, there's that dried-up old woman again. My God, what a sour look that woman has! How I dislike her.' The person posted by the side of this shrew to gather these pretty sayings pretended to know little about what was going on and enquired if it was Mme Gardel, to which the lady replied: 'Oh yes, but she's too old to play that rôle.'
>
> When, a little later, Mlle Bigottini made her entrance, the person posted by me or my friends asked who was the person playing the Negress, to which Mme Milon promptly replied: 'That is my sister, the

finest dancer of the Opéra.' When Mlle Saulnier made her entrance, Mme Milon, who was determined to belittle everything that might favour a work that was not her husband's, at once said: 'Just look at that great lump, Victoire, and all the faces she is making. How badly she acts!' And all this at the top of her voice.

Yesterday, during the ballet *Alexandre chez Apelles*, the shrew was talking to Mlle Chevigny, who was telling Mme Milon how she had resisted the entreaties of M. Gardel, who had wanted her to dance the *pas* she usually performed at the end of that ballet. This met with the full approval of Mme Milon, who said to her: 'Quite right too!' This simple particular is only mentioned to prove the accuracy of the man who was there to find out what that charming Mme Milon was saying. As she was whispering to Mlle Chevigny, a man who had just entered the stalls and had remained by the door said to Mme Milon: 'So you always like to run down Mme Gardel?' 'Yes,' she replied. 'I've had enough of that bag of bones.'

This is what happened at three performances, and to conclude this report on the silly remarks very typical of the woman who made them, it is perhaps necessary that our kind and good Director, M. Picard, should know that he is not spared either, and that his name is sometimes sullied by issuing from the lips of that foul-mouthed Mme Milon, who, after the scandalous scene she had made to Mlle A-d——, announced to those in the stalls: 'I have had a letter from that confounded ham of a Director whom we could well do without, but I don't care a damn for him or for the administration, and I'll wipe my behind with his letter.'

I can vouch for all these facts as if I had heard them myself.[9]

The altercation between Mme Milon and Mlle Audinot had compounded the scandal. Eulalie Audinot, a retired singer and Maximilien Gardel's sister-in-law, was firmly in the Gardel camp, and the spat between the two ladies was doubtless most colourful. But, however entertaining to those within earshot, it could not be countenanced, and Picard wrote to both ladies in identical terms:

> I have just this moment learnt that you created a scandalous scene during yesterday's performance at the Opéra. This is not the first time it has come to the administration's notice that you have been making derogatory remarks about some of the artistes. Yesterday they went

[9] Arch. Nat., AJ[13] 82. Mme Gardel to Picard, 13 May 1811.

too far, descending to the level of gross insults, which I like to think make you blush to remember ....

Were it not for the respect in which Milon is held by virtue of his position, his talent, his zeal and his conduct, I would have been forced to report the matter to the Superintendent, who might have decided to ban you from entering the Académie. I warn you, Madame, that if such a scene occurs again, I shall be forced to take such extreme measures.

Although Mlle Audinot made a prompt denial, there is no record of a response from Mme Milon. Perhaps she decided to remain silent, leaving it to her husband to make peace with the Director.[10]

[10] Arch. Nat., AJ[13] 82. Mme Gardel to Picard, 13 May 1811. Mlle Audinot to Picard, 17 May 1811.

24

'L'Enfant prodigue'

During the lull that followed the Wagram campaign, Napoleon was able to lead a more settled life. He was still keeping a watchful eye on the political situation in Europe, which for the moment seemed to be accepting his new order, but now, with his new Empress, he was spending more time on peaceful affairs closer to home. He had always taken a close personal interest in the affairs of the Opéra, and in the autumn of 1811 he instructed Rémusat to ask Gardel to submit proposals for a major new ballet. Gardel's response was to put forward two projects. The first was *Guillaume Tell*, a work he had long given up hope of ever presenting, and the other a new scenario entitled *L'Enfant prodigue*.

He had conceived *Tell* during the Revolution, and over the years had spent many hours polishing its scenario; it had even gone into production, but to his bitter disappointment had more than once been shelved. Now, when it seemed fated to remain forever unstaged, he had seen another chance for it. But this was hardly the moment to extol a liberator who threw off a foreign yoke, and, although disappointed, Gardel could not have been surprised when Napoleon preferred his other proposal: *L'Enfant prodigue*, a subject free of unfavourable political allusions.

Gardel had based his treatment of the biblical parable of the prodigal son on a recently published poem of epic proportions. He may well have had a copy of the poem in his hands before it was printed, and probably knew its author, Vincent Campenon, personally. A confirmed royalist, Campenon had escaped to Switzerland at the outset of the Revolution, but returned to France during the Consulate. Thanks to the influence of friends with connections, he had been placed in charge of the Office of Theatres at the Ministry of the Interior, but the leniency he showed in his task of examining plays displeased the First Consul and he was dismissed. Once again his friends came to the rescue, and he became Imperial Commissioner at the Opéra-Comique. Meanwhile, his reputation as a poet had been growing, and *L'Enfant prodigue* was his first major success, reflecting the state's more sympathetic attitude towards the Christian religion.

Campenon's poem made quite a stir when it came out in 1811, and gave rise to a number of stage versions of one kind or another. One of these, an *opéra-comique* by Gaveaux, was a miserable failure, but better fortune attended Gardel's ballet.

His project was included in the budget for 1811 and Napoleon gave it a special allocation of 60,000 francs. On 12 December Picard instructed Gardel to begin work on the production and to provide Isabey and Boutron with details of the scenic requirements. Apart from a few flats formerly used in *La Mort d'Adam* and *Les Mystères d'Isis*, the scenery was to be entirely new.

Gardel had very skilfully woven Campenon's lengthy poem (running to nearly 300 pages in its first edition) into three very contrasting acts, giving his characters, whom St Luke had left anonymous, the names bestowed upon them by the poet. From Campenon too had come the choice of Memphis as the scene of the prodigal son's sowing of wild oats, but for his birthplace Gardel had himself selected Goshen in the Nile delta. This curious choice had come about through Gardel's concern not to infringe more than necessary those Aristotelian unities of time and place that were still sanctified in the French classical theatre. Some bending of the rules was unavoidable, and, stickler that he was for the proprieties, Gardel offered his excuses and an explanation of a sort in the introduction to his scenario. There he suggested, a little lamely, that the 'short distance' (actually about fifty miles) between Goshen and Memphis made the speed at which the prodigal son would have to travel on foot between the last two acts 'less unbelievable', even if the twenty-four-hour time-span prescribed by the rule was unfortunately exceeded. Within the bounds of the plot such an infringement was inevitable, and Gardel's concern was characteristic not only of the care he took with his scenarios, but also of the respect with which he was wont to adapt another author's work.

Gardel's *L'Enfant prodigue* was given its first performance at the Opéra on 28 April 1812. It was warmly received; the receipts exceeded 8000 francs on the first night, and the praise awarded to its choreographer was unanimous.

The ballet divided itself naturally into three acts, neatly representing the exposition, the intrigue and the denouement. The first act, set in the region of Goshen, opens peacefully with the aged Ruben (Milon) sleeping before his tent, watched over by his family: his wife Nephtale (Chevigny), and his two sons, Pharan (S. Mérante) and Azaël (Aug. Vestris). Azaël is obviously his mother's favourite; she senses that he is fretting, but cannot bring him to confide in her. It being a feast day, Ruben leads his people in prayer. The girls perform a gentle dance with the shepherds. One of them, Jephtèle (Mme Gardel), cannot conceal her love for Azaël, but he is indifferent to her. Then, all of a sudden, it is noticed that he has vanished. Nephtale sends a servant in search, and Azaël is observed in the distance, ascending the nearby mountain. He is brought back; when questioned, he admits that he finds life in Goshen unbearably restrictive and has set his heart on going to Memphis. He asks for his father's blessing. Ruben is silent for a moment, and then gives orders to make ready for his son's departure. A camel is loaded with a generous supply of money. After Ruben has retired into his tent, Nephtale tries again to dissuade Azaël, but to no avail. Tearfully, she watches her son disappear from sight, and then, on a sudden impulse, sets off after him. Jephtèle, who has been observing her, realises that a sandstorm is brewing and goes in pursuit. At first it is feared that Nephtale has gone to accompany her son, but to everyone's relief Jephtèle returns, supporting the exhausted mother. In gratitude for saving Nephtale's life, Ruben adopts Jephtèle as his daughter.

In the second act the architectural splendour of Memphis formed a striking contrast to the rustic setting of the village. It is the feast-day of Apis, and when Azaël appears, accompanied by his father's old servant (Elie), three rogues single him out as a likely prey. After the servant has left him with entreaties to be careful, Azaël is looking around with amazement at the splendid scene when he is accosted by one of the rogues (Goyon), who plants a seed in his mind that he should dress more elegantly to enjoy the pleasures of the city. At the sight of the festival procession, Azaël is overwhelmed by the music and the colour, and no less by the beauty of the dancers. But his eyes then fall on a Moabite visitor (Godefroy) and his daughter, Lia (Bigottini). Azaël falls in love at first sight with Lia, who modestly responds to his admiration. He feels ashamed in his simple country clothes, but at that moment one of the rogues appears bearing an elegant new costume. To the sound of two contrasting marches – one solemn, to accompany the priests and dignatories, and the other light and gay to enliven the dances of the people before the idol of Apis – Azaël, now in his new clothes, looks around for Lia. Not seeing her, he makes his way to the temple, followed by the three rogues.

The scene changes to another quarter of the city, before the temple of Apis, with the Nile in the background. The procession enters the temple, leaving the revellers outside. Azaël sees Lia and her father making their way inside, and thrusts his way through the crowd to follow them. The three rogues remain outside, plotting to fleece Azaël in a game of dice. Azaël emerges from the temple with Lia, and timidly tells her of his love. At first she is embarrassed and seems to want to withdraw. Sensing his

37. Auguste Vestris as Azaël in *L'Enfant prodigue*. Engraving by Prud'hon from a drawing by Sébastien Coeuré. (Bibliothèque-Musée de l'Opéra: © Cliché BNF Paris)

38. *L'Enfant prodigue,* Act I. Costume sketches by François-Guillaume Ménageot. Left to right: Milon as Ruben, Chevigny as Nephtale, Auguste Vestris as Azaël, Mme Gardel as Jephtèle. (Bibliothèque-Musée de l'Opéra: © Cliché BNF Paris)

39. *L'Enfant prodigue,* Act II. Costume sketches by François-Guillaume Ménageot. Left to right: Bigottini as Lia, [Godefroy as Lia's father], Auguste Vestris as Azaël, [Elie as Ruben's servant]. (Bibliothèque-Musée de l'Opéra: © Cliché BNF Paris)

40. *L'Enfant prodigue*. Costume sketches by François-Guillaume Ménageot. Left figure: Marinette as the angel in Act III; third figure: Vestris as Azaël in his fine clothes, Act II. (Bibliothèque-Musée de l'Opéra: © Cliché BNF Paris)

41. *L'Enfant prodigue*. Design by Jean-Baptiste Isabey for Act II. (Bibliothèque-Musée de l'Opéra: © Cliché BNF Paris)

42. (above) Emilie Bigottini. From a portrait by Henri-François Riesner; drawn by Charles-Etienne Le Guay, lithographed by G. Engelmann. (Bibliothèque-Musée de l'Opéra)
43.(right) Emilie Bigottini. Portrait by Jean-Baptiste Isabey, painted during the Congress of Vienna, 1814. (Graphische Sammlung Albertina, Vienna: © Albertina, Wien)

55. Emilie Bigottini as Vittoria, disguised as *la folie*, in *Le Carnaval de Venise*. Engraving by Pierre Prud'hon from a drawing by Sébastien Coeuré. (Bibliothèque-Musée de l'Opéra)

56. *Proserpine*. Sketch for Act II, Scene 6 (Lake Spergus covered with swans), by Pierre-Luc-Charles Ciceri. (Bibliothèque-Musée de l'Opéra: © Cliché BNF Paris)
57. *Proserpine*. Sketch for Act II, Scene 9 (Mount Etna erupting; in a cloud, a chariot drawn by horses), by Pierre-Luc-Charles Ciceri. (Bibliothèque-Musée de l'Opéra: © Cliché BNF Paris)

ACADEMIE ROYALE

DE MUSIQUE.

On commencera à sept heures précises. -- Aujourd'hui dimanche 13 février 1820,

PAR EXTRAORDINAIRE,

LE CARNAVAL DE VENISE,

Ballet-pantomime en un acte de M. *Milon*, musique de M. *Kreutzer* et *Persuis*; suivi

DU ROSSIGNOL,

Opéra en un acte, paroles de M. *Etienne*, musique de M. *Lebrun*, divertissemens de M. *Gardel*.

Le Spectacle sera terminé par

LES NOCES DE GAMACHE,

Ballet-pantomime en deux actes de M. *Milon*, musique de M. *Lefebvre*.

CHANT : Mrs. Lays, Nourrit, Bonel, Trévaux; Mmes. Albert, Lebrun, Reine.

DANSE dans le *Carnaval* : Mrs. Albert, Ferdinand, Coulon, Capelle, Elie; Mmes. Bigottini, Courtin, Aimée, Virginie Hullin, Legros, Brocard, Perès, Hullin 3e., Leroux 1re., Leroux 2e., Bertrand 2e.

DANSE dans *le Rossignol*: Mrs. Ragaine, Richard 1er.; Mmes. Bertin, Nanine Narra, Seuriot 1re.

DANSE dans *les Noces de Gamache* : Mrs. Paul, Ferdinand, Montjoye, Mérante, Anatole, Capelle, Ragaine, Seuriot, Godefroy, L'enfant 1er., Gosselin, Lefebvre; Mmes. Fanny Bias, Delisle, Marinette Boissière, Elie, Virginie Hullin, Brocard 1re., Vigneron, Aubry, Perès.

MM. les Locataires de loges et Abonnés jouiront de leurs droits à cette représentation en remplacement de celle de demain lundi.

Demain lundi 14, *RELACHE*, à minuit BAL MASQUÉ.

S'adresser pour la location des Loges à la Salle de l'Académie royale de Musique.

C. BALLARD, Imprimeur du Roi, rue J.-J. Rousseau, n. 8.

58. Playbill for the last performance at the Salle Montansier, 13 February 1820, the night of the assassination of the Duc de Berry. (Bibliothèque-Musée de l'Opéra: © Cliché BNF Paris)

59. The carriage of the Duc de Berry turning from the Rue Richelieu into the Rue de Rameau. The side door, outside which he was assassinated, is just beyond the sentry box. (Simond, *Paris de 1800 à 1900*)

60. The assassination of the Duc de Berry. (Musée Carnavalet: © MVP/negative Desgraces) Louvel is seen being apprehended as if he had been running towards the Rue Lully. In fact, he tried to escape in the other direction.
61. The death of the Duc de Berry. Oil painting by François-Barthélémy Michel. (Musée Carnavalet: © MVP/negative Joffre) Since the ballet is shown still in progress, this must be seen as the Duke being attended to shortly after he was brought into the little salon.

opportunity, he passionately declares his love. Frightened, she is about to return to the temple, when Azaël holds her back. He threatens to kill himself if she will not listen to him. Confused, Lia runs back into the temple after throwing her belt to Azaël, who covers it with kisses. After the priests have left, he waits for Lia to come out again, believing she has rejected him. But when she joins him, it is to tell him she returns his love, but that their relationship can only continue if she is to be his wife. Forgetting his duties to his family and his tribe, he agrees, and she gives him her hand.

When her father emerges from the temple and learns what has happened, his fury knows no bounds. He curses his daughter and disowns her. Lia is distraught, realising she now has no support other than Azaël. She looks round for him, but cannot see him because he has become caught up in the revelling crowd. Meanwhile, anxiously searching for her, he has been set upon by four attractive young revellers, one of whom snatches away Lia's belt. Observing this incident, Lia becomes desperate; at the sight of Azaël apparently joining in the revelry and throwing her belt at the feet of one of the girls, she sees herself abandoned. In tears, she snatches the belt and flees. The revelry continues; the rogues, seeing Azaël now befuddled with wine, take advantage of him by proposing a game of dice. The dice are of course loaded, and he loses his fortune. Terrible news then puts an end to the revelry. The level of the Nile has fallen, and the land is threatened with ruin. It has been decreed that, on the occurrence of such a disaster, all foreigners are to be banished, and custom further requires that a young girl must be sacrificed to the river. In her dejected state Lia offers herself as the victim, and before anyone can stop her, runs to the river and throws herself in, still clutching the fatal belt. Azaël witnesses her sacrifice. The crowd look on him with horror. Restrained from following her and sharing her fate, he is chased out of the city.

Act III opens in the desert. A caravan of refugees has set up camp. His heart broken, Azaël is at the end of his strength. He falls unconscious on the sand, where he is discovered by some slaves. Realising he is alive, they send to the camp for help. But when their masters arrive, they turn out to be the three rogues. Recognising Azaël as the cause of their own misfortune, they tear off his clothes, dress him in the rags of a slave and leave him. Azaël's only wish now is to die. He is on the point of throwing himself into the river, when celestial music is heard and an angel descends to carry him into the air.

The scene changes to Ruben's tent at Goschen. Nephtale and Jephtèle are inconsolable at Azaël's absence. Ruben is beginning to regret his weakness in being over-generous to Azaël, and has to be reminded of his promise to pardon him if he repents. A messenger, whom Ruben has sent to obtain news of his son, is then seen returning, apparently with a slave, who turns out to be Azaël himself. Amid much rejoicing he falls at his father's feet in a state of great contrition. Azaël's attention is then caught by Jephtèle, and his father, after describing how she had saved his mother's life, tells him that if his repentance is sincere and lasting, Jephtèle will be his reward.

Transposing the parable to the stage unavoidably posed a problem, by virtue of its message that it behoves a sinner to repent and seek God's forgiveness. Inevitably such a message would be watered down in a dramatic presentation, as became clear to Geoffroy at the moment in the first act when Azaël tells his father that he intends to leave the family home to discover the wider world. 'The father conceals his sorrow,' Geoffroy told his readers:

> He even stretches his goodness to the point of providing his ungrateful son, who is about to abandon him, with money that merely encourages his licentiousness. This is set out in the Scriptures where, under the veil of allegory, the sole intention is to depict God's clemency. But when this parable is transferred to the stage, the spectator is always tempted to cast blame on a father who, far from restraining the demented hot-headedness of his son, is virtually inviting him to give in to it, and even providing him with the wherewithal to do so.

Azaël's departure, accompanied by a camel overladen with money-bags, somehow lacked interest. 'The son is odious,' Geoffroy went on, 'and the father too weak, although the mother's sorrow is touching and very well depicted by Mlle Chevigny.' Certainly it was all very 'religious and patriarchal', but the effect was a little cold, and some judicious pruning was clearly needed. 'Patriarchal customs are interesting when described on the page ... but on the stage they suffer the fate of pastorales, which are always deemed rather insipid.'

Any spectacular display of dancing in this act would have destroyed the atmosphere that Gardel was careful to create. Although Marie Gardel was featured in the dances of the maidens of Goshen and the shepherds, it was for her portrayal of Jephtèle that she would be remembered. She gave a believable study of a simple girl modestly harbouring a secret adoration. In Geoffroy's words, 'sweetness, modesty, propriety, a timid sensitivity pervades her whole being; she is innocence and perfection incarnate.'

Sauvo, in *Le Moniteur*, was also impressed by Chevigny's portrayal of the mother, particularly during the passage when she braves the storm to reach him and make a final plea to deflect him from his purpose – although he added the comment that 'effects such as these are magnified by the imagination when read, but are diminished in performance'. Writing in the *Journal de Paris*, Alphonse Martainville was impressed by the pastoral scene which opened the act, a shepherds' dance performed by twelve men and twelve women, led by three principals, Antonin, Alexandrine Rivière and Geneviève Gosselin. In company with Geoffroy, he was surprised by the ease and rapidity with which Ruben gave in to his son, but found the closing moments of the act, when Nephtale and the maidens bewail Azaël's desertion, very affecting.

The second act could hardly have offered a sharper contrast. The misfortunes that beset the prodigal son – falling in love, being robbed, then bereaved, expelled and turned into a slave all in the space of a single day, almost too much for anyone to bear – was played out in a festive setting that scintillated with colour and variety. At times the motley crowd of Egyptians, Moabites, Nubians and other foreign visitors would part to give space for dancers. Among these dancers, Albert and Clotilde were applauded as old favourites, but Beaupré and Geneviève Gosselin were almost unrecognisable in their make-up as 'black Egyptians'. But for all its splendour, bustling movement and drama, the act was not wholly satisfying. 'M. Gardel varies his *pas* and his movements to accord with their characters,' wrote Martainville,

> but unfortunately this public square in Memphis looks a little like the surroundings of the Palais-Royal at Carnival time, and the beauty of this act is regrettably spoilt by a few vulgar scenes. The allegory of the belt, while acting as an excuse for some charming dances, seems to belong more to [ancient mythology] than to be appropriate to this subject. Here, M. Gardel, who is always so meticulous when handling mythological customs, should have given more attention to those of the Hebrews.

Sauvo was also unsatisfied. In his opinion the act was a disappointment:

> The offer of rich clothing seemed a little mean, and the dual-purpose set was not perhaps a good choice. The Festival of Apis lacked grandeur, pomp and charm; there were not enough people, and insufficient thought had been given to linking the scenes and groups. The meeting

> between Lia and Azaël, the awakening of their love, Lia's avowal, the gift of her belt, which is then stolen by those other beauties to whom Azaël sacrifices it, his ingratitude, Lia's despair at believing herself deserted and the poor girl's suicide are scenes that both charm and impress, but pass all too quickly. The idea of the belt did not come up to the eloquence of the poem; it is here that [Gardel's] art really was mute, although he overcame the difficulty as well as he could. Nevertheless I believe it would have been better to have done things differently and rearranged the set and the action so that Azaël's magnificence and prodigality would have been more in tune with the title of the work, for in this act Azaël is certainly seen besotted and unfaithful and losing his fortune in a few throws of the dice; but we do not really see the 'prodigal son'.

This act introduced a second heroine in the person of Emilie Bigottini, for whom the rôle of Lia was her first major creation. Geoffroy seems to have been so taken by her as to give little thought to the broader merits or otherwise of the act. The tender Lia

> is cruelly punished for listening too much to the flutterings of her heart. This love affair becomes a tragedy – there is nothing here to encourage good girls ... Lia dances hardly at all, but her movements are very expressive; she is more warm-blooded than are the daughters of Goshen, her passions more quickly aroused. This rôle demands an elegant and noble presence, an animated and piquant expression, fiery glances. Mlle Bigottini enters well into the spirit of the part, and her talent contributes largely to the ballet's success.

In the last act the vision of the angel was acclaimed as a stunning effect. Coming after what Sauvo described as the 'distressing' scene in which the rogues strip Azaël of his clothing, the double flight by Marinette Boissière and Vestris, as the angel and the prodigal son, was 'so vaporous and magical' as 'really to give an impression of flight' such as had never been seen on the stage before. To Martainville, this final scene when Azaël returns home conveyed 'all the patriarchal pomp of ancient times, an enchanting setting of vineyards, harvesting and every other kind of country pursuit that offered an admirable contrast to the horrors of the desert.' Nephtale's recognition of her son seemed to him too long-drawn-out to be wholly convincing. To Martainville the scene was 'full of pathos', but Geoffroy was unimpressed, grumbling that 'pathos is not what people expect to look for in a ballet.' The ballet was brought to a close with a tableau of 'twenty or thirty groups of members of the tribe, arranged with marvellous artistry'. Wisely, Gardel had refrained from closing his ballet with a conventional *divertissement*, and avoided the cliché of a happy ending by leaving unresolved the question of whether Azaël would find happiness with Jephtèle.

The one character who remained central in all three acts was Azaël. At the age of fifty-two it was becoming more and more difficult for Auguste Vestris, who played it, to appear convincing as a *jeune premier*, but his dramatic skill was impressive enough for allowances to be made. As Sauvo explained, the ballet contained

> far fewer of those *tours de force*, perilous jumps and eternal pirouettes that in dancing are what trills are in singing, and in this respect Vestris very successfully set an example. In the first place, he acted the rôle of the prodigal son with an energy and natural expression that was quite remarkable, and from another point of view it would be fair to say that no one could have danced with more grace and correctness. There is no doubt he is fully aware of what a talent like his can gain even when his strength is on the wane; to lose the ability to astonish while preserving all that is needed to please is an honourable way to bow out.

Martainville described Vestris's 'talent for tragedy' as 'most astonishing', but Geoffroy, who was less easily carried away, tempered his praise by noting that he 'lacked the flower of youth that is essential to excuse the follies of the prodigal son.'[1]

On a more general level, Geoffroy was prompted by this ballet to express his thoughts on the place of pantomime in ballet, recognising it as essential if ballet was to continue to be a narrative art. In his second article, written after seeing *L'Enfant prodigue* again, he set down some ideas that led him to a strangely prescient conclusion, foreseeing how one day dance and pantomime might interlock in conveying action:

> In the ballet of *L'Enfant prodigue*, the pantomime is often quite separate from the dance. Some characters neither can nor should dance. Milon, for example, who plays the prodigal son's father to perfection, and Mlle Chevigny, who brings such energy and truth to depicting the alarm, sorrow and joy of a loving mother, would be breaking every rule if they had given way to all their groaning and grieving in strict time to the

[1] Quotations in this section are from *Journal de Paris*, 29 April 1812 (Martainville, signing himself M), *Moniteur*, 30 April 1812 (Sauvo) and *Journal de l'Empire*, 2 May 1812 (Geoffroy).

music. In that respect, the dance has not yet ventured to take the same liberties as has its sister art, music. Heroes and heroines of opera perform the saddest things in song, collapsing into grief and despair with all the pomp and circumstance of harmony, and dying as melodiously as they possibly can. This bizarre behaviour is only tolerated because music is accepted as the language of opera singers, but the dance has not yet come to terms with old age, misfortune and sorrow, even though it is one of the principal languages 'spoken' at the Opéra. So all those in despair, the old and the dying have to resort to pantomime; they are thus relieved of the need to be well turned-out and to assume correct positions, and for every good reason can dispense with turns, jumps and pirouettes.

Mme Gardel, who is so perfect a dancer and mime, can only perform those very modest dances that are compatible with the character of a girl from Goshen who is on the point of losing the object of her secret love. Mlle Bigottini, who conveys so beautifully the troubles of a young heart in which love is about to exercise its sway, has little dancing to do, and nor should she have, for she is too much bound up with her passion. The same can be said of the prodigal son who, in his varying fortunes, cannot often feel the need to dance. The ultimate degree of perfection would be to combine pantomime and dance so well that scenes in which only gesturing is now required would become *pas d'action*; but since such perfection would be suitable only to a limited number of principal dancers, it would be necessary to include as much dancing, movement, action and tableaux in ballets as possible, to shorten considerably those situations in which only gesture is used and to increase those in which *pas de deux, pas de trois, de quatre*, etc. are the real scenes.[2]

The score of *L'Enfant prodigue* – his second successive contribution to ballet – was composed and arranged by Henri-Montan Berton. By all accounts it was a workmanlike compilation, with numerous well-chosen borrowings and a fair amount of original music. The first act included the familiar prayer from Méhul's *opéra-comique, Joseph* (1807). A particularly interesting number in the second act was a *marche à deux sujets* with the dual purpose of accompanying both the procession of the priests of Apis and the revelry of the crowd. In this same act were an *allegretto* by Viotti (which may have been later replaced by a piece marked *allegretto sans lenteur* apparently taken from *Achille à Scyros*) and two borrowings

[2] *Journal de l'Empire*, 7 May 1812.

from Haydn: the second movement (*romance, allegretto*) from Symphony No. 87 (*'La Reine'*), which accompanied the love scene between Azaël and Lia, and, for the finale of the ballet, the *vivace* section of the first movement of Symphony No. 97. There were more borrowings in the last act: a *tempo di pastorale* by Paisiello, an *allegro* by Paër and, for Ruben's forgiving of his son, an appropriate passage from one of Sacchini's operas that was said to add pathos to that scene.

For all their reservations, the three major critics were unanimous in declaring the ballet to be a success. Picard, however, who was very conscious that the ballet had been personally sponsored by Napoleon, was on this occasion unduly sensitive to any criticism of it. At any other time he would certainly have taken a more balanced view, but his post depended on the goodwill of the Emperor and he had worked himself into such a state of anxiety over the reservations of Geoffroy, Martainville and Sauvo that he wrote a desperate letter to the Minister of Police:

> In offering the ballet *L'Enfant prodigue* to the public, the Académie Impériale de Musique was eager to carry out the wishes of His Majesty, who in approving this establishment's budget had given orders for the staging of this work, which he deigned to select from those presented to him; he even allocated special funds for this ballet's expenses.
>
> The first performance of this work took place last Tuesday. The public seemed satisfied, and the marks of its approval encourage the belief that it was a success. Today, Monseigneur, the critics seem to wish to destroy every vestige of prestige, and the newspapers, which are so to speak the leaders of opinion, bitterly censure the plan of the work and to all intents and purposes its performance. I know that 'every journalist pays his due to the devil', but nevertheless criticism must be just and mixed with a degree of indulgence. This indulgence is particularly due to a theatre that the Government supports and presents as a unique example of its kind. Such a motive, it seems to me, should recall to every critic's mind that an article written in a spirit of denigration strikes a harmful blow to this establishment by reducing receipts and thus adding to its expense.
>
> All these considerations have decided me, Monseigneur, to seek Your Excellency's protection in putting a stop, as far as is possible, to all the defamatory statements being spread about the Académie Impériale de Musique. It is said that the ballet has cost an enormous sum, but the fact is that the expenditure was fixed by His Majesty. Again, it is said that the Opéra does not bring in good receipts, whereas in fact receipts exceeded expenses in the first quarter of this year by 25,000 francs.

> The Committee of the Council of State has proof of this under its eyes, and His Majesty should not be unaware of it.
>
> Here I am not defending the ballet of *L'Enfant prodigue*. It has been delivered to the impartiality of the public, who will be its judge. What I want is that, like the opera *Les Bardes*, it will have its revenge on the critics in the strength of its receipts. But, as Director of the Académie, I must beg Your Excellency to be good enough to order the journalists to show more moderation in their articles and more indulgence for an establishment to which His Majesty deigns to give his special protection.[3]

Napoleon came to see *L'Enfant prodigue* for himself at its third performance on 5 May, bringing with him Marie-Louise. They came in time for the second act of the ballet, and stayed to the end, receiving a rapturous reception both on their arrival and when they left. Rémusat had taken special care to ensure that his master would not be bored. In a letter to Picard on the previous day, he had asked that the intervals should be kept as short as possible; that, to cope with the extensive costume changes between the first two acts, the number of dressers should be increased for this occasion only; and that the machinist Boutron should try to effect the scene changes as quickly as possible. 'I do not need to ask you,' Rémusat concluded, 'to tell Gardel to profit from the honest criticisms of his work by making such cuts as are deemed necessary.'[4]

Whether or not the Minister of Police bothered to rebuke the press, the ballet was certainly a success. It was to remain in the repertory until 1818, and to enjoy a brief revival in 1822–3. In Castil-Blaze's words, it 'brought consolation to our weeping Académie; the dance made up for the deficit caused by the failures of the lyric drama.'[5]

* * *

While Paris basked in the summer of 1812, the clouds of war were gathering in the east. Napoleon's hopes of a permanent understanding with the Tsar had proved illusory, and for some months he had been preparing for the conflict that was becoming increasingly inevitable. In May he left Paris for discussions with the Austrian Emperor and the King of Prussia to secure protection of his rear; and in June he joined the vast army of

[3] Arch. Nat., F^7 3492. Picard to Fouché, 1 May 1812.
[4] Arch. Nat., AJ^{13} 76. Rémusat to Picard, 4 May 1812.
[5] Castil-Blaze, *Académie*, II, 132.

more than half a million men that was mustering in Poland. On 24 June the Grande Armée crossed the Niemen. For weeks the great force pressed deeper into Russia, seeking battle, but not until September, when it had advanced 500 miles beyond the frontier, did a Russian army materialise before them. At Borodino both armies were mauled, but it was the Russians who withdrew, leaving the way to Moscow open. The occupation of that city proved an empty victory; nearly all the inhabitants had left, and such as remained put its largely wooden buildings to the torch. In St Petersburg the Tsar remained deaf to approaches for a peace, and after a month Napoleon decided to return to Poland and prepare for a new campaign in the spring. But he had not counted on the Russian winter. Unprotected against the biting cold and constantly harassed by Russian cavalry, the orderly march westwards quickly turned into a disastrous retreat. Casualties rose alarmingly, many more of them victims of cold than of enemy action. As the remnants of the once proud Grande Armée prepared to cross the Beresina, Napoleon received news of an attempted *coup d'état* in Paris. When the river was crossed – not by all his men, for many were left behind to surrender or were drowned – Napoleon decided to make post-haste for Paris.

News from the front had travelled slowly, most of it channelled through the bulletins of the army, but little by little the extent of the disaster filtered through to Paris. For many it may still have seemed remote, and the Parisians continued to take their pleasure in the theatre. A new opera, *Jérusalem délivrée* by Persuis, had been presented in August, and it was to this work, memorable only for the brilliance of Gardel's ballet scenes, that Napoleon looked to provide him with some much needed distraction when he attended the Opéra a week after his return to Paris. While Gardel served Napoleon well that evening, he was overwhelmed by a great personal worry: his son by Anne-Jaqueline Coulon, Henry-Pierre, a lieutenant in the Chasseurs, had been taken prisoner by the Russians, and his fate was unknown. Of the two men, Napoleon's troubles were to prove beyond even his extraordinary powers, but his ballet-master was to be more fortunate. Not long afterwards there came news that, unlike so many of his fellow officers in that disastrous campaign, his son had come through it safe and sound and was shortly to be united with his family.

25

Dancing to the Fall of the Empire

At fifty-five Gardel was no longer the powerful, active autocrat he had been fifteen to twenty years before, in Revolutionary times. The Napoleonic restructuring of the Opéra had circumscribed his responsibilities and made him as much a servant as a master. He had quite willingly accepted this change, which still left him securely in possession of the post of first *maître de ballet*. Nor, apparently, did he find his administrative duties unduly irksome, and his relationship with his superiors, Picard and Rémusat, remained relatively easy. He could usually count on their support for his creative endeavours, and setbacks were surprisingly few. He may have finally accepted that his *Guillaume Tell* was destined for oblivion, but when, in the summer of 1813, another grand project was summarily abandoned, the blow to his pride was shattering.

He had been anxious to follow up *L'Enfant prodigue* with another major work and had already chosen the subject, returning to the classical legends of the ancient world of which he was so fond. This time it was the tale of Meleager, one of the heroes of the Argonauts and the slayer of a monstrous boar that was laying waste his father's kingdom. Meleager presented the beast's hide to the beautiful Atalanta; when his uncles attempted to rob her of it, he slew them in his rage. From this rash action followed tragic consequences. Unknown to him, when he was a child the Fates had decreed that he would die when a certain log burning on the hearth was consumed, but his mother had preserved him by extinguishing the flames and hiding the log. Now, in her anger at learning that her son had killed her own brothers, she cast the log back on the fire and, as had been foretold, Meleager died.

It was this somewhat unlikely project that was firing Gardel's imagination in the early weeks of 1813, but other tasks were leaving him little time to work seriously on it. The most pressing of these distractions was Cherubini's new opera, *Les Abencérages*. For this colourful production set in fifteenth-century Moorish Spain, two *divertissements* had been required of him, in the first of which was to be inserted a Spanish fandango to the music of *Les Folies d'Espagne*, on which Gardel set much store. The inspiration for this had come after he discovered that both Albert and his *remplacement* Antonin were proficient in Spanish dances and could accompany themselves on the guitar. Realising what a novelty this would be to a Parisian audience, he conceived the idea of a *pas de quatre* for a star-studded quartet of two men and two women: Albert and Antonin, and his wife and Bigottini. When he put his idea to Cherubini, the composer could not have reacted more excitedly. It was just what was needed, he declared; the *pas* would provide a perfect centre-point for the *divertissement*. However, since Antonin was then the only male dancer at *remplacement* level, Cherubini advised Gardel to use only one male dancer, so that there would be an understudy if Albert should fall sick or be otherwise unavailable.

Gardel, who had been working out this number at the School of Dance's new quarters in the Menus-Plaisirs building in the Rue Richer, now had to break the news to Antonin that he would not be taking part. Even though the motive for the change was carefully explained, Antonin was convinced he was the victim of an injustice. Gardel tried to soften the blow by promising that Antonin would be Albert's understudy, and that, as compensation, he would be given a solo to the most beautiful melody in the opera.

He was true to his word, and on the evening of 2 March, when he set out for the Opéra after a visit to the Tuileries, he might have been entitled to feel he had handled an awkward situation with both tact and generosity. But when he arrived there shortly after the performance had ended, he found the place in turmoil. A most disgraceful scene had taken place during the ballet, *Les Noces de Gamache*. Antonin had well and truly taken his revenge by a reprehensible trick, secretly setting to work to enjoy for himself the first fruits of Gardel's novelty. To ensure the success of his plan, he had chosen as his accomplice Mme Courtin, the former Mlle Rivière who had recently married the Secretary of the Opéra. The music had been surreptitiously slipped into the orchestral parts of the score. Antonin and his partner had entered the stage enveloped in cloaks and concealed themselves behind a flat. Then, at the introductory chords, they removed their masks, darted into the centre of the stage, and proceeded to dance the very steps Gardel had designed. They were, of course, applauded to the echo, but when the curtain fell there was much to answer for. It must have required all the diplomacy of Courtin, who had been placed by his wife's involvement in a most awkward situation, to calm the anger of Milon and Albert. Only with difficulty was Milon able to prevent a blazingly angry Albert from doing physical harm to the infamous Antonin.

Gardel's demand that Antonin be punished could not be ignored. The young dancer was lucky not to have been dismissed on the spot, which would have been the case had he not been the only male *remplacement* in the company. The punishment handed out was short and sharp: he was condemned to four days' incarceration in the prison of L'Abbaye, being conducted to and from the Opéra to fulfil his duties.[1] It might have seemed a short sentence, but the incident may have spoilt his chances of ever being promoted to *premier sujet*.

Once the new Cherubini opera was behind him, Gardel picked up the threads of his Meleager project. At that point no scenario had been presented, all that was known to Picard and Rémusat being the theme on which it would be based. To Gardel's surprise, only a few days after the opera's première, Picard requested a costume schedule and details of the ballet's casting. This caught Gardel at a bad moment. Not only was he in need of a rest after an exceptionally busy few weeks working on the new opera as well as on revivals, but he was also in the process of moving house.[2] He was neither expecting, nor in the mood, to be pressed, for the ballet was scheduled to be presented in the autumn, still five months away. In any case, the request seemed unreasonable, as he expostulated:

> How can I decide on the number of the *pas* to be danced before the music has been selected, and when rehearsals have not given me the opportunity of making up my mind what accessories my ballet will require and how much time the dancing and the *divertissements* will have to take so as to balance the action? The Superintendent is as aware as you are, Monsieur, that the pantomime and the dances are not composed, as for a play, in the loneliness of one's study, and that it is only at the rehearsal stage that a firm judgement can be made as to what is to go into a *ballet d'action* to produce the appropriate effect.[3]

Rémusat asked Picard to calm him down, explaining that all he was asking for was an estimate of numbers so that he could have an idea of how much it would cost and what performance bonuses it would entail. Napoleon had apparently rapped Rémusat on the knuckles for allowing the expenses of the ballets in *Les Abencérages* to run over budget. 'What happened [on that evening],' wrote Rémusat to Picard, 'must teach us a lesson. It is no longer permissible to employ all the principal dancers as

[1] Arch.Nat., AJ[13] 1039. Gardel's report to Picard, undated, and Rémusat's order that Antonin be imprisoned, dated 3 March 1813. The incident is described in Castil-Blaze, *Académie*, II 136.

[2] He moved to 32 rue de Clichy.

[3] Arch. Nat., AJ[13]77. Gardel to Picard, 15 April 1813.

has been constantly done for the past few years, which not only results in enormous expenditure ... but also makes it exceedingly difficult to stage works, because if an artiste falls ill ... when all the others are being used, there is no one left to take over.'

Rémusat understood why Gardel could not give firm details of the costumes, but he did not see why he could not give some indications of the scenery requirements. However, although he had not yet seen the scenario, he was beginning to have doubts as to the suitability of the subject. In a letter to Picard suggesting that thought should be given to plans for next year's ballets, he asked that Gardel

> should not lose sight of the fact that people are a little tired of Greek and mythological ballets, and that he should look at modern history, the days of chivalry, or, if he wishes, faery for what will appeal to the public's rather bored taste. I think it might be a good idea, if possible, to give in the course of a year three or four short *ballets de genre* that would add variety to the repertory at little cost – provided, of course, that one grand ballet should be staged, but it should not be too pretentious.[4]

To leave himself free to finish the scenario, Gardel proposed that Milon should take over responsibility for the *divertissement* in the new opera of *Médée et Jason* that was about to go into production; even so he was unable to deliver it by 10 May as he had been asked. Rémusat, who was probably under pressure from Napoleon, then decided he could wait no longer, and proposed to his master that *Méléagre* should be accepted. Gardel, meanwhile, had been far from dilatory, having been burning the midnight oil to finish the scenario. Soon after it had been delivered, Picard told Gardel of a somewhat ominous conversation he had had with the Superintendent in the latter's box. Rémusat was complimentary about Gardel's skill in adapting the legend, but did not conceal his feeling that 'the subject was too sombre and too tragic for a ballet'.

When the scenario was considered, a number of criticisms were made, to which Gardel responded by making alterations. One objection was that offence might be caused by a scene in which Meleager's mother decides to bring about the death of her son. Gardel's solution to this was to show the Fates stealing the firebrand from its hiding-place and themselves throwing it into the flames, preventing the mother from snatching it back by means of 'whirlwinds of fire issuing from their mouths'. Another objec-

[4] Arch. Nat., AJ[13]77. Rémusat to Picard, 23 April 1813.

tion was that Meleager's murder of his uncles offended the rules of good taste; but Gardel did not agree, pointing out that his scenario did not specify the blood relationship and that the fight, which was not a murder as in the fable, took place offstage.

Gardel was under the impression that he had answered these objections satisfactorily when he was peremptorily informed that the ballet was not to be given. He was mortified, and unimpressed by the reason put forward: that it breached a recently-made regulation, of which he was unaware, that works requiring horses were no longer permitted. In his reply to Rémusat, he commented that had he been informed of the need to economise, he could have saved up to 20,000 francs on the scenery, and that he thought he had the right to expect the ban on horses to be lifted in his case.[5]

His objections went unheeded. The main reason for the abandonment of *Méléagre* was probably the gloominess of the subject, which might have been felt inappropriate for sustaining morale amid public grief for those who had not returned from Russia. Another factor may have been its expense. The matter of the horses was no doubt quite secondary, perhaps even an afterthought. Gardel would surely have sacrificed them had he been asked, for he would have been fully aware of the appalling losses of horses in the retreat from Moscow and the desperate need to replenish the new cavalry regiments being formed for the coming campaign.

There was also a concern over casting. As he wrote his scenario, Gardel must have had particular dancers in mind for the main characters; either Vestris or Albert would have made a very acceptable Meleager, and Atalanta would surely have been conceived for Marie Gardel, while for the protagonist's mother, there could be only one choice – Sophie Chevigny. But in March Chevigny had fallen during a performance of *Les Noces de Gamache* and severely damaged her foot. At first it was feared that she might be left with a permanent limp and would be forced to retire. Although she recovered to a degree that enabled her to resume her career towards the end of September, the pleasure had gone out of her performing and she had to restrict herself to pantomime rôles.

* * *

That summer Paris became excitedly aware that a new star was rising in the dance firmament – Geneviève Gosselin, who had been designated for

[5] Arch. Nat., AJ[13] 1023. Draft reply to Rémusat, undated. Also in this dossier are three versions of the draft scenario, and Gardel's note on the situation.

art. The difference in age between the two dancers is almost unobservable on the stage, but the difference between their talents strikes every experienced eye. Mlle Gosselin astonishes those who do not understand the art. Mme Gardel charms those who do.

In Geoffroy's eyes, Mlle Gosselin was no more than 'a dancer of whim and fantasy':

> [She] exerts an extraordinarily powerful attraction, but her appeal lies in a very extraordinary defect – abusing a suppleness that results from her physique and height, which are not correctly proportioned. There is a touch of the *grotteschi* in her style; her tilted and contorted manner, the uncoordinated movements that she forces on her body are astonishing, but not at all pleasing. Every art declines when artists seek to astonish rather than please, and blasé spectators like nothing better than to be astonished ... If Mlle Gosselin is to try to improve herself, she will have to begin by undoing what makes her reputation. Probably she will never perfect herself, for no one sacrifices applause when it is already being received, just to earn it again another day.[17]

The opposing point of view was most cogently put forward by the critic of the *Journal de Paris*, Martainville, who revealed what was perhaps the most extraordinary feature of Mlle Gosselin's technique, although by no means the only one:

> Several connoisseurs had noticed the unusual elegance of her movements, the finish of her steps, each executed with a most pronounced strength combined with the most gentle grace along with ... a restrained abandon and a modest voluptuousness that are the main characteristics of Mlle Gosselin's dancing. But the voices of the connoisseurs were drowned by the bravos lavished on the principal dancers. Finally the unnoticed dancer suddenly discovered, whether intentionally or by chance, that she could rise more often than usual on the point of her feet, presenting an elegant body supported, so to speak, on the big toe, or on a single toe-nail, and suddenly the public cried miracle. This pose is certainly not the most graceful part of Mlle Gosselin's talent, for *tours de force* are seldom graceful. But from the strength in the toe, one's attention strays to the skill of her feet, and from there to the vivacity of her legs, the rounded movements of her arms and the

[17] *Journal de l'Empire*, 31 July 1813.

> voluptuous set of her head. And one saw again the *lasciva puella* of Mlle Guimard in *Les Caprices de Galathée* with her creamy steps and childlike attitudes; one saw too the easy aplomb of Dauberval. And in Mlle Gosselin one recognised the phoenix of the dance, the present and future model for virtuosos of that kind ...
>
> Mlle Gosselin has taken the dance at the brilliant point to which Mme Gardel had brought it, with its finished footwork and precision and lightness of movement, and is now adding to it a dramatic effect, an expressive quality that stirs the spectator's senses and imagination.[18]

This skirmish between the old guard and the new died down almost as quickly as it had arisen. Both parties seemed to find common ground in accepting that Mlle Gosselin possessed a brilliance of technique never before approached, but it was conceded that she still had to acquire the interpretative skill and artistry of expression that only experience in pantomime rôles could provide. Time would have to tell whether she would pass this test; but meanwhile, with Antonin as her partner, she was featured in Milon's short *divertissement* in the new opera of *Médée et Jason*, and from 1 October was promoted to the grade of *remplacement*. This was to be only a stepping stone to further promotion the following year, when she was elevated to *premier sujet* with a substantial increase of salary to 8500 francs a year.

The sensation she had caused threw into the shade two promising débuts that had taken place some weeks earlier. The Opéra ballet was then grievously short of male principals who could compete with the abundance of female talent. Of the three *premiers sujets*, Vestris and Beaupré were nearing the end of their careers, and only Albert was in his prime. The situation was even more serious in that there was only one male dancer, Antonin, at *remplacement* level. But with the appearance that summer of Ferdinand and Paul, the prospects changed dramatically, for both were immediately engaged and would long remain pillars of the company.

Ferdinand was the older of the two. Originally destined for the navy, he had early discovered his vocation as a dancer, concealing his real name of Jean La Brunière de Médicis under the alias of Ferdinand, whether through family pressure or as a voluntary gesture in the family interest. He had come to Paris on Vestris's recommendation after dancing for several years in the provinces and, briefly, in Spain and Portugal. Paris now

[18] *Journal de Paris*, 23 July 1813.

saw him in a spectacular *pas de deux* with Geneviève Gosselin, composed by Vestris, in which the two dancers appeared to be competing with one another in a crescendo of feats, each more surprising than the last.

Antoine Paul too might have followed another career, for his father had had ambitions for his son to become a notary. But from the moment when, as a child, he saw Duport dance, he had only one dream – to emulate the great virtuoso. He came to Paris and entered Lebel's class at the School of Dance. Whoever it was who prepared him for his début, he revealed extraordinary qualities of elevation, rising effortlessly and with grace and displaying an aplomb remarkable for a lad of eighteen.

Later in the year, at the end of October, the younger Gosselin, Constance, was given her turn. Although tall like her sister Geneviève, she did not have the latter's unique physical qualities; but her teachers, first Lebel and later Coulon in the *classe de perfectionnement*, had formed her into a dancer of remarkable nobility and elegance. On her début she was noticeably suffering from extreme stage fright which affected her performance in her first *pas* in the *noble* style. However, she recovered her confidence when joined by Vestris in a lively *pas de deux* that exploited her elasticity as she bounded across the stage 'like a doe darting through a forest glade', leaving her partner striving as hard as he could to keep up with her. What a poetic idea, thought Martainville, 'to show future hopes going hand in hand with past memories.'[19]

*   *   *

To many, the dramas of the Opéra must have seemed very petty as news filtered through of the great struggle taking place on the plains of Germany. In April the Emperor had left to join his armies. Soon after, bulletins began to announce the first victories, but in reality the French were fighting against lengthening odds. Opposed by the armies of Russia and a reinvigorated Prussia, Napoleon was staking everything on a devastating victory on the Austerlitz model, but such a master stroke was to elude him, not least for want of sufficient cavalry. In June an armistice offered hope of a settlement, but no common ground could be found and hostilities were resumed; in August Austria joined the opposing coalition. With the French army in Spain in retreat, the situation was becoming desperate, but the decisive moment was still to come. In October, outside Leipzig, Napoleon found himself hemmed in by a much larger force, and for two

[19] *Journal de Paris*, 2 November 1813.

days a battle raged on an unprecedented scale. Napoleon managed to extricate his forces, but further heavy losses were inflicted as his men fell back towards the Rhine. Only by the exhaustion of the opposing armies was France spared from invasion before the year's end.

Throughout that summer and autumn of 1813 an air of unreality seemed to settle over Paris. There was little news from the theatre of war except such as was to be gleaned from the official bulletins, the tone of which changed ominously from announcements of victories to bold admissions of casualties and retreat. Families with menfolk at the front were filled with apprehension, and there was little that the Parisians could do but keep up their spirits and hope for a miracle.

The theatres had their part to play in maintaining morale, and it was during this autumn of apprehension that Milon began working on a new ballet. Its purpose was in no way propagandist, the ballet being designed solely to provide distraction for an hour or two from the realities of the moment. Pressed perhaps by Rémusat to produce what he called a *ballet de genre*, Milon came up with just that: a ballet set in the present about a girl who loses her reason through a disappointment in love and recovers it at the end to live happily ever after. Milon had not invented the plot, but had taken it, virtually intact, from a popular *opéra-comique* by Marsollier and Dalayrac, *Nina, ou la Folle par amour*, to the extent even of using the same title. The success of the *opéra-comique* had been largely due to the moving interpretation of Mme Dugazon in the title rôle. When it was first put on in 1786, the public was not accustomed to seeing a heroine presented in the grip of madness, but Mme Dugazon's interpretation had aroused no criticism on grounds of taste and was vividly remembered by those who had seen her. The plot had later been used by Paisiello, whose opera on the same theme had been well received in Paris in the early years of the Revolution.

With these antecedents, Milon's ballet enjoyed a built-in advantage when it was presented at the Opéra on 23 November 1813. The choreographer had followed Marsollier's original libretto quite faithfully, except that in his first act he had presented in pantomime the events leading up to Nina's insanity, which in the opera had merely been described in dialogue.

The first act of the ballet is set in the grounds of the Count's castle, where arrangements are in hand for a visit by the Governor. The festivities are being planned by the steward, Georges (Goyon), and Germeuil (Albert), who loves and is loved by the Count's daughter Nina (Bigottini). When the Count (Milon) makes his appearance, Germeuil asks for his consent to marry Nina, which is willingly granted. In due course the

ACADEMIE IMPERIALE DE MUSIQUE.

On commencera à 7 heures précises. --- *Aujourd'hui* mardi 23 novembre 1813,

OEDIPE A COLONE,

Opéra en trois actes, paroles de *M. Guillard*, musique de *Sacchini;* suivi de la 1re. représentation de

NINA,

OU LA FOLLE PAR AMOUR,

Ballet-pantomime en deux actes.

Mlle. *COPERE*, élève de *M. Coulon*, continuera ses débuts par le pas du premier acte de l'opéra.

Chant: Mrs. Dérivis, Nourrit, Albert, Duparc; Mmes. Branchu,

Danse dans l'Opéra: Mlle. Copère.

Danse dans le Ballet: Mrs. Milon, Vestris, Beaupré, Albert, Goyon, Antonin, Mérante, Elie, Paul, Ferdinand; Mmes. Gardel, Chevigny, Bigottini, Delisle, Courtin, Gosselin aînée, Masrelié cadette, Marinette, Aimée.

Incessamment la 6e. représent. de *Médée et Jason*, tragédie-lyrique en trois actes, retardée par indisposition.

S'adresser, pour la location des Loges, à M. DAMENCE, à la Salle de l'Académie impériale de Musique.

De l'Imprimerie de Ballard, rue J.-J. Rousseau, n°. 8.

Playbill for the first performance of Nina. *(Bibliothèque-Musée de l'Opéra: © Cliché BNF Paris)*

Governor (S. Mérante) arrives with his suite. He and the Count greet one another as old friends, and the Governor suggests strengthening the link between their families by marrying his son Blinval (Elie) to Nina. The Count is taken off guard by this unexpected request, which on reflection he feels he cannot refuse. The two fathers decide to keep their plan secret; but, unknown to them, Blinval has already left them to make his proposal to Nina. In great distress, she begs her father to reconsider, but he refuses and the steward is sent to ask Germeuil to leave the castle. To add to this mournful scene, another idyll is broken – that between the steward's daughter Georgette (M. Masrélier) and Victor (Ferdinand), the steward now deeming the latter too lowly a match for her.

Night then falls. Blinval and Germeuil come across one another and draw their swords. Germeuil is disarmed and is facing his rival with his chest bared, ready to be dispatched, when Nina comes running up, followed by the Count. In spite of Blinval's admission that he was the aggressor, Germeuil is peremptorily banished from the estate. He runs off in despair and throws himself into the sea. As a rescue party assembles to try to save the unfortunate young man, Nina falls to the ground in a faint.

When she regains consciousness, it is clear to all that she has lost her mind. She imagines herself dancing with Germeuil, but finding that he is not in her arms she searches wildly for him, becoming ever more frantic. She shrinks from her father and flees into the countryside.

In the second act Nina is discovered sleeping on a seat, watched over by her governess, the steward and the Count. The Count is led away as she begins to wake, for she now treats him as an object of horror. Finding herself alone, Nina imagines that her lover will be coming to her. Some young girls arrive to keep her company; in reply to her questioning, they tell her they have not seen him. The strains of a bagpipe announce Victor's arrival. The steward is still opposed to his marrying Georgette, but Nina tells him not to destroy his daughter's happiness. The Count comes forward and urges his steward to give his consent. At the sight of her father, Nina recoils and hastens away. At this point the Governor arrives, followed by Blinval and Germeuil, who has been saved from drowning. To Germeuil's astonishment, the Count welcomes him as a son. Nina is then seen returning, and everyone hides. Germeuil walks towards her; by slow degrees he leads her to recover her senses, and all ends happily.

Napoleon had returned to Saint-Cloud on 9 November, just a fortnight before the first performance. With so much on his hands – replacing losses for the coming campaign,[20] formulating proposals for a peace congress, imposing a ministerial shuffle – he gave himself an evening off on the 23rd to see the new ballet. Escorting Marie-Louise, he arrived to prolonged acclamation a few minutes before the curtain went up for the ballet, and stayed until the end.

Nina proved an immediate and resounding success. It may have contained 'a lot of acting but little dancing', falling, as Sauvo suggested, 'into the category of pantomime drama rather than ballet'; but Bigottini's brilliant rendering of the title rôle became the sensation of the season. It was not an emotionally searing display of histrionics, but a subtle, even gentle characterisation, so natural and deeply felt as to inspire identification with the heroine's misfortune. 'The art of pantomime,' commented Jouy, 'has perhaps never been carried further, and no one has made gesture speak with more sensitivity, grace and eloquence.'[21] Bigottini, added Sauvo, 'allowed not a single intention of the choreographer to be lost.'[22]

[20] To rebuild his depleted forces Napoleon had ordered 300,000 young men to be called to the colours. Rémusat made a plea that the young men at the Opéra, mostly no doubt dancers, should be exempted. General d'Hastrel was prepared to give orders to this effect, subject only to the Emperor's approval, which was presumably given. (Bibl.-Mus. de l'Opéra, Fonds Teneo, 1/16)

[21] Jouy, IV, 24.

[22] *Moniteur*, 25 November 1813.

Bigottini's Nina was unforgettable, a wonderfully rounded study, that for all its modest dimensions was to be counted among the greatest portrayals in pantomime. She moved many to tears by the depth and detail of her depiction of Nina's woes. To the future historian of the Opéra, Castil-Blaze, her performance was a revelation, inspiring him there and then with a determination to become a music critic.[23] Many years later, another worshipper at her shrine recalled his impressions of her performance, which over the years had remained crystal-clear in his memory:

> The sweet melancholy of love's suffering, the lingering hope that survives to offer consolation when reason is lost, the moment when happiness is restored to the betrothed girl on her recovery – all those delicate nuances of feeling that the actress had to express through the play of her features without the aid of words were rendered by Mlle Bigottini with wondrous skill. Her deftly calculated gestures betraying no sign of study, the graceful flow of her figure, the expression in her eyes, now animated, now languishing, and above all the absence of those forced poses that give away the alluring secrets of the dance – all this combined to present such a degree of perfection in the art of acting as was never attained by the actress of the Théâtre Italien [Mme Dugazon] even with the resources denied to that of the Opéra.[24]

The highlight of this remarkable performance, and what Martainville called 'the rôle's most difficult moment, [was] the transition from sanity to madness, performed in full view of the spectator. This situation, which had also been used in the ballet, *Jenny*, was rendered by Mlle Bigottini with the most energetic expression. I confess I was moved by it; she surpassed the impression that her talent had previously made on me.'[25]

Although it was Bigottini's Nina that was to be remembered above all else, her achievement was much enhanced by inspired performances in the other rôles by some of the Opéra's experienced mimes: Milon himself as a father placing his family's prestige above his daughter's happiness with such woeful consequences, to find himself reviled by her in her madness; Goyon, who gave a weighty portrayal of the Governor; Albert, whose intelligent and sensitive portrait of Germeuil was perfectly matched to Bigottini's Nina; and, not to be overlooked, Sophie Chevigny

[23] Castil-Blaze, *Académie*, II, 144.

[24] Touchard-Lafosse, IV, 231–2.

[25] *Journal de Paris*, 24 November 1813. Aumer's *Jenny* had been given at the Porte-Saint-Martin in 1806.

as Nina's governess, which was to be the last creation of her distinguished career.

Milon had placed his dances in the two fêtes, the first coming after the arrival of the Governor in Act I and the second bringing the ballet to its celebratory conclusion. Those in Act I were very varied. They began with a *pas de deux* by Vestris and Geneviève Gosselin as a village couple, which left the public somewhat nonplussed at seeing Vestris 'so preoccupied with admiring his partner that he gave no thought to what he himself should be doing, and carried his distraction so far as to end his pirouettes and whirlings with his back to the public. It is to Mlle Gosselin's crowning glory that she aroused such amazement in this great artiste who, ever since entering the Opéra, had upstaged so many ballerinas.'[26] This was followed by a minuet and gavotte danced by Bigottini, Albert, Elie and Marie Gardel, the last of whom took no part in the action but appeared solely as a dancer. Another cause of amusement was provided by Charles Beaupré in a sailor's dance which he performed with a salty verve. The dances at the end of Act II were of a more general nature, featuring Marie Gardel again and a *pas de deux* by Antonin and Mme Courtin, who had most surprisingly been forgiven for the scandal of the fandango earlier in the year, for which Antonin had been briefly gaoled.

The music for this ballet was provided by Louis Persuis, who wove in numerous borrowings from Dalayrac's score for the *opéra-comique* to emphasise the action and heighten the emotional impact of the dramatic scenes, particularly when Nina is discovered having lost her reason at the beginning of the second act. Two musical highlights in the score were solos for the harp and for the cor anglais, played respectively by Jean Vernier and Auguste Vogt.[27]

Nina was to survive until 1840. Until Bigottini retired in 1823 it remained exclusively hers, and she returned to make a final appearance in it in 1827 at Milon's retirement benefit. At that performance (the 180th) she was joined by three other dancers who had created their rôles – Milon, Albert and Ferdinand. Bigottini was succeeded by Amélie Legallois (1824), Caroline Brocard (1825), the actress Léontine Fay (1830), Amélie Perceval (1830) and Lise Noblet (1835). Its last performance, its 190th, took place in 1840, at Fanny Elssler's benefit prior to her departure for America. By then, however, it was only a travesty of what it once had been. Jules Janin dismissed it as 'deadly dull', losing patience with what

[26] *Journal de Paris*, 29 November 1813.

[27] After the Restoration of the Bourbons, the royal ballet-lover the Duc de Berry was so taken with Vogt's playing of this piece that he took lessons from the virtuoso himself.

he called 'the conventional gestures' of pantomime[28] – a remark that all too clearly reveals how much the art of pantomime had declined with the disappearance of the Gardel–Milon repertory. Théophile Gautier was impressed by Elssler's 'Shakespearean' reading of the part, but he too found the ballet unsatisfactory: 'feeble' was his word for it.[29] The fact was that the ballet, being placed at the end of an exceedingly long programme, had been insensitively cut. Not only had the gavotte been excised, but also the *pas* that Nina dances with Germeuil and repeats on her own at the onset of her insanity. As Charles Maurice noted, 'an oversight made nonsense of it when Fanny Elssler indicated her recollection of a dance that had not taken place'.[30]

* * *

Sophie Chevigny's accident had occurred in full view of the public in a performance of *Les Noces de Gamache* on a day traditionally devoted to festivity, Mardi Gras. Only two weeks earlier she had agreed to give up many of the rôles that were hers by virtue of her position as *premier sujet*. Devastating though her accident was, it only hastened a retirement that could not have been long deferred. She was already past forty, and her sparkling personality could no longer produce the illusion that she was much younger than her years. To Prince Clary, seeing her in 1810, she was 'too small and too thickset, but her grace makes you overlook her fat. Although a grandmother, and very ugly when seen close to, on stage she has a youth, a freshness, an unshakeable gaiety which has led Geoffroy, with every good reason, to call her "the voluptuous Chevigny". She is the very ideal of a pretty bacchante painted by Rubens.'[31]

In July 1813, after she had been absent for more than five months, Picard enquired when she expected to resume her service. In her reply she honestly told him that there could be no question of her being able to dance again, but if she could be of use in a purely pantomime capacity, she would be ready in about a month. For her return she proposed the rôle of Louise in *Le Déserteur*, but Picard had to explain that this was a part for a younger woman 'with a slender figure', and that Bigottini, who fitted this description, had already asked to play it.

Chevigny eventually made her return as the mother in *L'Enfant prodigue* towards the end of September, but by then her fate had been

[28] *Journal des débats*, 3 February 1840.
[29] *Presse*, 3 February 1840.
[30] *Courrier des théâtres*, 2 February 1840.
[31] Clary und Aldringen, 137–8.

decided. Any hope that she might be retained solely as a mime went unfulfilled, for Picard informed her she would be retired at the end of the following June. He offered a small crumb of comfort, adding that if she were able to resume her service 'as a dancer and a mime' before January, the Superintendent might cancel his instruction. She accepted her fate willingly enough, commenting sadly: 'At the instigation of my comrades and the *maîtres de ballet* I had offered my services as a mime, believing that I could still be of use in that difficult art. But seeing that the Superintendent is not very interested in that, or finds it easy to replace me, there is nothing I can do to prevent his orders being carried out.'[32]

Chevigny's retirement was a cause of great concern to Gardel, who appreciated far better than his masters the importance of maintaining the standards of pantomime. Several years after her retirement, he pleaded that her unrivalled understanding of pantomime be exploited by engaging her as a teacher:

> As a pantomime actress, Mlle Chevigny has not been surpassed in the rôles she has played, nor probably will she be for a long time. No one else has rendered with such perfection all the emotions required in the ballets *Ulysse*, *Cléopâtre*, *L'Enfant prodigue*, *Persée*, etc., etc. In a vocation that by its very nature is circumscribed, she has developed such a wide range of expression and effect that she has virtually no equal. As a model, she would be of the greatest use to young dancers with a leaning towards pantomime ... Would it not be possible in the interests of the Opéra ... to make an arrangement with her by which she would return to the Opéra on suitable terms solely to play pantomime rôles allotted to her by the *maîtres de ballet* in agreement with the management? In this way the public would not be deprived of the talent of this artiste, whose loss would be singularly felt in all her rôles; and at the same time her example and the advice she would agree to give to the young persons who seek it would form an excellent school of pantomime.[33]

Sadly this appeal fell on stony ground. When she retired she was not given the honour of a benefit, which in the normal course of events would have been her due, but in lieu was paid a lump sum of 10,000 francs in addition, of course, to her pension. She then withdrew into a dignified and uncomplaining retirement. As the years went by, memories

[32] Arch. Nat., AJ[13] 80. Chevigny to Picard, 19 September 1813.
[33] Arch. Nat., AJ[13] 80, 0[3] 1665. Gardel to the Council of the Opéra, apparently written in 1821.

of her brilliant characterisations dimmed and faded away, and by the time of her death, some time in the 1840s, she had been virtually forgotten.

The rejection of Gardel's request reflected the lack of any firm policy of instruction in the art of pantomime at the Opéra. It was not a subject included in the curriculum of the School of Dance, although it may have been touched upon in the perfection classes. Milon himself gave mime classes, presumably to selected pupils, but to a large extent young dancers learnt to act by the experience of studying their seniors in rehearsal and performing.

Carlo Blasis's later comments about French pantomime were to show the deterioration of standards that had taken place by the end of the 1820s. Expressing surprise that ballets of the quality of *L'Enfant prodigue, Le Retour d'Ulysse, Nina* and *Les Amours d'Antoine et de Cléopâtre* had not been followed in Paris by others of their kind, he surmised that 'the most plausible reason [was] the defective style of their pantomime, which is incapable of explaining sentiment and which fails even in those necessary gestures that are employed to indicate surrounding objects; consequently it cannot enter into detail, and its language is often obscure.'[34] He paid due tribute to some of the fine mimes in French ballets in his younger days – Auguste Vestris, Chevigny and Bigottini in particular – whose only failing was 'a want of sufficient gesture to express perfectly every circumstance ... Notwithstanding this, their description of sentiment was true; their features spoke, and their attitudes were gracefully conceived.' The fault, he concluded, lay with choreographers for '[neglecting] this department too much, or [lacking] sufficient talent to put Pantomime upon an equality with dancing.'[35] This stricture, it is presumed, was levelled not at Gardel and Milon, both of whom had by then retired, but at Aumer. Although French pantomime lacked the gestural profusion and power of the Italians, Gardel and Milon did their best to nurture it, and there can be no denying that the failure to take advantage of Chevigny's services as Gardel had urged was to impoverish the heritage of French pantomime.

[34] Blasis, 200.
[35] Blasis, 120–1.

26

Napoleon Falls, and Congress Dances

Napoleon could not afford to tarry in Paris that winter. By early January units of the Austrian and Prussian armies had already crossed the Rhine; and when the Emperor drove out of his capital later in the month, their advance guards were barely sixty miles from Paris. With a seemingly superhuman effort Napoleon had assembled another army in a matter of weeks, and in February, in an impressive burst of genius, won three victories in a row. But it was not enough to turn the tide, and inexorably the allied armies advanced on Paris, entering the city after a brief bombardment on the morning of 31 March. Caught off balance, Napoleon found himself isolated at Fontainebleau. No other course was open but to accept defeat and abdicate.

As the campaign moved into its final phase, the atmosphere in Paris was one of unreality. In the absence of reliable news, and as rumours proliferated, the public mood swung chaotically between jubilation and gloom. Yet the daily life of the city continued. Theatres remained open, and at the Opéra a wide range of ballets was presented. Money there was short, so there was little call for new productions. However, one novelty was offered to help lift morale and give a gleam of hope that all might turn out well: *L'Oriflamme*, a one-act opera recalling the Frankish king Charles Martel setting out on his heroic venture to save his people from the ravages of the Saracens.[1] In the context of Napoleon's desperate struggle to save his régime, it might have seemed strange to offer an image from France's royal past, but dynastic niceties were of little concern when a more immediate danger threatened – the approach of the Tsar's dreaded Cossacks.

With the enemy at its gates, Paris had become a city under siege. Streams of wounded soldiers were beginning to make their way back from the battlefields, jostling bemused groups of peasants trying to save their pathetic belongings and even their cattle from the invader. There

[1] *L'Oriflamme* was the last production at the Opéra to be reviewed by Geoffroy, who died later in February 1814.

was a fear that the city might be razed to the ground in retaliation for the burning of Moscow. And yet, on 29 March, the eve of the city's fall, the Opéra opened its doors as normal, and an enraptured, if distracted, audience applauded Vestris, Mme Gardel and Bigottini in *Paul et Virginie* as though little else in the world mattered. But next morning the call to arms was sounded, and cannon-fire could be heard from the hills of Montmartre. More and more casualties drifted back, and soon elements of the defending forces began retreating into the city. That evening Marshal Marmont sought an armistice.

On the morning of 31 March, the Tsar, the King of Prussia and the Austrian field marshals marched through Paris with their armies in parade order. As they entered the northern outskirts they were received in silence – but coming to the more elegant districts the reception became noticeably warmer, even enthusiastic.

One of the first public appearances by the Tsar and the King of Prussia was to attend the Opéra. *Le Triomphe de Trajan* was billed for the following day, 1 April; but owing to the indisposition of one of the singers, *La Vestale* had to be substituted at the last minute. This change greatly displeased the Tsar, to whom it had been suggested that *Trajan* would be seen as a singularly appropriate choice for honouring a conqueror. It took more than half an hour to smooth the ruffled feathers and persuade the Russian autocrat to enter his box with his compliant vassal, the King of Prussia. During the following weeks, before the return of Louis XVIII, the allied sovereigns presided over two command performances: the first on 15 April, when they were captivated by Bigottini in *Nina*, and the second on the 24th, when Vestris and Mme Gardel performed a Russian dance, and *Achille à Scyros* was performed.

* * *

Louis XVIII, who had been restored to the throne of his forebears, did not set foot on French soil until April was out. Ponderously overweight and painfully afflicted by gout, he was far from an inspiring figure; but nevertheless he was greeted with respect and relief, and here and there with enthusiasm from royalists now coming into the open. Within the Opéra the change of régime was barely noticeable. Gardel was honoured by being appointed *maître des ballets de la cour*, and on 17 May the King paid his first visit to the Opéra. He was accompanied by his brother and heir presumptive, the former Comte d'Artois, his niece the Duchesse d'Angoulême, sole survivor of the family of Louis XVI, and his nephew the Duc de Berry. Also in the audience were the Tsar, who had discreetly concealed his presence by occupying a *loge grillée*, and the King of Prussia.

No one could remember a more brilliant occasion at the Opéra. High-ranking officers, both French and allied, resplendent in uniforms of seemingly every imaginable colour, aglint with the stars and medals of their decorations and a profusion of gold braid, contrasted with the white gowns and bouquets of lilies of the ladies.

For the occasion Gardel had put together a celebratory *divertissement*, *Le Retour du lys*, consisting mainly of dances from different parts of Europe – a French minuet, an *anglaise*, an *allemande*, a *pas russe*, a *fandango* – all jumbled up 'without rhyme or reason ... a hotchpotch in which no one had given a moment's thought to including men and women of the market'.[2] But to be fair, it was never intended to last; after being shown to the general public three days later, it was seen no more.

The King made at least three more visits to the Opéra over the next eight months. In June he saw Bigottini in *L'Enfant prodigue*, shortly before she left to entertain the statesmen gathering in Vienna for the Congress. In November he graced a command performance, for which the entire amphitheatre was set aside for the royal party with a specially constructed box for himself in the centre – a merciful arrangement for a monarch whose gout made it difficult for him to stand unaided, let alone walk. It was noticed that several ladies of his household were in full mourning, but more colourful in his red uniform was the newly created Duke of Wellington, who watched the proceedings from one of the boxes. The ballet that evening, following *La Vestale*, was *Psyché*, which the King may have remembered from many years previously, before fleeing from Paris to escape the dangers of the Revolution. Had he done so, he must have seen Marie Miller, as she then was; but now, as Marie Gardel, she had become a little too old for the part, which had been confided, at the King's wish, to the new marvel, Geneviève Gosselin. *Psyché* was apparently a favourite ballet with him, as it was with Napoleon, and when he returned in January 1815 for another command performance, he saw it again.

On the change of régime, the official title of the Opéra had reverted to the Académie *Royale* de Musique. Picard still remained in his post as Director, but was now responsible to the Minister of the Royal Household, the Comte de Pradel, and his assistant, Des Entelles.[3] In the financial stringency imposed by Napoleon in the last months of the war, the artistes had been forced to sacrifice their *feux*. Funds continued to be

[2] *Journal de Paris*, 22 May 1814.
[3] Des Entelles was presumably the same official who had assisted Denis-Pierre-Jean Papillon de La Ferté in the Menus-Plaisirs during the last year of the old régime.

short under Louis XVIII, who was to prove less generous than his predecessor. The reduced budget meant that there was less provision for new productions. The only major creation in 1814 was Spontini's opera *Pélage*; no new ballet was to be presented, but the repertory was rich enough to satisfy the great influx of visitors, many from the British Isles, who now flocked to savour the delights of Paris which for so long had been but a receding memory, if not a legend. There was plenty to see, and the theatres did excellent business. At the Opéra, while not everyone found the French style of singing to their taste, the superiority of Paris in the field of dance was not to be denied. Provided that seats could be obtained – and prices were low by London standards – it was possible in 1814 to see a repertoire of ballets of astonishing variety: seven by Gardel (*Télémaque*, *Psyché*, *La Dansomanie*, *Achille à Scyros*, *Vénus et Adonis*, *Paul et Virginie* and *L'Enfant prodigue*), three by Milon (*Les Noces de Gamache*, *L'Enlèvement des Sabines* and *Nina*), and one (*Antoine et Cléopâtre*) by Aumer.

Exceptionally penetrating were the comments of two young Scottish visitors who stayed over until 1815. No ballet impressed them more than *L'Enfant prodigue*, which they had the good luck of seeing with Bigottini. The superiority over what London had to offer lay 'partly in the pre-eminent merits of the first-rate dancers'. Of Mme Gardel they honestly recorded: 'Her face is not handsome, but her figure is admirably formed for the display of her art, of which she is probably the most perfect mistress to be found in Europe.' To these unbiased young observers she was successfully holding her own against the young Bigottini, who, 'if she does not yet quite equal her rival in artificial accomplishments, ... at least attracts more admirers by her youth and beauty; by the exquisite symmetry of her form, and the natural grace and elegance of her movements'.[4]

Nor were these young Scots to be beguiled by *tours de force*, and their conclusions on the subject of French attitudes towards dancing were unexpectedly balanced:

> Many of the pirouettes, and other difficult movements, which are introduced into the *pas seuls*, *pas de deux*, &c. in which the great dancers display their whole powers, however wonderful as specimens of art, are certainly anything but eloquent or graceful. The applause in the French opera seemed to us to be in direct proportion to the difficulty, and to bear no relation whatever to the beauty of the performances. A Frenchman regards, with perfect indifference, dances which, to a

[4] Alison and Tyter, I 252.

stranger at least, appear performed with inimitable grace, because they are only common dances, admirably well executed; but when one of the male performers, after spinning about for a long time, with wonderful velocity, arrests himself suddenly and stands immovable on one foot; or when one of the females wheels round on the toes of one foot, folding her other limb nearly in a horizontal position – he breaks out into extravagant exclamations of astonishment and delight: '*Quel aplomb! Ah diable! Sacré Dieu!*' &c.

But although the principal dances at the Opera, and those on which the French chiefly pride themselves, are much injured, in point of beauty, by this artificial taste, the execution of the less laboured parts of these dances, and of nearly the whole of their common national dances, is quite free from this defect, and is, we should conceive, the most beautiful exhibition of the kind that is anywhere to be seen. It is only in a city where amusements of all kinds are sought for, not merely by way of relaxation, but as matters of serious interest and national concern, and where dancing, in particular, is an object of universal and passionate admiration, that such numbers of first-rate dancers can be found, as perform constantly at the Académie de Musique.[5]

In addition to accommodating the English invasion, Paris was filling up with returning *émigrés*, hopeful of obtaining lucrative posts under the new régime and of recovering property lost during the Revolution. In September the *Journal de Paris* championed what it called an '*émigré de la danse*.'[6] To call Baptiste Petit an *émigré* was not strictly correct, for he had been released from the Opéra in 1809 to accept a lucrative engagement in St Petersburg with his wife, Minette Duport. He had then returned to Paris to find the doors of the Opéra closed to him. Now, however, the change of régime had reawakened his hopes of being reinstated, and he had appealed directly to the King's brother. 'Being forced to remain in France on account of the war,' he explained, 'I have been deprived of my livelihood and been obliged to live like a foreigner in my own country.'[7] The way was then opened for him to make a series of début appearances. However, his expectations of an engagement as a *premier sujet* did not materialise, and he had to seek consolation in negotiating what was probably a more lucrative engagement for his wife and himself in London.

For the native Parisian that summer, there was the added interest in observing the younger dancers mature and essay their developing

[5] Alison & Tytler, I 253–5.
[6] *Journal de Paris*, 15 September 1814.
[7] Arch. Nat., AJ^{13} 80.

strengths and skills in new rôles. One of these was Fanny Bias, who returned in August after maternity leave, to play Eucharis in *Télémaque* for the first time. 'Lively and sprightly until Cupid strikes her with his arrow,' wrote Martainville, 'then anxious, pensive, almost melancholic when she realises the risks she must now take to find happiness with the man she loves – such are the sentiments that have to pass through Eucharis's mind, and which Mlle Bias conveyed with a power of expression that was skilfully varied and always convincing.'[8]

Five months later it was the turn of one of the senior ballerinas, Clotilde, to take on a rôle that a younger colleague had triumphantly made her own. This was the Moabite girl Lia, who is disgraced by her father for betrothing herself to the Prodigal Son, and who kills herself in the vain hope of appeasing the Nile. Bigottini, whose portrayal of this tragic heroine was engraved in the experience of all who had seen it, was then in Vienna, and it was a brave and selfless act of Clotilde to play the part so that Vestris, whose powers were on the wane, could be seen once more 'to remind us of the mime we have admired so often, and, every now and then, the dancer who was so applauded by our fathers'.[9]

* * *

With Louis XVIII comfortably but, as events were to show, by no means securely installed on his throne, the allied sovereigns departed from Paris and returned to their capitals, taking their armies with them. The political focus now shifted to Vienna, where, at the invitation of the Austrian Emperor, a great Congress had been called to settle the peace. During their stay in Paris, the Austrian delegation, like everyone else, had been dazzled by the splendours of the Paris ballet, and the Emperor, who was footing the bill for the Congress, consented to the engagement of some of the Opéra's principal dancers to divert the great gathering of sovereigns and statesmen who were expected to spend a month or two (so it was estimated) drawing up a peace treaty.

To preside over the pleasures of this extraordinary assemblage, even from behind the footlights, must have seemed the ultimate accolade for any artiste. Had France not been a defeated power, such an honour might have alighted by right of seniority on Mme Gardel. But the Opéra had little say in the matter, for the invitation came from Vienna, no doubt on the recommendation of Aumer, who, as ballet-master there, had plans to

[8] *Journal de Paris*, 4 August 1814.
[9] *Journal de Paris*, 4 October 1814.

revive *Les Amours d'Antoine et de Cléopâtre* and wanted Clotilde to appear in her original part of the Egyptian queen. But daunted perhaps by the prospect of an exceptionally exhausting season, Clotilde declined, and the invitation was addressed to the one ballerina with the 'star' potential to match such an awesomely important occasion – Emilia Bigottini.

Bigottini seemed to have all the qualities required to grace such an occasion. Not only was she a dancer of beguiling grace and elegance and a pantomime actress of unrivalled power, but she was also one of the great beauties of her time. A vision of how she appeared in the full glory of her career was vividly caught by her biographer, writing half a century after her death:

> Tall, slender, supple and slim, with a noble air of propriety and distinction, curling hair the colour of ebony and dark eyes shrouded by black lashes, a nose that was a little on the long side but very pure in outline, and a pretty mouth breaking into a mischievous smile, as can be seen in Vigneron's portrait: this conqueror of hearts exerted an ineffable attraction over all who came in contact with her. She was a tender soul, sentimental rather than voluptuous or, most certainly, wanton, yet capable of arousing and experiencing sensual pleasure. Her modest comportment, the languor of her expression, which seemed almost melancholy rather than ardent, and an allure that was so delicately welcoming were to captivate serious-minded men in search of affection, whether assumed or real, and in no way vulgar or flashy. It was soon realised that she was a woman of feeling and capable of a lasting attachment, for the bonds she forged were proof of her ability to give pleasure other than as a passing fancy.[10]

There was magic too, no doubt, in the aura that surrounded her as a woman whose private life was not constricted by the social conventions that ladies of high society were expected to observe. Bigottini was not only a ravishing beauty, but she had become a sexual icon in the eyes of the masculine society that frequented the world of the theatre. She had never married, and, although courted by a legion of admirers, she chose her lovers with care, requiring affection and loyalty as well as the provision of security both for herself and for her children. Her liaisons were generally enduring. Her first was with Napoleon's stepson, Eugène de Beauharnais. She was his first love too, and their relationship lasted for several years. They were separated when he became Viceroy of Italy in

[10] Félix-Bouvier, 8.

June 1805, and their affair ended amicably when he married a Bavarian princess in January of the following year.

Not long after their parting, she became the mistress of the fabulously wealthy Spanish grandee Casimir Pignatelli, Conde de Fuentes, whom she enticed away from Mlle Clotilde. By him she had her first child, a daughter, Armandine, born in Paris on 10 April 1807.

After the Count's death in 1810,[11] Bigottini formed a close friendship with Michel Duroc, the Grand Marshal of the Palace and one of the Emperor's closest friends. The relationship was none the less passionate for being childless,[12] and Bigottini was devastated when she learnt of her lover's death in battle near Görlitz in May 1813.

Duroc may have been briefly replaced in her affections by the dancer Albert, but by the time of the Congress of Vienna she was already the mistress of Franz Graf Pálffy, the director of the Hoftheater. He was to be the father of her second child, François-Jean-Charles, who was born on 28 August 1816.

Of course, even for a *premier sujet*, marriage into an Imperial family or to a millionaire grandee or a court official would have been beyond any reasonable bounds of possibility, and so it was understandable that she should expect some material provision in the interests of her security and that of her children. To cynical observers this might have seemed grasping, but there is not a shred of evidence that her protectors thought that the gifts and provision they made to her were anything more than her due.

Her realistic business sense was tempered by a sharp wit, which even Napoleon had once appreciated. It was probably after she had appeared at Saint-Cloud in *Paul et Virginie* in the summer of 1806 that the Emperor charged his friend Fontanes, then President of the Corps Législatif, with the task of sending her a mark of his satisfaction. In his innocence, Fontanes dispatched a beautifully bound set of the French classics. Some time afterwards Napoleon happened to ask Bigottini, who was not a great reader, whether she had been pleased with his gift.

'*Ma foi*, sire,' she replied, 'not very much.'

'Why was that?' the Emperor enquired.

[11] In the Dance Collection of the New York Public Library is a Power of Attorney dated 8 October 1810 by Dlle Jeanne Marie Antoinette Emilie Bigottini of 9 rue de Choiseul, Paris, in her capacity of natural and legal guardian of Armandine Alphonsine Pignatelly [*sic*], minor daughter of herself and the late Casimir Louis Gonzague Marie Alphonse Armand Pignatelli, Comte de Fuentes, granted to Antoine Vives of Valencia in respect of her entitlement under her father's estate.

[12] Félix-Bouvier suggested that Duroc fathered two children by her, including Odilon Duroc. In fact, Odilon was the son of the Grand Marshal's first cousin and was born in 1801 (see Jean de la Tour, *Duroc* (Paris, 1913), 313).

'Because,' came the answer, 'he paid me in *livres*, and I would have preferred to be paid in *francs*.'[13]

The administration of the Opéra at first wanted to treat Bigottini's visit to Vienna as a leave of absence under her contractual entitlement, but to this she strongly objected, arguing that the invitation coming from the Austrian Emperor himself meant that she would be going to Vienna as a representative of the Opéra. She left Paris towards the end of June, accompanied by Antonin and Aimée Petit[14], and within a week all three were working with Aumer. The court theatres in Vienna had only recently been reorganised, and opera and ballet were now the preserve of the recently constructed Kärnthnertor-Theater, which was not only the largest theatre in the city but also splendidly equipped. Aumer was already working on *Antonius und Klaeopatra*, but Bigottini was so impatiently expected that she and Antonin hurriedly learnt a torch dance, which they performed in a popular extravaganza on 16 July.

Cleopatra, which she first played on 1 August, was only one of many rôles that Vienna saw her perform. Aumer's activity was extraordinary. Seizing his opportunity, he presented Bigottini in a surprisingly varied range of parts during the five months of her engagement. Ballets and revivals followed in quick succession. Among his own ballets were *Zephir und Flora*, *Die Sklavenhändler* (in which she danced a *pas de châle* with another distinguished guest artist, André Deshayes), *Myrsil und Anteros* (in which she appeared as the goddess Diana) and his own version of the ballets in *La Vestale*. He also taught her rôles in two Dauberval revivals – Louise in *Le Déserteur* and Eucharis in *Telemachus*. But her greatest triumph was to come at the end of the season, when she appeared in *Nina*, which Aumer had restaged with her assistance. She was given the first performance, on 6 November, for her benefit, and played the title rôle fourteen times to packed houses until her farewell performance on 21 December.

Ballet was only one of the distractions that Vienna offered to the unprecedented array of kings, princes and diplomats within its walls. Originally estimated to last only a month or two, the Congress was to drag on until well into the following year, and one of the consequences was to extend the French dancers' absence from Paris to more than six months. 'The Congress,' observed the wry old Prince de Ligne, who would not live to see it end, 'makes no progress; it dances.' At night the very air seemed

[13] The former unit of currency, the *livre*, had been replaced by the *franc* in 1795.

[14] Anatole's sister, Aimée Petit, is not to be confused with Constance Gosselin, who was to marry Anatole in 1815 and thereafter be known as Mme Anatole.

to shimmer with the rhythm of the waltz as one ball followed another in a seemingly perpetual round of pleasure. Opportunities abounded too for more private adventures, nocturnal visits that were discreetly observed by the agents of the secret police. Mlle Aimée, it was reported, had made a useful conquest in Graf von Trauttmansdorff, but Bigottini's name was seldom mentioned in those comings and goings. It was well known that she was the mistress of Franz Graf Pálffy, but there was no suggestion of her resuming the friendship with her old flame Prince Eugène, who was in fact paying court to a pretty young French actress, Séraphine Lambert. However, when Bigottini took her benefit, he had the good taste to send her a valuable ring that told her she was not forgotten.

* * *

In January 1815 Geneviève Gosselin was promoted to the grade of *premier sujet*, and on 1 February Bigottini was welcomed back in *Nina*. Life seemed to be settling into a normal peacetime routine when, early in March, came startling news. Napoleon had escaped from Elba and landed in the south of France, with barely a thousand men. During the following two weeks, troops flocked to his standard as he made his way to Paris. On 19 March Louis XVIII faced reality; he was assisted into his carriage and driven north to the Belgian border, and the next day Napoleon was triumphantly borne into the Tuileries on the shoulders of cheering officers.

The Opéra resumed its imperial status as Milon was rehearsing a new ballet, *L'Epreuve villageoise*. This was no grand addition to the repertory, but a light piece aimed only at appealing to a wide public at a time when it was anticipated that Paris would be filled with visitors. Its modest scale was self-evident, for it was merely an adaptation of a popular *opéra-comique* by Grétry created as long ago as 1784, using its well-known tunes to accompany similar scenes in the ballet. It had, of course, been authorised before Napoleon's return. In giving his official blessing for its production, Louis XVIII's minister, the Comte de Blacas, had shown he shared the preference of his predecessor, Rémusat, for *ballets de genre*, telling Picard he 'would be delighted if the Opéra were sometimes to stage ballets that were a little less long and of a rustic nature.'[15]

Not that there was anything retrogressive in this. Indeed, there were precedents to be found in the works of such masters of the past as Dauberval and Maximilien Gardel, and few would disagree that a ballet repertory is the richer for mixing light works with weightier ones. Fur-

[15] Arch. Nat., AJ^{13} 94 (491).

thermore, Milon had already, and quite recently, achieved a resounding success in this genre with *Nina*, although he would certainly not have regarded *L'Epreuve villageoise* as anything more than a minor work, the purpose of which was simply to entertain.

Its action followed closely that of the *opéra-comique*, and several of Grétry's melodies were incorporated in Persuis's score to accompany similar passages in the ballet. The story revolved around a couple of lovers, Denise (Mme Courtin) and André (Albert). The young man is obsessed with the thought that his girl might not love him with a passion equal to his own. This drives him into furious bouts of jealousy, which, being an honest girl, she finds offensive; and they quarrel. Meanwhile, the roving eye of an elderly beau, Delafrance (Goyon), has alighted on Denise – notwithstanding that he is at the same time courting two experienced ladies of the village, Marton (Bigottini) and Lisette (Mme Gardel). When he tries to ingratiate himself with Denise's mother (M. Delisle), she sees through him and, in order to teach him a lesson, leads him to believe she will favour his suit. At the same time Denise sees a way of curing André of his obsessive jealousy. Delafrance sends Denise a bouquet accompanied by a note, but unfortunately André sees it being delivered and is convinced that his suspicions are well founded. Everyone then goes off to the village fair: Denise in the company of her mother and Delafrance, and André in the depths of despair. During the fair Denise observes Marton giving André a small object. Assuming it to be a gift of Marton's portrait, she angrily demands that André show it to her. He teases her by admitting that it is indeed a portrait of the person he loves most of all, but it turns out to be a mirror and when Denise looks at it, she sees her own face. The lovers are thus reconciled, and Delafrance, realising he has been duped, stamps off in a huff.

Milon had, as usual, prepared his dancers well for the mime scenes. Mme Courtin (the former Mlle Rivière) was a vivacious Denise, but Albert's André seemed a little too elegant and noble for a country boy. As for the two experienced ladies, Bigottini was chosen for the rôle of Marton presumably because it was the more dramatically demanding, with Marie Gardel, appearing for the first time in a secondary part, giving experienced support as her friend Lisette.

Milon had interwoven some entertaining dancing among the intricacies of the plot. The first act included a jolly dance for a group of villagers on their way to the fair, during which Denise is offered some flowers and is invited to join in – much to the annoyance of André, who cannot bear to see her dancing with anyone but himself. Later in the ballet was a scene in which, observed by Denise's mother who is hiding behind a bush,

Marton reminds Delafrance of the time they had once danced a minuet together, and the two of them – Bigottini and Goyon – drift into a gavotte before abandoning themselves to the voluptuous pleasure of a waltz.

The fairground scene was one of those intoxicating set pieces of revelry at which Milon was a past-master – a worthy companion piece to *Les Noces de Gamache*, suggestive of 'all the variety of a Kermess in Flanders coupled with the gaiety of a village festival in Provence.'[16] No doubt it was very carefully set, but it gave the impression of 'the most entertaining disorder' that led – after the performing monkey, Harlequin, Pierrot and Pantaloon had retired into the background – to a more formal final *divertissement* that included a brilliant *pas de trois* for Geneviève Gosselin, Paul and Ferdinand.

'And how are we to praise Mlle Gosselin?' wondered Martainville after seeing her that evening.

> She dances like no one else, and no one dances like her. She is the very ideal of the dance. It is true that to have risen to such a peak of perfection, she has had fewer difficulties to overcome than anyone else; the rapid precision of her movements has never been hindered by such obstacles to extending the range of movement that result from the formation of certain parts of the body. What Nature has withheld from Mlle Gosselin is a boon, for it might be said that before making her into a woman, Nature played a trick on her by making her into a dancer.[17]

More than any other comment on her exceptional gifts, this prolix passage offered a penetrating insight into the physical quality that gave Geneviève Gosselin an advantage over the other principal dancers of her time; for Martainville was clearly suggesting a physical conformation of an asexual nature – or, more specifically, that she had a boy's figure, like that of a young athlete, which gave her a technical potential beyond the scope of the more feminine bodies of her companions.

* * *

A few days later, on 18 April, Napoleon paid what was to be his last visit to the Opéra, which may have left him with a memory of Gosselin's Psyche, if ever he came to recall it during his lonely exile on St. Helena.[18]

[16] *Gazette de France*, 6 April 1815. Signed '*Le Souffleur émérite*'.
[17] *Journal de Paris*, 4 April 1815.
[18] The tally of ballets seen by Napoleon at the Opéra was as follows: *Le Jugement de Pâris* (four times); *Télémaque, Psyché, Le Retour de Zéphire, Vénus et Adonis* (three times); *Les Noces de Gamache* (twice);

However, when Milon's *Epreuve villageoise* was first seen on 4 April, France's long ordeal was not yet over. The allies had determined that Napoleon was to be given no mercy, and their armies began to reassemble in Belgium. Early in June Napoleon left Paris to stake his all on one last throw. On the 18th the opposing forces came to grips at Waterloo. By evening the fighting was over, and three days later Napoleon left his defeated troops to return to his bewildered capital, which until then had received only rumours of the disaster. This time it was the end, and for him there was no other course but to abdicate once again. On 8 July Louis XVIII returned to Paris; eight days later Napoleon surrendered to the captain of an English man-of-war and set sail on a voyage that was ultimately to take him to St Helena.

On 14 July a relieved Louis XVIII attended the Opéra to enjoy the comical fooleries of *La Dansomanie*, in which Geneviève Gosselin danced a *pas de deux* with Albert to variations on *La Charmante Gabrielle* and *Vive Henri Quatre* – two songs that had been adopted unofficially as anthems of the Bourbon régime.[19]

Later that month, on 25 July, Gardel and Milon presented their own tribute to the genial monarch, a short ballet – 'a sort of impromptu', as one critic called it – entitled *L'Heureux Retour*. They had divided their task between an opening scene with a slight storyline, for which Milon was responsible, and a final *divertissement* by Gardel. In earlier times such a tribute might have been more grandiose, with copious references to the ancient gods of Olympus; but in the wake of military defeat, the mood was more restrained. The restoration of the monarchy brought promise of peace, but aroused relief rather than enthusiasm. When the curtain rose, a street scene in Paris was revealed, gradually filling with National Guards and everyday characters gathering to welcome the returning King. Everyone is in the best of spirits except Caroline (Mme Courtin), a young woman grieving for her soldier lover, of whom no word has been heard since the great battle. A wounded Grenadier from the same regiment of the Old Guard (Milon) remembers him, but can throw no light on his fate. After a dramatic moment when Caroline cannot contain her fears, the batman of an English colonel arrives with a billeting order. Soon the colonel himself (Montjoie) appears, accompanied by a young

and *La Dansomanie*, *Acis et Galathée*, *Figaro*, *Paul et Virginie*, *Le Retour d'Ulysse*, *Alexandre chez Apelles*, *Vertumne et Pomone*, *Persée et Andromède*, *l'Enlèvement des Sabines*, *L'Enfant prodigue* and *Nina* (once). These figures do not include court performances (for which see Appendix F), nor, of course, any performances he might have attended before becoming ruler of France.

[19] *La Charmante Gabrielle*, although sometimes attributed to Henri IV, was probably composed by his Superintendent of Music, Eustache Du Caurroy. *Vive Henri Quatre* was another time-honoured royalist song, which later Tchaikowsky was to use for the apotheosis of *The Sleeping Beauty*.

French soldier, whose life he has saved – and who turns out to be none other than Caroline's sweetheart, Edouard (Elie).

A scene change now transports the audience to the Tuileries gardens for a grand *divertissement*, featuring most of the leading dancers and ending with a rousing finale to the strains of *Vive Henri Quatre*, thundered out to a triumphant rolling of drums and clashing of cymbals as rockets shoot into the air behind.

In the *divertissement* Geneviève Gosselin and Albert were given the place of honour, repeating their *pas de deux* to *La Charmante Gabrielle*. A host of others received their due share of applause: among the men, Antonin, Ferdinand, Paul, Montjoie; among the women, Gaillet, Fanny Bias, Aimée and, specially remarked, Marie Delisle, who appeared both as a fishwife in the first scene and as a Scottish girl in the second. For the true connoisseurs, forever on the lookout for budding talent, there were some fresh little faces among the children: yet another little Gosselin called Henriette, and two girls who were shortly to begin their ascent through the hierarchy, Amélie Legallois and Lise Noblet.

Except for the overture, which had been composed by Berton, the score had been patched together by Persuis, who had dipped generously into some of the popular songs of the day. The *Journal des débats* remarked that the music was all very well for a family outing, but that too much was heard of *Vive Henri Quatre* and *La Charmante Gabrielle*, which not only had been incorporated in the overture and the finale, but was played at the beginning of the evening, before the opening opera.[20] Other insertions included *Les Folies d'Espagne* and *God Save the King*, the latter being attributed on the score to Handel.

To an English lady who was present, there seemed to be an air of unreality in this curious celebration of the return of a gouty old monarch; what the war-weary nation really wanted was just to celebrate the coming of peace. Lady Granville gave a vivid account of the evening in a letter to her sister. 'Now for the cream of my story,' she began.

> We went to the Opéra. The house was full and brilliant beyond measure, and my brother in raptures, as I must say he is from morning till night. All nations, all embassies, all English men, and scarcely a reputable woman besides myself. Boxes for every King and Emperor of the known world. But what do you think they shout at, applaud, *pâment de rire* over? They dance the battle of Waterloo in all its details. The

[20] *Journal des débats*, 27 July 1815. Signed 'C'.

> Imperial Guard wounded form dejected groups, embrace the National Guard, whilst a smart English officer makes most brilliant entrées. This *héros de la pièce* ends the ballet with presenting a French officer whom he has taken prisoner to his mistress, who had imagined him lost. They both kneel to him and kiss the hem of his garment and dance a finale amidst bursts of applause.[21]

But, strange though it might seem to English eyes, there was much to enjoy in *L'Heureux Retour*. It was to be given twelve performances before the end of the year, and would survive until the summer of 1817.

Shortly after its first performance, dancers and connoisseurs alike were dismayed to learn that the genial Jean Goyon, who had created the rôle of the Dansomane and many other character parts (the last being Delafrance in *L'Heureux Retour*), had died after a short illness. For nearly thirty years he had been a stalwart member of the company. As a young man he had been difficult to handle, but in 1786 he had been good enough to be engaged by the London opera house, where his performance as the Beast in J.-B. Hus's *Zemira and Azor* had been the talk of the town for the frisson of horror that he projected when looking at his reflection in a mirror. He had returned to Paris to become one of the most versatile mimes of his generation.

As the year drew on, Louis Picard was beginning to realise that he had re-embraced the cause of Napoleon a little too hastily for a recently appointed Chevalier of the royal Order of St Louis, and in October he tendered his resignation as Director of the Opéra. However, this would not take effect until the end of the following March – a delay that would enable him to bow out with something of a flourish by presenting, as his swansong, one of the greatest triumphs in the history of ballet – Charles Didelot's *Flore et Zéphire*.

[21] Granville, I, 64-5.

Milon; but he reminded the Council that Didelot's ballet would incur expense, and that the Opéra was already committed to the production of his *Proserpine*, the rehearsals of which were scheduled to start in a few weeks.

Support for his views was, of course, a foregone conclusion, and in his report to the Grand Chamberlain, Picard added a few points that had presumably arisen in the discussion. He foresaw a danger of 'chicanery, intrigues and cabals' if outside choreographers were allowed to produce works at the Opéra, and pointed out that the ballet-masters had already shown great variety in building up the present repertory. If the public were tiring of grand ballets, the ballet-masters could be instructed to stage smaller-scale works at low cost, as had already been done in the case of *Nina* and *L'Epreuve villageoise*. Finally there was the problem of how to keep an outsider's work in the repertory after he had departed. 'The action and the *pas* of a ballet are not written down,' Picard reminded the Grand Chamberlain, 'but are carried only in the memory. Can one ballet-master be expected to be responsible for attending to the work of another choreographer?'[8]

Didelot was now growing anxious. He was meeting a wall of silence from the Grand Chamberlain, who presumably had more pressing concerns at a time when his Imperial master was gathering another army to inflict a decisive defeat on the allies. On 21 May, aware now of Gardel's opposition, he wrote again. Everything now seemed to be working against him, he complained: the Grand Chamberlain's reluctance to grant him an interview, Gardel's change of front, warning sounds from his friends – 'so many things ... that add to my anxiety and lead me to impose on Monseigneur's time out of fear, not of what might be said against me, but of what might be done to prevent me from responding and *above all, proving* my case.' He recognised that this was not a favourable moment to realise his ambition to return to the Opéra. In fact, his friends had advised him to wait until Gardel's retirement created a vacancy, but he had been impatient to return to France, and now, in desperation, he begged the Grand Chamberlain to decide his fate once and for all and put him out of his misery.[9]

By the time he wrote to the Grand Chamberlain again, he had seen Gardel's report to the Council, which he answered point by point:

1. *That by allowing M. Didelot to stage a ballet, the door is being opened to*

[8] Arch. Nat., AJ[13] 94. Picard to Montesquiou, undated, but presumably written on the day of the Council meeting, 5 May 1815.

[9] Arch. Nat.,O[3] 1639. Didelot to Montesquiou, 21 May 1815.

others, to the detriment of the ballet-masters, who cannot stage more than one or two works a year at the Opéra, which has budgeted accordingly.
But had any début been refused before mine? ... I have not requested an exception ... And can the cost of my little work prevent the ballet-masters from enjoying preferential treatment in budgeting? Furthermore, are débuts so rare? ...

Very well, let them be fixed at only one or two a year. Let there be allocated for these trials no more than the receipts from a first performance of a new ballet (after deduction of the usual expenses). I will willingly offer myself as an example for this rule. But what if such a work were to fail? So be it! The Opéra will merely have given two performances in the cause of art. But if it should succeed, it will be to everyone's gain, and the time and money spent on two début performances will not prevent the ballet-masters from presenting their own productions, for they will still have at least nine months for their works.

2. *That it is easy for outside choreographers to create a work and a few pleasing* pas *by compiling them from here, there and everywhere, but, once their ideas are exhausted, they might not produce a second. That having been absent for a long time, they will no longer have a feel for the taste of the public, nor any knowledge of the talents of the dancers at their disposal. That the talent of such choreographers is problematic. That the expenses incurred for those ballets that fail are as high as for those that succeed.*

This is merely insulting, and I shall reply only briefly with some facts. Let me stage a few ballets, let me be tested in rehearsal (even though twenty years of experience might seem to excuse me from such an examination) and it can then be seen which is the more *problematic* – my scorned talents or the impartiality and loyalty that force M. Gardel to prevent me from appearing. Much more to the point would be to try to avoid budgeting 60,000 francs for staging a single work, which is slowly ruining the Opéra, instead of abolishing débuts that are more likely to produce receipts and denigrating the reputation of those *choreographers* who are thereby deprived of the opportunity of showing their worth. In conclusion, it would be much better that a ballet-master should spend his time more profitably, by *creating* and exercising his imagination. In this way a sum reserved for a single work might give birth to three or four ...

3. *That to grant a début to M. Didelot, who has come back only to make money and who wishes to rob the ballet-masters of their greatest amenity, would be tantamount to rewarding him for desertion.*

At that time I was very young, I loved my art, and I saw nothing but obstacles and unpleasantness at the Opéra, where it was impossible to create anything. *Rose*, that lovely talent who has now gone to her grave, *Rose*, who had cast her lot in with mine, was no better treated than I. Basically, it was the unlawful action of the administration in forcing us to sacrifice a leave of absence that would have earned us 3000 louis [60,000 francs] which broke the terms of our contracts and decided us to leave the Opéra. We had given notice, and it had coolly given us a free hand to leave. If M. Gardel, who now sets himself up as the accuser of his former comrade, to whom *he had promised support*, needs to be reminded, we made it clear that we were abandoning the direction, not our comrades.

Am I the only one to have been exiled from the Opéra for trouble-making and misconduct? And are we to be punished twice over? Our salaries were withheld, a penalty was paid, proceedings were closed, and we settled our accounts with the establishment. Furthermore, I am no longer the youngster I was in '92; I am now a man who has made his mark, who has devoted himself to choreography, and whose talent is being condemned before it has even been examined; and against whom these gentlemen have become *judges* and *prosecutors*, dredging up a time-worn tale merely out of personal interest. I might add that I was a pensioner of the King of Sweden at the time when I was at the School of Dance in Paris; that I left at the age of fourteen; that after that time it was to Noverre, Vestris the father and Dauberval that I owe my talent, and that when I made my début in Paris, I had long ceased to belong to the School of Dance of the Opéra. So far as my returning is concerned: had I listened to my close friends, I would certainly have waited until M. Gardel's retirement before making an approach. This would have avoided *much unpleasantness*, but the desire to see my country once more – notwithstanding (as I can easily prove) that I could have gone elsewhere, and that I could not imagine that an artiste might still, after more than forty-five years of success, want to keep out the very persons whom he ought to be encouraging in order to find a suitable successor when the time comes to deprive the public of his rare talents – gave me reassurance and brought me to Paris. But why does not all this reassure M. Gardel too? His own merit, and the knowledge that if some dishonest wretch were to covet his place, the administration of the Opéra, being in his debt for many years of service, would be well able to keep him, should have made him take a more generous attitude.

4. It is necessary to appoint a third ballet-master, but at the second or even third level, who can be tried out in small things, divertissements *etc., and who can replace [a ballet-master] unable to attend to his duties. It is at that stage that a judgement can be made as to whether he can fill the place destined for him.*

So it is finally agreed that a third ballet-master is necessary; but 'necessary' here means, perhaps not nothing, but almost nothing. It is said that he is to replace those gentlemen should they be unable to attend to their duties. But it is possible that both MM. Gardel and Milon might be in that condition tomorrow. Can a third-rate talent be capable of taking their place? ... Such a choice certainly does credit to their foresight, but does not say much for their desire to do what is best for the administration. Consequently the public will have to make do with mediocrity when it could have been offered a better choice ... namely, between several persons of talent, without the door being closed to others who might have more. Everything in such a fine establishment as the Opéra has to be on a grand scale ... With three choreographers, everything must be done with the hand of a master, not that of an apprentice. The public must be well, not poorly, served, and its pleasures varied; only then will this theatre be a real Workshop of the Arts. It is only by removing defects, not by [perpetuating] a perverse system, that good will be done.

Is the Opéra the Museum of the Dance? ... In a Museum of Painting each artist hangs his picture, and in that of the Dance each recognised choreographer ought to be able to present his ballet. But then would there not be too many works? And could this be done without ruining the administration? Allow me to point out that men of recognised merit are not often to be found, and other [candidates] would only be admitted after having been tried out in rehearsal in *every branch of their art*, and subject to the conditions mentioned above. After this trial had been judged by the artistes, those who failed to attain the required standard should be allowed to display their talent at another theatre, which should be protected against being closed by intrigues and shady machinations within the Opéra (and by misleading the authorities) whenever talent should appear there ...[10] Would Gluck & Piccinni have been able to support the Opéra on their own? Can two ballet-masters maintain the dance? ...

[10] A reference to the closure of the Porte-Saint-Martin in 1805 following Henry's *Les Sauvages de la Floride*. See Chapter 17.

5. *If M. Didelot does not remain at the Opéra, the money spent on his ballet will be wasted.*

I undertake to allow my work to be performed twenty to twenty-five times should it have the good fortune to succeed, as it has elsewhere and at very little expense. This work is ready to be staged – fifteen days will suffice – and I am willing to bear the cost personally in the event of its being considered a 'compilation', as has been alleged, or even if it is judged to be bad.[11]

The boldness with which Didelot expressed himself in this defence suggests that at this point he felt he had nothing to lose. Apart from noticing that one of his points – the need for Gardel and Milon to have an assistant – had been partly conceded, he had now learnt that Gardel's *Proserpine* had been shelved for reasons of expense. So, perhaps as a last throw, he informed the Grand Chamberlain that he was putting his name forward for the post of assistant ballet-master, an appointment, as he hopefully explained, that would dispose of one problem, in that the production of his ballet would not infringe the Regulations. His ballet, he went on with a generosity he may later have regretted, 'would incur no expense, for I would willingly bear this personally, if necessary'.[12]

Picard's response was unhelpful, but not unexpected. He saw no urgency in appointing another ballet-master, and thought there were others who had a greater right to be considered than had Didelot.[13]

On 15 June, after his application had been rejected by the Grand Chamberlain, Didelot made an impassioned appeal to the Minister of the Interior, Lazare Carnot, the great 'organiser of victory' of Revolutionary times, who had now re-emerged, after many years in seclusion, to serve Napoleon in his hour of need:

At the very moment when the august presence of His Imperial Majesty is restoring liberal ideas, I find myself oppressed and deprived of the very benefits that are being reintroduced. Having exhausted every other means, I come to crave the indulgence once again of the Friend of Liberty and the Father of the Arts – in short, to place my petition before Your Excellency's eyes.

As a pupil of the Opéra who was banished, like many others, as a result of the sharp practice of the administration, and who has devoted

[11] Arch. Nat., O[3] 1710. 'Objections and Report made against my début and a survey of means to facilitate débuts economically'. Paper prepared by Didelot.
[12] Bibl.-Musée de l'Opéra, Dossier d'artiste (Didelot). Didelot to Montesquiou, 8 June 1815.
[13] Arch. Nat., AJ[13] 94. Picard's report to Montesquiou, 11 June 1815.

himself to choreography, I have returned after a long exile to offer my humble talent as a tribute to the source from which it derived. Desiring and expecting that I would not leave my country again and that I might perhaps enter the service of His Imperial Majesty, I presented a scenario, which was rejected on the ground that it resembled works that had already been given. I put forward facts to prove the error of this assertion, and offered to stage this trifle in fifteen days at hardly any expense, and even to indemnify the administration should I be taking an advantage. My ballet was then no longer criticised as being similar to any other, apart from a grand work not yet staged,[14] and the Comte de Montesquiou postponed my début. Distressed at having anticipated, in a trifle ten years before, a grand work which is still uncompleted and which now must be staged and performed before my own ballet, I offered a choice between two works of different types. And now, in the most flattering terms ... I have received a flat rejection from His Excellency the Comte de Montesquiou, and learn that in the meantime the ballet-masters have presented a report claiming that they alone have the right to compose works at the Académie Impériale de Musique.

Although Gluck and Piccinni were unable on their own to maintain the operatic repertory, two ballet-masters are asserting that between them they can maintain the ballet repertory, varying their style sufficiently to satisfy and attract a public crying out for novelty, and that they can bring in sufficient receipts to reduce the great burden that His Imperial Majesty is bearing for this great establishment.

Having first been vilified and then rejected, I have in vain requested a début such as has been granted as a matter of course to many other artistes before me: namely Hus, Gallet, Milon, Duport, Henry and most recently Aumer. I do not seek to take anyone's place, but only to make myself known, to be of use, and above all, if possible, to avoid leaving my country once more, even though I am in demand elsewhere.

Therefore, the aim of my humble petition, Monsieur le Comte, is to seek Your Excellency's favour to make myself known. Without a protector, without support, and with no recommendation other than my modest talent, my good character and a numerous family, I have humbly ventured to submit to Your Excellency the fate of an artiste who has been harshly treated and on whose account, for all their good will, the authorities have undoubtedly been misled.[15]

[14] This clearly refers to *Proserpine*, but there seems to have been no suggestion that its plot bore any resemblance to that of Didelot's ballet. However, the Opéra may have expressed doubt as to the wisdom of presenting two successive ballets with mythological subjects.

As it was, there was no time for Carnot to give this plea his full attention, if indeed any attention at all; for on the very day it was written Napoleon left Paris to join his armies in the north. When he returned nine days later, defeated at Waterloo, his authority had collapsed. In the few days left before he was replaced, Carnot could have had no time to concern himself with the problems of a disgruntled ballet-master. In any event, when Louis XVIII was restored for the second time, Didelot adopted a different approach – one for which his Russian recommendations may at last have had some weight.

Typically, the King had reinstated the structure of the Opéra in the form that had existed under the Old Régime, placing it under the supervision of the Minister of his Household, the Comte de Pradel, between whom and the Director was interposed the Intendant of the Menus-Plaisirs. In the ten years before the outbreak of the Revolution, the latter office had been effectively filled by Denis Papillon de La Ferté, who had been guillotined during the Terror. At the Restoration, his son Louis had been rewarded with the post, and it was he whom Didelot approached on 17 July, just nine days after the King's return to Paris. Conveniently forgetting his glowing reference to ideas of liberty in his recent application to Carnot, Didelot opened his letter to La Ferté with a flowery tribute to the restored monarchy:

> Under the auspices of the beautiful dawn that is breaking over France, and the justice with which the reign has already opened, I venture ... to request the favour of a début on the stage of the Opéra, as a composer of ballets.
>
> Although brought up in the French school and a former member of the Opéra, where many artistes have been permitted to compose ballets, I was nevertheless rejected by M. de Montesquiou on the pretext of a Regulation. But if one did exist, why was I not told at once? Why was I led to have hopes? After I had been asked for scenarios, after my début had been put off and then formally rejected, is it possible that, amid all the rejoicing at the happy turn of events, the Regulations should still prevent an artiste from briefly sharing in the public celebrations alongside his old comrades, particularly when he is seeking not to take anyone's place, but merely to make himself known?
>
> If, as has been alleged, my work, which has been well-known for the past twelve or sixteen years, bears a resemblance to ballets already given in Paris, it is for an enlightened public to judge whether I am

[15] Arch. Nat., O^3 1644 (6h). Didelot to Comte Carnot, 12 June 1815.

guilty of plagiarism. Furthermore, I have offered, and still offer, to have my work judged in rehearsal by the artistes, or to pay the modest expenses that may be incurred. As for the time it will take, I need only fifteen days to stage this trifle.

> Had it not been for the respected artiste[16] who kindly spoke to you and interested herself in my case, I would not have sought a protector. I would have assumed that my integrity and talent, ten years' service at the Russian Court and the eight I spent at the King's Theatre in London, added to my being well-known to the leading dancers in Paris (particularly those for whom I have worked, such as Deshayes, Laborie, Duport, Baptiste Petit, his wife, Vestris, Léon and so many others), would, when added to my zeal and desire to succeed, be ... a sufficient motive, worth more than any recommendation.[17]

Now at last Didelot had found an ally. On 28 July he forwarded to La Ferté the scenario of *Zéphire inconstant* with a brief explanation of why he had chosen the somewhat out-of-favour anacreontic genre. He added a plea that, if an opinion were to be sought on the recent production in London, the Intendant should ignore a version presented there in the current season and should assure himself that any assessment was based on the version Didelot had staged there eighteen months earlier.[18]

Didelot's enemies now shifted their ground, alleging that the flights that were to be a principal feature of his ballet – and the secret of which, with good reason, he was carefully guarding – were nothing new and resembled flights already seen at the Opéra. On learning what was being said behind his back, Didelot quickly dashed off another letter to La Ferté:

> Forgive my worrying you, but I have just learnt from M. Martin that someone has told you that my flying effects resemble those of the Opéra, or (as I think it would be more accurate to say) those that will be presented in times to come.
>
> I have the honour to assure you, Monsieur, that such an effect has never appeared on the stage of the Opéra. Alone and isolated, by means that are entirely invisible, it has produced a great effect every-

[16] This may have been Geneviève Gosselin, whose husband, the singer Martin, may have provided Didelot with a useful channel of information in his struggle to get his ballet accepted.

[17] Arch. Nat., O^3 1710. Didelot to La Ferté, 17 July 1815.

[18] Didelot, who had himself supervised his ballet, *Zéphire inconstant, puni et fixé*, in the London seasons of 1812 and 1814, is here disowning responsibility for a truncated version entitled *Zéphire et Flore* which had opened the season of 1815. No choreographer was credited, and the ballet-master, Armand Vestris, did not care to claim responsibility.

where. Zephyr, in his pursuit of Flora, seizes her in his arms in full view of the public, lifts her to make a circular flight at about 15 feet, and deposits her, still in full view of the public, on the altar of Hymen.

I have reason to believe that this is a ploy to steal this effect and deprive me of its novelty ...

Should you not be prepared to support an artiste who is relying only on your loyalty and who will be proud to be your protégé, I shall feel that this accusation of copying is again based on a desire to oust me, and that such an effect, which is seen in my work as a copy, will perhaps appear in someone else's work as original.[19]

La Ferté, with whom Didelot had established an excellent rapport, was already working on plans to reinvigorate the ballet repertory with new works. On 3 August he recommended to the Comte de Pradel that Gardel's *Proserpine* should be produced before the end of the year. However, since the scenery, music-copying and rehearsals would take several months, he urged Pradel to authorise *Zéphire inconstant*. 'The acceptance of this work is apparently desired by certain persons of the greatest eminence,' he added, 'and its composition and details make it likely that it will enjoy a brilliant success. Its staging will incur neither expense nor delay.' However, he felt bound to add that Gardel and Milon had entered an objection, which to La Ferté appeared to be based on 'a system of monopolies and exclusion' quite contrary to the interests of the Opéra and to the progress of art.[20]

The new Minister of the King's Household was a prudent man. While confirming the decision to proceed with the production of *Proserpine*, he asked La Ferté to consider with Picard whether the long-established custom whereby only the accredited ballet-masters had the right to stage ballets at the Opéra had any legally binding force:

Generally speaking, it cannot be denied that to attribute and restrict to a certain number of authors the right to compose for the theatre would be damaging to artistic progress. But it may be that this principle should not be strictly applied in the composition of ballets, the merit and success of which depend much less on the choice of subject than on their execution; and no doubt that is why the Article charging the ballet-masters with the task of composing ballets at this theatre has remained unchanged in the successive Regulations over the past

[19] Arch. Nat., O³ 1710. Didelot to La Ferté, 29 July 1815.
[20] Arch. Nat., O³ 1639. La Ferté to Pradel, 3 August 1815.

> twenty-five years. If such a principle is not legally enforceable under the Article, it is important to ensure that it can be waived without prejudice to the discipline and performance quality upon which the success of M. Didelot's ballet depends.[21]

La Ferté then submitted the question of accepting *Zéphire inconstant* to the Committee of the Opéra. This Committee – perhaps by a majority vote, for Gardel was a member – acknowledged the force of La Ferté's argument that it was in the Opéra's interests to encourage competition, and accepted that the Regulations did not give the ballet-masters an exclusive right to create all ballets presented at the Opéra. Financial stringency was now the order of the day, for the level of the nation's war reparations still remained to be settled,[22] and it was agreed to adopt a policy of 'producing short one-act ballets that are inexpensive in costumes, scenery and performers, and are simple to stage.'[23] *Zéphire inconstant* was considered to fulfil such conditions, despite the fact that it had two acts, and the Committee agreed that it should be accepted to fill the gap while waiting for *Proserpine*.

Gardel and Milon had given warning that its acceptance might give rise to insubordination within the company, but on this La Ferté took a firm line. Didelot himself might well have to face some unpleasantness, but that was for him to deal with, although the administration should be prepared to suppress any sign of insubordination. And as for the danger of splitting the public into two factions, it was considered that the resulting publicity might well work to the Opéra's advantage.[24]

On receipt of La Ferté's letter, Pradel searched for a formula to justify authorising Didelot's ballet, and on 17 August his decision was conveyed to the Intendant in a carefully worded letter:

> The Regulation charging the Heads of Ballet at the Opéra with composing ballets for this theatre does not in fact exclude, in special circumstances, the performance of works not composed by the Heads of Ballet. But custom, which until now has not been departed from, might appear to support such an exclusivity on the grounds that the performance of a new ballet needs to be directed and supervised by the author who has composed it, and that a master from outside the Académie

[21] Arch. Nat., O[3] 1644. Pradel to La Ferté, 8 August 1815.

[22] The nation's indemnity was finally settled at 700,000,000 francs, and would be paid off by 1818.

[23] Arch. Nat., O[3] 1639. La Ferté to Pradel, 1- August 1815 (second digit of date left uninserted).

[24] Arch. Nat.,O[3] 1639. La Ferté to Pradel, 1- August 1815 (second digit of date left uninserted).

Royale de Musique has difficulty in obtaining at that theatre the obedience given to the Heads of Ballet ...

It is only in this sense ... that I have been able to accept the possibility of indiscipline, the occasion and pretext for which disappears if the Heads of Ballet at the Académie Royale de Musique can be required to direct the production of new works that they have not composed.

That being the case, I no longer see any real disadvantage, whether from the points of view of art, the pleasure of the public, or the prosperity of the Académie Royale de Musique, in staging the ballet *Zéphir inconstant* at this theatre, and I have no hesitation in authorising its performance.[25]

Didelot was informed of this on 21 August, and asked to consult Boutron, the chief machinist, to prepare an estimate of the cost, which had yet to be approved. The first estimate (5 September) came out at 17,205 francs, which a week later was reduced to 12,611 francs largely by economising on the costumes. The item that Didelot fought hardest to preserve was the machinery for the flights; this was only marginally reduced to 3235 francs, mainly by omitting a minor part of the apparatus.[26]

Hardly had news of the authorisation of Didelot's ballet become known when Pradel found himself plagued by 'a number of persistent objections', which he professed to be ignoring. In particular, Gardel and Milon had submitted some further 'Observations':

At a time when we are celebrating the return of our legitimate sovereign, when every effort is being made to restore order in all parts of the kingdom, and when the infamy of anarchy is being buried once and for all, it is cruel to find ourselves victimised by intrigue and injustice. For at least thirty years we have been unremittingly faithful to our duties; we have made every sacrifice, in the department which we head, to support the great theatre of the Opéra. We have always been irreproachably conscientious and hard-working, and by our conduct have justified ... the esteem of the public and of our superiors. If we may be allowed to speak of talent, we merely ask one question. As composers of all the [ballet-pantomimes and] *divertissements* in the operas of the vast repertory of the Académie Royale de Musique, ... have we not given proof enough that our brushes were, and are still, capable of handling every type of work? So why is it necessary to open the door to

[25] Arch. Nat., O[3] 1644. Pradel to La Ferté, 17 August 1815.

[26] Arch. Nat., AJ[13] 94, O[3] 1710,O[3] 1639. Estimates.

all who cannot otherwise enter in order that they can upset the harmony of the Opéra ballet, and to sow discord there? Can it not be seen that once the door is opened, it will be difficult, not to put it more strongly, to refuse what has once been granted? And what then will become of the Opéra's accredited ballet-masters? Why infringe the Regulations so as to deprive two artistes of rights that have been conferred upon them, and disturb the tranquillity so necessary for their exacting labours and for the good of the service? Is it just a matter of gambling for a success? But do not [our own] works ... offer a guarantee of what can still be expected of our efforts?

We have already proved, in the Observations we have had the honour of submitting to the Intendant of the King's Menus-Plaisirs and to the Director, that this unjust decision was even more damaging to the administration than to the ballet-masters, in that it requires expenditure not comprised in the Budget and wastes time that would be better spent in staging works that will remain in the repertory; also, that additional and lengthy rehearsals for outside composers who are consequently not concerned with day-to-day administration would so exhaust the dancers that they would be unable to carry out their normal duties and would have to be replaced by inferiors, so that the public would become discontented and finally stay away.[27]

Didelot's troubles were far from over. Grumbles were arising within the company over the casting, in particular perhaps because of Didelot's choice of Geneviève Gosselin as Flora, a rôle to which Bigottini may have felt entitled by seniority. Pradel had been concerned not to antagonise Gardel unnecessarily, and he repeated to La Ferté his insistence on the right of the ballet-masters alone 'to direct the execution of all ballets authorised for production at the theatre to which they belong, and where the authority of an outside master might be contested or unrecognised'. Gardel and Milon, however, held themselves aloof, which no doubt conveyed a measure of their displeasure, although Didelot was probably happy to have a free hand. At the same time, he for his part was no doubt making demands to ensure that his ballet would be as perfect as he could make it. Pradel then began to worry about the expense. He was still trying to keep the cost within reasonable bounds, and finally, with some exasperation, he instructed La Ferté that he was not prepared to allocate more than 6000 francs, and that unless Didelot agreed to bear personally any excess over that figure, he was inclined to authorise the immediate

[27] Arch. Nat., O[3] 1639. 'Observations of the ballet-masters of the Opéra', received on 11 September 1815.

production of *Proserpine* 'and not to lay myself open to all the inconvenience that will apparently result from accepting *Zéphire inconstant*'.[28]

There is no suggestion that Didelot considered this financial arrangement unfair. The allocation was no more than the agreed estimate for Gardel's *Vénus et Adonis*, a ballet equivalent in scale to Didelot's. Admittedly some of the great pantomime ballets of the Napoleonic era had been far more costly – 80,000 francs had been allocated for *Persée et Andromède*, for example – but what was affordable by Napoleon in his wedding year was quite unrealistic in 1815. Didelot certainly made no objection to this suggestion, apart from asking that he should be charged with the excess only in the event of the ballet proving unsuccessful. Seeing the obstacles beginning to disappear, Didelot was immensely grateful for La Ferté's support. He assured him:

> I shall make every endeavour to justify the great efforts you have so kindly made in obtaining the order for my début, and to be a credit to my protector for supporting a reputation that certain spiteful parties have tried to denigrate.
>
> Please be good enough ... to give instructions for work on my new ballet to start immediately so that I can rehearse without interruption.
>
> May I also remind you that I am your protégé and have no other protector but you, and that so long as you are willing to support me, I shall be able to face every obstacle, but that without you I can only succumb?[29]

Didelot now had further discussions with the chief machinist Boutron and with Marche, the head tailor, as a result of which further reductions were made, bringing the estimated cost down to 9252.45 francs. On 6 October Pradel reminded Picard that the sum authorised for the ballet was 6000 francs, and informed him that Didelot's proposal that he should not be charged with the excess if his ballet was successful was not acceptable. Didelot may have felt this unfair, but clearly took the view that at this late stage further argument would have been counter-productive and so did not press the point. Pradel then gave his approval for rehearsals to be resumed without further delay. 'Its acceptance is now definite,' he told La Ferté. 'There is no need to discuss the objections or to deal with the complaints that have been directed against it.'[30]

[28] Arch. Nat., O^3 1644. Pradel to La Ferté, 22 September 1815.
[29] Arch. Nat., O^3 1710. Didelot to La Ferté, 26 September 1815.
[30] Arch. Nat., O^3 1644. Pradel to La Ferté, 6 October 1815.

28

Flore et Zéphire

What Paris was about to see would be the fourth version of a ballet, the origins of which stretched back twenty years to Didelot's earliest efforts in choreography. Its story had begun in 1795 in Lyons, to where Didelot had gone with his beloved Rose after the collapse of Mme Montansier's enterprise in her theatre in the Rue de la Loi. Lyons had suffered brutally during the Revolution, and life had barely returned to normal when the couple arrived there to dance at the Théâtre de la République. After revealing a talent for composition with several isolated *pas* in which the wife of the ballet-master, Coindé, was most advantageously and diplomatically served, Didelot was rewarded with the opportunity of producing a ballet.

For 'his first fruit in composition', as he called it, he planned a much longer work than that which was eventually presented towards the end of the year under the title of *La Métamorphose*. In its truncated form it consisted of two loosely connected episodes within a single act, a scene of satyrs and bacchantes and a miniature ballet in which Didelot and Rose appeared respectively as a faun and as Atalanta. Another episodic ballet scene based on the legend of Zephyr and Flora was disappointingly cut.

Fortunately Didelot did include the plot of the Zephyr and Flora episode as an appendix in the printed programme, revealing that flying effects were to be prominently featured even in this earliest sketch. The scene was to have opened as day was breaking. As Cupid lies asleep on a bed of roses, Zephyr was to appear in the half-light, floating in the air to greet the dawn before gently descending. 'This effect,' Didelot specified, 'must take place at the back of the set.' Following a scene with the Graces, Zephyr persuades Cupid to help him woo the nymph Chloris, and then rises again into the air to look down on his beloved. Cupid entices Chloris to his statue, where Zephyr confronts her and declares his passion. Aware of his reputation for inconstancy, she hesitates. Cupid then mischievously deprives Zephyr of his wings and gives them to Chloris, who flies into the air and disappears from view. Cupid insists that the furious Zephyr must swear to be faithful, an oath he will take only if Chloris is transformed into Flora in order to share the empire of the flowers with him. Chloris returns; hearing of Zephyr's oath, she can resist him no longer. Before returning his wings, she receives from him 'love's first kiss'. He then bears her away to Olympus to receive immortality from the hands of Jupiter.

The outlines of the ballet were thus drawn; even though it had not been performed, Didelot must presumably have been satisfied that the flights he contemplated were capable of being put into effect. When and where he had obtained the specialised knowledge for this he did not disclose: whether he had acquired the secret before coming to Lyons, or had worked it out with the machinist of the Théâtre de la République, Ravilly.

For Didelot, Lyons was probably never more than a stepping-stone in a journey to England that was already planned. The means by which he and Rose secured a contract as principal dancers at London's opera house and slipped out of France to face the winter storms in the Bay of Biscay and the Channel were secrets best kept to themselves at a time when the two countries were at war. They missed the early weeks of the season at the King's Theatre, but, still recovering from the fatigue of their journey, lost little time in appearing before the public. Although Onorati was titular ballet-master, Didelot was soon producing ballets of his own, one of which was *La Métamorphose*, presented under the title of *L'Amour vengé*. At the King's Theatre Didelot found a competent machinist, Cabanal, to judge from the impression made by 'the aerial passage of Cupid, who flew about the stage with great ease, with a retinue of little Loves'. On 7 July 1796 Didelot took his benefit, at which he was at last able to present his *Flore et Zéphire*, graced with a score by Cesare Bossi, a composer then resident in London. Cabanal again served him well. 'By an airiness of fancy,' an eye-witness reported, '[Didelot] makes all his *personnages* literally fly – for they are borne on the bosom of the air, in a very new and extraordinary manner'.[1]

Didelot was again in London for the following season, when *Flore et Zéphire* continued to enchant the public. In 1801 he was engaged in Russia, where he remained for the next ten years. Being preoccupied with new creations, his only opportunity to produce *Zéphire et Flore* (the names of the main characters having now been reversed) was for a single performance in 1804, when it was shown to Tsar Alexander I and his court at the Hermitage in St Petersburg. On his return to London, the ship carrying his luggage was wrecked in a storm while crossing the Baltic, and all the notes, drawings and music for his ballets, including Bossi's

[1] *True Briton*, 9 July 1796.

score for *Zéphire et Flore*, were lost. Undeterred, on his arrival in England he had another score composed by Frédéric Venua for a revised version that was presented at the King's Theatre in 1812 with a new title, *Zéphire inconstant, puni et fixé, ou les Noces de Flore*, to distinguish it from the version London had seen seventeen years earlier. Armand Vestris and Fortunata Angiolini played the title rôles and may have been persuaded to undertake the flying, for no substitution appears to have been observed. 'Zephyr and Flora,' it was recorded, 'both fly through the grove with so much ease as to make the illusion perfect.'[2]

The earlier history of the ballet was to be briefly and accurately told in Didelot's preface to the printed scenario of the Paris production of 1815, so as to refute rumours, as Didelot explained, that his ballet 'had been given almost in its entirety in several places under a different name than my own'. Such rumours had no doubt arisen from the fact that Jean Aumer had recently produced a ballet with the same title in Vienna, during the Congress.[3] Although the choreography and the production were no doubt Aumer's own, it may be that he had based it on Didelot's 1795 scenario, for he used the same somewhat unusual description – an 'episodic ballet' – as had Didelot. Louis Duport had also produced a ballet called *Zephir* in Vienna, but this was a version of Gardel's *Retour de Zéphire.*

* * *

Didelot's revised scenario for the London production of 1812 was no doubt what he submitted first to Montesquiou and later to Pradel on his arrival in Paris in 1815, and which became the basis of the production he began to prepare at the Opéra in the autumn of that year.

The period of rehearsals that began in October was to prove much longer than he had envisaged when he assured the two Ministers that it would take him no more than a couple of weeks to produce. What he overlooked was not only other demands on the dancers' time, but a chain of difficulties that beset him when he set to work. Looking back in later years, he spoke bitterly of 'the multiplicity of intrigues and obstacles' with which he had to cope.[4] Jean-Baptiste Hullin, father of the three talented little girls, also remembered 'the many obstacles placed in the path of the ballet, and a cabal so strong that sometimes, at Didelot's rehearsals, the ballet répétiteur failed to turn up and he, Hullin, took his place to oblige Didelot.'[5]

[2] *Morning Chronicle*, 8 April 1812.
[3] *Zephir und Flora*, first performed at the Hofoper, Vienna, on 16 August , 1814.
[4] Gluskhovsky, 165.
[5] Glushkovsky, 202.

Didelot was driven to the end of his tether and, when the ballet was nearly ready, a distressing scene took place over the set for the first act. According to Saint-Léon's account,

> a new forest backcloth was absolutely necessary, since it had to be so arranged that the wires for the flying were invisible to the public. The set was ordered in accordance with his wishes; but when it was finished, poor Didelot was surprised to see, at the rehearsal of a little opera that was to be performed before his ballet, his forest background being used for that aforesaid work before *Flore et Zéphire.* He protested with all his might against such an iniquity, shouting and bemoaning, but all to no avail.[6]

He worked himself up to such a pitch as to threaten to abandon the production, but his friends managed to talk him out of such a drastic step. At the end of the rehearsal 'he wanted to say a few words, but he was overcome by such violent emotion that his voice completely failed him. His chest seized up with cramp, and this dreadful condition, which was accompanied by a high fever, lasted several hours.'[7]

However, the records of the Opéra show that there was never any question of an entirely new set being designed for the first act. During the discussions in September about the financial provision for the ballet, Didelot must have seen the scenery specification, which clearly stated that the forest set from Sacchini's opera *Arvire et Evelina* (1788) would be used, although no doubt appropriately repainted. Also to be taken from store was a tree flat that had served for Piccinni's opera *Alcibiade solitaire*, which had been a miserable failure when shown the previous March; this was to be adapted so that it could conceal three persons from view – possibly stagehands controlling the flight. There was nothing sinister in using old stock; this was common practice, which applied even to Gardel.

Since a forest scene was not required for *Le Laboureur chinois*, the short opera that was to open the programme containing *Flore et Zéphire* (as it was henceforth to be called),[8] Saint-Léon's account is a little puzzling. If the rehearsal was a run-through of the whole programme, the set for the first act of *Zéphire* may have been in place to serve the opera as well as the ballet in order to save time. However, *Le Laboureur chinois* had its own

[6] Saint-Léon, note on Didelot, p.4.

[7] Mundt, 6.

[8] Although the ballet was always to be billed in Paris as *Flore et Zéphire*, the printed scenario bore the title *Zéphire et Flore*.

scenery and it is hardly conceivable that the Opéra would risk the disapproval of the public by skimping in such an obvious manner.

There is no doubt that Didelot was embittered by his experiences during the staging of *Flore et Zéphire* in Paris, but the opposition he had to face went deeper than 'jealousy and ill will' on Gardel's part. While Didelot maintained that his resignation from the Opéra in 1793 had been justified by the shabby treatment he had received from the administration, others noted that he had been quick to secure a more lucrative engagement and – what was even more damning in the eyes of his fellow dancers who had remained loyal to their country and the Opéra through the thick and thin of the years of revolution and war – he had then slipped away to dance in an enemy capital. He had done very well for himself in Russia, and had now returned on the coat tails of the occupation forces bearing recommendations that could hardly be ignored. In the aftermath of invasion and defeat, it must have been hard for many French dancers at the Opéra to view his arrival with equanimity, and the personnel might very well have closed ranks out of patriotism and made no secret of their feelings. Gardel himself had carefully withdrawn from any active opposition, but no doubt he observed Didelot's difficulties without much compassion and did little to curb the disaffection within the ranks that was motivated by other, deeper causes than mere loyalty to himself.

* * *

Didelot listened to his friends and persevered, and on 12 December 1815 the ballet was presented to the Paris public for the first time. Embellished with the royal coat of arms, the title page of the programme introduced Didelot as 'former first dancer of the Académie Royale de Musique and ballet-master of H.M. the Emperor of Russia'. His collaborators were also handsomely acknowledged, even if two of the names were misspelt, Venua appearing as Venna, and Ciceri as Cisery (revealing that his family name was being pronounced in the French manner, although it was of Italian origin).

The action of the ballet was described in some detail, as was customary. The curtain first rose to reveal a dense and picturesque wood. Zephyr (Albert) descends from the sky, carrying Cupid (F. Hullin) in his arms. When they alight, they go their separate ways in search of Flora. It is Zephyr who finds her, and he tells her of his love. Aware of his reputation for fickleness, Flora (G. Gosselin) resists his advances, and is about to leave when Zephyr plucks a beautiful flower, which she covets. He teases her with it and eventually gives it to her, but she slips away. Zephyr is incon-

ACADEMIE ROYALE
DE MUSIQUE.

On commencera à 7 heures précises. — *Aujourd'hui mardi 12 décembre 1815*,
La trente-huitième représentation

DU LABOUREUR
CHINOIS,

Opéra en un acte, paroles de *M.****, musique arrangée par *M. Lachnith*, divertissemens de *M. Milon*; suivi de la première de

FLORE
ET ZEPHIRE,

Ballet nouveau en deux actes.

CHANT : Mrs. Nourrit, Bonel, Bertin, Henrard, Prévost : Mme. Albert.
DANSE : Mrs. Albert, Beaupré, Anatole ; Mmes. Gosselin aînée fe. Martin, Delisle, Fanny Bias, Masrelié cadette, Marinette, Anatole-Gosselin, Berri aînée, Hullin 2e., Hullin 3e.

S'adresser, pour la location des loges, à M. DAMENCE, à la salle de l'Académie Royale de Musique.

BALLARD, Imprimeur du Roi, rue J.-J. Rousseau, n. 8.

Playbill for the first performance of Flore et Zéphire. *(Bibliothèque-Musée de l'Opéra: © Cliché BNF Paris)*

solable, and begs Cupid's help. Cupid laughingly agrees. But Zephyr is then distracted by a group of nymphs who are waking from their sleep. He is attracted to one of them, Cléise (M. Masrélier), who opens her eyes as she senses the gentle breeze from his wings. However, Cupid has already drawn his attention to another nymph, Aglaée (Julie Berry). As Zephyr hides, Cupid ascends a small mound and freezes into the stillness of a statue. Aglaée approaches carrying a pair of turtle doves. To her surprise the statue appears to gesture to the doves, and the sight of their billing and cooing is her 'first lesson of love'. Cupid and Zephyr rapidly change places, so that it is Zephyr who receives 'love's first kiss'. Aglaée draws back in surprise at the apparent metamorphosis of Cupid into a handsome young man. She wants to escape, but Zephyr holds her back. Accomplished in the art of seduction, Zephyr knows how to arouse her without frightening her, but Cupid is planning further mischief. Spirited away by Cupid's magic, Zephyr finds himself surrounded by a bevy of other nymphs – Aspasia (Boissière) with her lyre, the lively bacchante Erigone (M.M. Delisle) and the languorous Amynthe (Mme Anatole) –

who mock him for his duplicity. Cupid now warns Zephyr of Flora's approach. The nymphs try to hold him back, but Zephyr eludes them, flying away and bidding them an ironic farewell. The nymphs depart, swearing to be avenged for his desertion.

Act II opens with the entrance of Flora in search of Zephyr. Shepherdesses find her tending her roses, and she joins in their dances. She is then discovered by the vengeful nymphs, who complain bitterly of Zephyr's fickle behaviour and demand that he be banished. Although under no illusion about his wayward nature, Flora is greatly distressed. The nymphs are still pressing her to take her revenge when Cupid appears. They turn on him, accusing him of being a mischief-maker. Cupid protests his innocence. Seeing Zephyr approaching, he gives Cléise a veil and certain instructions on how to use it, and conceals Flora, to whom he also whispers a few words. He and the nymphs then depart.

Zephyr enters, skimming over the treetops and alighting on the ground. He is told that Flora has departed. Cupid now puts his plot into action. As instructed, Cléise feigns distress at being abandoned, and Zephyr is tempted to console her. When Cléise seems on the point of yielding, she covers herself with the veil and distracts Zephyr's attention so that he fails to notice Flora taking her place. Zephyr denies being interested in Flora, declaring that it is Cléise whom he loves. Flora then reveals her identity and berates him for his infidelity. He tries to escape, but the nymphs hold him back. Now captive, he has eyes only for Flora. Cupid then keeps his promise to the nymphs, and while Zephyr is on his knees begging forgiveness, strips him of his wings. Now it is Flora who will be given the power to fly. She departs, leaving Zephyr to his sorrow.

Zephyr reproaches Cupid for breaking his promise, but Cupid shows him Flora making a hurried return. Zephyr is so distraught at the loss of his wings that Cupid offers to lend him his own, and they hide. Flora descends, and, surprised at not finding Zephyr, calls to him. A fountain starts to play; above the jet Zephyr is seen hovering and displaying his wings. Cupid explains all to Flora, who tries to leave, more with the intention of tempting him to follow than of escaping. But Zephyr manages to seize her, lifts her into the air and places her before the altar that Hymen has prepared for them. Thus all ends happily. Venus (Mme Anatole) and her cortège come to Cythera, where Bacchus is awaiting them in his grotto; there the couple are wed, and Zephyr bears Flora to Olympus, to be invested by Jupiter with immortality.

* * *

Castil-Blaze's considered verdict, written in the 1830s, was that *Flore et Zéphire* 'did not come up to expectation; the inventiveness of the stage effects, which were being presented for the first time when it was new, and which shocked the audience into astonishment and admiration by their daring, are now commonplace; but the dances are delightful.'[9] Didelot had, of course, been well aware that the success of his ballet would depend very largely on the skill with which the flying was carried out. His first thought had been that the dancers playing Zephyr and Flora could be trained to perform it themselves; but Albert, who was to play Zephyr, was reluctant to take the risk, since such flying as had been done at the Opéra in the past had been done by understudies. Since such scenes were an indispensable part of his ballet, Didelot could not contemplate omitting them, and he saw no solution but to understudy Albert in the flying himself.[10] This was settled at an early stage, some time before rehearsals commenced, the costume specification specifically requiring a second costume to be made for a 'substitute Zephyr'.[11]

The flights were very much more complex than anything that had been seen at the Opéra before. There had been earlier flights: notably, Zephyr's rescue of Psyche from the rock in Gardel's ballet to soar with her into the wings; Henry's escape from the onslaught of Boreas and the winds in *L'Amour à Cythère*; and Azaël's aerial departure in the desert scene in *L'Enfant prodigue*. But they had been no more than exits lasting a few seconds that may have drawn a momentary gasp of surprise but certainly aroused no exhilaration at the sight of a man defying gravity. Didelot's flights for his Zephyr, on the other hand, were very much longer and were strictly choreographed so as to give the illusion, through carefully regulated movements of body and limbs, that Zephyr was indeed flying of his own volition. One critic reported:

> Here are no immortal gods descending from the flies in a chariot suspended by four strong ropes that one is supposed not to notice behind a few canvas clouds, but aerial creatures flying in space, now hovering, now darting forward again, forming elegant attitudes like those of the master sculptors of antiquity.[12]

[9] Castil Blaze, *La Danse*, 324.

[10] Glushkovsky, 202. Letter to F.A.Koni, October 1851. Slonimsky's assertion in his biography of Didelot that Albert 'refused point-blank' to fly is surely excessive. Much more likely is that the Opéra at the outset placed a fiat on its principal dancers taking such a risk.

[11] Arch. Nat., AJ[13] 94. Costume specification supporting estimate of 28 September 1815.

[12] *Gazette de France*, 15 December 1815. Signed '*Le Souffleur emérite*'.

Such was the control and co-ordination attainable by the special apparatus, that Didelot was able to carry another person without losing any of the effortless quality essential to preserve the illusion. His first flight, bearing the ten-year-old Félicité Hullin in his arms, was only a foretaste of a much greater feat to follow when he swooped around the stage with Flora to deposit her gently on the Temple of Hymen. And what was still more extraordinary was that few among the audience were aware that they were seeing, not Albert and Gosselin, but the forty-six-year-old choreographer himself and Mme Courtin.[13]

Didelot, who may well have performed the flights in most, at least, of all previous productions of the ballet, was perfectly familiar with the apparatus, which he had probably been instrumental in perfecting. He had brought the specification for it from Russia, as well as certain essential items such as the special harness, which almost certainly comprised loose-fitting elastic material.[14]

The specification for the work to be done by the Opéra, frustratingly incomplete, gives an idea of the apparatus. There were two rails running above the stage over the forest scene, which occupied the first four grooves, one at the first groove and the other at the fourth. The front rail was adapted from that used in *L'Enfant prodigue*, but extended to a length of 60 feet. Each rail carried a movable runner supplied with five pulleys. Four new drums were required for the wire, two for each flying machine, and together with various bits and pieces – clasp holders, rope, ironwork, pulleys, eight brass stands (two for each drum) and four iron cranking handles – the work to be carried out was priced at 800 francs. In addition, a ten-feet-high 'paralelle-groun' (*sic*: parallelogram?) had to be made at a cost of an additional 150 francs.[15]

The flyers were lifted off the ground by brass wires thin enough to appear invisible against the specially painted scenery. The wire itself may have been painted too, although there is no record of this.

The flying effects in *Flore et Zéphire* created an astonishing sensation, and people flocked to the Opéra to see it, their curiosity whetted by the descriptions in the press. The critic of the *Journal des débats* expressed his amazement when Zephyr appeared,

[13] It might appear extraordinary that the audience was taken in, but it should be borne in mind that stage lighting was much less strong in those times and, also, that the flying was not done in full lighting.

[14] Significantly, no harness was included in the Opéra's costume specification. Glushkovsky, 165, records that such a harness had been used in Didelot's *L'Amour et Psyché* in St Petersburg in 1809.

[15] Arch. Nat., AJ[13] 94.

first decade of the century and probably became acquainted with Didelot then. The score for the Paris production was also expanded with a number by Lefebvre and a popular song, *Réveillez-vous, belle endormie,* that accompanied the scene of Zephyr awakening the nymphs. Taken as a whole, the music struck the critics as only barely adequate. The *Journal de Paris* castigated it as 'very mediocre and feeble', and could not believe it was the work of a French composer; it was 'even inferior,' he added, rather gratuitously, 'to that of M. Bochsa, whose unfortunate facility is well known.'[31]

* * *

Notwithstanding the extraordinary success of his ballet, Didelot returned to Russia mortified by the rebuffs he had received before it was finally accepted, by Gardel's 'ill-will and jealousy', and by the animosity he had met during the rehearsals. The Opéra's parsimonious attitude in the matter of expenditure also rankled. In the event, however, the Opéra was to behave very honourably towards him in that matter, a gesture that Didelot preferred to ignore. In Russia, where he was to spend the rest of his life, he gave his listeners to understand he had been shabbily treated. It was probably on such sources that Saint-Léon based his story about a payment of 2000 francs that Louis XVIII ordered to be given to Didelot after the first performance. According to Didelot's version, when he called to collect this money, he was reminded that he owed some 2400 francs and that the King's gift would be withheld on account of his debt. So Didelot was still left with a debt of some 400 francs.

The facts, however, were somewhat different. Louis XVIII did not attend the première, although he was present at a later performance at the end of January, when Didelot was presented to him. An ex-gratia payment was indeed made to Didelot, not on that occasion but earlier in the month – and it was not a gift from the King but a voluntary gesture made, at the request of La Ferté, by the Comte de Pradel.

On 3 January 1816, after the first six performances had brought in gross receipts of nearly 49,000 francs, the cost of staging the ballet was finally worked out at 11,130.39 francs. Two days later La Ferté proposed to Pradel that it might be appropriate to waive Didelot's liability to pay the Opéra the excess of 5130.39 francs, taking into consideration the value

[31] *Journal de Paris*, 14 December 1815. The 26-year-old Nicolas Bochsa, who had been official harpist to Napoleon, had had a one-act *opéra-comique* produced at the Opéra-Comique the day before the first performance of *Flore et Zéphire*. It was not such a poor work as this comment suggests: it remained in the repertory there for thirty-seven years, longer than did Didelot's ballet at the Opéra.

of the addition to the Opéra's stock of scenery and costumes. Two ways of dealing with this were then considered: either to leave the indebtedness unclaimed or to write it off. La Ferté was in favour of the first alternative, but Pradel considered that this might create an awkward precedent and preferred making an ex-gratia payment of 6000 francs, which would remove any need to have the expenditure audited.[32]

La Ferté had hoped that this gesture might induce Didelot to consider returning to Paris on a future occasion to produce other ballets, but the wound to Didelot's pride was too deep. He left Paris in February to take up his post as ballet-master in Russia with few regrets. About the only friend he had made at the Opéra was his Zephyr, Albert, a dancer of unusual culture and sensitivity. It was his hope that Albert might be released to visit St Petersburg, no doubt to repeat his performance as Zephyr, and the Russian authorities lost no time in making approaches. In the course of these, one point had to be clarified. The ballerina whom Didelot wished to accompany Albert was not Geneviève Gosselin, as had been assumed, but her sister Constance, and this had to be made clear to the Opéra. On behalf of the Direction of the Imperial Theatres, Prince Tufiakin conveyed what must have been Didelot's opinion that Constance Gosselin had 'an even more distinguished talent than her sister', and Pozzo di Borgo, the Russian minister in Paris, was instructed to make the necessary arrangements.[33] The reasons behind this surprising switch were not explained. It is hardly likely that it resulted from a desire to recast the rôle of Flora in the *noble* style. Much more probable is that Didelot had serious doubts about Geneviève's stamina.

Significantly, on 20 February, not many days after Didelot's departure, a performance of *Flore et Zéphire* was cancelled because Geneviève Gosselin was unwell. The public was assured that there was nothing to be concerned about – her 'fatigue and failing strength' being attributed merely to 'overwork and the desire to justify the encouragement she had received at her début'. Such was the official story. Behind the scenes, however, there were probably more realistic fears, which had clearly not escaped Didelot's notice; for symptoms of consumption were in those times too familiar not to be recognised.

In the meantime the rôle of Flora was taken over by Fanny Bias, who proved a worthy substitute for her ailing predecessor. Although lacking Gosselin's exceptional qualities, she, like others of her generation, was attempting to master the newfangled trick – for it was still little more than

32 Arch. Nat., O^3 1746 (1p). Pradel to La Ferté, 23 January 1816.

33 Bibl.-Musée de l'Opéra, Fonds Deshayes, dossier 1. Letter from Tufiakin, 28 February (N.S.) 1816.

that – of *pointe* work. Sturdily built and sprightly by temperament, she was to become a favourite both with the Paris public and with the English visitors who were now crossing the Channel in droves to taste the pleasures of Parisian life. Among these cross-Channel islanders was the Irish poet, Thomas Moore, who immortalised her Flora in one of those comic jingles he was so adept at composing:

Fanny Bias in Flora – dear creature! – you'd swear,
 When her delicate feet in the dance twinkle round,
 That her steps are of light, that her home is the air,
And she only *par complaisance* touches the ground.[34]

For several years after Didelot's departure, Albert kept *Flore et Zéphire* in good shape purely out of friendship for its creator; but receiving no mark of appreciation from the Opéra for this voluntary gesture, he at last lost patience and suggested that a bonus might be appropriate. Meeting with a blunt rebuff, he withdrew, leaving the ballet to the mercy of others.[35] From that moment *Flore et Zéphire* began to wither.

Between 1820 and 1826, its annual total of performances fell from eleven to two. With no one to tend it, its weaknesses became more and more apparent. The anacreontic style was going out of favour, the flying effects had lost their novelty and the superficiality of the action could no longer be concealed. By 1824 it was only a shadow of its former self. In the view of an unkind critic, it had become 'the most soporific and boring piece in the entire choreographic repertory'. For this, perfidious Albion was blamed. 'Composed on the banks of the Thames,' he went on, 'this insipid ballet seems to exude the reek of fog.'[36]

When Fanny Bias died in 1825, it seemed that the days of *Flore et Zéphire* were numbered. But five years later, plans were laid for a revival. By then more of its choreographic detail had been forgotten, and it was recognised that a drastic reworking was needed to give it life. The task was first offered to Jean Coralli, who refused out of modesty, and finally it fell to Albert to teach the rôles, and to Aumer to arrange the ensembles. Although it was to prove a success for both Marie Taglioni, who was still to create the Sylphide that would bring her immortal fame, and her partner Jules Perrot, there was no concealing that it was something of a curiosity – an echo from the past that would soon be lost in the exotic dawn of Romanticism.

[34] Letter V.
[35] Arch. Nat., AJ[13] 125. Albert to Persuis, 18 and 27 July 1818.
[36] *Courrier des théâtres*, 4 May 1824.

29

Louis Henry as Hamlet and Samson

Nine years had now passed since the Théâtre de la Porte-Saint-Martin had been summarily closed and Louis Henry had fled to seek greener fields for the pursuit of his career. He had been accompanied in his flight by the Porte-Saint-Martin's leading ballerina, Marie Quériau, with whom he had formed a strong attachment. At that time Marie was a woman of twenty-seven, four years older than himself. For the past ten years she had been married to Charles-Bonaventure Quériau, whom she had met when he was managing the Grand-Théâtre in Marseilles, and by whom she had five children. The four youngest accompanied her and Henry on their flight to Italy; the eldest, Théodore, remained with his father, from whom Marie was, to all intents and purposes, separated. Henry apparently had little difficulty in securing engagements for them in the Carnival and Lent season of 1807/08 at La Scala, Milan – probably on a recommendation from Dominique Lefebvre, since they were featured in several of his ballets. Milan, however, was to be only a temporary stop; their final destination was Naples, where they were to settle to head the ballet company for seven successive seasons.

Of the many opera houses in Italy, the Teatro di San Carlo was second in importance only to La Scala. By a fortunate coincidence, Gaetano Gioja was on the point of leaving after four seasons as its ballet-master, and Henry, although he could claim only three ballets to his credit, managed to be appointed as his successor. What influence he drew upon to achieve his end may be surmised. Cambacérès had surely not forgotten his protégé, and with Naples now firmly within the orbit of French power under a Bonaparte king (Napoleon's brother Joseph), he would have been a most powerful sponsor. Whatever support Henry had managed to acquire, he was soon to wield such influence at the San Carlo that by 1815 he had become 'almost its master'.[1]

The three ballets Henry had produced in Paris were essentially French in style and content, for he had worked nowhere else. However, in Naples

[1] Arch. Nat., AJ^{13} 1039 (V). Pleadings in a family law suit, 1815.

he came under other influences, notably the more powerful style of mime by which the dancers expressed narrative, and the taste of the Neapolitans at large – to whom gesture was an indispensable feature of normal discourse, with its own complex vocabulary of signs and grimaces. Gioja, whom Henry had succeeded, was himself a Neapolitan, and his grand ballets such as *Cesare in Egitto* and the most recent, *Ero e Leandro*, were still fresh in people's memories as examples of how far pantomimic expression could be taken. To these circumstances Henry was only too willing to adapt, for they enabled him to provide his companion with splendid opportunities to exploit her interpretative talent. Further, the requirement of more complex narratives was a challenge, which he was to meet with varying degrees of success.

The subject of his first ballet for the Italian stage was Shakespeare's *Othello*, to which he added a fifth act to provide a happy ending.[2] Over the next seven years one creation followed another in impressive sequence; many had complicated plots, which were graphically conveyed by the skilled Italian mimes and eagerly absorbed by the Neapolitan public. Under his direction, and with Marie Quériau as the inevitable heroine, subjects such as William Tell, the deaths of Cleopatra, Samson and Delilah, and the murder of Abel, to name only a few, were enacted in dumb-show, interspersed with dances to the strains of the theatre's resident ballet composer, Count Robert von Gallenberg.

Napoleon's abdication in April 1814 sounded a warning to Henry that his position at the San Carlo was in jeopardy, for there was little likelihood that Murat[3] would retain the Neapolitan throne when the allied powers settled the terms of peace. Early in 1815 there came an important development in his life: Charles Quériau died of a stroke, and a few weeks later, to Henry's joy, Marie yielded to his desires. In the spring she told him she was pregnant. By then, Napoleon had escaped from Elba to seize back his throne, and Europe was again at war. But Napoleon's great gamble was to fail, and Murat, who had rashly attempted to regain his throne, was captured and shot.

To make the best of a difficult situation, Henry decided that Marie should have her child in Paris, where his family would care for her. His engagement at the San Carlo having expired, he set his sights on negotiating something suitably lucrative in London – most probably the post of ballet-master for the following year's opera season. So the two of them

[2] Created at the San Carlo on 14 May 1808, Henry's *Otello* predated Viganò's ballet on the same subject by some ten years.

[3] Napoleon had installed his brother-in-law Joachim Murat as King of Naples in 1808 when his brother Joseph was shifted to the throne of Spain.

packed their belongings and set out for Paris, where Henry stayed long enough to see Marie comfortably settled before continuing alone to Calais to board the Dover packet. On disembarking in the early hours of a December morning, drenched to the skin and unsteady on his legs, his first thought was to let her know of his safe arrival:

> My dear friend, I arrived at last in this town at 2 o'clock in the morning after the most horrible crossing ... It is quite true that the Mediterranean storms are nothing compared to those of the ocean ... I have been buffeted by the rain and the waves for nine consecutive hours ... I can assure you I was greatly relieved to know that you were on dry land ... I said to myself, Should I perish it will be because I wanted to seek the wherewithal to bring up the little creature whom I have not yet embraced, and to be of use to my nearest and dearest ... It must be admitted that the English ladies are very courageous; they were all at death's door, yet not one of them cried out. The English navigate their ships amazingly in the very face of danger, without shouting like the Neapolitans do ... When I disembarked I had so much water on my body that I must have weighed 300 lbs ... God protected me, deigning to do so again in his infinite mercy ... I send thousands of kisses to my daughter or son ...[4]

The news that Marie had borne him a son reached Henry in London some two weeks later. Unfortunately, his joy was tempered by the failure of his mission, and he returned empty-handed to Paris, where, having given up hope of being readmitted to the Opéra, he was presented with another opportunity. A year before, the Porte-Saint-Martin had been allowed to open its doors again, and, being naturally wary of the Opéra's reaction, the management had at first presented its dancers very discreetly.[5] A short pantomime by Duport, *Les Six Ingénues*, had produced no sign of hostility, and some weeks later this had been followed by a longer, more spectacular ballet by Jean Petipa, *Les Bergers de la Sierra Morena*.[6] In the summer a trio of Spanish dancers, Señor Luego and the Señoritas Ramos, had given Paris its first taste of the *escuela bolera*. So,

[4] Arch. Nat., AJ[13] 1039 (V). Henry to Marie Quériau, 6 December 1815.

[5] The *Almanach des Spectacles* of 1815 listed Rhenon as ballet-master, and Jean Petipa, Toussaint and Mmes Darcourt, Pierson and Aline-Dorlé as principal dancers.

[6] Jean Petipa was soon to become the father of two remarkable sons. Lucien (born in December 1815 and therefore almost the exact contemporary of Henry's recently born son) was for many years principal male dancer at the Opéra, where he produced several ballets, including *Namouna*. Marius (born in March 1818) became the great father-figure of late Imperial Russian ballet and is renowned for his association with Tchaikowsky.

when Henry returned to Paris, the Porte-Saint-Martin was already taking the first steps to recover its former reputation as an alternative centre for ballet; and his reappearance with Marie Quériau presented an opportunity that the theatre seized with little hesitation. Furthermore, Jean Petipa had recently returned to Marseilles, leaving the post of ballet-master fortuitously vacant.

Henry and Marie Quériau needed no recommendation, and within a very short time contracts had been signed and they were hard at work. The experience Henry had gained in Naples in handling complex themes was to be particularly appropriate; for the Porte-Saint-Martin's licence covered both melodrama and pantomime, and the content of the ballets he had to offer was heavily weighted in favour of the latter. Nevertheless, care still had to be taken to avoid the possibility of conflict with the Opéra, should it take steps to enforce any sort of monopoly; and an arrangement was reached whereby Henry's ballets would not be given on the Opéra's fashionable evenings.

Henry had brought with him the material for a tragic 'pantomime interspersed with dances' based on Shakespeare's *Hamlet*,[7] which he had probably been preparing for the San Carlo, since Gallenberg had already composed the music. He may have offered it to the King's Theatre during his visit to London. If the English reaction to a scenario that had taken considerable liberties with such a classical text had been negative, as might have been expected, the Porte-Saint-Martin had no such qualms. For *Hamlet*, which was presented to a Parisian public on 28 February 1816, and for other ballets that were to follow over the next nine months, Henry had at his disposal a resident company of dancers consisting of a handful of soloists and a *corps de ballet* of twenty-four. The principal rôles would, of course, be played by himself and Marie Quériau, while for the other mime parts he could rely on suitable members of the resident company, notably an actor called Defrêne, a master of make-up who specialised in the portrayal of villains.

Considerable liberties had been taken with Shakespeare's text, with which Henry may have been unfamiliar. His basic source, which he had adapted fairly freely, was no doubt the version that Jean-François Ducis had made for the Comédie-Française nearly fifty years before, and that more recently had been given a new lease of life by the inspired performance of Talma. In it the rôle of Polonius was suppressed; Ophelia was presented as Claudius's daughter with whom Hamlet is in love; and

[7] This would be Henry's third Shakespearean venture, following his *Otello* of 1808 and a *Romeo e Giulietta*, produced at the Fondo, Naples, in the summer of 1814.

Gertrude, Hamlet's mother, has not become the wife of his uncle, Claudius, with whom she had been implicated in the former king's murder. Also eliminated were the grave-digger and the mummers who, in Shakespeare's play, mime the circumstances of the crime before the court.

Henry's balletic version opened with Gertrude (Mme Quériau), the widowed Queen of Denmark, weeping before her husband's statue. Here she is found by her brother-in-law Claudius (Defrêne). Although they are lovers and have conspired together to murder the king, she is now overcome with remorse and implores Claudius to join her in seeking forgiveness. Her son Hamlet (Henry) enters, and Gertrude announces her decision to renounce the crown in his favour. Claudius, whose ambition is to become king, is taken aback. His daughter Ophelia (Mme Darcourt) then enters. She and Hamlet are in love, but when Gertrude seeks Claudius's consent to their marriage, he conceals his true feelings. Martial music then announces the arrival of troops victorious in the recent war; their valour is duly celebrated, and the festivities close with Gertrude formally announcing that she proposes to pass on the crown to Hamlet. Left alone, Hamlet prays before the statue. As he does so, his father's ghost (Lafitte) rises up to reveal that he was murdered by Claudius and Gertrude, and demands vengeance on them both. He hands Hamlet a dagger, enjoining him to use it only after being crowned king.

The second act is set in Gertrude's chamber. Claudius, Gertrude and Ophelia are at a loss to understand why Hamlet has not joined them, and a courtier is dispatched to look for him. They are informed that Hamlet has lost his reason, which seems confirmed when Hamlet enters, haggard and distraught. Distractedly he contemplates his father's portrait, recalling the terrible circumstances of his death. Disturbed at his behaviour, Gertrude and Claudius dismiss their retinue. Slowly Hamlet recovers; but he remains stupefied by the ghost's terrible demand that he kill both his mother and the father of the girl he loves. Asking to be left alone, he tries to convince himself that the ghost was after all only a wild figment of his imagination; but when his fingers rest on the dagger concealed under his doublet, he knows it was not. To lose no time in fulfilling the condition that the ghost has imposed, he decides to advance his coronation. As if scenting danger, Gertrude and Claudius press for delay, but Hamlet is obdurate. Claudius now realises he is lost unless he disposes of Hamlet and seizes the crown. The coronation procession forms, and Hamlet is declared king. Dismissing the courtiers, he draws his sword to attack Claudius, but Ophelia separates them. Hamlet gives orders for Claudius's arrest, but the latter is freed by his supporters.

The final act is set in the mausoleum of the Danish kings. After the ashes of the dead king have been deposited there, Hamlet accuses his mother of murdering his father. But just as she is on the point of confessing, Claudius arrives with his supporters. Hamlet is arrested and arraigned before the Senate. Gertrude attempts to defend him on grounds of insanity, but Hamlet insists he is sound of mind. He is found guilty and condemned to death. When Gertrude reveals Claudius's crime, no one believes her. Ophelia adds her plea for Hamlet to be spared, but Hamlet takes matters into his own hands, pulling out his dagger and killing Claudius. The latter's supporters attack Hamlet, but are scattered when, amid thunder and lightning, the floor opens and the ghost reappears. Gertrude falls dead. The ghost then accuses his murderers, declares Hamlet innocent and hands him the crown.

It was a bold stroke for Henry to open his season in Paris with a Shakespearean ballet, for the Bard of Avon was still regarded by the French as a barbarian. Classical tragedy, as it was regarded in France, was bound by the three unities of time, place and action that had supposedly been laid down by Aristotle – limitations wholly alien to Shakespeare. This, coupled with a few shortcomings in the production, led two critics to adopt a bantering tone, as if to suggest that the work hardly warranted serious consideration. Had they taken such an attitude in condemning a production at the Opéra, their ribaldry might have been infectious in the salons where theatrical affairs were discussed, and the ridiculed work might not have survived. The Porte-Saint-Martin, however, was a resort of popular entertainment with a clientele that was much less influenced by the views of society, and Henry's 'pantomime interspersed with dances' proved to be a decided box-office success. It clearly had an appeal to a broader public comfortable with the full-blooded genre of pantomime, as distinct from the Opéra's more refined genre of ballet-pantomime; and it achieved an astonishing tally of forty-eight performances by the time Henry's engagement came to an end in November.

The fairest assessment of it appeared in the *Journal de Paris*. While observing how coincidental it was that such a humourless piece should have been first presented on Ash Wednesday, its anonymous critic cited Noverre's *Médée et Jason* in support of his contention that the subject was a perfectly valid one for pantomime. To his mind, the adaptation of Shakespeare's tragedy showed great ingenuity, and the acting of Henry and Marie Quériau as Hamlet and Gertrude had certainly gripped the audience. Scenery and costumes came up to the Porte-Saint-Martin's standards, and Gallenberg's music had caught 'the colour of the subject'.

The dances, although not numerous, were designed with good taste, and Henry himself was praised for his vigour and grace.[8]

From the reviews of those who were not prepared to take the ballet seriously – notably Martainville in the *Quotidienne* and L.A. in the *Journal général des théâtres* – a certain insight can be gleaned into a few isolated passages of the action. To be fair, though, such descriptions must be taken for what they were: deliberate caricatures written with tongue in cheek to raise a cheap smile. Certainly Henry had not pleased everyone, but his effort could not be dismissed as unworthy.

The opening scene between Gertrude and Claudius was amusingly parodied by L.A.:

> When the curtain rises, Gertrude falls at the foot of a wooden statue, rises, throws herself down again, beating her hands on the pedestal for a long time, and finally, with a graceful pirouette, moves away.
>
> Seeing Claudius, Gertrude pulls a face. Claudius waves his arms, pointing at the sky, the earth, his heart, the wings and the prompter's box, but Gertrude pushes him away, throwing her arms into the air so forcefully that we thought she was going to try and imitate *Flore et Zéphire* and fly up into the air. Claudius seizes her by the arm, and shows her his own hand. We have no idea what Gertrude sees on his hand, but she performs a well-prepared *entrechat* with which she makes her escape from Claudius.
>
> That is all that can be understood in the introduction of this singular work. Fortunately the programme explains that the wooden statue ... is the effigy of the late king Hamlet; that by striking it hard Gertrude is expressing the remorse with which she is filled; that this lady is making a face at the sight of Claudius because he was her accomplice in the murder of Hamlet's father, and that the *entrechat* with which she recoils from her partner in crime signifies that she is repulsing Claudius with horror.

After Hamlet had entered to place some captured standards at the foot of the statue and fell to his knees ('a little heavily for a dancing prince') to be blessed by his mother, there followed a *divertissement*. This consisted for the most part of a *pas de trois* for Hamlet, Gertrude and Ophelia, the only dance in which the main characters took part. The two ladies, however, were little more than ancillary figures, for it was essentially a soliloquy for Hamlet, an outpouring of grief at his father's death. Before it

[8] *Journal de Paris*, 29 February and 14 March 1816.

began, Martainville could not help smiling at an amusing detail he had noticed:

> Like a young man familiar with the etiquette of the ballroom, [Hamlet] removes his fur boots, which he was to put on again when he had finished his *pas*. While the desolate son is giving vent to *entrechats* of mourning and pirouettes of sadness, the statue of his father, which is nothing more than a thin and badly painted plank, sways in time to show its sensitivity to Hamlet's wriggling despair.

Henry was still remembered in Paris as an outstanding dancer of the *noble* genre who had once contested the supremacy of Duport, and the *Journal de Paris* recognised his former 'vigour and grace'. L.A., however, was much more critical:

> Henry jumps and prances about very pretentiously, but without any lightness. His contortions and grimaces are dreadful, but if he thinks they are expressive, he is much mistaken. His dancing seems to be copied from that of the *grotteschi*. This dancer has been completely spoilt by his stay in Italy.

Martainville agreed. 'Henry,' he wrote, 'appeared stiff, stilted, lacking in grace and lightness; his gestures and his features also lacked expression. He seemed to be dancing in a bad mood.'

The apparition of the ghost, a white-clad figure rising from the bowels of the earth, drew faint praise from Martainville, who conceded that it might have been effective had it been better managed. The ghost's revelation of the crime committed by Claudius and Gertrude was made to Hamlet by means of a magic-lantern projection on a gauze. 'Never,' wrote L.A. in his comment on Hamlet's reaction to this revelation,

> have we seen anything more terrifying and at the same time amusing than the manner in which Hamlet expresses terror. Nose, mouth, chin, eyebrows, forehead, all are simultaneously set twitching; his hands seem to move independently of his arms, and he stamps his feet so violently that, on the day we saw this piece, all the dust rose from the stage and forced those in the proscenium boxes to retire for as long as M. Henry's fury lasted.

Martainville also left a description of Henry's histrionics, which rose to a peak in the coronation scene that closed the second act. 'He covers the stage in great tragic strides,' he wrote, 'falters, recovers, scares everyone around him, gives orders to be entertained by music and performs many other nonsensical tricks before momentarily calming down to accept the crown.' More antics were to come when Hamlet, once crowned, confronts Claudius and his mother with their crime. According to Martainville, there was something terrifying in this denunciation, even if its wild fury seemed somewhat excessive. The scene reached its climax when Henry seized an enormous two-handed sword, only to be disarmed before he could do any damage.[9]

Henry's *Hamlet* was certainly a brave attempt, but it fell short of the critical standards applied in Paris. Another reviewer called it a 'bizarre imitation' of the Shakespeare tragedy, and in all honesty could spare words of praise only for the machinist for his stage effects, and for Mme Quériau who, as he put it, had 'made Gertrude speak'.[10]

* * *

Marie Quériau had been delighted to discover how fondly she was remembered by many of her former admirers. Indeed, buried in the critical reviews of *Hamlet* had been an unmistakable demand for her to reappear in those soubrette rôles which, on her previous visit, she had so charmingly made her own – most notably, Lise in *La Fille mal gardée*, but also as the heroine of Aumer's sentimental ballet *Jenny*. All that had been ten years ago, and she was now thirty-six and recovering from her sixth pregnancy. Henry was no doubt anxious not to exhaust her, but such a demand could not be ignored. He compromised by preparing, at short notice, a slight one-act work entitled *Le Rosier*, which would not unduly tax her strength. Henri Darondeau, who had composed for Henry before, quickly produced a score, and the piece was presented on 3 April. Unfortunately its hasty staging was all too evident; not only was the plot trite, giving Marie little opportunity to build up a character, but even the choreography seemed stale and lacking in originality. Martainville, who might have been pleased if Henry had produced a worthwhile ballet in the French style, was left unsatisfied, limiting himself to remarking that 'one of her favourite attitudes is to hold herself on one leg while flinging the other to the level of her head with a sudden boldness that makes one realise that dancing also has its clichés.'[11]

[9] Quotations from the reviews of Martainville and L.A. are respectively from *Quotidienne*, 1 March 1816, and *Journal général des théâtres*, 3 March 1816.
[10] *Journal des débats*, 2 March 1816. Signed 'C'.
[11] *Quotidienne*, 8 April 1816.

Henry's engagement at the Porte-Saint-Martin was to continue until the first week of November, with a break of two months in June and July, much of which was taken up with rehearsals of another major production. This was to be another dramatic pantomime in the Italian tradition: *Samson*, a three-act adaptation of the biblical story that had already been tested on the Neapolitan public[12] and was presented at the Porte-Saint-Martin on 3 August, with Henry and Marie Quériau in the parts they had created.

For the Parisians at large, its plot was at least more familiar than that of *Hamlet*. Samson (Henry) and Delilah (Mme Quériau), the daughter (for purposes of the ballet) of the Philistine king (Defrêne), are to be married; but the general hostility against Samson becomes evident when, in the games accompanying the celebrations, he allows himself to be bound before realising his danger. Enraged, he breaks free and displays his massive strength by breaking open the city gates and disappearing into the countryside. Pursued by Philistine soldiers, he makes his way into the mountains. In answer to his prayers, an angel presents him with the jawbone of an ass. Brandishing it, he creates havoc and carnage among the Philistines. Finally, weary from his efforts and overcome by thirst, he casts the jawbone at a rock, from which water gushes forth. The Philistine women come to plead for peace and Delilah manages to soothe his anger. Their marriage then takes place, but the Philistine king harbours a hatred for Samson. He tells Delilah that it is her duty to avenge her race by killing him. After discovering that the secret of his strength lies in his hair, she drugs him but cannot bring herself to kill him. When chastised by her father, she reveals Samson's secret in the belief that his life will be spared. She is ordered to cut off his hair. Samson wakes, but no longer has the strength to defend himself. Condemned to death, he falls to his knees. His prayers are heard; miraculously his hair grows again. After breaking his chains, he brings the Philistine temple crashing down, only to die among its ruins.

In contrast to *Hamlet*, *Samson* caused little stir. The sympathetic critic of the *Journal de Paris* found the narrative too thin to support three acts, and the battle scenes too long, while C of the *Débats* was much more brutal. 'Samson is too much of an idiot, Delilah is odious, and King Phanor quite the most Cassandra-like of Philistines that can possibly be imagined,' he declared. 'It is reported that this pantomime delighted Naples, but that is not saying much.'[13]

[12] It had been staged at the San Carlo on 31 October 1810.

[13] *Journal de Paris*, 4 August 1816; *Journal des débats*, 5 August 1816.

As a spectacle it was magnificent, particularly in the final effect of the destruction of the Temple, but more than pruning was needed to make it palatable. The last two months of Henry's engagement were therefore largely given over to lighter works: *La Fille mal gardée* and a forgettable new ballet, *Le Mariage rompu*, which Henry presented on 19 October to a score by Alexandre Piccinni, the Porte-Saint-Martin's conductor and resident composer.

For once, Henry had not done Marie a favour, for a more ridiculous and contrived theme, spread over the three acts, it would be difficult to imagine. Suzette (Quériau), a village girl who happens to be the foster-sister of the daughter of the lord of the manor, emerges from the church after her wedding to her sweetheart Félix (Henry). She is then confronted with a crisis of identity. Mathurine, whom she has always believed to be her mother, confesses that in a moment of aberration she had exchanged the two babies, preferring the prettier of the two, and that Suzette is in fact the lord's daughter. The lord accepts her confession at face value, but on no account will he accept Félix as a son-in-law. So the unfortunate young peasant is hastily removed from the village, and the lord erects a tomb in the garden of the manor to make Suzette believe that Félix has died. Suzette falls into a depression so deep as to arouse fears for her health, and the lord, who is not without better feelings, relents. At a convenient moment Félix reappears, having escaped. Suzette swoons with surprise and joy, and the lord finally accepts the young man.

Absurd though this was, Marie Quériau was well served by the scene in which Suzette is brought to the brink of insanity. 'The play of her features, her gestures, her whole action conveyed that desperation of the mind that is akin to madness,' described Martainville. 'She reminded us of the truly sublime moments in the rôle of Jenny. I do not think pantomimic expression can be taken further.'[14]

When, a few weeks later, Henry and Marie Quériau returned to Italy to fulfil an engagement in Milan, they could have felt reasonably satisfied. Henry may have been disappointed by his treatment by the critics, but he was, of course, fully aware of the difference between French and Italian taste in ballet. He and Marie Quériau left France, consoled by the knowledge that, notwithstanding its critical reception, *Hamlet* had been a popular and financial success. But in the history of that ballet this was only the beginning, for within two years it would gain the distinction of having been applauded in three capitals: Paris at the Porte-Saint-Martin, Milan at La Scala, and finally at the San Carlo in his beloved Naples.

[14] *Quotidienne*, 20 October 1816. For *Jenny*, see Chapter 15.

By her side Albert, as Carlos, may have seemed a little restrained, but his handsome features, noble bearing and controlled acting made him the perfect romantic hero. In one sense he was a little outshone by Ferdinand, an excellent actor with a special gift for comedy, who played Fabricio as a kind of Figaro character. The latter's partner, the experienced soubrette Mme Courtin, was a perfect foil, playing Angelina with 'sparkling and impish coquetry.'[4]

Including the four principal characters and Auguste Vestris, who made an appearance as a gondolier, more than sixty dancers filled the stage in the Piazza scene. The main features of the dances interspersed in the action were a *pas de quatre* for the two principal couples and a harlequinade entitled *The Family of Harlequin*. Playing Harlequin at the age of fifty-one was the Opéra's most senior dancer after Vestris, Charles Beaupré; alongside him, as Harlequin's two sons, were the two younger Hullin girls, Félicité and Virginie. Punchinello appeared in the form of another old-timer, Isaac Branchu, a sad figure in real life as well as in character, who was very shortly to withdraw from the Opéra to pass his last years in advancing mental distress.[5]

When Branchu retired on pension at the end of 1816, he was succeeded in the part of Punchinello by Simon Mérante. Mérante, who made little impression in the part, then fell ill, and Georges Elie, younger brother of the man who stood in for Didelot for the flying in *Flore et Zéphire*, was selected to take it over. Finding no one ready to teach it to him, he timidly approached Mérante, who excused himself as being too ill to answer questions. Disconsolately making his way home after this wasted visit, he was passing the galleries of the Palais-Royal when his attention was caught by the barker of Séraphin's *Ombres chinoises* announcing that Punchinello was about to outdo his rivals and perform a dance of triumph. On a whim young Elie went inside, and was carried away by the grotesque movements of the cardboard figure whose shadow was projected on to a screen. It was a revelation, and he reshaped the dance into an interpretation that became famous and earned him the reputation that classed him among the most celebrated comic performers of his day.[6]

another air from *Le Tableau parlant*.

[4] Martainville in *Quotidienne*, 26 February 1816.

[5] Isaac Branchu was the first husband of the soprano Caroline Branchu, who created the rôle of Julia in Spontini's *La Vestale*. His illness may have been caused by a head wound received when serving as a soldier in 1794; a bullet had remained, undetected, embedded in the upper cavity of his nose for seventeen years before being spat out in a violent fit of coughing (*Opinion du parterre*, XIII, 344-6). He died in 1824.

[6] For many years he played the part of Alain in Aumer's 1827 reworking of Dauberval's *La Fille mal gardée* for the Opéra.

In the last act, Mme Gardel made what was to be one of the last appearances of her career, leading the Venetian noblewomen in the final *divertissement*.

Louis Persuis himself provided the music for this happy little ballet, in collaboration with Rodolphe Kreutzer. It had not been a very arduous task, for although the overture was original and effectively suggested the 'sounds of boisterous revelry that echo along the canals and in the streets of Venice', it included considerable borrowings from 'Gluck, Mozart, Paisiello, Grétry, Méhul, Boieldieu, etc.'[7] and, most strikingly, a popular Italian song, *Mamma, mamma cara*, which is still known today by the title of Milon's ballet.[8]

The expenditure on the ballet amounted to little more than 10,000 francs; only the scenery for the first act, possibly designed by Ciceri, was new.

The ballet's success at the first performance was encouraging, but not outstanding. When Milon's name was announced at the end, the applause continued for several minutes before the modest choreographer allowed himself to be dragged on to the stage, by which time some of the audience were already making their way out. The general impression at the time was that it fell short of *Nina* and *Les Noces de Gamache*, but it was nevertheless to survive longer than many a more ambitious ballet as an ideal piece to lighten the spirits after a tedious opera.

* * *

Sadly, the time had come for Marie Gardel to put away her ballet slippers and make her farewell from the stage she had graced for so long. Thirty years had passed since her début, and for twenty-seven of those she had been not merely a *premier sujet*, but the unchallenged queen of French ballet. For many her retirement would mark the passing of an era, for her husband had served the Opéra for fifteen years longer than she, and she had created the principal rôles in nearly every ballet he had staged. By any standard hers had been a most glorious reign, all the more remarkable in that she had never aroused any serious jealousy or rancour.

She made her last appearance before retiring at the end of June 1816 in what was perhaps her husband's most testing ballet, *Achille à Scyros*. Plans were then already being made for a grand benefit in her honour. It was to take place on 28 August, with seats priced from 20 francs for a

[7] *Gazette de Paris*, 28 February 1816.

[8] Paganini wrote a celebrated set of variations on it (his op. 10) in 1829, identifying the melody as the Neapolitan song given above. It seems, however, to have been written by Giovanni Cifolelli.

place in the *balcon* down to 6 francs for a side seat in the fourth tier. She was to be supported not only by her colleagues of the ballet, but by a distinguished cast of singers who were to appear in one of Grétry's most popular *opéras-comiques*, and by the leading soloists of the orchestra – the violinist Habeneck, the clarinettist Lefebvre, the horn-player Duvernoy and the harpist Vernier. Prominent among the audience were the Duc de Berry and his new Duchess in their box alongside the stage, and recognised in another box were the hawklike features of the British ambassador, the Duke of Wellington.

It was to be an evening to remember in more ways than one. The first of the two ballets given was *Le Jugement de Pâris*, revived after a lapse of five years with Bigottini and Albert in the rôles created by Mme Gardel herself (when still plain Mlle Miller) and Auguste Vestris. The other ballet was a work from the past that had not been seen for many a year, Maximilien Gardel's *Le Déserteur*. Now, almost thirty years after its first production at Fontainebleau, it was being given with Pierre and Marie Gardel in their original rôles: he as the young man falsely accused as a deserter, and she as his sweetheart who comes with the King's pardon just as the firing squad are raising their muskets. They were joined, in the rôles of the drunken Montauciel and the Cousin, by Auguste Vestris and Louis Milon; and in the final *divertissement* Marie Gardel, seemingly showing no sign of fatigue, danced a multiple *pas de deux* partnering each of the three in turn. The evening's entertainment was then brought to an end with a tarantella, and Marie Gardel came forward to make 'three deep curtseys, full of grace' to the cheering audience, many of whom had been in the theatre for six hours.

On an evening such as this, the audience came to pay tribute rather than to criticise, but an insertion in the third act of *Pâris* had been too curious not to be noticed: a *pas de deux* danced by Mme Courtin with a nineteen-year-old English dancer who seemed to have no qualification to appear on the stage of the Opéra. 'This fat, well-nourished young man,' as a critic described him, had, to say the least, a most curious style. A deficient turn-out gave a decidedly odd appearance to his *entrechats*, his posturing manner of performing pirouettes with elbows on hips seemed almost comical, and he had such a strange way of wriggling his hips that sent the spectators into gales of laughter.[9]

What was puzzling was that this insertion must have had the approval of the Gardels, of whom the young man was something of a protégé. His name was Oscar Byrne, and he came from a family of dancers and scene-

[9] *Journal de Paris*, 30 August 1816; *Journal des débats*, 31 August 1816.

painters well known on the London stage. The boy's father had become acquainted with the Comte de Blacas, the favourite of Louis XVIII, during his exile in England. After the Restoration Gardel had been persuaded, against his better judgement, to take him as a private pupil. By 1816 he may have felt he had done enough; and giving him an airing at the Opéra at his wife's benefit perhaps enabled him to extricate himself from a troublesome commitment.

Reports of how the audience had laughed at the poor boy's antics reached the London papers, and one writer cited the incident as an example of anti-English prejudice. Of course, it was nothing of the sort, and a correspondent honourably put the record straight by recalling having seen Oscar 'very heartily and very justly laughed at' at Drury Lane.[10]

* * *

Now that peace had returned, leading French dancers were once again in great demand as guest artists in foreign opera houses. During the war, London in particular had been starved of the superior talent that France provided in this field; but in 1816 the ballet company at the King's Theatre was headed by Armand Vestris as ballet-master and an impressive contingent of French dancers, including Baptiste Petit and his wife, the former Minette Duport, Charles Vestris and Arnaud Léon. Elsewhere in Europe, Mme Anatole had been given leave to delight the Berliners, and now, in August 1816, connoisseurs of the Opéra were shattered to learn that Bigottini and Albert had signed contracts with the Imperial Theatres in St Petersburg.

However, these engagements were still conditional on the Opéra's permission being granted, and the Comte de Pradel was determined that leaves of absence should be sparingly given and that the requirements of the Opéra must always be paramount. For the moment no action was taken on the Russian Embassy's request, and the continuing uncertainty only added to the public's alarm at the prospect of losing the Opéra's two principal dancers for several months – or perhaps even indefinitely if they were sufficiently tempted to remain. This anxiety was further increased by the news that Bigottini had placed one of her properties on the market. Happily, towards the end of October the problem was resolved by appealing to the couple's loyalty and also by a hint that the new Regulations would prevent a dancer's entering into a foreign engagement within three years of a previous one. They were also reminded that both dancers

[9] *Journal de Paris*, 30 August 1816; *Journal des débats*, 31 August 1816.

would be required for the new ballet that Milon was preparing and for a revival of *Psyché* planned for the following summer.

Milon found himself under pressure to complete work on his new ballet. In August 1816 he had called on his friend Lefebvre to write the music. Although he had composed for Milon on several previous occasions, Lefebvre seemed strangely reticent. It transpired that, having recently succeeded his father as music librarian, he was worried that Persuis might be offended at not being approached first. Not wanting to sour his relations with the Director, he wrote to Choron seeking reassurance:

> Yesterday I received a visit from M. Milon, who wants to work with me once again. I would willingly do so, but I still remember the risks I ran by achieving some success in this sort of work, and the bother caused me by *Pygmalion*, *Héro*, *Le Devin*, *Les Noces de Gamache*, *Vertumne et Pomone*, *Vénus et Adonis*, etc., although those works were done before M. Persuis came to power. I have only one ambition, to please my superiors and to keep my post, and I would prejudice myself if I were to ruffle a few feathers by accepting M. Milon's offer. I would rather refuse it than expose myself to new dangers.[11]

Lefebvre was no doubt wise to be wary, but Choron's orders were to do everything possible to hasten the production of the new ballet. In September it was the scene-designer Degotti's turn to be hounded. The ballet, he was told on 9 September, had to be ready by the 24th, just two weeks ahead; the dancers were rehearsing morning and evening, and if the ballet was not ready by then, the fault would be laid at Degotti's door and the Minister would be so informed.[12]

In the event the pressure on Degotti was lifted by an unexpected resistance on the part of the dancers to appear disguised as savages, and, what with one thing and another, the first performance was delayed by two months until 26 November 1816.

It was announced on the bills as *Les Sauvages de la mer du Sud*, a last-minute change from *Les Sauvages*, as it was entitled on the printed programme. The unnamed South Sea island could have been Tahiti, which in 1816 was in the process of being converted to Christianity by missionaries. The scenery for the ballet's single act was dominated by the idol of the local god Toya, clad in a robe, seen against the background of a bright

[10] *The Times*, 6, 10 and 11 September 1816.
[11] Arch. Nat., AJ[13] 109 (II). Lefebvre to Choron, 6 August 1816.
[12] Arch. Nat., AJ[13] 132. Choron to Degotti, 9 September 1816.

blue sea. To the left is the home of the heroine, Maheine (Bigottini), whose family abhor the primitive cult. She arouses the enmity of the priest Olikas (G. Elie), by resisting his advances; and when the time comes for a sacrificial virgin to be chosen, he points to her. At this point a violent storm breaks out and the natives scatter in terror.

Through the thunder the report of a distress cannon is heard. A blazing ship appears on the horizon, and soon a naval officer, Dorville (Albert), comes ashore from a rowing boat, followed shortly by his servant Casimir (Godefroy), who has floated to safety on a piece of wreckage. Casimir is wet through, and Dorville covers him with the idol's robe while his clothes dry. At that moment Dorville notices Maheine and releases her. Seeing Casimir in the idol's robe, she believes him to be the god himself come to life, and tries to appease him by dancing a few steps. To this Casimir responds with a French dance before toppling the idol into the sea and taking its place on the plinth. When the natives return, they take Dorville to be another victim demanded by their god. The situation becomes dangerous, and Maheine, knowing the natives' respect for dancing, presses Dorville to dance. His skill causes great wonderment. Olikas suspects trickery, but is chased away by the natives. Another French ship then arrives. Its captain assures the natives of his peaceful intent and invites them to abandon their superstitions in favour of the Christian God. Amid general rejoicing in the form of local and European dancing, the marriage of Maheine and Dorville is seen as an earnest of peace, and the lovers set sail for France.

Not even Bigottini and Albert could make much impression in what the *Débats* called 'a poor composition [full of] absurdities that one might have overlooked had they been accompanied by a few ingenious and novel scenes'.[13] Lefebvre's hastily written but modestly workmanlike score attracted a little praise, but he cannot have considered it in any way important. Even a special lighting effect for the sunrise, on which high hopes had been placed, had to be abandoned and replaced by a crude cut-out of red cloth lit from behind by an oil-lamp. The ballet limped on to its eighth performance before vanishing into oblivion. To add insult to injury, Milon was handed back the lens that had been specially ground for the sunrise effect, together with the bill, which Choron had refused to accept – notwithstanding that it had been ordered by the machinist, Gromaire. Being an honourable man, Milon paid it personally, although under protest, observing that it was 'something he had always regarded as impracticable'.[14]

[13] *Journal des débats*, 28 November 1816. Signed 'C'.
[14] Arch. Nat., AJ[13] 132. Milon to Choron, 27 February 1817.

31

The Duke and the Opera-Girl

Regularly noticed and pointed out by spectators at the Opéra in the early years of the Restoration was a round-faced, somewhat overweight young man who occupied the lowest of the proscenium boxes to the left of the stage. From his enjoyment of the ballet it was evident that he was a fervent lover of the dance.

Nor was his identity a secret, for Monseigneur Charles-Ferdinand, Duc de Berry, was not only a nephew of Louis XVIII, but to many the man upon whose virility rested the future of the Bourbon dynasty. For the very survival of the monarchy depended on a continuing provision of princes, and these were in short supply. Louis XVIII was old, infirm and childless, and the Duke was one of the two sons of his only brother, Monsieur, the former Comte d'Artois. When the King should die, the crown would pass to his brother or, if the latter had predeceased him, to his elder son, the Duc d'Angoulême. Angoulême had married the daughter of Louis XVI, the sole survivor of the tragic family imprisoned in the Temple; since there was no likelihood of offspring, the crown seemed bound to pass in due time to his younger brother, the Duc de Berry. The continuation of the main Bourbon line therefore depended upon his having a son.

Berry was a lusty playboy who saw himself as a military man, even though he had never distinguished himself in the field. During his exile in England he had formed a stable relationship with an Englishwoman, Amy Brown, whom he may well have married and by whom he had two daughters and probably also a son. Returning to France in 1814 in the wake of the allied armies, he had quickly discovered the delights of the Opéra – and one in particular, in the alluring form of a girl in the *corps de ballet*, who willingly accepted his invitations to supper in the private anteroom to his box.

For professional purposes she was known simply as Mlle Virginie. She was the daughter of a hairdresser, one Jean Oreille, who worked at the theatre; and it was probably through connections he made in the course of his duties that she was admitted into the children's class of the School of Dance. Her career in the *corps de ballet* had begun when she was thirteen, in 1808; her name first appeared in print in the programme of Aumer's *Amours d'Antoine et Cléopâtre*. And at that modest level she remained for the next six years. She apparently had no artistic pretensions, preferring to take advantage, under her father's wing, of the more remunerative opportunities that were available to the prettier girls in the *demimonde* of *filles d'Opéra*. In this way she became the mistress of one of the most valiant military heroes of the time, Marshal Bessières, who had commanded the cavalry of the Imperial Guard at Austerlitz and led the great charge that had won the day. In 1813 the Marshal, whom a sorrowing Napoleon was to liken to Bayard, the *chevalier sans peur et sans reproche*, was killed in battle. About a year later, when she caught the eye of the Duc de Berry, Virginie was free and available.

The Duchesse d'Abrantès, widow of another great soldier, General Junot, described Virginie as being 'as pretty as an angel and as stupid as a goose',[1] but the Duke was not seeking an intellectual companion. He became besotted with her and openly flaunted their liaison. 'A rumour has been spreading in Paris,' ran a police report, 'that the day before yesterday, the Demoiselle Virginie, the dancer of the Opéra, was driving in a barouche with the Duc de Berry at her side, and that on the previous day that same person had been seen in the Bois de Boulogne, escorted by the bodyguards of H.R.H. Monsieur, brother of the King.'[2] She was already a celebrity: police spies reported her presence at the Opéra-Comique in a box facing that of the royal family, and the circulation of a scurrilous pamphlet about the liaison, entitled *Les Amours de Paul et Virginie*.

On 3 March 1815, less than a year after their first meeting, Virginie gave birth to a healthy boy, who was given the name of Charles. The child's paternity was no secret, and the Comte de Reiset, referring to France's enormous losses in the recent wars, recalled how the prince was teased for the haste he had shown in contributing to the repopulation of the kingdom.

The Duke's conquests were legion; no pretty woman was safe from him. Although Virginie was his titular mistress, his amorous escapades ranged far and wide, and he did not take it kindly if one of his inamoratas was discovered to be sharing his favours with some other admirer. On one occasion Virginie nearly found herself trapped through an unfortunate misunderstanding on the part of the police. The Duke's roving eye had alighted on a certain lady at court, and what followed, as it was later recounted in a book based on the police archives, had all the elements of high farce:

[1] Castelot, 73, quoting the Duchesse d'Abrantès.

[2] Reiset, *Enfants*, 281, quoting police reports dated 15 September and 12 November 1814.

The Prince had the idea of having the beautiful Mme de M— shadowed. One of his men called at the Prefecture of Police, spoke to someone in authority, gave the necessary instructions, and then left.

Thereupon, a junior official was summoned and given the task of shadowing 'a mistress' of the Duc de Berry. He, in turn, in accordance with the hierarchical structure of the place, summoned a more lowly agent and entrusted him with the task of compiling a detailed report of the doings of His Royal Highness's 'mistress'.

But to this poor wretch, the existence of the proud and lofty Mme de M— lay beyond his ken. Along with everyone else of his class, he knew of only one mistress of the Prince, namely a certain adorable lady of the theatre. He thus overlooked the detail of his instructions, and being convinced that the pretty, high-spirited V— was the person he was to shadow, stuck to the poor girl like a dog to his bone. This fellow, although one of the most junior in the Prefecture, was an artful chap who would have been quite capable of carrying out his task had he not made the enormous blunder at the outset of mistaking the lady's identity. And such was the zeal and intelligence with which he set to work that, a week later, the Prince was presented with a detailed report disclosing in the most explicit terms numerous lapses of the divine bayadère from her vow of fidelity.

The shock, anger and disenchantment of the Prince on reading this evidence can be imagined. At first he wanted to kill his mistress, but then there followed what happens in this sort of situation when the man does not cease to be the lover. The girl countered the blunders of the police with tears, threatening to tear her lovely hair; and reclining on her couch in the attitude of Ariadne on the island of Naxos, she declared the informer to be a rogue in the pay of rivals or enemies.

The poor wretch of an informer was made out to have sold his pen. He was ostensibly dismissed, but in reality the Prefect of Police merely moved him to another brigade, and that was the end of the matter.[3]

This incident came as a great shock to Oreille, who was living very comfortably on his daughter's good fortune, having given up hairdressing to enjoy the benefits of a royal mistress's father. But once the danger had passed, his expectations that his daughter would retire into semi-respectability were revived.

[3] Peuchet, VI, 181–3.

'Monseigneur,' he was heard to confide in a crony, 'is too religious a man to allow my daughter to remain on the stage.'[4]

But just two days before the infant's birth, disaster had again threatened. Napoleon had escaped from Elba and landed in France. Within three weeks he was back in power in Paris, and Louis XVIII and the Duc de Berry had fled to Belgium. Jean Oreille was in a panic. Seeing his hopes of a comfortable and prosperous future vanishing, he began to rue the day when his daughter had surrendered to such an unsuitable admirer.

'What has finally set the seal on my dishonour,' he fumed, 'is to have a Bourbon in my family.'[5]

To her credit, however, Virginie remained devoted, and as soon as she was fit enough to travel, she joined her lover in the north, where he was garrisoned with a body of troops loyal to the King. As events turned out, the exile was to be short; for by July, with Napoleon safely dispatched to St. Helena, she and the Duke were back in Paris.

Dynastic necessity was now to complicate their relationship. If the main Bourbon line was to be assured, it was imperative to create a new generation of princes – a task that in the circumstances could fall only to the Duc de Berry, who had already given such ample proof of his fertility. By the end of 1815 a marriage had been arranged with the eldest granddaughter of the King of the Two Sicilies, Princess Marie-Caroline, and the royal marriage took place in June 1816.

Among the loose ends to be discreetly tied up were the problem of the Duke's offspring by Amy Brown and his affair with Virginie. The former was by far the more difficult, being complicated by uncertainty about whether the Duke had been legally married to Miss Brown. Virginie, however, was easier to deal with. The terms were to be kept secret, but the English ambassador, Sir Charles Stuart, somehow got wind of them and prepared a report for the Foreign Office:

> The dancer, Virginie, receives a pension of 6000 francs and her father 1000 écus. So she is well and truly dismissed. The child gives up the name of Charles-Louis. The Duc de Berry has formally promised to renounce all liaisons of this kind. He has been made to understand that if he is to gain the esteem and respect of the French, he must avoid scandals of the court of Louis XV and the Regency.[6]

[4] Castelot, 73.

[5] Castelot, 85.

[6] Reiset, *Enfants*, 286. This note was apparently purloined from the ambassador's desk by the rench police, and passed on to Comte Decazes, the Minister of Police.

It was no doubt part of this arrangement that she would leave the Opéra, and her name appeared for the last time in a ballet programme when *Flore et Zéphire* was produced in December 1815. The following May she was settled in a mansion in Paris, No. 6 rue Richepanse, which was to pass to her son when she died. In September the Duke signed a will leaving one-fifth of the proceeds of his 'private property including my pictures' to young Charles, acknowledging him as his natural son, and the remaining proportion to Amy Brown's two daughters.[7]

Louis XVIII had made it abundantly clear that he expected his nephew to cease his philanderings, settle down and concentrate on the task of producing a male heir. For a while the Duke was very attentive to his Italian bride, and towards the end of the year it became known that she was pregnant. An event so devoutly desired called for celebration, and as the moment of the birth approached the Opéra began to prepare its own contribution to the festivities. Between them, Gardel and Milon worked out a scenario for a modest ballet, and on 24 June 1817 Persuis issued an order calling on the entire company to pull together to ensure that it would be completely ready by 8 July.

This unusual urgency no doubt explained why both ballet-masters were responsible, for only once before had they collaborated in a ballet: in *L'Heureux Retour*, which had honoured Louis XVIII's return after the Hundred Days. The new ballet was ready in time, but since the birth was delayed, it was postponed to 14 July. On the 13th, the Duchess was delivered of a sickly infant, and, amid fears that the child might not survive, *Nina* was hastily substituted for the new ballet on the 14th. The next day the baby died.

Too much effort had gone into the work to discard it without a thought. The reference in it to a birth was, in fact, reasonably indirect, and after a suitable interval (when it could be interpreted as expressing a hope for a happy event to come) it was eventually given on 17 September 1817 under the title *Les Fiancées de Caserte*.

It was based on an ancient custom prescribed by a former King of Naples for a colony of silk workers in Caserta, whereby marriages were arranged at a ceremony in which proposals were made and accepted by the offer and exchange of roses. The action of the ballet centred on two sisters, Rosina (Bigottini) and Vittorina (Courtin), daughters of a silk dealer, Margarita (Delisle). Margarita has plans to marry Rosina to Paolino (A. Coulon), whose father, Geronimo (S. Mérante), has precipitately agreed to her proposal, unaware that his son is in love with

[7] Reiset, *Enfants*, 370. The holograph will is there illustrated.

Vittorina. The tearful protestations of the young couple move him to do what he can to extricate himself from his agreement. Meanwhile, the other daughter, Rosina, is being courted by a French officer, Dorlis (Albert), but under the rules Dorlis is not eligible to propose to her because he is not an Italian. Further, Margarita makes it clear that she will never consent to being parted from her daughter. Dorlis appeals to the Governor, who finally informs Margarita that Dorlis has agreed to be naturalised as a Neapolitan and remain in Caserta. All Margarita's objections are thus removed, and the ballet, which included a generous provision of dancing, closes with the ceremony of the exchange of roses, at which both sisters are betrothed to their lovers.

No one who saw one of the only two performances that were given of this work took it for anything more than an offering to welcome and encourage the Italian princess. It had never been intended to endure, and the *Journal de Paris* passed it over with only a brief notice:

> It certainly had some pleasing moments, such as the love passages between the two couples and the exchange of roses, which is charming, but the lack of invention and the all too obvious progress of the action cast a chill over some of the scenes. All the characters are too accommodating, and to quote a remark made of the works of Florian, it was 'a pastoral in sore need of a wolf'.[8]

The score was not without interest, being the first work to be heard at the Opéra by Gustave Dugazon, son of the celebrated actress. It was pleasingly graceful, and contained a striking horn solo accompanying one of the *pas de deux*. Equally impressive was the scenery that showed the coast of Calabria sparkling in the Mediterranean sun, painted by Pierre Ciceri.

Meanwhile, the Duke was hankering after the voluptuous attractions of Virginie. That winter it became common knowledge that, despite the assurances he had given to his uncle, he was seeing her again, not discreetly for which he might have been forgiven, but publicly, at a ball which she herself gave. The King was beside himself with fury, and his outburst could be heard outside in the Place du Carrousel. 'Anyone who marries at thirty-eight and does not settle down,' he bellowed at his nephew, 'only shows that he regards a wife as just another mistress. And what a moment to choose for such a scandal! ... In the old days an order would have been given to M. Lenoir, who would have flushed out the

[8] *Journal de Paris*, 19 September 1817.

young miss and told her that if her ball took place, she would spend the night at Sainte-Pélagie.'[9]

The Duke, however, was aware of how indispensable he was for the future of the dynasty, and knew perfectly well that as long as he could keep little Marie-Caroline content, his ageing uncle would in the end turn a blind eye. He was also well able to keep more than one woman happy, and in fact Virginie was far from being his only illicit love – her colleague at the Opéra, Caroline Brocard, had also enjoyed his favours, and no doubt there were others. However, Virginie's position as his established mistress was unchallenged and she clearly enjoyed the attention paid to her as the favourite of the man who, in the expected course of events, would one day be king.

As the second decade of the century drew towards its close, she shone in that louche penumbra that existed largely for the enjoyment of men to take outside the walls of high society – what a later generation would call the *demi-monde*. Her period of glory was destined to be brief. Only a glimpse of it survives, preserved in the memoirs of the Comte Marquiset, who recalled the impression she made upon him one evening at the theatre at Versailles:

> The beautiful Virginie, titular mistress of the Duc de Berry ... had booked the box in the very centre, facing the stage, and of course made her entrance like a duchess to the manner born – that is to say, after the curtain had risen. This was necessary to make an impression, and to show off to the public the most delightful gown in the world worn by the prettiest woman of the age.
>
> Virginie was accompanied by Monsieur her father, a dried-up, thin, corseted dummy wearing a light blue suit buttoned up to the neck, military-fashion, like a rolled-up umbrella. A self-important fidgety man giving himself airs. Curly-haired and pomaded, he wore his hat on the side of his head after the fashion of a wig-maker of the Faubourg-Saint-Denis, which he once was, and which honourable trade his daughter's new-found dignity no longer permits him to follow.
>
> The mistress of the Duc de Berry is a perfect beauty; her figure is remarkable, her dark eyes shine with both gentleness and vivacity, and her brown hair, being too tightly compressed in her hat, escapes in abundant tresses. Her features are not lacking in expression in a pleas-

[9] Daudet, 335–6. Lenoir was the Lieutenant of Police under the Old Régime who dealt with refractory dancers. The convent of Saint-Pélagie served as a women's prison, as well as rehabilitating repentant prostitutes.

> ing and captivating way, but her carriage and her manners still retain a flavour that betrays the *fille d'Opéra*, however much she tries to hide it. She has a loud voice and never stops gesticulating, often without moderation, and her gaiety as a woman in the public eye is conveyed by shrieks of laughter that are too loud to be in good taste.
>
> Five or six bodyguards went to pay court to her during the second piece, and the chatter and laughter of their small talk became at times so indiscreet that the pit began to murmur in protest.[10]

She was enjoying life while it lasted, happily heedless of what the future held.

[10] Marquiset, quoted in Reiset, *Enfants*, 288–90. Touchard Lafosse in his anecdotal history of the Opéra places this incident there, in the presence of the King, Monsieur and the Duc de Berry himself. As he described the incident, Virginie entered her box just as the audience was applauding the royal party, and, thinking the ovation was for her, acknowledged it. The audience egged her on with ironical *bravas* until a charitable spectator in the adjoining box disillusioned her.

32

Problems with Proserpine

With only the ephemeral offering to the Duchesse de Berry to its credit, the Opéra provided meagre fare for the followers of its ballet in 1817. The most notable event was a revival of *Psyché* with Bigottini. To succeed Mme Gardel in what many considered her finest rôle would have been a daunting task even for an experienced artiste, but to Bigottini it brought a splendid triumph. Not that she could ever dim the memory of her predecessor's unapproachable perfection and grace as a dancer, but she brought to the part a dramatic genius that was 'acclaimed as undoubtedly superior' to anything that had been seen in ballet before.[1]

The two ballerinas were separated in age by fourteen years, almost a generation, and, in a period of great change in both public taste and dance technique, this was inevitably reflected in their styles. But apart from their qualities as dancers, an even more striking point of contrast was to be found in their personal lifestyles. Marie Gardel had no pretensions to beauty, and her respectability, as wife and mother, had always been above reproach, while Emilie Bigottini exerted an unambiguous sexual attraction, her private life having long been a source of curiosity among Paris society. So it followed that while the older of the two appealed to both sexes alike, the younger kindled a stronger flame in the hearts of men, who found her dark southern beauty irresistibly seductive, and her figure no less enticing in the short ballet skirts then coming into vogue. Her appeal, for example, to the Irish poet Thomas Moore was overtly sexual:

> And when BIGOTTINI in PSYCHE dishevels
> Her black flowing hair, and by daemons is driven,
> Oh! who does not envy those rude little devils,
> That hold her, and hug her, and keep her from heaven?[2]

[1] *Journal des débats*, 25 June 1817.
[2] Moore, Letter V.

So perhaps it was not surprising that this tended to put some women on the defensive, a reaction that certainly seemed to have affected Lady Granville on seeing her that summer in *Le Carnaval de Venise*. 'Bigottini acts better than she dances,' she wrote rather dryly to her sister. 'I do not think her very handsome; her petticoats are five inches long.'[3]

Apart from worshipping at the shrine of Bigottini, connoisseurs of the ballet were consoled that summer by the appearance of two interesting newcomers. In June, Pauline Paul, younger sister of the promising virtuoso Antoine Paul, made a successful appearance that earned her an immediate engagement. This was followed a month later by the no less remarkable début of an ambitious young man of twenty-two who had gained laurels in Marseilles and Bordeaux. Charles Blazis, as he spelt his name in his application, was presented in a *pas de deux* with Mme Anatole-Gosselin.

The public was impressed and the Opéra was interested, but unfortunately his demands proved beyond what the administration was prepared to consider. He had at first wanted his engagement back-dated to June and to be given four months' paid leave from the end of November. This was clearly unacceptable, and, no doubt after consulting Gardel, Persuis was only disposed to offer him a contract from the following April; as far as salary was concerned, 2400 francs was thought sufficient, but Persuis was prepared to negotiate up to 3000 francs to secure his services. However, Blazis was demanding double that sum; the gap was too wide to be bridged, and the young man took his services elsewhere.[4] An international career of some distinction as a dancer and choreographer under the slightly modifed name of Carlo Blasis lay before him, but it was as a teacher and pedagogue that he would take his place in the history of his art. His two manuals, the *Traîté élémentaire* of 1821 and *The Art of Dancing* of 1828, were to break new ground in recording the technique and style of the French school in which he had been trained; but, ironically, he himself was never to work in Paris again.

However alluring, revivals and débuts could not conceal the stagnation that was setting in at the Opéra for want of a substantial ballet creation, and the attention of dance lovers was increasingly turning towards the Théâtre de la Porte-Saint-Martin, where ballet was establishing a strong foothold alongside the full-blooded melodramas that were becoming the rage. Henry's departure towards the end of 1816 had been immediately followed by the engagement of a young ballet-master who would remain

[3] Granville, I, 97. Letter to Lady Morpeth, May 1817.

[4] Arch.Nat., O[3] 1647 (August, September and October folders).

in charge of the ballet there until 1825, Frédéric Blache. His was a well-known name, for his father, Jean-Baptiste Blache, had been Dauberval's successor in Bordeaux and was recognised throughout France as the most celebrated choreographer working in the provinces. His son had come to Paris, not so much in his own right as being the authorised reproducer of his father's canon; and during 1817, when the Opéra could offer barely a single novelty, the Porte-Saint-Martin was to present no fewer than six ballets that had never been seen in the capital before.

The first offering, in January 1817, was *La Chaste Suzanne*, based on the apocryphal story of Susannah and the elders, and originally staged in Lyons. It was inspired by, if not based upon, a play of the same name produced at the Vaudeville at the time of Louis XVI's trial in 1793. It had then acquired notoriety because one of its lines – 'You are her accusers, you cannot be her judges' – was too near the bone in the highly charged political atmosphere of that time, and further performances had been banned by the Convention. Twenty-four years later the climate was calmer, and no such fate attended the ballet. The pairing of a ballerina playing Susannah with a boulevard actor pleading the cause of virtue as the prophet Daniel seemed somewhat incongruous to one critic; but the public took it in its stride. A Mlle Bégrand from Bordeaux portrayed the title rôle 'in a manner passably erotic',[5] particularly in the daring scene of Susannah taking her bath and being spied upon by the leering elders. Here, her costume was as flimsy as it could have been without running a risk of police intervention, and the vigorous miming of the elders, played by actors, gave every emphasis to the peril in which the heroine found herself. It was said that this scene alone was worth a fortune to the Porte-Saint-Martin.

The five ballets that followed in the course of 1817 were very varied in subject matter and offered a selection of works from different periods of the eminent choreographer's long career. All were highly successful, appealing to a public that was more easily pleased than that of the Opéra.

Les Meuniers, a simple comedy ballet, was the earliest work of all, first produced in 1787 in Montpellier. Ever since then it had remained a firm favourite, vying in popularity only with Dauberval's *La Fille mal gardée*. For Blache and his enormous family – he had fathered no fewer than thirty-two children – it was the cornerstone of his fortune, earning him more than 60,000 francs in royalties.

Almaviva et Rosina, as its title suggested, was a version of Beaumarchais's comedy, *Le Barbier de Séville*. It had first been given in

[5] *Journal des débats*, 11 August 1817.

Lyons, and on its revival in Paris many spectators must have compared it with Duport's similarly based *Figaro*, given at the Opéra eleven years before. Neither work, however, owed anything to the other. Blache's version was to be particularly remembered for its extraordinary mirror dance, which had no counterpart in Duport's ballet – a *pas de huit* with two couples on each side of a gauze drop representing the mirror, the four dancers behind reproducing with impressive precision the steps of the four in front.

L'Amour et la Folie, which was inspired by one of La Fontaine's fables, and *La Fille soldat* were both works from Blache's Bordeaux period.

Somewhat less successful was the spectacular *Haroun-al-Raschid*, the subject of which evoked memories of Boïeldieu's popular *opéra-comique*, *Le Calife de Bagdad*, telling of a caliph who disguises himself as a poor man to woo a fisherman's daughter and is nearly killed for his pains. His rescuer is a Spaniard whose betrothed has been taken prisoner and placed in the harem, from which he has unsuccessfully tried to obtain her release by bribing the chief eunuch, who took his money but cheated him by handing over an unwanted girl. To reward the Spaniard, the grateful caliph frees the heroine. If the action seemed dramatically somewhat weak, it was played with great zest; the dances were well arranged and the production was colourfully impressive, including a striking seascape on which a flotilla of small boats was shown in motion.

* * *

Meanwhile, Gardel was having a difficult year. He had been struggling with *Proserpine* for so long that at times he must have despaired of ever bringing it up to the standard he had set himself. And with his sixtieth birthday approaching, there was another worry on his mind: the looming prospect of retirement and the effect it would have on his finances. The arguments that Didelot had put forward two years earlier for the engagement of a third ballet-master had not been forgotten, and some time in 1817 the subject was resurrected by La Ferté and Persuis, who made it clear that it could no longer be a matter of training an apprentice; the situation called for an experienced ballet-master with successes to his credit. The discussion then moved to possible candidates, and eventually Gardel and Milon had to agree that the most suitable candidate was Jean Aumer, who was not only familiar with the company, but had convincingly demonstrated his potential at the Vienna Opera.

When Aumer was approached, he was more than interested, but, as he had to explain, he would not be free of his obligations to Vienna until the following summer. The negotiations then languished, not through any fault of Aumer's, but as a result of a failure of communication on the Opéra's part. Faced with an unexplained silence from Paris, Aumer found himself in a quandary, and when the Viennese authorities pressed him to sign a new contract, all he could do was to require a provision that he could give six months' notice of termination in the event of the Opéra requesting his services.[6]

Meanwhile, encouraged perhaps at hearing nothing further about the negotiations with Aumer, Gardel was concentrating his attention on the long-delayed project of *Proserpine*. This had been accepted in principle as long ago as the summer of 1813, and was originally scheduled for production before the end of that year. But when that time came, Napoleon's armies were in full retreat after the battle of Leipzig. *Proserpine* was then shelved – but only briefly, for in April 1815, during the Hundred Days, it was decided to produce it immediately following a new opera, *La Princesse de Babylone*. There was a short delay after Napoleon's defeat at Waterloo; but two months later, the Comte de Pradel, back in his ministry, confirmed his predecessor's decision. Progress then seemed to grind to a halt. The music still had to be written, and *Proserpine*'s production was deferred to that of *Flore et Zéphire*. Further delays ensued, and for one reason or another it was not until early in 1817 that the estimate of 19,038 francs for the scenery and costumes was approved, and Ciceri instructed to begin work on the sets.

That summer, as the weeks passed without any sign of progress, the Opéra was forced to exert pressure. Gardel was reminded that it was now six years since he had last produced a major ballet. It then transpired that he was in financial difficulties; that he wished to be given a benefit, and hoped that the Opéra would advance him 5000 francs on account to help him out. This gave the Opéra a lever, and in September 1817 it was formally agreed that the requested advance would be made on Gardel's undertaking to present two ballets in the course of 1818: *Proserpine* to be one, and the other a one-act ballet he had proposed under the title of *La Fête de Mathurine, ou la Servante justifiée*.[7]

Proserpine was planned on a scale not seen since Napoleon's time. By the end of 1817 the music was ready, work was proceeding well on the scenery and costumes, and the action was sufficiently worked out for rehearsals to begin. In February 1818 Gardel passed the printed proofs of

[6] Arch. Nat., AJ13 125. Aumer to Persuis, 26 July and 30 August 1817; Persuis to Aumer, 26 September 1817; Aumer to Persuis, 15 October 1817.

[7] Arch. Nat., O[3] 1647 (June, September 1817). Gardel had also proposed a three-act ballet, *La Fée Urgèle, ou la Cour d'Amour*, which was never to be produced.

the scenario, and at long last, on the 18th of that month, the curtain rose for the first performance.

As its title implied, the theme was based on the ancient legend of the daughter of Jupiter and Ceres, goddess of corn and the harvest. Proserpina was abducted by Pluto, god of the underworld, while gathering flowers. Ceres's hopes of recovering her daughter were to be of no avail because Proserpina had eaten a pomegranate in Pluto's realm. So great was Ceres's grief that Jupiter relented by allowing Proserpina to spend six months of the year with her mother and the remaining six with Pluto. This was the tale as told by the ancient writers, but Gardel had worked from another source, a recent epic poem by the historian Joseph Michaud. The original legend had thus passed through two adapters before reaching the form that the Opéra public was now to see re-enacted on the stage.

The first act was set in the sunny Sicilian countryside, dominated by two mountains, one of them the volcanic Mount Etna. Venus (M. Masrélier) is dismayed that Pluto (Montjoie), the god of the Underworld, has not come under her influence and taken a wife to share his realm. An eruption of the volcano brings Pluto from the bowels of the earth. At Venus's bidding, Cupid (J. Hullin) shoots a dart, which finds its mark, thus making Pluto susceptible to her plans. He is immediately smitten with the beauty of Proserpina (Bigottini), but Venus calms his ardour, telling him to bide his time and await a favourable moment to pay her court. Ceres (Clotilde), Proserpina's mother, then appears on her way to Olympus and, before continuing her journey, presents her daughter with a linen veil to wear as a symbol of chastity.

The second act finds Proserpina and her friend Cyane (Mme Courtin) asleep in a forest. At Venus's bidding, Cupid summons up the symbolic figures of Dreams to reveal to Proserpina the emptiness of a life without love. Venus causes Cyane to vanish, and assumes her form. In Proserpina's dream a band of lovers materialises, among whom is a girl who, notwithstanding the attentions of an admirer, cannot share in her companions' enjoyment. She tries to join in their dances, but finds no pleasure in them and is overcome by a feeling of weariness. Cupid then looses another of his darts, and at once she is transformed. During this dream scene, Venus has been observing the effect on Proserpina, who, on waking, is led away to see the dawn.

The scene changes to a hilly landscape in the region of Lake Spergus. Here Zephyr (Paul) is bidden to scatter sweet scents on the flowers and plants in preparation for Proserpina's arrival. Proserpina and Venus, the latter still disguised as Cyane, are joined by a band of nymphs. Proserpina is so overwhelmed by all the beauties of nature that Venus sends Cupid to alert Pluto that the moment for which he is waiting is nigh. She then points to a mound where some of the loveliest blooms remain unpicked. All of a sudden, as Proserpina approaches, it vanishes, and the nymphs are filled with terror at the sight of Pluto in his chariot, bearing Proserpina away. The real Cyane attempts to rescue her, but is left holding only her veil. Ceres returns to find her daughter gone. When she learns of the abduction, her anger is awesome; after uttering terrible threats, she departs to plead with Jupiter for her daughter's return.

Act III takes place in Pluto's palace. The demonic dances of his courtiers are stilled as he enters with Proserpina. At his order they pay her homage, but their terrifying aspect unnerves her. Observing her disquiet, Pluto commands them to withdraw and kneels at her feet, offering her the attributes of his power. Her fears begin to recede, as she realises that he is not the monster she had imagined. However, the thought of her mother's anguish and the recollection of her own abduction make her reluctant to yield. Strains of gentle music are then heard, and involuntarily she finds herself being led into the Elysian Fields. Here she begins to see her ravisher in a different light, as he reminds her of the dream in the forest. Pluto is uncertain whether he can ever win her, but his anxiety vanishes when Mercury comes to announce that Jupiter has decreed the marriage of Pluto and Proserpina and that Ceres has given her consent.

When the curtain fell on the last act, most of the audience could only respond half-heartedly, for the ballet had generally proved a disappointment. The dancers, who had given of their best, were warmly applauded, and on taking his call Gardel was able to bask for a moment in the enthusiasm they had generated. But neither the designer, Ciceri, nor the composer, Schneitzhoeffer, appeared. The audience then began to make their way out, leaving a small core of committed admirers still calling for Gardel. Eventually, and perhaps a little reluctantly, the ballet-master re-emerged from the wings. There were then shouts for Ciceri, but he was apparently unwilling to receive a tribute so obviously tardy and partial.

When he read the notices in the course of the next few days, Gardel could have been in little doubt that his ballet had been a failure. Praise from the *Journal de Paris*[8] had come like a cry in the wilderness; and the critic of the *Quotidienne* was also reasonably kind, calling it 'a success from several points of view', even though he found 'the action rather slow' and had to confess that his interest had occasionally flagged.[9] The

[8] *Journal de Paris*, 19 February 1818.
[9] *Quotidienne*, 20 February 1818.

other major papers, however, dismissed the work with little show of mercy.

Evariste Dumoulin in the *Constitutionnel* did try to couch his disappointment in terms that would not be too wounding, but made it clear that he considered the ballet flawed:

> M. Gardel has developed his action more or less successfully, but has neglected the substance for the form, and while his work is poor in invention, it is rich in details ... [It] would suffer much from a comprehensive examination, for it would be all too easy to show that the principal action begins too late and is not developed rapidly enough, so that the interest it arouses – the motive force of any theatrical production – drags, is weak, and often is non-existent.[10]

Martainville in the *Gazette de France* was the most scathing, accusing Gardel of having

> broken the rules of good taste by the use of ridiculously impracticable effects to support a feeble and trivial plot. It was a wretched piece with little drama, superfluous and poorly arranged in its details, lacking grace and originality, full of puerile and ridiculous effects and interminable dances without any point, and, to put it bluntly, boring, utterly boring ... [It] says nothing to the heart or to the imagination, and only occasionally pleases the eye.[11]

Le Moniteur was a shade more charitable. Gardel, wrote its critic, 'certainly did not offend ... the rules of good sense, but much of it lacked warmth, and the emptiness of the subject was apparent on several occasions despite the grace and elegance of the episodes that had to be thought up to fill out the three acts.'[12]

More scathing was the *Journal des débats*, which published a reasoned article explaining why, in its critic's view, the ballet had been found wanting. In the preface to his scenario, Gardel had quoted Michaud as saying that he hoped he had not transgressed the rules of taste and reason; and yet he, Gardel, had been guilty of this very failing. For all its splendour and perfectly performed dances, the ballet added nothing to his reputation, lacking both interest and vitality, and was saved only by the efforts of the performers. It could not be that the legend was an impossible

[10] *Constitutionnel*, 20 February 1818.
[11] *Gazette de France*, 22 February 1818.
[12] *Moniteur*, 19 February 1818.

subject for the stage, for Lully and Quinault had treated it in an opera that had survived for a good hundred years. But Gardel's adaptation of the legend had a fatal weakness in his presentation of the character of Pluto. In the ballet, that god was in no way terrifying, appearing more like a Syracusean shepherd than the tyrant of the Underworld, and the abduction scene was unconvincing: in what was one of the most brutal crimes of ancient mythology, he appeared 'in a most amiable and charming guise', with Proserpina offering only modest resistance.[13]

And another opportunity was lost in the depiction of Ceres, a rôle that, had it been given its due importance, might have provided a mime of the stature of the recently retired Chevigny with an opportunity to give a powerful display of histrionics. As Ovid had told the tale, Ceres's fury knew no bounds on learning of her daughter's abduction. She smashes the ploughshares, turns the land sterile and buries farmers and cattle alive. But in the ballet her maternal distress was limited to a few gestures directed against Cyane, and it was all over in a few seconds.

The principal actors were given few opportunities to shape their characters. Bigottini did what she could with the part of Proserpina, but the performance fell flat through no fault of hers, or indeed of the other leading players – Clotilde, Masrélier, Montjoie – who accompanied her in the pantomime scenes. The only moment of excitement came in the final *divertissement* when young Antoine Paul gave a display of controlled strength and effortless lightness as he skimmed the stage in the purely dancing part of Zephyr.

Visually, the production was on the whole impressive. In designing the scenery, Ciceri had shown such skill that no one noticed that much of it had previously served in other works. The set showing Lake Spergus in the second act was an unqualified triumph, looking as fresh as new, with a fleet of swans sailing majestically over its surface – an effect only slightly marred by the shadows thrown on to the backcloth behind.

This was only one of a profusion of effects that Gardel, in his enthusiasm, had demanded of the machinist. Unfortunately, Gromaire – he who had been responsible for Mlle Aubry's accident ten years before – lacked the skill and experience of his predecessor, Boutron, and failed to manage the scene changes in Acts II and III with the smooth efficiency required to maintain the illusion. From the scenic point of view, *Proserpine* was an exceptionally complex production, requiring a multiplicity of effects in addition to rapid changes of scene. The eruption of Mount Etna was well managed, but the operation of the chariots of Ceres and Pluto left much

[13] *Constitutionnel*, 20 February 1818. Signed C.

to be desired. In the second act the sunrise effect was spoilt because the stagehands whose task was to move the lamps manually found it impossible to do so without jerking. And in the same act, the effect of a rosebud opening to reveal Cupid shooting his dart, and then closing again – designed by a mechanic named Bursay at a cost of about 200 francs – appeared contrived and ridiculous.

The one contribution about which there was no controversy was the music. Jean-Madeleine Schneitzhoeffer was a name new to most connoisseurs, and one that became immediately memorable primarily because no one could pronounce his name. He was the son of a senior member of the orchestra, and *Proserpine* was to be the first of a succession of ballet scores that he would write for the Opéra over the next sixteen years. From the opening bars of the overture, the musically aware realised that a promising new talent had arisen. The dream scene and the dances in Pluto's court revealed him in two very contrasting moods, and his melodies for the dances were most happily crafted and varied. Without exception, the critics were impressed by his variety of invention and sensitivity to the demands of the action, describing the score as 'very beautifully constructed, very dramatic' ... 'energetic, tender and graceful' ... 'expressive and melodious' ... 'well adapted'.[14] It was a most promising début; the only criticism to be voiced was that he had ignored the convention of using borrowed melodies to help the audience follow the mime passages, but in this departure he was moving with, if not ahead of, the times.

Strangely enough, in light of the critical disapproval, the ballet continued to draw the public. Interest in it had been quite exceptional, and the box-office receipts on the first night amounted to 8682 francs, a figure that had only been exceeded by *Les Amours d'Antoine et de Cléopâtre*. Judged merely on the returns, it could be counted a success, but Gardel and the powers at the Opéra must have been all too aware that, artistically, it was not.

A week after the première Persuis received a letter from his Minister, Pradel, enclosing a paper entitled 'A Few Observations on the Ballet *Proserpine*', which he passed on to Gardel. The identity of its author was not disclosed, and if Gardel had any suspicion, he was careful to keep it to himself.[15] But to be told by an amateur how to do his job certainly touched a tender nerve, and perhaps it was only because his critic was

[14] *Journal de Paris*, 20 February 1818; *Gazette de France* (Martainville), 22 February 1818; *Quotidienne*, 20 February 1818; *Constitutionnel* (Evariste D[umoulin]), 20 February 1818.

[15] The only clue may be the handwriting of the draft of these Observations to be found in box O3 1649 at the Archives Nationales.

apparently a man of some importance that he took the trouble to respond.

With many of his observations he disagreed. The suggestion that Pluto would have been a more interesting character had he been shown as a lover rather than a ravisher, he most firmly rejected. Also turned down was the proposal that the ballet should open with a scene showing Jupiter ordering Venus to influence Proserpina in favour of Pluto, so that the motive behind Venus's actions was explained at the outset. This, Gardel explained, he had himself considered, but discarded in order not to overload the ballet with mechanical effects. Also rejected were a suggestion that Pluto should take part in the dream scene (on the ground that it would introduce an element of reality that would make nonsense of it) and a proposal that the abduction should be effected at Cupid's command, with Pluto seen both in the act of seizing Proserpina and in that of carrying her off. To this Gardel put forward a very practical objection. That the abduction had been less effective than it should have been was not at issue, but as Gardel explained, he had been anxious to avoid a mishap that might have aroused laughter. To show a chariot making a rapid start from a stationary position, he pointed out from experience, almost inevitably caused the occupants to lose their balance.

However mortified he was at the reception of his work, Gardel was not blind to the need to make revisions, but this he would only do in his own way. Persuis understood this, and gently prodded him, writing a soothing letter that at the same time made a few gentle suggestions for him to consider:

> In sending you a few Observations that had been made to me about the ballet *Proserpine*, my intention was in no way to force you to adopt ideas that ran counter to your own. You alone have the right to improve your work wherever you feel changes are required. I look forward to receiving the new dénouement that you have sketched. By the way, I am far from accepting all the opinions of the author of the Observations.
>
> For example, I do not think that Pluto ought to appear as a lover rather than a ravisher. Undoubtedly it is the character of a ravisher that must predominate. However, I see no objection, if it would add a little charm to the scene, to making Pluto appear first as a lover and only deciding to use violence after having tried gentle means. This accords better with the way of nature, and is in no way contrary to Pluto's character, as depicted for the stage, and in the way you have

> outlined it by showing, in the third act, this god being respectful and attentive towards Proserpina.
>
> The way you have ended the first act pleased the audience. But, on the other hand, the idea of the critic who would like the appearance of Pluto ... to be linked in some way to the phenomenon of the volcano is very good.
>
> For the reason you give, and also because the moment of Proserpina's awakening has not yet come, it should not be she who is wounded by Cupid's arrow. So would it not be possible to give the dream a more pronounced character, i.e. to make it a little more fantastic so that the spectator cannot confuse it with scenes of real characters?
>
> It also seems to me that the substitution of the false Cyane for the real one adds a little obscurity and confusion into the action. I would like, if possible, to do away with this incident.
>
> But of all this, Monsieur, I leave you to be the final judge, realising that no one is more able to make the best decision, and I am happy to leave you to make such improvements to your work as seem to you appropriate.[16]

This letter was written a week before Good Friday, and it was suggested that revisions might be made in time for the reopening after the Easter break. But Gardel was averse to interrupting the ballet's run, and it was agreed that the changes should be introduced during the course of the next few performances. When, in the middle of May, Constance Anatole and Aimée Petit briefly took over the rôles of Proserpina and Cyane in the absence of Bigottini and Mme Courtin, who were both unwell, the *Journal de Paris* recorded that a number of cuts had been made. The decision not to interrupt the performances proved to be wise, for by the end of 1818 the ballet had reached its eighteenth performance. It was given seven times more the following year, the last on 10 November 1819. Its disappearance thereafter would come about through no conscious decision. Three months after that performance, the opera house was closed and the personnel moved into temporary and smaller quarters while a new theatre was being built. *Proserpine* would be too complex a production to adapt for a smaller stage, and by the time the new opera house in the Rue Le Peletier was opened, it had too few advocates for it to be revived.

[16] Arch. Nat., O^3 1649. Persuis to Gardel, 13 March 1818.

33

A Flurry of Farewells

As the decade of the 1810s drew to a close, it was difficult to foresee what course the ballet of the Opéra would take in the years ahead. With money short, and the semi-fiasco of *Proserpine* still smarting in Gardel's mind, spectacular ballets were decidedly out of favour. More to be favoured, so far as the administration was concerned, was the simpler, less costly form of the *ballet de genre*, with its unassuming and often inconsequential plot, told movingly or farcically as the case might require, in pantomime, and coupled with a generous provision of dances. This form was no new phenomenon, for it was based on a respectable tradition reaching back at least to Maximilien Gardel's *Déserteur* and Dauberval's *Fille mal gardée*, and could claim a number of more recent successes such as Pierre Gardel's *Dansomanie* and Milon's *Noces de Gamache*, *Carnaval de Venise* and *Nina*.

The prospect of Gardel's retirement also had to be faced, for with his departure a veritable era would come to a close. He had dominated the ballet as no choreographer had done before him or would do for many years ahead, but he had prepared no successor to take over his sceptre. It could of course be assumed that Milon would remain for some years longer to act as a link between the past and the future, but the matter of Aumer's engagement as third ballet-master, which had been decided upon to meet this eventuality, had not yet been finalised. Two weeks after Aumer had signed a conditional engagement with the Vienna Opera, a contract arrived from Paris for his signature. Aumer had immediately written to explain his reasons for signing that new contract with Vienna, and how he had insisted upon a condition giving him power to terminate it should the Opéra require his services. And there, for many months, the matter had rested, with Aumer holding on to the contract, unsigned, until he received a response to his letter.

In the summer of 1818, concerned at the continuing silence from the Opéra, he was preparing to go to Paris to discuss the matter with Persuis and to propose staging his ballet *Aline*, which had been a proven success in Vienna. But a week before he was to set out, disturbing news reached him. Persuis, he was told, was furious with him for breaking his word, and the Opéra had now asked Albert to stage a ballet. Aumer at once wrote a placating letter to Persuis, but a few weeks later fell ill and was ordered by his doctor to take the waters.[1]

In fact, Aumer need not have feared that Albert would be preferred to him. The Opéra had indeed given Albert the opportunity of staging a ballet, but it was to be a work of very modest dimensions, for which Albert had concocted a contrived little plot with a Swiss setting that achieved little more than to provide a frame for his dances. This trial work, for it was no more than that, was presented under the title *Le Séducteur du village* on 3 July 1818.

The principal character, as the title implied, is a wealthy young libertine called Alphonse (Montjoie), whose roving eye has alighted on Claire (Bigottini), the daughter of Farmer Edmond (Milon). It becomes apparent that he cannot resist a pretty face when his eye falls upon the shy and innocent Edmée (Bias). However, his thoughts soon return to Claire, who, to his bafflement, rejects his advances. His cynical friend Julien (S. Mérante) then suggests taking the bold step of abducting her. Meanwhile, an old flame, the coquettish Gemmie (Marinette), annoyed at being cast off, decides to teach Alphonse a lesson. Now the reason for Claire's resistance is revealed: she has a sweetheart, Mectal (Albert). Alphonse, learning to his dismay that she is to be married the next day, returns to resume his unwelcome attentions. By chance Edmée again crosses his path. He cannot resist the opportunity of making a new conquest, and she is on the point of yielding when Gemmie comes to her rescue by crying out a word of warning.

Incorrigible, Alphonse has not abandoned his pursuit of Claire, who most firmly rejects him. Julien now presses him to abduct her, and the two concoct a plot, which is overheard by Farmer Edmond's farm-boy, Guillaume (Ferdinand). By pretending to offer help, Guillaume is taken into their confidence and warns his master what is going on. Farmer Edmond decides that the plot must be nipped in the bud, and that Claire and Mectal must be married at once. Meanwhile Alphonse, who is lying in wait with some of his cronies, is discovered by Edmée and Gemmie, who keep him occupied by their chatter until the wedding procession emerges from the farmhouse. Realising he has been outwitted, Alphonse can do no more than accept defeat with good grace.

Some critics overlooked the triviality of this plot, but it was abundantly clear that Bigottini's genius for characterisation was quite wasted in the

[1] Arch. Nat., AJ[13] 125. Aumer to Persuis, 15 October 1817; 22 July and 1 September 1818.

part of Claire. However, the composition of the dances won general approval. Albert himself was deservedly acclaimed for his part in them, but he left one critic thinking he had more ideas in his legs than in his head.[2]

Both scenery and music met with approval: Ciceri's Swiss scene was praised as appropriately 'romantic', and Schneitzhoeffer's score, with its references to Swiss folksongs, was 'as pleasing as that of *Proserpine*, and easier on the ear'.[3] Furthermore, the composer had obliged certain critics of the earlier score by incorporating, as the scenario directed, two *airs parlants*: the song *Blondinette joliette, de l'amour crains la douce loi* to accompany Gemmie's warning shout to Edmée, and the air *Ecoute-moi, je t'en supplie* from Dalayrac's *opéra-comique, Picaros et Diego*, that added emphasis to Alphonse's fervent appeal to Claire to listen to his blandishments.

Unmemorable though it was, *Le Séducteur du village* enjoyed a short-lived popularity after being reduced from two acts to one. The spirited dances that Albert had created for it moved one critic to observe that danseuses' skirts seemed to be becoming shorter and that the flesh-coloured pantaloons worn beneath them increasingly close-fitting.[4] This was a revealing observation in more ways than one, for of late there had been a noticeable trend towards purely technical achievement in Coulon's perfection class. Only the year before, Gardel had voiced his disapproval when, attending the examination of the pupils, he had been shocked to see them performing difficult steps that he felt were beyond their capabilities. To his mind such displays of strength and technical difficulty turned the examination into a sort of contest, making it difficult for an examiner to judge the pupils' qualities and to reach a fair assessment of their promise. In his report, he had suggested that Coulon should concentrate more on placement and turning, *pointe* work, a good turn-out, stretching the knees and seeing that 'the movements of the head, arms and body are constantly in perfect harmony with the steps of the legs, however difficult'.[5]

* * *

Within a few days of Albert's merry and inconsequential little ballet, a shadow passed over the Opéra. Word was circulating that Geneviève Gosselin, the white hope of French ballet, had died at her country home at Charenton-Saint-Maurice, on the outskirts of Paris.

[2] *Quotidienne*, 5 June 1818.
[3] Martainville in *Gazette de France*, 5 June 1818.
[4] *Almanach des spectacles*, second year, 59–60.
[5] Arch. Nat., AJ^{13} 110.

More than three years had passed since exhaustion had caused her to interrupt her career just when she had appeared in her first important creation, the rôle of Flora. After a few performances in *Flore et Zéphire* her strength had begun to fail, and she was ordered to rest. The Opéra had never lost hope that she might recover to develop her extraordinary talent. It was at first thought that she had merely overtaxed her strength. She was kept on the company roll for as long as possible, but after a year the seriousness of her condition had to be faced and she was retired at the end of June 1817. A few months later, Gardel and Milon gloomily reported: 'Mlle Gosselin is not in a fit state to perform her duties, and [we] fear that the pain she is suffering will prevent her from doing so for a long time.'[6] Even then hopes were not abandoned that through some miracle she might recover; to give her encouragement, the Opéra assured her that if she were able to resume her career at the beginning of 1819, the period of her absence would be ignored for the purposes of her pension entitlement and that meanwhile she would be retained on the company's strength in an honorary capacity.[7] But in reality there could be no hope, for there was then no known cure for the tuberculosis that was ravaging her lungs.[8]

It must have been hard for those who had loved and cared for her during her illness to recognise in the still and wasted body the vital young dancer with the build and strength of a young athlete and the lightness of a doe, who possessed such harmony and control of movement and such astonishing physical accomplishments to have sent the most hardened connoisseurs into ecstasy. What hopes and aspirations had been destroyed by the cruel rupture of a career at the very moment of its flowering!

Aside from her brilliant promise as a dancer, she was to be remembered for her virtue, in an age when society regarded dancers little higher than courtesans – although she doubtless had had to guard her honour against proposals that were made to all in her profession by men of fashion and privilege, haunting the theatre in search of mistresses.

One of these, M. Puységur, a former emigré in the service of the King, had assiduously courted her in the days after Napoleon's fall. But she had resisted this vain, elderly peacock, who dressed so bizarrely like an *incroyable* of old and chattered away about little else than beauty and the latest gossip. He proved to be harmless enough, even if he liked to boast at

[6] Arch. Nat., AJ[13] 111 (VIII). Gardel and Milon to Persuis, 14 September 1817.
[7] Arch. Nat., O[3] 1648.
[8] The assertion that she had died in childbirth, made by Nérée-Desarbres in his *Deux Siècles de l'Opéra* (Paris, 1868), is without foundation.

dinner parties that he had had an affair with her and that she had jilted him for a singer.[9]

Her husband, whom she married in 1815, was no ordinary singer. Jean-Blaise Martin, a man about thirty years her senior, was a theatrical celebrity in his own right. As the leading singer of the Opéra-Comique, he possessed such a distinctive voice, extending over three octaves and covering both a tenor's and a baritone's compass, that it was to be given a category of its own, which has been known ever since as '*bariton Martin*'. Nor was he admired simply as a virtuoso; he had studied acting under Talma and Mme Dugazon, and by the combination of his dramatic and musical gifts he had established a reputation unequalled in his particular sphere.

Theirs was a marriage bonded by love of music, for Geneviève had been reared in a family whose fortunes depended on her father's skill as a luthier. The marriage had also opened up another dimension, for there was the prospect that, under her husband's guidance, she might develop a gift of interpretation that would add the laurels of a mime to those she had gained through her unique gifts as a dancer. But this was never to be put to the test. Flora, her only important rôle, had given her little opportunity to show her acting skill.

When she died, three and a half years had passed since she had last danced on the stage. Memories of her had already begun to fade, and other dancers had come to the fore in her place. Her death received only brief mentions in the press; there were no considered obituary notices. Her name would surface a decade later on the Paris début of another extraordinary dancer, Marie Taglioni; but in the meantime it sank into near oblivion, commemorated only by a moving epitaph published in an ephemeral theatrical almanac:

Pleurez, nymphes légères,
Dont les pas charment l'oeil!
Pleurez, jeunes bergères,
Therpsichore est en deuil.
Son élève chérie,
Dans l'âge des amours,
A la parque ennemie
Abandonne ses jours:
Aux arts elle est ravie
Malgré tous les secours;

[9] Granville, I, 101.

Malgré nos voeux pour elle,
Atropos qui l'appelle,
Rend nos soins superflus;
Rien n'émeut la cruelle,
Et Gosselin n'est plus.[10]

* * *

Gardel was now punctiliously engaged in meeting his obligation to Persuis by preparing his second promised creation for 1818. For this he had saved himself considerable trouble by resurrecting an earlier project, which had lain in his files for at least five years.[11] This was a modest one-act *ballet de genre, La Servante justifiée*, which was put together that summer and given its first performance on 30 September. Its plot had a long genealogy, originating in a love tale in Marguerite d'Angoulême's *Heptaméron*. It had been borrowed first by La Fontaine, then by Favart for an *opéra-comique*, and more recently by the German dramatist Kotzebue for a short comedy presented in a French translation at the Variétés in 1807 under the title of *C'était moi*. It was this last piece that had been Gardel's immediate source, for that title had been his original choice for the ballet.

The story told of a wealthy and somewhat shameless young farmer, Mathurin (Albert), who has taken a fancy to the family servant, Alix (Bigottini). A busybody of a neighbour, the widow Cateau (Mme Courtin), witnesses what appears to be a compromising scene between the two of them, which ends by their hastily hiding at the approach of Mathurin's wife, Mathurine (Mme Anatole). The old gossip is all agog to spread the scandal, but no one is around to listen to her except the drum major of the village band, who cannot hear her through the blare of his musicians. She then decides to go into the nearby town, whither Mathurine has departed on some business. Fortunately for Mathurin, she misses his wife, who has returned by a different route before her. This gives Mathurin the time and opportunity to put things right. That he can

[10] Weep, light-footed nymphs,/ Whose very steps charm the eye!/ Weep, young shepherdesses,/ For Terpsichore is in mourning./ Her favourite pupil,/ Still in the flower of youth,/ To hostile Fate/ Has offered up her life:/ Snatched from the arts,/ Despite every attention:/ And our prayers notwithstanding,/ When Atropos summons her,/ All treatment is of no avail;/ The cruel one is not to be moved,/ And Gosselin is no more. *Almanach des spectacles*, second year, 59–60.

[11] Arch. Nat., AJ[13] 1024. A cast list gives the names of the dancers he had in mind for the leading parts as follows: Chevigny (who retired in 1813) as Mathurine, Vestris as Mathurin, Mlle Delisle as Alix, Mme Gardel as Cateau. Gardel's synopsis has the title *C'était moi*, and his early scenario (written in 1813 or earlier) was entitled *La Fête de Mathurine*.

do so is facilitated by the striking likeness between Mathurine and Alix, and by the fact that Mathurine has given Alix a dress similar to her own. So when his wife returns, Mathurin manages to arrange to repeat with her the earlier scene with Alix, which Cateau had witnessed. Thus, when Cateau returns and begins to tell her story, Mathurine innocently tells her that it was she, not Alix, who had been with Mathurin. Mathurin is thus let off the hook, and the ballet ends with a feast of dancing to celebrate his wife's birthday. Only Cateau is discontented, furious that a juicy titbit of scandal has eluded her.

The idea of showing the hero getting away with his dalliance with the maid might have been thought somewhat shocking to be offered to an audience containing a considerable proportion of ladies; but Gardel skilfully avoided this danger, helped not only by the absence of dialogue, but also by the device of playing the dalliance scenes behind a light gauze. This had the effect of distracting the audience's attention from Albert and Bigottini to Mme Courtin's very droll performance as the village gossip – though as a consequence of this gesture towards decency, the scene lost part of its point. Martainville, who was generally unimpressed by the ballet, found 'the erotic scene and its counterscene ... sketched with so little skill as to be rendered ineffective'.[12]

The dancers, however, did their best to bring the piece to life. The principal characters were, of course, in sure hands, and Milon presented a splendid cameo as the drum major that was particularly admired by military men. 'His swagger, saluting and manner of dancing were characteristic of his rank,' wrote Sauvo in *Le Moniteur*. 'It was a portrait by Horace Vernet to the life.'[13]

The ballet was thus largely saved by the dancers, and Martainville, for all his severity, conceded that it had not been a failure. Indeed, it was to retain a place in the repertory until 1826, but a revival five years later made it clear that it had by then outlived its time.

* * *

Three benefit performances – those of Beaupré, Gardel and Clotilde – following one another within a few months seemed to presage the end of an era in the unfolding story of French ballet. It might well have been said that all three beneficiaries were irreplaceable, but in the hard light of reality their contributions were already enshrined in the tradition of their art.

[12] *Gazette de France*, 2 October 1818.
[13] *Moniteur*, 2 October 1818.

At the age of sixty, Charles Beaupré was retiring after nearly thirty years of assiduous service during which he had established a reputation as a character dancer of rare insight and power. Gardel held him in such esteem that, a year before his retirement, in the hope of tempting him to remain a little longer, he recommended that a new grade should be introduced – that of *premier danseur bouffon*. This, he suggested, would 'reward (and I speak with the future in mind) a good *danseur sérieux*, if one should appear, or a true *comique* – a Dauberval, in fact, if good luck should send you one.'[14] But the suggestion went unheeded, and Beaupré was pensioned off at the end of 1818. At his benefit in December, he gave his admirers an idea of what they would lose on his retirement by acting in a comedy before being giving his last performance as Sancho Panza, the rôle he had created nearly two decades ago in Milon's *Noces de Gamache*, and in which he would be remembered for as long as the ballet lasted.

Gardel's benefit was a much more solemn affair, as might have befitted the farewell of the man who had been at the helm of the Opéra ballet through three decades of fair weather and foul, but in fact his retirement was to be deferred for a number of years yet. To pay due honour to his extraordinary achievement, the Comédie-Française and the Opéra joined forces. The evening opened with a performance of Racine's *Athalie* that was doubly remarkable in that Talma would be making his first appearance as the High Priest Joad, and because it would be performed with Gossec's seldom-heard choruses. Then followed the contribution of the ballet, for which Gardel had chosen not one of his great mythological works, but the joyful *Dansomanie*, in which there was a wonderful surprise – the reappearance, for this occasion only, of his wife and muse. For a fleeting few minutes, the connoisseurs relished, for the last time, Marie Gardel's 'inimitable grace, her *pas glissés* and her enticing lightness'[15] as she danced the *pas russe* with Ferdinand 'wickedly well ... as though wishing to chide the public for allowing her to retire so prematurely.'[16]

The other senior figure to bow out gracefully was Clotilde, the survivor of that little band of ballerinas who had burst upon Paris two decades before, in the early years of the Revolution. At her benefit in May, she too appeared as if time had stood still, playing Calypso in *Télémaque*.

The very elusiveness of her artistry, added to the fading memories of the manners of the Old Régime, would make it difficult for a successor to capture the essence of the *noble* style which she had received from the hands of the '*diou de la danse*' himself. Although Mme Anatole would

[14] Arch. Nat., AJ[13] 110 (I). Report by Gardel to Persuis, 18 June 1817.
[15] *Journal de Paris*, 10 March 1819.
[16] *Journal des débats*, 10 March 1819.

prove a competent successor in that genre, neither she nor anyone else would ever reproduce the majestic presence, the commanding dignity and the stately walk for which Clotilde had been renowned.

The eminent critic Geoffroy, who had been brought up and spent his early manhood under the Old Régime, had put his finger on the secret of Clotilde's magic when he explained that her style had been formed 'at a time when more attention was paid to the essentials of dancing and to the observance of rules which younger dancers are too inclined to sacrifice to their vaulting ambitions.'[17]

This magic had depended on an imposing presence that was to prove inimitable, and on conveying an image of the purest classical beauty that in real life she did not possess. To an honest admirer, who compared her stage persona 'in hunting attire with a knee-length skirt' to the celebrated statue of the goddess Diana in the Louvre, she was 'too tall and noticeably too thin, but so well formed and majestic that she appears beautiful, even though her features are not.'[18]

As always happens on the retirement of a great artiste, there was an elusive personal cachet that could never be handed on. But on Clotilde's departure another thread had snapped: the direct link with Gaétan Vestris. Her loss was thus doubly felt, and the images she left on the memories of her admirers were all the more keenly and nostalgically treasured. One such admirer was the great novelist Stendhal, who recollected how on several occasions – 'and what beautiful days they were for me!' – he had found himself in her dressing-room at the Opéra and had been privileged, a mere boy in the fourth class, 'to watch her dress and undress'.[19]

And another, writing in a new age when Taglioni and Elssler held sway in the ballet, could still call to mind a portrait as precise in its detail as if it had been composed in the heat of the actual experience, remembering Clotilde as

> a tall and beautiful dancer with a serious and voluptuous expression and a body as supple as a willow branch. At that time, people would call Mlle George a beautiful statue and Cl[otilde] a beautiful creature. Her blonde hair, like pure gold, crowned a broad forehead beneath which were set two sapphire-blue eyes. Her head was delicately balanced, like an egret's, on a long, elegant, proud neck. Connoisseurs from that time still speak of her with tears in their eyes, nostalgically

[17] *Journal de l'Empire*, 21 December 1812.
[18] Clary und Aldringen, 138, 252.
[19] Stendhal, 110.

> recalling a beauty long vanished and a certain indescribable motion of the hips that gave to Cl[otilde]'s entire body a quivering effect that was indescribably voluptuous. When she raised her arms and went into a *plié* in preparation for a pirouette, the manner in which she lifted her arms revealed all the curves of her bust, while the *plié* itself, which caused the hips of that delectable woman to protrude, was a sight for sore eyes![20]

She was not destined to enjoy a long and happy retirement, falling a victim to cancer and dying, after many months of pain, in 1826 at the age of fifty. So little then remained of the riches she had once enjoyed that the reported extent of her admirers' generosity might well be questioned. At her death her effects were valued at little more than 800 francs, while her annuity of 5400 francs from Pignatelli died with her. Boïeldieu, who had never divorced her, formally renounced his rights to the small inheritance so that it could be shared between her two daughters.

* * *

Amid such a glut of benefits, some might have wondered why one of the most eminent of veterans had apparently been overlooked. Somewhat unwillingly, Auguste Vestris had been retired after a dancing career of extraordinary length at the end of September 1816. It was a decision he had long dreaded, for he had been incapable of setting aside any savings for his old age; he had always spent his money as it came, and was ever short of ready cash. Overnight his salary of 10,000 francs was replaced by a pension of 4000 francs. His appointment as a teacher to take the second division of the perfection class went some way to alleviate his distress, but crises continued to arise, and on one occasion he was briefly imprisoned for debt before friends came to his rescue. In 1823 he married a young wife, who may have brought some order into his financial affairs. Private lessons helped too: his Danish pupil, August Bournonville, who had been recommended by Gardel, paid 60 francs a month for this privilege.

The delay in organising his benefit was due primarily to his inability to make the arrangements that were the beneficiary's responsibility. It was up to him to agree the date with the Opéra, as well as to select the programme and approach fellow artistes whom he hoped would donate their services. The delay would not have concerned the Opéra had he not been

[20] Vernières, 307.

advanced 5000 francs, to be deducted from the anticipated receipts. In 1821 Courtin was instructed to try to settle a date; if he was unable to stir the old dancer into action, he was to warn him that the Opéra might have to withhold the debt from his salary and pension.[21] Another five years were to pass before the benefit took place in 1826. Sadly, the delay had worked against his interests, for the proceeds – just marginally above 8750 francs – were little more than a quarter of what Gardel had netted eight years before.

Even Gardel had financial worries; only months after his highly successful benefit he was forced to petition the King for help. Many of his grievances applied equally to Vestris. Both had lost their royal emoluments in the first year of the Revolution, and both could grumble about the losses they had then suffered by their salaries being paid in assignats that had become virtually worthless – a poor reward for remaining at their posts when less loyal colleagues had been emigrating. To Gardel this seemed particularly hard when he had given forty-four years of service and 'in the disastrous course of the Revolution [had] sustained the Opéra on [his] own with [his] ballets'.[22] But these were ancient grievances. His present difficulties were the result not of extravagance, as the Opéra had thought, but of a long-drawn-out lawsuit and his son's education.[23]

Apart from the three benefit nights, 1819 had been an uneventful year. No new ballet had been given, and a revival of Duport's *Acis et Galathée* had been a failure. In the autumn a dying Persuis had resigned as Director, to be replaced by the violinist Viotti, but this change had little effect on day-to-day affairs. With every effort being concentrated on the new Spontini opera, *Olympie*, the ballet seemed to be vegetating: Aumer was not expected in Paris until the following June, and there seemed little in prospect to enliven the evenings of the connoisseurs. And so the New Year of 1820 dawned – waiting, it might be said, for Aumer, and unaware of the tragedy that lay ahead.

[21] Arch. Nat., AJ^{13} 111. Intendant to Courtin, 27 January 1821.

[22] Arch. Nat., O^{3} 1650.

[23] Bibl. de l'Arsenal, Ro. 9968. Auctioneer's précis of a letter from Gardel dated 11 October 1818. The reference to Henry-Pierre as the son in question poses a mystery, for he was then a serving soldier in his thirties. The précis may be at fault, for the reference would seem to make more sense if it had referred to his younger son Achille, who was then eighteen.

34

The Last Night

For the tragic finale that was to bring the history of the opera house in the Rue de Richelieu to its abrupt close, the focus shifted from the illusionary world of the stage to a crowded, stuffy and dimly lit salon behind one of the proscenium boxes. On the last Sunday of the 1820 Carnival, 13 February, the auditorium had filled with a chattering, laughing throng who had come to enjoy a jolly evening in the last few hours of revelry before Lent. Ballet was to be the major offering in a programme comprising a suitably short opera, *Le Rossignol*, and not one but two of the most entertaining comedy ballets the Opéra had on offer, *Le Carnaval de Venise* and *Les Noces de Gamache*.

Many eyes that evening must have turned to the box, prominently situated between the two proscenium pillars on the left of the stage, which belonged to that fervent supporter of the ballet, the Duc de Berry; but when the curtain rose on *Le Carnaval de Venise* it was still unoccupied, and remained so until the end of the first interval. As the curtain was about to rise for the opera, the Duke and his Duchess were alighting from their carriage at the side entrance in the Rue Rameau. During the second interval, they paid a visit to the box of the Duc d'Orléans, and as they were making their way back along the corridor, one of the box doors suddenly opened, striking the Duchess on her arm. For a reason that would become known before the night was out, the Duke seemed very concerned. Would the Duchess like to go back to the Elysée? he enquired; but no, she expressed the wish to see the last ballet.

During the brief interlude between the two acts of *Les Noces de Gamache*, the Duchess complained of feeling tired. It was decided that she would return home, leaving the Duke to see the rest of the performance. He accompanied her out of the box, and they made their way to where their carriage stood waiting. A footman lowered the steps and the Duke helped his wife into the carriage, murmuring a brief farewell before turning to go back into the theatre.

Just at that moment a man came running from the direction of the Rue de Richelieu, colliding first with the footman and then bumping into the

Duke's aide-de-camp who, taking him for a clumsy man in a hurry, shouted angrily: 'Hey, look where you're going!'

The Duke, who had his back to the stranger, found himself grasped by the right shoulder and felt a violent blow to the left side of his chest. To his horror his hand closed on the hilt of a knife protruding from his clothing. He realised at once what had happened, for the fear of an assassin could never have been far from the mind of the man on whom rested the future of the dynasty.

'I've been assassinated!' he cried. 'That man has killed me!'

Alarmed by the commotion, the Duchess pushed open the carriage door and was about to jump out when her lady-in-waiting grabbed hold of her dress. A footman came forward to help her, but ignoring the Duke's plea to stay where was, she broke free, leapt to the ground and ran to where he lay, supported by his equerry, his gentleman-in-waiting and the footmen. Between them they carried him back into the lobby and placed him on a bench. He was still conscious, but in great distress. As they were unbuttoning his jacket, he gasped: 'I'm done for! A priest, send for a priest! Come, my wife, let me die in your arms.'

He fumbled with the hilt of the knife as if trying to shift it, and with the help of the lady-in-waiting he managed to pull it out. As he fainted with the pain, the Duchess threw herself across his body, his blood flowing copiously on to her dress.

Meanwhile, the sentry and several members of the Opéra's guard had gone in pursuit of the assailant, who had fled towards the Rue de Richelieu. The chase ended in the Arcade Colbert, where a lad from a nearby café had the presence of mind to stand in his way and catch him in his arms. His pursuers were at his heels, and the man was promptly handed over to the sentry and brought back to the Opéra.

The Duke was carried up the stairs and into the private salon of his box, where he was gently placed in an armchair. He was having difficulty breathing. 'I'm suffocating! Give me some air,' he pleaded. To create a draught, the door leading to the box was opened, and suddenly the little room was filled with the festive music and applause as the ballet drew to a close. In the desperation of the moment, no one seemed conscious of this bizarre accompaniment to the desperate struggle to save a life.

By now the Duke had regained consciousness, and was told that his attacker, who was then being interrogated in a nearby room, had been caught. The Duke seemed concerned to know whether he was a foreigner; on being told that he was not, he groaned and remarked: 'It is too cruel to have to die at the hand of a Frenchman!'

No time had been lost seeking medical assistance, although neither of the two honorary surgeons usually on duty could be found. A young surgeon named Drogard was first on the scene, and was soon followed by others. A Dr Blancheton, who lived nearby, took charge, cleaning the wound and, ignoring the Duke's objections that any assistance was useless in his plight, having him bled in his right arm. Blancheton tried to reassure him that the wound was not deep, but the Duke, having tried himself to pull out the six-inch dagger which had been driven into his chest up to the hilt, knew better. A little later two more medical men arrived, Bougon and Lacroix, sent by the Duke's father, Monsieur. Bougon now bent down to suck the wound to release more blood, ignoring the Duke's anxiety that the blade might have been poisoned.

The small room was now filling rapidly. As well as the doctors, the Duc d'Orléans had appeared, and in the background were the Roullets, a couple who were among the most useful of those present, undertaking errands and performing all sorts of other services as the night wore on. It had been Roullet, the Opéra's publisher and keeper of the bookstall in the Foyer where programmes could be bought, who had first gone in search of a doctor. His wife, the box-keeper in charge of the King's box, acted as a sort of nurse in attendance, for whom no task was too menial – cutting the Duke's clothing to reveal the wound, helping to move him, and producing a little pharmacy chest containing vinegar to bathe his forehead and orange blossom for a sweet drink to quench his thirst. She seemed quite indefatigable in spite of being partly crippled,[1] and was the unsung heroine of that dreadful night.

There was a great stir when the Bishop of Chartres appeared to take the dying man's confession. He found the Duke being prepared for another bleeding, with the Duchess protesting volubly at such unnecessary cruelty. 'I am here, Monseigneur,' this cleric announced, seating himself importantly at the bedside as the doctors went on with their work to locate a vein. Now the urgency was to find a ligature. The Duchess and her lady-in-waiting offered their garters, but these, being elastic, were of no use, and it was the Duchess's belt that eventually served the desired purpose. By now the Duke was beginning to lose consciousness, seeming unable to distinguish his wife from all the faces looking down at him.

As the room was becoming unbearably crowded, the doctors enquired whether another room was available. By chance the salon connected with the offices of the administration, where Courtin, the administrator,

[1] Roullet used to trundle her himself to and from the Opéra in a wheelchair, which he would attach to a column in the Arcade Colbert. The journey from their home on the Left Bank took the best part of an hour.

was still on duty. In no time a room was tidied up and a trestle-bed belonging to the Secretary-General, Grandsire, was made up for the Duke, who was carefully carried in and placed on it.

More members of the royal family were now turning up. First to arrive was the Duke's brother, Angoulême, who was to kneel by the bedside for the rest of the night; and shortly after him his father was announced. The Duke seemed obsessed with thoughts of his assailant. 'What did I do to that man?' he asked in bewilderment. 'Might it be someone I unwittingly offended?' 'No, no,' his father assured him, having perhaps received a report of Louvel's interrogation. 'You never offended that man, he had no personal hatred towards you.' 'It was a madman then?' the Duke replied before enquiring when the King would be coming. 'I may not have time to ask for the man to be pardoned.'

At this point, as if there were not already enough doctors around, the celebrated Dupuytren, consultant surgeon to the King, came to examine the wound and give a pronouncement. Gathering the other doctors around him, he held a whispered consultation, at the end of which he announced that the wound would have to be enlarged, as that was the only way of emptying the chest of blood. Asked where he felt the greatest pain, the Duke seemed at first not to understand, but when the Duchess repeated the question, he placed her hand on his chest. 'There?' she asked. 'Yes,' he replied, 'I'm suffocating.'

Monsieur wanted his daughter-in-law to leave while the painful operation was carried out. 'My father,' she retorted, 'do not force me to disobey you.' Then, turning to the doctors, she added: 'Gentlemen, do your duty.' She remained holding his hand as the knife went into the wound, and it was at this moment that the dying man was heard to say to her: 'My friend, do not let yourself be overwhelmed by sorrow. Take care of the child you are bearing.' A murmur arose from those within earshot, for these were words of hope, being the first indication that she was pregnant and that there was a chance of a male heir.

The exploration of the wound revealed no more than that it was mortal, and now suddenly, in a loud voice that everyone could hear, the Duke began to confess his sins and to call out for his natural daughters.

'Charles, dear Charles,' his wife pleaded, 'calm yourself. I shall take care of them as if they were my own.'

He then turned to his brother. 'I am sorry for the sorrow I have caused you by our little disagreements,' he said. 'Look after my family. Promise me you will not let them be forgotten.'

After a short while two shy little girls, dressed in yellow cashmere overcoats, were noticed at the back of the room. They were the Duke's two daughters, Charlotte and Louise, whom he had fathered during his exile in England. The royal family knew of their existence, and they were established quite openly in Paris. The little girls came forward to the bedside, and the Duke spoke to them in English. It was an affecting moment. The Duchess took them into her arms, and, turning to her own baby daughter, invited them to kiss their little sister.

The Duke then motioned his brother to lower his head, whispering a few words in his ear that no one else could hear. What was then said was never divulged, but it was generally believed to be a request to look after another child of his: Charles, his two-year-old son by Virginie Oreille.

The Curé of Saint-Roch had meanwhile arrived with the sacraments, having made his way from his church on foot through a crowd of masked revellers returning from balls and other amusements of the town. After the Sacrament had been administered, the doctors still persevered. The atmosphere was oppressive, and at the sight of so many people crowded around his bed, the Duke despairingly remarked: 'What a lot of useless people there are shut up in this place!'

The patient was now bled a second time. It was then found that there were no more vases to take away the slops. Mme Roullet again obliged, exploring the building in search of a drain. Finding none, she took the last expedient of emptying the contents of her basin out of the window with a warning cry of '*Gare l'eau*'. The dirty water cascaded on to the roof of the Duke's carriage, some of it splattering on to the patient coachman's cloak.

The arrival of the old King at five o'clock was a moment that all who witnessed it would remember. He was carried into the room where his nephew lay and, after being helped out of his portable chair, hobbled to the bedside. By now the Duke's spirits were very low, and little strength was left in him. Still obsessed by the fate of his assailant, his first words to his uncle were a plea for his pardon.

'Nephew,' replied the King, 'you will, I hope, survive this dreadful event. So let us speak of that later. The matter is an important one, and has to be investigated.'

The King gestured to Dupuytren and, discreetly whispering in Latin, enquired about his nephew's condition. He was told there was no hope, no hope at all. It was clear that the end was nigh. As if sensing this, the Duchess at last broke down. She was led into the next room, but soon recovered her composure and returned at the moment when, at his request, the Duke was being eased round to face the wall.

Dupuytren suggested to the King that he might wish to be spared the painful moment that was approaching.

'I have no fear of the sight of death,' the King told him. 'And I still have a duty to perform for my nephew.'

When death came, the Duchess could not at first take it in. Dupuytren had to hold the mirror of the King's snuff box to the dead man's mouth and show her that it was unclouded. Then, supported by the eminent surgeon, the King leant over the body and closed his nephew's eyes.[2]

So passed the Duc de Berry, not on a battlefield as in his unfulfilled dreams he might have hoped, but at the scene, one might say, of many of his conquests, and on a trestle-bed belonging to the Secretary-General of the Opéra, Grandsire. By a curious coincidence this bed had served the Duke once before in much happier circumstances. Grandsire had been in Cherbourg at the time of the Duke's landing there following Napoleon's first abdication in 1814, and when it was discovered that all the beds in the Prefecture had been taken up, he had been honoured to lend his own for the use of the prince who was returning from his long exile.[3]

It was commonly believed among those in the know that the Duke's fatal decision not to accompany the Duchess home that evening was made because he was expecting one of the danseuses in the last act of *Les Noces de Gamache* to give him a prearranged sign that she would come to him after the ballet. It was later rumoured that Virginie was the object of his desire that evening, and a touching but apocryphal image arose that during his long agony a young woman in ballet costume was seen to slip into the room and fall to her knees weeping by his bedside, and had to be spirited away. But in fact Virginie had retired from the ballet four years before. If this rumour had any foundation, which is doubtful, it was more likely that the Duke had been seeking tenderer flesh, possibly the sixteen-year-old Amélie Legallois, whose relationship with the Duke was disclosed eleven years later by a London scandal-sheet.[4]

For several years Virginie had been set up by the Duke in a comfortable establishment near the Madeleine, where he had continued to visit her. At the time of his death, she was pregnant by him again, and would bear him a second son, Ferdinand, the following October – just eleven days after the Duchesse de Berry was delivered of the baby prince known to history as the Comte de Chambord. It must have been the birth of Virginie's second child that inspired a poetaster to compose the following verse, which was gleefully passed around Paris that winter:

[2] This description is based mainly upon two contemporary accounts, the official story as told by Chateaubriand and the curious, rambling memoir of Pierre-Nicolas Roullet. The latter work was suppressed, nearly every copy being seized and destroyed, but a few copies escaped the net, including the one now in the Bibliothèque Nationale; it was reprinted in 1861.

[3] Grandsire's letter was printed in the *Journal des débats* of 17 February 1820.

[4] *Satirist*, 31 July and 7 August 1831.

Le bon Duc fut des plus féconds.
Il était pour la bagatelle:
C'était là son unique fonds.
Le Cour s'en formalisa-t-elle,
Quand vint ce petit prince-là?
'Pour le coup, voilà la merveille,
Dit Louis Dix-huit à Du Cayla:
Nos enfants sont faits par l'Oreille!'[5]

Virginie was to survive her royal lover by more than half a century, dying in October 1875 at the age of eighty. The Duc d'Angoulême apparently honoured his promise, for the two boys were ennobled by Louis XVIII and granted the right to expand their plebeian name into 'Oreille de Carrière'. Charles, who was the elder, became a soldier, serving briefly in the Austro-Hungarian army, and predeceased his mother, dying in 1856; one of his sons, Charles-Casimir Oreille de Carrière, followed in his grandmother's footsteps by choosing a theatrical career, becoming an opera singer of modest renown. Ferdinand, Virginie's second son, briefly outlived his mother, but left no offspring.

The other principal player in the drama of 13 February 1820 – the assassin, Pierre-Joseph Louvel – had been taken to the Conciergerie after his preliminary interrogation at the Opéra. He maintained to the very end that he had no accomplice and had received no payment to carry out his crime. He was driven by a consuming obsession to rid France of the Bourbons. Formally tried by the Court of Peers in June, he was inevitably found guilty, and guillotined the following morning on the Place de Grève.

To the Comtesse de Boigne, writing many years after the event, there seemed something inevitable, not to say appropriate in a curious way, in the Duc de Berry's end:

> It is impossible to believe that that savage Louvel, who had for a long time been hunting down the Prince, would not have found another opportunity to strike. The Duc de Berry's irregular way of life led him almost daily, and without an escort, to places where it would seem much easier to locate him.

[5] The Duke was one of the most fertile of men./ Devoted to the sport of philandering,/ Which for him was the sole interest in life./ And was the Court surprised/ When that little prince came along?/ 'This time it's really a miracle,'/ Said Louis Eighteen to Du Cayla:/ 'Our children come out through the ear [Oreille].' *Intermédiaire*, XLVI (10 December 1902), 850. The Comtesse du Cayla was Louis XVIII's platonic companion in his last years. Their relationship became known in the latter half of 1820.

> If a similar catastrophe had happened at a danseuse's front door, at the moment when he was getting out of his cabriolet, it would have had a very different effect on the public than the image of him falling into the arms of his young wife, all splattered with his blood, in a place where he was surrounded by all the proprieties of his rank. In this respect there was something providential in such a great misfortune.[6]

Another victim of the assassination was the theatre that had provided the setting. The Archbishop of Paris had insisted – as a precondition, it was believed, of allowing the Sacrament to be given in such ungodly surroundings – that the building would be used no more as a theatre. Indeed, not another performance was given on its stage; the decision was taken to demolish it and erect in its place an expiatory chapel to the memory of the Duke. The demolition gang soon set to work, preserving as much as possible to incorporate in a new theatre to be built elsewhere. The site eventually chosen was on the Rue Le Peletier, stretching back to incorporate the Hôtel de Choiseul on the Rue Drouot, which would provide room for much-needed administrative offices. Originally envisaged only as a temporary home, it was to prove more durable than its two predecessors, serving with distinction until it was burnt down in 1873. As for the site of the previous house, the expiatory chapel was never built, and after the Revolution of 1830 it was laid out into the charming little square, with its Visconti fountain, that today faces the entrance to the Bibliothèque Nationale.

*   *   *

The combination of the abrupt closing of the theatre, Gardel's semi-retirement, and the imminent arrival of a new ballet-master were to mark the opening of a new era in the evolution of French ballet. Generally, the progress of artistic evolution cannot, like the reigns of kings, be precisely divided into periods, but here for once a boundary line could be firmly fixed. Although the day-to-day activity continued smoothly on its way, changes were in process that would transform the ballet by giving it a new aesthetic – a development that would come about imperceptibly but inexorably through the evolution of artistic attitudes and public taste, and to which the term Romanticism would be attached. Only when the time was ripe to survey this evolution in proper perspective and make historical sense of it would an assessment of ballet's progression become

[6] Boigne, 30.

possible. It then became clear that 1820 was indeed a watershed, marking a division that went far beyond the accidental consequence that a theatre had to be sacrificially demolished.

Although still at its early, formative, stage, a radical shift in tastes and attitudes was already under way. The end of the Napoleonic adventure had made pompous productions inspired by the mythology or history of the classical past no longer politically relevant. At the same time the stratification of the Opéra's public was changing, with an increasing proportion coming from families of the *haute bourgeoisie* and the nouveaux riches, who were less constrained by tradition than the privileged classes of old. But the most potent influence for change was to be the new directions being taken by writers and artists of the younger generation who were beginning to probe sources previously untapped for their inspiration. Soon every art would be affected by this trend, and in the years ahead much heat would be expended in what became fundamentally a generation clash between a conservative, backward-looking element supporting the tenets of what they called Classicism and a swelling band of ardent young iconoclasts who would gather under the banner of Romanticism.

In 1820 the age over which Gardel had presided in the field of ballet for forty years – a period unsurpassed for its length and the spread of French dominance – was about to pass into history. And history has so far not been kind. The impact of the Romantic ballet was such that it cast into the shadows what had gone before. But that earlier flowering, and a flowering it truly was at its apogee, is important not only for the understanding of what came after, but for its own very considerable achievements. Moreover, ballet in Paris had for the first time become accepted as an equal partner with the opera – indeed, as we have seen, at times a predominant partner.

35

Farewell to the Master

The Archbishop's demand that the theatre in the Rue de Richelieu should no longer be used as a place of entertainment caused a hiatus in the Opéra's activities. Whether or not Gardel's retirement was being mooted at this time, for him this sudden break coincided with an unwelcome reduction of his responsibilities. Although the Opéra's willingness to retain him as first ballet-master for a further seven years with no reduction of salary was to bring him much-needed financial relief, the curtailment of his duties in that he would produce no more ballets apart from those incidental to operas was a most bitter blow to his self-esteem. Of course, whenever one of his ballets was revived, he would be placed in charge, but his hopes of adding to his canon were to remain unfulfilled. Of no avail was his reworking of his ballet *Méléagre et Atalante*, which was favourably considered for production in 1823, only to be again discarded; and an amusing piece of whimsy called *Le Bal masqué*, in which Lise Noblet and Pauline Montessu come to the ball dressed as Camargo and Sallé, did not reach fruition either.

Although he had laurels enough to rest upon, this demotion, as he saw it, remained a nagging wound. In an attempt to seek a less hurtful explanation for his exclusion than failing powers of invention, he looked back to the days under Napoleon when his star was at its zenith, and tried to convince himself that his misfortune was due to being politically out of favour with the restored Bourbon régime. Being by nature undemonstrative and aloof, he kept his feelings very much to himself, although young August Bournonville, when he frequented the ballet-master's home in the 1820s, sensed the underlying depression and bitterness that was eating into the old man's soul.

By then Gardel had visibly aged. 'He was already an old man when I became acquainted with him,' wrote Bournonville, 'and very different in appearance from those portraits that show him as a young man dressed in the extravagant attire of the Republic, with a powdered wig and flowing shirt frills. He now wore a dark brown wig, and with the passing of time his hooked nose had turned to a bright red, giving him an expression that was more supercilious than ever. His imperturbable aloofness was just as I heard it described in earlier times, although it did not preclude cordiality and humour in daily intercourse. But when on duty in the theatre, it was often so chilling that it could make the boldest foot shake. Consequently, he was far more respected than popular with the company.'[1]

Between the proud old master and his protégé there developed a warm affection. In his letters home Bournonville frequently wrote of Gardel's kindness, telling how he had been honoured with an invitation to accompany him to the Opéra in his carriage, and on another occasion been trusted with the loan of several violin-concerto scores. It had been his hope that Gardel, who had been his father's teacher, might take him on too as a pupil; but the ballet-master explained that his dance studio had been dismantled, recommending him instead to Auguste Vestris – an inspired referral, as it would turn out. A few months later, Gardel expressed the wish to see young Bournonville dance, and for this critical test Vestris taught his young pupil one of the master's own *pas* – that which Vestris himself had danced in *Persée*. Not surprisingly, Bournonville found it 'very difficult'.[2]

Being perceived as Gardel's protégé opened many doors, but nowhere did Bournonville meet a warmer welcome than in the home of the master himself. There Bournonville came to know the Gardels well; but the account of Gardel that he left in his memoirs is frustratingly cursory. He referred to Gardel's 'uncommonly fine education (in comparison with that of his contemporary colleagues)' and his exceptional gifts as a musician, but the man himself barely comes to life in his pages. Was Bournonville shy of penetrating the reserve of a man he described as by nature cold and ostensibly phlegmatic, or was he being circumspect? We shall never know.

However, Bournonville did afford a glimpse into the intimacy of the Gardel home, where he became acquainted with a number of celebrated figures of the time. Presiding over this select company was she whom Bournonville called 'the treasure of the household': Marie Gardel, still sylphlike of figure, her lightness and grace untouched by the passing of time. Bournonville recalled:

> Just as she had once enraptured the public by her graceful and perfect dancing, so, too, she now knew how to diffuse about her an atmos-

[1] Bournonville, *Theatre Life*, 453.
[2] Bournonville, *Lettres*, I, 31.

phere of comfort and pleasure, and many a time by an encouraging word inspired the young dancer to risk the ultimate effort. Just such a compliment from her lips gave me, too, a strong incentive to pass with success the examination required in order to obtain a début. I know of no honour that has so lifted my spirits as when the jury, '*à l'unanimité*', declared me worthy to perform at the Théâtre de l'Académie Royale de Musique, and when Gardel, speaking on behalf of the administration, offered me an engagement as soloist with Europe's most renowned ballet![3]

Bournonville was too young to have seen Gardel's ballets in their pristine condition, with the exception of the last, *La Servante justifiée.* When he had first come to Paris with his father in 1820, he missed few performances at the Opéra, seeing also *Le Jugement de Pâris* (this no less than eight times), *La Dansomanie* and *Paul et Virginie*; but since performances were then being given in the restricted surroundings of the Théâtre Favart, he was not seeing them in their full splendour. When he returned to Paris five years later, the Gardel repertory had further diminished, and such ballets as had survived had probably lost a little more of their original polish. It is in this context that Bournonville's comments on Gardel's ballets have to be understood. While allowing that *Télémaque*, *Pâris*, *Psyché*, *La Dansomanie*, *L'Enfant prodigue* and *Proserpine* (incidentally, not all of which he had seen) were 'original creations and marked an epoch in the higher genre of ballet', he gave it as his opinion that Gardel 'did not possess true genius but had an infinite amount of taste and experience'.[4] Nevertheless, he conceded that such Gardel ballets as he had seen 'bore the stamp of perfection', even if for dramatic effect Milon moved him more in *Nina* and *Clari* (a ballet created in 1820).

During these final years of Gardel's career, Bournonville frequently observed him at work, rehearsing *divertissements* for operas, and was immensely impressed. 'No one,' he wrote, 'was able to rival him in the scenic arrangement of grand operas, wherein dancing and magnificent pageantry played an important rôle ... One did not know what to admire most: his inexhaustible wealth of invention or the well-calculated use of time and energies at his excellent rehearsals.'[5]

Certainly the old master still had much to offer, and between 1820 and his retirement in 1827, Gardel contributed to the production of no fewer than fifteen new operas, culminating with two important works – *Le Siège*

[3] Bournonville, *Theatre Life*, 453.
[4] Bournonville, *Theatre Life*, 19.
[5] Bournonville, *Theatre Life*, 452.

de Corinthe and *Moïse* – by the new musical genius who had risen in the operatic firmament, Rossini.

On 23 February 1829, little more than eighteen months after his retirement, Gardel was given the honour of a benefit, for which he revived his most celebrated ballet, *Psyché*. Preceding it, the soprano Maria Malibran had donated her services in an act from Guglielmi's opera *Romeo e Giulietta*, before hurrying into the auditorium to applaud the ballet from a centre box. In the thirty-six years since its creation, *Psyché* had accumulated more performances than any other ballet at the Opéra; this would be its 560th but, sadly, the last.[6] Specially for the occasion he had prepared the sensational young ballerina Marie Taglioni in the title rôle, which was still identified with his wife in the memories of older habitués. Although the ballet was showing its age, Taglioni made a strong impression in the famous dancing-lesson scene, in which she was paired with the experienced Mme Anatole as Terpsichore. However, the effect of this interesting revival was blunted by a mechanical hitch, when the *gloire* that was to carry Jupiter, Venus, Cupid and Psyche to Mount Olympus failed to take off, leaving those abashed immortals having to 'take a short cut into the wings' to a burst of ironic applause.[7] Despite this mishap, however, the evening served its purpose, leaving Gardel with a welcome windfall of 22,550 francs.

Sadly, Gardel's retirement was to be clouded by bereavement and ill health. A few months before his benefit he had lost his only sister, Agathe, whose passing had come as a stabbing reminder of his own mortality. 'Having been subjected over the last two years to all the blows that my unfortunate fate held in store for me,' he wrote to a friend, 'I have now just received the most painful one of all.'[8]

Not long afterwards, his health, which until then had been quite robust, began to deteriorate. In the first winter of his retirement he was laid low for several weeks with a bout of pneumonia. A few years later, his doctors diagnosed a gallstone in his bladder, for which the only cure was an operation to crush it so that it could be washed out of his system – performed without anaesthetic. He had already undergone four such operations when, in May 1833, his wife, who was caring for him with the utmost devotion, suddenly collapsed and almost instantly died. Within days of this brutal bereavement he had to endure yet another operation; and there is no knowing whether that was the last. As the years passed, it would become clear that he was too frail to live on his own, and he then

[6] Up to the present time, only two other ballets, *Coppélia* and *Giselle*, have passed this record.
[7] *Figaro*, 27 February 1829.
[8] Maurice, I, 410.

gave up his apartment at 58 Rue de Clichy to be cared for by his daughter Rose and her husband Stéphan Crétu[9] in the area of Montmartre, then still in the countryside, known as 'the village of Orsel'.

In 1837 he received another bitter blow. His son by Anne-Jacqueline Coulon, Henry-Pierre, the veteran of the retreat from Moscow, died at the age of fifty of a lung complaint. As the first-born, Henry-Pierre must have been a son of whom his father was especially proud. In the course of a military career of some distinction, he had endured his fair share of combat. As a sub-lieutenant in the mounted Chasseurs of the Imperial Guard, he had fought in Spain, receiving a savage cut in the face from an English sabre in the battle of Beneventa. Bearing this honourable scar, he had been promoted to full lieutenant in time to accompany the Grand Army into Russia. Captured at Mohilev during the terrible retreat, he had returned to take part in the campaign of France. At the Restoration he transferred his loyalties to Louis XVIII, who appointed him a Chevalier of the Legion of Honour. By the time of his retirement, he had risen to the rank of Major.

Gardel had now lost both of the children whom Anne-Jacqueline Coulon had borne him, Henry-Pierre's sister, Anne-Charlotte, who had married the conductor Habeneck, having died in January 1817. But his second family by Marie Gardel, Rose and Achille, survived to surround him with the care and comfort he needed in his declining years; and it was in Rose's house, overlooking the city that had been the scene of his triumphs, that he slipped peacefully away on 9 November 1840, at the age of eighty-two. He was buried two days later in the Cemetery of Montmartre.[10]

* * *

Gardel undoubtedly died a disappointed man, for his ballets, the product of a lifetime of creation, had been swept aside to give place to a repertoire of a younger generation. They had fallen victim to the new vogue of Romanticism, which had given ballet a new aesthetic so potent that past achievements were all too readily overlooked in the excitement of the moment. To what extent Gardel was able to accept and understand this new trend may never be known, but there was really no need for him to

[9] Stéphan Crétu may have been the son of the actor, Anthelme Crétu, who was the associate of Mlle Montansier.

[10] The date of death, 18 October, given in encyclopaedias and other authorities, is incorrect. Gardel's grave no longer exists, the family having acquired a burial plot only for a term of years, which have long since expired.

despair. For without the cumulative legacy of the past, and specifically that of Gardel and the infrastructure laid down in his time, the sunburst of the Romantic ballet would not have been possible.

However, the disappearance of the repertory of Gardel and Milon was no more than the fate that lay in store for virtually every choreographer on his retirement. For there was then no accepted method of recording a ballet, nor was it the custom for a ballet-master to care for the works of a predecessor or even a colleague. Indeed, the very concept that a ballet could attain immortality as a classic was foreign.

Enough has been written in these pages to reveal the vast scope of Gardel's ballets, ranging from major works on classical themes that included his most daring achievement, *Achille à Scyros*, to the comedy of *La Dansomanie*, the sentiment of *Paul et Virginie* and his experiment with a biblical episode in *L'Enfant prodigue*. Together, they form an extraordinary output of stage presentations, but their scenarios also deserve attention on literary grounds, as texts. Before embarking on his dance career in Paris in the reign of Louis XV, their author had received a sound education in his native city, Nancy, grounded upon Latin and rhetoric. By his upbringing he was to remain, all his life, essentially a man of the Enlightenment, and this is abundantly revealed in his scenarios, which usually passed through a lengthy process of revision before he was satisfied by the clarity with which the motivations that underpinned the silent acting of his dancer-actors were explained.

With the ballets of his associate, Louis Milon, and the occasional offering by a younger choreographer, a repertory was maintained in the Gardel years that bears favourable comparison with that of the Romantic period that immediately followed. This is vividly illustrated by statistics that, while not being proffered as the only yardstick for comparison, at least dispel any illusion that the period preceding the Romantic era was a barren one in the field of ballet. Taking the 'Gardel years' as being from 1790, when he produced his first ballet, to 1819, and the 'Romantic era' as covering the years from 1820 to 1850, the figures are revealing. During the Gardel years a total of 40 new ballets were presented, against 46 in the Romantic era. Of the 40 new ballets in the Gardel years, 10 were performed more than 100 times; and of those, one ballet passed its 500th performance, one its 400th and another its 200th. Of the 46 new ballets in the Romantic era, only 7 were performed more than 100 times, of which *Giselle* alone can match the most frequently performed ballet of Gardel's. Another interesting point of comparison is in the aggregate number of ballets performed during the two periods; here the Gardel years show a higher total, 3251 performances as against 2341 in the Romantic era.

When Gardel died, nine years had passed since anyone had seen one of his ballets; and possibly too much of the detail of their choreography had been forgotten for them to be revived with any acceptable level of fidelity. However, not quite all had vanished, even if what has survived is precious little. Today, nearly two centuries on, there remain a few little nuggets that Gardel's colleague Léon Michel described in words in his teaching notebooks: a gavotte from *La Dansomanie*, a *pas* from *Psyché*, an '*air de début*' for Mlle Gosselin, and an extract from the ballet in *La Vestale*.[11]

The progress ballet had made under Gardel's rule was of great significance. In the course of forty years it had progressed from a charming, lightweight diversion to being accepted as a serious theatre art in its own right, capable of handling a wide variety of subject matter, and at moments even attaining a level of grandeur. Leading composers of the time such as Cherubini, Méhul, Catel and Steibelt had viewed ballet as not unworthy of their collaboration. Scene design, too, was playing an increasingly important part under the impulse of such artists as Degotti, Isabey and Ciceri.

But the most important advances had come in the area of dance technique. Although brought up in the *noble* style of the Old Régime, Gardel was wise enough to countenance the developments in style and technique that made their appearance during the Revolution and the First Empire. Prominent among these developments were pirouettes of ever increasing virtuosity, and a shift of the basic placing to the three-quarter *pointe*, which changed in a most fundamental way the whole style of the dancer's performance.

Writing in 1816, and looking back to the days of his youth, Jean-Etienne Despréaux, Guimard's husband and himself a trained dancer, mourned the disappearance of the style of his younger days:

> Dancing today bears no resemblance to what I myself saw from 1770 to 1790 or '92. The lower-class public in red bonnets who took over the pit and Nicolet's boulevard dancers who have been introduced on to the stage of the Opéra have made us forget the grace that gave the moving spectacle of the Opéra its gloss. Talent in dancing does not lie in knowing how to perform all kinds of steps in time to some rhythm or other ... Speed is only a slight advantage.

But dazzling *tours de force* were what the public increasingly wanted, and what Duport and Paul, with their eye-catching pirouettes and jumps,

[11] Bibl.-Mus. de l'Opéra, C2675 (1-3).

gave them. Their female counterparts were also drawn towards technical display. Guimard had danced in a *terre á terre* style that was always firmly based upon grace of movement; and, as her husband declared, 'disapproved of the present custom of raising the foot to the level of the hip'. Movements such as that, he went on, dislocated the body, were ungraceful, and were done only to astonish the pit.[12] Despréaux was not more specific, but it was possible he had in mind the astonishing ability of Geneviève Gosselin to perform what then appeared as marvels on the very tips of her toes – a feat, the future significance of which still lay concealed, that was to herald the vast extension of the ballerina's technique known collectively as '*pointe* work'.

The only area in the complex art of ballet in which a decline might have been observed was pantomime. This subject continued to be taught by Milon until his retirement in 1826, but although dancers must have been instructed in it in some fashion after that, it seems to have been somewhat haphazard. In Gardel's time the company had included several exceptionally gifted silent actors – Milon, Goyon, Elie, Branchu and Beaupré among the men, and Chevigny and Bigottini among the women – but during the Romantic period, the pantomime content of the ballets, which in Gardel's time had taken up a considerable proportion of performance time, would become less prominent. One reason for this was no doubt the diminishing relevance of pantomime on the popular stage, where theatres no longer needed to rely on silent acting to evade restrictions on their repertoires.

In Gardel's time ballet began to appeal to a broadening segment of the public. Emigration during the Revolution and men of new wealth had brought fresh blood into the audiences of the Opéra, while theatres such as the Porte-Saint-Martin and the Gaîté began to provide ballet with an alternative arena, appealing to a more popular public. Indeed, in the aftermath of the Revolution of 1830, the Porte-Saint-Martin would even provide the Opéra with three of the most eminent choreographers of the Romantic period, Jean Coralli, Joseph Mazilier and Jules Perrot.

Also, as its status grew in the broader context of the French theatre, ballet became increasingly a subject for critical appraisal. The specialised ballet critic would not appear until the next century, but as newspapers and journals began to proliferate and attract a progressively wider readership, more and more critics began to write about ballet. The most eminent critic of the Napoleonic period, Julien-Louis Geoffroy, whose essays on a broad range of subjects appeared in the *Journal des débats*, wrote

[12] Goncourt, *Guimard*, 249–50, quoting a letter from Despréaux dated 2 December 1816.

copiously on new operas and ballets. Other contributions were made by lesser, but no less informative, commentators: François Sauvo in the *Moniteur*, Jacques Salgues in the *Courrier de l'Europe*, Evariste Dumoulin in the *Constitutionnel* and Alphonse Martainville in the *Journal de Paris* – the last of whom had the honour of being introduced, sympathetically, in Balzac's great novel *Les Illusions perdus*. It is often through their descriptions that a paragraph, a sentence or even a phrase is to be discovered that enables the past to come alive in the reader's imagination nearly two centuries later.

Towering over the period, and fully deserving the right for it to be named after him, was Pierre Gardel. Few ballet-masters have bestridden the age in which they worked in more magisterial fashion than he. He became a legend in his lifetime, and something of his aura shines through the words of Charles Maurice in a recollection written shortly after the master's death:

> No director or author has ever enjoyed, as did Gardel in our own times, the respect that authority can impose on those who are submitted to it. There was a time when this celebrated ballet-master invariably came to rehearsal wearing a black suit, with his hair powdered and a sword by his side. At his approach artistes and dance pupils formed into two lines, between which the master choreographer passed like a king receiving tribute from his subjects. Today that would be considered ridiculous. But look what has happened to discipline.[13]

A tall story perhaps, but not too tall to leave us with an image of that somewhat remote figure, respected rather than loved, who steered French ballet so ably and so firmly through a most violent period in the nation's history and who brought that art to maturity. In company with Noverre, he is entitled to be considered as one of the founding fathers of the art to which he devoted his very existence.

[13] Maurice, I, 112.

Appendix A

Ballets created at the Paris Opéra, September 1793 – December 1819

A = act(s)
B = Ballet
BAn = Ballet anacréontique
BC = Ballet comique
BH = Ballet héroique
BP = Ballet pantomime
BPF = Ballet pantomime folie
BPH = Ballet pantomime historique
BV = Ballet vaudeville
D = Divertissement
DP = Divertissement pantomime
FP = Folie pantomime
s = scenes

Date of first performance at Opéra	*Title of ballet*	*Description*	*Choreographer*	*Composer*	*Scene designer*	*Costume designer*	*Principal dancers*	*A: Number of performances*	*B: Years in repertory*	*C: Average receipts over first 10 or fewer perfs*
								A	*B*	*C*
12 Dec. 1793	Les Muses, ou le Triomphe d' Amour	BAn, 1a	J.B. Hus	Ragué	Fontaine, Porfillion		Vestris; Miller, Saulnier, Clotilde	3	1793	
4 Dec. 1799	Héro et Léandre	BP, 1a	Milon	Lefebvre			Vestris; Gardel, Duport, Clotilde, Chevigny	26	1799 –1802	4017
14 June 1800	La Dansomanie	FP, 1a	Gardel	Méhul	Degotti	Berthélémy	Vestris, Goyon, Branchu, Gardel; Gardel, Clotilde	245	1800–26	5028
20 Aug. 1800	Pygmalion	BP, 2a	Milon	Lefebvre	Degotti		Vestris, Beaulieu, Duport; Gardel, Chameroy, Saulnier	18	1800–05	2872

Date of first performance at Opéra	*Title of ballet*	*Description*	*Choreographer*	*Composer*	*Scene designer*	*Costume designer*	*Principal dancers*	*A: Number of performances*	*B: Years in repertory*	*C: Average receipts over first 10 or fewer perfs*
								A	*B*	*C*
18 Jan. 1801	Les Noces de Gamache	BPH, 2a	Milon	Lefebvre	Degotti, Protain	Berthélémy	Aumer, Beaupré, Vestris; Chevigny, Chameroy	160	1801–41	4750
3 Mar. 1802	Le Retour de Zéphire, ou la Vallée de Tempé	B, 1a	Gardel	Steibelt			Deshayes; Gardel, Clotilde, Chevigny, Saulnier	108	1802–22	3545
14 Jan. 1803	Daphnis et Pandrose, ou la Vengeance de l' Amour	BP, 2a	Gardel	[Méhul]	Degotti, Protain		Vestris; Gardel, Clotilde, Aimée Vestris, Millière	6	1803	4540
2 June 1803	Lucas et Laurette	B, 1a	Milon	Lefebvre			Vestris, Goyon; Gardel, Chevigny	2	1803	2578
23 Oct. 1804	Une Demi-heure de caprice, ou Mélzi et Zénor	D, 1a	Gardel				Vestris; Gardel, Delisle	5	1804	3581

Date of first performance at Opéra	*Title of ballet*	*Description*	*Choreographer*	*Composer*	*Scene designer*	*Costume designer*	*Principal dancers*	*A: Number of performances B: Years in repertory C: Average receipts over first 10 or fewer perfs*		
								A	*B*	*C*
18 Dec. 1804	Achille à Scyros	BP, 3a	Gardel	Cherubini	Degotti, Protain, Moench	Berthélémy	Duport, Gardel, Milon; Gardel, V. Saulnier	65	1804–20	4760
10 May 1805	Acis et Galathée	BP, 1a	Duport	Darondeau, Gianella			Duport, Lefebvre; Duport, Chevigny	25	1805–19	5497
29 Oct. 1805	L' Amour à Cythère	BP, 2a	Henry	Gaveaux			Henry, St-Amand; Gardel, Millière, Collomb	9	1805–07	2165
30 May 1806	Figaro	BP, 3a, 4s	Duport				Duport, St-Amand, Hullin; Duport, Collomb	14	1806–07	4184
24 June 1806	Paul et Virginie	BP, 3a	Gardel	Kreutzer			St-Amand, Vestris; Gardel, M. & V(II). Saulnier, Bigottini	111	1806–28	3492

Date of first performance at Opéra	Title of ballet	Description	Choreographer	Composer	Scene designer	Costume designer	Principal dancers	A	B	C
								A: Number of performances B: Years in repertory C: Average receipts over first 10 or fewer perfs		
20 July 1806	L' Hymen de Zéphyre, ou le Volage fixé	D, 1a	Duport				Duport; Duport, Collomb, V. Hullin, Rosière	9	1806–08	3081
27 Feb. 1807	Le Retour d' Ulysse	BH, 3a	Milon	Persuis			Milon, St-Amand; Clotilde, Chevigny	20	1807–09	2247
8 Mar. 1808	Les Amours d' Antoine et de Cléopâtre	BH, 3a	Aumer	Kreutzer	Degotti, Isabey		Vestris; Chevigny, Clotilde	20	1808-14	4109
4 Oct. 1808	Vénus et Adonis	B, 1a	Gardel	Lefebvre			Vestris, Montjoie, Aumer; Clotilde	89	1808–21	3789
20 Dec. 1808	Alexandre chez Appelles	BH, 2a	Gardel	Catel	Degotti, Daguerre		Vestris, Aumer, Milon; Gardel	35	1808–12	3169
26 Dec. 1809	La Fête de Mars	DP, 1a	Gardel	Kreutzer	Ciceri, Boquet		Vestris, Albert; Gardel, Chevigny	3	1809–10	3692

Date of first performance at Opéra	*Title of ballet*	*Description*	*Choreographer*	*Composer*	*Scene designer*	*Costume designer*	*Principal dancers*	*A: Number of performances B: Years in repertory C: Average receipts over first 10 or fewer perfs*		
								A	*B*	*C*
24 Jan. 1810	Vertumne et Pomone	BP, 1a	Gardel	Lefebvre		Marche	Vestris; Gardel	4	1810	3524
8 June 1810	Persée et Andromède	BP, 3a	Gardel	Méhul	Protain f., Lebe-Gigun, Mathis, Desroches	Ménageot	Vestris, Albert; Gardel, Clotilde, Chevigny	20	1810–12	
25 June 1811	L' Enlèvement des Sabines	BPH, 3a	Milon	Berton	Isabey	Ménageot	Vestris, Milon; Gardel, Clotilde, Chevigny	44	1811–18	3856
28 Apr. 1812	L' Enfant prodigue	BP, 3a	Gardel	Berton	Isabey	Ménageot	Vestris; Gardel, Chevigny, Bigottini	49	1812–23	4308
23 Nov. 1813	Nina, ou la Folle par amour	BP, 2a	Milon	Persuis after Dalayrac	Ciceri, Daguerre		Albert, Milon, Elie 1; Bigottini, Chevigny	190	1813–40	3720
17 May 1814	Le Retour des lys	D	Gardel	[Persuis]				2	1814	

Date of first performance at Opéra	Title of ballet	Description	Choreographer	Composer	Scene designer	Costume designer	Principal dancers	A: Number of performances A	B: Years in repertory B	C: Average receipts over first 10 or fewer perfs C
4 Apr. 1815	L' Epreuve villageoise, ou André et Denise	BC, 2a	Milon	Persuis after Grétry			Albert, S. Mérante, Milon; Courtin, Bigottini, Gardel, Delisle	96	1815–28	2509
25 July 1815	L' Heureux Retour	B, 1a	Milon, Gardel	Persuis, Kreutzer, Berton	Daguerre and others		Albert, Elie 1; Courtin, Gosselin	16	1815–17	4924
12 Dec. 1815	Flore et Zéphire	BAn, 2a	Didelot	Venua	Ciceri	Marche	Albert; Gosselin	173	1815–31	8420
22 Feb. 1816	Le Carnaval de Venise, ou la Constance à l' épreuve	BP, 2a	Milon	Persuis, Kreutzer	Ciceri, Daguerre		Albert, Ferdinand; Bigottini, Courtin	166	1816–38	3500
26 Dec. 1816	Les Sauvages de la mer du sud	B, 1a	Milon	Lefebvre	Degotti		Albert, Godefroi, Elie 1, S. Mérante; Bigottini	8	1816–17	3098

Date of first performance at Opéra	*Title of ballet*	*Description*	*Choreographer*	*Composer*	*Scene designer*	*Costume designer*	*Principal dancers*	*A: Number of performances* *B: Years in repertory* *C: Average receipts over first 10 or fewer perfs* *A*	*B*	*C*
17 Sep. 1817	Les Mariages de Caserte, ou l' Echange des roses	B, 1a	Gardel, Milon	Dugazon	Ciceri		Albert, A. Coulon; Bigottini, Courtin	2	1817	2627
18 Feb. 1818	Proserpine	BP, 3a	Gardel	Schneitz-hoeffer	Ciceri	Berthélémy	Montjoie, Paul; Bigottini, Courtin	25	1818–19	4513
3 June 1818	Le Séducteur au village, ou Claire et Mectal	BP, 2a	Albert	Schneitz-hoeffer	Ciceri		Albert, Montjoie, S. Mérante; Bigottini, Bias	16	1818	2408
30 Sep. 1818	La Servante justifiée	BV, 1a	Gardel	Kreutzer	Degotti		Albert, S. Mérante; Bigottini, Anatole, Courtin	75	1818–31	4128

Appendix B

Opera divertissements *produced at the Paris Opéra, 1794–1819*

1794

18 Feb.	*Horatio Coclès* (Méhul) No choreographer credited.
4 Mar.	*Toulon soumis* (Rochefort) No choreographer credited.
3 Apr.	*La Réunion du 10 août, ou l'Inauguration de la République française* (Porta). Ballets by Gardel. Act I: danced chorus at end. Act II opened with chorus and ballet of the Heroines, seated on gun carriages, and ended with a Ballet and Hymn to Liberty. Act III ended with a Grand Ballet. Act V ended with a General Ballet.
22 Aug.	*Denys le tryan, maître d'école à Corinthe* (Grétry). Ended with a grand ballet. No choreographer credited
1 Sep.	*La Rosière républicaine, ou la Fête de la Raison* (Grétry). Final ballet by Gardel.

1797

17 Jan.	*Anacréon* (Grétry). Ballets in Act II by Gardel.
1 July	*Alceste* (Gluck, 1776). New ballets by Gardel included a *pas* to an *andante* by Haydn, and another to the first part of Viotti's third violin concerto.

1798

14 July	*Apelle et Campaspe* (Ehler). No choreographer credited.
18 Dec.	*Olimpie* (Kalkbrenner). No choreographer credited.

1799

5 Apr.	*La Caravane du Caïre* (Grétry, 1784). New ballets by Gardel.
31 Dec.	*Armide* (Gluck, 1777). New ballets by Gardel to musical insertions by Widerkehr, Ehler (a *symphonie concertante*) and Vogel.

1800

24 July	*Praxitèle* (Mme Devismes). No choreographer credited.
10 Oct.	*Les Horaces* (Porta). Ballets by Gardel, who also arranged the combat scene.

1801

12 Apr.	*Astynax* (Kreutzer). From the sixth performance, included a *pas de deux* to a movement from one of Kreutzer's violin concertos.
20 Aug.	*Les Mystères d'Isis* (Mozart, arranged by Lachnith). Ballets by Gardel.
7 Nov.	*Le Casque et les colombes* (Grétry). Choreography by Gardel.

1802

29 Mar. *Proserpine* (Paisiello). Ballets by Gardel.
4 May *Sémiramis* (Catel). Ballets by Gardel.

1803

6 Apr. *Saül* (arr. Kalkbrenner and Lachmith). *Divertissement* by Milon.
9 Aug. *Mahomet II* (Jadin). Ballet by Gardel.
4 Oct. *Anacréon chex Polycrate* (Cherubini). Ballet by Gardel (in which Mme Gardel declaimed a few words of recitative).

1804

8 Feb. *Le Connétable de Clisson* (Porta). Ballet by Gardel.
8 July *Ossian* (Le Sueur). Ballets by Gardel and Milon.

1805

10 Apr. *La Prise de Jéricho* (arr. Kalkbrenner and Lachnith). *Divertissement* by Milon.
17 Sep. *Don Juan* (Mozart). Ballet by Gardel.

1806

6 Apr. *Nephtali* (Blangini). Ballet by Gardel, who was also in overall charge of the production.
19 Aug. *Castor et Pollux* (Winter). Ballet *La Naissance de Vénus* by Gardel.

1807

2 Jan. *L'Inauguration du temple de la Victoire* (Le Sueur, Persuis). Ballets by Gardel.
23 Oct. *Le Triomphe de Trajan* (Persuis, Le Sueur). Ballets by Gardel, apart from one *pas de trois* by L. Duport.
15 Dec. *La Vestale* (Spontini). Ballets by Gardel.

1808

24 May *Aristippe* (Kreutzer). Ballets by Gardel.

1809

21 Mar. *La Mort d'Adam* (Le Sueur). Ballet in Act I by Gardel. Ballet in Act II by Milon.
28 Nov. *Fernand Cortez* (Spontini). Ballets by Gardel.

1810

23 Mar. *Abel* (Kreutzer). Ballet by Gardel.

8 Aug. *Les Bayadères* (Catel). *Divertissements* by Gardel and Milon.

1811

27 Mar. *Le Triomphe du mois de mars* (Kreutzer). Ballet by Gardel.

16 Apr.	*Sophocle* (Fiocchi). Ballets by Gardel and Milon.
14 June	*Armide* (Gluck, 1777). Ballets by Gardel.
17 Dec.	*Les Amazones* (Méhul). Ballets by Milon.

1812

26 May	*Oenone* (Kalkbrenner). Contained 'one very wretched ballet'. No choreographer credited.
15 Sep.	*Jérusalem délivrée* (Persuis). Ballet by Gardel.

1813

5 Feb.	*Le Laboureur chinois* (various, arr. Berton: Mozart, Haydn, Simon Mayer). Ballet by Milon.
6 Apr.	*Les Abencérages* (Cherubini). Ballets by Gardel.

1814

1 Feb.	*L'Oriflamme* (Méhul, Paër, Berton, Kreutzer). *Divertissements* by Gardel.
23 Aug.	*Pélage* (Spontini). Ballet by Gardel.

1815

30 May	*La Princesse de Babylone* (Kreutzer). Ballet by Gardel.

1816

23 Apr.	*Le Rossignol* (Le Brun). Ballet by Gardel.
21 June	*Les Deux Rivaux* (Spontini, Persuis, Berton, Kreutzer). Ballet by Gardel.
30 July	*Nathalie* (Reicha). Ballet by Gardel.

1817

4 Mar.	*Roger de Sicile* (Berton). Ballets by Milon.

1818

19 Jan.	*Zéloïde* (Le Brun). Ballet by Milon.
29 June	*Zirphile et Fleur de myrte* (Catel). Ballet by Gardel.

1819

22 Dec.	*Olympie* (Catel). Ballet by Gardel.

Appendix C

Principal dancers at the Paris Opéra, 1793–1820

Female

Anatole, Mme *See* Gosselin, Constance-Hyppolite
Bias, Anne-Françoise, *dite* Fanny 1807–25
b. 3 June 1789; d. 6 September 1825
Bigottini, Emilie[-Jeanne-Marie-Antoinette de la Wateline] 1801–23
b. Toulouse, 16 April 1784; d. Paris, 28 April 1858
Chameroy, Louise 1791–92, 1796–1802
b. 5 May 1779; d. Paris, 13 [or 15?] October 1802
Chevigny, Geneviève-Sophie 1790–1804, 1806–14
b. Paris, 12 May 1772; d. during the 1840s
Clotilde[-Augustine Mafleuret] 1793–1818
b. Paris, 1 March 1776; d. Paris, 15 December 1826
Collomb, Magdeleine, *dite* Emilie 1791–1808
b. 15 October 1768; d. Paris, May 1840
Coulon, Anne-Jacqueline 1778–1801
b. 1764; d. June 1831
Courtin, Mme *See* Rivière, Marie-Alexandrine
Courtois, *See* Louise
Delisle, Marie-Marguerite Verdélisle, *dite* 1792–1820
b. 28 October 1782; d. February 1840
Delisle, Marie-Sophie 1802–04
b. c. 1786
Duchemin-Lavoisier, Elisabeth-Louise 1791–97
Duport, Marie-Adélaïde, *dite* Minette 1799–1809
b. c. 1784
Félicité [Saint-Denier, Françoise-] 1799–1816
Gardel (*née* Houbert, *dite* Miller), Marie-Elisabeth-Anne 1786–1816
b. Auxonne, 4 April 1770; d. Paris, 18 May 1833
Gosselin, Constance-Hyppolite 1813–29
b. 5 January 1794
Gosselin, Geneviève-Adélaïde 1809–18
b. 17 October 1791; d. Charenton-Saint-Maurice, 17 June 1818
Hullin, Félicité 1815–16
b. c. 1805
Hullin, Joséphine 1815–18, 1828–29
b. c. 1809; d. Paris, July 1838
Hullin, Virginie 1804–08
b. c. 1799; d. 1829
Hutin, Alexandrine 1792–98, 1803–08
d. June 1820

Louise [Courtois] 1794–1805
d. May 1806
Masrélier, Marie-Jeanne-Véronique 1799–1820
b. 5 October 1784; alive in 1841
Masrélier, Geneviève-Jacqueline 1799–1816
b. 11 September 1782; dead by 1841
Millière, Marie Brigot, *dite* 1792–1808
b. Paris, 1780/81
Pérignon (née Gervais), Marie-Eve 1779–1802
b. 1763; probably dead by 1809
Rivière, Marie-Alexandrine 1801–20
b. 17 July 1786
Rose [Marie-Rose Pole] 1786–93
d. St Petersburg, March/April 1803
Saulnier, Marie-Jeanne Artaud, *dite* Mimi 1796–1814
b. c. 1779; d. before 1841
Saulnier, Victoire 1784–94
b. c. 1769
Saulnier, Victoire [Jeanne-Victoire Vanneaux de Fondouse, *née* Artaud, *dite*] 1804–20
b. 5 June 1783; alive in 1840
Taglioni, Luigia 1799–1806
b. 1785
Vestris, Anne-Catherine Augier, *dite* Aimée, wife of Auguste Vestris 1793–1809
b. 1774; d. Paris, August 1809

Male

Albert, François Decombe, *dit* 1808–31, 1842–43
b. Bordeaux, 4 April 1787; d. Fontainebleau, 19 July 1865
Anatole, Auguste-Anatole Petit, *dit* 1807–20
b. 5 March 1789
Antonin, Antoine Ricquier, *dit* 1801–15 or –16
Aumer, Jean-Louis 1797–1809; 1820–31 (as ballet-master)
b. Strasbourg, 21 April 1774; d. Saint-Martin-en-Bosc, July 1833
Baptiste [Petit] 1804–09
b. 1784
Beaulieu, Jean-Baptiste, N. Renaud *dit* 1797–1811
b. 1779; d. 6 July 1811
Beaupré, Charles-Florentin Richer de la Rigaudière, *dit* 1789–1819
b. 8 July 1764; d. April 1842
Branchu, Isaac 1792–1816
b. Geneva, 10 October 1773; d. 4 November 1824
Coulon, Antoine-Louis 1816–32
b. 19 July 1796; d. 3 September 1849
Coulon, Jean-François (Teacher), 1807–27
b. 15 January 1774; d. May 1836

Deshayes, André-Jean-Jacques 1792–98, 1800–02
b. 24 January 1776; d. Batignolles, 19 December 1846
Didelot, Charles-Louis-Frédéric 1788, 1791–93
b. Stockholm, 1769; d. Kiev, 7/19 November 1837
Duport, Louis-Antoine [1797–99,] 1800–08
b. Paris, c. 1783; d. Paris, 19 October 1853
Elie, Georges-Antoine Roussy, *dit* 1817-48
b. Paris, 15 October 1800
Elie [elder brother of Georges]
b. 1786, d. 1817
Ferdinand, Jean-Alexis Labrunière de Médicis *dit* 1813–33
b. Bordeaux, 3 November 1791; d. Bordeaux, 1837
Frédéric [Schreuder] 1782–93
Gardel, Pierre[-Gabriel] 1771–1796 (as dancer); 1787–1827 (as ballet-master)
b. Nancy, 4 February 1758; d. Montmartre, 9 November 1840
Goyon, Jean 1786–1815
d. July 1815
Henry, Louis-Xavier-Stanislas Bonnachon, *dit* 1802–07
b. Versailles, 5 March 1784; d. Naples, 4 November 1834
Huard, Alexis 1779–84, 1786–98
Laborie, Louis 1786–89, 1791–94
b. c. 1768
Mérante, Simon-Alexandre 1808–30
b. Paris, 8 March 1783; alive in 1850
Michel[-Saint-Léon], Léon 1803–16
b. 25 July 1777; d. April 1853
Milon, Louis-Jacques 1790–1826 (as dancer or mime), 1800–26 (as ballet-master)
b. Gravachon (Seine), 18 April 1766; d. Neuilly-sur-Seine, 25 or 26 November 1849
Montjoie, Louis-Stanislas 1807–42
b. La Chaud-fond, Switzerland, 15 December 1790; d. Saint-Germain-en-Laye, May 1865
Nivelon, Louis 1777–99
b. Paris, 15 August 1760; d. Saint-Martin (Eure), July 1837
Paul, Antoine 1813–31
b. Marseilles, 21 December 1798; d. Anet, November 1871
Saint-Amant, Pierre-Charles-Martin 1796–1809
b. c. 1779; d. 2 June 1809
Taglioni, Filippo 1799–1802
b. Milan, 5 November 1777; d. Como, 11 February 1871
Vestris, Armand 1800–03
b. 3 May 1787; d. Vienna, 17 May 1825
Vestris, Charles 1812
Vestris, [Jean-Marie-]Auguste [1772, 1773,] 1775–1816
b. Paris, 27 March 1760; d. Paris, 5 December 1842

Appendix D

Ballets performed at the Théâtre de la Porte-Saint-Martin, 1802–19

First perf.	Title	Choreographer	Composer	Years in repertory	Number of perfs.
20.11.02	*Les Jeux d'Egl*	Dauberval		1802–04	53
13.10.03	*La Fille mal gardée*	Dauberval		1803–19	254
7.12.03	*Le Déserteur*	Dauberval		1803–05	41
22.5.04	*Annette et Lubin*	Dauberval		1804–06	24
17.7.04	*Le Page inconstant*	Dauberval		1804, 07	64
6.3.05	*Rosina et Lorenzo*	Aumer		1805	7
22.5.05	*Les Vendangeurs*	J.B. Blache		1805–06, 19	39
20.3.06	*Jenny*	Aumer	Darondeau	1806–07	81
28.6.06	*Les Deux Créoles*	Aumer	Darondeau	1806–07	65
1.12.07	*La Joûte*	E. Hus		1807, 16	46
6.6.07	*Les Sauvages de la Floride*	Henry	Darondeau	1816	27
27.7.07	*Les Deux petits Savoyards*	Henry	Darondeau & A. Piccinni	1816	14
7.1.15	*Les Six Ingénues*	Duport	A. Piccinni	1815, 19	51
16.3.15	*Les Bergers de la Sierra Morena* (aka *Une Nuit d'été*)	J. Petipa	A. Piccinni	1815, 19	51
28.2.16	*Hamlet*	Henry	Gallenberg	1816	47
3.4.16	*Le Rosier*	Henry	Darondeau	1816	48
3.8.16	*Samson*	Henry	Gallenberg	1816	14
19.10.16	*Le Mariage rompu*	Henry		1816	18
2.1.17	*La Chaste Suzanne*	J.B. Blache	arr. A. Piccinni	1817–19	97
14.2.17	*Les Meuniers*	J.B. Blache		1817, 19	17
19.4.17	*Almaviva et Rosina*	J.B. Blache		1817–18	51
7.8.17	*L'Amour et la Folie*	J.B. Blache		1817–18	38
27.10.17	*Haroun-al-Raschid*	J.B. Blache		1817–18	27
12.11.18	*La Fille soldat*	J.B. Blache		1818–19	58
2.8.19	*La Double Fête du village*	J.B. Blache		1819	24

NOTE: The five Dauberval ballets presented between 1802 and 1804 and Blache's *Les Vendangeurs* were produced by Aumer. The Blache ballets presented between 1817 and 1819 were produced by his son, F.A. Blache.

Appendix E

Ballets given at other Paris theatres, 1794–1819

(Ch = choreographer; M = musician; the theatre where the ballet was presented appears at the end of each entry in parenthesis.)

13.3.94	*La Journée de l'amour* (Ch: Gallet, M: Mengozzi) Cast included Didelot, Laborie, Rochefort; Rose [Pole], Rochefort, Simonet (Théâtre National)
20.8.94	*La Fête américaine* (Ch: Peicam, M: Waller) (Opéra-Comique)
28.9.94	*Le Ballet de l'amour* (Ch: Gallet) Cast: Didelot, Laborie; Rose [Pole] (Egalité)
24.10.94	*Les Pirates vaincus par les français* (Ch: Peicam)
6.11.94	*La Guingette nationale* (Ch: Goujy) (Lycée des Arts)
8.5.99	*Pigmalion* (Ch: Milon, M: Lefebvre) With Alexis, L. Duport; E. Bigottini, M. Duport (Ambigu-Comique)
16.6.99	*Le Déserteur* (Ch: Dauberval, revived by E.Hus) (Gaîté)
5.6.00	*Le Jour de noces, ou l'enlèvement* (Ch: Carlo Taglioni) (Gaîté)
29.7.00	*L'Amant statue, ou l'Ecole hollandaise* (Ch: Carlo Taglioni) (Gaîté)
20.6.04	*Les Vendageurs du Médoc* (Ch: E. Hus) (Gaîté)
16.7.07	*Le Barbier au village* (Ch: Hullin) (Gaîté)
30.4.12	*La Botte de sept lieus, ou l'Enfant précoce* (Ch: Hullin, M: A. Piccinni) (Gaîté)
15.5.12	*Lise et Colin dans leur ménage, ou la suite de la Fille mal gardée* (Ch: Jacquinot, M: Foignet) (Jeux-Gymnastiques)
28.12.16	*La Rencontre imprévue* (Ch: Anatole Petit) (Théâtre de la Société de la rue de Paradis)

Appendix F

Ballets produced by Pierre Gardel for operas presented at the Imperial Court, 1809–11

Date	Palace	Title	Composer
12.1.09 26.1.09	Tuileries	*Numa Pompilio*	Paër
2.2.09 16.2.09	Tuileries	*La morte di Cleopatra*	Nasolini
2.3.09	Tuileries	*Diane et Endymion*	Stefano Vestris
9.3.09	Tuileries	*Romeo e Giulietta*	Zingarelli
30.10.09	Fontainebleau	*Pimmalione*	Cherubini
24.1.11	Tuileries	*Pirro*	Paisiello
16.6.11	Tuileries	*Didon abandonnata*	Paër

Appendix G

Identified borrowings from Haydn in ballet scores of the Paris Opéra, 1793–1819

Symphonies

No. 41	4th mvt.	*Le Retour d'Ulysse* (252)
No. 49	2nd mvt.	*Le Jugement de Pâris* (E348)
No. 67	1st mvt.	*Daphnis et Pandrose* (125)
	4th mvt.	*Le Retour d'Ulysse* (252)
No. 73	3rd mvt.	*Le Jugement de Pâris* (E348)
No. 82	2nd mvt.	"
No. 85	2nd mvt.	*Armide* (73)
	4th mvt.	*Héro et Léandre* (71)
No. 87	2nd mvt.	*L'Enfant prodigue* (343)
No. 90	2nd mvt.	*Héro et Léandre* (71)
No. 92	2nd mvt.	*Le Volage fixé* (219)
No. 94	2nd mvt.	*Achille à Scyros* (168)
No. 97	1st mvt.	*Le Jugement de Pâris* (E348)
	"	*L'Enfant prodigue* (343)
	2nd mvt.	*Héro et Léandre* (71)

Quartets

Op. 33/3	2nd mvt.	*Achille à Scyros* (168)

References in parentheses are to pages in the text of this book, except where preceded by E, in which cases they relate to *The Ballet of the Enlightenment*.

Other borrowings from Haydn, so far unidentified, are to be found in Pierre Laurent's ballet *L'Ile d'amour* (1790, E313) and in the ballet music for the operas *Démophon* (1789, E425) and *Les Mystères d'Isis* (106).

Dauberval also borrowed from the symphonies of Haydn, and used a popular song entitled *La Jeune et gentille Lisette* in the second act of *La Fille mal gardée* (1789) with the same theme that Haydn used in the second movement of his Symphony No. 85.

Bibliography

Alison, Sir H. & Tytler, P. F. *Travels in France during the Years 1814–15* (Edinburgh, 1816)

Allévy, Marie-Antoinette *La Mise-en-scène en France dans la première moitié du dix-neuvième siècle* (Paris, 1938)

Amanton, Claude-Nicolas *Notice sur Madame Gardel* (Auxerre, 1835)

Anon. *Le Monde d'amour, histoires galantes: l'Opéra, ses déesses et ses danseuses* (Geneva, n.d., c.1860)

Anon. *Paris pendant l'année 1795* (London, 1795)

Archives Nationales *Danseurs et ballets de l'Opéra de Paris* (Paris, 1988)

Aulard, François-Victor-Alphonse *Paris pendant le réaction thermidorienne et sous la Directoire* (Paris, 1898–1902)

— *Paris sous le Consulat* (Paris, 1903–11)

— *Paris sous le Premier Empire* (Paris, 1912–24)

Avrillon, Mlle [C.M.C. de Villemarest] *Mémoires de Mademoiselle Avrillon sur la vie privée de Joséphine, sa famille et sa cour* (Paris, 1833)

Babault and others *Annales dramatiques, ou Dictionnaire générale des théâtres* (Paris, 1808–12)

Baron, M.A. *Lettres à Sophie sur la danse* (Paris, 1825)

Bartlet, Elizabeth C. 'Grétry and the Revolution' (*Grétry et l'Europe de l'Opéra-Comique*, ed. Philippe Vendrix (Liège, 1992), pp. 47–110)

[Beffroy de Reigny] *Dictionnaire néologique des hommes et des choses* (Paris, Year IX)

Berchoux, J. *La Danse, ou les dieux de l'Opéra* (Paris, 1806)

Bergman, Gösta M. *Lighting in the Theatre* (Stockholm, 1977)

Berry, Mary *Extracts from the Journals and Correspondence of Miss Berry, 1783–1852* (London, 1866)

Blasis, Carlo *The Code of Terpsichore* (London, 1830)

Blok, L.D. *Klassicheskii Tanets: istoriya i sovremennost'* (Moscow, 1987)

Boigne, Anna-Adélaïde, Comtesse de *Mémoires de la comtesse de Boigne, née Osmond*, ed. Jean-Claude Berchet (Paris, 1989)

Boisson, F. A. *Les Douze Colonnes de Louis: l'histoire inconnue du Grand-Théâtre de Bordeaux* (Bordeaux, 1964)

Bonet de Treiches, Joseph-Balthazar *De l'Opéra en l'an XII* (Paris, 1803)

Borgnis, M. J.-A. *Traité complet de mécanique appliqué aux arts* (Paris, 1820)

Bouchenot-Déchin, Patricia *La Montansier* (Paris, 1993)

Bouquet, Marie-Thérèse *Il Teatro di Corte dalle origini al 1788* (Vol. I of *Storia del Teatro Regio di Torino*, coordinated by Alberto Basso) (Turin, 1976)

Bournonville, August *Lettres à la maison de son enfance*, ed. Nils Schiørring and Svend Kragh-Jacobsen (Copenhagen, 1969–78)

— *Mit Theaterliv* (Copenhagen, 1848-77) – English edition, *My Theatre Life*, trans. Patricia McAndrew (London, 1979)

Brenet, Michel *Grétry, se vie et ses oeuvres* (Paris, 1884)

Brévau, Bruno *Les Changements de la vie musicale Parisienne de 1774 à 1799* (Paris, 1980)

Brown, Frederick *Theatre and Revolution* (New York, 1980)

Capon, Gaston *Les Vestris: le 'diou' de la danse et sa famille (1730–1808)* (Paris, 1908)

Castelot, André *Le Duc de Berry et son double mariage* (Paris, 1951)

Castil-Blaze *L'Académie impériale de musique... de 1645 à 1855* (Paris, 1855)

— *La Danse et les ballets depuis Bacchus jusqu'à Mademoiselle Taglioni* (Paris, 1832)

Cazenove d'Arlens, Constance de *Deux Mois à Paris et à Lyon sous le Consulat: Journal... (février–avril 1803)* (Paris, 1903)

Chapman, John V. 'Auguste Vestris and the Expansion of Technique' *Dance Research Journal* (New York), Vol. 19 No. 1, Summer 1987, pp. 11–18

— 'Forgotten Giant: Pierre Gardel' *Dance Research* (London), Vol. V No. 1, Spring 1987, pp. 3–20

— 'The Paris Opéra Ballet School, 1798–1827' *Dance Chronicle* (New York), Vol. 12 No. 2, 1989, pp. 196–220

— 'Silent Drama to Silent Dream: Parisian Ballet Criticism, 1800–1830' *Dance Chronicle* (New York), Vol. 11 No. 3, 1988, pp. 365–80

Chazin-Bennahum, Judith *Dance in the Shadow of the Guillotine* (Carbondale and Edwardsville, Illinois, 1988)

— 'Anacreon's Triple Threat to French Eighteenth Century Ballet' *Proceedings, Society of Dance History Scholars*, Towson, Maryland, 1984, pp. 88–94)

— *Livrets of Ballets and Pantomimes during the French Revolution* Doctoral dissertation, University of New Mexico, 1981

Chénier, Marie-Joseph *Oeuvres posthumes de M.J. Chénier* (Paris, 1824–6)

Chéruzel, Maurice *Jean-Georges Noverre, levain de la danse moderne* (Saint-Germain-en-Laye, 1994)

Christout, Marie-Françoise '*Danse et Révolution: historique et thématique*' *Corps Ecrit*, Vol. 28, Oct.–Dec. 1988, pp. 55–62

Clary und Aldringen, Prince Karl Joseph von *Souvenirs: trois mois à Paris lors du mariage de Napoléon et de Marie-Louise* (Paris, 1914)

Clément, Charles *Léopold Robert d'après sa correspondance inédite* (Paris, 1875)

Collins, Herbert F. *Talma: a Biography of an Actor* (London, 1964)

Collomb, Emilie *Agenda. 1805–09* (Manuscript, Bibliothèque-Musée de l'Opéra, Paris, Fonds Collomb 7)

[Compan, Charles] *Dictionnaire de la danse* (Paris, 1787)

Constant *Mémoires ... sur la vie privée de Napoléon* (Paris, 1830)

Couvreur, Manuel '*La Folie à l'Opéra-Comique: deux grelots de Momus aux larmes de Nina*' (*Grétry et l'Europe de l'Opéra Comique*, ed. Philippe Vendrix (Liège, 1992), pp. 201–220)

Darroussat, Séverine *François-Nicolas Delaistre (1746–1832)* Master's thesis, Paris IV-Sorbonne University, 1999

Dartois-Lapeyre, Françoise '*Napoléon, l'Opéra et la danse*' (*Napoléon, de l'histoire à la légende*, Paris, 2000, pp. 117–53)

Daudet, Ernest *Louis XVIII et le duc Decazes* (Paris, 1899)

Demuth, Norman *French Opera* (Horsham, 1963)

Des Granges, Charles-Marc *Geoffroy et la critique dramatique sous le Consulat et l'Empire (1800–14)* (Paris, 1897)

Deshayes, André-Jean-Jacques *Idées générales sur l'Académie royale de musique et particulièment sur la danse* (Paris, 1822)

Despréaux, Jean-Etienne *Mes Passe-temps* (Paris, 1806)

Divova, Elisaveta Petrovna *Journal et souvenirs de Madame Divoff* – Introduction and notes by S. Kaznakoff (Paris, 1929)

Donnet, A. & Orgiazzi *Architechnographie des théâtres* (Paris, 1820)

Du Fayl, Ezvar *L'Académie Nationale de Musique, 1671–1877* (Paris, 1878)

Dufrane, Louis *Gossec: sa vie, ses oeuvres* (Paris & Brussels, 1927)

Duport, Louis *Réponse de M. Duport, artiste de l'Académie Impériale de Musique, à un pamphlet intitulé Opinion d'un habitué ... dans l'affaire de M. Duport* (Paris, [1804])

Estrées, Paul d' *Le Théâtre sous la Terror (Théâtre de la Peur), 1793–94* (Paris, 1913)

Falcone, Francesca 'The Evolution of the Arabesque in Dance' *Dance Chronicle* (New York), Vol. 22, 1999, pp. 71–118

Fauville, Henri *La France de Bonaparte vue par les visiteurs anglais* (Aix-en-Provence, 1989)

Favre, Georges *Boieldieu, sa vie, son oeuvre* (Paris, 1944)

— '*La Danseuse Clotilde Mafleurai: première femme d'Adrien Boïeldieu*' *Revue musicale* (Paris), Vol. 195, Jan. 1940, pp. 1–11; Vol. 197, Apr. 1940, pp. 204–18

Ferrero, Mercedes Viale *La scenografia dalle origini al 1936* (Vol. III of *Storia del Teatro Regio di Torino*, coordinated by Alberto Basso) (Turin, 1980)

Félix-Bouvier *Une danseuse de l'Opéra – La Bigottini* (Paris, 1909)

Firmin-Didot, Albert *Souvenirs de J.-E. Despréaux, ancien danseur de l'Opéra et poète chansonnier, 1748–1820* (Issoudun, 1894)

Fischer, Carlos *Les Costumes de l'Opéra* (Paris, 1931)

Fournel, Victor *Curiosités théâtrales* (Paris, 1859)

Fournier, August *Die Geheimpolizei auf dem Wiener Kongress, eine Auswahl aus ihren Papieren* (Vienna and Leipzig, 1913)

Fribourg, André '*L'Eglise et l'Opéra: histoire de Mlle Chameroy*' *La Revue de Paris*, 1908, pp. 67–9

Gatti, Carlo *Il Teatro alla Scala nella storia e nell'arte (1778–1963)* (Milan, 1964)

Gautier, Théophile *Gautier on Dance*, ed. and trans. by Ivor Guest (London, 1986)

Geoffroy, Julien-Louis *Cours de littérature dramatique* (Paris, 1825)

Glushkovskii, Adam Pavlovich *Vospominanya Baletmeistera* (Leningrad & Moscow, 1940)

Goncourt, Edmond *La Guimard* (Paris, 1892)

— & Jules de *Histoire de la société française pendant la Révolution* (Paris, 1854)

Gourret, Jean *Ces Hommes qui ont fait l'Opéra, 1669–1984* (Paris, 1984)

Granville, Harriet, Countess of *Letters...1810–1845*, ed. Hon. F. Leveson Gower (London, 1894)

Greathead, Bertie *An Englishman in Paris: 1803*, ed. J.P.T. Bury and J.C. Barry (London, 1953)

Guest, Ivor *Le Ballet de l'Opéra de Paris* (Paris, 2001)

— *The Ballet of the Enlightenment* (London, 1996)

— 'Comedy Ballet in the Neo-Classical Era: *La Fille mal gardée* and *La Dansomanie*' (*Gustavian Opera*, ed. Inger Mattsson, Royal Swedish Academy of Music (Stockholm, 1991), pp. 449–64)

— '*La Dansomanie*' *Dancing Times* (London), No. 902, Nov. 1985, pp. 127–9

Hadamovsky, Franz *Die Wiener Hoftheater (Staatstheater)* Part II: 1811–1974 (Vienna, 1975)

Hall, John R. *The Bourbon Restoration* (London, 1909)

Hammond, Sandra Noll 'Clues to Ballet's Technical History from the Early Nineteenth-Century Ballet Lesson' *Dance Research* (London), Vol. III No. 1, Autumn 1984, pp. 53–66

— 'The *Gavotte de Vestris*: a Dance of Three Centuries' *Proceedings, Society of Dance History Scholars*, Towson, Maryland, 1984, pp. 47–52

— 'Searching for the Sylph: Documentation of Early Developments in *Pointe* Technique' *Dance Research Journal* (New York), Vol. 19 No. 2, Winter 1987–88, pp. 27–31

— 'Windows into Romantic Ballet: Context and Structure of Four Early Nineteenth-Century *Pas de deux*' *Proceedings, Society of Dance History Scholars*, New York City, 1997, pp. 137–44

Hastings, Baird *Choreographer and Composer* (Boston, 1983)

[Hatin, F.] *Le Livre du centenaire du Journal des Débats, 1789–1889* (Paris, 1889)

Hauterive, Ernest d' *La Police secret du premier Empire* (Paris, 1922)

Hemmings, F.W.J. *Theatre and State in France, 1760–1905* (Cambridge, 1994)

Hillairet, Jacques *Evocation du vieux Paris* (Paris, 1952)

Holmström, Kirsten Gram *Monodrama, Attitudes, Tableaux Vivants: studies on some trends of theatrical fashion, 1770–1815* (Stockholm, 1967)

Honour, Hugh *Neo-classicism* (London, 1968)

Houssaye, Arsène *Princesses de comédie et déesses d'opéra* (Paris, 1860)

Hugo, Valentine J. '*Tableau de la danse au théâtre pendant la Révolution française (1789–1795)*' *Revue Musicale* (Paris), Mar. 1922, pp. 222–30; Apr. 1922, pp. 44–50; May 1922, pp. 127–46

Isherwood, Robert M. *Farce and Fantasy: Popular Entertainment in Eighteenth-Century Paris* (New York, 1986)

Johnson, James H. *Listening in Paris* (Berkeley, California, 1995)

Jouy, Etienne de *L'Hermite de la Chaussée d'Antin, ou Observations sur les moeurs et les usages parisiens au commencement du XIXe siècle* (Paris, 1814)

Jullien, Adolphe *Histoire du costume au théâtre* (Paris, 1880)

— *Paris dilettante au commencement du siècle* (Paris, 1884)

Jürgensen, Knud Arne *The Bournonville Tradition: the First Fifty Years, 1829–1879* (London, 1997)

Kennedy, Emmet *A Cultural History of the French Revolution* (New Haven, Connecticut, and London, 1987)

Kirstein, Lincoln *Movement and Metaphor: Four Centuries of Ballet* (New York, 1971)

Krasovskaya, Vera M. *Zapadnoevropeiskii baletnii teatr: ocherki istorii, tom. 3: Preromantizm* (Leningrad, 1983)

Labat-Poussin, Brigitte *Archives du Théâtre National de l'Opéra (AJ*[13] *1 à 1446)* (Paris, 1977)

La Garde-Chambonas, Comte de *Souvenirs du Congrès de Vienne, 1814–1815* (Paris, 1901)

Lagrave, Henri; Mazouer, Charles; and Regaldo, Marc *La Vie théâtrale à Bordeaux des origines à nos jours* Vol. I (Paris, 1985)

Lajarry, S. Champion aîné *Une actrice au paradis* (Paris, 1836)

Lajarte, Théodore de *Bibliothèque musicale de l'Opèra* (Paris, 1878)

— *Les Curiosités de l'Opéra* (Paris, 1883)

La Laurencie, Lionel de '*Les Débuts de Viotti comme directeur de l'Opéra en 1819*' *Revue de musicologie* (Paris), Vol. 11, Aug. 1924, pp. 110–22

Lanzac de Laborie '*L'Opéra il y a cent ans*' *Revue hebdomadaire* (Paris), Sep.–Oct. 1912

— *Paris sous Napoléon: spectacles et musées* (Paris, 1913)

Lecomte, L.-Henry *Histoire des théâtres de Paris: le Théâtre National, le Théâtre de l'Egalité, 1793–1794* (Paris, 1907)

— *Napoléon et le monde dramatique* (Paris, 1912)

Lefeuve, Charles *Histoire de Paris, rue par rue, maison par maison* (Paris, 1873)

Lejeune, André & Wolff, Stéphane *Les Quinze Salles de l'Opéra* (Paris, 1955)

Lemaistre, J.G. *A Rough Sketch of Modern Paris, or Letters on Society, Manners, Public Curiosities, and Amusements, in that capital, written during the last twelve months of 1801 and the first five of 1802* (London, 1803)

Levinson, Andrei *Meister des Balletts* (Potsdam, 1923)

Lifar, Serge *Auguste Vestris, 'Le Dieu de la Danse'* (Paris, 1950)

London Stage, 1660–1800, The Part V (1776–1800), ed. Charles Beecher Hogan (Carbondale, Illinois, 1960–80)

Louis, Maurice A.-L. *Danses populaires et ballets d'Opéra* (Paris, 1965)

Luce de Lancival, Jean-Charles-Julien *Achille à Scyros* (2nd edn, Paris, 1807)

Lynham, Deryck *The Chevalier Noverre, Father of Modern Ballet* (London, 1950)

Magri, Gennaro *Theoretical and Practical Treatise on Dancing*, trans. Mary Skeaping, with Anna Ivanovna and Irmgaard E. Berry; ed. Irmgaard E. Berry and Annalisa Fox (London, 1988)

Marquiset, Comte Alfred *A travers ma vie: souvenirs classés et annotés*, ed. Armand Marquiset (Paris, 1904)

Maurice, Charles *Epaves: théâtre – histoire – anecdotes – mots* (Paris, 1865)

— *Histoire anecdotique du théâtre* (Paris, 1856)

Meglin, Joellen A. '*Sauvages*, Sex-Roles and Semiotics: representations of Native Americans in the French Ballet, 1736–1837' *Dance Chronicle* (New York), Vol. 23 Nos 2 and 3, 2000, pp. 87–132, 275–320

Mercier, Louis-Sébastien *Le Nouveau Paris*, ed. Jean-Claude Bonnet (Paris, 1994)

Michel, Marcelle *L'Apogée et la décadence du ballet sous la Révolution et l'Empire* Doctoral thesis, University of Paris, 1955

— *Geoffroy et la critique chorégraphique* Thesis, University of Paris, 1955

Mongrédien, Jean *French Music from the Enlightenment to Romanticism, 1789–1830* (Portland, Oregon, 1996)

Moore, Lillian *The Duport Mystery*, *Dance Perspectives* (New York) Vol. 7, 1960

Moore, Thomas *The Fudge Family in Paris* (London, 1818)

Mosnier, H. *Un Ancien Conventionnel Directeur de l'Opéra, Bonet des Treiches* (Paris, 1891)

Mundt, N. 'Biografiya Karla-Ludoviks Didlo' *Repertuar russkogo teatra* (St. Petersburg), Vol. I No. 3, 1840, pp. 1–8

Napoleon I *Correspondance* (Paris, 1858–69)

— *Lettres inédites (An VIII – 1815)*, ed. Léon Lecestre (Paris, 1897)

Nérée-Desarbres *Deux Siècles à l'Opéra* (Paris, 1868)

Noiray, Michel '*L'Opéra de la Révolution (1790–1794): un "tapage de chien"?*' (*La Carmagnole des muses*, ed. Jean-Claude Bonnet (Paris, 1988), pp. 359–79)

Noverre, Jean-Georges *Lettres sur la danse et les ballets* (Lyon and Stuttgart, 1760)

— *Lettres sur la danse, les ballets et les arts* (St Petersburg, 1804)

— *Lettres sur les arts imitateurs en général et sur la danse en particulier* (Paris and The Hague, 1807)

Oman, Carole *Napoleon's Viceroy: Eugène de Beauharnais* (London, 1966)

[Ourry & Sauvan] *Petite Chronique de Paris faisant suite aux mémoires de Bachaumont* (Paris, 1819)

Ozouf, Mona *Festivals and the French Revolution* (Cambridge, Massachusetts, 1988)

Packenham, Simona *In the Absence of the Emperor: London–Paris, 1814–15* (London, 1968)

Paris, Isabelle, Comtesse de *La Reine Marie-Amélie, grand-mère de l'Europe* (Paris, 1998)

Paul, Sir John *Journal of a Party of Pleasure* (London, 1803)

Pélissier, Paul *Histoire administrative de l'Académie Nationale de Musique et de Danse* (Paris, 1906)

Pendle, Karin '*L'Opéra-Comique à Paris de 1762 à 1789*' (*L'Opéra-Comique en France au XVIII*[e] *siècle*, ed. Philippe Vendrix (Liège, 1992), pp. 79–177)

Peuchet, Jacques *Mémoires tirés des archives de la Police de Paris* (Paris, 1838)

Peyronnet, Pierre *La Mise-en-scène au XVIII*[e] *siècle* (Paris, 1974)

Pierre, Constant *L'Ecole de chant à l'Opéra* (Paris, 1896)

Pitou, Spire *The Paris Opéra* Vol. II: 1715–1815; Vol. III: 1815–1914 (Westport, Connecticut, 1985, 1990)

Plunkett, Joseph de *Fantômes et souvenirs de la Porte-St-Martin* (Paris, 1946)

Pougin, Arthur *Dictionnaire historique et pittoresque du théâtre* (Paris, 1885)

— *Un directeur d'opéra au dix-huitième siècle* (Paris, 1914)

— *Méhul: sa vie, son génie, son caractère* (Paris, 1889)

Prod'homme, J.-G. '*François-Joseph Gossec (1734–1829): la vie – les oeuvres – l'homme et l'artiste*' *Euterpe* (Paris), Vol. 8, Sep. 1949, pp. 3–113

— *L'Opéra (1669–1925)* (Paris, 1925)

Prudent, H. & Gaudet, P. *Les Salles de spectacle construites par Victor Louis à Bordeaux, au Palais-Royal et à la Place Louvois* (Paris, 1903)

Prudhomme, Louise-Marie *Histoire générale et impartiale des erreurs, des fautes et des crimes commis pendant la Révolution Française* (Paris, 1797)

Prudhommeau, Germaine *Les Premiers Ballets de Pierre Gardel* Paper, unpublished, given at the international congress *La Recherche en danse* (Paris, 1986)

— '*Les Retentissements de la Révolution sur l'Opéra de Paris*' *Révolution et Danse*, actes du Colloque de l'A.E.H.D. (Paris, 1990), pp. 63–73

Quatrelles L'Epine, *Cherubini (1760–1842): notes et documents inédits* (Lille, 1913)

Radicchio, Giuseppe & D'Oria, Nicole Sajous *Les Théâtres de Paris pendant la Révolution* (Paris, 1990)

Reichardt, Johann Friedrich *Un Hiver à Paris sous le Consulat* (Paris, 1896)

Reiset, Marie-Antoine, Vicomte de *Les Enfants du duc de Berry* (Paris, 1905)

Rémusat, Mme de *Lettres, 1804–14* (Paris, 1881)

— *Mémoires. 1802–14* (Paris, 1880)

Ribeiro, Aileen *Fashion in the French Revolution* (London, 1988)

Ritorni, Carlo *Commentarii della vita e delle opere coreodrammatiche di Salvatore Vigano* (Milan, 1838)

Root-Bernstein, Michèle *Boulevard Theatre and Revolution in Eighteenth-Century Paris* (Ann Arbor, Michigan, 1984)

Roqueplan, Nestor *Les Coulisses de l'Opéra* (Paris, 1855)

Rougemont, Martine de *La Vie théâtrale en France au XVIIIe siècle* (Paris, 1988)

Roullet, [Pierre-Nicholas] *Notice historique des évènements qui se sont passés dans l'administration de l'Opéra la nuit du 13 février 1820* (Paris, 1820)

Royer, Alphonse *Histoire de l'Opéra* (Paris, 1875)

Saint-Léon, Arthur Michel *La Sténochorégraphie... avec portraits et biographies des plus célèbres maîtres de ballets anciens et modernes* (Paris, 1852)

Saunders, Edith *Napoleon and Mademoiselle George* (London, 1958)

Sévelinges, Charles-Louis de *Le Rideau levé, ou la petite revue des grands théâtres* (Paris, 1818)

Simond, Charles *Paris de 1800 à 1900 d'après les estampes et mes memoires du temps* (Paris, 1900)

Slonimsky, Yuri *Didlo: vekhi tvorcheskoi biografii* (Leningrad & Moscow, 1958)

Smith, Marian 'Borrowings and Original Music: a Dilemma for the Ballet-Pantomime Composer' *Dance Research* (London), Vol. VI No. 2, Autumn 1988, pp. 3–29

— 'Musical Scores as Dance Sources' *Proceedings, Society of Dance History Scholars*, Provo, Utah, 1994, pp. 89–94

Smith, William C. *The Italian Opera and Contemporary Ballet in London, 1789–1820* (London, 1953)

Stendhal *Souvenirs d'égotisme, autobiographie, lettres inédites* (Paris, 1892)

Swift, Mary Grace *A Loftier Flight: the life and accomplishments of Charles-Louis Didelot, balletmaster* (Middletown, Connecticut, 1974)

Taigny, Edmond *J.B. Isabey: sa vie et ses oeuvres* (Paris, 1859)

Testa, Alberto *Chronologia dei balli, 1740–1936* (Vol. V, Part III of *Storia del Teatro Regio di Torino*, coordinated by Alberto Basso) (Turin, 1988)

Touchard-Lafosse, G. *Chroniques secrètes et galantes de l'Opéra, 1667–1845* (Paris, 1846)

— *La Pudeur et l'Opéra* (Paris, 1835)

Valberkh, Ivan *Iz Archiva Baletmeistera*, ed. Yuri Slonimsky (Moscow & Leningrad, 1948)

Vernières, Jules '*Les Coulisses de l'Opéra*' *Revue de Paris*, Vol. XXXI, July 1836, pp. 303–22

Villani, Antonio and others *Il Teatro de San Carlo* (Naples, 1987)

Warner, Mary-Jane Evans *Gavottes and Bouquets: a comparative study of changes in dance style between 1700 and 1850* Doctoral dissertation, Ohio State University, 1974

Wicks, C. Beaumont *The Parisian Stage* Vol. I: 1800–1815; Vol. II, 1816–1830 (University of Alabama, 1950, 1953)

Wild, Nicole *Décors et Costumes du XIXe siècle* Vol. I: L'Opéra de Paris (Paris, 1987)

— *Dictionnaire des théâtres parisiens au XIXe siècle* (Paris, 1989)

Winter, Marian Hannah *The Pre-Romantic Ballet* (London, 1974)

ENCYCLOPAEDIAS

Biographical Dictionary of Actors, Actresses, Musicians, Dancers, Managers and Other Stage Personnel in London, 1660–1800 (Highfill, Burnim, Kalman & Langhans) (Carbondale & Edwardsville, Illinois, 1973–93)

Biographie universelle ancienne et moderne (Michaud) (Paris, 1854-)

Biographie universelle des musiciens (Fétis) (Paris, 1860–5)

Calendrier historique et chronologique des théâtres pour l'année 1794 (seconde de la République) (Paris, 1793–4)

Dictionnaire de biographie française (Roman d'Amat) (Paris, 1933–)

Enciclopedia dello spettacolo (Amico & Savio) (Rome, 1954–62)

Galerie biographique des artistes dramatiques des Théâtres Royaux (Paris, 1826)

Grand Dictionnaire universel du XIXe siècle (Larousse) (Paris, 1866–76)

Grande Encyclopédie, La (Paris 1885–1910)

International Dictionary of Ballet (Bremser) (New York & London, 1993)

International Encyclopedia of Dance (Cohen) (Detroit, London & Washington, 1998)

New Grove Dictionary of Music and Musicians (Sadie) (London, 1980)

JOURNALS, PERIODICALS

Affiches, annonces et avis divers, 1793

Almanach des spectacles, 1816–21

Ami des arts, 1797

Censeur dramatique, 1797–8

Constutionnel, 1815–20

Courrier de l'Europe et des spectacles, 1807–11

Courrier des spectacles, 1797–1807

Fanal, 1819–20

Gazette de France, 1805–20

Gazette de Paris, 1789–93

Gazette nationale, see *Moniteur*

Intermédiaire des chercheurs et curieux, passim

Journal de Paris, 1777–1820
Journal des débats, 1800–20 (as *Journal de l'Empire*, 1805–14, 1815)
Journal des spectacles, 1793–4
Journal des théâtres, 1794–5
Journal des théâtres et des fêtes nationales, 1794–5
Moniteur universel, 1793–1820
Publiciste, 1797–1810
Observateur des spectacles, 1802–3
Opinion du parterre, 1802–13
Quotidienne, 1797; 1814–20
Spectacles de Paris, 1751–94

Index

BALLETS

OPERAS

Vestale, La (Spontini), 40, 268-270, 296, 368, 374, 429, 481, 492

LITERARY WORKS